READ
Reason
Write

AN ARGUMENT TEXT AND READER

READ Reason Write

AN ARGUMENT TEXT AND READER

EIGHTH EDITION

Dorothy U. Seyler

Boston   Burr Ridge, IL   Dubuque, IA   New York   San Francisco   St. Louis
Bangkok   Bogotá   Caracas   Kuala Lumpur   Lisbon   London   Madrid   Mexico City
Milan   Montreal   New Delhi   Santiago   Seoul   Singapore   Sydney   Taipei   Toronto

The McGraw·Hill Companies

McGraw-Hill Higher Education
        A Division of The McGraw-Hill Companies

1 2 3 4 5 6 7 8 9 0 DOC/DOC 0 9 8 7 6

ISBN 978-0-07-353320-9
MHID 007-353320-3

Editor in Chief: *Emily Barrosse*
Publisher: *Lisa Moore*
Sponsoring Editor: *Christopher Bennem*
Marketing Manager: *Tamara Wederbrand*
Developmental Editor: *Joshua Feldman*
Production Editor: *Chanda Feldman*
Manuscript Editor: *Jennifer Gordon*
Design Manager: *Gino Cieslik*
Art Editor: *Ayelet Arbel*
Production Supervisor: *Randy Hurst*
Composition: *10/12 Palatino by Carlisle Publishing Services*
Printing: *PMS 307, 45# New Era Matte, R. R. Donnelley & Sons, Inc.*

Cover: © Alan Schein/zefa/Corbis (Supreme Court), ©Bettmann/CORBIS (Martin Luther King,
Jr.), The Dallas Morning News (Jazz), © George Tames/The New York Times (John F. Kennedy),
Hulshizer-AP-World Wide Photos (Statue of Liberty), © Joseph Sohm; Visions of America/
CORBIS (Constitution), © Kevin Lamarque /Reuters/Corbis (Flags), © Reuters/CORBIS (Tanks),
© Rick Fowler/Corbis (Protestor), © Saul Loeb/epa/epa/Corbis (Man in Chair).

Credits: The credits section for this book begins on page 758 and is considered an extension of the
copyright page.

The Internet addresses listed in the text were accurate at the time of publication. The inclusion of a
Web site does not indicate an endorsement by the authors or McGraw-Hill, and McGraw-Hill
does not guarantee the accuracy of the information presented at these sites.

Library of Congress Cataloging-in-Publication Data
Seyler, Dorothy U.
    Read, reason, write / Dorothy U. Seyler.--8th ed.
        p. cm.
    Includes bibliographical references and index.
    ISBN 978-0-07-353320-9
    1. English language—Rhetoric. 2. Persuasion (Rhetoric) 3. College readers. 4. Report
  writing. I. Title.
PE1408.S464 2006
808' .0427—dc22

                                                                        2006049980

www.mhhe.com

About the Author

DOROTHY U. SEYLER is Professor of English at Northern Virginia Community College. A Phi Beta Kappa graduate of the College of William and Mary, Dr. Seyler holds advanced degrees from Columbia University and the State University of New York at Albany. She taught at Ohio State University, the University of Kentucky, and Nassau Community College before moving with her family to Northern Virginia.

She has coauthored *Introduction to Literature* in its second edition. She is the author of *Understanding Argument*, *Doing Research* (second edition), *The Reading Context* and *Steps to College Reading* (both in their third editions), and *Patterns of Reflection* (now in its sixth edition). In addition, Professor Seyler has published articles in professional journals and popular magazines. She enjoys tennis and golf, traveling, and writing about both sports and travel.

Contents

Preface

I have written in previous prefaces to *Read, Reason, Write* that being asked to prepare a new edition is much like being asked back to a friend's house: Although you count on it, you are still delighted when the invitation comes. Well, the seventh edition kept old friendships and made new ones as well, so here I am, writing a preface to the eighth edition, more than twenty years after first presenting this text to college students and their instructors. Over these years, *Read, Reason, Write* has grown in size—most books have—but also in stature within the teaching community and in its value to students. Of course, neither this text nor I am getting older, only better, as this eighth edition demonstrates!

Although some important new material strengthens the eighth edition, the essential character of *Read, Reason, Write* remains the same. This text still combines instruction in critical reading and analysis, argument, and research strategies with a rich collection of readings providing practice for these skills and new ideas and insights for readers. A key purpose of *Read, Reason, Write* remains to help students develop into better writers of the kinds of papers they are most often required to write, both in college and in the workplace: summaries, analyses, reports, arguments, and documented essays. To fulfill this key purpose, the text must do more than provide instruction and opportunities for practice; the text must demonstrate to student writers that these seemingly disparate skills connect in important ways. *Read, Reason, Write* remains a new kind of text because it shows students the interrelatedness of reading, analytic, argumentative, and research skills and seeks, in connecting these skills, always to extend each student's critical thinking ability.

FEATURES OF *READ, REASON, WRITE*

- An emphasis on good reading skills for effective arguing and writing.
- Instruction, models, and practice in understanding reading context and analyzing elements of style.
- Instruction, models, and practice in writing summaries and book reviews.
- Focus on argument as contextual: written (or spoken) to a specific audience with the expectation of counterarguments.
- Explanations and models of various types of arguments that bridge the gap between an understanding of logical structures and the ways we actually write arguments.

- Presentation of Aristotelian, Toulmin, and Rogerian models of argument as useful guides to analyzing the arguments of others and organizing one's own arguments.
- In-depth discussion of logical argument, including extensive coverage of induction and deduction.
- Guidelines and revision boxes throughout the text that provide an easy reference for students.
- Instruction, models, and practice in researching and evaluating sources and in composing and documenting researched papers.
- A rich collection of readings, both timely and classic, that provide examples of the varied uses of language and strategies for argument.
- A brief but comprehensive introduction to reading and analyzing literature, found in the Appendix.

NEW FEATURES IN THE EIGHTH EDITION

This new edition maintains the key features of previous editions while adding new material that will make the eighth edition even more helpful to both students and instructors. The significant additions are:

- A much greater emphasis on visual argument throughout the text. Each chapter now opens with a visual—cartoon or photograph—with questions for reading and thinking about the visual.
- Two color inserts adding more visuals. The first, in Chapter 7, provides examples of different types of visuals for analysis in this chapter on using visuals in argument.
- A second color insert, in Chapter 13, the chapter on the media. These eight images are famous photographs from the Vietnam era up to our time.
- A total of 111 readings, plus seven student essays. Fifty-six of the readings are new, and some of those from the seventh edition are now in new places in the text. One of the seven student sample essays is new.
- Of the eleven chapters in the anthology section of the text, two chapters are entirely new, and the others have been refocused and refreshed with some new readings.
- Some of the new topics for reading and discussion include the social impact of modern technology, especially the small electronics; the role of bloggers in our understanding of the news; copyright issues and Google's plans for a digital library; the politics of science; and the impact of Katrina on our thinking about society and government.
- A streamlining of the section on research, with greater emphasis on electronic searches.

ACKNOWLEDGMENT

No book of value is written alone. I am pleased to acknowledge the contributions of others in shaping this text. My thanks are due—as always—to the library staff at the Annandale Campus of Northern Virginia Community College, especially to Marian Delmore, Ruth Stanton, and Ellen Westman, who have helped me locate needed information and have kept me current with the new technology for research. I would also like to thank students Ian Habel, Garrett Berger, Chris Brown, Laura Mullins, Monica Mitchell, Connie Childress, and Alan Peterson, whose essays grace this text. They should be proud of the skill and effort they put into their writing.

I appreciate as well the many good suggestions of the following reviewers of the eighth edition:

Craig R. Barrette
Brescia University

Karen S. Burge
Wichita State University

Glenn Davis
St. Cloud State University

Linda George
Pittsburgh Technical Institute

Ruth Haber
Worcester College

Brenda Helmbrecht
California Polytechnic State University

Tom Hodgkin
Northwestern Connecticut Community College

Ray Lacina
Delta College

Jeff Olma
Florida Community College at Jacksonville

Samuel Olorounto
New River Community College

Donna Potratz
MiraCosta College

Nelson C. Sager
Sul Ross State University

Anne A. Smith
Northwest Mississippi Community College

Mark N. Taylor
Berry College

Sandy Zapp
Paradise Valley Community College

My former editor Steve Pensinger needs to be remembered for steering me through four editions of this book. I am also grateful to Tim Julet and Alexis Walker for guidance through the fifth edition and to Chris Narozny, development editor of the sixth edition. My hat's off to Lisa Moore, executive editor for the sixth and seventh editions, to Christopher Bennem, sponsoring editor for the eighth edition, and to Joshua Feldman, the hardworking and dedicated developmental editor of both the seventh and eighth editions. I have been blessed with a chorus of voices enriching this text throughout its life: May you all live long and prosper!

I'll close by once again dedicating this text to my daughter Ruth who, despite her own career and interests, continues to give generously of her time, reading possible essays for each new edition. My wish for all students: May you come to understand, as Ruth does, that it is the liberal education that makes continued growth of the human spirit both possible and pleasurable.

Dorothy U. Seyler

Northern Virginia Community College

Critical Reading
and Analysis

PhotoEdit

Read: What is the situation in the photo—who are the two figures, where are they, how do they differ?

Reason: What ideas are suggested by the photo?

Reflect/Write: Why might this visual have been chosen for Chapter 1?

Writers and Their Sources

READING, WRITING, AND THE CONTEXTS OF ARGUMENT

Arguments are everywhere! Do you agree? Well, what about textbooks, you counter. They are designed to inform, not to present an argument. True—to a degree. On the other hand, the author makes choices about what's important to include and how students should go about the business of learning the material of a particular course. Even writing primarily designed to inform says to readers: Do it my way! Think about these ideas as I would! Well, what about novels or personal essays, you "argue." Surely they are not arguments. A good point—to a degree. The ideas about human life and experience that appear in works we can label "expressive" are more subtle, more indirect, than the points we meet head-on in an argument. Still, expressive writing gives us ideas or ways of seeing the world. Perhaps we need to recognize that writing strategies and purposes spread along a continuum; they do not fit into neat categories.

You can accept the larger scope of argument and still expect that in your current course on argument—or critical thinking—you probably will not be asked to write a short story or a personal essay. You might, though, be asked to write a summary or a style analysis, so you will need to think about how those writing tasks connect to the world of argument. Count on this: You will be asked to write! Why work on your writing skills? Here are some good answers to this question:

- Communication skills are the single most important skill sought by employers.
- The better a writer you become, the better reader you will become.
- The more confident a writer you become, the more efficiently you will handle written assignments in all your courses.
- The more you write, the more you will learn about who you are and what really matters to you.

You are about to face a variety of writing assignments. Pay close attention to each one so that you will know what sort of writing your instructor expects. To help you learn the conventions of different types of writing for different audiences, this text includes a variety of articles: informative essays, editorials, articles from scholarly journals, book reviews. Always think about what role each assignment calls for. Are you expected to be a student demonstrating knowledge, a citizen arguing for tougher drunk-driving laws, or a scholar presenting the results of research? Any writer—including you—will take on different roles, writing for different audiences, using different strategies to reach each audience. There are many kinds of argument and many ways to argue successfully.

RESPONSES TO SOURCES

If this is a text about *writing* arguments, why does it contain so many readings, you may wonder. There are good reasons for the collection of readings you find here:

- College and the workplace will demand that you learn complex information and ideas through reading. This text will give you practice in reading more challenging works.
- You will need to read to learn and to think critically about what you read.
- In the world of argument, your reading will serve as a basis for writing. You will be writing based in some way on a source or sources you have been assigned or have selected in response to an assignment. The focus of attention shifts from you to your subject, a subject others have debated before you. You will need to understand the issue, think carefully about the views of others on the issue, and only then develop your own response.

To understand how critical thinkers may respond to sources, let's examine "The Gettysburg Address," Abraham Lincoln's famous speech dedicating the Civil War battlefield. We can use this document to see the various ways writers respond—in writing—to the writing of others.

THE GETTYSBURG ADDRESS | ABRAHAM LINCOLN

Fourscore and seven years ago our fathers brought forth on this continent a new nation, conceived in liberty and dedicated to the proposition that all men are created equal. Now we are engaged in a great civil war, testing whether that nation, or any nation so conceived and so dedicated, can long endure. We are met on a great battlefield of that war. We have come to dedicate a portion of that field as a final resting place for those who here gave their lives that that nation might live. It is altogether fitting and proper that we should do this. But, in a larger sense, we cannot dedicate—we cannot consecrate—we cannot hallow—this ground. The brave men, living and dead, who struggled here have consecrated it far above our poor power to add or to detract. The world will little note nor long remember what we say here, but it can never forget what they did here. It is for us, the living, rather to be dedicated here to the unfinished work which they who fought here have thus far so nobly advanced. It is rather for us to be here dedicated to the great task remaining before us—that from these honored dead we take increased devotion to that cause for which they gave the last full measure of devotion; that we here highly resolve that these dead shall not have died in vain; that this nation, under God, shall have a new birth of freedom; and that government of the people, by the people, for the people shall not perish from the earth.

What Does It Say? How Could It Be Summarized or Paraphrased? THE RESPONSE TO CONTENT

Instructors often ask students to *summarize* or *paraphrase* their reading of a complex chapter, a supplementary text, a difficult poem, or a series of journal articles on library reserve. Frequently, book report assignments specify that summary and evaluation be combined. Your purpose in writing a summary is to show your understanding of the work's main ideas and of the relationships among those ideas. If you can put what you have read into your own words and focus on the text's chief points, then you have command of that material. Here is a sample restatement of Lincoln's "Address":

> Our nation was initially built on a belief in liberty and equality, but its future is now being tested by civil war. It is appropriate for us to dedicate this battlefield, but those who fought here have dedicated it better than we. We should dedicate ourselves to continue the fight to maintain this nation and its principles of government.

Sometimes it is easier to recite or quote famous or difficult works than to state, more simply and in your own words, what has been written. The ability to summarize or paraphrase reflects both reading and writing skills. For more coverage of writing summaries, see pages 13–16; for more coverage of paraphrases, see pages 16–17.

How Is It Written?
How Does It Compare with Another Work?   THE ANALYTIC RESPONSE

Summary requirements are often combined with analysis or evaluation, as in a book report. Most of the time you will be expected to *do something* with what you have read, and to summarize or paraphrase will be insufficient. Frequently you will be asked to analyze a work—that is, to explain the elements of structure and style that a writer has chosen. You will want to examine sentence patterns, organization, metaphors, and other techniques selected by the writer to convey attitude and give force to ideas. Developing your skills in analysis will make you both a better reader and a better writer.

Many writers have examined Lincoln's word choice, sentence structure, and choice of metaphors to make clear the sources of power in this speech.* Analyzing Lincoln's style, you might examine, among other elements, his effective use of *tricolon:* the threefold repetition of a grammatical structure, with the three points placed in ascending order of significance.

> Lincoln uses two effective tricolons in his brief address. The first focuses on the occasion for his speech, the dedication of the battlefield: "we cannot dedicate—we cannot consecrate—we cannot hallow. . . ." The best that the living can do is formally dedicate; only those who died there for the principle of liberty are capable of making the battlefield "hallow." The second tricolon presents Lincoln's concept of democratic government, a government "of the people, by the people, for the people." The purpose of government—"for the people"—resides in the position of greatest significance.

A second type of analysis, a comparison of styles of two writers, is a frequent variation of the analytic assignment. By focusing on similarities and differences in writing styles, you can see more clearly the role of choice in writing and may also examine the issue of the degree to which differences in purpose affect style. One student, for example, produced a thoughtful and interesting study of Lincoln's style in contrast to that of Martin Luther King, Jr., as revealed in his "I Have a Dream" speech (see pages 705–08):

> Although Lincoln's sentence structure is tighter than King's and King likes the rhythms created by repetition, both men reflect their familiarity with the King James Bible in their use of its cadences and expressions. Instead of saying eighty-seven years ago, Lincoln, seeking solemnity, selects the biblical expression "Fourscore and seven years ago." Similarly, King borrows from the Bible and echoes Lincoln when he writes "Five score years ago."

---

*See, for example, Gilbert Highet's essay, "The Gettysburg Address," in *The Clerk of Oxenford: Essays on Literature and Life* (New York: Oxford UP, 1954), to which I am indebted in the following analysis.

Is It Logical?
Is It Adequately Developed?
Does It Achieve Its Purpose? THE JUDGMENT OR EVALUATION RESPONSE

Even when the stated purpose of an essay is "pure" analysis, the analysis implies a judgment. We analyze Lincoln's style because we recognize that "The Gettysburg Address" is a great piece of writing and we want to see how it achieves its power. On other occasions, judgment is the stated purpose for close reading and analysis. The columnist who challenges a previously published editorial has analyzed the editorial and has found it flawed. The columnist may fault the editor's logic or lack of adequate or relevant support for the editorial's main idea. In each case the columnist makes a negative judgment about the editorial, but that judgment is an informed one based on the columnist's knowledge of language and the principles of good argument.

Part of the ability to judge wisely lies in recognizing each writer's purpose. It would be inappropriate to assert that Lincoln's address is weakened by its lack of facts about the battle. The historian's purpose is to record the number killed or to analyze the generals' military tactics. Lincoln's purpose was different.

> As Lincoln reflected upon this young country's being torn apart by civil strife, he saw the dedication of the Gettysburg battlefield as an opportunity to challenge the country to fight for its survival and the principles upon which it was founded. The result was a brief but moving speech that appropriately examines the connection between the life and death of soldiers and the birth and survival of a nation.

These sentences establish a basis for an analysis of Lincoln's train of thought and use of metaphors, but this analysis, and positive judgment, is grounded in an understanding of Lincoln's purpose and the context in which he spoke.

How Does It Help Me to Understand
Other Works, Ideas, Events? THE RESEARCH RESPONSE

Frequently you will read not to analyze or evaluate but rather to use the source as part of learning about a particular subject. Lincoln's address is significant for the Civil War historian both as an event of that war and as an influence on our thinking about that war. "The Gettysburg Address" is also vital to the biographer's study of Lincoln's life or to the literary critic's study either of famous speeches or of the Bible's influence on English writing styles. Thus Lincoln's brief speech is a valuable source for students in a variety of disciplines; it becomes part of their research process. Able researchers study it carefully, analyze it thoroughly, place it in its proper historical, literary, and personal contexts, and use it to develop their own arguments.

To practice reading and responding to sources, study the following article by Ellen Goodman. The exercises that follow will check your reading skills and your understanding of the various responses to reading just discussed. Use the prereading questions to become engaged with each text.

IN PRAISE OF A SNAIL'S PACE | ELLEN GOODMAN

Author of *Close to Home* (1979), *At Large* (1981), and *Keeping Touch* (1985), collections of her essays, Ellen Goodman has been a feature writer for the Boston *Globe* since 1967 and a syndicated columnist since 1976. The following column was published August 13, 2005.

PREREADING QUESTIONS Why might someone write in praise of snail mail? What does Goodman mean by "hyperactive technology"?

1   CASCO BAY, Maine—I arrive at the island post office carrying an artifact from another age. It's a square envelope, handwritten, with a return address that can be found on a map. Inside is a condolence note, a few words of memory and sympathy to a wife who has become a widow. I could have sent these words far more efficiently through e-mail than through this "snail mail." But I am among those who still believe that sympathy is diluted by two-thirds when it arrives over the Internet transom.

2   I would no more send an e-condolence than an e-thank you or an e-wedding invitation. There are rituals you cannot speed up without destroying them. It would be like serving Thanksgiving dinner at a fast-food restaurant.

3   My note goes into the old blue mailbox and I walk home wondering if slowness isn't the only way we pay attention now in a world of hyperactive technology.

4   Weeks ago, a friend lamented the trouble she had communicating with her grown son. It wasn't that her son was out of touch. Hardly. They were connected across miles through e-mail and cell phone, instant-messaging and text-messaging. But she had something serious to say and feared that an e-mail would elicit a reply that said: I M GR8. Was there no way to get undivided attention in the full in-box of his life? She finally chose a letter, a pen on paper, a stamp on envelope.

5   How do you describe the times we live in, so connected and yet fractured? Linda Stone, a former Microsoft techie, characterizes ours as an era of "continuous partial attention." At the extreme end are teenagers instant-messaging while they are talking on the cell phone, downloading music and doing homework. But adults too live with all systems go, interrupted and distracted, scanning everything, multi-technological-tasking everywhere.

6   We suffer from the illusion, Stone says, that we can expand our personal bandwidth, connecting to more and more. Instead, we end up overstimulated, overwhelmed and, she adds, unfulfilled. Continuous partial attention inevitably feels like a lack of full attention.

7   But there are signs of people searching for ways to slow down and listen up. We are told that experienced e-mail users are taking longer to answer, freeing themselves from the tyranny of the reply button. Caller ID is used to find out who we don't have to talk to. And the next "killer ap," they say, will be e-mail software that can triage the important from the trivial.

8   Meanwhile, at companies where technology interrupts creativity and on-line contact prevents face-to-face contact, there are no e-mail-free Fridays. At

others, there are bosses who require that you check your BlackBerry at the meeting door.

If a ringing cell phone once signaled your importance to a client, now that client is impressed when you turn off the cell phone. People who stayed connected 10 ways, 24-7, now pride themselves on "going dark." 9

"People hunger for more attention," says Stone, whose message has been welcomed even at a conference of bloggers. "Full attention will be the aphrodisiac of the future." 10

Indeed, at the height of our romance with e-mail, "You've Got Mail" was the cinematic love story. Now e-mail brings less thrill—"who will be there?" And more dread—"how many are out there?" Today's romantics are couples who leave their laptops behind on the honeymoon. 11

As for text-message flirtation, a young woman ended hers with a man who wrote, "C U L8R." He didn't have enough time to spell out Y-O-U? 12

Slowness guru Carl Honore began "In Praise of Slowness" after he found himself seduced by a book of condensed classic fairy tales to read to his son. One-minute bedtime stories? We are relearning that paying attention briefly is as impossible as painting a landscape from a speeding car. 13

It is not just my trip to the mailbox that has brought this to mind. I come here each summer to stop hurrying. My island is no Brigadoon: WiFi is on the way, and some people roam the island with their cell phones, looking for a hot spot. But I exchange the Internet for the country road. 14

Georgia O'Keeffe once said that it takes a long time to see a flower. No technology can rush the growth of the leeks in the garden. All the speed in the Internet cannot hurry the healing of a friend's loss. Paying attention is the coin of this realm. 15

Sometimes, a letter becomes the icon of an old-fashioned new fashion. And sometimes, in this technological whirlwind, it takes a piece of snail mail to carry the stamp of authenticity. 16

QUESTIONS FOR READING AND REASONING

1. What has Goodman just done? How does this action serve the author as a lead-in to her subject?

2. What is Goodman's main idea or thesis?

3. What examples illustrate the problem the author sees in our times? What evidence does Goodman present to suggest that people want to change the times?

4. What general solutions does Goodman suggest?

QUESTIONS FOR REFLECTING AND WRITING

1. How do the details at the beginning and end of the essay contribute to Goodman's point? Write a paragraph answer to this question. Then consider: Which one of the different responses to reading does your paragraph illustrate?

2. Goodman quotes Stone's description of our times as one of "continuous partial attention." Do you agree that this phrase aptly sums up our era? Why or why not? If you agree, do you think this is a problem? Why or why not?

3. "The Gettysburg Address" is a valuable document for several kinds of research projects. For what kinds of research projects would Goodman's essay be useful? List several possibilities; be prepared to discuss your list with classmates.

ACTIVE READING: USE YOUR MIND!

Reading is not about looking at black marks on a page—or turning the pages as quickly as we can. Reading means constructing meaning from the marks on the page, getting a message. We read with our brains, not our eyes and hands! This concept is often underscored by the term *active reading.* To help you always achieve active reading, not passive page turning, follow these guidelines.

GUIDELINES for Active Reading

- **Understand your purpose in reading.** Do not just start turning pages to complete an assignment. Think first about your purpose. Are you reading for knowledge on which you will be tested? Focus on your purpose as you read, asking yourself, "What do I need to learn from this work?"

- **Reflect on the title before reading further.** Titles are the first words writers give us. Take time to look for clues in a title that may reveal the work's subject and perhaps the writer's approach or attitude as well. Henry Fairlie's title "The Idiocy of Urban Life," for example, tells you both Fairlie's subject (urban or city living) and his position (urban living is idiotic).

- **Become part of the writer's audience.** Not all writers have you and me in mind when they write. As an active reader, you need to "join" a writer's audience by learning about the writer, about the time in which the piece was written, and about the writer's expected audience. For readings in this text you are aided by introductory notes; be sure to study them.

- **Predict what is coming.** Look for a writer's main idea or purpose statement. Study the work's organization. Then use this information to anticipate what is coming. When you read "There are three good reasons for requiring a dress code in schools," you know the writer will list *three* reasons.

- **Concentrate.** Slow down and give your full attention to reading. Watch for transition and connecting words that show you how the parts of a text connect. Read an entire article or chapter at one time—or you will need to start over to make sense of the entire piece.

- **Annotate as you read.** The more senses you use, the more active your involvement. That means marking the text as you read (or taking notes if the material is not yours). Underline key sentences, such as the writer's thesis. Then, in the margin, indicate that it is the thesis. With a series of examples (or reasons), label them and number them. When you look up a word's definition, write the definition in the margin next to the word. Draw diagrams to illustrate concepts; draw arrows to connect example to idea. Studies have shown that students who annotate their texts get higher grades. Do what successful students do.

- **Keep a reading journal.** In addition to annotating what you read, you may want to develop the habit of writing regularly in a journal. A reading journal gives you a place to note impressions and reflections on your reading, your initial reactions to assignments, and ideas you may use in your next writing.

EXERCISE: Active Reading

Read the following selection, noting the annotations that have been started for you. As you read, add your own annotations. Then write a journal entry—four to five sentences at least—to capture your reactions to the following column.

POLITICAL ADS AND THE VOTERS THEY ATTRACT | RICHARD MORIN

A journalist with the *Washington Post,* Richard Morin writes a regular Sunday column titled "Unconventional Wisdom" that presents interesting new information from the social sciences. The following column appeared November 23, 2003.

Even though it pains me to report it, those negative political advertisements designed to scare the pants off us appear to work quite well. But here's a surprise—so do those positive ads filled with happy children and cascading violins. `1` `topic`

`Note: Both types of ads work—why?`

What's the connection? Both depend on manipulating the emotions of viewers. `2`

What's more, emotion-drenched political ads are most effective among sophisticated voters, who probably would be the most chagrined to learn that they're suckers for political mudslinging and cheerleading, claims Ted Brader, a political science professor and researcher at the Institute for Social Research at the University of Michigan. `3`

"Emotions are so central to what makes us tick," Brader said. "Political scientists for years have basically ignored them. But if you think about what causes us to do anything in life, political or otherwise, there are always strong emotions involved." `4`

His study, which he is expanding into a book, began as research for his PhD at Harvard University. Brader recruited 286 voting-age men and women in 11 Massachusetts communities during the weeks leading up to the 1998 Democratic gubernatorial primary. The race pitted incumbent Attorney General Scott Harshbarger against former state senator Patricia McGovern. `5`

Test subjects were randomly assigned to one of four groups. Each group watched a half-hour local news broadcast that featured one of four seemingly genuine 30-second campaign ads that Brader had prepared. Two ads were `6` positive in tone and two were negative. The names of the candidates were alternated so that each one was featured an equal number of times in the ads.

7   The scripts for the two positive ads were identical. What was different were the accompanying sounds and images. One ad featured uplifting "cues"—symphonic music and warm, colorful images of children intended to inspire an even more enthusiastic reaction to the upbeat message—while the other used bland visual and audio enhancements.

8   The scripts for the two negative ads also were the same. But one featured tense, discordant music and grainy pictures of crime scenes to create a sense of fear. The other ad lacked the scary special effects.

9   The test subjects answered a survey before and after the experiment that measured, among other things, interest in the campaign and candidate preference. And yes, after the study the participants were let in on the secret. "They were 'debriefed' after their participation and given a written explanation that the political ads they saw were completely fictitious, made by me for the study and not by the candidates, and there was not necessarily any connection between what is said in the ads and the candidates' actual positions," Brader said.

10   It's good that he did eventually 'fess up, because the enhanced ads worked better than Brader or his faculty advisers suspected they would. When enthusiasm cues were added to a positive script, the test subjects' self-reported likelihood to vote on Election Day was a whopping 29 percentage points higher than those of subjects who saw the positive ad without the emotion-enhancing cues.

11   The negative ad with fear-inducing cues was particularly effective in persuading viewers to vote for the candidate promoted in the ad. Nearly 10 percent of those who saw the "fear" ad switched allegiance, and 20 to 25 percent were less certain of their choice after seeing their favored candidate dragged through the mud.

12   Those exposed to fear cues also could remember more details of related news stories shown in the broadcast. It also made them more likely to want to obtain more information about the candidates, suggesting one benefit to negative ads: "They may scare people into thinking" about political campaigns, Brader said.

13   Brader also found that better-informed, better-educated voters were more susceptible to fear-inducing and enthusiasm-enhancing ads than less-knowledgeable voters. "That really contradicts the traditional claim that emotional appeals work primarily on the ignorant masses," or those who are otherwise easily led, he said.

14   Why are smarties so susceptible to emotional ads? Brader doesn't know. It could be, he said, that such ads "resonate with people who are already emotional about politics to begin with because they have a vested interest."

15   For political consultants, this is news they can use. "Candidates should aim positive ads at their base of support and fear ads at undecided and opposing voters," Brader advised. "Front-runners, incumbents in times of peace and prosperity, and members of the majority party in a district should rely principally on enthusiasm. Their opponents—trailing candidates, challengers, members of the minority party—should be drawn to the use of fear."

UNDERSTANDING YOUR SOURCES

Readers expect accurate, fair, and sensitive uses of sources. An inaccurate summary does not serve its purpose. A passage that is misquoted or quoted out of context makes readers question your credibility. So, after reading and annotating, develop your understanding of a source more fully by doing a preliminary analysis that answers the following questions:

1. *What is the work's primary purpose? Does it combine purposes?* Remember that texts can be classified as expressive (evoking feelings), expository (imparting information), or persuasive (arguing for a position). We can also distinguish between a serious purpose and a humorous one, remembering that humor can be used to advance a serious topic. However, purposes shade into one another. Arguments appeal to emotions, and passionate fiction can teach us about human life and experience. You may assume that a textbook's primary purpose is to give information, but keep in mind that the textbook can take a position on various conflicts within the field.

2. *What is the thesis, the main idea of the work?* Often the best way to understand a text's thesis is to first ask, "What is the subject?" Then ask, "What does the author assert about that subject, or want me to understand about that subject?" Stating the thesis as a complete sentence will help you move from subject to assertion. You may find one or two sentences that state the work's thesis, but keep in mind that sometimes the thesis is implied, not stated.

3. *How is the thesis developed and supported?* Consider: Does the writer present a series of examples to illustrate the main idea? Or blend reasons and evidence to develop an argument? Does the writer organize chronologically? Set up a contrast pattern or make an analogy? Explain causes? Observing both the type of support and its organization will help you see how the parts fit together. When you "know what it says," you can write a summary or begin to analyze or judge the work.

WRITING SUMMARIES

Preparing a good summary is not always as easy as it looks. *A summary briefly restates, in your own words, the main points of a work in a way that does not misrepresent or distort the original.* A good summary shows your grasp of main ideas and your ability to express them clearly. You need to condense the original while giving all key ideas appropriate attention. As a student you may be assigned a summary to:

- Show that you have read and understood assigned works.
- Complete a test question.
- Have a record of what you have read for future study or to prepare for class discussion.
- Explain the main ideas in a work that you will also examine in some other way, such as in a book review or a refutation essay.

When assigned a summary, pay careful attention to word choice. Avoid judgment words, such as: "Brown then proceeds to develop the *silly* idea that. . . ." Follow these guidelines for writing good summaries.

GUIDELINES for Writing Summaries

- **Write in a direct, objective style, using your own words.** Use few, if any, direct quotations, probably none in a one-paragraph summary.
- **Begin with a reference to the writer (full name) and the title of the work and then state the writer's thesis.** (You may also want to include where and when the work was published.)
- **Complete the summary by providing other key ideas.** Show the reader how the main ideas connect and relate to one another.
- **Do not include specific examples, illustrations, or background sections.**
- **Combine main ideas into fewer sentences than were used in the original.**
- **Keep the parts of your summary in the same balance as you find in the original.** If the author devotes about 30 percent of the essay to one idea, that idea should get about 30 percent of the space in your summary.
- **Select precise, accurate verbs to show the author's relationship to ideas.** Write Jones *argues*, Jones *asserts*, Jones *believes*. Do not use vague verbs that provide only a list of disconnected ideas. Do *not* write Jones *talks about*, Jones *goes on to say*.
- **Do not make any judgments about the writer's style or ideas.** Do *not* include your personal reaction to the work.

EXERCISE: Summary

With these guidelines in mind, read the following two summaries of Ellen Goodman's "In Praise of a Snail's Pace" (see pages 8–9). Then answer the question: What is flawed or weak about each summary? To aid your analysis, (1) underline or highlight all words or phrases that are inappropriate in each summary, and (2) put the number of the guideline next to any passage that does not adhere to that guideline.

SUMMARY 1

I really thought that Goodman's essay contained some interesting ideas about modern technology. She talks about mailing a letter instead of using e-mail or text-messaging. She thinks it's better to do this when someone dies. Goodman says that we don't pay attention, and some people think cell phones should be turned off. But it would be hard for me to turn off my phone.

SUMMARY 2

In Ellen Goodman's "In Praise of a Snail's Pace" (August 13, 2005), she talks about problems with today's use of electronic communication devices—not technical problems but how people feel about communicating this way. She is on vacation in Maine to slow down, and she starts by saying that she has used a letter rather than e-mail to send a sympathy message. She wonders if e-mail is appropriate for personal messages. She says our times are "connected and yet fractured." We don't pay attention to others and get into multi-tasking. We should turn off our phones and take time to look at flowers.

Although we can agree that the writers of these summaries have read and basically understood most of Goodman's essay, we can also find weaknesses in each summary. The second summary can be greatly improved by eliminating some details, combining some ideas, and refocusing on the main idea. Here is a much-improved version of summary 2:

REVISED SUMMARY 2

In Ellen Goodman's column "In Praise of a Snail's Pace" (syndicated August 13, 2005), she asserts that we need to slow down and give more personal attention to others. We have embraced modern communications technology, believing that this makes us more connected to others, but the connection is impersonal and distant. Many, along with Goodman, see text-messaging and 24/7 electronic "connections" as interfering with the personal attention that makes relationships meaningful. She suggests that we turn off the electronic gadgets, slow down in our personal lives, and give the people who matter to us our full attention.

At times you may need to write a summary of a page or two rather than one paragraph. Frequently, long reports are preceded by a one-page summary. A longer summary may become part of an article-length review of an important book. Or instructors may want a longer summary of a lengthy or complicated article or text chapter. The following is an example of a summary of a lengthy article on cardiovascular health.

SAMPLE LONGER SUMMARY

In her article "The Good Heart," Anne Underwood (*Newsweek,* October 3, 2005) explores recent studies regarding heart disease that, in various ways, reveal the important role that one's attitudes have on physical health, especially the health of the heart. She begins with the results of a study published in the *New England Journal of Medicine* that examined the dramatic increase in cardiovascular deaths after an earthquake in Los Angeles in 1994. People who were not hurt by the quake died as a result of the fear and stress brought on by the event. As Underwood explains in detail, however, studies continue to show that psychological and social factors affect coronaries even more than sudden shocks such as earthquakes. For example, according to Dr. Michael Frenneaux, depression "at least doubles an otherwise healthy person's heart-attack risk." A Duke University study showed that high levels of hostility also raised the risk of death by heart disease. Another study showed that childhood traumas can increase heart disease risks by 30 to 70 percent. Adults currently living under work and family stress also increase their risks significantly.

How do attitudes make a difference? A number of studies demonstrate that negative attitudes, anger, and hostile feelings directly affect the chemistry of the body in ways that damage blood vessels. They also can raise blood pressure. Less directly, people with these attitudes and under stress often eat more, exercise less, and are more likely to smoke. These behaviors add to one's risk. Some physicians are seeking to use this information to increase the longevity of heart patients. They are advising weight loss and exercise, yoga and therapy, recognizing, as Underwood concludes, that "the heart does not beat in isolation, nor does the mind brood alone."

Observe the differences between the longer summary of Anne Underwood's article and the paragraph summary of Ellen Goodman's column:

- Some key ideas or terms may be presented in direct quotation.
- Results of studies may be given in some detail.
- Appropriate transitional and connecting words are used to show how the parts of the summary connect.
- The author's name is often repeated to keep the reader's attention on the article summarized, not on the author of the summary.

WRITING PARAPHRASES

Although the words *summary* and *paraphrase* are sometimes used interchangeably, they are not exact synonyms. Summary and paraphrase are alike in that they are both written responses to sources. They differ in *how* they respond and *why. Like a summary, a paraphrase is an objective restatement of someone's writing, but the purpose of a paraphrase is to clarify a complex passage or to include material from a source in your own writing.*

When using sources for research, you will incorporate some of their information and ideas in your own paper, in your own words, and with proper documentation. Usually each paraphrased passage is fairly brief and is blended in with your own thinking on the topic. Paraphrasing clearly and accurately—and documenting correctly—takes some practice. Much more discussion, together with examples and opportunities for practice, can be found in the section on research. (See pages 274–306.)

When your purpose is to clarify a poem, a complex philosophical passage, or prose filled with figurative language, your paraphrase will be longer, maybe longer than the original. Here is an example: first a passage from British philosopher Bertrand Russell's "A Free Man's Worship," followed by a paraphrase. As you read Russell's passage, underline words or phrases you find confusing. Then, as you read the paraphrase, look back to the original to see how the writer has restated Russell's ideas.

FROM "A FREE MAN'S WORSHIP" | BERTRAND RUSSELL

[F]or Man, condemned to-day to lose his dearest, tomorrow himself to pass through the gate of darkness, it remains only to cherish, ere yet the blow falls, the lofty thoughts that ennoble his little day; disdaining the coward terrors of the slave to Fate, to worship at the shrine that his own hands have built; undismayed by the empire of chance, to preserve a mind free from the wanton tyranny that rules his outward life; proudly defiant of the irresistible forces that tolerate, for a moment, his knowledge and his condemnation, to sustain alone, a weary but unyielding Atlas [someone bearing a heavy load, as Atlas did, holding up the sky on his shoulders], the world that his own ideals have fashioned despite the trampling march of unconscious power.

Paraphrase of the Passage by Russell

All that we can do, before we lose our loved ones and then face our own death, is to place value on the important ideas that mark humans as special creatures and give meaning to our lives. We must reject any fear of dying that would make us slaves to Fate and instead be proud of what we have accomplished. We must not be distressed by the powers of chance or blind luck. We must not let their control over much that happens to us keep us from maintaining a mind that is free, a mind that we use to think for ourselves. Keeping our minds free and embracing knowledge are ways to defy the powers of the universe over which we have no control. And so, even though we may at times grow weary of battling the blind forces of the universe, we continue to find strength in the interior world that we have shaped by our ideals.

Note, first, that the paraphrase is longer than the original. The goal is to clarify, not to highlight main ideas only. Second, the paraphrase clarifies the passage by turning Russell's one long sentence into several sentences and using simpler language. When you can state a writer's ideas in your own words, you have really understood the writer's ideas.

When you are asked the question "What does it say?" think about whether you need a summary or a paraphrase. When an instructor asks you to state, in your own words, the meaning of Lincoln's long concluding sentence in "The Gettysburg Address," the instructor wants a paraphrase. When an instructor asks you what an assigned essay is about, the instructor wants a summary.

ACKNOWLEDGING SOURCES INFORMALLY

You must always identify sources you are using and make clear to readers how you are using them. Even when you are not writing a formally documented paper, you must identify each source by author and title and make clear your relationship to each source. What follows are some of the conventions of writing you need to use when writing about sources.

Referring to People and Sources

Readers in academic, professional, and other serious contexts expect writers to follow specific conventions of style when referring to authors and to various kinds of sources. Study the following guidelines and examples and then mark the next few pages for easy reference—perhaps by turning down a corner of the first and last pages.

References to People

- In a first reference, give the person's full name (both the given name and the surname): *Ellen Goodman, Robert J. Samuelson.* In second and subsequent references, use only the last name (surname): *Goodman, Samuelson.*
- Do not use Mr., Mrs., or Ms. Special titles such as President, Chief Justice, or Doctor may be used in the first reference with the person's full name.
- Never refer to an author by her or his first name. Write *Dickinson,* not *Emily; Whitman,* not *Walt.*

References to Titles of Works

Titles of works must *always* be written as titles. Titles are indicated by capitalization and by either quotation marks or underlining. (In handwritten or typed papers, italic type is represented by underlining. Nonpublished works, such as your essays for courses, should contain underlining, not italic type.)

Guidelines for Capitalizing Titles

- The first and last words are capitalized.
- The first word of a subtitle is capitalized.
- All other words in titles are capitalized except
  - Articles (*a, an, the*).
  - Coordinating conjunctions (*and, or, but, for, nor, yet, so*).
  - Prepositions (*in, for, about*).

Titles Requiring Quotation Marks

Titles of works published within other works—within a book, magazine, or newspaper—are indicated by quotation marks.

Essays	"The Real Pregnancy Problem"
Short stories	"The Story of an Hour"
Poems	"To Daffodils"
Articles	"Choose Your Utopia"
Chapters	"Writers and Their Sources"
Lectures	"Crazy Mixed-Up Families"
TV episode	"Resolved: Drug Prohibition Has Failed" (one debate on the television show Firing Line)

Titles Requiring Underlining (Italics *in Print*)

Titles of works that are separate publications and, by extension, titles of items such as works of art and films are underlined.

Plays	<u>A Raisin in the Sun</u>
Novels	<u>War and Peace</u>
Nonfiction books	<u>Read, Reason, Write</u>
Book-length poems	<u>The Odyssey</u>
Magazines	<u>U.S. News & World Report</u>
Journals	<u>New England Journal of Medicine</u>
Newspapers	<u>New York Times</u>
Films	<u>The Wizard of Oz</u>
Paintings	<u>The Birth of Venus</u>
Recordings	<u>Eine Kleine Nachtmusik</u>
TV programs	<u>Nightline</u>

Read the following article (published October 3, 2005, in *Time* magazine) and respond by answering the questions that follow. Observe, as you read, how the author refers to the various sources he uses to develop the article and how he presents material from those sources. We will use this article as a guide to handling quotations.

THE GEEK SHALL INHERIT THE EARTH | LEV GROSSMAN

PREREADING QUESTIONS What does the term *geek* mean? Does the term have positive or negative associations for you?

There was a time—yes, my children, the legends are true—when J.R.R. Tolkien was not cool. Really. Very much not cool. Also video games, and Spider-Man, and the X-Men. There was a time, not even that long ago, when you could get beaten up by jocks in the woods behind the backstop for being down with the X-Men. Not that this happened to me personally. Friend of mine. Friend of mine's cousin, actually. Lives in Canada. You wouldn't know him. 1

The point is, things like that don't happen so much anymore. Over the past few years, an enormous shift has taken place in American culture, a disturbance in the Force, a rip in the fabric of space-time. What was once hopelessly geeky—video games, fantasy novels, science fiction, superheros—has now, somehow, become cool. 2

It's as if the economic hegemony of the geek in the 1990s, when high tech and the Internet were driving the economy, has somehow been converted into a cultural hegemony. Rappers and athletes trick out their Hummers with Xboxes. Supermodels insist in interviews that they used to be losers in high school. Jon Cryer—Jon Cryer? Duckie from *Pretty in Pink*?—has a hit TV show. Did we lose a war with Nerdistan? 3

4　Just ask two of the ringleaders of this bloodless, prom-dateless coup: archgeek Joss Whedon, the man behind *Buffy the Vampire Slayer* and the science-fiction movie *Serenity,* which opens this Friday; and Neil Gaiman, creator of the classic comic book *Sandman* and author of the fantasy novel *Anansi Boys,* which comes out this month. Gaiman also has a movie opening this Friday, the *Dark Crystal*–flavored fantasy *Mirrormask.* "It will be national geek day!" he says.

5　Whedon and Gaiman agree that the line between dork and non-dork has become hopelessly blurred. "When I started doing *Sandman,* I could look at a group of people lined up to get my autograph, and I knew who was my fan and who was somebody's mum there to get a signature," says Gaiman, who's English. "It doesn't work that way anymore. They're people. They're us. That's what they look like."

6　"They're a lot more attractive than I am, actually," Whedon deadpans. "Which kind of disturbs and upsets me."

7　For the ectomorphs among us, it's a great time to be alive. *Napoleon Dynamite* is a cult hit. There are women, it is said, who find *The O.C.*'s Seth Cohen sexy, and men who feel the same way about bespectacled *SNL*er Tina Fey, to say nothing of emerging *Harry Potter* hottie Emma Watson. And Orlando Bloom—hello? Dude's an elf? There are even "nerd-core" hip-hop artists, like Atlanta-based mc chris, whose *Fett's Veete* is rapped entirely from the point of view of the bounty hunter from the *Star Wars* movies. "Say my name is Boba Fett, I know my s___ is tight/Start not actin' right, you're frozen in carbonite . . ."

8　It's not hard to see how this happened. It's partly good business: nerds are highly employable, bursting with disposable income, and the entertainment industry has discovered them as a prime demographic to be marketed to, the same way it discovered teenage girls after *Titanic.* On a deeper level, there's something about the nerd's principled disdain for (or inability to abide by, same difference) ordinary social conventions that strikes Americans—a nation of nonconformists—as noble.

9　What's not clear is whether nerds are all that thrilled to be embraced by the same mainstream America that used to make them eat grass during gym class. (Again: *or so I've heard.*) "We're in this weird world," Gaiman says bemusedly. "*Anansi Boys* is coming out, and it's a fantasy novel, and it's being published as a mainstream thing. It should have been 10,000 copies, just for people who love them, who would have had to go to a science-fiction specialty shop with a cat in it just to find it."

10　Now that everybody wants to get down with the dorks, will they vanish altogether, assimilated into the mainstream the way the Borg assimilated Seven of Nine on *Star Trek: Voyager*? Will their colorful indigenous culture be lost forever, drowned in an ocean of weenie wannabes?

11　Not quite yet. "I miss a little of that element. The danger of, Oh, I'm holding this science-fiction magazine," says Whedon, who's currently slated to direct a Wonder Woman movie. "That's pretty much gone. We've been co-opted by the Man." He sighs, then brightens up a bit. "Although when I walk into a restaurant with a stack of comic books, I still do get stared at a little bit." Thank God for that. If he's lucky, maybe they'll even beat him up behind the backstop.

QUESTIONS FOR READING AND REASONING

1. What is Grossman's subject? What is his thesis? Where does he state it?
2. What reasons does Grossman offer to explain how geeks have "become cool"?
3. What examples of dorks does Grossman use to show their shift to mainstream acceptance and popularity? Who is the most famous geek of all—whom Grossman does not mention?
4. Do the nerds seem happy to be part of the cultural mainstream?
5. How does the author establish that he is a geek?
6. Explain the last sentence of the essay.
7. How does Grossman refer to the sources he uses?

PRESENTING DIRECT QUOTATIONS: A GUIDE TO FORM AND STYLE

Although most of your papers will be written in your own words and style, you will sometimes use direct quotations. Just as there is a correct form for references to people and to works, there is a correct form for presenting borrowed material in direct quotations. Study the guidelines and examples and then mark these pages, as you did the others, for easy reference.

Reasons for Using Quotation Marks

We use quotation marks in four ways:

- To indicate dialogue in works of fiction and drama.
- To indicate the titles of some kinds of works.
- To indicate the words that others have spoken or written.
- To separate ourselves from or call into question particular uses of words.

The following guidelines apply to all four uses of quotation marks, but the focus will be on the third use.

A Brief Guide to Quoting

1. Quote accurately. Do not misrepresent what someone else has written. Take time to compare what you have copied with the original, paying particular attention to spelling and punctuation.
2. Put *all* words taken from a source in quotation marks. (To take words from a source without making it clear that they are not your words is to plagiarize, a form of stealing punished in academic and professional communities.) Never change words. Always indicate deleted words with spaced dots (. . .). If you need to add words to make the meaning of a passage clear, place the added words in [square brackets], not (parentheses).

3. *Always* make the source of quoted words clear. If you do not provide the author of the quoted words, readers will have to assume that you are calling those words into question—the fourth reason for quoting. Observe that Grossman introduces his two sources, Joss Whedon and Neil Gaiman, in paragraph 4 and then repeats either Whedon or Gaiman with every quotation so that readers always know who is being quoted.

4. If you want to quote words from an author (for example, Whedon) quoted by another author (Grossman), you must make clear that you are getting Whedon's words from Grossman's article, not directly from Whedon:

   ORIGINAL: "We've been co-opted by the Man."

   INCORRECT: Speaking of dorks becoming mainstream, Whedon says that "we've been co-opted by the Man."

   CORRECT: One of Whedon's observations about the mainstreaming of dorks, quoted by Grossman, is that "we've been co-opted by the Man."

5. Place commas and periods *inside* the closing quotation mark—even when only one word is quoted:

   Grossman explains that the video games and science fiction that used to be part of the world of geeks only has now "become cool."

6. Place colons and semicolons *outside* the closing quotation mark:

   Lev Grossman argues that dorks have become mainstream in his essay "The Geek Shall Inherit the Earth": "What was once hopelessly geeky . . . has now, somehow, become cool"; however, he is not sure that all of the geek writers are entirely pleased to be mainstream.

7. Do not quote unnecessary punctuation. When you place quoted material at the end of a sentence you have written, use only the punctuation needed to complete your sentence:

   ORIGINAL: "Did we lose a war with Nerdistan?"

   INCORRECT: Grossman refers to Jon Cryer and Duckie as successful geeks and muses that perhaps "we lost a war with Nerdistan?".

   CORRECT: Grossman refers to Jon Cryer and Duckie as successful geeks and muses that perhaps "we lost a war with Nerdistan."

8. When the words you quote make up only part of your sentence, do not capitalize the first quoted word, even if it was capitalized in the original source. *Exception:* The passage you quote follows an introduction that ends with a colon:

   INCORRECT: Grossman observes that "What was once hopelessly geeky—video games, fantasy novels, science fiction, superheroes—has now, somehow, become cool."

CORRECT:	Grossman observes that "what was once hopelessly geeky—video games, fantasy novels, science fiction, superheroes—has now, somehow, become cool."
ALSO CORRECT:	Grossman explores a change in the place of geeks in modern American culture: "What was once hopelessly geeky—video games, fantasy novels, science fiction, superheroes—has now, somehow, become cool."

9. Use single quotation marks (the apostrophe key on your keyboard) to identify quoted material within quoted material:

   Grossman points out that "there are even 'nerd-core' hip-hop artists."

10. Depending on the structure of your sentence, use a colon, a comma, or no punctuation before a quoted passage. A colon provides a formal introduction to quoted passages. Use it sparingly for emphasis or to introduce a long quotation. (See the last example in item 8.) Use a comma *only* when your sentence structure requires it. Quoted words presented in a "that" clause are *not* preceded by a comma.

ORIGINAL:	"What is not clear is whether nerds are all that thrilled to be embraced by the same mainstream America that used to make them eat grass during gym class."
CORRECT:	"What is not clear," Grossman asserts, "is whether nerds are all that thrilled to be embraced by the same mainstream America that used to make them eat grass during gym class."
ALSO CORRECT:	Grossman wonders if nerds "are all that thrilled to be embraced by the same mainstream America that used to make them eat grass during gym class."

11. To keep direct quotations as brief as possible, omit irrelevant portions. Indicate missing words with ellipses (three spaced dots: . . .). For example: Grossman asserts that "what was once hopelessly geeky . . . has now, somehow, become cool." Some instructors want the ellipses placed in square brackets—[. . .]—to show that you have added them to the original, not that the ellipses were part of the original. Modern Language Association (MLA) style does not require the square brackets unless you are quoting a passage that already has ellipses as part of the passage. In that case, brackets would distinguish your omission from an omission in the original material.

12. Think about your reader.

   - When you quote, give enough context to make the quoted material clear.
   - Do not put so many bits and pieces of quoted passages into one sentence that your reader gets tired trying to follow the ideas.
   - Make sure that your sentences are both complete and correctly constructed. Quoting is not an excuse to write fragments or badly constructed sentences.

> **NOTE:** All examples of quoting given above are in the present tense. We write that "Grossman notes," "Grossman believes," "Grossman asserts." Even though his article was written in the past, we use the present tense to describe his ongoing ideas. (See Chapter 12 for a variation of this convention.)

FOR DEBATE

As you read the following article, practice active reading, including annotating the essay. Concentrate first on what the author has to say but also observe the structure or organization of the essay and the author's use of quotations and references to authors and works.

CENTURY OF FREEDOM | ROBERT J. SAMUELSON

A graduate of Harvard University, Robert Samuelson began his career as a reporter and is now a columnist whose articles are syndicated in many newspapers each week and biweekly in *Newsweek* magazine. Although he often writes about economics, Samuelson also examines political and cultural issues, especially those that have a connection to economic issues, as he does in the following column published December 22, 1999.

PREREADING QUESTIONS Why is the fate of freedom in this century "fragile"? What are some of the problems we may face trying to meet new ideas of freedom?

1   What 20th-century development most altered the human condition? There is no shortage of candidates: the automobile, antibiotics, the airplane, computers, contraceptives, radio and television, to name a few. But surely the largest advance in human well-being involves the explosion of freedom. In a century scarred by gulags, concentration camps and secret-police terror, freedom is now spreading to an expanding swath of humanity. It is not only growing but also changing—becoming more ambitious and ambiguous—in ways that might, perversely, spawn disappointment and disorder in the new century.

2   In 1900 this was unimaginable. "Freedom in the modern sense [then] existed only for the upper crust," says political sociologist Seymour Martin Lipset of George Mason University. There were exceptions—America certainly, but even its freedom was curtailed. In 1900 women could vote in only four western states. Not until the ratification of the 19th Amendment in 1920 could all women vote. In the South, a web of laws prevented black Americans from voting. It took the Voting Rights Act of 1965 to change that.

3   Elsewhere the picture was bleaker. In 1900 empires dotted the world. The British Empire contained roughly 400 million people, about a quarter of the world's population. Lesser empires were still enormous: the Austro-Hungarian, the Ottoman, the French and others. Human subjugation was the rule, not the exception.

Consider the situation now. In 1999 Freedom House—a watchdog group   4
based in Washington—classified as "free" 88 of the world's 191 countries, with
2.4 billion people or about 40 percent of the total. These nations enjoyed free
elections and traditional civil rights of speech, religion and assembly. Of
course, there are shades of gray. In this twilight zone Freedom House placed
53 countries with 1.6 billion people, because either elections or civil liberties
were compromised. Russia was "partially free"; China was "not free."

Still, the world's frame of reference has fundamentally altered. Even in   5
societies where freedoms are abused, their absence usually becomes an issue.
But freedom has not simply spread. It's also evolved, especially in the United
States. The freedom that Americans expect as they enter the 21st century is
not the same as the freedom they expected as they entered the 20th.

Traditional freedom historically meant liberation from oppression. But now   6
freedom increasingly involves "self-realization." People need, it's argued, to be
freed from whatever prevents them from becoming whoever they want to be.
There's a drift toward "positive liberty" that emphasizes "the things that government ought to do for us," says sociologist Alan Wolfe of Boston College.
This newer freedom blends into individual "rights" (for women, minorities, the
disabled) and "entitlements" (for health care, education and income support)
deemed essential for self-realization.

The broader freedom is not just American. In a new book, *Development as*   7
Freedom, the Nobel-Prize-winning economist Amartya Sen argues that "the
expansion of freedom is both the primary end and . . . principal means of development" in poorer countries. But Sen's freedom eclipses the classic political and economic freedoms. It includes "social opportunities" (expanded
education and health care), "transparency guarantees" (a lack of corruption)
and more "entitlements" (to ensure basic decency and prevent "abject misery"). Indeed, it seems to include almost anything that might advance human
well-being.

In some ways, freedom's explosion connects the century's two great con-   8
stants: war and economic progress. Deaths in World War I and World War II
are crudely reckoned at 10 million and as many as 60 million, respectively. But
these vast tragedies ultimately paid some dividends for common people, because they doomed colonial empires. Also, the nature of the wars emphasized
freedom. They were too destructive to be mere contests of nations. They had
to be about ideals. The Cold War—an ideological conflict—conveyed the
same message.

If war expanded freedom, prosperity embellished it. Since 1900 the world's   9
population has roughly quadrupled, from almost 1.6 billion to 6 billion. Meanwhile, the global production of goods and services—from food and steel to air
travel and health care—has risen 14 to 15 times, estimates economist Angus
Maddison for the Organization for Economic Cooperation and Development
in Paris. As nations grew wealthier, traditional freedom wasn't enough. People
ascended what psychologist Abraham Maslow called the human hierarchy of
needs—from food and shelter to self-esteem and spiritual needs, such as

justice and beauty. People could not (it was said) be "free" without realizing these larger yearnings.

10   Freedom's fate in the next century is fragile, in part because the very notion is now so ill-defined. Classic freedom—coupling the opportunity for success with the danger of failure—hardly ensures personal fulfillment or social order. "On the one hand, you're told you're free," says Lipset. "But on the other, you're a potential loser. And if you lose, you don't feel free." The traditional freedoms of belief and lifestyle also require, if they are not to foster anarchy, tolerance and self-restraint.

11   But at least traditional freedom is universal. Everyone can, in theory, enjoy the freedoms of speech, religion, assembly and property. This sort of freedom promises the absence of coercion. By contrast, the new freedoms of individual "rights" and "entitlements" are increasingly exclusive, can involve social competition for benefits and may mean the subtle (or not so subtle) coercion of one group by another—all tending to weaken a sense of community. The "rights" of women, gays and the disabled cannot be directly enjoyed by men, straights or the nondisabled. Financing entitlements means taxes—a form of collective coercion—by which taxpayers subsidize beneficiaries.

12   Freedom, always a combustible concept, promises to become more so, because in a world of television and the Internet, ideas glide almost spontaneously across cultural and political boundaries. The eagerness of the West to export its ideals may increasingly collide with the willingness and capacity of others to abandon or modify their own. What we value, they may fear or mishandle. Freedom is a great blessing. But it has never been easy—and never will be.

QUESTIONS FOR READING

1.   What is Samuelson's subject? What is his thesis? Is there one sentence that you think works as the essay's thesis? If so, did you underline it when annotating?

2.   Look again at paragraph 1. There is more than one sentence that could be a thesis statement. Which one is the better choice for the author's main idea? Why?

3.   How did the century's wars contribute to freedom?

4.   What is the traditional idea of freedom? What is the newer concept of freedom all about?

QUESTIONS FOR REASONING AND ANALYSIS

1.   What kind of support does Samuelson provide for the idea of the "century of freedom"? What general plan or organization does the author use?

2.   In paragraph 11, Samuelson puts the words *rights* and *entitlements* in quotation marks. Why? What point does he want to make with that strategy?

3.   This essay was written before September 11, 2001. How might the author have written the final paragraph after that date? Explain your suggested revision.

QUESTIONS FOR REFLECTING AND WRITING

1. Which of the problems mentioned in paragraphs 10, 11, and 12 most threaten freedom in the twenty-first century, in your view? Why?

2. Do you agree with Samuelson that freedom was the most significant development in the twentieth century? If so, why? If not, what development would you argue for instead? Explain and support your view. If you write, refer correctly to the author and title and present any direct quotations from Samuelson in correct form.

THEIR HEARTS AND MINDS? | DAVID RIEFF

A graduate of Princeton University, David Rieff is a senior fellow at the World Policy Institute, a contributing editor of *The New Republic* magazine, and the author of numerous articles and books, including *Slaughterhouse: Bosnia and the Failure of the West* (1995) and *At the Point of a Gun: Democratic Dreams and Armed Intervention* (2005). The following essay appeared in the *New York Times Magazine*, September 4, 2005.

PREREADING QUESTIONS How does winning "their hearts and minds" differ from "winning the war"? How are they the same?

1 With its bitter echoes of Vietnam, the expression "hearts and minds" is one that many Americans understandably use ironically rather than seriously. But if the last three years have demonstrated anything, it is that hearts and minds are essential to defeating the insurgencies that United States forces face in Iraq and, increasingly, again in Afghanistan. Whatever you think about the Iraq war, or the fight against Islamic terrorism more broadly, the move among American policymakers away from military solutions and toward political ones can only be a good thing.

2 President Bush's appointment of his longtime confidante Karen Hughes as under secretary of state for public diplomacy and public affairs, and of Dina Powell, an Egyptian-American Washington highflier, as her deputy, is perhaps the clearest sign that the administration is finally getting serious about beliefs as well as bullets. Certainly, the agenda Hughes outlined during her Senate confirmation hearings in July was ambitious. "We're involved," she told the Foreign Relations Committee, "in a generational and global struggle of ideas." She added: "I recognize the job ahead will be difficult. Perceptions do not change easily or quickly."

3 Refreshing though it was for its candor, Hughes's statement neglected the larger question: Is hostility toward the United States based largely on misperceptions of America's actions and intentions or on a genuine dislike of the power America wields around the world? It would be wonderful, of course, if the bin Ladens and al-Zarqawis drew their support primarily from the miseducation of young people in radical madrasas and the misinformation that the administration believes to be dished out on Al Jazeera. But in their equation of

hatred with ignorance, Hughes, and the rest of the Bush administration, including the president himself, may be falling into a determinist trap. Their profound belief that American ideals *should* prevail leads them to assume that these ideals *must* prevail if only they are communicated well enough.

4   To believe this, however, you must believe that there is an inevitable progress to history—a progress toward freedom. The president said as much in his second Inaugural Address, arguing that it was the United States' mission to spread such freedom throughout the world. His view is shared by many Americans. But non-Americans have become increasingly wary of this mission. Is it possible to persuade them that, as Hughes put it in her Senate testimony, the United States is "a tremendous force for good"?

5   Between the end of World War II and the fall of the Berlin Wall, a large number of people in Western Europe, the Soviet empire and elsewhere did believe this. (Latin America was, of course, the great exception.) The Bush administration has often expressed its confidence that the American mission in Iraq will eventually succeed, just as the occupations of Germany and Japan and the struggle with Soviet communism succeeded. The problem is that despite the old cliché about history repeating itself, history rarely repeats itself.

6   Able officials like Karen Hughes do not seem to have come to grips with the difficulties of waging a war of ideas against the exponents of a radically unfamiliar worldview. The administration is doubtless right to insist that, like the communists before them, the Islamists are marked by their contempt for individual liberty and by their willingness to commit mass murder in the name of some radiant future. But there is an essential distinction—one that may make the strategy that worked against the Soviet empire impotent with regard to the jihadists. Communism was a version of modernity. It valued education—above all, scientific education—and it insisted on gender equality. The United States was also committed to modernity. The conflict was thus a clash between two systems that shared certain fundamental presuppositions. And given the rank inferiority of the communist version, the belief that democracy and capitalism could and would prevail made sense.

7   But the conflict with jihadism is a contest between modernity and antimodernity, and, as we are discovering to our cost, obscurantism has a far larger constituency and a far more powerful hold on the popular imagination, certainly in the Islamic world, than most people imagined a generation ago. Jihadists have the advantage of speaking to a Muslim population that already shares many of their beliefs, whereas communists had to indoctrinate many of their constituents from scratch. Add to this the fact that, in countries like Egypt, a version of modernity has largely failed to provide ordinary people with a decent life, and the appeal of the fundamentalists is neither so difficult to explain nor so irrational as it sometimes appears.

8   Restating America's case more eloquently would certainly be a good thing. But the assumption that everyone in the world will gravitate toward a variation on American democracy if given half a chance is more likely based on wishful thinking (and, doubtless, good intentions) than on a sound and sober reading

of history. In her Senate testimony, Karen Hughes said that "people will choose freedom over tyranny and tolerance over extremism every time." Would that it were true. Of course people crave freedom, but Karen Hughes's idea of it and the Ayatollah al-Sistani's idea of it are very different. As for people unfailingly choosing tolerance, the historical perspective suggests that this has been the exception rather than the rule. An American public diplomacy that convinces itself otherwise has little chance of success, no matter how influential the person at its helm and how many resources she has at her disposal.

QUESTIONS FOR READING

1. What is the specific occasion, or event, that is the basis for the author's article?
2. What is Rieff's subject? Why is "Karen Hughes" not the appropriate answer?
3. What, according to the author, do Hughes and President Bush believe about American ideals? To win the hearts and minds of Iraqis, what must we do better?
4. How was the battle with communism after World War II different from the battle with Islamic jihadists today? List the specific differences explained by Rieff.

QUESTIONS FOR REASONING AND ANALYSIS

1. What is Rieff's thesis, the claim of his argument? Where does he present it most clearly?
2. Does Rieff prefer a military solution rather than a war for hearts and minds? How do you know?
3. Rieff writes that "of course people crave freedom." If that is so, then why is it so difficult to bring freedom and democracy to Iraq?
4. Rieff asserts that the "historical perspective" shows that people do not prefer "tolerance over extremism every time." What are some examples from history to support his statement?

QUESTIONS FOR REFLECTING AND WRITING

1. Rieff asserts that the battle in Iraq is between "modernity and antimodernity." What does he mean by this distinction? List specifics that are represented by each of these more general terms.
2. Do you agree with the author that the battle for hearts and minds will not be easy because of differences in beliefs and values? Why or why not?
3. Look again at Robert Samuelson's "Century of Freedom." Are there any points of agreement between Samuelson and Rieff? How does Rieff's discussion add to Samuelson's earlier essay? Do you think that Samuelson would agree or disagree with the key points of Rieff's argument?

1. Bill Gates has argued that e-books will replace paper books in the not-too-distant future. What are the advantages of e-books? What are the advantages of paper books? Are there any disadvantages to either type of book? Which would you prefer? How would you argue for your preference?

2. Write a one-paragraph summary of either David Rieff's or Robert Samuelson's essay. Be sure that your summary clearly states the author's main idea, the claim of his argument. Take your time and polish your word choice.

3. Read actively and then prepare a one-and-a-half-page summary of Linda J. Waite's "Social Science Finds: 'Marriage Matters'" (pages 566–73). Your readers want an accurate and balanced but much shorter version of the original because they will not be reading the original article. Explain not only what the writer's main ideas are but also how the writer develops her essay. That is, what kind of research supports the article's thesis? Pay close attention to your word choice.

GOING ONLINE

Robert Samuelson refers to the organization Freedom House. Check out its website (**www.freedomhouse.org**). For what kinds of projects might material at this Web site be useful? Select either an essay or a chart from the site, read it, and then write a brief summary.

Read: What is the situation? Who are the two men? Where are they?

Reason: What did drive the civilization mad? What is the clue that will answer the question?

Reflect/Write: What makes this cartoon clever?

CHAPTER 2

Responding Critically to Sources

In some contexts, the word *critical* carries the idea of harsh judgment: "The manager was critical of her secretary's long phone conversations." In other contexts, though, the term means to evaluate carefully. When we speak of the critical reader or critical thinker, we have in mind someone who reads actively, who thinks about issues, and who makes informed judgments. Here is a profile of the critical reader or thinker:

TRAITS OF THE CRITICAL READER/THINKER

- **Focused on the facts.**
  Give me the facts and show me that they are relevant to the issue.
- **Analytic.**
  What strategies has the writer/speaker used to develop the argument?
- **Open-minded.**
  Prepared to listen to different points of view, to learn from others.

- **Questioning/skeptical.**
  What other conclusions could be supported by the evidence presented?
  How thorough has the writer/speaker been?
  What persuasive strategies are used?
- **Creative.**
  What are some entirely different ways of looking at the issue or problem?
- **Intellectually active, not passive.**
  Willing to analyze logic and evidence.
  Willing to consider many possibilities.
  Willing, after careful evaluation, to reach a judgment, to take a stand on issues.

EXAMINING THE CONTEXT OF A SOURCE

Reading critically requires preparation. Instead of "jumping into reading," begin by asking questions about the work's total context. You need to be able to answer the following four questions before—or while—you read.

Who Is the Author?

Key questions to answer include:

- *Does the author have a reputation for honesty, thoroughness, and fairness?* Read the biographical note, if there is one; ask your instructor about the author; learn about the author in a biographical dictionary or online; try *Book Review Digest* (in your library or online) for reviews of the author's books.
- *Is the author writing within his or her area of expertise?* People can voice opinions on any subject, but they cannot transfer expertise from one subject area to another. A football player endorsing a political candidate is a citizen with an opinion, not an expert on politics.
- *Is the author identified with a particular group or set of beliefs? Does the biography place the writer in a particular institution or organization?* For example, a member of a Republican administration may be expected to favor a Republican president's policies. A Roman Catholic priest may be expected to take a stand against abortion. These kinds of details provide hints, but you should not decide, absolutely, what a writer's position is until you have read the work with care. Be alert to reasonable expectations, but avoid stereotyping a writer.

What Kind of Audience Is Addressed?

Understanding the intended audience can help you answer two questions: the depth and sophistication of the work and a possible bias or slant.

- *Does the writer expect a popular audience, a general but educated audience, or a specialized audience that will share professional expertise or cultural, political, or religious preferences?* Often you can judge the expected audience by noting the kind of publication in which an article appears or the publisher of the book. For example, *Reader's Digest* is written for a mass audience; *Psychology Today, Science,* or *Newsweek* aim for a general but more knowledgeable reader. By contrast, articles in the *New England Journal of Medicine* are written by medical doctors and research scientists for a specialized audience.

- *Does the writer expect readers who are likely to be favorable to the writer's views?* Some newspapers are fairly consistently liberal, whereas others are usually politically conservative. (Do you know the political leanings of your local paper?) The particular interests of the *Christian Science Monitor* and *Ms.* should be considered when you read articles from these sources. Remember: All arguments are "slanted" or "biased"—that is, they take a stand. That's okay. You just need to read with an awareness of a writer's particular background and interests.

What Is the Author's Purpose in Writing?

Is the piece informative or persuasive in intent? Designed to entertain or to be inspiring? Think about the title; read a book's preface to learn of the author's goals; pay attention to tone as you read.

What Are the Writer's Sources of Information?

Some questions to ask about sources include: Where was the information obtained? Is it still valid? Are sources clearly identified? Be suspicious of writers who want us to believe that their unnamed "sources" are "reliable." Pay close attention to dates. A biography of King George III published in 1940 may still be the best source. An article urging the curtailing of county growth based on population statistics from the 1980s is no longer reliable.

EXERCISES: Examining the Context

1. What can you judge about the reliability or bias of the following? Consider author, audience, and purpose.
    a. An article on the Republican administration, written by a former campaign worker for a Democratic presidential candidate.
    b. A discussion, published in the Boston *Globe,* of the Patriots' hope for the next Super Bowl.
    c. A letter to the editor about conservation, written by a member of the Sierra Club. (What is the Sierra Club? Study some of its publications or check out its website to respond to this topic.)
    d. A column in *Newsweek* on economics. (Look at the business section of *Newsweek.* Your library has the magazine.)
    e. A 1948 article in *Nutrition Today* on the best diets.

     f.   A biography of Benjamin Franklin published by Oxford University Press.

     g.   A *Family Circle* article about a special vegetarian diet written by a doctor. (Who is the audience for this magazine? Where is it sold?)

     h.   A pamphlet by Jerry Lewis urging you to contribute to a fund to combat muscular dystrophy.

     i.   A discussion of abortion in *Ms.* magazine.

     j.   An editorial in your local newspaper entitled "Stop the Highway Killing."

2.   Analyze an issue of your favorite magazine. Look first at the editorial pages and articles written by the staff, then at articles contributed by other writers. Answer these questions for both staff writers and contributors:

     a.   Who is their audience?

     b.   What is the purpose of the articles and of the entire magazine?

     c.   What type of article dominates the issue?

     d.   Describe their style and tone. How appropriate are the style and tone?

3.   Select one environmental Web site and study what is offered. The EnviroLink Network (**www.envirolink.org**) will lead you to many sites. Another possibility is the Nature Conservancy (**www.tnc.org**). Write down the name of the site you chose and its uniform resource locator (URL). Then answer these questions:

     a.   Who is the intended audience?

     b.   What seems to be the primary purpose or goal of the site?

     c.   What type of material seems to dominate the site?

     d.   For what kinds of writing assignments might you use material from the site?

UNDERSTANDING ATTITUDE

Critical readers read for implication and are alert to tone or nuance. When you read, think about not just *what* is said but *how* it is said. Consider the following excerpt:

> What happened to the War on Drugs? Did Bush—the old man, not the son— think that we actually *won* that war? Or did he confuse the War on Drugs with the stupid Gulf War he's so proud of winning? Well, he never did understand "the vision thing."

First, we recognize that the writer's subject is the War on Drugs, an expression used to refer to government programs to reduce drug use. Second, we understand that the writer does not believe that the war has been won; rather, we still have a drug problem that we need to address. We know this from the second sentence, the rhetorical question that we answer by thinking that maybe Bush thought the drug problem had been solved but the writer—and we—know better. What else do you observe in this passage? What is the writer's attitude toward George Bush? Note the writer's language. The former president is "the old man." He is proud of winning a "stupid" war. He, by implication, is stupid to think that he helped win the War on Drugs. And, finally, we are reminded of Bush's own words that he didn't have a vision of what he wanted to do as president.

How would you rewrite the passage to make it more favorable to Bush? Here is one version that students wrote to give the passage a positive attitude toward Bush:

> What has happened to the War on Drugs? Did some members of President George Bush's administration think that government policies had been successful in reducing drug use? Or did the administration change its focus to concentrate on winning the Gulf War? Perhaps, in retrospect, President Bush should have put more emphasis on the war against drugs.

The writers have not changed their position that the War on Drugs has not been won—yet they have greatly altered our outlook on the subject. This version suggests that the failure to win the drug war was the fault of Bush's administration, not of Bush himself, and that perhaps the failure is understandable given the need to focus attention on the Gulf War. In addition, references to the former president treat him with dignity. What is the difference in the two passages? Only the word choice.

Denotative and Connotative Word Choice

The students' ability to rewrite the passage on the War on Drugs to give it a positive attitude tells us that, although some words may have similar meanings, they cannot always be substituted for one another without changing the message. Words with similar meanings have similar *denotations*. Often, though, words with similar denotations do not have the same connotations. A word's *connotation* is what the word suggests, what we associate the word with. The words *house* and *home,* for example, both refer to a building in which people live, but the word *home* suggests ideas—and feelings—of family and security. Thus the word *home* has a strong positive connotation. *House* by contrast brings to mind a picture of a physical structure only because the word doesn't carry any "emotional baggage."

We learn the connotations of words the same way we learn their denotations—in context. Most of us, living in the same culture, share the same connotative associations of words. At times, the context in which a word is used will affect the word's connotation. For example, the word *buddy* usually has positive connotations. We may think of an old or trusted friend. But when an unfriendly person who thinks a man may have pushed in front of him says, "Better watch it, *buddy,*" the word has a negative connotation. Social, physical, and language contexts control the connotative significance of words. Become more alert to the connotative power of words by asking what words the writers could have used instead.

> **NOTE:** Writers make choices; their choices reflect and convey their attitudes. *Studying the context in which a writer uses emotionally charged words is the only way to be sure that we understand the writer's attitude.*

EXERCISES: Connotation

1. For each of the following words or phrases, list at least two synonyms that have a more negative connotation than the given word:
   a. child
   b. persistent
   c. thin
   d. a large group
   e. scholarly
   f. trusting
   g. underachiever
   h. quiet

2. For each of the following words, list at least two synonyms that have a more positive connotation than the given word:
   a. notorious
   b. fat
   c. politician
   d. old (people)
   e. fanatic
   f. reckless
   g. sot
   h. cheap

3. Read the following paragraph and decide how the writer feels about the activity described. Note the choice of details and the connotative language that make you aware of the writer's attitude.

   Needing to complete a missed assignment for my physical education class, I dragged myself down to the tennis courts on a gloomy afternoon. My task was to serve five balls in a row into the service box. Although I thought I had learned the correct service movements, I couldn't seem to translate that knowledge into a decent serve. I tossed up the first ball, jerked back my racket, swung up on the ball—clunk—I hit the ball on the frame. I threw up the second ball, brought back my racket, swung up on the ball—ping—I made contact with the strings, but the ball dribbled down on my side of the net. I trudged around the court, collecting my tennis balls; I had only two of them.

4. Write a paragraph describing an activity that you liked or disliked without saying how you felt. From your choice of details and use of connotative language, convey your attitude toward the activity. (The paragraph in exercise 3 is your model.)

5. Select one of the words listed below and explain, in a paragraph, what the word connotes to you personally. Be precise; illustrate your thoughts with details and examples.
   a. nature
   b. mother
   c. romantic
   d. nerd
   e. playboy
   f. artist

COLLABORATIVE EXERCISES: On Connotation

1. List all of the words you know for *human female* and for *human male*. Then classify them by connotation (positive, negative, neutral) and by level of usage (formal, informal, slang). Is there any connection between type of connotation and level of usage? Why are some words more appropriate in some social contexts than in others? Can you easily list more negative words used for one sex than for the other? Why?

2. Some words can be given a different connotation in different contexts. First, for each of the following words, label its connotation as positive, negative, or neutral. Then, for each word with a positive connotation, write a sentence in which the word would convey a more negative connotation. For each word with a negative connotation, write a sentence in which the word would suggest a more positive connotation.

   a. natural   d. free
   b. old   e. chemical
   c. committed   f. lazy

3. Each of the following groups of words might appear together in a thesaurus, but the words actually vary in connotation. After looking up any words whose connotation you are unsure of, write a sentence in which each word is used correctly. Briefly explain why one of the other words in the group should not be substituted.

   a. brittle, hard, fragile   d. strange, remarkable, bizarre
   b. quiet, withdrawn, glum   e. thrifty, miserly, economical
   c. shrewd, clever, cunning

Recognizing Tone

Closely related to a writer's attitude is the writer's tone. We can describe a writer's attitude toward the subject as positive, negative, or (rarely) neutral. Attitude is the writer's position on, or feelings about, his or her subject. The way that attitude is expressed—the voice we hear and the feelings conveyed through that voice—is the writer's *tone*. Writers can choose to express attitude through a wide variety of tones. We may reinforce a negative attitude through an angry, somber, sad, mocking, peevish, sarcastic, or scornful tone. A positive attitude may be revealed through an enthusiastic, serious, sympathetic, jovial, light, or admiring tone. We cannot be sure that just because a writer selects a light tone, for example, the attitude must be positive. Humor columnists such as Dave Barry often choose a light tone to examine serious social and political issues. Given their subjects, we recognize that the light and amusing tone actually conveys a negative attitude toward the topic.

COLLABORATIVE EXERCISES: On Tone

With your class partner or in small groups, examine the following three paragraphs, which are different responses to the same event. First, decide on each writer's attitude. Then describe, as precisely as possible, the tone of each paragraph.

1. It is tragically inexcusable that this young athlete was not examined fully before he was allowed to join the varsity team. The physical examinations given were unbelievably sloppy. What were the coach and trainer thinking of not to insist that each youngster be examined while undergoing physical stress? Apparently they were not thinking about our boys at all. We can no longer trust our sons and our daughters to this inhumane system so bent on victory that it ignores the health—indeed the very lives—of our children.

2. It was learned last night, following the death of varsity fullback Jim Bresnick, that none of the players was given a stress test as part of his physical examination. The oversight was attributed to laxness by the coach and trainer, who are described today as being "distraught." It is the judgment of many that the entire physical education program must be reexamined with an eye to the safety and health of all students.

3. How can I express the loss I feel over the death of my son? I want to blame someone, but who is to blame? The coaches, for not administering more rigorous physical checkups? Why should they have done more than other coaches have done before or than other coaches are doing at other schools? My son, for not telling me that he felt funny after practice? His teammates, for not telling the coaches that my son said he did not feel well? Myself, for not knowing that something was wrong with my only child? Who is to blame? All of us and none of us. But placing blame will not return my son to me; I can only pray that other parents will not have to suffer so. Jimmy, we loved you.

ANALYZING STYLE

We have begun the process of understanding attitude by becoming more aware of context and connotation and more alert to tone. Tone is created and attitude conveyed primarily through word choice and sentence structure but also through several other techniques.

Word Choice

In addition to responding to a writer's choice of connotative language, observe the *level of diction* used. Are the writer's words primarily typical of conversational language or of a more formal style? Does the writer use slang words or technical words? Is the word choice concrete and vivid or abstract and intellectual? These differences help to shape tone and affect our response to what we read. Lincoln's word choice in "The Gettysburg Address" (see page 5) is formal and abstract. Lincoln writes: "on this continent" rather than "in this land," "we take increased devotion" rather than "we become more committed." Another style, the technical, will be found in some articles in this text. The social scientist may write that "the child . . . is subjected to extremely punitive discipline," whereas a nonspecialist, more informally, might write that "the child is controlled by beatings or other forms of punishment."

One way to create an informal style is to choose simple words: *land* instead of *continent*. To create greater informality, a writer can use contractions: *we'll* for *we will*. There are no contractions in "The Gettysburg Address."

> **NOTE:** In your academic and professional writing, you should aim for a style informal enough to be inviting to readers but one that, in most cases, avoids contractions or slang words.

Sentence Structure

The eighteenth-century satirist Jonathan Swift once said that writing well was a simple matter of putting "proper words in proper places." Writers need to think not just about the words they choose but also about their arrangement into sentence patterns. Studying a writer's sentence patterns will reveal how they affect style and tone. When analyzing these features, consider the following questions:

1. *Are the sentences generally long or short, or varied in length?*
Are the structures primarily:

- *Simple* (one independent clause)
  In 1900 empires dotted the world.
- *Compound* (two or more independent clauses)
  Women make up only 37 percent of television characters, yet women make up more than half of the population.
- *Complex* (at least one independent and one dependent clause)
  As nations grew wealthier, traditional freedom wasn't enough.

Sentences that are both long and complex create a more formal style. Long compound sentences joined by *and* do not increase formality much because such sentences are really only two or more short, simple patterns hooked together. On the other hand, a long "simple" sentence with many modifiers will create a more formal style. The following example, from an essay on leadership by Michael Korda, is more complicated than the sample compound sentence above:

- *Expanded simple sentence*
  [A] leader is like a mirror, reflecting back to us our own sense of purpose, putting into words our own dreams and hopes, transforming our needs and fears into coherent policies and programs.

In "The Gettysburg Address" three sentences range from 10 to 16 words, six sentences from 21 to 29 words, and the final sentence is an incredible 82 words. All but two of Lincoln's sentences are either complex or compound-complex sentences. By contrast, in "Century of Freedom," Robert Samuelson, who does have a number of longish sentences, especially when he is quoting others, includes a paragraph (5) with five sentences. These five sentences are composed of 9, 13, 6, 8, and 25 words. The second and fifth sentences are complex in structure—note the greater number of words as well—but the other three are all simple sentences.

2. *Does the writer use sentence fragments (incomplete sentences)?*
Although many instructors struggle to rid student writing of fragments, professional writers know that the occasional fragment can be used effectively for emphasis. Science fiction writer Bruce Sterling, thinking about the "melancholic beauty" of a gadget no longer serving any purpose, writes:

- Like Duchamp's bottle-rack, it becomes a found objet d'art. A metallic fossil of some lost human desire. A kind of involuntary poem.

The second and third sentences are, technically, fragments, but because they build on the structure of the first sentence, readers can add the missing words *It becomes* to complete each sentence. The brevity, repetition of structure, and involvement of the reader to "complete" the fragments all contribute to a strong conclusion to Sterling's paragraph.

3. *Does the writer seem to be using an overly simplistic style? If so, why?*

Overly simplistic sentence patterns, just like an overly simplistic choice of words, can be used to show that the writer thinks the subject is silly or childish or insulting. In one of her columns, Ellen Goodman objects to society's over-simplifying of addictions and its need to believe in quick and lasting cures. She makes her point with reference to two well-known examples—but notice her technique:

- Hi, my name is Jane and I was once bulimic but now I am an exercise guru . . .
- Hi, my name is Oprah and I was a food addict but now I am a size 10.

4. *Does the writer use parallelism (coordination) or antithesis (contrast)?*

When two phrases or clauses are parallel in structure, the message is that they are equally important. Look back at Korda's expanded simple sentence. He coordinates three phrases, asserting that a leader is like a mirror in these three ways:

- Reflects back our purpose
- Puts into words our dreams
- Transforms our needs and fears

Antithesis creates tension. A sentence using this structure says "not this" but "that." Lincoln uses both parallelism and antithesis in one striking sentence:

- The world will little note nor long remember
      <u>what</u> we say here,
   but it [the world] can never forget
      <u>what</u> they did here.

Metaphors

When Korda writes that a leader is like a mirror, he is using a *simile*. When Lincoln writes that the world will not remember, he is using a *metaphor*—actually *personification*. Metaphors, whatever their form, all make a comparison between two items that are not really alike. The writer is making a *figurative comparison*, not a literal one. The writer wants us to think about some ways in which the items are similar. Metaphors state directly or imply the comparison; similes express the comparison using a connecting word; personification always compares a nonhuman item to humans. The exact label for a metaphor is not as important as:

- Recognizing the use of a figure of speech
- Identifying the two items being compared
- Understanding the point of the comparison
- Grasping the emotional impact of the figurative comparison.

> **REMEMBER:** We need to pay attention to writers' choices of metaphors. They reveal much about their feelings and perceptions of life. And, like connotative words, they affect us emotionally even if we are not aware of their use. Become aware. Be able to "open up"—explain—metaphors you find in your reading.

EXERCISE: Opening Up Metaphors

During World War II, E. B. White, the essayist and writer of children's books, defined the word *democracy* in one of his *New Yorker* columns. His definition contains a series of metaphors. One is: Democracy "is the hole in the stuffed shirt through which the sawdust slowly trickles." We can open up or explain the metaphor this way:

> Just as one can punch a hole in a scarecrow's shirt and discover that there is only sawdust inside, nothing to be impressed by, so the idea of equality in a democracy "punches" a hole in the notion of an aristocratic ruling class and reveals that aristocrats, underneath, are ordinary people, just like you and me.

Here are two more of White's metaphors on democracy. Open up each one in a few sentences.

> Democracy is "the dent in the high hat."
> Democracy is "the score at the beginning of the ninth."

Organization and Examples

Two other elements of writing, organization and choice of examples, also reveal attitude and help to shape the reader's response. When you study a work's organization, ask yourself questions about both placement and volume. Where are these ideas placed? At the beginning or end—the places of greatest emphasis—or in the middle, suggesting that they are less important? With regard to volume, ask yourself, "What parts of the discussion are developed at length? What points are treated only briefly? *Note:* Sometimes simply counting the number of paragraphs devoted to the different parts of the writer's subject will give you a good understanding of the writer's main idea and purpose in writing.

Repetition

Well-written, unified essays will contain some repetition of key words and phrases. Some writers go beyond this basic strategy and use repetition to produce an effective cadence, like a drum beating in the background, keeping time to the speaker's fist pounding the lectern. In his repetition of the now-famous phrase "I have a dream," Martin Luther King, Jr., gives emphasis to his vision of an ideal America (see pages 705–08). In the following paragraph a student tried her hand at repetition to give emphasis to her definition of liberty:

> Liberty is having the right to vote and not having other laws which restrict that right; it is having the right to apply to the university of your choice without being rejected because of race. Liberty exists when a gay man has the right to a teaching position and is not released from the position when the news of his orientation is disclosed. Liberty exists when a woman who has been offered a job does not have to decline for lack of access to day care for her children, or when a 16-year-old boy from a ghetto can get an education and is not instead compelled to go to work to support his needy family.

These examples suggest that repetition generally gives weight and seriousness to writing and thus is appropriate when serious issues are being discussed in a forceful style.

Hyperbole, Understatement, and Irony

Grace Lichtenstein chose as the title of her book on college sports: *Playing for Money.* Now, college athletes do play, but presumably not for money. The title emphasizes that these "games" are serious business, not "play," for the athletes, coaches, and colleges. The bringing together of words that presumably do not go together—"play" and "money"—ironically underscores the problems in college athletics that Lichtenstein examines.

Quotation Marks, Italics, and Capital Letters

Several visual techniques can also be used to give special attention to certain words. A writer can place a word or phrase in quotation marks and thereby question its validity or meaning in that context. Ellen Goodman writes, for example:

- I wonder about this when I hear the word "family" added to some politician's speech.

Goodman does not agree with the politician's meaning of the word *family,* as she reveals in her essay, but we know this immediately from her use of quotation marks. The expression *so-called* has the same effect:

- There has been a crackdown on the Chinese people's *so-called* liberty.

Italicizing (underscoring when typing) a key word or phrase also gives added emphasis. Dave Barry, in his essay printed below, uses italics for emphasis:

- Do you want appliances that are smarter than you? Of course not. Your appliances should be *dumber* than you, just like your furniture, your pets and your representative in Congress.

Capitalizing words not normally capitalized has the same effect of giving emphasis. As with exclamation points, writers need to use italics or capitalization sparingly, or the emphasis sought through contrast will be lost.

EXERCISES: Recognizing Elements of Style

1. Name the technique or techniques used in each of the following passages. Then briefly explain the idea of each passage.
    a. We are becoming the tools of our tools. (Henry David Thoreau)
    b. The bias and therefore the business of television is to *move* information, not collect it. (Neil Postman)
    c. If guns are outlawed, only the government will have guns. Only the police, the secret police, the military. The hired servants of our rulers. Only the government—and a few outlaws. (Edward Abbey)
    d. Having read all the advice on how to live 900 years, what I think is that eating a tasty meal once again will surely doom me long before I reach 900 while not eating that same meal could very well kill me. It's enough to make you reach for a cigarette! (Russell Baker)
    e. If you are desperate for a quick fix, either legalize drugs or repress the user. If you want a civilized approach, mount a propaganda campaign against drugs. (Charles Krauthammer)
    f. Oddly enough, the greatest scoffers at the traditions of American etiquette, who scorn the rituals of their own society as stupid and stultifying, voice respect for the customs and folklore of Native Americans, less industrialized people, and other societies they find more "authentic" than their own. (Judith Martin)
    g. Text is story. Text is event, performance, special effect. Subtext is ideas. It's motive, suggestions, visual implications, subtle comparisons. (Stephen Hunter)
    h. This flashy vehicle [the school bus] was as punctual as death: seeing us waiting at the cold curb, it would sweep to a halt, open its mouth, suck the boy in, and spring away with an angry growl. (E. B. White)
2. Read the following essay by Dave Barry. Use the questions that precede and follow the essay to help you determine Barry's attitude toward his subject and to characterize his style.

REMOTE CONTROL | DAVE BARRY

A humor columnist for the *Miami Herald* since 1983, Dave Barry is now syndicated in more than 150 newspapers. A Pulitzer Prize winner in 1988, Barry has written several books, including *Dave Barry Slept Here* (1989). The following column appeared in March 2000.

PREREADING QUESTIONS   What is Barry's purpose in writing? What does he want to accomplish in this column—besides being funny?

1   Recently the *Washington Post* printed an article explaining how the appliance manufacturers plan to drive consumers insane.

2   Of course they don't *say* they want to drive us insane. What they *say* they want to do is have us live in homes where "all appliances are on the Internet, sharing information" and appliances will be "smarter than most of their owners." For example, the article states, you could have a home where the dishwasher "can be turned on from the office" and the refrigerator "knows when it's out of milk" and the bathroom scale "transmits your weight to the gym."

3   I frankly wonder whether the appliance manufacturers, with all due respect, have been smoking crack. I mean, did they ever stop to ask themselves *why* a consumer, after loading a dishwasher, would go to the office to start it? Would there be some kind of career benefit?

4   YOUR BOSS: What are you doing?

5   YOU (tapping computer keyboard): I'm starting my dishwasher!

6   YOUR BOSS: That's the kind of productivity we need around here!

7   YOU: Now I'm flushing the upstairs toilet!

8   Listen, appliance manufacturers: We don't *need* a dishwasher that we can communicate with from afar. If you want to improve our dishwashers, give us one that senses when people leave dirty dishes on the kitchen counter, and shouts at them: *"Put those dishes in the dishwasher right now or I'll leak all over your shoes!"*

9   Likewise, we don't need a refrigerator that knows when it's out of milk. We already have a foolproof system for determining if we're out of milk: We ask our wife. What we could use is a refrigerator that refuses to let us open its door when it senses that we are about to consume our fourth Jell-O Pudding Snack in two hours.

10   As for a scale that transmits our weight to the gym: Are they *nuts?* We don't want our weight transmitted to our own *eyeballs!* What if the gym decided to transmit our weight to all these other appliances on the Internet? What if, God forbid, our refrigerator found out what our weight was? We'd never get the door open again!

11   But here is what really concerns me about these new "smart" appliances: Even if we like the features, we won't be able to use them. We can't use the appliance features we have *now.* I have a feature-packed telephone with 43 buttons, at least 20 of which I am afraid to touch. This phone probably can communicate with the dead, but I don't know how to operate it, just as I don't know how to operate my TV, which has features out the wazooty and requires *three* remote controls. One control (44 buttons) came with the TV; a second (39 buttons) came with the VCR; the third (37 buttons) was brought here by the cable man, who apparently felt that I did not have enough buttons.

12   So when I want to watch TV, I'm confronted with a total of 120 buttons, identified by such helpful labels as PIP, MTS, DBS, F2, JUMP and BLANK. There are three buttons labeled power, but there are times—especially if my son and his friends, who are not afraid of features, have changed the settings—when I honestly cannot figure out how to turn the TV on. I stand there, holding three

remote controls, pressing buttons at random, until eventually I give up and go turn on the dishwasher. It has been, literally, years since I have successfully recorded a TV show. That is how "smart" my appliances have become.

And now the appliance manufacturers want to give us even *more* features. 13 Do you know what this means? It means that some night you'll open the door of your "smart" refrigerator, looking for a beer, and you'll hear a pleasant, cheerful voice—recorded by the same woman who informs you that Your Call Is Important when you call a business that does not wish to speak with you personally—telling you: "Your celery is limp." You will not know how your refrigerator knows this, and, what is worse, you will not know who else your refrigerator is telling about it ("Hey, Bob! I hear your celery is limp!"). And if you want to try to make the refrigerator *stop*, you'll have to decipher Owner's Manual instructions written by and for nuclear physicists ("To disable the Produce Crispness Monitoring feature, enter the Command Mode, then select the Edit function, then select Change Vegetable Defaults, then assume that Train A leaves Chicago traveling westbound at 47 mph, while Train B . . .").

Is this the kind of future you want, consumers? Do you want appliances 14 that are smarter than you? Of course not. Your appliances should be *dumber* than you, just like your furniture, your pets and your representatives in Congress. So I am urging you to let the appliance industry know, by phone, letter, fax and e-mail, that when it comes to "smart" appliances, you vote no. You need to act quickly. Because while you're reading this, your microwave oven is voting YES.

QUESTIONS FOR READING AND REASONING

1. After thinking about Barry's subject and purpose, what do you conclude to be his thesis? Does he have more than one main idea?

2. How would you describe the essay's tone? Serious? Humorous? Ironic? Angry? Something else? Does a nonserious tone exclude the possibility of a degree of serious purpose? Explain your answer.

QUESTIONS FOR REFLECTING AND WRITING

1. What passages in the article do you find funniest? Why?

2. What strategies does Barry use to create tone and convey attitude? List, with examples, as many as you can.

WRITING ABOUT STYLE

What does it mean to "do a style analysis"? A style analysis answers the question "How is it written?" Let's think through the steps in preparing a study of a writer's choice and arrangement of language.

Understanding Purpose and Audience

A style analysis is not the place for challenging the ideas of the writer. A style analysis requires the discipline to see how a work has been put together *even if you disagree with the writer's views.* You do not have to agree with a writer to appreciate his or her skill in writing. A style analysis may imply, or even express, a positive evaluation of the author's writing—but that is not the same as agreeing or disagreeing with the author's ideas.

If you think about audience in the context of your purpose, you should conclude that a summary of content does not belong in a style analysis. Why? Because we write style analyses for people who have already read the work. Remember, though, that your reader may not know the work in the detail that you know it, so you will need to give examples to illustrate the points of your analysis.

Planning the Essay

First, organize your analysis according to elements of style, not according to the organization of the work. Scrap any thoughts of "hacking" your way through the essay, commenting on the work paragraph by paragraph. This approach invites summary rather than analysis. It also means that you have not selected an organization that supports your purpose in writing. Think of an essay as like the pie in Figure 2.1. We could divide the pie according to key ideas—if we were summarizing. But we can also carve the pie according to elements of style, the techniques we have discussed in this chapter. This is the general plan you want to follow for your essay.

So, you need to select those techniques you think are most important in creating the writer's attitude and to discuss them one at a time. Do not try to include the entire pie; instead, select three or four elements to examine in

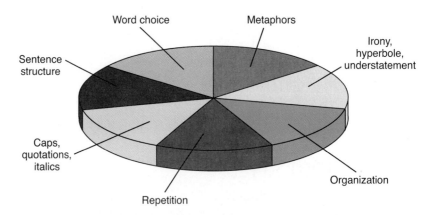

FIGURE 2.1 Analyzing Style

some detail. If you were asked to write an analysis of the Dave Barry column, for example, you might select his use of italics and quotation marks, his use of hyperbole, and his use of irony. These are three techniques that stand out in Barry's writing.

Drafting the Style Analysis

If you were to select three elements of style, as in the Dave Barry example above, your essay might look something like this:

Paragraph 1: Introduction	1. Attention-getter 2. Author, title, publication information of article/book 3. Brief explanation of author's subject 4. Your thesis—that you will be looking at style
Paragraph 2: First body paragraph	Analysis of italics and quotation marks. (See below for more details on body paragraphs.)
Paragraph 3: Second body paragraph	1. Topic sentence that introduces analysis of hyperbole 2. Three or more examples of hyperbole 3. Explanation of how each example connects to the author's thesis—that is, how the example of hyperbole works to convey attitude. This is your analysis; don't forget it!
Paragraph 4: Third body paragraph	Analysis of irony—with same three parts as illustrated above.
Paragraph 5: Conclusion	Restate your thesis: We can understand Barry's point through a study of these three elements of his style.

A CHECKLIST FOR REVISION

When revising and polishing your draft, use these questions to complete your essay.

- ☐ Have I handled all titles correctly?
- ☐ Have I correctly referred to the author?
- ☐ Have I used quotation marks correctly when presenting examples of style? (Use the guidelines in Chapter 1 for these first three questions.)

☐ Do I have an accurate, clear presentation of the author's subject and thesis?

☐ Do I have enough examples of each element of style to show my readers that these elements are important?

☐ Have I connected examples to the author's thesis? That is, have I shown my readers how these techniques work to develop the author's attitude?

To reinforce your understanding of style analysis, read the following essay by Ellen Goodman, answer the questions that follow, and then study the student essay that analyzes Goodman's style.

CHOOSING FAMILIES | ELLEN GOODMAN

Author of *Close to Home* (1979), *At Large* (1981), and *Keeping Touch* (1985), collections of her essays, Ellen Goodman has been a feature writer for the Boston *Globe* since 1967 and a syndicated columnist since 1976. She has won a Pulitzer Prize for distinguished commentary. The following column was published on November 24, 1988.

PREREADING QUESTIONS What is Goodman's subject? Why is it incorrect to say that her subject is Thanksgiving?

1   BOSTON—They will celebrate Thanksgiving the way they always do, in the Oral Tradition. Equal parts of food and conversation. A cornucopia of family.

2   These are not restrained people who choose their words and pick at their stuffing. These are people who have most of their meals in small chicken-sized households. But when they come together, they feast on the sounds as well as tastes of a turkey-sized family.

3   Indeed, their Thanksgiving celebrations are as crowded with stories as their tables are with chairs. Arms reach indelicately across each other for second helpings, voices interrupt to add relish to a story. And there are always leftovers too enormous to complete, that have to be wrapped up and preserved.

4   But what is it that makes this collection of people a family? How do we make a family these days? With blood? With marriage? With affection? I wonder about this when I hear the word "family" added to some politician's speech like gravy poured over the entire plate. The meaning is supposed to be obvious, self-evident. It is assumed that when we talk about family we are all talking about the same thing. That families are the same. But it's not that simple.

5   For the past eight years, the chief defender of the American family has lived in the White House. But Reagan's own family has always looked more like our contemporary reality than his traditional image. There has been marriage and divorce among the Reagans, adoption and blending, and more than one estrangement. There is a mother, this holiday season, who hasn't talked to her daughter for more than a year.

The man who will take his place as head of this family ideology has 6
wrapped himself in a grandfatherly image. Yet Bush's family is also extended in
ways that are common but not always comforting to other Americans.

As young people, George and Barbara Bush left home again and again, 7
setting up temporary quarters in 17 cities. Now they have five children scattered in an equal number of states: Texas and Florida, Colorado, Virginia and
Connecticut. Theirs, like many of ours, do not live at home, but come home,
for the holidays.

We hold onto a particular primal image of families—human beings created 8
from the same genetic code, living in the same area code. We hold onto an
image of *the* family as something rooted and stable. But that has always been
rare in a country where freedom is another word for mobility, both emotional
and physical.

In America, families are spliced and recombined in as many ways as DNA. 9
Every year our Thanksgiving tables expand and contract, place settings are removed and added. A guest last year is a member this year. A member last year
may be an awkward outsider this year. How many of our children travel between alienated halves of their heritage, between two sets of people who
share custody of their holidays?

Even among those families we call stable or intact, the ride to the airport 10
has become a holiday ritual as common as pumpkin pie. Many parents come
from retirement homes, many children from college, many cousins from jobs
in other Zip Codes. We retrieve these people, as if from a memory hole, for
reunions.

What then makes a family, in the face of all this "freedom"? It is said that 11
people don't choose their parents. Or their aunts and uncles. But in a sense
Americans do choose to *make* a family out of these people. We make room for
them in our lives, choose to be with them and preserve that choice through a
ritual as simple as passing seconds at a table.

All real families are made over time and through tradition. The Oral Tradi- 12
tion. We create a shared treasure trove of history, memories, conversation.
Equal parts of food and conversation. And a generous serving of pleasure in
each other's company.

QUESTIONS FOR READING, REASONING, AND WRITING

1. What is Goodman's attitude toward families; that is, what does she assert about
   families in this column? Is there one sentence that states her thesis? If so, which
   one? If not, write a thesis for the essay.

2. Characterize Goodman's style. Analyze her word choice, metaphors, sentence
   structure, organization, and use of the Reagan and Bush families as examples.
   How does each contribute to our understanding of her point?

3. Why are Goodman's metaphors especially notable? Open up—or explain—three
   of her metaphors.

STUDENT ESSAY

GOODMAN'S FEAST OF STYLE

Alan Peterson

Thanksgiving is a time for "families" to come together, eat a big meal, share their experiences and each other's company. In her November 24, 1988, article "Choosing Families," which appeared on Thanksgiving Day in the Washington Post, Ellen Goodman asks the question: "Who makes up these families?" By her definition, a family does not consist of just "blood" relatives; a family contains acquaintances, friends, relatives, people who are "chosen" to be in this year's "family." An examination of Goodman's essay reveals some of the elements of style she uses to effectively ask and answer her question.

Goodman's clever organization compels the reader to read on. She begins by focusing on a Thanksgiving dinner scene, referring to families and households in terms of food. After setting the table by evoking the reader's memories of Thanksgivings past, Goodman asks the central question of her essay: "[W]hat is it that makes this collection of people a family" (49)? Goodman argues that the modern meaning of family has evolved so much that the traditional definition of family is no longer the standard. To clarify modern definitions, she provides examples of famous families: First Families. After suggesting that the Reagans have been the "chief defender of the American family" (49) for the last eight years, she points out that the Reagans, with their divorces, their adoptions, their estrangements, are anything but the traditional family they wish to portray. Rather, the Reagans represent the human traits that define the "contemporary reality" (49) of today's families. Next, President Bush's family is examined. Goodman points out that the Bushes' five children live in five different states, and that Barbara and George Bush, as young people,

Introduction includes author, title, and date of article.

Student's thesis.

Analysis of Goodman's organization.

*Page reference given, according to MLA style.**

---

*This essay illustrates formal documentation according to the Modern Language Association (MLA).

set up "temporary quarters in 17 cities" (50). She develops an answer to her question in the ensuing paragraphs. She observes that families today are disjointed, nontraditional, different from one another. She refers to families that are considered "stable or intact" (50) and shows how even those families can be spread out all over the country. In her closing paragraphs she repeats the question "What makes a family?" Then, after another reference to Thanksgiving dinner, she concludes the article by stating her main point: "All real families are made over time and through tradition" (50). Goodman's organization—a question, some examples, several answers, and strong confirmation—powerfully frames her thesis.

In an essay written about a theme as homespun as family and Thanksgiving celebrations, a reader would not expect the language to be too formal. Choosing her words carefully, Goodman cultivates a familiar and descriptive, yet not overly informal style. Early in the essay, Goodman uses simple language to portray the Thanksgiving meal. She refers to voices interrupting, arms reaching, leftovers that have to be wrapped up. Another effective technique of diction Goodman employs is the repetition of words and sounds. She points out that the Bushes, as young people, "left home again and again" (50). She defines the image we have of families as that of people created from the same "genetic code, living in the same "area code," and of cousins in "other Zip Codes" (50). Then, characterizing the reality of the configuration of today's American families, Goodman states: "A guest last year is a member this year," while a "member last year may be an awkward outsider this year" (50). An additional example of repetition appears in the first and last paragraphs. Goodman repeats the sentence fragment "Equal parts of food and conversation" (50). This informal choice of words opens and closes her essay, cleverly setting the tone in the beginning and reiterating the theme at the end.

Analysis of Goodman's word choice and repetition.

Perhaps the most prevalent element of style present in Goodman's piece, and a dominant characteristic of her essay style, is her use of metaphors. From the opening sentences all the way through to the end, this article is full of

Analysis of Goodman's metaphors.

metaphors. Keeping with the general focus of the piece (the essay appeared on Thanksgiving Day), many of the metaphors liken food to family. Her references include "a cornucopia of family," "chicken-sized households" and a "turkey-sized family," people who "feast on the sounds as well as the tastes," and voices that "add relish to a story" (49). She imparts that a politician can use the word "family" like "gravy poured over the entire plate" (49). Going to the airport to pick up family members of these disjointed American families has become "a holiday ritual as common as pumpkin pie" (50). Goodman draws parallels between the process of "choosing" people to be with and the simple ritual of passing seconds at the table. Indeed, the essay's mood emphasizes the comparison of and inextricable bond between food and family.

Ellen Goodman's "Choosing Families" is a thought-provoking essay on the American family. She organizes the article so that readers are reminded of their own Thanksgiving experiences and consider who is included in their "families."

<aside>Conclusion restates Goodman's position and student's thesis.</aside>

After asking "What is it that makes this collection of people a family?" Goodman provides election-year examples of prominent American families, then an explanation of "family" that furnishes her with an answer. Her word choice and particularly the repetition of words and sounds make reading her essay a pleasure. The metaphors Goodman uses link in readers' minds the images of Thanksgiving food and the people with whom they spend the holiday. Her metaphors underscore the importance she places on having meals with the family, which is the one truly enduring tradition for all people. Perhaps the most important food-and-family metaphor comes in the last sentence: "a generous serving of pleasure in each other's company" (50).

Work Cited

Goodman, Ellen. "Choosing Families." Washington Post. 24 Nov. 1988. Rpt. in Read, Reason, Write: An Argument Text and Reader. 8th ed. Ed. Dorothy U. Seyler. New York: McGraw-Hill, 2008. 50–51.

COMBINING SUMMARY, ANALYSIS, AND EVALUATION: THE REVIEW

Writing a good review requires combining skills you have been working on: critical reading, accurate summary, analysis of style, and evaluation of the work—book or film—in the context of the writer or director's subject, intended audience, and comparative success. Let's look again at steps in the writing process as they apply to writing a review.

Knowing Your Audience

Try to imagine writing your review for your classmates, not just your instructor. Try not to focus on this assignment as writing to be graded. Rather, think about why we turn to reviews: What do readers want to learn? They want to know if they should read the book or see the film. Your job is to help readers make that decision.

Understanding Your Purpose

Your purpose, then, is to provide clear, accurate information and a fair evaluation of both the material covered (or not covered) and the presentation of that material. Balance is important. You do not want most of your review to be summary, with just a few sentences of evaluation "stuck on" at the end. You also do not want a detailed summary of the work's beginning followed by skimpy coverage of the rest. This lack of balance may suggest to readers that you have not read or seen the entire work. Just remember: When reviewing a novel or movie, do not explain the entire plot. You do not want to give away the ending!

Establishing a General Plan

First, study the work carefully. Be sure that you can write a complete and accurate summary, even if you need to leave some of the plot details out of your review. Second, the analysis part of your review needs two elements: comment on the work's structure and special features plus discussion of the writer's (or director's) style. How is the work put together? For a nonfiction book, how many chapters or sections are there, and what does each cover? Does the book contain visuals? An index? For a film, how does the story unfold? What actors are in the lead roles? What special effects are used? These are the kinds of questions readers expect a review to answer.

Your analysis of style needs to be connected to the work's intended audience. For example, is the biography informally written or heavily documented with notes and references? What is the level of formality of the book? What is the age level or knowledge level of the author's expected audience? Films are rated for age groups. Books can also be rated for age and level of knowledge of the subject.

Your summary and analysis can point the way to a fair and sensible evaluation. If, for example, you have many problems understanding a book aimed at a general audience, then it is fair to say that the author has not successfully reached his or her audience. If, on the other hand, you selected a book to review that was designed for specialists, then your reading challenge is not relevant to a fair judgment. All it allows you to do is point out that the book is tough going for a nonspecialist (or a movie sequel, for example, is hard to follow in spots for those who did not see the original film). Your evaluation should include an assessment of content and presentation. Did the book or film fulfill its intended purpose? Was it as thorough as you expected in the light of other works on the same or a similar topic? (A study of American literature in the 1920s, for instance, that fails to mention Ernest Hemingway would surely be evaluated as incomplete and thus flawed.)

Drafting the Review

There is no simple formula for combining summary, analysis, and evaluation in a review. Some instructors simplify the task by requiring a two-part review: summary first and then analysis and evaluation. If you are not so directed, then some blending of the three elements will be expected. Often reviews begin with an opening that is both an attention-getter and a broad statement of the work's subject or subject category. (This is a *biography* of Franklin; this is a *female action-hero* flick.) An evaluation in general terms follows to complete the opening paragraph. Then the reviewer uses a "summary–analysis–evaluation" pattern, providing details of content and presentation and then assessing the work.

Here are two reviews for you to study. The first one, by Lynda Ransdell, has been annotated for you. As you read the second review, add your own annotations.

ANNOTATED REVIEW

Opening includes author, title, and general evaluation.

Dr. Cynthia Pemberton's new book, *More Than a Game: One Woman's Fight for Gender Equity in Sport,* is destined to become a classic in sport sociology, sport history, and women's studies. The author chronicles the trials and tribulations of Dr. Pemberton's Title IX battle at Linfield College, a small liberal arts college in Oregon. She uses an effective writing style to tell a painful and fascinating story that begins with her naivete about the potential impact of questioning gender equity at her college, and ends with her decision to move on to a different career as an educator and administrator in higher education. Throughout the book, Pemberton describes the different types of roadblocks encountered—and how she dealt with those roadblocks. The subtle discrimination is shocking. The strength of her character in dealing with these roadblocks is impressive. One of my favorite parts of the book is how she effectively disarms the myth that men's minor sports are being dropped because women's sports are being added—due to Title IX. In reality, women's sports are much less powerful than men's major sports, yet we continue to receive the blame

Summary with evaluation of style.

Reviewer's comment on the book's subject.

for dropping men's athletic teams. In reality, excesses in major men's sports such as football and basketball contribute to belt-tightening in high school and college athletics.

The book made me laugh and cry—always a good sign when searching for the ultimate book to read—or, when searching for the ultimate book to make an impact on students who are unfamiliar with Title IX. Mostly, I could relate to her stories—given my background as a former small college coach and faculty member.

Evaluation.

The target audience for this book includes educators, coaches, athletes, and administrators at any level. Additionally, anyone interested in studying women's sports or pursuing a Title IX case will love this book. It is a "must read" for students studying the humanistic, realistic, and not so glamorous side of Title IX. It should help educate those preparing to file a Title IX grievance, or those who have not had to fight a battle in women's athletics. It will dramatically open the eyes of those who take women's contemporary participation opportunities, training facilities, and coaching for granted.

Analysis—book's target audience—plus evaluation.

The passion, courage, and knowledge used to write this book solidify Dr. Cynthia Pemberton's status as one of the premier experts on Title IX in the U.S.

Ends with strong evaluation.

STUDENT REVIEW

WINCHESTER'S ALCHEMY: TWO MEN AND A BOOK

Ian Habel

One can hardly imagine a tale promising less excitement for a general audience than that of the making of the Oxford English Dictionary (OED). The sensationalism of murder and insanity would have to labor intensely against the burden of lexicography in crafting a genuine page-turner on the subject. Much to my surprise, Simon Winchester, in writing The Professor and the Madman: A Tale of Murder, Insanity, and the Making of The Oxford English Dictionary, has succeeded in producing so compelling a story that I was forced to devour it completely in a single afternoon, an unprecedented personal feat.

The Professor and the Madman is the story of the lives of two apparently very different men and the work that brought them together. Winchester begins by recounting the circumstances that led to the incarceration of Dr. W. C. Minor, a well-born, well-educated, and quite insane American ex-Army surgeon. Minor, in a fit of delusion, had murdered a man whom he believed to have crept into his Lambeth hotel room to torment him in his sleep. The doctor is tried and whisked off to the Asylum for the Criminally Insane, Broadmoor.

The author then introduces readers to the other two main characters: the OED itself and its editor James Murray, a low-born, self-educated Scottish philologist. The shift in narrative focus is used to dramatic effect. The natural assumption on the part of the reader that these two seemingly unrelated plots must eventually meet urges us to read on in anticipation of that connection. As each chapter switches focus from one man to the other, it is introduced by a citation from the OED, reminding us that the story is ultimately about the dictionary. The citations also serve to foreshadow and provide a theme for the chapter. For example, the OED definition of *murder* heads the first chapter, relating to the details of Minor's crime.

Winchester acquaints us with the shortcomings of seventeenth- and eighteenth-century attempts at compiling a comprehensive dictionary of the English language. He takes us inside the meetings of the Philological Society, whose members proposed the compilation of the dictionary to end all dictionaries. The OED was to include examples of usage illustrating every shade of meaning for every word in the English language. Such a mammoth feat would require enlisting thousands of volunteer readers to comb the corpus of English literature in search of illustrative quotations to be submitted on myriad slips of paper. These slips of paper on each word would in turn be studied by a small army of editors preparing the definitions.

It is not surprising that our Dr. Minor, comfortably tucked away at Broadmoor, possessing both a large library and seemingly infinite free time, should become one of those volunteer readers. After all, we are still rightfully assuming some connection of the book's two plot lines. Yet what sets Dr. Minor apart from his fellow volunteers (aside from the details of his incarceration) is the remarkable efficiency with which he approached his task. Not content merely to fill out slips of paper for submission, Minor methodically indexed every possibly useful mention of any word appearing in his personal library. He then asked to be kept informed of the progress of the work, submitting quotations that would be immediately useful to editors. In this way he managed to "escape" his cell and plunge himself into the work of contemporaries, to become a part of a major event of his time.

Minor's work proved invaluable to the OED's staff of editors, led by James Murray. With the two plot lines now intertwined, readers face such questions as "Will they find out that Minor is insane?" "Will Minor and Murray ever meet?" and "How long will they take to complete the dictionary?" The author builds suspense regarding a meeting of Minor and Murray by providing a false account of their first encounter, as reported by the American press, only to shatter us with the fact that this romantic version did not happen. I'll let Winchester give you the answers to these questions, while working his magic on you, drawing you into this fascinating tale of the making of the world's most famous dictionary.

ANALYZING TWO OR MORE SOURCES

Scientists examining the same set of facts do not always draw the same conclusions; neither do historians and biographers agree on the significance of the same documents. How do we recognize and cope with these disparities? As critical readers we analyze what we read, pose questions, and refuse to believe everything we find in print or hear on television. To develop these skills in recognizing differences, instructors frequently ask students to contrast the views of two or more writers. In psychology class, for example, you may be asked to contrast the views of Sigmund Freud and John B. Watson on child development. In a communications course, you may be asked to contrast the moderator styles of two talk-show hosts. We can examine differences in content or presentation, or both. Here are guidelines for preparing a contrast of sources.

GUIDELINES for Preparing a Contrast Essay

- **Work with sources that have something in common.** Think about the context for each, that is, each source's subject and purpose. (It would not make much sense to contrast a textbook chapter, for example, with a TV talk show because their contexts are so different.)

- **Read actively to understand the content of the two sources.** Tape films, radio, or TV shows so that you can listen/view them several times, just as you would read a written source more than once.

- **Analyze for differences, focusing on your purpose in contrasting.** If you are contrasting the ideas of two writers, for example, then your analysis will focus on ideas, not on writing style. To explore differences in two news accounts, you may want to consider all of the following: the impact of placement in the newspaper/magazine, accompanying photographs or graphics, length of each article, what is covered in each article, and writing styles. Prepare a list of specific differences.

- **Organize your contrast.** It is usually best to organize by points of difference. If you write first about one source and then about the other, the ways that the sources differ may not be clear for readers. Take the time to plan an organization that clearly reveals your contrast purpose in writing. To illustrate, a paper contrasting the writing styles of two authors can be organized according to the following pattern:

  Introduction: Introduce your topic and make clear your purpose to contrast styles of writer A and writer B.

  A1
  > Sentence structures of writer A and writer B
  B1

  A2
  > Word choice of writer A and writer B
  B2

  A3
  > Metaphors used by writer A and writer B
  B3

  Conclusion: Explain the effect of the differences in style of the writers.

- **Illustrate and discuss each of the points of difference for each of the sources.** Provide examples and explain the impact of the differences in level of formality or connotation.

- **Always write for an audience who may be familiar with your general topic but not with the specific sources you are discussing.** Be sure to provide adequate context (names, titles of works, etc.).

EXERCISES: Analyzing Two Sources

Whenever two people choose to write on the same topic, there are bound to be differences in choice of specifics and emphasis—and that's before there are differences in philosophy and political or social perspective. If the medium is different—such as a novel and a movie version of the novel—further differences built into each medium will be present. When we are seeking information and analysis of a subject, we are wise to use more than one source for our information. When we explore a similar subject treated in different media, we can learn much about the particular characteristics of each medium in addition to the possibly different points of view of, for example, writer and film director.

What follows is a review of the 2005 film of Jane Austen's novel *Pride and Prejudice*. Read and annotate the review.

1.   Then find another review of the same film, either searching on the Internet or in your library's electronic databases. Think about differences in content, attitude, and evaluation. What details or elements of the film get the most attention from each writer? Is there a difference in tone? Prepare a list of points of difference you would include in a comparative analysis. Organize your selected points of difference and list details you would use to develop each point as if you were planning to draft an essay. Be prepared to explain and defend your choice of outline.
2.   View the movie yourself and write your own review of the film. Then compare your review to the one printed here—or to another one that you find. Examine the two reviews by following the guidelines given above.
3.   View the 2005 version of the movie and the earlier film version mentioned in the review (with Greer Garson and Laurence Olivier). Contrast the two film versions, following the guidelines given above.
4.   Read the novel and view the 2005 film version. Contrast the novel and the film version, following the guidelines given above.

KNIGHTLEY, IN SHINING ARMOUR | PETER RAINER

Peter Rainer is film critic for the *Christian Science Monitor*. His review was published there on November 10, 2005.

"She is tolerable but not handsome enough to tempt me," says the imperious Mr. Darcy (Matthew MacFadyen) to his friend Charles Bingley (Simon Woods) in the latest—and one of the best—adaptations of Jane Austen's *Pride and Prejudice*. The woman in question, Elizabeth Bennet (Keira Knightley, who triumphantly comes into her own here), has overheard his indiscretion. The glint in her eyes tells us she will soon have her say—not to mention her way.

2   And so she does, setting in motion one of the great romances in the canon. *Pride and Prejudice* has been adapted for TV five times—most notably in the 1995 BBC miniseries starring Jennifer Ehle and Colin Firth—but only once before as a movie, 65 years ago, starring Greer Garson and Laurence Olivier.

3   The new version is directed by Joe Wright, making his feature debut. He claims not to have read Austen's classic before reading the script that novelist Deborah Moggach fashioned for him, and this turns out to be a good thing: Approaching the book unburdened by the usual academic baggage, he frees it up for the screen. And he does so without ever losing sight of the emotional richness at the heart of the novel. This version is no dumbed-down escapade catering to the youth market. If young audiences respond to it at all—as I am sure they will—it will be because Wright has brought out the vigor in Austen's romance in a way that the other adaptations I've seen never quite accomplished.

4   Elizabeth is 20 in the movie, Darcy 28, and they look and act it—though MacFadyen's Darcy had his brooding Heathcliff side. (Garson and Olivier were 32 and 33 when their movie was shot, and their rectitude made them seem even older.) Elizabeth's four sisters, including the Bingley-smitten Jane (Rosamund Pike) and the 15-year-old cad-magnet Lydia (Jena Malone), are likewise the same ages that Austen intended. As seen from this youthful perspective, *Pride and Prejudice* has some of the same surprise that *Romeo and Juliet* does when it's cast properly. These lovers are practically kids. They seem to be experiencing their ardor for the first time.

5   The spiritedness is rooted by Wright's rich eye for the intricacies of romantic complication as it plays out against a landscape of country estates and formal gardens. His compositions are painterly but never static. Most adaptations of the novel have been set in the early and (from a production design standpoint) stuffier 19th century rather than, as here, in the late 18th, when Austen wrote the initial manuscript—at 21—of what later became *Pride and Prejudice*.

6   This period accuracy is reflected in the Bennets' rather ramshackle estate, which sometimes resembles a hippie crash pad laced with finery. Mrs. Bennet (the marvelous Brenda Blethyn), the flibbertigibbet mother of her eligible brood, understands full well that her daughters must land husbands who will elevate their station in life. Mr. Bennet (the equally marvelous Donald Sutherland), the bemused patriarch, has a special feeling for Elizabeth, the brightest of the bunch. Her loss to him, even to a prize catch like Darcy, is the basis for one of the late, great scenes in the movie, an occasion for sweet sorrow.

7   Austen has sometimes been criticized for a narrowness of vision—mostly by critics with no vision at all. Lurking just beneath the surface of her comedy of manners are the crushing subtleties of class distinction and the desperation of those who would rise above it. In the end, the finest achievement of Wright's movie is that it fully captures what Martin Amis, writing on *Pride and Prejudice*, said of Austen: "Money is a vital substance in her world; the moment you enter it you feel the frank horror of moneylessness, as intense as the tacit horror of spinsterhood." All that, and a great love story, too. Grade: A.

FOR READING AND ANALYSIS

Now read, analyze, and be prepared to discuss the following two essays.

WATCH YOUR LANGUAGE | ANDREW VACHSS

Andrew Vachss is an attorney whose only clients are children. He also writes mystery novels and maintains a dramatic and useful website. The following article, with the subtitle lead: "If you want to fight against the abuse of children," originally appeared in *Parade* magazine, June 5, 2005.

PREREADING QUESTIONS Based on the title and subtitle lead-in and what you know about the author, what do you expect this essay to be about? How important is the language we use to label or "name" an action?

School counselor put on probation for fondling teen

Court papers detail girls' lives
Child prostitutes were abused by pimps, records say

Mayor accused of molestation

Student details affair with teacher

Child prostitute ring nets prison terms for 3 people

Years ago, I participated in 1 the rescue of a child from bondage. Destiny (not her real name) was 13. She had been re-peatedly raped by a pair of predators to "educate" her. Then, along with several other young girls, she was forced to sell herself to strangers. Each day, she woke to the threat of disfiguring brutality if she failed to bring in sufficient money that night. Later, it was reported that "pimps" had been arrested, and "a number of child prostitutes were taken into custody."

What was wrong with calling 2 Destiny a "child prostitute"? After all, she was a child, and she was engaged in prostitution. First, the word itself implies a judgment of character. Don't we call people who sell out their moral convictions in exchange for personal gain "whores"? More important, prostitution implies a *willing* exchange. Ultimately, the term "child prostitution" implies that little children are "seductive," that they "volunteer" to have sex with adults in exchange for cash (which, of course, the children never see).

The difference between calling Destiny a "child prostitute" and a "prosti- 3 tuted child" is not purely semantic. It is more than the difference between a hard truth and a pernicious lie. It not only injures the victims; it actively gives aid and comfort to the enemy. By allowing the term "child prostitution" to gain a foothold in our language, we lose ground that can never be recovered. Look at the following examples:

- A judge spares a predatory pedophile a long prison sentence on the grounds that "it takes two to tango." Another grants work-release to a sex offender, declaring that the 5-year-old victim was "unusually promiscuous."

- A teacher is arrested for sexual intercourse with a minor student in her class. The newspapers describe the conduct as "a forbidden love affair."

- A young actor, in an interview given before his drug-overdose death, describes how he "lost his virginity" when he was 3 or 4 years old.

4 How have such grotesque distortions taken control of our language? To answer that question, we must first ask another: Who profits? Who benefits from pervasive cultural language that trivializes violence against children?

5 Pedophiles are very familiar with the power of language. They would have us believe that child pornography is a free-speech issue. They know that if they succeed in placing "child prostitution" anywhere on the continuum of voluntary sexual activity, they will have established a beachhead from which to launch future assaults.

6 We must understand that such language is no accident—it is the deliberate product of cultural lobbyists. There is a carefully orchestrated campaign to warp public perception, a perception that affects everything from newspaper coverage to legislation and even jury verdicts.

7 If they can get us to accept that children consent to sex for money, it will be easier to sell the idea that they can consent to sex for "love." But an adult male who sexually abuses little boys is no more "homosexual" than one who victimizes little girls is "heterosexual." They are both predatory pedophiles. There is no such thing as a child prostitute; there are only prostituted children.

8 When we use terms such as "lose one's virginity" in referring to adult sex acts with children instead of calling it "rape," or when we say that teachers "have affairs" with their pupils instead of saying that the teachers sexually exploit them, the only beneficiaries are the predators who target children.

9 This is not about political correctness. It is about telling the truth. In any culture, language is the undercurrent that drives the river of public perception. That undercurrent has been polluted for too long. If we really want to protect our children, it's time to watch our language.

WHAT WORDS REALLY SAY

When it comes to child abuse, the language we use can distort the reality of the crime and create a roadblock to justice. The next time you hear a news report, keep in mind what the following terms actually mean . . . and the consequences of the conduct described.

PEDOPHILE

An individual with intense, recurrent sexually arousing fantasies and urges toward prepubescent children. Those who decide to act on such feelings can be termed "predatory pedophiles." The predatory pedophile is as dangerous as cancer and as camouflaged in approach. His presence becomes known only by the horrendous damage left in his wake. Predatory pedophiles most often operate inside a child's "circle of trust." He (or she) may be a teacher, a doctor, a scout leader, a police officer, an athletic coach, a religious counselor, or a child-care professional. They are protected not only by our ignorance of their presence but also by our unwillingness to confront the truth.

FONDLING

Nonpenetrative sexual misconduct with a child, often resulting in severe emotional damage to the victim.

MOLESTATION

Sexual assault of a child, often resulting in both physical and emotional damage.

NONVIOLENT INCEST

The rape by extortion of a child by a family member, creating a climate of oppression and fear in the child's daily life that inevitably results in profound long-term damage.

INTERGENERATIONAL LOVE

The sexual exploitation of a child under the guise of a consensual relationship. This pedophiles' perversion of the word "love" is routinely promoted in all their literature as "harmless" or even "beneficial" to the victim.

CHILD PROSTITUTE

A child, often held captive against his or her will, who is physically and/or emotionally coerced into performing sex acts with adults for the profit of others.

QUESTIONS FOR READING

1. What is Vachss's topic? (Be more precise than "language use.")
2. Explain the author's definition of "child prostitute." Why is this label inappropriate for Destiny, in the author's view?
3. What does Vachss mean by the label "predatory pedophiles"?
4. Who gains from the distorted language shown in the box? What do they gain?

QUESTIONS FOR REASONING AND ANALYSIS

1. What is Vachss's thesis? Where does he state it?
2. Analyze the author's word choice, examples, and metaphors. How do these strategies contribute to Vachss's argument?
3. How would you characterize the essay's tone? How is the tone created?

QUESTIONS FOR REFLECTING AND WRITING

1. How did you answer the second prereading question? After reading Vachss's essay, do you think that you should answer the question differently? Why or why not?
2. Do you agree with the author that our language does distort the truth, putting children at risk? Why or why not?
3. What, if anything, do you want the courts to do with predatory pedophiles? With online child pornography? Why?

I HAVE A CHIP, BUT IT'S NOT ON MY SHOULDER | CATHERINE GETCHES

Catherine Getches is a freelance writer living in northern California. She often writes about cultural issues. The following essay was published in the *Washington Post* on September 18, 2005.

PREREADING QUESTIONS Does Getches really mean that she doesn't have a chip on her shoulder? Do you look forward to microchip implants?

Can a microscopic tag be implanted in a person's body to track his every movement? There's actual discussion about that. You will rule on that—mark my words—before your tenure is over.

> –Sen. Joseph Biden,
> to Judge John Roberts
> at his confirmation hearings, Sept. 12

1   I can't wait for the day when we all have microchips implanted in our heads. It's exciting to be so close—pet owners are already implanting VeriChips in their animals to help track them down, motorists have OnStar on call to pinpoint their location in case of emergency, and by 2006 the State Department plans to put Radio Frequency Identification (RFID) tags into new U.S. passports to keep track of us.

We're already scrutinized by surveillance cameras at stoplights and in 2
public places, and the reauthorized USA Patriot Act gives the feds even more
opportunities to search my house. So I say, why bother with all the inevitable
lawsuits and legislative hot air? Let's skip to the next logical step. I hereby volunteer to be an RFID guinea pig. Just insert the chip discreetly beneath my
scalp, so I can get started on my easy-as-E-ZPass existence.

Think of all the advantages: While you're stuck in line at the supermarket, 3
the better-than-barcode technology embedded in my brain will allow the
cashier not just to know who I am and where I've been, but charge my groceries
directly to my account. Just a tilt of the neck, and I'm sailing on through. No
more fussing with my wallet or wondering which of my overburdened credit
cards to use. This is what self-checkout was meant to be.

The possibilities make my head spin. Imagine the time savings if the chip 4
could transmit video, too. That way, whenever I walk into an airport or a gun
show or an office, the security folks will see I'm there, what I'm wearing and
carrying—the perfect combination of anonymity and total exposure. Sure, I'd
miss those backhanded pat downs in the airport security line, and the pleasant
chats with the TSA officers while they root through my dirty laundry. But there's
something intangible, even appealing, about being seen invisibly, knowing
screeners can probe much deeper, without any effort on my part. (You know,
invasions of privacy can be kind of flattering, too, like when a speeding ticket
arrives in the mail and right there next to the amount of the fine is, surprise, a
photo of my face!)

The beauty of virtual mugging is omnipresent when anyone with a scanner 5
has access to my personal data: my name, medical history, habits, tastes, not
only where I bank but what I might want to buy, based on my shopping history.
With my head constantly transmitting, companies will be able to triangulate
much more than my location. Some critics refer to RFID as "spy chips," but I
like to think of it this way: I'm the star of my own virtual reality show.

My bad sense of direction is eradicated with electronic eavesdropping. 6
Once I'm one with OnStar, how can I ever really be lost if someone is always
watching me? Sure, the parking ticket guy will have X-ray vision of my guilty
pleasures as well as my driving record (maybe he'll think it's cool that I order old "Magnum P.I." episodes via Netflix), but it's so worth it when the
McDonald's drive-through captures my frequency, knows the value meal I
like and charges my credit card—with the entire transaction taking place in
my head.

Spammers already know my name and e-mail address, so I'm sure I won't 7
find it strange when a police officer pulls me over and brings up a book I recommended last week on Amazon.com. I never wanted to carry a purse in the
first place, and now my checkbook-free-lifestyle will liberate me. Instead of un-
loading the contents of my bag and hunting for I.D. at the nightclub, bouncers
can frisk all the digital data they want. Nightlife for me will be streamlined-VIP,
as back-room bartenders zap drinks to my card, adding a whole new meaning
to American Express.

8   Besides, why would I want to stand in line behind animals for this kind of technology? Pets have enjoyed "smart" labels for 15 years. And it's not just the Irish setter next door who has it so good: Beer kegs, library books, Calvin Klein clothing, baseball tickets and Gillette razors are all equipped with RFID. Now there is talk of laser-coded fruit—Wal-Mart has placed orders for apples and oranges with tags etched into their wax or tattooed on their skin. (Please, oh please, don't let a banana beat me to bar-coded bliss.)

9   Here's what I say to anyone who balks and brings up civil liberties or "Big Brother": First, I don't even like that show and second, most people who say they want privacy have a double standard. At U.S.-Canadian border crossings, drivers willingly undergo background checks, fingerprinting, interviews, and photographs as part of the Nexus pass commuters' program—complete exposure for a wait-free crossing. But then the same types get all indignant at giving up a Zip code to the Macy's cashier. Recently, I read that Google's CEO doesn't like being googled. Now *that* makes my head hurt.

10   Once I'm equipped with my personal transponder, I'm hoping for more free time. I'm already thinking of ways to spice it up for my voyeurs—mostly trying to pose and look good for the surveillance cameras, popping up everywhere. Some protesters stage "distraction" plays in front of them, but who wants to share the attention?

11   Now, if I can only figure out how to get advance notice so I can make sure the house is clean before the agents arrive to search it. There has to be a radio frequency that vaporizes dust mites.

QUESTIONS FOR READING

1. What is Getches's subject? What was the occasion for her writing?
2. What are the specific situations that will be easier with a RFID implant?
3. What are possible disadvantages? How does the author dismiss these?

QUESTIONS FOR REASONING AND ANALYSIS

1. What is the author's primary strategy for conveying attitude? What is Getches's attitude toward tracking chip implants? What examples and word choice help to convey her attitude?
2. What, then, is Getches's thesis?

QUESTIONS FOR REFLECTING AND WRITING

1. Do you enjoy and appreciate the strategy Getches uses? Or, does it bother you? If you appreciate it, what makes it clever? If you are bothered, why?
2. Do you think that chip implants have any advantages? If so, what are they? If not, why not?

SUGGESTIONS FOR DISCUSSION AND WRITING

1. Analyze the style of one of the essays from Section 4 of this text. Do not comment on every element of style; select several elements that seem to characterize the writer's style and examine them in detail. Remember that style analyses are written for an audience familiar with the work, so summary is not necessary.

2. Many of the authors included in this text have written books that you will find in your library. Select one that interests you, read it, and prepare a review of it that synthesizes summary, analysis, and evaluation. Prepare a review of about 300 words; assume that the book has just been published.

3. Choose two newspaper and/or magazine articles that differ in their discussion of the same person, event, or product. You may select two different articles on a person in the news, two different accounts of a news event, an advertisement and a *Consumer Reports* analysis of the same product, or two reviews of a book or movie. Analyze differences in both content and presentation and then consider why the two accounts differ. Organize by points of difference and write to an audience not necessarily familiar with the articles.

4. Choose a recently scheduled public event (the Super Bowl, the Olympics, a presidential election, the Academy Award presentations, the premiere of a new television series) and find several articles written before and several after the event. First compare articles written after the event to see if they agree factually. If not, decide which article appears to be more accurate and why. Then examine the earlier material and decide which was the most and which the least accurate. Write an essay in which you explain the differences in speculation before the event and why you think these differences exist. Your audience will be aware of the event but not necessarily aware of the articles you are studying.

The World of Argument

DILBERT: © Scott Adams/Dist. by United Feature, Syndicate, Inc.

Read: What is the situation? Who is the speaker in frame one? What has he just finished? What is the response of the others in frames two and three?

Reason: Are we to understand that there was absolutely no content? What point is Scott Adams, the cartoonist, making about PowerPoint presentations?

Reflect/Write: Do you agree with the cartoonist's assessment of PowerPoint presentations? Why or why not?

CHAPTER 3

Understanding _{the} Basics of Argument

In this section we will explore the processes of thinking logically and analyzing issues to reach informed judgments. Remember: Mature people do not need to agree on all issues to respect one another's good sense, but they do have little patience with uninformed or illogical statements masquerading as argument.

CHARACTERISTICS OF ARGUMENT

Argument Is Conversation with a Goal

When you enter into an argument (as speaker, writer, or reader), you become a participant in an ongoing debate about an issue. Since you are probably not the first to address the issue, you need to be aware of the ways that the issue has been debated by others and then seek to advance the conversation, just as you would if you were having a more casual conversation with friends. If the time of the movie is set, the discussion now turns to whose car to take or where to meet. If you were to just repeat the time of the movie, you would add nothing useful to the conversation. Also, if you were to change the subject to a movie you saw last week, you would annoy your friends by not offering useful information or showing that you valued the current conversation. Just as with your conversation about the movie, you want your argument to stay focused on the issue, to respect what others have already contributed, and to make a useful addition to our understanding of the issue.

Argument Takes a Stand on an Arguable Issue

A meaningful argument focuses on a debatable issue. We usually do not argue about facts. "Professor Jones's American literature class meets at 10:00 on Mondays" is not arguable. It is either true or false. We can check the schedule of classes to find out. (Sometimes the facts change; new facts replace old ones.) We also do not debate personal preferences for the simple reason that they are just that—personal. If the debate is about the appropriateness of boxing as a sport, for you to declare that you would rather play tennis is to fail to advance the conversation. You have expressed a personal preference, interesting perhaps, but not relevant to the debate.

Argument Uses Reasons and Evidence

Some arguments merely "look right." That is, conclusions are drawn from facts, but the facts are not those that actually support the assertion, or the conclusion is not the only or the best explanation of those facts. To shape convincing arguments, we need more than an array of facts. We need to think critically, to analyze the issue, to see relationships, to weigh evidence. We need to avoid the temptation to "argue" from emotion only, or to believe that just stating our opinion is the same thing as building a sound argument.

Argument Incorporates Values

Arguments are based not just on reason and evidence but also on the beliefs and values we hold and think that our audience may hold as well. In a reasoned debate, you want to make clear the values that you consider relevant to the argument. In an editorial defending the sport of boxing, one editor wrote that boxing "is a sport because the world has not yet become a place in which the qualities that go into excellence in boxing [endurance, agility, courage] have no value" (*Washington Post,* February 5, 1983). But James J. Kilpatrick also appeals to values when he argues, in an editorial critical of boxing, that we should not want to live in a society "in which deliberate brutality is legally authorized and publicly applauded" (*Washington Post,* December 7, 1982). Observe, however, the high level of seriousness in the appeal to values. Neither writer settles for a simplistic personal preference: "Boxing is exciting," or "Boxing is too violent."

Argument Recognizes the Topic's Complexity

Much false reasoning (the logical fallacies discussed in Chapter 5) results from a writer's oversimplifying an issue. A sound argument begins with an understanding that most issues are terribly complicated. The wise person approaches such ethical concerns as abortion or euthanasia or such public policy issues as tax cuts or trade agreements with the understanding that there are many philosophical, moral, and political issues that complicate discussions of these topics. Recognizing an argument's complexity may also lead us to an understanding that there can be more than one "right" position. The thoughtful arguer respects the views of others, seeks common ground when possible, and often chooses a conciliatory approach.

THE SHAPE OF ARGUMENT: THE ARISTOTELIAN MODEL

Still one of the best ways to understand the basics of argument is to reflect on what the Greek philosopher Aristotle describes as the three "players" in any argument: the *writer* (or *speaker*), the *argument itself,* and the *reader* (or *audience*). Aristotle calls the argument itself the *logos*—the assertion and support for that assertion. A successful argument needs a logical and convincing *logos*. An argument also implies an audience, those whose views on our topic we want to influence. Aristotle calls this part of argument *pathos*. Good arguers need to be alert to the values and attitudes of their audience and to appeal effectively to the emotions of that audience. However, Aristotle also explains that part of our appeal to an audience rests in the *logos*, our logic and evidence. An "argument" that is all emotional appeal will not move thoughtful audiences.

Finally (and for Aristotle the most important of the three players) is the writer/speaker, or *ethos*. No argument, Aristotle asserts, no matter how logical seeming, no matter how appealing emotionally, will succeed if the audience rejects the arguer's credibility, the writer's "ethical" qualities. As members of the audience we need to believe that the arguer is a person of knowledge, honesty, and goodwill.

As Figure 3.1 illustrates, we argue in a specific context of three interrelated parts. We present support for a concrete assertion, thesis, or claim to a specific audience whose demands and expectations and character we have given thought to when shaping our argument. And we present ourselves as informed, competent, and reliable so that our audience will give serious attention to our

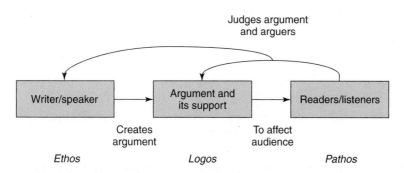

FIGURE 3.1 Aristotelian Structure of Argument

argument. Remember: Your audience evaluates *you* as a part of their evaluation of your argument. Lose your credibility and you lose your argument.

THE SHAPE OF ARGUMENT: THE TOULMIN MODEL

British philosopher Stephen Toulmin adds to what we have learned from Aristotle by focusing our attention on the basics of the argument itself. First, consider this definition of argument: *An argument consists of evidence and/or reasons presented in support of an assertion or claim that is either stated or implied.* For example:

CLAIM:	We should not go skiing today
EVIDENCE:	because it is too cold.
EVIDENCE:	Because some laws are unjust,
CLAIM:	civil disobedience is sometimes justified.
EVIDENCE:	It's only fair and right for academic institutions to
CLAIM:	accept students only on academic merit.

The basics of a complete argument, Toulmin asserts, are actually a bit more complex than these examples suggest. Each argument has a third part that is not stated in the preceding examples. This third part is the "glue" that connects the support—the evidence and reasons—to the argument's claim and thus fulfills the logic of the argument. Toulmin calls this glue an argument's *warrants*. These are the principles or assumptions that allow us to assert that our evidence or reasons— what Toulmin calls the *grounds*—do indeed support our claim. (Figure 3.2 illustrates these basics of the Toulmin model of argument.)

Look again at the sample arguments to see what warrants must be accepted to make each argument work:

CLAIM:	We should not go skiing today.
EVIDENCE:	It is too cold.
ASSUMPTIONS (WARRANTS):	When it is too cold, skiing is not fun; the activity is not sufficient to keep one from becoming uncomfortable. AND: Too cold is what is too cold for me.
CLAIM:	Civil disobedience is sometimes justified.
EVIDENCE:	Some laws are unjust.
ASSUMPTIONS (WARRANTS):	To get unjust laws changed, people need to be made aware of the injustice. Acts of civil disobedience will get people's attention and make them aware that the laws need changing.
CLAIM:	Academic institutions should accept students only on academic merit.
EVIDENCE:	It is fair and right.
ASSUMPTIONS (WARRANTS):	Fair and right are important values. AND: Academic institutions are only about academics.

CLAIM:	Academic institutions should accept students only on academic merit.
EVIDENCE:	It is only fair and right.
WARRANT:	(1) Fair and right are important values. (2) Academic institutions are only about academics.

FIGURE 3.2 The Toulmin Structure of Argument

Assumptions play an important role in any argument, so we need to be sure to understand what they are. Note, for instance, the second assumption operating in the first argument: The temperature considered uncomfortable for the speaker will also be uncomfortable for her companions—an uncertain assumption. In the second argument, the warrant is less debatable, for acts of civil disobedience usually get media coverage and thus dramatize the issue. The underlying assumptions in the third example stress the need to know one's warrants. Both warrants will need to be defended in the debate over selection by academic merit only.

COLLABORATIVE EXERCISE: Building Arguments

With your class partner or in small groups, examine each of the following claims. Select two, think of one statement that could serve as evidence for each claim, and then think of the underlying assumption(s) that complete each of the arguments.

1. Professor X is not a good instructor.
2. Americans need to reduce the fat in their diets.
3. Tiger Woods is a great golfer.
4. Physical education classes should be graded pass/fail.
5. College newspapers should be free of supervision by faculty or administrators.

THE LANGUAGE OF CLAIMS AND SUPPORT

What kinds of statements function as claims and as support?

- Claims: usually either inferences or judgments, for these are debatable assertions.
- Support: facts, opinions based on facts (inferences), or opinions based on values, beliefs, or ideas (judgments) or some combination of the three.

Let's consider what kinds of statements each of these terms describes.

> **NOTE:** Placing such qualifiers as "I believe," "I think," or "I feel" in an assertion does not free you from the need to support that claim. The statement "I believe that President Clinton was a great president" calls for an argument based on evidence and reasons.

Facts

Facts are statements that are verifiable. Factual statements refer to what can be counted or measured or confirmed by reasonable observers or trusted experts.

> There are twenty-six desks in Room 110.
>
> In the United States about 400,000 people die each year as a result of smoking.

These are factual statements. We can verify the first by observation—by counting. The second fact comes from medical records. We rely on trusted record-keeping sources and medical experts for verification. By definition, we do not argue about the facts. Usually. Sometimes "facts" change, as we learn more about our world. For example, only in the last thirty years has convincing evidence been gathered to demonstrate the relationship between smoking and various illnesses of the heart and lungs. And sometimes "facts" are false facts. These are statements that sound like facts but are incorrect. For example: Agassi has won more Wimbledon titles than Sampras. Not so.

Inferences

Inferences are opinions based on facts. Inferences are the conclusions we draw from an analysis of facts.

> There will not be enough desks in Room 110 for upcoming fall-semester classes.
>
> Smoking is a serious health hazard.

Predictions of an increase in student enrollment for the coming fall semester lead to the inference that most English classes scheduled in Room 110 will run with several more students per class than last year. The dean should order new desks. Similarly, we infer from the number of deaths that smoking is a health problem; statistics show more people dying from tobacco than from AIDS, or murder, or car accidents, causes of death that get media coverage but do not produce nearly as many deaths.

Inferences vary in their closeness to the facts supporting them. That the sun will "rise" tomorrow is an inference, but we count on its happening, acting as if it is a fact. However, the first inference stated above is based not just on the fact of twenty-six desks but on another inference—a projected increase in student enrollment—and two assumptions. The argument looks like this:

FACT:	There are twenty-six desks in Room 110.
INFERENCE:	There will be more first-year students next year.
ASSUMPTIONS:	1. English will remain a required course.
	2. No additional classrooms are available for English classes.
CLAIM:	There will not be enough desks in Room 110 for upcoming fall-semester classes.

This inference could be challenged by a different analysis of the facts supporting enrollment projections. Or, if additional rooms can be found, the dean will not need to order new desks. Inferences can be part of the support of an argument, or they can be the claim of an argument.

Judgments

Judgments are opinions based on values, beliefs, or philosophical concepts. (Judgments also include opinions based on personal preferences, but we have already excluded these from argument.) Judgments concern right and wrong, good and bad, better or worse, should and should not:

No more than twenty-six students should be enrolled in any English class.

Cigarette advertising should be eliminated, and the federal government should develop an antismoking campaign.

To support the first judgment, we need to explain what constitutes overcrowding, or what constitutes the best class size for effective teaching. If we can support our views on effective teaching, we may be able to convince the college president that ordering more desks for Room 110 is not the best solution to an increasing enrollment in English classes. The second judgment also offers a solution to a problem, in this case a national health problem. To reduce the number of deaths, we need to reduce the number of smokers, either by encouraging smokers to quit or not to start. The underlying assumption: Advertising does affect behavior.

EXERCISE: Facts, Inferences, and Judgments

Compile a list of three statements of fact, three inferences, and three judgments. Try to organize them into three related sets, as illustrated here:

- Smoking is prohibited in some restaurants.
- Secondhand smoke is a health hazard.
- Smoking should be prohibited in all restaurants.

We can classify judgments to see better what kind of assertion we are making and, therefore, what kind of support we need to argue effectively.

FUNCTIONAL JUDGMENTS (guidelines for judging how something or someone works or could work)

Tiger Woods is the best golfer to play the game.

Antismoking advertising will reduce the number of smokers.

AESTHETIC JUDGMENTS (guidelines for judging art, literature, music, or natural scenes)

The sunrise was beautiful.

The Great Gatsby's structure, characters, and symbols are perfectly wedded to create the novel's vision of the American dream.

ETHICAL JUDGMENTS (guidelines for group or social behavior)

Lawyers should not advertise.

It is discourteous to talk during a film or lecture.

MORAL JUDGMENTS (guidelines of right and wrong for judging individuals and for establishing legal principles)

Taking another person's life is wrong.

Equal rights under the law should not be denied on the basis of race or sex.

Functional and aesthetic judgments generally require defining key terms and establishing criteria for the judging or ranking made by the assertion. How, for example, do we compare golfers? On the amount of money won? The number of tournaments won? Or the consistency of winning throughout one's career? What about the golfer's quality and range of shots? Ethical and moral judgments may be more difficult to support because they depend not just on how terms are defined and criteria established but on values and beliefs as well. If taking another person's life is wrong, why isn't it wrong in war? Or is it? These are difficult questions that require thoughtful responses.

EXERCISES: Understanding Assumptions, Facts, False Facts, Inferences, and Judgments

1. Categorize the judgments you wrote for the previous exercise (page 79) as either aesthetic, moral, ethical, or functional. Alternatively, compile a list of three judgments that you then categorize.
2. For each judgment listed for exercise 1, generate one statement of support, either a fact or an inference or another judgment. Then state the warrant (underlying assumption) required to complete each argument.
3. Read the following article and then complete the exercise that follows. This exercise tests both careful reading and your understanding of the differences among facts, inferences, and judgments.

PARADISE LOST | RICHARD MORIN

Richard Morin, a journalist with the *Washington Post,* writes a regular Sunday column titled "Unconventional Wisdom," a column presenting interesting new information from the social sciences. The following article was Morin's column for July 9, 2000.

1   Here's my fantasy vacation: Travel back in time to the 1700s, to some languid South Pacific island paradise where ripe fruit hangs heavy on the trees and the native islanders live in peace with nature and with each other.

2   Or at least that was my fantasy vacation until I talked to anthropologist Patrick Kirch, one of the country's leading authorities on the South Pacific and

director of the Phoebe Hearst Museum of Anthropology at the University of
California at Berkeley.

The South Seas islands painted by Paul Gauguin and celebrated by Robert 3
Louis Stevenson were no Gardens of Eden, Kirch writes in his riveting new
history of the South Pacific, *On the Road of the Winds*. Many of these islands
witnessed episodes of environmental depredation, endemic warfare and
bloody ritual long before seafaring Europeans first visited. "Most islands of the
Pacific were densely populated by the time of European contact, and the
human impact on the natural ecosystem was often disastrous—with wholesale
decimation of species and loss of vast tracts of land," he said.

Kirch says we can blame the French for all the loose talk about a tropical 4
nirvana. "French philosophers of the Enlightenment saw these islands, especially Tahiti, as the original natural society where people lived in a state of
innocence and food fell from the trees," he said. "How wrong they were."

French explorer Louis Antoine de Bougainville visited Tahiti for two 5
weeks in 1769 and thought he discovered a paradise awash in social tolerance and carefree sex. Bougainville's breathless description of Tahiti became
the basis for Jean Jacques Rousseau's concept of *l'homme naturel*—the
noble savage.

Savage, indeed. Even as Bougainville poked around their craggy volcanic 6
island, Rousseau's "noble savages" were busy savaging each other. The Tahitians were in the midst of a bitter civil war, complete with ritual sacrifice to
their bloodthirsty war god, Oro. On Mangaia in the Cook Islands, Kirch discovered ovens and pits filled with the charred bones of men, women, and
even children.

And forget that free-love nonsense. Dating, mating and reproduction were 7
tricky business throughout the South Seas several hundred years ago. To keep
the population in check, the residents of tiny Tikopia in the Santa Cruz Islands
practiced infanticide. Abortion also was common. And to "concentrate" their
bloodlines, Kirch said, members of the royal class in Hawaii married their brothers and sisters. If they only knew . . .

Not all South Seas islands were little cesspools. On some of the smaller 8
islands, early Polynesians avoided cultural collapse by adopting strict population control measures, including enforced suicide. "Some young men were
encouraged to go to sea and not return," he said.

Perhaps the best example of the havoc wrought by the indigenous peo- 9
ples of the South Pacific is found on desolate Easter Island, home of the monolithic stone heads that have gazed out from the front of a thousand travel
brochures. Until recently, researchers believed that Easter Island's open,
grassy plains and barren knife-point volcanic ridges had always been, well,
grassy plains and barren ridges.

Not true, says Kirch. The island was once covered with dense palm and 10
hardwood forests. But by the 1700s, when the first Europeans arrived, these
forests had been burned by the islanders to clear land for agriculture, transforming lush groves into semi-tropical tundra. "On Easter Island, the ultimate extinction of the palm and other woody plants had a further

consequence: the inability to move or erect the large stone statues" because there were no logs to use as rollers to move the giant heads from the quarries, Kirch writes.

11   The stone carvers' society collapsed, as did Easter Island culture. By the time Dutch explorer Jacob Roggeveen arrived on Easter Sunday in 1722, residents had taken to living in underground caves for protection from the social chaos that had enveloped their island home.

12   When viewed today, Kirch says, the monoliths remain an "imposing stone text that suggests a thousand human sagas." They also carry a lesson to our age, he argues—warning us "to achieve a sustainable relationship with our planet"—or else.

Label each of the following sentences as F (fact), FF (false fact), I (inference), or J (judgment).

_____ 1. In the 1700s native South Pacific islanders lived in peace and harmony.

_____ 2. It is foolish to romanticize life on South Sea islands.

_____ 3. French philosopher Rousseau based his idea of the noble savage on the Tahitians.

_____ 4. The stone statues on Easter Island suggest many stories.

_____ 5. In the past, noble Hawaiians married within their families.

_____ 6. Tahitians were savage people.

_____ 7. Some South Pacific islanders used to practice abortion and infanticide.

_____ 8. Easter Island has always had grassy plains and barren ridges.

_____ 9. Finding and using sustainable strategies will help preserve the environment.

_____ 10. People should not marry family members.

LEARNING MORE ABOUT THE TOULMIN MODEL OF ARGUMENT

Philosopher Stephen Toulmin was particularly interested in the great range in the strength or probability of various arguments. Some kinds of arguments are stronger than others because of the language or logic they use. Other arguments must, necessarily, be heavily qualified for the claim to be supportable. Toulmin developed his language to provide a strategy for analyzing the degree of probability in a given argument and to remind us of the need to qualify some kinds of claims. You have already seen how the idea of warrants, or assumptions, helps us think about the "glue" that presumably makes a given argument work. Additional Toulmin terms and concepts help us analyze the arguments of others and prepare more convincing arguments of our own.

Claims

A claim is what the argument asserts or seeks to prove. It answers the question "What is your point?" In an argumentative speech or essay, the claim is the speaker or writer's main idea or thesis. Although an argument's claim "follows" from reasons and evidence, we often present an argument—whether written or spoken—with the claim stated near the beginning of the presentation. We can better understand an argument's claim by recognizing that we can have claims of fact, claims of value, and claims of policy.

Claims of Fact

Although facts usually support claims, we do argue over some facts. Historians and biographers may argue over what happened in the past, although they are more likely to argue over the significance of what happened. Scientists also argue over the facts, over how to classify an unearthed fossil, for example, or whether the fossil indicates that the animal had feathers. For example:

> CLAIM: The small, predatory dinosaur *Deinonychus* hunted its prey in packs.

This claim is supported by the discovery of several fossils of *Deinonychus* close together and with the fossil bones of a much larger dinosaur. Their teeth have also been found in or near the bones of dinosaurs that have died in a struggle.

Assertions about what will happen are sometimes classified as claims of fact, but they can also be labeled as inferences supported by facts. Predictions about a future event may be classified as claims of fact:

> CLAIM: The United States will win the most gold medals at the 2004 Olympics.

> CLAIM: I will get an A on tomorrow's psychology test.

What evidence would you use today to support each of these claims? (And, did the first one turn out to be correct?)

Claims of Value

These include moral, ethical, and aesthetic judgments. Assertions that use such words as *good* or *bad, better* or *worse,* and *right* or *wrong* will be claims of value. The following are all claims of value:

> CLAIM: Pete Sampras is a better tennis player than Andre Agassi.

> CLAIM: *Adventures of Huckleberry Finn* is one of the most significant American novels.

> CLAIM: Cheating hurts others and the cheater too.

> CLAIM: Abortion is wrong.

Arguments in support of judgments demand relevant evidence, careful reasoning, and an awareness of the assumptions one is making. Support for claims of value often include other value statements. For example, to support the claim that censorship is bad, arguers often assert that the free exchange of ideas is good and necessary in a democracy. The support is itself a value statement. The arguer may believe, probably correctly, that most people will more readily agree to the support (the free exchange of ideas is good) than to the claim (censorship is bad).

Claims of Policy

Finally, claims of policy are assertions about what should or should not happen, what the government ought or ought not to do, how to best solve social problems. Claims of policy debate, for example, college rules, state gun laws, or federal aid to Africans suffering from AIDS. The following are claims of policy:

> CLAIM: College newspapers should not be controlled in any way by college authorities.
>
> CLAIM: States should not have laws allowing people to carry concealed weapons.
>
> CLAIM: The United States must provide more aid to African countries where 25 percent or more of the citizens have tested positive for HIV.

Claims of policy are often closely tied to judgments of morality or political philosophy, but they also need to be grounded in feasibility. That is, your claim needs to be doable, to be based on a thoughtful consideration of the real world and the complexities of public policy issues.

Grounds (or Data or Evidence)

The term *grounds* refers to the reasons and evidence provided in support of a claim. Although the words *data* and *evidence* can also be used, note that *grounds* is the more general term because it includes reasons or logic as well as examples or statistics. We determine the grounds of an argument by asking the question "Why do you think that?" or "How do you know that?" When writing your own arguments, you can ask yourself these questions and answer by using a *because* clause:

> CLAIM: Smoking should be banned in restaurants
>
> because
>
> GROUNDS: secondhand smoke is a serious health hazard.
>
> CLAIM: Pete Sampras is a better tennis player than Andre Agassi
>
> because
>
> GROUNDS: 1. he has been ranked number one longer than Agassi,
>
> 2. he has won more tournaments than Agassi, and
>
> 3. he has won more major tournaments than Agassi.

Warrants

Why should we believe that your grounds do indeed support your claim? Your argument's warrants answer this question. They explain why your evidence really is evidence. Sometimes warrants reside in language itself, in the meanings of the words we are using. If I am *younger* than my brother, then my brother must be *older* than I am. In a court case attempting to prove that Jones murdered Smith, the relation of evidence to claim is less assured. If the police investigation has been properly managed and the physical evidence is substantial, then Smith may be Jones's murderer. The prosecution has—presumably beyond a reasonable doubt—established motive, means, and opportunity for Smith to commit the murder. In many arguments based on statistical data, the argument's warrant rests on complex analyses of the statistics—and on the conviction that the statistics have been developed without error. In some philosophical arguments, the warrants are the logical structures (often shown mathematically) connecting a sequence of reasons. Still, without taking courses in statistics and logic, you can develop an alertness to the "good sense" of some arguments and the "dubious sense" of others. You know, for example, that good SAT scores are a predictor of success in college. Can you argue that you will do well in college because you have good SATs? No. We can determine only a statistical probability. We cannot turn probabilities about a group of people into a warrant about one person in the group. (In addition, SAT scores are only one predictor. Another key variable is motivation.)

What is the warrant for the Sampras claim?

CLAIM:	Pete Sampras is a better tennis player than Andre Agassi.
GROUNDS:	The three facts listed above.
WARRANT:	It is appropriate to judge and rank tennis players on these kinds of statistics. That is, the better player is one who has held the number one ranking for the longest time, has won the most tournaments, and also has won the most major tournaments.

Backing

Standing behind an argument's warrant may be additional *backing*. Backing answers the question "How do we know that your evidence is good evidence?" You may answer this question by providing authoritative sources for the data used (for example, the Census Bureau or the U.S. Tennis Association). Or, you may explain in detail the methodology of the experiments performed or the surveys taken. When scientists and social scientists present the results of their research, they anticipate the question of backing and automatically provide a detailed explanation of the process by which they acquired their evidence. In criminal trials, defense attorneys challenge the backing of the prosecution's argument. They question the handling of blood samples sent to labs for DNA testing, for instance. The defense attorneys want jury members to doubt the *quality* of the evidence, perhaps even to doubt the reliability of DNA testing altogether.

This discussion of backing returns us to the point that one part of any argument is the audience. To create an effective argument, you need to assess the potential for acceptance of your warrants and backing. Is your audience likely to share your values, your religious beliefs, or your scientific approach to issues? If you are speaking to a group at your church, then backing based on the religious beliefs of that church may be effective. If you are preparing an argument for a general audience, then using specific religious assertions as warrants or backing probably will not result in an effective argument.

Qualifiers

Some arguments are absolute; they can be stated without qualification. *If I am younger than my brother, then he must be older than I am.* Most arguments need some qualification; many need precise limitations. If, when playing bridge, I am dealt eight spades, then my opponents and partner together must have five spade cards—because there are thirteen cards of each suit in a deck. My partner *probably* has one spade but *could be* void of spades. My partner *possibly* has two or more spades, but I would be foolish to count on it. When bidding my hand, I must be controlled by the laws of probability. Look again at the smoking ban claim. Observe the absolute nature of both the claim and its support. If second-hand smoke is indeed a health hazard, it will be that in *all* restaurants, not just in some. With each argument we need to assess the need of qualification that is appropriate to a successful argument.

Sweeping generalizations often come to us in the heat of a debate or when we first start to think about an issue. For example: *Gun control is wrong because it restricts individual rights.* But on reflection surely you would not want to argue against all forms of gun control. (Remember: An unqualified assertion is understood by your audience to be absolute.) Would you sell guns to felons in jail or to children on the way to school? Obviously not. So, let's try the claim again, this time with two important qualifiers:

> QUALIFIED   Adults without a criminal record should not be restricted in the
> CLAIM: purchase of guns.

Others may want this claim further qualified to eliminate particular types of guns or to control the number purchased or the process for purchasing. The gun-control debate is not about absolutes; it is all about which qualified claim is best.

Rebuttals

Arguments can be challenged. Smart debaters assume that there are people who will disagree with them. They anticipate the ways that opponents can challenge their arguments. When you are planning an argument, you need to think about how you can counter or rebut the challenges you anticipate. Think of yourself as an attorney in a court case preparing your argument *and* a defense of the other attorney's challenges to your argument. If you ignore the important role of rebuttals, you may not win the jury to your side.

USING TOULMIN'S TERMS TO ANALYZE ARGUMENTS

Terms are never an end in themselves; we learn them when we recognize that they help us to organize our thinking about a subject. Toulmin's terms can aid your reading of the arguments of others. You can "see what's going on" in an argument if you analyze it, applying Toulmin's language to its parts. Not all terms will be useful for every analysis because, for example, some arguments will not have qualifiers or rebuttals. But to recognize that an argument is *without qualifiers* is to learn something important about that argument.

First, here is a simple argument broken down into its parts using Toulmin's terms:

GROUNDS: Because Dr. Bradshaw has an attendance policy,

CLAIM: students who miss more than seven classes will

QUALIFIER: most likely (last year, Dr. Bradshaw did allow one student, in unusual circumstances, to continue in the class) be dropped from the course.

WARRANT: Dr. Bradshaw's syllabus explains her attendance policy, a

BACKING: policy consistent with the concept of a discussion class that depends on student participation and consistent with the attendance policies of most of her colleagues.

REBUTTAL: Although some students complain about an attendance policy of any kind, Dr. Bradshaw does explain her policy and her reasons for it the first day of class. She then reminds students that the syllabus is a contract between them; if they choose to stay, they agree to abide by the guidelines explained on the syllabus.

This argument is brief and fairly simple. Let's see how Toulmin's terms can help us analyze a longer, more complex argument. Read actively and annotate the following essay while at the same time noting the existing annotations using Toulmin's terms. Then answer the questions that follow the article.

LET THE ZOO'S ELEPHANTS GO | LES SCHOBERT

The author has spent more than thirty years working in zoos, primarily in care of elephants. He has been a curator of both the Los Angeles and North Carolina zoos. His argument was published October 16, 2005, in the *Washington Post*.

PREREADING QUESTIONS What are some good reasons to have zoos? What are some problems associated with them?

The Smithsonian Institution is a national treasure, but when it comes to elephants, its National Zoo is a national embarrassment.   1

In 2000 the zoo euthanized Nancy, an African elephant that was suffering   2
from foot problems so painful that standing had become difficult for her. Five

Toulmin's terms:

years later the zoo has announced that Toni, an Asian elephant, is suffering from arthritis so severe that she, too, may be euthanized.

Grounds.

3   The elephants' debilitating ailments are probably a result of the inadequate conditions in which they have been held. The same story is repeated in zoos across the country.

Backing.

4   When I began my zoo career 35 years ago, much less was known about elephants than is known today. We now understand that keeping elephants in tiny enclosures with unnatural surfaces destroys their legs and feet. We have learned that to breed naturally and rear their young, elephants must live in herds that meet their social requirements. And we have come to realize that controlling elephants through domination and the use of ankuses (sharply pointed devices used to inflict pain) can no longer be justified.

Claim.

5   Zoos must change the concept of how elephants are kept in captivity, starting with how much space we allot them. Wild elephants may walk 30 miles a day. A typical home range of a wild elephant is 1,000 square miles. At the National Zoo, Toni has access to a yard of less than an acre. Zoo industry standards allow the keeping of elephants in as little as 2,200 square feet, or about 5 percent of an acre.

Grounds.

6   Some zoos have begun to reevaluate their ability to house elephants. After the death of two elephants in 2004, the San Francisco Zoo sent its surviving elephants to a sanctuary in California. This year the Detroit Zoo closed its elephant exhibit on ethical grounds, and its two surviving elephants now thrive at the California sanctuary as well.

Rebuttal to counterargument.

7   But attitudes at other zoos remain entrenched. To justify their outdated exhibits, some zoos have redefined elephant longevity and natural behavior. For example, National Zoo officials blame Toni's arthritis on old age. But elephants in the wild reproduce into their fifties, and female elephants live long after their reproductive cycles cease. Had she not been captured in Thailand at the age of 7 months, Toni, at age 39, could have had decades more of life as a mother and a grandmother. Instead, she faces an early death before her 40th birthday, is painfully thin and is crippled by arthritis.

Claim, qualified (options explained). Grounds.

8   The National Zoo's other elephants face the same bleak future if changes are not made. A preserve of at least 2 square miles—1,280 acres, or almost eight times the size of the National Zoo—would be necessary to meet an elephant's physical and social needs. Since this is not feasible, the zoo should send its pachyderms to a sanctuary. One such facility, the Elephant Sanctuary in Tennessee, offers 2,700 acres of natural habitat over which elephants can roam and heal from the damage caused by zoo life. The sanctuary's soft soil,

Grounds.

varied terrain, freedom of choice and freedom of movement have restored life to elephants that were suffering foot and joint diseases after decades in zoos and circuses.

Claim restated. Warrant (states values).

9   The National Zoo has the opportunity to overcome its troubled animal-care history by joining progressive zoos in reevaluating its elephant program. The zoo should do right by its elephants, and the public should demand nothing less.

QUESTIONS FOR READING

1. What is the occasion that had led to the writing of this article?
2. What is Schobert's subject?
3. State his claim in a way that shows that it is a solution to a problem.

QUESTIONS FOR REASONING AND ANALYSIS

1. What type of evidence (grounds) does the author provide?
2. What are the nature and source of his backing?
3. What makes his opening effective?
4. What values does Schobert express? What assumption does he make about his readers?

QUESTIONS FOR REFLECTING AND WRITING

1. Are you surprised by any of the facts about elephants presented by Schobert? Do they make sense to you, upon reflection?
2. Should zoos close down their elephant houses? Why or why not?
3. Are there any alternatives to city zoos with small elephant houses besides elephant sanctuaries?

USING TOULMIN'S TERMS AS A GUIDE TO STRUCTURING ARGUMENTS

You have seen how Toulmin's terms can help you to analyze and see what writers are actually "doing" in their arguments. You have also observed from both the short and the longer argument that writers do not usually follow the terms in precise order. Indeed, you can find both grounds and backing in the same sentence, or claim and qualifiers in the same paragraph, and so on. Still, the terms can help you to sort out your thinking about a claim you want to support. The following exercises will provide practice in your use of these terms to plan an argument.

EXERCISES: Using Toulmin's Terms to Plan Arguments

1. In groups or on your own, build an outline for the claim: "It is foolish to romanticize life on South Sea islands." Use information from Richard Morin's article "Paradise Lost" (pages 80–82) for some of your grounds. Set up your plan on a page (or more) with each of Toulmin's terms listed down the left margin and your plan for the parts of the argument opposite each appropriate term. (Be sure to refer to Morin and his article when you use information from "Paradise Lost"; the references are your *backing*.)
2. Select one of the following claims, or one of your own if your instructor approves, and plan an argument, listing as many grounds as you can and paying

attention to possible rebuttals of counterarguments. Use the same format as
described in the previous exercise. Expect your outline to be one to two pages.

a.   Professor X is (or is not) a good teacher.
b.   Colleges should (or should not) admit students only on the basis of
     academic merit.
c.   Americans need (or do not need) to reduce the fat in their diets.
d.   Physical education classes should (or should not) be graded pass/fail.
e.   Public schools should (or should not) have dress codes.
f.   Helmets for bicyclists should (or should not) be mandatory.
g.   Sales taxes on cigarettes should (or should not) be increased.
h.   All cigarette advertising should (or should not) be prohibited.

FOR DEBATE

HOW BINGEING BECAME THE NEW COLLEGE SPORT | BARRETT SEAMAN

A graduate of Hamilton College and trustee of the college, Barrett Seaman was an
editor of *Time* magazine for many years, working at a variety of bureaus abroad and
covering the Reagan administration as well. His book *Binge: What Your College
Student Won't Tell You* was published in 2005. Seaman gathered material for his book
by living in college dorms and observing today's students. His essay, based on his
book, appeared in *Time* on August 29, 2005.

PREREADING QUESTIONS What specifically, does the term *binge* mean to you? Do
you engage in behavior you would describe as bingeing? If so, why?

1   In the coming weeks, millions of students will begin their fall semester of
college, with all the attendant rituals of campus life: freshman orientation, reg-
istering for classes, rushing by fraternities and sororities and, in a more recent
nocturnal college tradition, "pregaming" in their rooms.

2   Pregaming is probably unfamiliar to people who went to college before
the 1990s. But it is now a common practice among 18-, 19- and 20-year-old students who cannot legally buy or consume alcohol. It usually involves sitting in
a dorm room or an off-campus apartment and drinking as much hard liquor as
possible before heading out for the evening's parties. While reporting for my
book *Binge*, I witnessed the hospitalization of several students for acute alcohol poisoning. Among them was a Hamilton College freshman who had consumed 22 shots of vodka while sitting in a dorm room with her friends. Such
hospitalizations are routine on campuses across the nation. By the Thanksgiving break of the year I visited Harvard, the university's health center had admitted nearly 70 students for alcohol poisoning.

3   When students are hospitalized—or worse yet, die from alcohol poisoning,
which happens about 300 times each year—college presidents tend to react by
declaring their campuses dry or shutting down fraternity houses. But tighter

enforcement of the minimum drinking age of 21 is not the solution. It's part of the problem.

Over the past 40 years, the U.S. has taken a confusing approach to the 4 age-appropriateness of various rights, privileges and behaviors. It used to be that 21 was the age that legally defined adulthood. On the heels of the student revolution of the late '60s, however, came sweeping changes: the voting age was reduced to 18; privacy laws were enacted that protected college students' academic, health and disciplinary records from outsiders, including parents; and the drinking age, which had varied from state to state, was lowered to 18.

Then, thanks in large measure to intense lobbying by Mothers Against 5 Drunk Driving, Congress in 1984 effectively blackmailed states into hiking the minimum drinking age to 21 by passing a law that tied compliance to the distribution of federal-aid highway funds—an amount that will average $690 million per state this year. There is no doubt that the law, which achieved full 50-state compliance in 1988, saved lives, but it had the unintended consequence of creating a covert culture around alcohol as the young adult's forbidden fruit.

Drinking has been an aspect of college life since the first Western universi- 6 ties in the 14th century. My friends and I drank in college in the 1960s—sometimes a lot but not so much that we had to be hospitalized. Veteran college administrators cite a sea change in campus culture that began, not without coincidence, in the 1990s. It was marked by a shift from beer to hard liquor, consumed not in large social settings, since that is now illegal, but furtively and dangerously in students' residences.

In my reporting at colleges around the country, I did not meet any presi- 7 dents or deans who felt that the 21-year age minimum helps their efforts to curb the abuse of alcohol on their campuses. Quite the opposite. They thought the law impeded their efforts since it takes away the ability to monitor and supervise drinking activity.

What would happen if the drinking age was rolled back to 18 or 19? 8 Initially, there would be a surge in binge drinking as young adults savored their newfound freedom. But over time, I predict, U.S. college students would settle into the saner approach to alcohol I saw on the one campus I visited where the legal drinking age is 18: Montreal's McGill University, which enrolls about 2,000 American undergraduates a year. Many, when they first arrive, go overboard, exploiting their ability to drink legally. But by midterms, when McGill's demanding academic standards must be met, the vast majority have put drinking into its practical place among their priorities.

A culture like that is achievable at U.S. colleges if Congress can muster the 9 fortitude to reverse a bad policy. If lawmakers want to reduce drunk driving, they should do what the Norwegians do: throw the book at offenders no matter what their age. Meanwhile, we should let the pregamers come out of their dorm rooms so that they can learn to handle alcohol like the adults we hope and expect them to be.

QUESTIONS FOR READING

1. What is Seaman's subject? Be precise; binge drinking is not sufficient.
2. What does the term *pregaming* mean? Why do college students do this?
3. What serious consequences can result from pregaming?
4. What is the history of the drinking age in the United States? What, in the author's view, has been an unintended result of the current drinking age?

QUESTIONS FOR REASONING AND ANALYSIS

1. What is Seaman's claim? Where does he state it?
2. What purpose does McGill University serve for Seaman?
3. How does the author participate and rebut possible counterarguments?
4. What is the major assumption underlying the author's argument for lowering the drinking age?

QUESTIONS FOR REFLECTING AND WRITING

1. Do you agree that there is plenty of evidence of binge drinking, and of its serious consequences among college students? If so, do you agree that this is a problem that can and must be addressed? If so, do you agree that Seaman's solution is the best way to address the problem?
2. At what point—if anywhere—do you disagree with the author? If you disagree, explain why. If you accept all of the steps in his argument, defend your position.

DON'T MAKE TEEN DRINKING EASIER | JOSEPH A. CALIFANO, JR.

Joseph Califano is a lawyer and former secretary of Health, Education, and Welfare (1977–1979). The author of nine books, he is founder and currently president of the National Center on Addiction and Substance Abuse at Columbia University. His rebuttal to T. R. Reid's article was published in the *Washington Post* on May 11, 2003.

PREREADING QUESTIONS Given what you know about Joseph Califano, what do you expect his position to be?

1   T. R. Reid's May 4 [2003] op-ed piece, "Let My Teenager Drink," is a dangerous example of what happens if we let anecdote trump facts. Reid jumps from the comfort he derives from his 16- and 17-year-old daughters "out drinking Saturday night" at a neighborhood pub in London, where it is legal, to the conclusion that the English and Europeans have far fewer problems with teen drinking than we do in the United States, where the age to legally buy alcohol is 21.

2   Let's start with the facts. In 2001 the Justice Department released an analysis comparing drinking rates in Europe and the United States. The conclusion:

American 10th-graders are less likely to use and abuse alcohol than people of the same age in almost all European countries, including Britain. British 15- and 16-year-olds were more than twice as likely as Americans to binge drink (50 percent vs. 24 percent) and to have been intoxicated within the past 30 days (48 percent vs. 21 percent). Of Western European nations, only Portugal had a lower proportion of young people binge drinking, which is defined as having five or more drinks in a row.

That same year, in a study of 29 nations, including Eastern and Western 3 Europe, the World Health Organization found that American 15-year-olds were less likely than those in 18 other nations to have been intoxicated twice or more. British girls and boys were far likelier than their U.S. counterparts to have been drunk that often (52 and 51 percent vs. 28 and 34 percent).

Then there are the consequences of teen drinking. This month a Rand 4 study that followed 3,400 people from seventh grade through age 23 reported that those who had three or more drinks within the past year, or any drink in the past month, were likelier to use nicotine and illegal drugs, to have stolen items within the past year and to have problems in school. In a report issued last December, the American Medical Association found that teen drinking—not bingeing, just drinking—can seriously damage growth processes of the brain and that such damage "can be long term and irreversible." The AMA warned that "short term or moderate drinking impairs learning and memory far more in youth than in adults" and that "adolescents need only drink half as much to suffer the same negative effects." This exhaustive study concluded that teen drinkers "perform worse in school, are more likely to fall behind and have an increased risk of social problems, depression, suicidal thoughts and violence."

Alcohol is a major contributing factor in the three leading causes of teen 5 death—accidents, homicide and suicide—and increases the chances of juvenile delinquency and crime. Studies at the National Center on Addiction and Substance Abuse at Columbia University have found that teenagers who drink are more likely than those who do not to have sex and have it at an earlier age and with multiple partners.

There are many reasons why teens drink, but I doubt that states setting the 6 drinking age at 21 is one of them. Focus groups of young women suggest that the increase in their binge drinking is related to their wanting to "be one of the boys" and to reduce inhibition, particularly because of the pressure many feel to have sex. Few understand that, on average, one drink has the impact on a woman that it takes two drinks to have on a man. Adolescents of both sexes who have low self-esteem or learning disabilities, or who suffer eating disorders, are at higher risk of drinking.

As for the alcohol industry's role: The Center on Alcohol Marketing and 7 Youth at Georgetown University recently revealed that during the past two years, those under 21 heard more beer and liquor commercials on the radio than did adults. The Kaiser Family Foundation Teen Media Monitor, released in February, identified Coors Light and Budweiser beers as two of the five largest advertisers on the most popular television shows for teen boys. For the alcohol industry, it's a good long-term investment, because underage drinkers are likelier to become heavy adult drinkers and grow up to become that 9 percent of adult drinkers who consume 46.3 percent of the alcohol sold in the United States. If Mr. Reid thinks that politicians are hanging tough on the drinking age of 21 in order to "garner support and contributions from interest groups," I suggest he take a look at the political contributions from the alcohol industry to keep the price down by killing tax increases (and in this Congress to roll taxes back) and to prevent content and caloric labeling of its products.

8   Fortunately, overwhelming majorities of teens in the United States (84 percent) and adults (83 percent) favor keeping the legal drinking age of 21. Rather than paint rosy but unrealistic pictures of life in countries where teens can legally buy alcohol, we need to get serious about preventing underage drinking. We need to address the many factors that influence teens to drink: genetics, family situation, peer pressure, schools, access to alcohol, alcohol advertising targeting teens. The best place to start is to help parents understand the consequences of their teen's drinking.

QUESTIONS FOR READING

1. What is Califano's initial purpose in writing?
2. How do American teens compare with European teens in terms of alcohol consumption, binge drinking, and intoxication?
3. What are the consequences of teen drinking?
4. What are some of the causes of teen drinking?
5. How do American adults and teens feel about this country's drinking age?

QUESTIONS FOR REASONING AND ANALYSIS

1. Analyze Califano's argument using Toulmin's terms.
2. Analyze the author's organization. What does he do first? Second? And so on? How does his organization help his rebuttal?
3. Evaluate Califano's argument. What kind of evidence (grounds) does he use? Is it effective?

QUESTIONS FOR REFLECTING AND WRITING

1. Do you agree with Califano? If so, then presumably you accept the legal drinking age of 21—right? If you disagree with Califano, what are your counterarguments?
2. Usually, what kind of argument works best with you, one based on personal experience and anecdote or one based on statistics?

SUGGESTIONS FOR DISCUSSION AND WRITING

1. What are some problems caused by college students' drinking? You may be able to offer some answers to this question based on your knowledge and experience. You may also want to go **online** for some statistics about college drinking and health and safety risks. Drawing on both experience and data, what claim can you support?

2. Compare the style and tone in Seaman's and Califano's essays. Has each one written in a way that works for the author's approach to this issue? Be prepared to explain your views or develop them into a comparative analysis of style.

3. Explore further into the strongly debated issue of zoos. Check your library's electronic databases for recent articles. If you are near a zoo, take a look at the animals and the zoo's programs and schedule an interview with one of the curators. Where does your new information lead you? Can you defend a position on zoos?

GOING ONLINE

A good starting place for online research about college drinking and health and safety risks is at **www.collegedrinkingprevention.gov**, or conduct your own search.

© Bettmann/CORBIS

Read: Who is the figure? What is he doing?

Reason: Where does the figure appear to be?
What are the details of the context that
you infer?

Reflect/Write: The photo seems so "ordinary." What
gives it significance?

CHAPTER 4

Writing Effective Arguments

The basics of good writing remain much the same for works as seemingly different as the personal essay, the argument, and the researched essay. Good writing is focused, organized, and concrete. Effective essays are written in a style and tone that are suited to both the audience and the writer's purpose. These are sound principles, all well known to you. But how, exactly, do you achieve them when writing argument? This chapter will help you answer that question.

KNOW YOUR AUDIENCE

Too often students plunge into writing without thinking much about audience, for, after all, their "audience" is only the instructor who has given the assignment, just as their purpose in writing is to complete the assignment and get a grade. These views of audience and purpose are likely to lead to badly written arguments. First, if you are not thinking about readers who may disagree with you, you may not develop the best defense of your claim—which may need a rebuttal to possible counterarguments. Second, you may ignore your essay's needed introductory material on the assumption that the instructor, knowing the assignment, has a context for understanding your writing. To avoid these pitfalls, use the following questions to sharpen your understanding of audience.

Who Is My Audience?

If you are writing an essay for the student newspaper, your audience consists—primarily—of students, but do not forget that faculty and administrators also read the student newspaper. If you are preparing a letter-to-the-editor refutation of a recent column in your town's newspaper, your audience will be the readers of that newspaper—that is, adults in your town. Some instructors give assignments that create an audience such as those just described so that you will practice writing with a specific audience in mind.

If you are not assigned a specific audience, imagine your classmates, as well as your instructor, as part of your audience. In other words, you are writing to many readers in the academic community. These readers are intelligent and thoughtful, expecting sound reasoning and convincing evidence. These readers also represent varied values and beliefs, as they are from diverse cultures and experiences. Do not confuse the shared expectations of writing conventions, sound reasoning, and accuracy in presenting data with shared beliefs.

What Will My Audience Know about My Topic?

What can you expect a diverse group of readers to know? Whether you are writing on a current issue or a centuries-old debate, you must expect most readers to have some knowledge of the issues. Their knowledge does not free you from the responsibility of developing your support fully, though. In fact, their knowledge creates further demands. For example, most readers know the main arguments on both sides of the abortion issue. For you to write as if they do not—and thus to ignore the arguments of the opposition—is to produce an argument that probably adds little to the debate on the subject.

On the other hand, what some readers "know" may be little more than an overview of the issues from TV news—or the emotional outbursts of a family member. Some readers may be misinformed or prejudiced, but they embrace their views enthusiastically nonetheless. So, as you think about the ways to develop and support your argument, you will have to assess your readers' knowledge and sophistication. This assessment will help you decide how much background information to provide or what false facts need to be revealed and dismissed.

Where Does My Audience Stand on the Issue?

Expect readers to hold a range of views, even if you are writing to students on your campus or to an organization of which you are a member. It is not true, for instance, that all students want coed dorms or pass/fail grading. And, if everyone already agrees with you, you have no reason to write. An argument needs to be about a topic that is open to debate. So:

- Assume that some of your audience will probably never agree with you but may offer you grudging respect if you compose an effective argument.
- Assume that some readers do not hold strong views on your topic and may be open to convincing, if you present a good case.
- Assume that those who share your views will still be looking for a strong argument in support of their position.
- Assume that if you know you hold an unpopular position your best strategy will be a conciliatory approach. (See page 104–105 for a discussion of the conciliatory argument.)

How Should I Speak to My Audience?

Your audience will form an opinion of you based on how you write and how you reason. The image of argument—and the arguer—that we have been creating in this text's discussion is of thoughtful claims defended with logic and evidence. However, the heated debate at yesterday's lunch does not resemble this image of argument. Sometimes the word *persuasion* is used to separate the emotionally charged debate from the calm, intellectual tone of the academic argument. Unfortunately, this neat division between argument and persuasion does not describe the real world of debate. The thoughtful arguer also wants to be persuasive, to win over the audience. And highly emotional presentations can contain relevant facts in support of a sound idea. Instead of thinking of two separate categories—argument and persuasion—think instead of a continuum from the most rigorous logic at one end to extreme flights of fantasy on the other. Figure 4.1 suggests this continuum with some kinds of arguments placed along it.

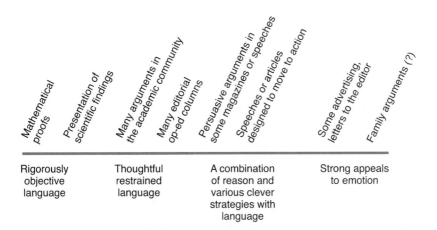

FIGURE 4.1 A Continuum of Argumentative Language

Where should you place yourself along the continuum in the language you choose and the tone you create? You will have to answer this question with each specific writing context. Much of the time you will choose "thoughtful, restrained language" as expected by the academic community, but there may be times that you will use various persuasive strategies. Probably you will not select "strong appeals to emotion" for your college or workplace writing. Remember that you have different roles in your life, and you use different *voices* as appropriate to each role. Most of the time, for most of your arguments, you will want to use the serious voice you normally select for serious conversations with other adults. This is the voice that will help you establish your credibility, your *ethos*.

Irony or Sarcasm?

As you learned in Chapter 2, irony is a useful rhetorical strategy for giving one's words greater emphasis by actually writing the opposite of what you mean. Many writers use irony effectively to give punch to their arguments. Irony catches our attention, makes us think, and engages us with the text. Sarcasm is not quite the same as irony. Irony can cleverly focus reader attention on life's complexities. Sarcasm is more often vicious than insightful, relying on harsh, negative word choice. Probably in most of your academic work, you will want to avoid sarcasm, and you will want to think carefully about the effect of any strongly worded appeal to your readers' emotions. Better to persuade your audience with the force of your reasons and evidence than to lose them because of the static of nasty language. But the key, always, is to know your audience and understand how best to present a convincing argument to that specific group.

UNDERSTAND YOUR WRITING PURPOSE

There are many kinds of arguments. As you consider possible topics, think about what you actually want to *do* with each topic—beyond wanting to write convincingly in defense of your claim. Different types of arguments require different approaches, or different kinds of evidence. It helps to be able to recognize what kind of argument you are contemplating. Here are some useful ways to classify arguments:

- **Inductive argument or investigative paper similar to those in the social sciences.** If you are given an assignment to collect evidence in an organized way to support a claim about advertising strategies or violence in children's programming, then you will be writing an investigative paper, presenting evidence that you have gathered and analyzed to support your claim.
- **Claim of values, or position paper.** If you are given the assignment to argue for your position on euthanasia, trying juveniles as adults, or national identification cards, you need to recognize that this assignment calls for a claim of values. You will be writing a rather philosophical argument, presenting reasons in support of a complex, controversial issue. You will need to pay close attention to your warrants or assumptions.

- **A definition argument.** If you are asked to consider the qualities or traits we should look for in a president or professor, you are really being asked to define "a good president" or "a good professor." Some of your points may seem quite concrete—practical—to you, but your specifics are really tied to an ideal you imagine, and that ideal is best understood as a definition.
- **A problem/solution argument, or claim of policy.** If you are given the broad subject: "What should we do about _____?" and you have to fill in the blank, you are being asked to recommend solutions to a current problem. What should we do about students' disruptive behavior? About gridlock on your town's streets? These kinds of questions ask for different types of answers than do questions about what traits make a good president or who are the greatest athletes.
- **A refutation or rebuttal of someone else's argument.** If you are given the assignment to find a letter to the editor, newspaper editorial, or essay in your textbook with which you disagree, you are being asked to prepare a refutation essay, a specific challenge to a specific argument. You know, then, that you will repeatedly refer to the work you are rebutting, so you will need to know that work thoroughly.

Understand at the beginning of your planning just what kind of argument you have chosen, and you will write more effectively.

MOVE FROM TOPIC TO CLAIM TO POSSIBLE SUPPORT

When you write a letter to the editor of a newspaper, you have chosen to respond to someone else's argument that has bothered you. In this writing context, you already know your topic and, probably, your claim as well. You also know that your purpose will be to refute the article you have read. In composition classes, the context is not always so clearly established, but you will usually be given some guidelines with which to get started.

Selecting a Topic

Suppose that you are asked to write an argument that is in some way connected to First Amendment rights. Your instructor has limited and focused your topic choice and purpose. Start thinking about possible topics that relate to freedom of speech and censorship issues. To aid your topic search and selection, use one or more invention strategies:

- Brainstorm (make a list).
- Freewrite (write without stopping for 10 minutes).
- Map or cluster (connect ideas to the general topic in various spokes, a kind of visual brainstorming).
- Read (in this case, look through the text for ideas).

Your invention strategies lead, let us suppose, to the following list of possible topics:

Administrative restrictions on the college newspaper
Hate speech restrictions or codes
Deleting certain books from high school reading lists
Controls and limits on alcohol and cigarette advertising
Restrictions on violent TV programming
Dress codes/uniforms

Looking over your list, you realize that the last item, dress codes/uniforms, may be about freedom but not freedom of speech, so you drop it from consideration. All of the other topics have promise. Which one do you select? Two considerations should guide you: interest and knowledge. First, your argument is likely to be more thoughtful and lively if you choose an issue that matters to you. You can also appreciate the usefulness of information and ideas on the topic. But, unless you have time for study, you are wise to choose a topic about which you already have some information and ideas. To continue the example, let's suppose that you decide to write about television violence because you are concerned about violence in American society, and you have given this issue some thought. It is time to phrase your topic as a tentative thesis or claim.

Drafting a Claim

Good claim statements will keep you focused in your writing—in addition to establishing your main idea for readers. Give thought, then, both to your position on the issue and to the wording of your claim. *Claim statements to avoid:*

- Claims using vague words such as *good* or *bad.*

  VAGUE: TV violence is bad for us.

  BETTER: We need more restrictions on violent TV programming.

- Claims in loosely worded "two-part" sentences.

  UNFOCUSED: Campus rape is a serious problem, and we need to do something about it.

  BETTER: College administrators and students need to work together to reduce both the number of campus rapes and the fear of rape.

- Claims that are not appropriately qualified.

  OVERSTATED: Violence on television is making us a violent society.

  BETTER: TV violence is contributing to viewers' increased fear of violence and insensitivity to violence.

- Claims that do not help you focus on your purpose in writing.

> **UNCLEAR PURPOSE:**   Not everyone agrees on what is meant by violent TV programming.

(Perhaps this is true, but more important, this claim suggests that you will define violent programming. Such an approach would not keep you focused on a First Amendment issue.)

> **BETTER:**   Restrictions on violent TV programs can be justified.

(Now your claim directs you to the debate over restrictions of content.)

Listing Possible Grounds

As you learned in Chapter 3, you can generate grounds to support a claim by adding a "because" clause after a claim statement. We can start a list of grounds for the topic on violent TV programming in this way:

> We need more restrictions on violent television programming *because*

- Many people, including children and teens, watch many hours of TV (get stats).
- People are affected by the dominant activities/experiences in their lives.
- There is a connection between violent programming and desensitizing and fear of violence and possibly more aggressive behavior in heavy viewers (get detail of studies).
- Society needs to protect young people.

You have four good points to work on, a combination of reasons and inferences drawn from evidence.

Listing Grounds for the Other Side or Another Perspective

Remember that arguments generate counterarguments. Continue your exploration of this topic by considering possible rebuttals to your proposed grounds. How might someone who does not want to see restrictions placed on television programming respond to each of your points? Let's think about them one at a time:

> We need more restrictions on violent television programming because

1. *Many people, including children and teens, watch many hours of TV.*

Your opposition cannot really challenge your first point on the facts, only its relevance to restricting programming. The opposition might argue that if parents think their children are watching too much TV, they should turn it off. The restriction needs to be a family decision.

2. *People are affected by the dominant activities/experiences in their lives.*

It seems common sense to expect people to be influenced by dominant forces in their lives. Your opposition might argue, though, that many people have the TV on for many hours but often are not watching it intently for all of that time. The more dominant forces in our lives are parents and teachers and peers, not the TV. The opposition might also argue that people seem to be influenced to such different degrees by television that it is not fair or logical to restrict everyone when perhaps only a few are truly influenced by their TV viewing to a harmful degree.

3. *There is a connection between violent programming and desensitizing and fear of violence and possibly more aggressive behavior in heavy viewers.*

Some people are entirely convinced by studies showing these negative effects of violent TV programming, but others point to the less convincing studies or make the argument that if violence on TV were really so powerful an influence, most people would be violent or fearful or desensitized.

4. *Society needs to protect young people.*

Your opposition might choose to agree with you in theory on this point—and then turn again to the argument that parents should be doing the protecting. Government controls on programming restrict adults, as well as children, whereas it may only be some children who should watch fewer hours of TV and not watch adult "cop" shows at all.

Working through this process of considering opposing views can help you see

- Where you may want to do some research for facts to provide backing for your grounds
- How you can best develop your reasons to take account of typical counter-arguments.
- If you should qualify your claim in some ways.

Considering the Rogerian or Conciliatory Argument

Psychologist Carl Rogers asserts that the most successful arguments take a conciliatory approach. The characteristics of this approach include:

- Showing respect for the opposition in the language and tone of the argument
- Seeking common ground by indicating specific facts and values that both sides share
- Qualifying the claim to bring opposing sides more closely together

In their essay "Euthanasia—A Critique," authors Peter A. Singer and Mark Siegler provide a good example of a conciliatory approach. They begin their essay by explaining and then rebutting the two main arguments in favor of euthanasia. After stating the two arguments in clear and neutral language, they write this in response to the first argument:

> We agree that the relief of pain and suffering is a crucial goal of medicine. We question, however, whether the care of dying patients cannot be improved without resorting to the drastic measure of euthanasia. Most physical pain can

be relieved with the appropriate use of analgesic agents. Unfortunately, despite widespread agreement that dying patients must be provided with necessary analgesia, physicians continue to underuse analgesia in the care of dying patients because of concern about depressing respiratory drive or creating addiction. Such situations demand better management of pain, not euthanasia.

In this paragraph, Singer and Siegler accept the value of pain management among dying patients. They go even further and offer a solution to the problem of suffering among the terminally ill—better pain management by physicians. They remain thoughtful in their approach and tone throughout, while sticking to their position that legalizing euthanasia is not the solution.

Chris Brown, in the sample student essay on pages 179–81, provides a good example of a conciliatory argument. Read it and note examples of the three elements of the conciliatory argument outlined by Carl Rogers. Consider how you can use this approach to write more effective arguments. It will help you avoid "overheated" language and maintain your focus on what is doable in a world of differing points of view. There is the expression that "you can catch more flies with honey than with vinegar." Using "honey" instead of "vinegar" might also make you feel better about yourself.

Planning Your Approach

Now that you have thought about arguments on the other side, you decide that you want to argue for a qualified claim that is also more precise:

> To protect young viewers, we need restrictions on violence in children's programs and ratings for prime-time adult shows that clearly establish the degree of violence in those shows.

This qualified claim responds to two points of the rebuttals. Our student hasn't given in to the other side but has chosen to narrow the argument to emphasize the protection of children, an area of common ground.

Next, it's time to check some of the articles in this text or go online to get some data to develop points 1 and 3. You need to know that 99 percent of homes have at least one TV; you need to know that by the time young people graduate from high school they have spent more time in front of the TV than in the classroom. Also, you can find the average number of violent acts by hour of TV in children's programs. Then, too, there are the various studies of fearfulness and aggressive behavior that will give you some statistics to use to develop the third point. Be sure to select reliable sources and then cite the sources you use. Citing sources is not only required and right; it is also part of the process of establishing your credibility and thus strengthening your argument.

Finally, how are you going to answer the point about parents controlling their children? You might counter that in theory this is the way it should be—but in fact not all parents are at home watching what their children are watching, and not all parents care enough to pay attention. However, all of us suffer from the consequences of those children who are influenced by their TV watching to become more aggressive or fearful or desensitized. These children grow up to become the adults the rest of us have to interact with, so the problem becomes one for the society as a whole to solve, not individual parents. If you had not disciplined yourself to go through the process of listing possible rebuttals, you may not have thought through this part of the debate.

DRAFT YOUR ARGUMENT

Many of us can benefit from a step-by-step process of invention—such as we have been exploring in the last few pages. In addition, the more notes you have from working through the Toulmin structure, the easier it will be to get started on your draft. Many students report that they can control their writing anxiety when they generate detailed notes. A page or two of notes that also suggest an organizational strategy can remove that awful feeling of staring at a blank page or blank computer screen.

In the following chapters on argument, you will find specific suggestions for organizing the various kinds of arguments we listed in the section on understanding your writing purpose. But you can always rely on one of the following two basic organizations for argument, regardless of the specific type of argument:

PLAN 1: ORGANIZING AN ARGUMENT

Attention-getting opening (why the issue is important, or current, etc.)

Claim statement

Reasons and evidence in order from least important to most important

Challenge to potential rebuttals or counterarguments

Conclusion that reemphasizes claim

PLAN 2: ORGANIZING AN ARGUMENT

Attention-getting opening

Claim statement (or possibly leave to the conclusion)

Order by arguments of opposing position, with your challenge to each

Conclusion that reemphasizes (or states for the first time) your claim

GUIDELINES for Drafting

- **Try to get a complete draft of an essay in one sitting, so that you can "see" the whole piece.**
- **If you can't think of a clever opening, state your claim and move on to the body of your essay.** After you draft your reasons and evidence, a good opening may occur to you.

- **If you find that you need something more in some parts of your essay, leave space there as a reminder that you will need to return to that paragraph later.**
- **Try to avoid using either a dictionary or thesaurus while drafting.** Your goal is to get the ideas down. You will polish later.
- **Learn to draft at your computer.** Revising is so much easier that you will be more willing to make significant changes if you work at your PC. If you are handwriting your draft, leave plenty of margin space for additions or for directions to shift parts around.

REVISE YOUR DRAFT

If you have drafted at the computer, begin revising by printing a copy of your draft. Most of us cannot do an adequate job of revision by looking at a computer screen. Then remind yourself that revision is a three-step process: rewriting, editing, and proofreading.

Rewriting

You are not ready to polish the writing until you are satisfied with the argument. Look first at the total piece. Do you have all the necessary parts: a claim, support, some response to possible counterarguments? Examine the order of your reasons and evidence. Do some of your points belong, logically, in a different place? Does the order make the most powerful defense of your claim? Be willing to move whole paragraphs around to test the best organization. Also reflect on the argument itself. Have you avoided logical fallacies? Have you qualified statements when appropriate? Do you have enough support? The best support for your argument?

Consider development: Is your essay long enough to meet assignment requirements? Are points fully developed to satisfy the demands of readers? One key to development is the length of your paragraphs. If most of your paragraphs are only two or three sentences, you have not developed the point of each paragraph satisfactorily. It is possible that some paragraphs need to be combined because they are really on the same subtopic. More typically, short paragraphs need further explanation of ideas or examples to illustrate ideas. Compare the following paragraphs for effectiveness:

First Draft of a Paragraph from an Essay on Gun Control

One popular argument used against the regulation of gun ownership is the need of citizens, especially in urban areas where the crime rate is higher, to possess a handgun for personal protection, either carried or kept in the home. Some citizens may not be aware of the dangers to themselves or their families when they purchase a gun. Others, more aware, may embrace the myth that "bad things only happen to other people."

Revised Version of the Paragraph with Statistics Added

> One popular argument used against the regulation of gun ownership is the need of citizens, especially in urban areas where the crime rate is higher, to possess a handgun for personal protection, whether it is carried or kept in the home. Although some citizens may not be aware of the dangers to themselves or their families when they purchase a gun, they should be. According to the Center to Prevent Handgun Violence, from their Web page "Firearm Facts," "guns that are kept in the home for self-protection are 22 times more likely to kill a family member or friend than to kill in self-defense." The Center also reports that guns in the home make homicide three times more likely and suicide five times more likely. We are not thinking straight if we believe that these dangers only apply to others.

A quick trip to the Internet has provided this student with some facts to support his argument. Observe how he has referred informally but fully to the source of his information. (If your instructor requires formal MLA documentation in all essays, then you will need to add a Works Cited page and give a full reference to the Web site. See pages 306–09.)

Editing

Make your changes, print another copy, and begin the second phase of revision: editing. As you read through this time, pay close attention to unity and coherence, to sentence patterns, and to word choice. Read each paragraph as a separate unit to be certain that everything is on the same subtopic. Then look at your use of transition and connecting words, both within and between paragraphs. Ask yourself: Have you guided the reader through the argument? Have you shown how the parts connect by using appropriate connectors such as *therefore, in addition, as a consequence, also,* and so forth?

Read again, focusing on each sentence, checking to see that you have varied sentence patterns and length. Read sentences aloud to let your ear help you find awkward constructions or unfinished thoughts. Strive as well for word choice that is concrete and specific, avoiding wordiness, clichés, trite expressions, or incorrect use of specialized terms. Observe how Samantha edited one paragraph in her essay "Balancing Work and Family":

Draft Version of Paragraph

vague reference
agreement.

wordy.

short sentences.

> Women have come a long way in equalizing themselves, but inequality within marriages do exist. One reason for this can be found in the media. Just last week America turned on their televisions to watch a grotesque dramatization of skewed priorities. On Who Wants to Marry a Millionaire, a panel of women vied for the affections of a millionaire who would choose one of them to be his wife. This show said that women can be purchased. Also that men must provide and that money is worth the sacrifice of one's individuality. The show also suggests that physical attraction is more important than the building of a complete relationship. Finally, the show says that women's true value lies in

their appearance. <u>This</u> is a dangerous message to send to both men and women viewers.

vague reference.

Edited Version of Paragraph

Although women have come a long way toward equality in the workplace, inequality within marriages can still be found. The media may be partly to blame for this continued inequality. Just last week Americans watched a grotesque dramatization of skewed priorities. On <u>Who Wants to Marry a Millionaire</u>, a panel of women vied for the affections of a millionaire who would choose one of them to be his wife. Such displays teach us that women can be purchased, that men must be the providers, that the desire for money is worth the sacrifice of one's individuality, that physical attraction is more important than a complete relationship, and that women's true value lies in their appearance. These messages discourage marriages based on equality and mutual support.

Samantha's editing has eliminated wordiness and vague references and has combined ideas into one forceful sentence. If you have a good argument, you do not want to lose readers because you have not taken the time to polish your writing.

A Few Words about Words and Tone

You have just been advised to check your word choice to eliminate wordiness, vagueness, clichés, and so on. Here is a specific checklist of problems often found in student papers with some ways to fix the problems.

- *Eliminate clichés.* Do not write about "the fast-paced world we live in today" or the "rat race." First, do you know for sure that the pace of life for someone who has a demanding job is any faster than it was in the past? Using time effectively has always mattered. Also, clichés suggest that you are too lazy to find your own words.

- *Avoid jargon.* In the negative sense of this word. Specialists in any group have their own "language." That's one meaning of jargon. The negative meaning refers to nonspecialists who fill their writing with "heavy-sounding terms" to give the appearance of significance. Watch for any overuse of "scientific" terms such as *factor* or *aspect,* or other vague, awkward language.

- *Avoid language that is too informal for most of your writing contexts.* What do you mean when you write: *"Kids* today watch too much TV"? Alternatives include *children, teens, adolescents.* These words are both less slangy and more precise.

- *Avoid nasty attacks on the opposition.* Change "those jerks who are foolish enough to believe that TV violence has no impact on children" to language that explains your counterargument without attacking those who may disagree with you. After all, you want to change the thinking of your audience, not make them resent you for name-calling.

- *Avoid all discriminatory language.* In the academic community and the adult workplace, most people are bothered by language that belittles any one group. This includes language that is racist or sexist or reflects negatively on the older or disabled persons or those who do not share your sexual orientation or religious beliefs. Just don't do it!

Proofreading

You also do not want to lose the respect of readers because you submit a paper filled with "little" errors—errors in punctuation, mechanics, and incorrect word choice. Most readers will forgive one or two little errors but will become annoyed if they begin to pile up. So, after you are finished rewriting and editing, print a copy of your paper and read it slowly, looking specifically at punctuation, at the handling of quotations and references to writers and to titles, and at those pesky words that come in two or more "versions": *to, too,* and *two; here* and *hear; their, there,* and *they're*; and so forth. If instructors have found any of these kinds of errors in your papers over the years, then focus your attention on the kinds of errors you have been known to make. Refer to Chapter 1 for handling references to authors and titles and for handling direct quotations. Use a glossary of usage in a handbook for homonyms (words that sound alike but have different meanings), and check a handbook for punctuation rules. Take pride in your work and present a paper that will be treated with respect. What follows is a checklist of the key points for writing good arguments that we have just examined.

A CHECKLIST FOR REVISION ■·■

- ☐ Have I selected an issue and purpose consistent with assignment guidelines?
- ☐ Have I stated a claim that is focused, appropriately qualified, and precise?
- ☐ Have I developed sound reasons and evidence in support of my claim?
- ☐ Have I used Toulmin terms to help me study the parts of my argument, including rebuttals to counterarguments?
- ☐ Have I taken advantage of a conciliatory approach and emphasized common ground with opponents?
- ☐ Have I found a clear and effective organization for presenting my argument?
- ☐ Have I edited my draft thoughtfully, concentrating on producing unified and coherent paragraphs and polished sentences?
- ☐ Have I eliminated wordiness, clichés, jargon?
- ☐ Have I selected an appropriate tone for my purpose and audience?
- ☐ Have I used my word processor's spell check and proofread a printed copy with great care?

FOR ANALYSIS AND DEBATE

WE NEED A HIGHER QUALITY OUTRAGE | DEBORAH TANNEN

University Professor and professor of linguistics at Georgetown University, Deborah Tannen has written popular books on the use of language by "ordinary" people. Among her many books are *Talking from 9 to 5* (1994) and *I Only Say This Because I Love You* (2004). The following article was published October 22, 2004, in the *Christian Science Monitor.*

PREREADING QUESTIONS Should we avoid disagreements over politics for fear of offending someone? Or, should we have serious debates that include disagreements?

We need to ratchet up the level of opposition in our public and private 1
discourse.

This statement may seem surprising, coming from someone who wrote a 2
book, *The Argument Culture,* claiming that the rise of opposition is endangering our civil life. Why do I now say we need more? The key is what I call "agonism": ritualized opposition, a knee-jerk, automatic use of warlike formats.

Agonism obliterates and obfuscates real opposition. When there's a ruckus 3
in the street outside your home, you fling open the window and see what's happening. But if there's a row outside every night, you shut the window and try to block it out. That's what's happening in our public discourse. With all the shouting, we have less, rather than more, genuine opposition—the kind that is the bedrock on which democracy rests.

Agonism grows out of our conviction that opposition is the best, if not 4
the only, path to truth. In this view, the best way to explore an idea is a debate that requires opponents to marshal facts and arguments for one side, and ignore, ridicule, or otherwise undermine facts and arguments that support the other side.

Many journalists prize two types of agonism: One is the value of attack over 5
other modes of inquiry, such as analyzing, integrating, or simply informing. The other is a seemingly laudable search for "balance," which results in reporting accusations without examining their validity.

Legitimate opposition is quashed when dissension from public policy is 6
branded "hate speech" or unpatriotic. True hate speech stirs passions against members of a group precisely because of their membership in that group. Expressing passionate opposition to—even hatred for—the policies of elected officials is a legitimate, necessary form of engagement in public life. Candidates and individuals may differ—indeed, must differ—on public policy, such as whether invading Iraq enhanced or hampered American security. But questioning the patriotism of those who believe the invasion was a mistake quashes legitimate debate.

We can know others' policies, but we cannot know their motives. Accusing 7
opponents of venal motives makes it easy to dismiss valid criticism. One can

decry the fact that many of the contracts for rebuilding Iraq were awarded to Halliburton without claiming that the war was undertaken in order to enrich the company the vice president once led. One can argue that having received medals for heroic deeds in the Vietnam war does not equip John Kerry to execute the war in Iraq without seeking to discredit not only his, but all, Purple Hearts. One can argue that the president is using the Sept. 11 attacks to bolster his public profile without going so far as to claim (as does a message circulating on the Internet) that he played a role in authorizing those attacks. And one can validly defend the way the war was conducted without accusing one's critics of undermining the war efforts.

8   Agonism leads to the conviction that fights are riveting to watch. Together with ever-diminishing budgets and corporate demands for ever-greater profits, this conviction tempts TV producers to quickly assemble shows by finding a spokesperson for each side—the more extreme, the better—and letting them slug it out. This format leaves no forum for the middle ground, where most viewers are. The result is that the extremes define the issues, problems seem insoluble, and citizens become alienated from the political process.

9   A single-minded devotion to "balance" also creates the illusion of equivalence where there is none. For example, as shown repeatedly by journalist Ross Gelbspan as well as in a recent article by Maxwell and Jules Boykoff in the academic journal *Global Environment Change*, news coverage of global warming actually ends up being biased because news reports of scientists' mounting concern typically also feature prominently one of the few "greenhouse skeptics" who declare the concern bogus. This "balanced" two-sides approach gives the impression that scientists are evenly divided, whereas in fact the vast majority agree that the dangers of global climate change are potentially grave.

10   Take, too, the current bemoaning of negativity in the presidential campaign. Given the devotion to "balance," reports tend to juxtapose negative statements from both sides. But negativity comes in many forms. Attacks on an opponent's character distract attention from the issues that will be decided in the election. Attacks on an opponent's proposed and past policies are appropriate; we need more of such attention to policy.

11   The preoccupation with balance plays a role here, too. If the goal is only ensuring balance, then journalists can feel their work is done when they have reported accusations flung from each side, abnegating the responsibility to examine the validity of the attacks.

12   Ironically, while the press is busy gauging who's ahead and who's behind in the contest, significant opposition is left out. Martin Walker, of United Press International, notes that when President Bush addressed the United Nations last month, newspapers in every country other than our own—including our British allies and papers such as the French *Le Figaro*, which supported the invasion of Iraq—reported the event as a duel, with President Bush on one side and UN Secretary-General Kofi Annan or the international community on the other. The American press, whether they are supportive or critical of the president's speech, ignored the oppositional context and reported on his speech alone.

This downplaying of genuine opposition is mirrored in our private conversations. In many European countries, heated political discussions are commonplace and enjoyed; most Americans regard such conversations as unseemly arguments, so they avoid talking politics—especially with anyone whose views differ, or are unknown, lest they inadvertently spark a conflict or offend someone who disagrees.

As a result, we aren't forced to articulate—and therefore examine—the   14
logic of our views, nor are we exposed to the views of those with whom we disagree. And if young people don't hear adults having intense, animated political discussions, the impression that politics has no relevance to their lives is reinforced. Surely this contributes to the woefully low voter turnout among young Americans.

The Yugoslavian-born poet Charles Simic has said, "There are moments in   15
life when true invective is called for, when it becomes an absolute necessity, out of a deep sense of justice, to denounce, mock, vituperate, lash out, in the strongest possible language."

We have come to such a moment. Leaving aside invective, vituperation,   16
and mockery, I believe that we need space for peaceful yet passionate outrage. The challenges we face are monumental. Among them are the spread of nuclear weapons, the burgeoning number of individuals and groups who see the United States as a threat, and the question of how far to compromise our liberties and protections in the interest of security.

On the domestic side, the challenges include the impending insolvency   17
of Medicare and social security, the rising number of working Americans with no health insurance, and the question of whether the checks and balances provided by the three branches of government should be strengthened or weakened.

In the face of challenges of these proportions, we can no longer afford to   18
have voices of true opposition muted by the agonistic din.

QUESTIONS FOR READING

1. What is Tannen's subject? Be precise.
2. What does the term *agonism* mean? What is the typical response to agonism?
3. What are the two types of agonism embraced by journalists?
4. What are the characteristics of "attack" journalism? What are the consequences of this approach to the news? What is the problem with the "balanced" approach to reporting the news?

QUESTIONS FOR REASONING AND ANALYSIS

1. Examine Tannen's examples of "attack" journalism. What makes them effective?
2. Analyze her two examples of "balanced" journalism. What makes them effective? Observe that the author does not state a presidential preference. Is it possible to infer her preference?

3. Analyze the author's conclusion—her last four paragraphs. Study her lists of problems and her word choice. Is this an effective ending? Does she drive home her point and get the reader's attention focused on the problem she has examined? Why or why not?

QUESTIONS FOR REFLECTING AND WRITING

1. Look again at Tannen's list of problems at the conclusion of her argument. Would you make the same list of problems that we need to be debating? If not, what would you add? Delete? Why?
2. Does Tannen's objection to the balanced approach to reporting make sense to you? Agree or disagree and defend your choice.
3. Which form of agonism might most distort issues for the public? Why? Defend your choice.

IN DEFENSE OF VOLUNTARY EUTHANASIA | SIDNEY HOOK

A philosopher, educator, and author, Sidney Hook (1902–1989) taught philosophy at New York University and was a senior research fellow at the Hoover Institution. He published numerous articles and books on philosophy throughout his busy career, and his autobiography, *Out of Step: An Unquiet Life in the Twentieth Century*, appeared in 1987. The following argument for euthanasia, incorporating his personal experience with grave illness, was published in the *New York Times* in 1987.

PREREADING QUESTIONS Have you lost a loved one who suffered at the end of his or her life? If so, how has that experience shaped your thinking on the issue? Do you have a position on doctor-assisted suicide? If so, what is your view?

1   A few short years ago, I lay at the point of death. A congestive heart failure was treated for diagnostic purposes by an angiogram that triggered a stroke. Violent and painful hiccups, uninterrupted for several days and nights, prevented the ingestion of food. My left side and one of my vocal cords became paralyzed. Some form of pleurisy set in, and I felt I was drowning in a sea of slime. At one point, my heart stopped beating; just as I lost consciousness, it was thumped back into action again. In one of my lucid intervals during those days of agony, I asked my physician to discontinue all life-supporting services or show me how to do it. He refused and predicted that someday I would appreciate the unwisdom of my request.

2   A month later, I was discharged from the hospital. In six months, I regained the use of my limbs, and although my voice still lacks its old resonance and carrying power I no longer croak like a frog. There remain some minor disabilities and I am restricted to a rigorous, low sodium diet. I have resumed my writing and research.

3   My experience can be and has been cited as an argument against honoring requests of stricken patients to be gently eased out of their pain and life. I cannot agree. There are two main reasons. As an octogenarian, there is a reasonable likelihood that I may suffer another "cardiovascular accident" or

worse. I may not even be in a position to ask for the surcease of pain. It seems to me that I have already paid my dues to death—indeed, although time has softened my memories they are vivid enough to justify my saying that I suffered enough to warrant dying several times over. Why run the risk of more?

Secondly, I dread imposing on my family and friends another grim round of misery similar to the one my first attack occasioned.   4

My wife and children endured enough for one lifetime. I know that for them the long days and nights of waiting, the disruption of their professional duties and their own familial responsibilities counted for nothing in their anxiety for me. In their joy at my recovery they have been forgotten. Nonetheless, to visit another prolonged spell of helpless suffering on them as my life ebbs away, or even worse, if I linger on into a comatose senility, seems altogether gratuitous.   5

But what, it may be asked, of the joy and satisfaction of living, of basking in the sunshine, listening to music, watching one's grandchildren growing into adolescence, following the news about the fate of freedom in a troubled world, playing with ideas, writing one's testament of wisdom and folly for posterity? Is not all that one endured, together with the risk of its recurrence, an acceptable price for the multiple satisfactions that are still open even to a person of advanced years?   6

Apparently those who cling to life no matter what, think so. I do not.   7

The zest and intensity of these experiences are no longer what they used to be. I am not vain enough to delude myself that I can in the few remaining years make an important discovery useful for mankind or can lead a social movement or do anything that will be historically eventful, nor less event-making. My autobiography, which describes a record of intellectual and political experiences of some historical value, already much too long, could be posthumously published. I have had my fill of joys and sorrows and am not greedy for more life. I have always thought that a test of whether one had found happiness in one's life is whether one would be willing to relive it—whether, if it were possible, one would accept the opportunity to be born again.   8

Having lived a full and relatively happy life, I would cheerfully accept the chance to be reborn, but certainly not to be reborn again as an infirm octogenarian. To some extent, my views reflect what I have seen happen to the aged and stricken who have been so unfortunate as to survive crippling paralysis. They suffer, and impose suffering on others, unable even to make a request that their torment be ended.   9

I am mindful too of the burdens placed upon the community, with its rapidly diminishing resources, to provide the adequate and costly services necessary to sustain the lives of those whose days and nights are spent on mattress graves of pain. A better use could be made of these resources to increase the opportunities and qualities of life for the young. I am not denying the moral obligation the community has to look after its disabled and aged. There are times, however, when an individual may find it pointless to insist on the fulfillment of a legal and moral right.   10

11   What is required is no great revolution in morals but an enlargement of imagination and an intelligent evaluation of alternative uses of community resources.

12   Long ago, Seneca observed that "the wise man will live as long as he ought, not as long as he can." One can envisage hypothetical circumstances in which one has a duty to prolong one's life despite its costs for the sake of others, but such circumstances are far removed from the ordinary prospects we are considering. If wisdom is rooted in knowledge or the alternatives of choice, it must be reliably informed of the state one is in and its likely outcome. Scientific medicine is not infallible, but it is the best we have. Should a rational person be willing to endure acute suffering merely on the chance that a miraculous cure might presently be at hand? Each one should be permitted to make his own choice—especially when no one else is harmed by it.

13   The responsibility for the decision, whether deemed wise or foolish, must be with the chooser.

QUESTIONS FOR READING

1.   What subject is introduced in Hook's opening two paragraphs? What strategy does he use as an introduction?

2.   What have some people seen in his experience? For what two reasons does Hook disagree with them?

3.   When others observe the pleasures of life the author can still experience, what are Hook's responses? Summarize his reasons for not wanting to continue to live on in his 80s.

QUESTIONS FOR REASONING AND ANALYSIS

1.   What is Hook's position on euthanasia? Where does he state his claim?

2.   Analyze the nature of the author's argument. What kind of evidence does he provide?

3.   Hook writes of "intelligent evaluation," of "wisdom," "knowledge," and "a rational person." How would you describe his philosophy? What does he value as essential to being human?

QUESTIONS FOR REFLECTION AND WRITING

1.   Hook argues that he should be free to make choices about his life—or death— as long as he does not harm others. Do you agree with this philosophy, in general? Do you agree that it applies to the choice of euthanasia? Why or why not?

2.   What is your position on euthanasia? What are your reasons?

EUTHANASIA—A CRITIQUE | PETER A. SINGER AND MARK SIEGLER

A graduate of the University of Toronto Medical School and holding a master's in public health from Yale University, Dr. Peter A. Singer is assistant professor of medicine and associate director of the Center for Bioethics at the University of Toronto. He is the author of many articles on bioethics, end-of-life care, and euthanasia. Dr. Mark Siegler obtained his medical degree from the University of Chicago, where he is director of the Center of Clinical Medical Ethics. Siegler is a recognized authority in the field of clinical medical ethics, having written more than 100 articles, six books, and the chapters on clinical ethics in two standard texts on internal medicine. In the following article, published in the *New England Journal of Medicine* on June 20, 1990, the authors provide a good review of the issues that are central to the debate on euthanasia and present their views on this issue.

PREREADING QUESTIONS Do you have a current position on doctor-assisted suicide? If so, what is your view? If not, do you think the issue deserves more thought on your part? Why or why not? If you have a position, what are the main sources of influence: family, friends, religious beliefs?

A vigorous medical and political debate has begun again on euthanasia, a practice proscribed 2500 years ago in the Hippocratic oath.[1-4] The issue has been publicized recently in three widely divergent settings: a journal article, a legislative initiative in California, and public policy in the Netherlands. 1

The case of "Debbie" shows that euthanasia can be discussed openly in a respected medical journal. "It's Over, Debbie" was an anonymous, first-person account of euthanasia, published on January 8, 1988, in the *Journal of the American Medical Association*,[5-8] that stimulated widespread discussion and elicited spirited replies. Later in 1988, perhaps as a result, the Council on Ethical and Judicial Affairs of the American Medical Association reaffirmed its opposition to euthanasia.[9] 2

In California, a legislative initiative[10,11] has shown that in the near future euthanasia may be legalized in certain U.S. jurisdictions. A bill proposing a California Humane and Dignified Death Act was an attempt to legalize euthanasia through the referendum process, which allows California voters to approve controversial issues directly. Public-opinion polls reported that up to 70 percent of the electorate favored the initiative, and many commentators flatly predicted that the initiative would succeed. Nevertheless, the signature drive failed, collecting only 130,000 of the 450,000 required signatures. Attributing the failure to organizational problems, the proponents vowed to introduce the legislation again in California and in other states in 1990. 3

Experience in the Netherlands has shown that a liberal democratic government can tolerate and defend the practice of euthanasia. Although euthanasia is technically illegal in the Netherlands, in fact it is part of Dutch public policy today.[1,12-16] There is agreement at all levels of the judicial system, including the 4

Supreme Court, that if physicians follow the procedural guidelines issued by a state commission, they will not be prosecuted for performing euthanasia.[16] The Dutch guidelines emphasize five requirements: an explicit, repeated request by the patient that leaves no doubt about the patient's desire to die; very severe mental or physical suffering, with no prospect of relief; an informed, free, and consistent decision by the patient; the lack of other treatment options, those available having been exhausted or refused by the patient; and consultation by the doctor with another medical practitioner (and perhaps also with nurses, pastors, or others).[13] The usual method of performing euthanasia is to induce sleep with a barbiturate, followed by a lethal injection of curare.[1] An estimated 5000 to 10,000 patients receive euthanasia each year in the Netherlands.[16]

5   In view of these developments, we urge physicians to consider some reasons for resisting the move toward euthanasia. This article criticizes the main arguments offered by proponents and presents opposing arguments. The case for euthanasia is described in detail elsewhere.[10,17]

CRITIQUE OF THE CASE FOR EUTHANASIA

6   In the debate about euthanasia, imprecision of language abounds. For the purposes of this article, euthanasia is defined as the deliberate action by a physician to terminate the life of a patient. The clearest example is the act of lethal injection. We distinguish euthanasia from such other acts as the decision to forgo life-sustaining treatment (including the use of ventilators, cardiopulmonary resuscitation, dialysis, or tube feeding—the issue raised in the Cruzan case[18]); the administration of analgesic agents to relieve pain; "assisted suicide," in which the doctor prescribes but does not administer a lethal dose of medication; and "mercy killing" performed by a patient's family or friends. The Dutch guidelines described above and the terms proposed in the California initiative represent two versions of euthanasia.

7   The case for euthanasia is based on two central claims.[10,17] First, proponents argue that patients whose illnesses cause them unbearable suffering should be permitted to end their distress by having a physician perform euthanasia. Second, proponents assert that the well-recognized right of patients to control their medical treatment includes the right to request and receive euthanasia.

Relief of Suffering

8   We agree that the relief of pain and suffering is a crucial goal of medicine.[19] We question, however, whether the care of dying patients cannot be improved without resorting to the drastic measure of euthanasia. Most physical pain can be relieved with the appropriate use of analgesic agents.[20] Unfortunately, despite widespread agreement that dying patients must be provided with necessary analgesia,[21] physicians continue to underuse analgesia in the care of dying patients because of concern about depressing respiratory drive or creating addiction. Such situations demand better management of pain, not euthanasia.

9   Another component of suffering is the frightening prospect of dying shackled to a modern-day Procrustean bed, surrounded by the latest forms of high

technology. Proponents of euthanasia often cite horror stories of patients treated against their will. In the past, when modern forms of life-saving technology were new and physicians were just learning how to use them appropriately, such cases occurred often; we have begun to move beyond that era. The law, public policy, and medical ethics now acknowledge the right of patients to refuse life-sustaining medical treatment, and a large number of patients avail themselves of this new policy.[22-24] These days, competent patients may freely exercise their right to choose or refuse life-sustaining treatment; to carry out their preferences, they do not require the option of euthanasia.

We acknowledge that some elements of human suffering and mental   10
anguish—not necessarily related to physical pain—cannot be eliminated completely from the dying process. These include the anticipated loss of important human relationships and membership in the human community, the loss of personal independence, the feeling of helplessness, and the raw fear of death. Euthanasia can shorten the duration of these emotional and psychological hardships. It can also eliminate fears about how and when death will occur. Finally, euthanasia returns to the patient a measure of control over the process of dying. These are the benefits of euthanasia, against which its potential harms must be balanced.

Individual Rights

The second argument in favor of euthanasia is based on the rights of the   11
individual. Proponents contend that the right of patients to forgo life-sustaining medical treatment should include a right to euthanasia. This would extend the notion of the right to die to embrace the concept that patients have a right to be killed by physicians. But rights are not absolute. They must be balanced against the rights of other people and the values of society. The claim of a right to be killed by a physician must be balanced against the legal, political, and religious prohibitions against killing that have always existed in society generally and in medicine particularly. As the President's Commission for the Study of Ethical Problems in Medicine and Biomedical and Behavioral Research has observed, "Policies prohibiting direct killing may also conflict with the important value of patient self-determination. . . . The Commission finds this limitation on individual self-determination to be an acceptable cost of securing the general protection of human life afforded by the prohibition of direct killing."[22] We agree. In our view, the public good served by the prohibition of euthanasia outweighs the private interests of the persons requesting it.

THE CASE AGAINST EUTHANASIA

The arguments against euthanasia are made from two perspectives: pub-   12
lic policy and the ethical norms of medicine.

Euthanasia Is Perilous Public Policy

Proponents of euthanasia use the concept of individual rights to support   13
their claim, but this same concept can be used for the opposite purpose. The argument against euthanasia on grounds of civil rights involves a consideration of the rights not just of those who would want euthanasia themselves but of all

citizens. As public policy, euthanasia is unacceptable because of the likelihood, or even the inevitability, of involuntary euthanasia—persons being euthanized without their consent or against their wishes.

14   There are four ways in which the policy of voluntary euthanasia could lead to involuntary euthanasia. The first is "crypthanasia" (literally, "secret euthanasia").[15] In the Netherlands, for instance, it is alleged that vulnerable patients are euthanized without their consent. Dutch proponents of euthanasia disavow these reports and claim that they are unrelated to the toleration of voluntary euthanasia. We suggest, however, that a political milieu in which voluntary euthanasia is tolerated may also foster involuntary euthanasia and lead to the killing of patients without consent. The second way in which involuntary euthanasia may occur is through "encouraged" euthanasia, whereby chronically ill or dying patients may be pressured to choose euthanasia to spare their families financial or emotional strain.[25] The third way is "surrogate" euthanasia. If voluntary euthanasia were permissible in the United States, the constitutional guarantees of due process, which tend to extend the same rights to incompetent as to competent patients, might permit euthanizing incompetent patients on the basis of "substituted judgment" or nebulous tests of "burdens and benefits." Finally, there is the risk of "discriminatory" euthanasia. Patients belonging to vulnerable groups in American society might be subtly coerced into "requesting" euthanasia. In the United States today, many groups are disempowered, disenfranchised, or otherwise vulnerable: the poor, the elderly, the disabled, members of racial minorities, the physically handicapped, the mentally impaired, alcoholics, drug addicts, and patients with the acquired immunodeficiency syndrome. In a society in which discrimination is common and many citizens do not have access even to basic health care, the legalization of euthanasia would create another powerful tool with which to discriminate against groups whose "consent" is already susceptible to coercion and whose rights are already in jeopardy.

15   The proponents of euthanasia contend that procedural safeguards, such as the five provisions of the Dutch guidelines noted above, will prevent involuntary euthanasia. They claim further that society permits many dangerous activities if adequate procedural safeguards are provided to reduce risk and protect the public. We agree that safeguards would reduce the risk of involuntary euthanasia, but they would not eliminate it entirely. In the case of euthanasia, safeguards have not been adequately tested and shown to be effective. Even in their presence, we are concerned that patients could be euthanized without their consent or even against their wishes. Even one case of involuntary euthanasia would represent a great harm. In the current era of cost containment, social injustice, and ethical relativism, this risk is one our society should not accept.

Euthanasia Violates the Norms of Medicine

16   In addition to being perilous as public policy, euthanasia violates three fundamental norms and standards of medicine. First, as noted above, it diverts attention from the real issues in the care of dying patients—among

them, improved pain control, better communication between doctors and patients, heightened respect for the patient's right to choose whether to accept life-sustaining treatment, and improved management of the dying process, as in hospice care. The hospice movement has demonstrated that managing pain appropriately and allowing patients control over the use of life-sustaining treatments reduce the need for euthanasia.

Second, euthanasia subverts the social role of the physician as healer. His- 17 torically, physicians have scrupulously avoided participating in activities that might taint their healing role, such as capital punishment or torture. Physicians should distance themselves from euthanasia to maintain public confidence and trust in medicine as a healing profession.

Third, euthanasia strikes at the heart of what it means to be a physician.[26] 18 Since the time of Hippocrates, the prohibition against it has been fundamental to the medical profession and has served as a moral absolute for both patients and physicians. This prohibition has freed physicians from a potential conflict of interest between healing and killing and in turn has enabled patients to entrust physicians with their lives. It has enabled physicians to devote themselves singlemindedly to helping patients achieve their own medical goals. This prohibition may even have encouraged medical research and scientific progress, because physicians, with the consent of patients, are motivated to perform risky, innovative procedures that are aggressive and sometimes painful, with a total commitment to benefit the patient.

CONCLUSIONS

Pressure to legalize euthanasia will surely increase in an era of spiraling 19 health care costs, but it must be resisted. Euthanasia represents a development that is dangerous for many vulnerable patients and that threatens the moral integrity of the medical profession. Physicians must become more responsive to the concerns of patients that underlie the movement for euthanasia and must provide better pain management, more compassionate terminal care, and more appropriate use of life-sustaining treatments. But physicians need to draw the line at euthanasia. They and their professional associations should defend the integrity of medicine by speaking out against the practice. Finally, even if euthanasia is legalized in some jurisdictions, physicians should refuse to participate in it, and professional organizations should censure any of their members who perform euthanasia.

REFERENCES
[1]Angell M. Euthanasia. N Engl J Med 1988; 319:1348–50.
[2]Singer PA. Should doctors kill patients? Can Med Assoc J 1988; 138:1000–1.
[3]Kinsella TD, Singer PA, Siegler M. Legalized active euthanasia: an Aesculapian tragedy. Bull Am Coll Surg 1989; 74(12):6–9.
[4]Wanzer SH, Federmann DD, Adelstein SJ, et al. The Physician's responsibility toward hopelessly ill patients: A second look. N Engl J Med 1989; 320:844–9.

[5]It's over, Debbie. JAMA 1988; 259:272.

[6]Vaux KL. Debbie's dying: mercy killing and the good death. JAMA 1988; 259:2140–1.

[7]Gaylin W, Kass LR, Pellegrino ED, Siegler M. 'Doctors must not kill.' JAMA 1988; 259:2139–40.

[8]Lundberg GD. 'It's over, Debbie' and the euthanasia debate. JAMA 1988; 259:2142–3.

[9]The Council on Ethical and Judicial Affairs of the American Medical Association. Euthanasia. Report: C (A-88). AMA council report. Chicago: American Medical Association, 1988:1.

[10]Risley RL. A humane and dignified death: a new law permitting physician aid-in-dying. Glendale, Calif.: Americans Against Human Suffering, 1987.

[11]Parachini A. Mercy, murder, & mortality: perspectives on euthanasia: the California Humane and Dignified Death Initiative. Hastings Cent Rep 1989; 19(1):Suppl:10–2.

[12]Pence GE. Do not go slowly into that dark night: mercy killing in Holland. Am J Med 1988; 84:139–41.

[13]Rigter H, Borst-Eilers E, Leenen HJJ. Euthanasia across the North Sea. BMJ 1988; 297:1593–5.

[14]Rigter H. Mercy, murder, & morality: euthanasia in the Netherlands: distinguishing facts from fiction. Hastings Cent Rep 1989; 191(1):Suppl:31–2.

[15]Fenigsen R. Mercy, murder & morality: perspectives on euthanasia: a case against Dutch euthanasia. Hastings Cent Rep 1989; 19(1):Suppl:22–30.

[16]de Wachter MAM. Active euthanasia in the Netherlands. JAMA 1989; 262:3316–9.

[17]Humphry D., Wickett A. The right to die: understanding euthanasia. New York: Harper & Row, 1986.

[18]Angell M. Prisoners of technology: the case of Nancy Cruzan. N Eng J Med 1990; 322:1226–8.

[19]Cassell EJ. The nature of suffering and the goals of medicine. N Engl J Med 1982; 306:639–45.

[20]Foley KM. The treatment of cancer pain. N Engl J Med 1985; 313:84–95.

[21]Angell M. The quality of mercy. N Engl J Med 1982; 306:98–9.

[22]President's Commission for the Study of Ethical Problems in Medicine and Biomedical and Behavioral Research. Deciding to forgo life-sustaining treatment: a report on the ethical, medical, and legal issues in treatment decisions. Washington, D.C.: Government Printing Office, 1983.

[23]The Hastings Center. Guidelines on the termination of life-sustaining treatment and the care of the dying: a report. Briarcliff Manor, N.Y.: Hastings Center, 1987.

[24]Emanuel EJ. A review of the ethical and legal aspects of terminating medical care. Am J Med 1988; 84:291–301.

[25]Kamisar Y. Some non-religious views against proposed "mercy-killing" legislation. Minn Law Rev 1958; 42:969–1042.

[26]Kass LR. Neither for love nor money: why doctors must not kill. Public Interest 1989; 94(winter):25–46.

QUESTIONS FOR READING

1. What debate do the authors join in with their essay?

2. How many people in the Netherlands apparently employ euthanasia each year? Summarize the required guidelines physicians must follow to use euthanasia there without prosecution.

3. How do Singer and Siegler define *euthanasia?* What is not included in their definition?

4. What are the two reasons of those who argue for euthanasia? Summarize the authors' rebuttal of each reason.

5. What two approaches do the authors take in arguing against euthanasia?

6. Why is euthanasia bad public policy? What could voluntary euthanasia lead to? What characteristics of modern society make, in the authors' view, legalizing euthanasia too risky?

7. What do the authors want physicians to do?

QUESTIONS FOR REASONING AND ANALYSIS

1. What do the authors want to accomplish in their opening references to the article on "Debbie," the California initiative, and the practice of euthanasia in the Netherlands?

2. Analyze the essay's organization, indicating the paragraphs that belong in each part.

3. What do the authors accomplish in paragraph 10?

4. What is Singer and Siegler's claim?

QUESTIONS FOR REFLECTING AND WRITING

1. Do you agree that interest in euthanasia is increasing? What evidence would you cite to support your answer?

2. Which of the two arguments supporting euthanasia is the most convincing, in your view? Which of the arguments against euthanasia is the most convincing? Why?

3. Where do you stand on the issue of legalizing euthanasia? Be prepared to defend your position.

1. Do you agree with Singer and Siegler that we live in an "era of cost containment, social injustice, and ethical relativism"? Why or why not? The authors do not cite evidence for this assertion. Develop an argument either in support of this claim or to challenge it.

2. The two articles on euthanasia make for interesting comparisons beyond their differing positions on the issue. Do a comparative analysis of the style, format, and choice of evidence in the two essays. Consider: How is each essay effective in its context of audience and purpose? Why would neither essay be effective with the other one's audience?

3. Where do you stand on the issue of euthanasia? Be prepared to defend your position.

GOING ONLINE

You may want to go online to find information on euthanasia beyond what is available in the chapter's essays. You can start your search at these sites: www.religioustolerance.org/euthanas.htm; www.finalexit.org; www.euthanasia.com.

Rob Rogers: © The Pittsburgh Post-Gazette/Dist. by United Features Syndicate, Inc.

Read: Who are the figures in the cartoon? What is the situation? Who is speaking the lines?

Reason: How are we to read the lines? What is the idea expressed by the drawing?

Reflect/Write: What makes the cartoon clever? Which readers will be most amused? Who will not be amused?

CHAPTER 5

Learning More about Argument: Induction, Deduction, Analogy, and Logical Fallacies

You can build on your knowledge of the basics of argument, examined in Chapter 3, by understanding some traditional forms of argument: induction, deduction, and analogy. It is also important to recognize arguments that do not work.

INDUCTION

Induction is the process by which we reach inferences— opinions based on facts, or on a combination of facts and less debatable inferences. The inductive process moves from particular to general, from support to assertion. We base our inferences on the facts we have gathered and studied. In general, the more evidence, the more convincing the argument. No one wants to debate tomorrow's sunrise; the evidence for counting on it is too convincing. Most inferences, though, are drawn from less evidence, so we need to examine inductive arguments closely to judge their reasonableness.

The pattern of induction looks like this:

EVIDENCE: There is the dead body of Smith. Smith was shot in his bedroom between the hours of 11:00 P.M. and 2:00 A.M., according to the coroner. Smith was shot by a .32-caliber pistol. The pistol left in the bedroom contains Jones's fingerprints. Jones was seen, by a neighbor, entering the Smith home at around 11:00 the night of Smith's death. A coworker heard Smith and Jones arguing in Smith's office the morning of the day Smith died.

CLAIM: Jones killed Smith.

The facts are presented. The jury infers that Jones is a murderer. Unless there is a confession or a trustworthy eyewitness, the conclusion is an inference, not a fact. This is the most logical explanation; that is, the conclusion meets the standards of simplicity and frequency while accounting for all of the known evidence.

The following paragraph illustrates the process of induction. In their book *Discovering Dinosaurs,* authors Mark Norell, Eugene Gaffney, and Lowell Dingus answer the question "Did dinosaurs really rule the world?"

> For almost 170 million years, from the Late Triassic to the end of the Cretaceous, there existed dinosaurs of almost every body form imaginable: small carnivores, such as *Compsognathus* and *Ornitholestes,* ecologically equivalent to today's foxes and coyotes; medium-sized carnivores, such as *Velociraptor* and the troodontids, analogous to lions and tigers; and the monstrous carnivores with no living analogs, such as *Tyrannosaurus* and *Allosaurus.* Included among the ornithischians and the elephantine sauropods are terrestrial herbivores of diverse body form. By the end of the Jurassic, dinosaurs had even taken to the skies. The only habitats that dinosaurs did not dominate during the Mesozoic were aquatic. Yet, there were marine representatives, such as the primitive toothed bird *Hesperornis.* Like penguins, these birds were flightless, specialized for diving, and probably had to return to land to reproduce. In light of this broad morphologic diversity [number of body forms], dinosaurs did "rule the planet" as the dominant life form on Earth during most of the Mesozoic [era that includes the Triassic, Jurassic, and Cretaceous Periods, 248 to 65 million years ago].

Observe that the writers organize evidence by type of dinosaur to demonstrate the range and diversity of these animals. A good inductive argument is based on a sufficient volume of *relevant* evidence. The basic shape of this inductive argument is illustrated in Figure 5.1.

CLAIM:	Dinosaurs were the dominant life form during the Mesozoic Era.
GROUNDS:	The facts presented in the paragraph.
ASSUMPTION (WARRANT):	The facts are representative, revealing dinosaur diversity.

FIGURE 5.1 The Shape of an Inductive Argument

Observe the inductive process in the following section from Mark A. Norell and Xu Xing's "The Varieties of Tyrannosaurs."

THE VARIETIES OF TYRANNOSAURS | MARK A. NORELL AND XU XING

Popular images often portray tyrannosaurs as solitary animals, or speedy, or 1 both. Arguably the best evidence for such behavior is trackways, which are essentially snapshots of individual events. Trackways have indicated herding in sauropods, preserved the moment of a kill, and even suggested that some theropod dinosaurs hunted in packs. Unfortunately, only a couple of tyrannosaur trackways have been recovered, and some are not particularly informative.

Other evidence, though, suggests tyrannosaurs were gregarious. For ex- 2 ample, some tyrannosaur excavations have yielded multiple individuals. One of those is a quarry that Barnum Brown excavated in the Red Deer River area of what is now Dinosaur Provincial Park in Alberta, Canada. The quarry was re-excavated by Philip J. Currie of the Royal Tyrrell Museum of Paleontology in Drumheller, Alberta. Currie's analysis of collections both old and new showed that several *Albertosaurus* individuals of various ages and sizes were preserved together. Because no other dinosaur species were preserved with those animals, Currie surmised that they died at the same time, perhaps while crossing a dangerous river. Although the find is not definitive evidence for pack behavior, it and other similar depositions of multiple tyrannosaurs are at least highly suggestive that such behavior took place.

As for the speed of tyrannosaurs, some fantastic claims have suggested the 3 huge animals could reach sprinterlike speeds. But those claims fail to take account of some basic issues in the physics of movement of large animals. John R. Hutchinson, now at the University of London's Royal Veterinary College, and his colleagues digitally modeled the hind limb and hips of a *T. rex* [*see "A Weighty Matter," by Adam Summers, June 2002*]. By varying the controllable factors in the model such as posture and the total weight of the animal, Hutchinson was able to calculate how big the muscles of the hind limb must have been for the animal to move at various speeds.

4   His simulations clearly showed that *T. rex* adults could never have run much faster than twenty-five miles an hour. Going faster would have tied up such a high percentage of the total body mass in the hindlimb muscles that the rest of the animal would have been emaciated.

5   In fact, the fastest runners were probably juvenile *T. rex*'s and other smaller tyrannosaurs. That suggests the various tyrannosaur species would have exploited different prey in areas where they lived together—just as cheetahs, leopards, and lions do in Africa today. The speed analysis also suggests that *T. rex* and other big species would have gone from speedy youth to lumbering adulthood.

QUESTIONS FOR ANALYSIS

1. What, specifically, are the authors' two topics?
2. Underline all statements that are inferences, number them, and then identify the evidence given for each inference.
3. What general inference about our understanding of dinosaurs do the authors imply?

COLLABORATIVE EXERCISE: Induction

With your class partner or in small groups, make a list of facts that could be used to support each of the following inferences:

1. Whole-wheat bread is nutritious.
2. Fido must have escaped under the fence during the night.
3. Sue must be planning to go away for the weekend.
4. Students who do not hand in all essay assignments fail Dr. Bradshaw's English class.
5. The price of Florida oranges will go up in grocery stores next year.

DEDUCTION

Although induction can be described as an argument that moves from particular to general, from facts to inference, deduction cannot accurately be described as the reverse. Deductive arguments are more complex. *Deduction is the reasoning process that draws a conclusion from the logical relationship of two assertions, usually one broad judgment or definition and one more specific assertion, often an inference.* Suppose, on the way out of American history class, you say, "Abraham Lincoln certainly was a great leader." Someone responds with the expected question "Why do you think so?" You explain: "He was great because he performed with courage and a clear purpose in a time of crisis." Your explanation contains a conclusion and an assertion about Lincoln (an inference) in support. But behind your explanation rests an idea about leadership,

CLAIM:	Lincoln was a great leader.
GROUNDS:	1. People who perform with courage and clear purpose in a crisis are great leaders.
	2. Lincoln was a person who performed with courage and a clear purpose in a crisis.
ASSUMPTION (WARRANT):	The relationship of the two reasons leads, logically, to the conclusion.

FIGURE 5.2 The Shape of a Deductive Argument

in the terms of deduction, a *premise.* The argument's basic shape is illustrated in Figure 5.2.

Traditionally, the deductive argument is arranged somewhat differently from these sentences about Lincoln. The two reasons are called *premises;* the broader one, called the *major premise,* is written first and the more specific one, the *minor premise,* comes next. The premises and conclusion are expressed to make clear that assertions are being made about categories or classes. To illustrate:

MAJOR PREMISE:	All people who perform with courage and a clear purpose in a crisis are great leaders.
MINOR PREMISE:	Lincoln was a person who performed with courage and a clear purpose in a crisis.
CONCLUSION:	Lincoln was a great leader.

If these two premises are correctly, that is, logically, constructed, then the conclusion follows logically, and the deductive argument is *valid.* This does not mean that the conclusion is necessarily *true.* It does mean that if you accept the truth of the premises, then you must accept the truth of the conclusion, because in a valid argument the conclusion follows logically, necessarily. How do we know that the conclusion must follow if the argument is logically constructed? Let's think about what each premise is saying and then diagram each one to represent each assertion visually. The first premise says that all people who act a particular way are people who fit into the category called "great leaders":

The second premise says that Lincoln, a category of one, belongs in the category of people who act in the same particular way that the first premise describes:

If we put the two diagrams together, we have the following set of circles, demonstrating that the conclusion follows from the premises:

We can also make negative and qualified assertions in a deductive argument. For example:

PREMISE:	No cowards can be great leaders.
PREMISE:	Falstaff was a coward.
CONCLUSION:	Falstaff was not a great leader.

Or, to reword the conclusion to make the deductive pattern clearer: No Falstaff (no member of this class) is a great leader. Diagramming to test for validity, we find that the first premise says no A's are B's:

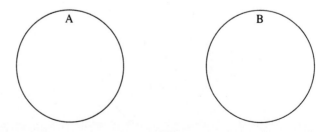

The second premise asserts all C's are A's:

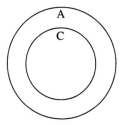

Put together, we see that the conclusion follows necessarily from the premises: No C's can possibly be members of class B.

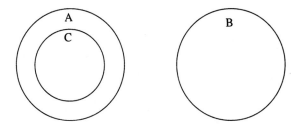

We can, in addition, shape a deductive argument with a qualified premise and conclusion.

PREMISE: All boys in my class are seniors.

PREMISE: Some boys in my class are football players.

CONCLUSION: Some seniors are football players
                            or
                Some football players are seniors.

Diagramming to test the argument's validity, we observe that, indeed, the conclusion follows from the premises:

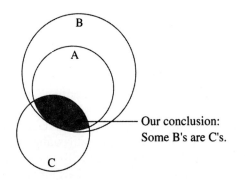

Our conclusion:
Some B's are C's.

Some deductive arguments merely look right, but the two premises do not lead logically to the conclusion that is asserted. We must read each argument carefully or diagram each one to make certain that the conclusion follows from the premises. Consider the following argument: *Unions must be communistic because they want to control wages.* The sentence contains a conclusion and one reason, or premise. From these two parts of a deductive argument we can also determine the unstated premise, just as we could with the Lincoln argument: *Communists want to control wages.* If we use circles to represent the three categories of people in the argument and diagram the argument, we see a different result from the previous diagrams:

Diagramming the argument reveals that it is invalid; that is, it is not logically constructed because the statements do not require that the union circle be placed inside the communist circle. We cannot draw the conclusion we want from any two premises, only from those that provide a logical basis from which a conclusion can be reached.

We must first make certain that deductive arguments are properly constructed or valid. But suppose the logic works and yet you do not agree with the claim? Your complaint, then, must be with one of the premises, a judgment or inference that you do not accept as true. Consider, as an example, the following argument:

MAJOR PREMISE:	(All) dogs make good pets.
MINOR PREMISE:	Fido is a dog.
CONCLUSION:	Fido will make a good pet.

This argument is valid. (Diagram it; your circles will fit into one another just as with the Lincoln argument.) However, you are not prepared to agree, necessarily, that Fido will make a good pet. The problem is with the major premise. For the argument to work, the assertion must be about *all* dogs, but we know that not all dogs will be good pets.

When composing a deductive argument, your task will be to defend the truth of your premises. Then, if your argument is valid (logically constructed), readers will have no alternative but to agree with your conclusion. If you disagree with someone else's logically constructed argument, then you must show why one of the premises is not true. Your counterargument will seek to discredit one (or both) of the premises. The Fido argument can be discredited by your producing examples of dogs that have not made good pets.

A deductive argument can serve as the core of an essay, an essay that supports the argument's claim by developing support for each of the premises. Since the major premise is either a broad judgment or a definition, it will need to be defended on the basis of an appeal to values or beliefs that the writer expects readers to share. The minor premise, usually an inference about a particular situation (or person), would be supported by relevant evidence, as with any inductive argument. You can see this process at work in the Declaration of Independence. Questions follow the Declaration to guide your analysis of this famous example of the deductive process.

THE DECLARATION OF INDEPENDENCE |

In Congress, July 4, 1776
The unanimous declaration of the thirteen
United States of America

When in the course of human events, it becomes necessary for one people to   1
dissolve the political bands which have connected them with another, and to assume among the powers of the earth, the separate and equal station to which the Laws of Nature and of Nature's God entitle them, a decent respect to the opinions of mankind requires that they should declare the causes which impel them to the separation.

We hold these truths to be self-evident, that all men are created equal, that   2
they are endowed by their Creator with certain unalienable rights, that among these are life, liberty and the pursuit of happiness. That to secure these rights, governments are instituted among men, deriving their just powers from the consent of the governed. That whenever any form of government becomes destructive of these ends, it is the right of the people to alter or to abolish it, and to institute new government, laying its foundation on such principles and organizing its powers in such form, as to them shall seem most likely to effect their safety and happiness. Prudence, indeed, will dictate that governments long established should not be changed for light and transient causes; and accordingly all experience hath shown, that mankind are more disposed to suffer, while evils are sufferable, than to right themselves by abolishing the forms to which they are accustomed. But when a long train of abuses and usurpations, pursuing invariably the same object evinces a design to reduce them under absolute despotism, it is their right, it is their duty, to throw off such government, and to provide new guards for their future security. Such has been the patient sufferance of these Colonies; and such is now the necessity which constrains them to alter their former systems of government. The history of the present King of Great Britain is a history of repeated injuries and usurpations, all having in direct object the establishment of an absolute tyranny over these States. To prove this, let facts be submitted to a candid world.

3   He has refused his assent to laws, the most wholesome and necessary for the public good.

4   He has forbidden his Governors to pass laws of immediate and pressing importance, unless suspended in their operation till his assent should be obtained; and when so suspended, he has utterly neglected to attend to them.

5   He has refused to pass other laws for the accommodation of large districts of people, unless those people would relinquish the right of representation in the Legislature, a right inestimable to them and formidable to tyrants only.

6   He has called together legislative bodies at places unusual, uncomfortable, and distant from the depository of their public records, for the sole purpose of fatiguing them into compliance with his measures.

7   He has dissolved representative houses repeatedly, for opposing with manly firmness his invasions on the rights of the people.

8   He has refused for a long time, after such dissolutions, to cause others to be elected; whereby the legislative powers, incapable of annihilation, have returned to the people at large for their exercise; the State remaining in the meantime exposed to all the dangers of invasion from without and convulsions within.

9   He has endeavoured to prevent the population of these States; for that purpose obstructing the laws of naturalization of foreigners; refusing to pass others to encourage their migration hither, and raising the conditions of new appropriations of lands.

10   He has obstructed the administration of justice, by refusing his assent to laws for establishing judiciary powers.

11   He has made judges dependent on his will alone, for the tenure of their offices, and the amount and payment of their salaries.

12   He has erected a multitude of new offices, and sent hither swarms of officers to harass our people, and eat out their substance.

13   He has kept among us, in times of peace, standing armies without the consent of our legislatures.

14   He has affected to render the military independent of and superior to the civil power.

15   He has combined with others to subject us to a jurisdiction foreign to our constitution, and unacknowledged by our laws; giving his assent to their acts of pretended legislation:

16   For quartering large bodies of armed troops among us:

17   For protecting them, by a mock trial, from punishment for any murders which they should commit on the inhabitants of these States:

18   For cutting off our trade with all parts of the world:

19   For imposing taxes on us without our consent:

20   For depriving us, in many cases, of the benefits of trial by jury:

21   For transporting us beyond seas to be tried for pretended offences:

22   For abolishing the free system of English laws in a neighbouring Province, establishing therein an arbitrary government, and enlarging its boundaries so as to render it at once an example and fit instrument for introducing the same absolute rule into these Colonies:

For taking away our Charters, abolishing our most valuable laws, and altering fundamentally the forms of our governments: 23

For suspending our own Legislatures, and declaring themselves invested with power to legislate for us in all cases whatsoever. 24

He has abdicated government here, by declaring us out of his protection and waging war against us. 25

He has plundered our seas, ravaged our coasts, burnt our towns, and destroyed the lives of our people. 26

He is at this time transporting large armies of foreign mercenaries to complete the works of death, desolation and tyranny, already begun with circumstances of cruelty and perfidy scarcely paralleled in the most barbarous ages, and totally unworthy the head of a civilized nation. 27

He has constrained our fellow citizens taken captive on the high seas to bear arms against their country, to become the executioners of their friends and brethren, or to fall themselves by their hands. 28

He has excited domestic insurrections amongst us, and has endeavoured to bring on the inhabitants of our frontiers, the merciless Indian savages, whose known rule of warfare, is an undistinguished destruction of all ages, sexes, and conditions. 29

In every stage of these oppressions we have petitioned for redress in the most humble terms; our repeated petitions have been answered only by repeated injury. A prince whose character is thus marked by every act which may define a tyrant is unfit to be the ruler of a free people. 30

Nor have we been wanting in attention to our British brethren. We have warned them from time to time of attempts by their legislature to extend an unwarrantable jurisdiction over us. We have reminded them of the circumstances of our emigration and settlement here. We have appealed to their native justice and magnanimity, and we have conjured them by the ties of our common kindred to disavow these usurpations, which would inevitably interrupt our connections and correspondence. They too have been deaf to the voice of justice and of consanguinity. We must, therefore, acquiesce in the necessity, which denounces our separation, and hold them, as we hold the rest of mankind, enemies in war, in peace friends. 31

We, therefore, the Representatives of the United States of America, in General Congress assembled, appealing to the Supreme Judge of the world for the rectitude of our intentions, do, in the name, and by the authority of the good people of these Colonies, solemnly publish and declare, That these United Colonies are, and of right ought to be Free and Independent States; that they are absolved from all allegiance to the British Crown, and that all political connection between them and the State of Great Britain, is and ought to be totally dissolved; and that as Free and Independent States, they have full power to levy war, conclude peace, contract alliances, establish commerce, and to do all other acts and things which Independent States may of right do. And for the support of this declaration, with a firm reliance on the protection of Divine Providence, we mutually pledge to each other our lives, our fortunes, and our sacred honor. 32

QUESTIONS FOR ANALYSIS

1. What is the Declaration's central deductive argument? State the argument in the shape illustrated above: major premise, minor premise, conclusion. Construct a valid argument. If necessary, draw circles representing each of the three terms in the argument to check for validity. (*Hint:* Start with the claim "George III's government should be overthrown.")
2. Which paragraphs are devoted to supporting the major premise? What kind of support has been given?
3. Which paragraphs are devoted to supporting the minor premise? What kind of support has been given?
4. Why has more support been given for one premise than the other?

EXERCISES: Completing and Evaluating Deductive Arguments

Turn each of the following statements into valid deductive arguments. (You have the conclusion and one premise, so you will have to determine the missing premise that would complete the argument. Draw circles if necessary to test for validity.) Then decide which arguments have premises that could be supported. Note the kind of support that might be provided. Explain why you think some arguments have insupportable premises. Here is an example:

PREMISE: All Jesuits are priests.

PREMISE: No women are priests.

CONCLUSION: No women are Jesuits.

Since the circle for women must be placed outside the circle for priests, it must also be outside the circle for Jesuits. Hence the argument is valid. The first premise is true by definition; the term *Jesuit* refers to an order of Roman Catholic priests. The second premise is true for the Roman Catholic Church, so if the term *priest* is used only to refer to people with a religious vocation in the Roman Catholic Church, then the second premise is also true by definition.

1. Mrs. Ferguson is a good teacher because she can explain the subject matter clearly.
2. Segregated schools are unconstitutional because they are unequal.
3. Michael must be a good driver because he drives fast.
4. The media clearly have a liberal bias because they make fun of religious fundamentalists.

ANALOGY

The argument from analogy is an argument based on comparison. Analogies assert that since A and B are alike in several ways, they must be alike in another way as well. The argument from analogy concludes with an inference, an assertion of a significant similarity in the two items being compared. The other similarities serve as evidence in support of the inference. The shape of an argument by analogy is illustrated in Figure 5.3.

Although analogy is sometimes an effective approach to an issue because clever, imaginative comparisons are often moving, analogy is not as rigorously logical as either induction or deduction. Frequently an analogy is based on only two or three points of comparison, whereas a sound inductive argument presents many examples to support its conclusion. Further, to be convincing, the points of comparison must be fundamental to the two items being compared. An argument for a county leash law for cats developed by analogy with dogs may cite the following similarities:

- Cats are pets, just like dogs.
- Cats live in residential communities, just like dogs.
- Cats can mess up other people's yards, just like dogs.
- Cats, if allowed to run free, can disturb the peace (fighting, howling at night), just like dogs.

Does it follow that cats should be required to walk on a leash, just like dogs? If such a county ordinance were passed, would it be enforceable? Have you ever tried to walk a cat on a leash? In spite of legitimate similarities brought out by the analogy, the conclusion does not logically follow because the arguer is overlooking a fundamental difference in the two animals' personalities. Dogs can be trained to a leash; most cats (Siamese are one exception) cannot be so trained. Such thinking will produce sulking cats and scratched owners. But the analogy, delivered passionately to the right audience, could lead community activists to lobby for a new law.

Observe that the problem with the cat-leash-law analogy is not in the similarities asserted about the items being compared but rather in the underlying assumption that the similarities logically support the argument's conclusion. A good analogy asserts many points of comparison and finds likenesses that are essential parts of the nature or purpose of the two items being compared. The best way to challenge another's analogy is to point out a fundamental difference in the nature or purpose of the compared items. For all of their similarities, when it comes to walking on a leash, cats are *not* like dogs.

GROUNDS:	A has characteristics 1, 2, 3, and 4.
	B has characteristics 1, 2, and 3.
CLAIM:	B has characteristic 4 (as well).
ASSUMPTION (WARRANT):	If B has three characteristics in common with A, it must have the key fourth characteristic as well.

FIGURE 5.3 The Shape of an Argument by Analogy

EXERCISES: Analogy

1. Analyze the following analogies. List the stated and/or implied points of comparison and the conclusion in the pattern illustrated on page 139. Then judge each argument's logic and effectiveness as a persuasive technique. If the argument is not logical, state the fundamental difference in the two compared items. If the argument could be persuasive, describe the kind of audience that might be moved by it.

    a. College newspapers should not be under the supervision or control of a faculty sponsor. Fortunately, no governmental sponsor controls the *New York Times,* or we would no longer have a free press in this country. We need a free college press, too, one that can attack college policies when they are wrong.

    b. Let's recognize that college athletes are really professional and start paying them properly. College athletes get a free education, and spending money from boosters. They are required to attend practices and games, and—if they play football or basketball—they bring in huge revenues for their "organization." College coaches are also paid enormous salaries, just like professional coaches, and often college coaches are tapped to coach professional teams. The only difference: the poor college athletes don't get those big salaries and huge signing bonuses.

    c. Just like any business, the federal government must be made to balance its budget. No company could continue to operate in the red as the government does and expect to be successful. A constitutional amendment requiring a balanced federal budget is long overdue.

2. Read and analyze the following analogy by Zbigniew Brzezinski. The questions that follow his article will aid your analysis.

WAR AND FOOTBALL | ZBIGNIEW BRZEZINSKI

Former national security advisor to President Jimmy Carter, Dr. Brzezinski is an expert on politics and foreign affairs. He has published many books and articles, including *The Grand Chessboard: American Primacy and Its Geostrategic Imperative* (1997), and currently works at the Center for Strategic and International Studies. His article on football was published in the *Washington Post* on January 7, 2000.

1   I discovered American football late in life. Initially, I thought the game was a bore. When I saw my first football match after coming to America as a child reared on soccer, I was even appalled. Why are all these men, helmeted and wearing protective gear, bending over and then piling on top of one another? I was mystified by their conspiratorial huddling. And when I first heard the referee announce "penalty declined," I remember turning to my American guide and naively noting that it was chivalrous of the rewarded team to have done so.

2   After my appointment to the White House in the mid-'70s, I was favored by invitations to sit in the Redskins' owner's box—and the Washington thing to do, of course, was to go. Before long it dawned on me: The game is unique in

the manner it translates into sport all the main ingredients of real warfare. Henceforth I was hooked.

Consider the following parallels: 3

- The owners of the teams are like heads of state. Some are nasty dicta-   4 tors, some merely preside like monarchs. Some posture and are loud-mouths, but all are treated with a deference worthy of kings. The senior Cooke—my occasional and very regal host—both reigned and ruled; his son merely reigned. The new, post-Cooke owner conveys an intelligent passion for football, reminiscent of President Nixon, that will probably benefit the team.

- The coaches are the CinCs, to use Washington jargon. They set the over-   5 all strategy and supervise its tactical implementation in the course of combat. In constant wireless contact with their forces as well as with their scouting experts (a k a intelligence), examining instant play photos (a k a overhead imagery) and consulting their deputies for offensive and defensive operations, they are clearly the commanders in chief. Some are like Gen. Eisenhower; others remind you of Gen. MacArthur. The truly victorious ones (e.g., Gibbs or Parcells) reflect the needed ability to simultaneously inspire, intimidate and innovate.

- The quarterbacks, as is often noted, are the field commanders. They   6 make last-minute tactical decisions on the basis of direct observation of hostile deployments, and they're expected, when necessary, to impro-vise tactically, though in the context of their CinCs' overall strategy. Some hustle and take risks; some stay put and just grind away. Again, shades of Gen. Patton or of Gen. Westmoreland.

- The teams engage in offensive and defensive maneuvers, as in real war.   7 They rely either on a concentration of power (especially in ground at-tacks), on flanking attacks or on sudden deployment behind enemy lines (passing). Deception, speed and force are the required ingredients for success. Skill, precision and iron discipline are instilled by intense training.

- Good intelligence is also essential. Hence much effort is spent on the   8 constant monitoring of the enemy's tactics, with specialists (high in the stands, equipped with long-distance observation equipment) seeking to spot potential weaknesses while identifying also the special strengths of the opponent. Timely strategic as well as tactical adjustments (especially during halftime) are often a key to the successful completion of the cam-paign (a k a game).

- As in real combat, teams suffer casualties, and these can cripple even a   9 strong team. It is especially important to protect the field commander-quarterbacks; they are a key target of enemy action since their loss can be especially disruptive.

- Last but not least, the home front also plays a role. Systematic motiva-   10 tion of the morale of civilians (the spectators) can play an important role in stirring the combatants into greater passion while demoralizing the enemy. The home-field advantage is thus the equivalent to fighting in the defense of your own homeland.

11   Once I understood the above, the mindless piles of bodies, the strange posturing of grown men and the armored uniforms all came to make sense to me. A great game. Like a war.

QUESTIONS FOR READING

1. What were Brzezinski's initial views of American football?
2. What are the points of comparison between football and war? State these in summary form in your own words.

QUESTIONS FOR REASONING AND ANALYSIS

1. The author's subject is clear, as is his use of analogy as a strategy. But, what is his purpose in writing? What does he want readers to conclude from his analogy? (Consider: How do you read the last two sentences? What are most people's attitudes toward war?)
2. What, then, is Brzezinski's thesis, the claim of his argument?
3. What elements of style add to the analogy's effectiveness? How would you describe the essay's tone?

QUESTIONS FOR REFLECTING AND WRITING

1. What kinds of readers are least likely to be moved by the author's analogy? Why?
2. If you do not accept Brzezinski's analogy, how would you counter it?

ARGUMENTS THAT DO NOT WORK: LOGICAL FALLACIES

A thorough study of argument needs to include a study of logical fallacies because so many "arguments" fail to meet standards of sound logic and good sense. Before examining specific types of arguments that do not work, let's consider briefly why people offer arguments that aren't sensible.

Causes of Illogic

Ignorance

One frequent cause for illogical debate is simply a lack of knowledge of the subject. Some people have more information than others, either from formal study or from wide-ranging experiences. The younger you are, the less you can be expected to know about or understand complex issues. On the other hand, if you want to debate a complex or technical issue, then you cannot use ignorance as an excuse for producing a weak argument. To illustrate: Following the 1992 riots in Los Angeles, then press secretary Marlin Fitzwater asserted that welfare programs of the 1960s and 1970s caused the riots. When reporters asked which programs, Fitzwater responded that he did not have a list with him! Instead of ducking the need for evidence, you want to read as much as you can, listen carefully to discussions, ask questions, and, when called on to write, select topics about which you have knowledge or which you are willing to study before writing.

Egos

Ego problems are another cause of weak arguments. Those with low self-esteem often have difficulty in debates because they attach themselves to their ideas and then feel personally attacked when someone disagrees with them. Usually the next step is a defense of their views with even greater emotion and irrationality, even though self-esteem is enhanced when others applaud our knowledge and thoughtfulness, not our irrationality.

Prejudices

A third cause of irrationality is the collection of prejudices and biases that we carry around, having absorbed them "ages ago" from family and community. Prejudices range from the worst ethnic, religious, or sexist stereotypes to political views we have adopted uncritically (Democrats are all bleeding hearts; Republicans are all rich snobs), to perhaps less serious but equally insupportable notions (if it's in print, it must be right; if it's not meat and potatoes, it is not really dinner). People who see the world through distorted lenses cannot possibly assess facts intelligently and reason logically from them.

A Need for Answers

Finally, many bad arguments stem from a human need for answers—any answers—to the questions that deeply concern us. We want to control our world because that makes us feel secure, and having answers makes us feel in control. This need can lead to illogic from oversimplifying problems, from refusing to settle for qualified answers to questions.

The causes of illogic lead us to a twofold classification of bad arguments: logical fallacies that result from (1) oversimplifying the issue or from (2) ignoring the issue by substituting emotion for reason.

Fallacies That Result from Oversimplifying

Errors in Generalizing

Errors in generalizing include overstatement and hasty or faulty generalization. All have in common an error in the inductive pattern of argument. The inference drawn from the evidence is unwarranted, either because too broad a generalization is made or because the generalization is drawn from incomplete or incorrect evidence. *Overstatement* occurs when the argument's assertion is an unqualified generalization—that is, it refers to all members of a category or class, although the evidence justifies an assertion about only some of the class. Overstatements often result from stereotyping, giving the same traits to everyone in a group. Overstatements are frequently signaled by words such as *all, every, always, never,* and *none.* But remember that assertions such as "children love clowns" are understood to refer to "all children," even though the word *all* does not appear in the sentence. It is the writer's task to qualify statements appropriately, using words such as *some, many,* or *frequently,* as appropriate. Overstatements are discredited by finding only one exception to disprove the assertion. One frightened child who starts to cry when the clown approaches will destroy the argument. Here is another example:

- Lawyers are only interested in making money.

  (What about lawyers who work to protect consumers, or public defenders who take care of those unable to pay for a lawyer?)

  Hasty or faulty generalizations may be qualified assertions, but they still oversimplify by arguing from insufficient evidence or by ignoring some relevant evidence. For example:

- Political life must lead many to excessive drinking. In the last six months the paper has written about five members of Congress who have either confessed to alcoholism or have been arrested on DUI charges.

  (Five is not a large enough sample from which to generalize about *many* politicians. Also, the five in the newspaper are not a representative sample; they have made the news because of their drinking.)

Forced Hypothesis

The *forced hypothesis* is also an error in inductive reasoning. The explanation (hypothesis) offered to account for a particular situation is "forced," or illogical, because either (1) sufficient evidence does not exist to draw any conclusion or (2) the evidence can be explained more simply or more sensibly by a different hypothesis. This logical fallacy often results from failure to consider other possible explanations. You discredit a forced hypothesis by providing alternative conclusions that are more sensible or just as sensible as the one offered. Consider the following example:

- Professor Redding's students received either A's or B's last semester. He must be an excellent teacher.

  (The grades alone cannot support the conclusion. Professor Redding could be an excellent teacher; he could have started with excellent students; he could be an easy grader.)

Non Sequitur

The term *non sequitur,* meaning literally "it does not follow," could apply to all arguments that do not work, but the term is usually reserved for those arguments in which the conclusions are not logically connected to the reasons, those arguments with the "glue" missing. In a hasty generalization, for example, there is a connection between support (five politicians in the news) and conclusion (many politicians with drinking problems), just not a convincing connection. With the *non sequitur* there is no recognizable connection, either because (1) whatever connection the arguer sees is not made clear to others or because (2) the evidence or reasons offered are irrelevant to the conclusion. For example:

- Donna will surely get a good grade in physics; she earned an A in her biology class.

  (Doing well in one course, even one science course, does not support the conclusion that the student will get a good grade in another course. If Donna is not good at math, she definitely will not do well in physics.)

Slippery Slope

The *slippery slope* argument asserts that we should not proceed with or permit A because, if we do, the terrible consequences X, Y, and Z will occur. This type of argument oversimplifies by assuming, without evidence and usually by ignoring historical examples, existing laws, or any reasonableness in people, that X, Y, and Z will follow inevitably from A. This kind of argument rests on the belief that most people will not want the final, awful Z to occur. The belief, however accurate, does not provide a sufficiently good reason for avoiding A. One of the best-known examples of slippery slope reasoning can be found in the gun-control debate:

- If we allow the government to register handguns, next it will register hunting rifles; then it will prohibit all citizen ownership of guns, thereby creating a police state or a world in which only outlaws have guns.

  (Surely no one wants the final dire consequences predicted in this argument. However, handgun registration does not mean that these consequences will follow. The United States has never been a police state, and its system of free elections guards against such a future. Also, citizens have registered cars, boats, and planes for years without any threat of these belongings being confiscated.)

False Dilemma

The *false dilemma* oversimplifies an issue by asserting only two alternatives when there are more than two. The either–or thinking of this kind of argument can be an effective tactic if undetected. If the arguer gives us only two choices and one of those is clearly unacceptable, then the arguer can push us toward the preferred choice. For example:

- The Federal Reserve System must lower interest rates, or we will never pull out of the recession.

  (Clearly, staying in a recession is not much of a choice, but the alternative may not be the only or the best course of action to achieve a healthy economy. If interest rates go too low, inflation can be triggered. Other options include the government's creating new jobs and patiently letting market forces play themselves out.)

False Analogy

When examining the shape of analogy, we also considered the problems with this type of argument. (See page 139.) Remember that you challenge a false analogy by noting many differences in the two items being compared or by noting a significant difference that has been ignored.

Post Hoc Fallacy

The term *post hoc,* from the Latin *post hoc, ergo propter hoc* (literally, "after this, therefore because of it") refers to a common error in arguments about cause. One oversimplifies causation by confusing a time relationship with cause. Reveal the illogic of *post hoc* arguments by pointing to other possible causes:

- We should throw out the entire city council. Since the members were elected, the city has gone into deficit spending.

  (Assuming that deficit spending in this situation is bad, was it caused by the current city council? Or did the current council inherit debts? Or is the entire region suffering from a recession?)

EXERCISES: Fallacies That Result from Oversimplifying

1. Here is a list of the fallacies we have examined so far. Make up or collect from your reading at least one example of each fallacy.
   a. Overstatement
   b. Stereotyping
   c. Hasty generalization
   d. Forced hypothesis
   e. *Non sequitur*
   f. Slippery slope
   g. False dilemma
   h. False analogy
   i. *Post hoc* fallacy

2. Explain what is illogical about each of the following arguments. Then name the fallacy represented. (Sometimes an argument will fit into more than one category. In that case name all appropriate terms.)
   a. Everybody agrees that we need stronger drunk-driving laws.
   b. The upsurge in crime on Sundays is the result of the reduced rate of church attendance in recent years.
   c. The government must create new jobs. A factory in Illinois has laid off half its workers.
   d. Steve has joined the country club. Golf must be one of his favorite sports.
   e. Blondes have more fun.
   f. You'll enjoy your Volvo; foreign cars never break down.
   g. Gary loves jokes. He would make a great comedian.

h. The economy is in bad shape because of the Federal Reserve Board. Ever since they expanded the money supply, the stock market has been declining.
i. Either we improve the city's street lighting, or we will fail to reduce crime.
j. DNA research today is just like the study of nuclear fission. It seems important, but it's just another bomb that will one day explode on us. When will we learn that government must control research?
k. To prohibit prayer in public schools is to limit religious practice solely to internal belief. The result is that an American is religiously "free" only in his own mind.
l. Professor Johnson teaches in the political science department. I'll bet she's another socialist.
m. Coming to the aid of any country engaged in civil war is a bad idea. Next we'll be sending American troops, and soon we'll be involved in another Vietnam.
n. We must reject affirmative action in hiring or we'll have to settle for incompetent employees.

3. Examine the logic in this famous passage from Lewis Carroll's *Alice in Wonderland.* What logical fallacy does the king commit?

The King turned pale, and shut his note-book hastily. "Consider your verdict," he said to the jury, in a low trembling voice.

"There's more evidence to come yet, please your Majesty," said the White Rabbit, jumping up in a great hurry: "this paper has just been picked up."

"What's in it?" said the Queen.

"I haven't opened it yet," said the White Rabbit; "but it seems to be a letter, written by the prisoner to—to somebody."

"It must have been that," said the King, "unless it was written to nobody, which isn't usual, you know."

"Who is it directed to?" said one of the jurymen.

"It isn't directed at all," said the White Rabbit; "in fact, there's nothing written on the *outside*." He unfolded the paper as he spoke, and added, "It isn't a letter, after all: it's a set of verses."

"Are they in the prisoner's handwriting?" asked another of the jurymen.

"No, they're not," said the White Rabbit, "and that's the queerest thing about it." (The jury all looked puzzled.)

"He must have imitated somebody else's hand," said the King. (The jury all brightened up again.)

"Please, your Majesty," said the Knave, "I didn't write it, and they can't prove that I did: there's no name signed at the end."

"If you didn't sign it," said the King, "that only makes the matter worse. You *must* have meant some mischief, or else you'd have signed your name like an honest man."

There was a general clapping of hands at this: it was the first really clever thing the King had said that day.

"That *proves* his guilt, of course," said the Queen, "so, off with—"

"It doesn't prove anything of the sort!" said Alice. "Why, you don't even know what they're about!"

Fallacies That Result from Ignoring the Issue

There are many arguments that divert attention from the issue under debate. Of the six discussed here, the first three try to divert attention by introducing a separate issue or "sliding by" the actual issue; the following three seek diversion by appealing to the audience's emotions or prejudices. In the first three the arguer tries to give the impression of presenting an argument; in the last three the arguer charges forward on emotional manipulation alone.

Begging the Question

To assume that part of your argument is true without supporting it is to *beg the question*. Arguments seeking to pass off as proof statements that must themselves be supported are often introduced with such phrases as "the fact is" (to introduce opinion), "obviously," and "as we can see." For example:

- Clearly, lowering grading standards would be bad for students, so a pass/fail system should not be adopted.

  (Does a pass/fail system lower standards? No evidence has been given. If so, is that necessarily bad for students?)

Red Herring

The *red herring* is a foul-smelling argument indeed. The debater introduces a side issue, some point that is not relevant to the debate:

- The senator is an honest woman; she loves her children and gives to charities.

  (The children and charities are side issues; they do not demonstrate honesty.)

Straw Man

The *straw man* argument attributes to opponents erroneous and usually ridiculous views that they do not hold so that their position can be easily attacked. We can challenge this illogic by demonstrating that the arguer's opponents do not hold those views or by demanding that the arguer provide some evidence that they do:

- Those who favor gun control just want to take all guns away from responsible citizens and put them in the hands of criminals.

  (The position attributed to proponents of gun control is not only inaccurate but actually the opposite of what is sought by gun-control proponents.)

Ad Hominem

One of the most frequent of all appeals to emotion masquerading as argument is the *ad hominem* argument (literally, argument "to the man"). Sometimes the debate turns to an attack of a supporter of the issue; other times, the illogic is found in name-calling. When someone says that "those crazy liberals at the

ACLU just want all criminals to go free," or a pro-choice demonstrator screams at those "self-righteous fascists" on the other side, the best retort may be silence, or the calm assertion that such statements do not contribute to meaningful debate.

Common Practice or Bandwagon

To argue that an action should be taken or a position accepted because "everyone is doing it" is illogical. The majority is not always right. Frequently when someone is defending an action as ethical on the ground that everyone does it, the action isn't ethical and the defender knows it isn't. The bandwagon argument is a desperate one. For example:

- There's nothing wrong with fudging a bit on your income taxes. After all, the superrich don't pay any taxes, and the government expects everyone to cheat a little.

  (First, not everyone cheats on taxes; many pay to have their taxes done correctly. And if it is wrong, it is wrong regardless of the number who do it.)

Ad Populum

Another technique for arousing an audience's emotions and ignoring the issue is to appeal *ad populum,* "to the people," to the audience's presumed shared values and beliefs. Every Fourth of July, politicians employ this tactic, appealing to God, mother, apple pie, and "traditional family values." As with all emotional gimmicks, we need to reject the argument as illogical.

- Good, law-abiding Americans must be sick of the violent crimes occurring in our once godly society. But we won't tolerate it anymore; put the criminals in jail and throw away the key.

  (This does not contribute to a thoughtful debate on criminal justice issues.)

EXERCISES: Fallacies That Result from Ignoring the Issue

1. Here is a list of fallacies that result from ignoring the issue. Make up or collect from your reading at least one example of each fallacy.
   a. Begging the question
   b. Red herring
   c. Straw man
   d. *Ad hominem*
   e. Common practice or bandwagon
   f. *Ad populum*
2. Explain what is illogical about each of the following arguments. Then name the fallacy represented.
   a. Gold's book doesn't deserve a Pulitzer Prize. She has been married four times.
   b. I wouldn't vote for him; many of his programs are basically socialist.
   c. Eight out of ten headache sufferers use Bayer to relieve headache pain. It will work for you, too.

   d.   We shouldn't listen to Colman McCarthy's argument against liquor ads in college newspapers because he obviously thinks young people are ignorant and need guidance in everything.
   e.   My roommate Joe does the craziest things; he must be neurotic.
   f.   Since so many people obviously cheat the welfare system, it should be abolished.
   g.   She isn't pretty enough to win the contest, and besides she had her nose "fixed" two years ago.
   h.   Professors should chill out; everybody cheats on exams from time to time.
   i.   The fact is that bilingual education is a mistake because it encourages students to use only their native language and that gives them an advantage over other students.
   j.   Don't join those crazy liberals in support of the American Civil Liberties Union. They want all criminals to go free.
   k.   Real Americans understand that free trade agreements are evil. Let your representatives know that we want American goods protected.

3.   Examine the following letter to the editor by Christian Brahmstedt that appeared in the *Washington Post* on January 2, 1989. If you think it contains logical fallacies, identify the passages and explain the fallacies.

HELP THOSE WHO HELP, NOT HURT, THEMSELVES

1   In the past year, and repeatedly throughout the holiday season, the *Post* has devoted an abnormally large share of newsprint to the "plight" of the vagrants who wander throughout the city in search of free handouts: i.e., the "homeless."

2   As certain as taxes, the poor shall remain with civilization forever. Yet these "homeless" are certainly not in the same category as the poor. The poor of civilization, of which we have all been a part at one time in our lives, are proud and work hard until a financial independence frees them from the category. The "homeless" do not seek work or pride. They are satisfied to beg and survive on others' generosity.

3   The best correlation to the "homeless" I have witnessed are the gray squirrels on Capitol Hill. After feeding several a heavy dose of nuts one afternoon, I returned the next day to see the same squirrels patiently waiting for a return feeding. In the same fashion, the "homeless" are trained by Washington's guilt-ridden society to continue begging a sustenance rather than learning independence.

4   The *Post* has preached that these vagrants be supported from the personal and federal coffers—in the same manner as the squirrels on Capitol Hill. This support is not helping the homeless; it is only teaching them to rely on it. All of our parents

struggled through the depression as homeless of a sort, to arise and build financial independence through hard work.

5   The "homeless" problem will go away when, and only when, Washingtonians refuse to feed them. They will learn to support themselves and learn that society demands honest work for an honest dollar.

6   It would be better for Washington citizens to field their guilt donations to the poor, those folks who are holding down two or more jobs just to make ends meet, rather than throwing their tribute to the vagrants on the sewer grates. The phrase "help those who help themselves" has no more certain relevance than to the "homeless" issue.

EXERCISES: Analyzing Arguments

1.   Analyze the following letter to the editor titled "Beer Commercials Do No Harm," published on January 28, 1989, and written by James C. Sanders, president of the Beer Institute. How effectively does Sanders make his case? How convincing is the evidence that he presents? Do you accept his warrant that his evidence is authoritative? If not, what do you think he should have included in the letter? Try to answer these questions in detail to be prepared for class discussion.

BEER COMMERCIALS DO NOT HARM

1   With respect to the letter to the editor of Jan. 13 concerning the banning of beer commercials, we believe it is appropriate to respond. While the tragedy of drunk driving and other abuses of alcohol beverages is of concern to us all, there are much broader problems and solutions that must be addressed.

2   First, we must consider the empirical evidence on the effect or lack of effect of alcohol beverage advertising and its impact on abuse. There exists a substantial body of evidence that suggests that the only impact of alcohol beverage advertising is that of brand preference, shifting those who choose to drink to a particular beverage or brand name.

3   There exists no sound evidence that alcohol beverage advertising has an adverse impact on abuse. Alcohol beverage advertising does not promote

excessive consumption, influence nondrinkers to become drinkers or induce young people to drink.

4   In fact, studies show that parents and peers, respectively, are the major contributors to a young person's decision to consume or not to consume. Furthermore, studies have shown that "the best controlled studies show no overall effect of alcohol advertising on consumption."

5   Another related issue is the right to commercial free speech. The alcohol beverage industry—specifically, the beer and wine industries—advertises on television legal products whose responsible, moderate consumption is enjoyed by the majority of our population. This is not to disregard a certain percentage of citizens who should not consume our product—specifically, underage persons and alcoholics.

6   The alcohol beverage industry is concerned and involved in programs that educate, inform and support positive, realistic solutions to alcohol abuse. We are working with many organizations whose goals are to reduce the problems associated with the misuse of our products. Radical or empirically unsound approaches to alcohol problems serve only to divert us from sound, positive solutions.

2. Analyze the logical fallacies in the following student essay. Make notes of specific problems to be prepared for class discussion.

DEATH

In the editorial section of the *Washington Post* I came across an article titled "New York on the Brink." The article is about New York thinking and trying to impose the death penalty. The editors are against the death sentence, and I disagree with them.

The death sentence is obviously a moral and political issue. But is it right to let killers just serve time and be released back into society after taking someone's life? The death penalty has been around as long as man. It is needed to get rid of the murderers and keep the innocent safe and secure.

The article says that President George Bush's speech in New York urging a mandatory federal death penalty for the killing of law enforcement officers is unfair.

Why is that unfair? The police are out to protect the innocent. It is unfair not to serve justice on those individuals. If a criminal goes around killing the protectors of law and peace, who knows what they can and will do to the common citizens.

Another thing to think about is the overcrowding of prisons. There is very little room for prisoners these days. The author didn't even think of that. By ridding society of the killers, it will make room for other criminals to serve time. I wonder if the author is willing to pay extra taxes to build new prisons.

The author also argues that the death penalty doesn't prevent murders from happening. There have always been murderers throughout history, and there will always be murders. But I think that I would think twice about killing someone if I knew that I would die as well. But there will always be people who take the chance. The death penalty would just get rid of those who do them.

The author's final argument is that sanctioned killing is as abhorrent as murder. I think the author would have a change of heart if someone close to him or her was murdered. It is only fair that the murderer pay the same price as the victim.

It is time that people start to open their eyes and realize that it is a life and death world out there. And the only way to change the suffering of the law abiders is to get rid of the law breakers. The death penalty is the price a free society pays to stay free.

EVALUATING THE ARGUMENTS OF OTHERS: THE REFUTATION ESSAY

When your primary purpose in writing is to challenge someone's argument rather than to present your own argument, you are writing a *refutation*. A good refutation demonstrates, in an orderly and logical way, the weaknesses of logic or evidence in the argument, or it both analyzes weaknesses and builds a counterargument. Refutations can challenge a specific, written argument, but they can also challenge a prevailing attitude or belief that is, in the writer's view, contrary to the evidence. The sample refutation that follows shows the first purpose. It is annotated to show you how the author puts together his refutation. But first, study the following guidelines to prepare a good refutation essay:

GUIDELINES for Preparing a Refutation Essay

1. **Read accurately.** Make certain that you have understood your opponent's argument. If you assume views not expressed by the writer and accuse the writer of holding those illogical views, you are guilty of the straw man fallacy, of attributing and then attacking a position that the person does not hold. Look up terms and references you do not know and examine the logic and evidence thoroughly.

2. **Pinpoint the weaknesses in the original argument.** Analyze the argument to determine, specifically, what flaws the argument contains. If the argument contains logical fallacies, make a list of the ones you plan to discredit. Examine the evidence presented. Is it insufficient, unreliable, or irrelevant? Decide, before drafting your refutation, exactly what elements of the argument you intend to challenge.

3. **Write your thesis.** After analyzing the argument and deciding on the weaknesses to be challenged, write a thesis which establishes that your disagreement is with the writer's logic, assumptions, or evidence, or a combination of these.

4. **Draft your essay, using the following three-part organization:**

   a. *The opponent's argument.* Usually you should not assume that your reader has read or remembered the argument you are refuting. Thus at the beginning of your essay, you need to state, accurately and fairly, the main points of the argument to be refuted.

   b. *Your thesis.* Next make clear the nature of your disagreement with the argument you are refuting.

   c. *Your refutation.* The specifics of your counterargument will depend upon the nature of your disagreement. If you are challenging the writer's evidence, then you must present the more recent evidence to explain why the evidence used is unreliable or misleading. If you are challenging assumptions, then you must explain why they do not hold up. If your thesis is that the piece is filled with logical fallacies, then you must present and explain each fallacy.

GENDER GAMES | DAVID SADKER

A professor of education at American University, David Sadker has written extensively on educational issues, especially on the treatment of girls in the classroom. He is the author of *Failing at Fairness: How Our Schools Cheat Girls* (1995). "Gender Games" appeared in the *Washington Post* on July 31, 2000. Read, study the annotations, and then answer the questions that follow.

Attention-getting opening.

1   Remember when your elementary school teacher would announce the teams for the weekly spelling bee? "Boys against the girls!" There was nothing like a gender showdown to liven things up. Apparently, some writers never left this elementary level of intrigue. A spate of recent books and articles takes us back to the "boys versus girls" fray but this time, with much higher stakes.

May's *Atlantic Monthly* cover story, "Girls Rule," is a case in point. The magazine published an excerpt from *The War Against Boys* by Christina Hoff Sommers, a book advancing the notion that boys are the real victims of gender bias while girls are soaring in school.

Sommers and her supporters are correct in saying that girls and women have made significant educational progress in the past two decades. Females today make up more than 40 percent of medical and law school students, and more than half of college students. Girls continue to read sooner and write better than boys. And for as long as anyone can remember, girls have received higher grades than boys.

But there is more to these selected statistics than meets the eye. Although girls continue to receive higher report card grades than boys, their grades do not translate into higher test scores. The same girls who beat boys in the spelling bees score below boys on the tests that matter: the PSATs crucial for scholarships, the SATs and the ACTs needed for college acceptances, the GREs for graduate school and even the admission tests for law, business and medical schools.

Many believe that girls' higher grades may be more a reflection of their manageable classroom behavior than their intellectual accomplishment. Test scores are not influenced by quieter classroom behavior. Girls may in fact be trading their initiative and independence for peer approval and good grades, a trade-off that can have costly personal and economic consequences.

The increase in female college enrollment catches headlines because it heralds the first time that females have outnumbered males on college campuses. But even these enrollment figures are misleading. The female presence increases as the status of the college decreases. Female students are more likely to dominate two-year schools than the Ivy League. And wherever they are, they find themselves segregated and channeled into the least prestigious and least costly majors.

In today's world of e-success, more than 60 percent of computer science and business majors are male, about 70 percent of physics majors are males, and more than 80 percent of engineering students are male. But peek into language, psychology, nursing and humanities classrooms, and you will find a sea of female faces.

Higher female enrollment figures mask the "glass walls" that separate the sexes and channel females and males into very different careers, with very different paychecks. Today, despite all the progress, the five leading occupations of employed women are secretary, receptionist, bookkeeper, registered nurse and hairdresser/cosmetologist.

Add this to the "glass ceiling" (about 3 percent of Fortune 500 top managers are women) and the persistence of a gender wage gap (women with advanced degrees still lag well behind their less-educated male counterparts) and the crippling impact of workplace and college stereotyping becomes evident.

Even within schools, where female teachers greatly outnumber male teachers, school management figures remind us that if there is a war on boys,

2 Claim to be refuted.

3 What's right about the opponent's argument.

4 1st point of refutation.

5 2nd point of refutation.

6 3rd point of refutation.

7

8

9

10

women are not the generals. More than 85 percent of junior and senior high school principals are male, while 88 percent of school superintendents are male.

11   Despite sparkling advances of females on the athletic fields, two-thirds of athletic scholarships still go to males. In some areas, women have actually lost ground. When Title IX was enacted in 1972, women coached more than 90 percent of intercollegiate women's teams. Today women coach only 48 percent of women's teams and only 1 percent of men's teams.

12   If some adults are persuaded by the rhetoric in such books as *The War Against Boys*, be assured that children know the score. When more than 1,000 Michigan elementary school students were asked to describe what life would be like if they were born a member of the opposite sex, more than 40 percent of the girls saw positive advantages to being a boy: better jobs, more money and definitely more respect. Ninety-five percent of the boys saw no advantage to being a female.

13   *The War Against Boys* attempts to persuade the public to abandon support for educational initiatives designed to help girls and boys avoid crippling stereotypes. I hope the public and Congress will not be taken in by the book's misrepresentations. We have no time to wage a war on either our boys or our girls.

QUESTIONS FOR READING

1. What work, specifically, is Sadker refuting? What is the claim presented by this work?
2. What facts about girls does Sadker grant to Sommers?
3. What facts about girls create a different story, according to Sadker?

QUESTIONS FOR REASONING AND ANALYSIS

1. What is Sadker's claim? What is he asserting about girls?
2. What does Sadker think about the whole idea of books such as Sommers's?

QUESTIONS FOR REFLECTING AND WRITING

1. What statistic is most startling to you? Why?
2. Do you agree that Sadker's statistics are more significant in telling us how women are doing in school, sports, and work? If you disagree with Sadker, how would you counter his argument?
3. Think about your high school experiences. Do you think that teachers are waging a war against boys? What evidence do you have to support your views?

EXERCISE: Analyzing an Argument

Read the following article by Robert Bork and analyze his evidence and logic. As a part of your analysis, answer these questions:

1.   What kind of argument is this?
2.   What is Bork's claim?
3.   What kinds of grounds does he present?
4.   What is the tone of his argument? (Do you think that he expects readers to agree with him?)
5.   Has he supported his claim to your satisfaction or not?
6.   Do you find any logical fallacies in his argument? If so, how would you challenge them?

ADDICTED TO HEALTH | ROBERT H. BORK

A conservative legal scholar currently at the American Enterprise Institute for Policy Research, Robert Bork has been acting attorney general and solicitor general of the U.S. Court of Appeals. His appointment to the Supreme Court, rejected by the Congress, has led to a book by Bork on the whole affair and to other books and articles on legal and public policy issues. The following appeared in the *National Review* on July 28, 1997.

Government efforts to deal with tobacco companies betray an ultimate 1 ambition to control Americans' lives.

When moral self-righteousness, greed for money, and political ambition 2 work hand in hand they produce irrational, but almost irresistible, policies. The latest example is the war on cigarettes and cigarette smokers. A proposed settlement has been negotiated among politicians, plaintiffs' lawyers, and the tobacco industry. The only interests left out of the negotiations were smokers, who will be ordered to pay enormous sums with no return other than the deprivation of their own choices and pleasures.

It is a myth that today's Americans are a sturdy, self-reliant folk who will 3 fight any officious interference with their liberties. That has not been true at least since the New Deal. If you doubt that, walk the streets of any American city and see the forlorn men and women cupping their hands against the wind to light cigarettes so that they can get through a few more smokeless hours in their offices. Twenty-five percent of Americans smoke. Why can't they demand and get a compromise rather than accepting docilely the exile that employers and building managers impose upon them?

The answer is that they have been made to feel guilty by self-righteous 4 non-smokers. A few years back, hardly anyone claimed to be seriously troubled by tobacco smoke. Now, an entire class of the morally superior claim to be able to detect, and be offended by, tobacco smoke several offices away from their own. These people must possess the sense of smell of a deer or an Indian guide. Yet they will happily walk through suffocating exhaust smoke from buses rather than wait a minute or two to cross the street.

No one should assume that peace will be restored when the last cigarette 5 smoker has been banished to the Alaskan tundra. Other products will be pressed into service as morally reprehensible. If you would know the future, look at California—the national leader in health fanaticism. After a long day in

Los Angeles flagging a book I had written, my wife and I sought relaxation with a drink at our hotel's outdoor bar. Our anticipation of pleasure was considerably diminished by a sign: "Warning! Toxic Substances Served Here." They were talking about my martini!

6   And martinis are a toxic substance, taken in any quantity sufficient to induce a sense of well-being. Why not, then, ban alcohol or at least require a death's head on every martini glass? Well, we did once outlaw alcohol; it was called Prohibition. The myth is that Prohibition increased the amount of drinking in this country; the truth is that it reduced it. There were, of course, some unfortunate side effects, like Al Capone and Dutch Schultz. But by and large the mobsters inflicted rigor mortis upon one another.

7   Why is it, then, that the end of Prohibition was welcomed joyously by the population? Not because alcohol is not dangerous. Not because the consumption of alcohol was not lessened. And not in order to save the lives of people with names like Big Jim and Ice Pick Phil. Prohibition came to an end because most Americans wanted to have a drink when and where they felt like it. If you insist on sounding like a law-and-economics professor, it ended because we thought the benefits of alcohol outweighed the costs.

8   That is the sort of calculation by which we lead our lives. Automobiles kill tens of thousands of people every year and disable perhaps that many again. We could easily stop the slaughter. Cars could be made with a top speed of ten miles an hour and with exteriors the consistency of marshmallows. Nobody would die, nobody would be disabled, and nobody would bother with cars very much.

9   There are, of course, less draconian measures available. On most highways, it is almost impossible to find anyone who observes the speed limits. On the theory of the tobacco precedent, car manufacturers should be liable for deaths caused by speeding; after all, they could build automobiles incapable of exceeding legal speed limits.

10   The reason we are willing to offer up lives and limbs to automobiles is, quite simply, that they make life more pleasant (for those who remain intact)— among other things, by speeding commuting to work, by making possible family vacations a thousand miles from home, and by lowering the costs of products shipped from a distance. The case for regulating automobiles far more severely than we do is not essentially different from the case for heavy regulation of cigarettes or, soon, alcohol.

11   But choices concerning driving, smoking, and drinking are the sort of things that ought to be left to the individual unless there are clear, serious harms to others.

12   The opening salvo in the drive to make smoking a criminal act is the proposed settlement among the cigarette companies, plaintiffs' lawyers, and the states' attorneys general. We are told that the object is to protect teenagers and children (children being the last refuge of the sanctimonious). But many restrictions will necessarily affect adults, and the tobacco pact contains provisions that can only be explained as punishment for selling to adults.

13   The terms of the settlement plainly reveal an intense hatred of smoking. Opposition to the pact comes primarily from those who think it is not severe

enough. For example, critics say the settlement is defective in not restricting the marketing of cigarettes overseas by American tobacco companies. Connecticut's attorney general, Richard Blumenthal, defended the absence of such a provision: "Given our druthers we would have brought them to their knees all over the world, but there is a limit to our leverage." So much for the sovereignty of nations.

What the settlement does contain is bad enough. The pact would require the companies to pony up $60 billion; $25 billion of this would be used for public-health issues to be identified by a presidential panel and the rest for children's health insurance. Though the purpose of the entire agreement is punitive, this slice is most obviously so. 14

The industry is also required to pay $308 billion over 25 years, in part to repay states for the cost of treating sick smokers. There are no grounds for this provision. The tobacco companies have regularly won litigation against plaintiffs claiming injury on the grounds that everybody has known for the past forty years that smoking can cause health problems. This $308 billion, which takes from the companies what they have won in litigation, says, in effect, that no one assumed the risk of his own behavior. 15

The provision is groundless for additional reasons. The notion that the states have lost money because of cigarettes ignores the federal and state taxes smokers have paid, which cover any amount the states could claim to have lost. Furthermore, a percentage of the population dies early from smoking. Had these people lived longer, the drain on Medicare and Medicaid would have been greater. When lowered pension and Social Security costs are figured in, it seems certain that government is better off financially with smoking than without it. If we must reduce the issue to one of dollars, as the attorneys general have done, states have profited financially from smoking. If this seems a gruesome and heartless calculation, it is. But don't blame me. The state governments advanced the financial argument and ought to live with its consequences, however distasteful. 16

Other provisions of the settlement fare no better under the application of common sense. The industry is to reduce smoking by teenagers by 30 percent in five years, 50 percent in seven years, and 60 percent in ten years. No one knows how the industry is to perform this trick. But if those goals are not met, the industry will be amerced $80 million a year for each percentage point it falls short. 17

The settlement assumes teenage smoking can be reduced dramatically by requiring the industry to conduct an expensive anti-smoking advertising campaign, banning the use of people and cartoon characters to promote cigarettes, and similar tactics. It is entirely predictable that this will not work. Other countries have banned cigarette advertising, only to watch smoking increase. Apparently the young, feeling themselves invulnerable, relish the risk of smoking. Studies have shown, moreover, that teenagers are drawn to smoking not because of advertising but because their parents smoke or because of peer pressure. Companies advertise to gain or maintain market share among those who already smoke. 18

19   To lessen the heat on politicians, the pact increases the powers of the Food and Drug Administration to regulate tobacco as an addictive drug, with the caveat that it may not prohibit cigarette smoking altogether before the year 2009. The implicit promise is that the complete prohibition of cigarettes will be seriously contemplated at that time. In the meantime, the FDA will subject cigarettes to stricter and stricter controls on the theory that tobacco is a drug.

20   Another rationale for prohibiting or sharply limiting smoking is the supposed need to protect non-smokers from secondhand smoke. The difficulty is that evidence of causation is weak. What we see is a possible small increase in an already small risk which, as some researchers have pointed out, may well be caused by other variables such as misclassification of former smokers as non-smokers or such lifestyle factors as diet.

21   But the tobacco companies should take little or no comfort from that. Given today's product-liability craze, scientific support, much less probability, is unnecessary to successful lawsuits against large corporations.

22   The pact is of dubious constitutionality as well. It outlaws the advertising of a product it is legal to sell, which raises the problem of commercial speech protected by the First Amendment. The settlement also requires the industry to disband its lobbying organization, the Tobacco Institute. Lobbying has traditionally been thought to fall within the First Amendment's guarantee of the right to petition the government for the redress of grievances.

23   And who is to pay for making smoking more difficult? Smokers will have the price of cigarettes raised by new taxes and by the tobacco companies' costs of complying with the settlement. It is a brilliant strategy: Smokers will pay billions to have their pleasure taken away. But if the tobacco settlement makes little sense as public policy, what can be driving it to completion? The motivations are diverse. Members of the plaintiff's bar, who have signally failed in litigation against tobacco to date, are to be guaranteed billions of dollars annually. The states' attorneys general have a different set of incentives. They are members of the National Association of Attorneys General, NAAG, which is commonly, and accurately, rendered as the National Association of Aspiring Governors.

24   So far they have got what they wanted. There they are, on the front pages of newspapers all over the country, looking out at us, jaws firm, conveying images of sobriety, courage, and righteousness. They have, after all, done battle with the forces of evil, and won—at least temporarily.

25   Tobacco executives and their lawyers are said to be wily folk, however. They may find ways of defeating the strictures laid upon them. It may be too soon to tell, therefore, whether the tobacco settlement is a major defeat or a victory for the industry. In any case, we can live with it. But whenever individual responsibility is denied, government control of our behavior follows. After cigarettes it will be something else, and so on *ad infinitum*. One would think we would have learned that lesson many times over and that we would have had enough of it.

FOR DEBATE AND ANALYSIS

"JUDICIAL ACTIVISM" TO BE THANKFUL FOR | COLBERT I. KING

A native Washingtonian, Colby King has held a number of positions in the government, including special agent for the State Department, and in banking, including at the World Bank. King joined the *Washington Post*'s editorial board in 1990, began writing a weekly column in 1995, and became deputy editor of the editorial page in 2000. In 2003 he won a Pulitzer Prize for commentary. The following column was published October 29, 2005.

PREREADING QUESTIONS Why does King put the expression "judicial activism" in quotation marks? (In what ways do many people use the phrase? Does King agree with them?)

The celebration of Rosa Parks's extraordinary contribution to America pre-   1
sents an excellent opportunity for me to summon all the strength at my command so that I may shout at the top of my lungs: "Thank God Almighty for
liberal judicial activism." I suppose this makes me a heretic in a town where radical right dogma reigns supreme, especially after the trashing of White House
counsel and now withdrawn Supreme Court nominee Harriet Miers. But I'll still
pay tribute to activist judges. After all, it was a default by elected leaders that
led an "activist" Supreme Court to decide in 1956 that it was unconstitutional
to require that Rosa Parks and other black passengers in Montgomery, Ala., sit
at the back of buses solely because of their race.

This celebration of Parks's life is also a chance to set the record straight.   2
The culprits in Parks's case weren't limited to the white bus driver who told her
to give up her seat to a white man or the white police officer who arrested her.
The folks who really degraded Parks and other black bus riders were the
Alabamans who put and kept Jim Crow laws on the books. Had it been left up
to them, the arrests of Rosa Parks and other African Americans would have
continued. And of course we can't leave out Alabama's white majority, which
either liked or was indifferent to segregation.

When the Montgomery Improvement Association, led by a 26-year-old   3
preacher, Dr. Martin Luther King Jr., tried to negotiate a bus desegregation plan
with the city commission and the bus company, all it got in return was resistance—
oh, yes, and a stick of dynamite thrown into King's home. Thus the lawsuit.

Alabama argued then, as do conservatives today, that courts have no busi-   4
ness second-guessing decisions of states and cities that are acting within their
own laws. But the Supreme Court, looking at the Constitution, saw something
else. True, there was not one word in the Constitution about the operation of
bus companies or the seating of passengers. But "activist" high court justices,
bless their souls, examining the due process and equal protection clauses of
the 14th Amendment, found violations of the rights of black passengers that
Alabama was either too blind or too unrepentant to see.

5   It wasn't the first time.

6   The year before Rosa Parks took her stand by keeping her seat, the Supreme Court reviewed the legal precedent established decades either in *Plessy v. Ferguson,* which blessed the "separate but equal" doctrine. Settled law though *Plessy* may have been, the "liberal" Supreme Court under Chief Justice Earl Warren ruled in *Brown v. Board of Education* that school segregation "solely on the basis of race" violated the equal protection clause of the 14th Amendment.

7   Make no mistake: It was within the power of state legislatures and Congress to put a halt to racial discrimination in public education. Had they wanted to or had they been commanded by a popular majority to bring about equal access to educational opportunity, legislators could have done so. Instead they allowed that abomination called *Plessy* to stand, leaving it up to nonviolent protests and judicial tests to challenge racial discrimination in public education.

8   So on the occasion of Rosa Parks's death, I also pay tribute to "activist" justices such as Warren, William O. Douglas, William Brennan and Thurgood Marshall, NAACP lawyer and later a justice. They are and will always be among my heroes.

9   (I'll pause here to allow my conservative colleagues to get hold of themselves.)

10   To continue. Were it not for "liberal, activist" courts, who knows how long it would have been before:

- Rosa Parks could have sat anywhere she wanted on a bus?
- Miscegenation laws would have been invalidated?
- Illegally obtained evidence would have been deemed inadmissible in court?
- Citizens accused of a crime would have been provided a lawyer if they couldn't afford one?
- Citizens would have to be informed of their rights, including the right to remain silent and the right to counsel, before being questioned by police?
- Public school boards would have been stopped from writing and adopting prayers for students to recite?
- All citizens would have been guaranteed a constitutional "right to privacy"?

11   Who are the opponents of "liberal judicial activism"? There's no one-size-fits-all description. But some of the loudest voices belong to those who never liked the civil rights movement or the series of landmark cases that expanded rights under the Warren Court. They never saw a court-ordered desegregation remedy they could stand or a states' rights doctrine that didn't trump the rights of racial minorities.

12   They are the sort of folks who believed Arkansas Gov. Orville Faubus had a point when he used state troopers to block nine black students from entering Little Rock's Central High School even though it was under a federal court's

desegregation order. They tend to disparage any and all decisions they don't like as the personal preferences of high-handed judges exceeding their jurisdiction. To them, anyone who spends time knocking down barriers faced by folks who are not white and male is automatically suspect.

Which explains why I knew Harriet Miers was doomed with conservatives. 13 Last Sunday *The Post* published a story by Jo Becker and Sylvia Moreno that said that as president of the State Bar of Texas, Miers vowed to make the bar "inclusive of women and minorities." Miers, according to the story, "championed the cause of increasing the number of female and minority lawyers in the bar's own leadership ranks and in law firms across the state, writing that 'we are strongest capitalizing on the benefits of our diversity.'" To the right wing, them's fightin' words.

The mere idea that Miers supported a bar resolution that encouraged 14 Texas law firms to hire more minority lawyers and that set aside a specific number of seats on the bar's board of directors for women and minorities was enough to make conservatives do back flips. Too much like the thinking of a "liberal activist judge."

In my book, however, Harriet Miers's determination to tear down racial and 15 sexual barriers in Texas legal circles is a mark in her favor. Who knows? It might even have made Rosa Parks smile.

QUESTIONS FOR READING

1. What is the occasion for King's writing?
2. What decision did the Supreme Court make in 1956? In 1955?
3. Who was responsible for the situation in the 1950s that led to the Supreme Court actions?
4. Who are the people objecting to "activist judges" today?
5. Why could King predict that the Miers nomination was doomed?

QUESTIONS FOR REASONING AND ANALYSIS

1. What is King's claim? Is it stated or implied in the essay?
2. King provides a long list of laws in paragraph 10; what does he gain by this list? (Consider both its length and the specifics listed.)
3. What kinds of readers does the author expect to distress? How does he try to deal with them? What common ground does he expect opponents to accept?

QUESTIONS FOR REFLECTING AND WRITING

1. In what sense can this argument be described as a refutation?
2. Do you value the laws listed in paragraph 10? If no, why not? If yes, do you then approve of "activist judges"? If you do not approve, how do you account for what King would see as a disconnect in your logic?

DIVERSITY GETS BENCHED | RUTH MARCUS

After attending law school, Ruth Marcus switched careers to journalism. She was first a reporter for the *Washington Post* and is now one of its editorial writers. The column here was published November 1, 2005.

PREREADING QUESTIONS Who are the nine Supreme Court justices? What diversity currently exists on the Supreme Court?

1   Well, that certainly mixes things up. The first Supreme Court vacancy went to a white Catholic judge who went to Harvard College and Harvard Law School. The second, chances are, will be filled by a white Catholic judge who went to college at Princeton and law school at Yale.

2   At this rate, a WASP male from Stanford is going to look like a diversity pick.

3   Now, I have nothing against white guys, Catholics, judges or Ivy Leaguers—or Stanford WASPs for that matter. And I thought the president make a mistake in nominating Harriet Miers to take the place of Justice Sandra Day O'Connor. The Miers pick represented the elevation of gender over quality; instead of adding to the sense that it is normal and appropriate to have women on the high court, the choice make it look as if presidents have to make sacrifices to scrounge up female nominees. Like almost every woman I know, of every ideological stripe, I was relieved when she withdrew.

4   But I also find it disturbing that the drive for diversity has been so quickly, so blithely abandoned: *Been there, tried that, now we can pick who we REALLY want.* Diversity at the expense of quality is no virtue, but quality without diversity is nonetheless a vice.

5   To test this notion, just imagine an all-male, all-white Supreme Court. No president looking at a high court vacancy would consider that acceptable in this day and age, nor should he—or she. A court with a lone female justice—or, for that matter, a lone African American justice, or no Hispanic justice at all—isn't all that much better.

6   Justice Antonin Scalia, in an interview last month with CNBC, dismissed the suggestion that having people of different races, religions and genders on the court has any effect on the outcome. "As far as the product of the court is concerned, it makes no difference at all," Scalia said. "I don't think there's . . . a female legal answer to a question and a male legal answer to the same question. That's just silly."

7   Perhaps when it's phrased that way, but no one cries silly when it's suggested that having people on the court from different life experiences—politicians, perhaps, or private law practice—could add a valuable perspective to those who have spent most of their career on the bench.

8   Why, to take an example that Samuel Alito confronted as an appeals court judge, wouldn't a female judge bring a potentially different perspective to the question of whether married women can be required to notify their husbands before obtaining an abortion? You don't have to be a woman to imagine the harm that could ensue from mandating such marital communications by a

reluctant spouse. But it might help; see, e.g., the difference between Alito's clinical dissent on the issue and the Supreme Court plurality that included O'Connor.

And even Scalia acknowledges, albeit somewhat grudgingly, the symbolic importance of diversity. "I suppose, from the standpoint of . . . having the whole country feel that the court is an institution that, in fact, represents the whole country, I think there's something to be said for having people of different backgrounds on it," he said. 9

I was on my way to law school when O'Connor was nominated in 1981, and the event seemed at once ridiculously tardy and deeply significant. By that time, women were no rarity in law schools, and it never occurred to me that my gender would present any handicap in either law or journalism. But it was also impossible not to notice that women were far less likely to speak up in class than men, and that it wasn't until the final semester of my final year that I had a female professor. O'Connor's addition to the high court signified both that change had come and that more was on the way. 10

Twelve years and a different career path later, on a sun-drenched June afternoon, I stood in the Rose Garden as President Bill Clinton announced his selection of Ruth Bader Ginsburg. Reporters aren't supposed to have feelings—certainly not White House reporters for *The Post*—but it was hard not to when Ginsburg, stepping to the microphone, said Clinton's choice of her to be the second female justice "contributes to the end of the days when women, at least half the talent pool in our society, appear in high places only as one-at-a-time performers." 11

I suspect that this, in the end, is what women in the workplace want—to be not solo representatives of their gender but simply part of the mix. Justice Ginsburg, unfortunately, may have been premature in proclaiming that that day had come. 12

QUESTIONS FOR READING

1. What is Marcus's subject? Be precise. "The Supreme Court" is not precise enough.
2. What seemed to be the primary purpose of the Miers nomination? Why was the author (and many women) relieved when she withdrew?
3. What is Justice Scalia's view of diversity on the Court? How does the author respond to his views?
4. What did Marcus see in the appointment of Sandra Day O'Connor? What was the significance of Ruth Bader Ginsburg's appointment?

QUESTIONS FOR REASONING AND ANALYSIS

1. What is Marcus's claim? State her argument as a syllogism. (Start with the conclusion: Judge Alito should not be appointed to the Supreme Court.)
2. What is clever about the author's title? Find several other cleverly worded sentences and explain why they are clever.
3. Describe the author's tone; how does it help her argument?

QUESTIONS FOR REFLECTING AND WRITING

1. Marcus's argument is one of values, not of data. Has she presented her reasons convincingly? Why or why not?

2. How important is diversity in the workplace? In schools/colleges? In positions of leadership? Explain and defend your position.

1. a. Develop one of the following analogies, listing as many similarities as you can and thinking as you write about a conclusion your analogy reasonably leads to.

   Life is like a ride on the starship *Enterprise*.
   Students are like the early explorers to the North Pole.
   Humans are like spiders in a web.
   The mind is like a vast ocean.
   Modern science is like magic.

   b. Exchange your list with a classmate and check each other's analogies to see if there is a fundamental difference that negates the argument. Some comparisons or a conclusion may need revision.

   c. Develop your analogy (revised if necessary) into a short essay. The conclusion of your analogy is your essay's claim.

2. Think of your own analogy to develop an argument on student needs, student rights, or student responsibilities. Follow the guidelines for the first assignment above.

3. Select an editorial, op-ed column, a letter to the editor, or one of the essays in this text as an argument with which you disagree. Prepare a refutation of your opponent's logic or evidence or both. Follow the guidelines for writing a refutation found on page 154.

Read: Who are the speakers? What is the situation?

Reason: What is the point of the cartoon? What does Dana Summers, the cartoonist, want readers to think about?

Reflect/Write: Why does this cartoon make a good opening for a chapter on definition arguments and arguments based on values?

CHAPTER 6

Reading, Analyzing, and Writing Definition Arguments and Position Papers

This chapter focuses on two forms of argument, definition and the position paper, that may seem more abstract than the forms we've discussed previously. But let's remember what we've learned about argument: We enter into an ongoing conversation with others—and with the views already expressed on the issue. So even the seemingly more abstract and general definition arguments and claims of value in position papers need to be grounded in what has already been expressed "out there." For nearly any form of argument, presenting your stance within the proper context is essential.

THE DEFINITION ARGUMENT: DEBATING THE MEANING OF WORDS

"Define your terms!" someone yells in the middle of a heated debate. Although yelling may not be the best strategy, the advice is sound for writers of argument. People disagree more than we may think over the meaning of words. We cannot let words mean whatever we want and still communicate, but we do need to realize that many words have multiple meanings. Words also differ in their connotations, in the emotional associations we attach to them. For some, civil disobedience is illegal behavior; for others, it's patriotism in action.

When to Define

There are two occasions for defining words as a *part* of your argument. First, you need to define any technical terms that may not be familiar to your readers—or that readers may not understand as fully as they think they do. David Norman, early in his book on dinosaurs, writes:

> Nearly everyone knows what some dinosaurs look like, such as *Tyrannosaurus,* *Triceratops,* and *Stegosaurus.* But they may be much more vague about the lesser known ones, and may have difficulty in distinguishing between dinosaurs and other types of prehistoric creatures. It is not at all unusual to overhear an adult, taking a group of children around a museum display, being reprimanded sharply by the youngsters for failing to realize that a woolly mammoth was not a dinosaur, or—more forgivably—that a giant flying reptile such as *Pteranodon,* which lived at the time of the dinosaurs, was not a dinosaur either.
>
> So what exactly is a dinosaur? And how do paleontologists decide on the groups they belong to?

Norman answers his questions by explaining the four elements that all dinosaurs have, by constructing a definition of *dinosaur.*

Second, you need to define any word you are using in a special way. If you were to write: "We need to teach discrimination at an early age," you should add: "by *discrimination* I do not mean prejudice. I mean discernment, the ability to see differences." (*Sesame Street* has been teaching children this good kind of discrimination for many years.)

Sometimes we turn to definition because we believe that a word is being used incorrectly. Columnist George Will once argued that we should forget *values* and use instead the word *virtues*—that we should seek and admire virtues, not values. At some point in discussions such as these, our purpose shifts. Instead of using definition as one step in the argument, definition becomes the central purpose of the argument. This is the third use of definition: An extended definition *is* the argument.

GUIDELINES for Evaluating Definition Arguments

When reading definition arguments, what should you look for? The basics of good argument apply to all arguments: a clear statement of claim, qualified if appropriate, a clear explanation of reasons and evidence, and enough relevant evidence to support the claim. How do we recognize these qualities in a definition argument? Use the following points as guides to evaluating:

- **Why is the word being defined?** Has the writer convinced you of the need to understand the word's meaning or change the way the word is commonly used?

- **How is the word defined?** Has the writer established his or her definition, clearly distinguishing it from what the writer perceives to be objectionable definitions? It is hard to judge the usefulness of the writer's position if the differences in meaning remain fuzzy. If George Will is going to argue for using *virtues* instead of *values*, he needs to be sure that readers understand the differences he sees in the two words.

- **What strategies are used to develop the definition?** Can you recognize the different types of evidence presented and see what the writer is doing in his or her argument? This kind of analysis can aid your evaluation of a definition argument.

- **What are the implications in accepting the author's definition?** Why does George Will want readers to embrace *virtues* rather than *values*? Will's argument is not just about subtle points of language; his argument is about attitudes that affect public policy issues. Part of any evaluation of a definition argument must include our recognition of—and assessment of—the author's definition.

- **Is the definition argument convincing?** Do the reasons and evidence lead you to agree with the author, to accept the idea of the definition and its implications as well?

Preparing a Definition Argument

In addition to the guidelines for writing arguments presented in Chapter 4, you can use the following advice specific to writing definition arguments.

Planning

1. **Think:** Why do you want to define your term? To add to our understanding of a complex term? To challenge the use of the word by others? Know your purpose.

2. **Think:** How are you defining the word? What are the elements/parts/steps in your definition? Some brainstorming notes are probably helpful to keep your definition concrete and focused.

3. **Think:** What strategies will you use to develop and support your definition? Defining gives you a purpose, but it does not automatically suggest ways to develop your argument. Consider using several of these possible strategies for development:

   - *Word origin or history of usage.* The word's original meaning can be instructive. If the word has changed meaning over time, explore these changes as clues to how the word can (or should) be used, especially if you are going to object to the term's current use.
   - *Descriptive details.* Illustrate with specifics. List the traits of a leader or patriot or courageous person. Explain the behaviors that make a wise or courteous person. Describe the situations that show the existence of liberty. Use negative traits as well as positive ones. That is, show what is *not* covered by the word.
   - *Comparison and/or contrast.* Clarify and limit your definition by contrasting it with words of similar meanings. For example, what are the differences between courtesy and manners or knowledge and wisdom or neighborhoods and communities?
   - *Examples.* Illustrate your definition with actual or hypothetical examples. Churchill, Lincoln, and Franklin D. Roosevelt could all be used as examples of leaders. You can also create a hypothetical ideal candidate for Congress or for student government president.
   - *Function or use.* A frequent strategy for defining is explaining an item's use or function: A pencil is a writing instrument. A similar approach can give insight into more general or abstract terms as well. For example, what do we have—or gain—by emphasizing virtues instead of values? What does a community *do* that a neighborhood does not do?
   - *Metaphors.* Consider using figurative comparisons. When fresh—not clichés—they add vividness and punch to your writing.

Drafting

1. Begin with an opening paragraph or two that introduces your subject in an interesting way. Possibilities include the occasion that has led to your writing—explain for instance, a misunderstanding about your term's meaning that you want to correct.

2. Do *not* begin by quoting or paraphrasing a dictionary definition of the term. "According to Webster . . ." is a tired approach lacking reader interest. If the dictionary definition were sufficient, you would have no reason to write an entire essay to define the term.

3. State your claim—your definition of the term—early in your essay, if you can do so in a sentence or two. If you do not state a brief claim, then establish your purpose in writing early in your essay. (You may find that there are too many parts to your definition to combine into one or two sentences.)

4. Use several specific strategies for developing your definition. Select several strategies from the list above and organize your approach around these

strategies. That is, you can develop one paragraph of descriptive details, another of examples, another of contrast with words that are not exactly the same in meaning.

5. Consider specifically refuting the error in word use that led to your decision to write your own definition. If you are motivated to write based on what you have read, then make a rebuttal part of your definition argument.

6. Consider discussing the implications of your definition. You can give weight and value to your argument by defending the larger significance of readers' embracing your definition.

A CHECKLIST FOR REVISION ■-■-□-■-□-■-□-■-□-■-□-■-□-■-□-■-□-■-□-■-□-■-□-■-□-■-□-■-□-■

☐ Do I have a good understanding of my purpose? Have I made this clear to readers?

☐ Have I clearly stated my definition? Or clearly established the various parts of the definition that I discuss in separate paragraphs?

☐ Have I organized my argument, building the parts of my definition into a logical, coherent structure?

☐ Have I used specifics to clarify and support my definition?

☐ Have I used the basic checklist for revision in Chapter 4 (see page 110)?

STUDENT ESSAY

PARAGON OR PARASITE?

Laura Mullins

Do you recognize this creature? He is low maintenance and often unnoticeable, a favorite companion of many. Requiring no special attention, he grows from the soil of pride and rejection, feeding regularly on a diet of ignorance and insecurity, scavenging for hurt feelings and defensiveness, gobbling up dainty morsels of lust and scandal. Like a cult leader clothed in a gay veneer, disguising himself as blameless, he wields power. Bewitching unsuspecting but devoted groupies, distracting them from honest self-examination, deceiving them into believing illusions of grandeur or, on the other extreme, unredeemable worthlessness, he breeds jealousy, hate, and fear; thus, he thrives. He is Gossip.

Attention-getting introduction.

Clever extended metaphor.

Subject introduced.

One of my dearest friends is a gossip. She is an educated, honorable, compassionate, loving woman whose character and judgment I deeply admire and respect. After sacrificially raising six children, she went on to study medicine and become a doctor who graciously volunteers her expertise. How, you may be wondering, could a gossip deserve such praise? Then you do not understand the word. My friend is my daughter's godmother; she is my gossip,

Etymology of gossip and early meanings.

or *god-sib,* meaning sister-in-god. Derived from Middle English words *god,* meaning spiritual, and *sip/sib/syp,* meaning kinsman, this term was used to refer to a familiar acquaintance, close family friend, or intimate relation, according to the *Oxford English Dictionary.* As a male, he would have joined in fellowship and celebration with the father of the newly born; if a female, she would have been a trusted friend, a birth-attendant or midwife to the mother of the baby. The term grew to include references to the type of easy, unrestrained conversation shared by these folks.

Current meanings.

As is often the case with words, the term's meaning has certainly evolved, maybe eroded from its original idea. Is it harmless, idle chat, innocuous sharing of others' personal news, or back-biting, rumor-spreading, and manipulation? Is it a beneficial activity worthy of pursuit, or a deplorable danger to be avoided?

Good use of sources to develop definition.

In her article "Evolution, Alienation, and Gossip" (for the Social Issues Research Centre in Oxford, England), Kate Fox writes that "gossip is not a trivial pastime; it is essential to human social, psychological, and even physical well-being." Many echo her view that gossip is a worthy activity, claiming that engaging in gossip produces endorphins, reduces stress, and aids in building intimate relationships. Gossip, seen at worst as a harmless outlet, is encouraged in the workplace. Since much of its content is not inherently critical or malicious, it is viewed as a positive activity. However, this view does nothing to encourage those speaking or listening to evaluate or examine motive or purpose; instead, it seems to reflect the "anything goes" thinking so prevalent today.

Conversely, writer and high school English and geography teacher Lennox V. Farrell of Toronto, Canada, in his essay titled "Gossip: An Urban Form of Sorcery," presents gossip as a kind of "witchcraft . . . based on using unsubstantiated accusations by those who make them, and on uncritically accepting these by those enticed into listening." Farrell uses gossip in its more widely understood definition, encompassing the breaking of confidences, inappropriate sharing of indiscretions, destructive tale-bearing, and malicious slander.

What, then, is gossip? We no longer use the term to refer to our children's godparents. Its current definition usually comes with derogatory implications. Imagine a backyard garden: you see a variety of greenery, recognizing at a glance that you are looking at different kinds of plants. Taking a closer look, you will find the gossip vine; inconspicuously blending in, it doesn't appear threatening, but ultimately it destroys. If left in the garden it will choke and then suck out life from its host. Zoom in on the garden scene and follow the creeping vine up trees and along a fence where two neighbors visit. You can overhear one woman saying to the other, "I know I should be the last to tell you, but your husband is being unfaithful to me." (Caption from a cartoon by Alan De la Nougerede.)

Good use of metaphor to depict gossip as negative.

The current popular movement to legitimize gossip seems an excuse to condone the human tendency to puff-up oneself. Compared in legal terms, gossip is to conversation as hearsay is to eyewitness testimony; it's not credible. Various religious doctrines abhor the idea and practice of gossip. An old Turkish proverb says, "He who gossips to you will gossip of you." From the Babylonian Talmud, which calls gossip the three-pronged tongue, destroying the one talking, the one listening, and the one being spoken of, to the Upanishads, to the Bible, we can conclude that no good fruit is born from gossip. Let's tend our gardens and check our motives when we have the urge to gossip. Surely we can find more noble pursuits than the self-aggrandizement we have come to know as gossip.

Conclusion states view that gossip is to be avoided—the writer's thesis.

THE POSITION PAPER: EXAMINING CLAIMS OF VALUES

We studied the refutation argument in Chapter 5 and the definition argument earlier in this chapter. A third type of argument to understand is the claim of value that we frequently call the position paper.

Characteristics of the Position Paper

The position paper or claim of value may be the most difficult of argument assignments simply because it is often perceived to be the easiest. Let's think about this kind of argument:

- The claim of value is more general or abstract or philosophical than other types of arguments.
- It makes a claim about what is right or wrong, good or bad, for us as individuals or as a society. Topics can vary from capital punishment to pornography to endangered species.
- A claim of value is developed in large part by a logical sequencing of reasons. But a support of principles also depends on relevant facts. Remember the long list of specific abuses listed in the Declaration of Independence (pages 135–37).
- A successful claim of value argument requires more than a forceful statement of personal beliefs.

GUIDELINES for Analyzing a Claim of Value

When reading position papers, what should you look for? Again, the basics of good argument apply here as well as with definition arguments. To analyze claims of values specifically, use the following questions as guides:

- **What is the writer's claim?** Is it clear?
- **Is the claim qualified if necessary?** Some claims of value are broad philosophical assertions ("Capital punishment is immoral and bad public policy"). Others are qualified ("Capital punishment is acceptable only in crimes of treason").
- **What facts are presented?** Are they credible? Are they relevant to the claim's support?
- **What reasons are given in support of the claim?** What assumptions are necessary to tie reasons to claim? Make a list of reasons and assumptions and analyze the writer's logic. Do you find any fallacies?
- **What are the implications of the claim?** For example, if you argue for the legalization of all recreational drugs, you eliminate all "drug problems" by definition. But what new problems may be created by this approach? Consider more car accidents and reduced productivity for openers.
- **Is the argument convincing?** Does the evidence provide strong support for the claim? Are you prepared to agree with the writer, in whole or in part?

Supporting a Claim of Value

In addition to the guidelines for writing arguments presented in Chapter 4, you can use the following advice specific to writing position papers or claims of value.

Planning

1. **Think:** What claim, exactly, do you want to support? Should you qualify your first attempt at a claim statement?
2. **Think:** What grounds (evidence) do you have to support your claim? You may want to make a list of the reasons and facts you would consider using to defend your claim.
3. **Think:** Study your list of possible grounds and recognize the assumptions (warrants) and backing for your grounds.
4. **Think:** Now make a list of the grounds most often used by those holding views that oppose your claim. This second list will help you prepare counterarguments to possible rebuttals, but first it will help you test your commitment to your position. If you find the opposition's arguments persuasive and cannot think how you would rebut them, you may need to rethink your position. Ideally, your two lists will confirm your views but also increase your respect for opposing views.
5. **Consider:** How can I use a conciliatory approach? With an emotion-laden or highly controversial issue, the conciliatory approach can be an effective strategy. Conciliatory arguments include:
   - The use of nonthreatening language
   - The fair expression of opposing views
   - A statement of the common ground shared by opposing sides.

   You may want to use a conciliatory approach when: (1) you know your views will be unpopular with at least some members of your audience; (2) the issue is highly emotional and has sides that are "entrenched" so that you are seeking some accommodations rather than dramatic changes of position; (3) you need to interact with members of your audience and want to keep a respectful relationship going. The sample student essay on gun control illustrates a conciliatory approach.

Drafting

1. Begin with an opening paragraph or two that introduces your topic in an interesting way. Possibilities include a statement of the issue's seriousness or reasons why the issue is currently being debated—or why we should go back to reexamine it. Some writers are spurred by a recent event that receives media coverage; recounting such an event can produce an effective opening. You can also briefly summarize points of the opposition that you will challenge in supporting your claim.

2.   Decide where to place your claim statement. Your best choices are either early in your essay or at the end of your essay, after you have made your case. The second approach can be an effective alternative to the more common pattern of stating one's claim early.

3.   Organize evidence in an effective way. One plan is to move from the least important to the most important reasons, followed by rebuttals to potential counterarguments. Another possibility is to organize by the arguments of the opposition, explaining why each of their reasons fails to hold up. A third approach is to organize logically. That is, if some reasons build on the accepting of other reasons, you want to begin with the necessary underpinnings and then move forward from those.

4.   Provide a logical defense of or specifics in support of each reason. You have not finished your task by simply asserting several reasons for your claim. You also need to present facts or examples for or a logical explanation of each reason. For example, you have not defended your views on capital punishment by asserting that it is right or just to take the life of a murderer. Why is it right or just? Executing the murderer will not bring the victim back to life. Do two wrongs make a right? These are some of the thoughts your skeptical reader may have unless you explain and justify your reasoning. *Remember:* Quoting another writer's opinion on your topic does not provide proof for your reasons. It merely shows that someone else agrees with you.

5.   Maintain an appropriate level of seriousness for an argument of principle. Of course, word choice must be appropriate to a serious discussion, but in addition be sure to present reasons that are also appropriately serious. For example, if you are defending the claim that music CDs should not be subject to content labeling because such censorship is inconsistent with First Amendment rights, do not trivialize your argument by including the point that young people are tired of adults controlling their lives. (This is another issue for another paper.)

A CHECKLIST FOR REVISION

☐   Do I have a clear statement of my claim? Is it qualified, if appropriate?

☐   Have I organized my argument, building the parts of my support into a clear and logical structure that readers can follow?

☐   Have I avoided logical fallacies?

☐   Have I found relevant facts and examples to support and develop my reasons?

☐   Have I paid attention to appropriate word choice, including using a conciliatory approach if that is a wise strategy?

☐   Have I used the basic checklist for revision in Chapter 4 (see page 110)?

STUDENT ESSAY

EXAMINING THE ISSUE OF GUN CONTROL

Chris Brown

The United States has a long history of compromise. Issues such as representation in government have been resolved because of compromise, forming some of the bases of American life. Americans, however, like to feel that they are uncompromising, never willing to surrender an argument. This attitude has led to a number of issues in modern America that are unresolved, including the issue of gun control. Bickering over the issue has slowed progress toward legislation that will solve the serious problem of gun violence in America, while keeping recreational use of firearms available to responsible people. To resolve the conflict over guns, the arguments of both sides must be examined, with an eye to finding the flaws in both. Then perhaps we can reach some meaningful compromises.

Gun advocates have used many arguments for the continued availability of firearms to the public. The strongest of these defenses points to the many legitimate uses for guns. One use is protection against violence, a concern of some people in today's society. There are many problems with the use of guns for protection, however, and these problems make the continued use of firearms for protection dangerous. One such problem is that gun owners are not always able to use guns responsibly. When placed in a situation in which personal injury or loss is imminent, people often do not think intelligently. Adrenaline surges through the body, and fear takes over much of the thinking process. This causes gun owners to use their weapons, firing at whatever threatens them. Injuries and deaths of innocent people, including family members of the gun owner, result. Removing guns from the house seems to be the only solution to these sad consequences.

Introduction connects ambivalence in American character to conflict over gun control.

Student organizes by arguments for no gun control.

1. Guns for protection.

Responding to this argument, gun advocates ask how they are to defend themselves without guns. But guns are needed for protection from other guns. If there are no guns, people need only to protect themselves from criminals using knives, baseball bats, and other weapons. Obviously the odds of surviving a knife attack are greater than the odds of surviving a gun attack. One reason is that a gun is an impersonal weapon. Firing at someone from 50 feet away requires much less commitment than charging someone with a knife and stabbing repeatedly. Also, bullet wounds are, generally, more severe than knife wounds. Guns are also more likely to be misused when a dark figure is in one's house. To kill with the gun requires only to point and shoot; no recognition of the figure is needed. To kill with a knife, by contrast, requires getting within arm's reach of the figure.

2. Recreational uses.   There are other uses of guns, including recreation. Hunting and target shooting are valid, responsible uses of guns. How do we keep guns available for recreation? The answer is in the form of gun clubs and hunting clubs. Many are already established; more can be constructed. These clubs can provide recreational use of guns for responsible people while keeping guns off the streets and out of the house.

3. Second Amendment rights.   The last argument widely used by gun advocates is the constitutional right to bear arms. The fallacies in this argument are that the Constitution was written in a vastly different time. This different time had different uses for guns, and a different type of gun. Firearms were defended in the Constitution because of their many valid uses and fewer problems. Guns were mostly muskets, guns that were not very accurate beyond close range. Also, guns took more than 30 seconds to load in the eighteenth century and could fire only one shot before reloading. These differences with today's guns affect the relative safety of guns then and now. In addition, those who did not live in the city at the time used hunting for food as well as for recreation; hunting was a necessary component of life. That is not true today. Another use of guns in the eighteenth century was as protection from animals. Wild animals such as bears and cougars were much more common. Settlers, explorers, and hunters needed protection from these animals in ways not comparable with modern life.

Finally, Revolutionary America had no standing army. Defense of the nation and of one's home from other nations relied on local militia. The right to bear arms granted in the Constitution was inspired by the need for national protection as well as by the other outdated needs previously discussed. Today America has a standing army with enough weaponry to adequately defend itself from outside aggressors. There is no need for every citizen to carry a musket, or an AK-47, for the protection of the nation. It would seem, then, that the Second Amendment does not apply to modern society.

To reach a compromise, we also have to examine the other side of the issue. Some gun-control advocates argue that all guns are unnecessary and should be outlawed. The problem with this argument is that guns will still be available to those who do not mind breaking the law. Until an economically sound and feasible way of controlling illegal guns in America is found, guns cannot be totally removed, no matter how much legislation is passed. This means that if guns are to be outlawed for uses other than recreational uses, a way must be found to combat the illegal gun trade that will evolve. Tough criminal laws and a large security force are all that can be offered to stop illegal uses of guns until better technology is available. This means that, perhaps, a good resolution would involve gradual restrictions on guns, until eventually guns were restricted only to recreational uses in a controlled setting for citizens not in the police or military.

Student establishes a compromise position.

Both sides on this issue have valid points. Any middle ground needs to offer something to each side. It must address the reasons people feel that they need guns for protection, allow for valid recreational use, and keep guns out of the hands of the public, except for properly trained police officers. Time and money will be needed to move toward the removal of America's huge handgun arsenal. But, sooner or later a compromise on the issue of gun control must be made to make America a safer, better place to live.

Conclusion restates student's claim.

FOR DEBATE

SETTING LIMITS ON TOLERANCE | CHARLES KRAUTHAMMER

A graduate of Harvard Medical School and board certified in psychiatry, Charles Krauthammer is a syndicated columnist and a regular on the political talk show *Inside Washington*. He has won a Pulitzer Prize for political commentary. The following column appeared August 12, 2006.

PREREADING QUESTIONS Should the president approve of surveillance of citizens to fight the war on terror? Should known terrorists be refused admittance into the United States?

1   In 1977, when a bunch of neo-Nazis decided to march through Skokie, a suburb of Chicago heavily populated with Holocaust survivors, there was controversy as to whether they should be allowed. I thought they should. Why? Because neo-Nazis are utterly powerless.

2   Had they not been—had they been a party on the rise, as in late-1920s Germany—I would have been for not only banning the march but also for practically every measure of harassment and persecution from deportation to imprisonment. A tolerant society has an obligation to be tolerant. Except to those so intolerant that they themselves would abolish tolerance.

3   Call it situational libertarianism: Liberties should be as unlimited as possible—unless and until there arises a real threat to the open society. Neo-Nazis are pathetic losers. Why curtail civil liberties to stop them? But when a real threat—such as jihadism—arises, a liberal democratic society must deploy every resource, including the repressive powers of the state, to deter and defeat those who would abolish liberal democracy.

4   Civil libertarians go crazy when you make this argument. Beware the slippery slope, they warn. You start with a snoop in a library, and you end up with Big Brother in your living room.

5   The problem with this argument is that it is refuted by American history. There is no slippery slope, only a shifting line between liberty and security that responds to existential threats.

6   During the Civil War, Abraham Lincoln went so far as to suspend habeas corpus. When the war ended, America returned to its previous openness. During World War II, Franklin Roosevelt interned an entire ethnic group. His policies were soon rescinded (later apologized for) and shortly afterward America embarked on a period of unprecedented expansion of civil rights. Similarly, the Vietnam-era abuses of presidential power were later exposed and undone by Congress.

7   Our history is clear. We have not slid inexorably toward police power. We have fluctuated between more and less openness depending on need and threat. And after the Sept. 11 mass murders, America awoke to the need for a limited and temporary shrinkage of civil liberties to prevent more such atrocities.

8   Britain is just now waking up, post-7/7. Well, at least its prime minister is. His dramatic announcement that Britain will curtail its pathological openness to those who would destroy it—by outlawing the fostering of hatred and in-

citement of violence and expelling those engaged in such offenses—was not universally welcomed.

His own wife made a speech a week after the *second* London attacks loftily 9 warning against restricting civil liberties. "It is all too easy to respond in a way that undermines commitment to our most deeply held values and convictions and cheapens our right to call ourselves a civilized nation," declared Cherie Blair. You need only read Tony Blair's 12-point program to appreciate how absurd was his wife's defense of Britain's pre-7/7 civil liberties status quo.

For example, point 3: "Anyone who has participated in terrorism, or has 10 anything to do with it anywhere, will be automatically refused asylum in our country." What sane country grants asylum to terrorists in the first place?

Point 5, my favorite, declared "unacceptable" the remarkable fact that a 11 man accused of the 1995 Paris metro bombing has successfully resisted extradition across the Channel *for 10 years.*

Blair's proposals are progress, albeit from a very low baseline—so low a 12 baseline that the mere announcement of his intent to crack down had immediate effect. Within three days, the notorious Sheik Omar Bakri Mohammed, a Syrian-born cleric who has been openly preaching jihad for 19 years, skipped the country and absconded to Beirut.

Not only had Bakri been allowed to run free the whole time, but he had 13 collected more than 300,000 pounds in welfare, plus a 31,000-pound gift from the infidel taxpayers: a Ford Galaxy (because of a childhood leg injury).

It took 52 dead for at least the prime minister to adopt situational libertar- 14 ianism. Or as Blair put it, "The rules of the game are changing," declaring his readiness, finally, to alter the status quo in the name of elementary self-defense.

Before departing Britain, Bakri complained that it would be unfair to have 15 him deported from the country he reviled: "I have wives, children, sons-in-law, daughters-in-law. It would be hard on my family if I was deported."

Wives, no less. Point 10 of Blair's plan would establish a commission to try 16 to get immigrants to adopt more of the local mores.

QUESTIONS FOR READING

1. How does the example in the opening paragraph serve to introduce Krauthammer's subject?
2. What does the author mean by "situational libertarianism"?
3. What is the current reason for restricting civil liberties? How do some people respond to curtailing liberties?
4. What has been Britain's response to their July 7, 2005, terrorist bombing?

QUESTIONS FOR REASONING AND ANALYSIS

1. What is Krauthammer's claim? Where does he state it?
2. What is the counterargument expected by Krauthammer? How does he rebut this argument?

3. Paragraphs 8 through 16 are about Britain's response to their 9/11. How does the author use this discussion to advance his argument?

4. Describe the author's tone at the end. How does he want readers to respond?

QUESTIONS FOR REFLECTING AND WRITING

1. Do you agree that a liberal democracy must restrict civil liberties in order to defeat those who would abolish liberal democracy? Can one give up one's values to save them and be sure of finding them again? Do good ends justify repressive means? Reflect on these questions. Be able to defend your position.

2. Should immigrants be encouraged (required?) to adopt their new country's mores? Should they be allowed to live in violation of the country's laws? Explain and defend your position.

YOU CAN'T FIGHT TERRORISM WITH RACISM | COLBERT I. KING

A native Washingtonian, Colby King has held a number of positions in the government, including special agent for the State Department, and in banking, including at the World Bank. King joined the *Washington Post*'s editorial board in 1990, began writing a weekly column in 1995, and became deputy editor of the editorial page in 2000. In 2003 he won a Pulitzer Prize for commentary. His column on fighting terrorism was published July 30, 2005.

PREREADING QUESTIONS Should police and airport security personnel use profiling to protect against terrorism? If profiling were used, would you be a suspect? Does how you answer the second question affect how you answer the first one?

1   During my day job I work under the title of deputy editorial page editor. That entails paying more than passing attention to articles that appear on the op-ed page. Opinion writers, in my view, should have a wide range in which to roam, especially when it comes to edgy, thought-provoking pieces. Still, I wasn't quite ready for what appeared on the op-ed pages of Thursday's *New York Times* or Friday's *Post*.

2   A *New York Times* op-ed piece by Paul Sperry, a Hoover Institution media fellow ["It's the Age of Terror: What Would You Do?"], and a *Post* column by Charles Krauthammer ["Give Grandma a Pass; Politically Correct Screening Won't Catch Jihadists"] endorsed the practice of using ethnicity, national origin and religion as primary factors in deciding whom police should regard as possible terrorists—in other words, racial profiling. A second *Times* column, on Thursday, by Haim Watzman ["When You Have to Shoot First"] argued that the London police officer who chased down and put seven bullets into the head of a Brazilian electrician without asking him any questions or giving him any warning "did the right thing."

3   The three articles blessed behavior that makes a mockery of the rights to which people in this country are entitled.

4   Krauthammer blasted the random-bag-checks program adopted in the New York subway in response to the London bombings, calling it absurd and a waste of effort and resources. His answer: Security officials should concentrate

on "young Muslim men of North African, Middle Eastern and South Asian origin." Krauthammer doesn't say how authorities should go about identifying "Muslim men" or how to distinguish non-Muslim men from Muslim men entering a subway station. Probably just a small detail easily overlooked.

All you need to know is that the culprit who is going to blow you to bits, 5 Krauthammer wrote, "traces his origins to the Islamic belt stretching from Mauritania to Indonesia." For the geographically challenged, Krauthammer's birthplace of the suicide bomber starts with countries in black Africa and stops somewhere in the Pacific Ocean. By his reckoning, the rights and freedoms enjoyed by all should be limited to a select group. Krauthammer argued that authorities should work backward and "eliminate classes of people who are obviously not suspects." In the category of the innocent, Krauthammer would place children younger than 13, people older than 60 and "whole ethnic populations" starting with "Hispanics, Scandinavians and East Asians . . . and women," except "perhaps the most fidgety, sweaty, suspicious-looking, overcoat-wearing, knapsack-bearing young women."

Of course, by eliminating Scandinavians from his list of obvious terror suspects, 6 Krauthammer would have authorities give a pass to all white people, since subway cops don't check passengers' passports for country of origin. As for sweaty, fidgety, knapsack-bearing, overcoat-wearing young women who happen to be black, brown or yellow? Tough nuggies, in Krauthammer's book. The age-60 cutoff is meaningless, too, since subway cops aren't especially noted for accuracy in pinning down stages of life. In Krauthammer's worldview, it's all quite simple: Ignore him and his son; suspect me and mine.

Sperry also has his own proxy for suspicious characters. He warned security 7 and subway commuters to be on the lookout for "young men praying to Allah and smelling of flower water." Keep your eyes open, he said, for a "shaved head or short haircut" or a recently shaved beard or moustache. Men who look like that, in his book, are "the most suspicious train passengers."

It appears to matter not to Sperry that his description also includes huge 8 numbers of men of color, including my younger son, a brown-skinned occasional New York subway rider who shaves his head and moustache. He also happens to be a former federal prosecutor and until a few years ago was a homeland security official in Washington. Sperry's profile also ensnares my older brown-skinned son, who wears a very short haircut, may wear cologne at times, and has the complexion of many men I have seen in Africa and the Middle East. He happens to be a television executive. But what the hell, according to Sperry, "young Muslim men of Arab or South Asian origin" fit the terrorist profile. How, just by looking, can security personnel identify a Muslim male of Arab or South Asian origin goes unexplained.

Reportedly, after Sept. 11, 2001, some good citizens of California took out 9 after members of the Sikh community, mistaking them for Arabs. Oh, well, what's a little political incorrectness in the name of national security. Bang, bang—oops, he was Brazilian. Two young black guys were London bombers: one Jamaican, the other Somalian. Muslim, too. Ergo: Watch your back when around black men—they could be, ta-dum, Muslims.

10   So while advocates of racial profiling would have authorities subject men and women of black and brown hues to close scrutiny for criminal suspicions, they would look right past:

- White male Oklahoma bomber Timothy McVeigh, who killed 168 people, including 19 children, and damaged 220 buildings.
- White male Eric Rudolph, whose remote-controlled bomb killed a woman and an off-duty police officer at a clinic, whose Olympic Park pipe bomb killed a woman and injured more than 100, and whose bombs hit a gay club and woman's clinic.
- White male Dennis Rader, the "bind, torture, kill" (BTK) serial killer who terrorized Wichita for 31 years.
- D.C.-born and Silver Spring-raised white male John Walker Lindh, who converted to Islam and was captured in Afghanistan fighting for the Taliban.
- The IRA bombers who killed and wounded hundreds; the neo-fascist bombers who killed 80 people and injured nearly 300 in Bologna, Italy; and the truck bombings in Colombia by Pedro Escobar's gang.

11   But let's get really current. What about those non-Arab, non-South Asians without black or brown skins who are bombing apartment buildings, train stations and theaters in Russia. They've taken down passenger jets, hijacked schools and used female suicide bombers to a fare-thee-well, killing hundreds and wounding thousands. They are Muslims from Chechnya, and would pass the Krauthammer/Sperry eyeball test for terrorists with ease. After all, these folks hail from the Caucasus; you can't get any more Caucasian than that.

12   What the racial profilers are proposing is insulting, offensive and—by thought, word and deed, whether intentional or not—racist. You want estrangement? Start down that road of using ethnicity, national origin and religion as a basis for police action and there's going to be a push-back unlike any seen in this country in many years.

QUESTIONS FOR READING

1. What kind of argument is this? How do the opening paragraphs make the type of argument clear?
2. What are Krauthammer's views on random searches? Who should be targeted? Who ignored?
3. What are Sperry's views? Who would he profile?

QUESTIONS FOR REASONING AND ANALYSIS

1. What is King's claim? Where does he state it?
2. How does the author refute the arguments of Krauthammer and Sperry? List his points of rebuttal, both practical and value-based.

3. In paragraphs 10 and 11, King lists those who would not be stopped based on profiling. What is effective about the list. How might Krauthammer and Sperry respond to King's list?

4. Woven into the careful quoting and specific examples are lines that create a hard-edged tone to King's refutation. Find these lines and explain their effect.

QUESTIONS FOR REFLECTING AND WRITING

1. Has King effectively refuted Krauthammer and Sperry? Why or why not?

2. How is King's argument also a response to Krauthammer's column in this chapter? Who, in your view, has the better argument? Why?

1. Charles Krauthammer and Colbert King seem far apart on the issue of appropriate government action in the war on terror. How can they be brought closer together? Find and argue for common ground, creating a conciliatory argument.

2. Chris Brown, in the student essay, writes a conciliatory argument seeking common ground on the volatile issue of gun control. Write your own conciliatory argument on this issue, offering a different approach than Brown, but giving credit to Brown for any ideas that you borrow from his essay. Alternatively, write a refutation of Brown's essay.

3. In the other student essay, Laura Mullins defines the term *gossip*. Select one of the following words to define and prepare your own extended definition argument, using at least three of the strategies for defining that you find in Laura's essay. For each word in the list, you see a companion word in parentheses. Use that companion word as a word that you contrast with the word you are defining. (For example, how does gossip differ from conversation? How do manners differ from courtesy?) You can advance your definition if you can make fine distinctions among words similar in meaning.

    | courtesy (manners) | hero (star) |
    | wisdom (knowledge) | community (neighborhood) |
    | patriotism (chauvinism) | freedom (liberty) |

Mike Luckovich © Atlanta-Journal Constitution/Dist. by Creators.com

Read: This famous photograph was frequently reprinted and referred to in congressional debates in 1964. What is its subject?

Reason: What details make it dramatic? What message does it send?

Reflect/Write: How does the photo make you feel? What does it lead you to contemplate?

CHAPTER 7

Reading, Analyzing, and Using Visuals and Statistics in Argument

We live in a visual age. Many of us go to movies to appreciate and judge the film's visual effects. The Internet is awash in pictures and colorful icons. Perhaps the best symbol of our visual age is *USA Today*, a paper filled with pictures in color and many tables and other graphics as a primary way of presenting information. *USA Today* has forced the more traditional papers to add color photos to compete. We also live in a numerical age. Lisa Mundy, writing in "A Date to Remember," observes that using the expression 9/11 to refer to the events of September 11, 2001, says something about our times: "We are all digital thinkers now, accustomed to looking at our calendars, our watches, and seeing numerals." This chapter brings together these markers of our times as they are used in argument—and as argument—for we find statistics and visuals used as part of argumentative books and essays, but we also need to remember that cartoons and advertisements are arguments in and of themselves.

RESPONDING TO VISUAL ARGUMENTS

Many arguments bombard us today in visual forms. Two such visual arguments are political cartoons and advertising. Most major newspapers have a political cartoonist whose drawings appear regularly on the editorial page. (Some comic strips are also political in nature, at least some of the time.) These cartoons are designed to make a political point in a visually clever and amusing way. (That is why they are both "cartoons" and "political" at the same time.) Their uses of irony and caricatures of known politicians make them among the most emotionally powerful, indeed stinging, of arguments.

Advertisements are among the most creative and powerful forms of argument today. Remember that ads are designed to take your time (for shopping) and your money. Their messages need to be powerful to motivate you to action. With some products (what most of us consider necessities), ads are designed to influence product choice, to get us to buy brand A instead of brand B. With other products, ones we really do not need or which may actually be harmful to us, ads need to be especially clever. Some ads do provide some information (car X gets better gas mileage than car Y). Other ads (perfume ads, for example) take us into a fantasy land so that we will spend $50 on a small but pretty bottle. Another type of ad is the "image advertisement," an ad that assures us that a particular company is top-notch. If we admire the company, we will buy its goods or services.

Here are guidelines for reading visual arguments with insight. You can practice these steps with the exercises that follow.

GUIDELINES for Reading Political Cartoons

- **What scene is depicted?** Identify the situation.
- **Identify each of the figures in the cartoon.** Are they current politicians, figures from history or literature, the "person in the street," or symbolic representations?
- **Who speaks the lines in the cartoon?**
- **What is the cartoon's general subject?** What is the point of the cartoon, the claim of the cartoonist?

GUIDELINES for Reading Advertisements

- **What product or service is being advertised?**
- **Who seems to be the targeted audience?**
- **What is the ad's primary strategy?** To provide information? To reinforce the product's or company's image? To appeal to particular needs or desires?

For example, if an ad shows a group of young people having fun and drinking a particular beer, to what needs/desires is the ad appealing?

- **Does the ad use specific rhetorical strategies such as humor, understatement, or irony?**
- **What is the relation between the visual part of the ad (photo, drawing, typeface, etc.) and the print part (the text, or copy)?** Does the ad use a slogan or catchy phrase? Is there a company logo? Is the slogan or logo clever? Is it well known as a marker of the company? What may be the effect of these strategies on readers?
- **What is the ad's overall visual impression?** Consider both images and colors used.

EXERCISES: Analyzing Cartoons and Ads

1. Analyze the cartoon below and the *Dilbert* cartoon in the color insert, using the guidelines listed previously. You may want to jot down your answers to the questions to be well prepared for class discussion.

2. Review the cartoons that open Chapters 2, 3, 5, 6, 8, 14, 16, 17, 20, and 21. Select the one you find most effective. Analyze it in detail to show why you think it is the cleverest.

3. Analyze the ads on pages 194 and 195 and in the color insert, again using the guidelines listed previously. After answering the questions listed with the guidelines, consider these as well: Will each ad appeal effectively to its intended audience? If so, why? If not, why not?

THEY'D RATHER BE IN COLORADO.

Taking the same dull vacation can start eating away at you after a while. So why not try Colorado? The mountains. The magic. The plains. The people. The history. The culture. The fun. The sheer exhilaration of something new. Something you can't experience anywhere else.
Call us or give our Web site a nibble.

COLORADO
1-800-COLORADO · WWW.COLORADO.COM

Courtesy of the National Federation of Coffee Growers of Columbia

READING GRAPHICS

Graphics—photographs, diagrams, tables, charts, and graphs—present a good bit of information in a condensed but also visually engaging format. Graphics are everywhere: in textbooks, magazines, newspapers. It's a rare training session or board meeting that is conducted without the use of graphics to display information. So, you want to be able to read graphics and create them, when appropriate, in your own writing. Here are general guidelines for reading all types of graphics. The guidelines will use Figure 7.1 to illustrate points; study the figure repeatedly as you read through the guidelines.

GUIDELINES for Reading Graphics

1. **Locate the particular graphic referred to in the text and study it at that point in your reading.** Graphics may not always be placed on the same page as the text reference. Stop your reading to find and study the graphic; that's what the writer wants you to do. Find Figure 7.1 on this page.

2. **Read the title or heading of the graphic.** Every graphic, except photographs, is given a title. What is the subject of the graphic? What kind of information is provided? Figure 7.1 shows differences in suicide rates by race, gender, and age.

3. **Read any notes, description, and the source information at the bottom of the graphic.** Figure 7.1 came from the U.S. Bureau of the Census for 1994. Critical questions: What is this figure showing me? Is the information coming from a reliable source? Is it current enough to still be meaningful?

4. **Study the labels—and other words—that appear as part of the graphic.** You cannot draw useful conclusions unless you understand exactly what is being shown. Observe in Figure 7.1 that the four bars for each age group (shown along the horizontal axis) represent white males, black males, white females, and black females, in that order, for each age category.

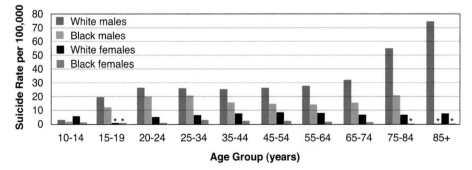

FIGURE 7.1 Differences in Suicide Rate According to Race, Gender, and Age (Source: Data from the U.S. Bureau of the Census, 1994).

5. **Study the information, making certain that you understand what the numbers represent.** Are the numerals whole numbers, numbers in hundreds or thousands, or percentages? In Figure 7.1 we are looking at suicide *rates per 100,000 people* for four identified groups of people at different ages. So, to know exactly how many white males between 15 and 19 commit suicide, we need to know how many white males between 15 and 19 there are (or were in 1994) in the United States population. The chart does not give us this information. It gives us *comparative rates* per 100,000 people in each category and tells us that almost 20 in every 100,000 of white males between 15 and 19 commit suicide.

6. **Draw conclusions.** Think about the information in different ways. Critical questions: What does the author want to accomplish by including these figures? How are they significant? What conclusions can you draw from Figure 7.1? Answer the following questions to guide your thinking.

   a. Which of the four compared groups faces the greatest risk from suicide over his or her lifetime? Would you have guessed this group? Why or why not? What might be some of the causes for the greatest risk to this group?

   b. What is the greatest risk factor for increased suicide rate—race, gender, age, or a combination? Does this surprise you? Would you have guessed a different factor? Why?

   c. Which group, as young teens, is at greatest risk? Are you surprised? Why or why not? What might be some of the causes for this?

Graphics provide information, raise questions, explain processes, engage us emotionally, make us think. Study the various graphics in the exercises that follow to become more expert in reading and responding critically to visuals.

EXERCISES: Reading and Analyzing Graphics

1. Study the pie charts in Figure 7.2 and then answer the following questions.
   a. What is the subject of the charts?

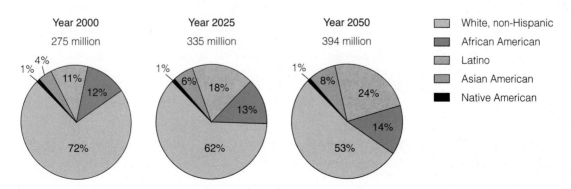

FIGURE 7.2 The Shifting of U.S. Racial-Ethnic Mix (Sources: U.S. Bureau of the Census. *Current Population Reports* P25:1130, 1996 James Henslin. *Sociology: A Down-to-Earth Approach*, 5th ed.).

b. In addition to the information within the pie charts, what other information is provided?

c. Which group increases by the greatest relative amount? How would you account for that increase?

d. Which figure surprises you the most? Why?

2. Study the line graph in Figure 7.3 and then answer the following questions.

a. What two subjects are treated by the graph?

b. In 2000 what percentage of men's income did women earn?

c. During which five-year period did men's incomes increase by the greatest amount?

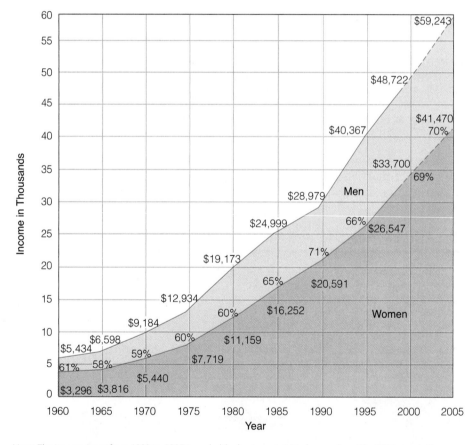

Note: The income jump from 1990 to 1995 is probably due to a statistical procedure. The 1995 source (for 1990 income) uses "median income," while the 1997 source (for 1995 income) merely says "average earnings." How the "average" is computed is not stated. For a review of this distinction, see Table 5.2. Broken lines indicate the author's estimates.

FIGURE 7.3 What Percentage of Men's Income Do Women Earn? The Gender Gap Over Time (Source: James M. Henslin, *Sociology*, 5th ed.).

	1970		2000	
	MEN	**WOMEN**	**MEN**	**WOMEN**
Estimated life expectancy	67.1	74.1	74.24	79.9
% high school graduates	53	52	87	88
% of BAs awarded	57	43	45	55
% of MAs awarded	60	40	45	55
% of PhDs awarded	87	13	61	39
% in legal profession	95	5	70	30
Median earnings	$26,760	$14,232	$35,345	$25,862
Single parents	1.2 million	5.6 million	n/a	n/a

FIGURE 7.4 Men and Women in a Changing Society (Sources: for 1970: *1996 Statistical Abstract*, U.S. Dept. of Commerce, Economics and Statistics Administration, Bureau of the Census. 2000 data: National Center for Education Statistics http://nces.ed.gov/fastfacts).

  d. Does the author's prediction for the year 2005 suggest that income equality for women will have taken place?

  e. Are you bothered by the facts on this graph? Why or why not?

3. Study the table in Figure 7.4 and then answer the following questions.

  a. What is being presented and compared in this table?

  b. What, exactly, do the numerals in the second line represent? What, exactly, do the numerals in the third line represent? (Be sure that you understand what these numbers mean.)

  c. For the information given in lines 2, 3, 4, and 5, in which category have women made the greatest gains on men?

  d. See if you can complete the missing information in the last line. Where will you look to find out how many men and women are single parents in 2000?

  e. Which figure surprises you the most? Why?

4. Maps, as you can see from color plate 3, can be used to show all kinds of information, not just the locations of cities, rivers, or mountains. Study the map and then answer the questions that follow.

  a. What, exactly, does the map show? Why does it not "look right"?

  b. How many electoral votes did each candidate win?

  c. How are the winning states for each candidate clustered? What conclusions can you draw from observing this clustering?

  d. What advice would you give to each party to ensure that party's presidential win in 2008?

  e. How would the map look if it were drawn to show population by state? Would the red states look bigger or smaller?

5. Review the photos opening Chapters 1 and 15 and answer the following questions for each one.

  a. What does each photo show us? What details make each one dramatic?

  b. Both photos appeared in a sociology textbook. What message does each one send to viewers? Why would a sociologist select them for a college text?

THE USES OF AUTHORITY AND STATISTICS

Most of the visuals you have just studied provide a way of presenting statistics—data that many today consider essential to defending a claim. One reason you check the source information accompanying graphics is that you need to know—and evaluate—the authority of that source. When a graphic's numbers have come from the Census Bureau, you know you have a reliable source. When the author writes that "studies have shown . . . ," you want immediately to become suspicious of the authority of the data. All elements of the arguments we read—and write—need to be evaluated. They all contribute to the writer's credibility, or lack thereof.

Judging Authorities

We all know that movie stars and sports figures are not authorities on cereals and soft drinks. But what about *real* authorities? When writers present the opinions or research findings of authorities as support for a claim, they are saying to readers that the authority is trustworthy and the opinions valuable. But what they are asserting is actually an assumption or warrant, part of the glue connecting evidence to claim. Remember: Warrants can be challenged. If the "authority" can be shown to lack authority, then the logic of the argument is destroyed. Use this checklist of questions to aid your evaluation of authorities.

☐ *Is the authority actually an authority on the topic under discussion?* When a famous scientist supports a candidate for office, he or she speaks as a citizen, not as an authority.

☐ *Is the work of the authority still current?* Times change; expertise does not always endure. Galileo would be lost in the universe of today's astrophysicists. Be particularly alert to the dates of information in the sciences in general, in genetics and the entire biomedical field, in health and nutrition. It is almost impossible to keep up with the latest findings in these areas of research.

☐ *Does the authority actually have legitimate credentials?* Are the person's publications in respected journals? Is he or she respected by others in the same field? *Just because it's in print does not mean it's a reliable source!*

☐ *Do experts in the field generally agree on the issue?* If there is widespread disagreement, then referring to one authority does not do much to support a claim. This is why you need to understand the many sides of a controversial topic before you write on it, and you need to bring knowledge of controversies and critical thinking skills to your reading of argument. This is also why writers often provide a source's credentials, not just a name, unless the authority is quite famous.

☐ *Is the authority's evidence reliable, so far as you can judge, but the interpretation of that evidence seems odd, or seems to be used to support strongly held beliefs?* Does the evidence actually connect to the claim? A respected authority's work can be stretched or manipulated in an attempt to support a claim that the authority's work simply does not support.

EXERCISES: Judging Authorities

1. Jane Goodall has received worldwide fame for her studies of chimpanzees in Gombe and for her books on those field studies. Goodall is a vegetarian. Should she be used as an authority in support of a claim for a vegetarian diet? Why or why not? Consider:
   a. Why might Goodall have chosen to become a vegetarian?
   b. For what arguments might Goodall be used as an authority?
   c. For what arguments might she be used effectively for emotional appeal?
2. Suppose a respected zoologist prepares a five-year study of U.S. zoos, compiling a complete list of all animals at each zoo. He then updates the list for each of the five years, adding births and deaths. When he examines his data, he finds that deaths are one and one-half times the number of births. He considers this loss alarming and writes a paper arguing for the abolishing of zoos on the grounds that too many animals are dying. Because of his reputation, his article is published in a popular science magazine. How would you evaluate his authority and his study?
   a. Should you trust the data? Why or why not?
   b. Should you accept his conclusions? Why or why not?
   c. Consider: What might be possible explanations for the birth/death ratio?

Understanding and Evaluating Statistics

There are two useful clichés to keep in mind: "Statistics don't lie, but people lie with statistics" and "There are lies, damned lies, and statistics." The second cliché is perhaps a bit cynical. We don't want to be naïve in our faith in numbers, but neither do we want to become so cynical that we refuse to believe any statistical evidence. What we do need to keep in mind is that when statistics are presented in an argument they are being used by someone interested in winning that argument.

Some writers use numbers without being aware that the numbers are incomplete or not representative. Some present only part of the relevant information. Some may not mean to distort, but they do choose to present the information in language that helps their cause. There are many ways, some more innocent than others, to distort reality with statistics. Use the following guidelines to evaluate the presentation of statistical information.

GUIDELINES for Evaluating Statistics

Make yourself aware of the ways data can be misleading in both the arguments you read and those you write by examining these questions.

- **Is the information current and therefore still relevant?** Crime rates in your city based on 1990 census data probably are no longer relevant, certainly not current enough to support an argument for increased (or decreased) police department spending.

- **If a sample was used, was it randomly selected and large enough to be significant?** Sometimes in medical research, the results of a small study are publicized to guide researchers to important new areas of study. When these results are reported in the press or on TV, however, the small size of the study is not always made clear. Thus one week we learn that coffee is bad for us, the next week that it is okay.
- **What information, exactly, has been provided?** When you read "Two out of three chose the Merit combination of low tar and good taste," you must ask yourself "Two-thirds of how many altogether?"
- **How have the numbers been presented?** And what is the effect of that presentation? Numbers can be presented as fractions, whole numbers, or percentages. Writers who want to emphasize budget increases will use whole numbers—billions of dollars. Writers who want to de-emphasize those increases select percentages. Writers who want their readers to respond to the numbers in a specific way add words to direct their thinking: "a *mere* 3 percent increase" or "the *enormous* $5 billion increase."

EXERCISES: Reading Tables and Charts and Using Statistics

1. Figure 7.5, a table from the *Statistical Abstract of the United States, 2002,* shows U.S. family income data from 1980 to 2000. Percentages and median income are given for all families and then, in turn, for white, black, and Hispanic families. Study the data and then complete the exercises that follow.
   a. In a paper assessing the advantages of a growing economy, you want to include a paragraph on family income growth to show that a booming economy helps everyone, that "a rising tide lifts all boats." Select data from the table that best support your claim. Write a paragraph beginning with a topic sentence and including your data as support. Think about how to present the numbers in the most persuasive form.
   b. Write a second paragraph with the following topic sentence: "Not all Americans have benefited from the boom years" or "a rising tide does not lift all boats." Select data from the table that best support this topic sentence and present the numbers in the most persuasive form.
   c. Exchange paragraphs with a classmate and evaluate each other's selection and presentation of evidence.
2. Go back to Figure 7.1 (p. 196) and reflect again on the information that it depicts. Then consider what conclusions can be drawn from the evidence and what the implications of those conclusions are. Working in small groups or with a class partner, decide how you want to use the data to support a point.
3. Figure 7.6, another table from the *Statistical Abstract,* presents mean earnings by degree earned. First, be sure that you know the difference between mean and median (used in Figure 7.5). Study the data and reflect on the conclusions you can draw from the statistics. Consider: Of the various groups represented, which group most benefits from obtaining a college degree—as opposed to having only a high school diploma?

YEAR	NUMBER OF HOUSE- HOLDS (1,000)	PERCENT DISTRIBUTION							MEDIAN INCOME (DOLLARS)
		UNDER $15,000	$15,000-$24,999	$25,000-$34,999	$35,000-$49,999	$50,000-$74,999	$75,000-$99,999	$100,000 AND OVER	
ALL HOUSEHOLDS[1]									
1980	82,368	20.2	15.5	14.0	18.9	18.7	7.5	5.2	35,238
1985	88,458	19.6	15.1	13.7	17.7	18.3	8.7	6.8	36,246
1990	94,312	18.4	14.1	13.7	17.2	18.8	9.1	8.7	38,446
1995	99,627	18.3	14.9	13.1	16.4	18.3	9.4	9.6	38,262
1998	103,874	17.1	13.4	13.1	15.5	18.8	10.2	12.0	41,032
1999	104,705	16.0	13.8	12.4	15.8	18.5	10.5	13.2	42,187
2000	106,418	16.0	13.4	12.5	15.5	18.9	10.4	13.4	42,151
WHITE									
1970	57,575	19.4	14.6	16.3	21.8	18.5	5.8	3.7	35,148
1980	71,872	18.1	15.1	14.1	19.5	19.7	8.0	5.6	37,176
1985	76,576	17.6	14.7	13.8	18.2	19.2	9.2	7.4	38,226
1990	80,968	16.0	13.9	13.8	17.6	19.6	9.6	9.3	40,100
1995	84,511	16.4	14.6	13.0	16.7	19.1	9.8	10.4	40,159
1998	87,212	15.2	13.0	13.0	15.7	19.6	10.7	12.9	43,171
1999	87,671	14.2	13.6	12.2	16.0	19.1	11.1	13.8	43,932
2000	88,543	14.4	13.0	12.6	15.4	19.4	11.0	14.2	44,232
BLACK									
1980	8,847	37.6	18.9	13.7	14.4	10.7	3.4	1.3	21,418
1985	9,797	35.9	18.7	13.4	14.1	11.4	4.5	1.9	22,742
1990	10,671	35.4	15.8	13.7	14.6	12.7	4.7	3.1	23,979
1995	11,577	32.3	17.8	13.8	14.5	12.4	6.0	3.1	25,144
1998	12,579	30.5	17.0	13.6	14.5	13.4	6.1	4.9	26,751
1999	12,849	28.1	15.9	13.8	14.6	14.4	6.6	6.7	28,848
2000	13,355	26.0	16.5	12.9	16.8	15.2	6.5	6.1	30,436
HISPANIC[2]									
1980	3,906	26.2	20.1	16.2	17.0	14.0	4.2	2.2	27,161
1985	5,213	28.1	18.8	15.4	16.8	13.1	5.3	2.5	26,803
1990	6,220	26.1	18.2	15.7	16.9	14.1	5.2	3.8	28,671
1995	7,939	28.9	20.3	14.9	14.5	13.1	4.6	3.8	25,668
1998	9,060	24.7	17.1	16.3	15.7	14.6	6.0	5.6	29,894
1999	9,319	21.1	18.4	15.5	16.8	15.1	7.3	5.8	31,761
2000	9,663	18.9	18.3	14.7	17.7	17.4	7.4	5.8	33,455

[1]Includes other races not shown separately.
[2]Persons of Hispanic origin may be of any race.

FIGURE 7.5 Money Income of Households—Percent Distribution by Income Level, Race, and Hispanic Origin, in Constant (2000) Dollars: 1980 to 2000. (Source: U.S. Census Bureau. Statistical Abstract of the United States, 2002).

CHARACTERISTIC	TOTAL PERSONS	NOT A HIGH SCHOOL GRADUATE	HIGH SCHOOL GRADUATE ONLY	SOME COLLEGE, NO DEGREE	ASSO- CIATE'S	BACHE- LOR'S	MASTER'S	PROFES- SIONAL	DOCTORATE
All persons[1]	32,356	16,121	24,572	26,958	32,152	45,678	55,641	100,987	86,833
Age:									
25 to 34 years old	29,901	16,916	24,040	26,914	28,088	39,768	46,768	58,043	60,852
35 to 44 years old	36,900	18,894	27,444	34,219	35,370	50,153	56,816	100,240	94,936
45 to 54 years old	41,465	19,707	28,883	36,935	37,508	54,922	62,158	116,327	87,659
55 to 64 years old	38,577	22,212	27,558	32,240	35,703	50,141	57,580	132,326	97,214
65 years old and over	24,263	12,121	18,704	19,052	17,609	30,624	35,639	104,055	78,333
Sex:									
Male	40,257	18,855	30,414	33,614	40,047	57,706	68,367	120,352	97,357
Female	23,551	12,145	18,092	20,241	25,079	32,546	42,378	59,792	61,136
White	33,326	16,623	25,270	27,674	32,686	46,894	55,622	103,450	87,746
Male	41,598	19,320	31,279	34,825	41,010	59,606	68,831	123,086	97,076
Female	23,756	12,405	18,381	20,188	24,928	32,507	41,845	57,314	64,080
Black	24,979	13,569	20,991	24,101	28,772	37,422	48,777	75,509	(B)
Male	28,821	16,391	25,849	27,538	31,885	42,530	54,642	(B)	(B)
Female	21,694	10,734	16,506	21,355	26,787	33,184	44,761	(B)	(B)
Hispanic[2]	22,096	16,106	20,704	23,115	29,329	36,212	50,576	64,029	(B)
Male	24,970	18,020	23,736	27,288	36,740	42,733	60,013	(B)	(B)
Female	18,187	12,684	16,653	18,782	22,695	29,249	41,118	(B)	(B)

LEVEL OF HIGHEST DEGREE

B Base figure too small to meet statistical standards for reliability of a derived figure.
[1] Includes other races, not shown separately.
[2] Persons of Hispanic origin may be of any race.

FIGURE 7.6 Mean Earnings by Highest Degree Earned: 1999. In dollars. For persons 18 years old and over with earnings. Persons as of March the following year. (Source: U.S. Census Bureau. *Statistical Abstract of the United States*, 2002).

WRITING THE INVESTIGATIVE ARGUMENT

The first step in writing an investigative argument is, of course, to select a topic to study. Composition students, even if not highly skilled in research procedures, can write successful investigative essays on the media, on campus issues, or on various local concerns. Although you begin with a topic—not a claim—since you have to gather evidence before you can see what it means, you should select a topic that holds your interest and that you may have given some thought to before choosing to write. For example, you may have noticed some clever ads for jeans or beer, or perhaps you are bothered by plans for another shopping area along a major street near your home. Either one of these topics can lead to an effective investigative, or inductive, argument.

Gathering and Analyzing Evidence

Let's reflect on strategies you will need to use to gather evidence for a study of magazine ads for a particular kind of product (the topic of the sample student paper that follows).

- Select a time frame and a number of representative magazines.
- Have enough magazines to render at least twenty-five ads on the product you are studying.
- Once you decide on the magazines and issues to be used, pull *all* ads for your product. Your task is to draw useful conclusions based on adequate data objectively collected. You can't leave some ads out and have a valid study.
- Study the ads, reflecting on the inferences they allow you to draw. The inferences become the claim of your argument. You may want to take the approach of classifying the ads, that is, grouping them into categories by the various appeals used to sell the product.

More briefly, consider your hunch that your area does not need another shopping mall. What evidence can you gather to support a claim to that effect? You could locate all existing strip or enclosed malls within a 10-mile radius of the proposed new mall site, visit each one, and count the number and types of stores already available. You may discover that there are plenty of malls but that the area really needs a grocery store or a bookstore. So instead of reading to find evidence to support a claim, you are creating the statistics and doing the analysis to guide you to a claim. Just remember to devise objective procedures for collecting evidence so that you do not bias your results.

Planning and Drafting the Essay

You've done your research and studied the data you've collected; how do you put this kind of argument together? Here are some guidelines to help you draft your essay.

GUIDELINES for Writing an Investigative Argument

- **Begin with an opening paragraph that introduces your topic in an interesting way.** Possibilities include beginning with a startling statistic or explaining what impact the essay's facts will have on readers.

- **Devote space early in your paper to explaining your methods or procedures, probably in your second or third paragraph.** For example, if you have obtained information through questionnaires or interviews, recount the process: the questions asked, the number of people involved, the basis for selecting the people, and so on.

- **Classify the evidence that you present.** Finding a meaningful organization is part of the originality of your study and will make your argument more forceful. It is the way you see the topic and want readers to see it. If you are studying existing malls, you might begin by listing all of the malls and their locations. But then do not go store by store through each mall. Rather, group the stores by type and provide totals.

- **Consider presenting evidence in several ways, including in charts and tables as well as within paragraphs.** Readers are used to visuals, especially in essays containing statistics.

- **Analyze evidence to build your argument.** Do not ask your reader to do the thinking that is your job. No data dumps! Explain how your evidence *is* evidence by discussing the connection between facts and the inferences they support.

Analyzing Evidence: The Key to an Effective Argument

This is the thinking part of the process. Anyone can count stores or collect ads. What is your point? How does the evidence you have collected actually support your claim? You must take your readers by the hand and guide them through the evidence. Consider this example:

In a study of selling techniques used in computer ads in business magazines, a student, Brian, found four major selling techniques, one of which he classifies as "corporate emphasis." Brian begins his paragraph on corporate emphasis thus:

> In the technique of corporate emphasis, the advertiser discusses the whole range of products and services that the corporation offers, instead of specific elements. This method relies on the public's positive perception of the company, the company's accomplishments, and its reputation.

Brian then provides several examples of ads in this category, including an IBM ad:

> In one of its eight ads in the study, IBM points to the scientists on its staff who have recently won the Nobel Prize in physics.

But Brian does not stop there. He explains the point of this ad, connecting the ad to the assertion that this technique emphasizes the company's accomplishments:

> The inference we are to draw is that IBM scientists are hard at work right now in their laboratories developing tomorrow's technology to make the world a better place in which to live.

Preparing Graphics

Tables, bar charts, and pie charts are particularly helpful ways to present statistical evidence you have collected for an inductive argument. One possibility is to create a pie chart showing your classification of ads (or stores or questions on a questionnaire) and the relative amount of each item. For example, suppose you find four selling strategies. You can show in a pie chart the percentage of ads using each of the four strategies.

Computers help even the technically unsophisticated prepare simple charts, but even if that seems beyond your skill level, you can always do a simple table. When preparing graphics, keep these points in mind:

- Every graphic must be referred to in the text at the appropriate place— where you are discussing the information in the visual. Graphics are not disconnected attachments to an argument. They give a complete set of data in an easy-to-digest form, but some of that data you must discuss in the essay itself.
- Every graphic (except photographs) needs a label. Use Figure 1, Figure 2, and so forth. Then refer to each graphic by its label.
- Every graphic needs a title. Always place a title after Figure 1 (and so forth), on the same line, at the top of your visual.
- In a technically sophisticated world, hand-drawn graphics are not acceptable. Underline the graphics' title line, or place the visual within a box. (Check the tool bar at the top of your screen.) Type elements within tables. Use a ruler or compass to prepare graphics, or learn to use the graphics programs in your computer.

A CHECKLIST FOR REVISION

- ☐ Have I stated a claim that is precise and appropriate to the data I have collected?
- ☐ Have I fully explained the methodology I used in collecting my data?
- ☐ Have I selected a clear and useful organization?
- ☐ Have I presented and discussed enough specifics to show readers how my data support my conclusions?
- ☐ Have I used graphics to present the data in an effective summary form?
- ☐ Have I revised, edited, and proofread my paper?

STUDENT ESSAY

BUYING TIME

Garrett Berger

Introduction connects to reader.

Chances are you own at least one wristwatch. Watches allow us immediate access to the correct time. They are indispensable items in our modern world, where, as the saying is, time is money. Today the primary function of a wristwatch does not necessarily guide its design; like clothes, houses, and cars, watches have become fashion statements and a way to flaunt one's wealth.

Student explains his methodology of collecting ads. Paragraph concludes with his thesis.

To learn how watches are being sold, I surveyed all of the full-page ads from the November issues of four magazines. The first two, GQ and Vogue, are well-known fashion magazines. The Robb Report is a rather new magazine that caters to the overclass. Forbes is of course a well-known financial magazine. I was rather surprised at the number of advertisements I found. After surveying 86 ads, marketing 59 brands, I have concluded that today watches are being sold through five main strategies: DESIGN/BRAND appeal, CRAFTSMANSHIP, ASSOCIATION, FASHION appeal, and EMOTIONAL appeal.

Discussion of first category.

In most DESIGN/BRAND appeal ads, only a picture and the brand name are used. A subset of this category uses the same basic strategy with a slogan or phrases to emphasize something about the brand or product. A Mont Blanc ad shows a watch profile with a contorted metal link band, asking the question, "Is that you?" The reputation of the name and the appeal of the design sell the watch. Rolex, perhaps the best-known name in high-end watches, advertises, in Vogue, its "Oyster Perpetual Lady-Datejust Pearlmaster." A close-up of the watch face showcases the white, mother-of-pearl dial, sapphire bezel, and diamond-set band. A smaller, more complete picture crouches underneath, showing the watch on its side. The model name is displayed along a gray band that runs near the bottom. The Rolex crest anchors the bottom of the page. Forty-five ads marketing 29 brands use the DESIGN/BRAND strategy. A large picture of the product centered on a solid background is the norm.

CRAFTSMANSHIP, the second strategy, focuses on the maker, the horologer, and the technical sides of form and function. Brand heritage and a unique, hand-crafted design are major selling points. All of these ads are targeted at men, appearing in every magazine except <u>Vogue</u>. Collector pieces and limited editions were commonly sold using this strategy. The focus is on accuracy and technical excellence. Pictures of the inner works and cutaways, technical information, and explanations of movements and features are popular. Quality and exclusivity are all-important.

Discussion of second category.

A Cronoswiss add from <u>The Robb Report</u> is a good example. The top third pictures a horologer, identified as "Gerd-R Lange, master watchmaker and founder of Cronoswiss in Munich," directly below. The middle third of the ad shows a watch, white-faced with a black leather band. The logo and slogan appear next to the watch. The bottom third contains copy beginning with the words: "My watches are a hundred years behind the times." The rest explains what that statement means. Mr. Lange apparently believes that technical perfection in horology has already been attained. He also offers his book, <u>The Fascination of Mechanics</u>, free of charge along with the "sole distributor for North America" at the bottom. A "Daniel Roth" ad from the same magazine displays the name across the top of a white page; towards the top, left-hand corner a gold buckle and black band lead your eye to the center, where a gold watch with a transparent face displays its inner works exquisitely. Above and to the right, copy explains the exclusive and unique design accomplished by inverting the movement, allowing it to be viewed from above.

Detailed examples to illustrate second category.

The third strategy is to sell the watch by establishing an ASSOCIATION with an object, experience, or person, implying that its value and quality are beyond question. In the six ads I found using this approach, watches are associated with violins, pilots, astronauts, hot air balloons, and a hero of the free world. This is similar to the first strategy, but relies on a reputation other than that of the maker. The watch is presented as being desirable for the connections created in the ad.

Discussion of third category.

Rarmigiani ran an ad in <u>The Robb Report</u> featuring a gold watch with a black face and band illuminated by some unseen source. A blue-tinted violin rises in the background; the rest of the page is black. The brief copy reads: "For those who think a Stradivarius is only a violin. The Parmigiani Toric Chronograph is only a wristwatch." "The Moon Watch" proclaims an Omega ad from <u>GQ</u>. Inset on a white background is a picture of an astronaut on the moon saluting the American flag. The silver watch with a black face lies across the lower part of the page. The caption reads: "Speedmaster Professional. The first and only watch worn on the moon." Omega's logo appears at the bottom.

Discussion of
fourth category.

The fourth strategy is to present the watch simply as a FASHION statement. In this line of attack, the ads appeal to our need to be current, accepted, to fit in and be like everyone else, or to make a statement, setting us apart from others as hip and cool. The product is presented as a necessary part of our wardrobes. The watch is fashionable and will send the "right" message. Design and style are the foremost concerns; "the look" sells the watch.

Techno Marine has an ad in <u>GQ</u> which shows a large close-up of a watch running down the entire length of the left side of the page. Two alternate color schemes are pictured on the right, separating small bits of copy. At the bottom on the right are the name and logo. The first words at the top read: "Keeping time—you keep your closet up to the minute, why not your wrist? The latest addition to your watch wardrobe should be the AlphaSport." Longines uses a similar strategy in <u>Vogue</u>. Its ad is divided in half lengthwise. On the left is a black-and-white picture of Audrey Hepburn. The right side is white with the Longines' logo at the top and two ladies' watches in the center. Near the bottom is the phrase "Elegance is an Attitude." Retailers appear at the bottom. The same ad ran in <u>GQ</u>, but with a man's watch and a picture of Humphrey Bogart. A kind of association is made, but quality and value aren't the overriding concerns. The point is to have an elegant attitude like these fashionable stars did, one that these watches can provide and enhance.

The fifth and final strategy is that of EMOTIONAL appeal. The ads using this approach strive to influence our emotional responses and allege to influence the emotions of others towards us. Their power and appeal are exerted through the feelings they evoke in us. Nine out of ten ads rely on a picture as the main device to trigger an emotional link between the product and the viewer. Copy is scant; words are used mainly to guide the viewer to the advertiser's desired conclusions.

Discussion of fifth category.

A Frederique Constant ad pictures a man, wearing a watch, mulling over a chess game. Above his head are the words "Inner Passion." The man's gaze is odd; he is looking at something on the right side of the page, but a large picture of a watch superimposed over the picture hides whatever it is that he is looking at. So we are led to the watch. The bottom third is white and contains the maker's logo and the slogan "Live your Passion." An ad in <u>GQ</u> shows a man holding a woman. He leans against a rock; she reclines in his arms. Their eyes are closed, and both have peaceful, smiling expressions. He is wearing a Tommy Hilfiger watch. The ad spans two pages; a close-up of the watch is presented on the right half of the second page. The only words are the ones in the logo. This is perhaps one of those pictures that are worth a thousand words. The message is he got the girl because he's got the watch.

Even more than selling a particular watch, all of these ads focus on building the brand's image. I found many of the ads extremely effective at conveying their messages. Many of the better-known brands favor the comparatively simple DESIGN/BRAND appeal strategy, to reach a broader audience. Lesser-known, high-end makers contribute many of the more specialized strategies. We all count and mark the passing hours and minutes. And society places great importance on time, valuing punctuality. But these ads strive to convince us that having "the right time" means so much more than "the time."

Strong conclusion; the effect of watch ads.

FOR READING AND ANALYSIS
MONGREL AMERICA | GREGORY RODRIGUEZ

A senior fellow at New America Foundation, Gregory Rodriguez is currently working on a book on America's changing views on race as a result of Mexican immigration. His essay, published in the January/February 2003 issue of *Atlantic Monthly,* was one of several written by New America Foundation scholars examining "the state of the union."

PREREADING QUESTIONS What does Rodriguez mean by "mongrel" America? What are some of the ways in which immigrants of the last thirty years have changed this country?

1   Are racial categories still an important—or even a valid—tool of government policy? In recent years the debate in America has been between those who think that race is paramount and those who think it is increasingly irrelevant, and in the next election cycle this debate will surely intensify around a California ballot initiative that would all but prohibit the state from asking its citizens what their racial backgrounds are. But the ensuing polemics will only obscure the more fundamental question: What, when each generation is more racially and ethnically mixed than its predecessor, does race even mean anymore? If your mother is Asian and your father is African-American, what, racially speaking, are you? (And if your spouse is half Mexican and half Russian Jewish, what are your children?)

2   Five decades after the end of legal segregation, and only thirty-six years after the Supreme Court struck down anti-miscegenation laws, young African-Americans are considerably more likely than their elders to claim mixed heritage. A study by the Population Research Center, in Portland, Oregon, projects that the black intermarriage rate will climb dramatically in this century, to a point at which 37 percent of African-Americans will claim mixed ancestry by 2100. By then more than 40 percent of Asian-Americans will be mixed. Most remarkable, however, by century's end the number of Latinos claiming mixed ancestry will be more than two times the number claiming a single background.

3   Not surprisingly, intermarriage rates for all groups are highest in the states that serve as immigration gateways. By 1990 Los Angeles County had an intermarriage rate five times the national average. Latinos and Asians, the groups that have made up three quarters of immigrants over the past forty years, have helped to create a climate in which ethnic or racial intermarriage is more accepted today than ever before. Nationally, whereas only eight percent of foreign-born Latinos marry non-Latinos, 32 percent of second-generation and 57 percent of third-generation Latinos marry outside their ethnic group. Similarly, whereas only 13 percent of foreign-born Asians marry non-Asians, 34 percent of second-generation and 54 percent of third-generation Asian-Americans do.

4   Meanwhile, as everyone knows, Latinos are now the largest minority group in the nation. Two thirds of Latinos, in turn, are of Mexican heritage. This is significant in itself, because their sheer numbers have helped Mexican-Americans do more than any other group to alter the country's old racial thinking. For in-

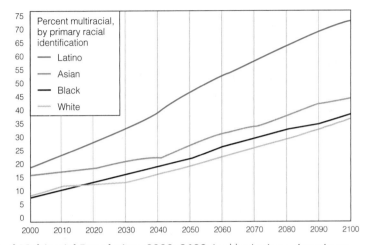

Projected Multiracial Population, 2000–2100 Led by Latinos, Americans are intermarrying and producing mixed-race children at a rapid rate.

stance, Texas and California, where Mexican-Americans are the largest minority, were the first two states to abolish affirmative action: when the collective "minority" populations in those states began to outnumber whites, the racial balance that had made affirmative action politically viable was subverted.

Many Mexican-Americans now live in cities or regions where they are a majority, changing the very idea of what it means to be a member of a "minority" group. Because of such demographic changes, a number of the policies designed to integrate nonwhites into the mainstream—affirmative action in college admissions, racial set-asides in government contracting—have been rendered more complicated or even counterproductive in recent years. In California cities where whites have become a minority, it is no longer clear what "diversity" means or what the goals of integration policies should be. The selective magnet-school program of the Los Angeles Unified School District, for example, was originally developed as an alternative to forced busing—a way to integrate ethnic-minority students by encouraging them to look beyond their neighborhoods. Today, however, the school district is 71 percent Latino, and Latinos' majority status actually puts them at a disadvantage when applying to magnet schools.

But it is not merely their growing numbers (they will soon be the majority in both California and Texas, and they are already the single largest contemporary immigrant group nationwide) that make Mexican-Americans a leading indicator of the country's racial future; rather, it's what they represent. They have always been a complicating element in the American racial system, which depends on an oversimplified classification scheme. Under the pre-civil-rights formulation, for example, if you had "one drop" of African blood, you were fully black. The scheme couldn't accommodate people who were part one thing and part another. Mexicans, who are a product of intermingling—both cultural and genetic—between the Spanish and the many indigenous peoples of North and Central America, have a history of tolerating and even reveling in such ambiguity. Since the conquest of Mexico, in the sixteenth century, they have practiced mestizaje—racial and cultural synthesis—both in their own country and as they came north. Unlike the English-speaking settlers of the western frontier, the Spaniards were willing everywhere they went to allow racial and cultural mixing to blur the lines between themselves and the natives. The fact that Latin America is far more heavily populated by people of mixed ancestry than Anglo America is the clearest sign of the difference between the two outlooks on race.

7   Nativists once deplored the Mexican tendency toward hybridity. In the mid-nineteenth century, at the time of the conquest of the Southwest, Secretary of State James Buchanan feared granting citizenship to a "mongrel race." And in the late 1920s Representative John C. Box, of Texas, warned his colleagues on the House Immigration and Naturalization Committee that the continued influx of Mexican immigrants could lead to the "distressing process of mongrelization" in America. He argued that because Mexicans were the products of mixing, they harbored a relaxed attitude toward interracial unions and were likely to mingle freely with other races in the United States.

8   Box was right. The typical cultural isolation of immigrants notwithstanding, those immigrants' children and grandchildren are strongly oriented toward the American melting pot. Today two thirds of multiracial and multiethnic births in California involve a Latino parent. Mexicanidad, or "Mexicanness" is becoming the catalyst for a new American cultural synthesis.

9   In the same way that the rise in the number of multiracial Americans muddles U.S. racial statistics, the growth of the Mexican-American mestizo population has begun to challenge the Anglo-American binary view of race. In the 1920 census Mexicans were counted as whites. Ten years later they were reassigned to a separate Mexican "racial" category. In 1940 they were officially reclassified as white. Today almost half the Latinos in California, which is home to a third of the nation's Latinos (most of them of Mexican descent), check "other" as their race. In the first half of the twentieth century Mexican-American advocates fought hard for the privileges that came with being white in America. But since the 1960s activists have sought to reap the benefits of being nonwhite minorities. Having spent so long trying to fit into one side or the other of the binary system, Mexican-Americans have become numerous and confident enough to simply claim their brownness—their mixture. This is a harbinger of America's future.

10   The original melting-pot concept was incomplete: it applied only to white ethnics (Irish, Italians, Poles, and so forth), not to blacks and other nonwhites. Israel Zangwill, the playwright whose 1908 drama *The Melting Pot* popularized the concept, even wrote that whites were justified in avoiding intermarriage with blacks. In fact, multiculturalism—the ideology that promotes the permanent coexistence of separate but equal, cultures in one place—can be seen as a by-product of America's exclusion of African-Americans from the melting pot; those whom assimilation rejected came to reject assimilation. Although the multicultural movement has always encompassed other groups, blacks gave it its moral impetus.

But the immigrants of recent decades are helping to forge a new American   11
identity, something more complex than either a melting pot or a confederation
of separate but equal groups. And this identity is emerging not as a result of
politics or any specific public policies but because of powerful underlying cultural forces. To be sure, the civil-rights movement was instrumental in the initial assault on racial barriers. And immigration policies since 1965 have tended
to favor those immigrant groups—Asians and Latinos—who are most open to
intermarriage. But in recent years the government's major contribution to the
country's growing multiracialism has been—as it should continue to be—a retreat from dictating limits on interracial intimacy and from exalting (through
such policies as racial set-asides and affirmative action) race as the most important American category of being. As a result, Americans cross racial lines
more often than ever before in choosing whom to sleep with, marry, or raise
children with.

Unlike the advances of the civil-rights movement, the future of racial iden-   12
tity in America is unlikely to be determined by politics or the courts or public
policy. Indeed, at this point perhaps the best thing the government can do is to
acknowledge changes in the meaning of race in America and then get out of
the way. The Census Bureau's decision to allow Americans to check more than
one box in the "race" section of the 2000 Census was an important step in this
direction. No longer forced to choose a single racial identity, Americans are now
free to identify themselves as mestizos—and with this newfound freedom we
may begin to endow racial issues with the complexity and nuance they deserve.

QUESTIONS FOR READING

1. What are the projected numbers of mixed ancestry for African Americans, Asian
    Americans, and Latinos?
2. Where are intermarriage rates the highest currently?
3. What is America's largest minority?
4. Where will Mexican Americans soon be the majority group?
5. What kinds of programs have these demographic changes affected?
6. What has long been the attitude of Mexicans toward racial mixing?
7. What is the difference between the melting pot and multiculturalism?
8. What is the new racial identity, and what are emerging attitudes toward the iden-
    tifying of race in America?

QUESTIONS FOR REASONING AND ANALYSIS

1. What is Rodriguez's subject? What is his claim—what is changing, what is caus-
    ing the change, and what is Rodriguez's attitude toward the changes?
2. What *type* of argument is this? That is, what kind of evidence does Rodriguez
    use to support his claim?

3.   Why should the changes in demographics that Rodriguez examines change government policies? How does the author support his view on these changes?

4.   Evaluate Rodriguez's argument. Do his predictions seem credible? Are the changes he describes consistent with your experiences?

QUESTIONS FOR REFLECTING AND WRITING

1.   What group is least likely to agree with the authors' conclusions about policy change? Has Rodriguez convinced you of the appropriateness of eliminating such policies as affirmative action and racial set-asides? Why or why not?

2.   Is the ongoing blending of cultures good for families? Good for the country? Why or why not? Be prepared to defend your position—with good evidence and good reasons, not with emotion and illogic.

DISCIPLINE AND PUNISH | ANNETTE FUENTES

Annette Fuentes has worked as a reporter, editor, and columnist for various New York City newspapers, and she has been an adjunct professor at the Columbia School of Journalism. She usually writes on health and social policy issues as a freelance journalist. The following article was published December 15, 2003, in *The Nation*.

PREREADING QUESTIONS Examine the school bus image. What does it look like? What does this suggest to you about the essay's subject and the author's attitude?

1   Bryson Donaldson, 12, was horsing around at his Muskogee, Oklahoma, school one morning last fall, mimicking the cops-and-robbers scenario that is as American as apple pie and Al Pacino. Bryson pointed his finger like a gun at a classmate and in a flash was hit with a five-day suspension. The principal singled out Bryson, the only African-American in his grade, for punishment, patting him down and scanning his sixth-grader's frame with a metal detector. He was placed in an alternative program for "bad" students, serving two days of his sentence until his mother brought in the NAACP. Bryson had been a straight-A student, but that changed. "He has nightmares now," Diane Donaldson said last June. "I had to take him to a psychiatrist. It is to the point where we have to struggle to go to school every day."

2   Daniel Brion, 14, was an eighth grader with a bright mind, a diagnosis of ADHD (attention deficit hyperactivity disorder) and a typical adolescent's jubilation as summer approached this past May. Walking down the hall of his Lexington, Kentucky, school, Daniel remarked that he wished the school would burn down and take the principal with it. His words were overheard and translated to said principal thusly: Daniel had gasoline and was recruiting a gang to burn down the school. Without notifying Daniel or his parents, the principal brought in the police to investigate Daniel's comments. Two weeks later, Daniel was yanked out of math class and interrogated by an officer who read him his Miranda rights. "The whole thing is like Franz Kafka's *The Trial*," said Dr. Gail Brion, his mother. "They were ready to arrest him on charges of terrorist threats."

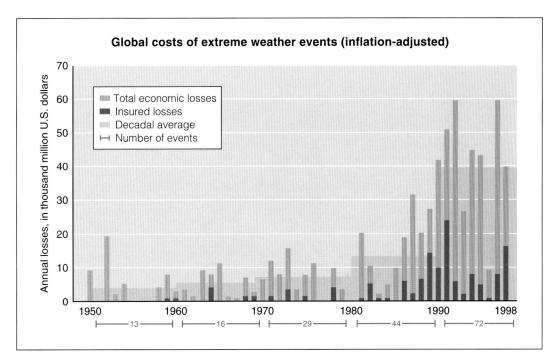

Global costs of extreme weather events (inflation-adjusted)

Legend:
- Total economic losses
- Insured losses
- Decadal average
- ⊢⊣ Number of events

Y-axis: Annual losses, in thousand million U.S. dollars

X-axis: 1950, 1960, 1970, 1980, 1990, 1998

Number of events: 13, 16, 29, 44, 72

DATA SOURCE: Intergovernmental Panel on Climate Changes

Estimated Number of Adults and Children Living with HIV/AIDS, by Country.

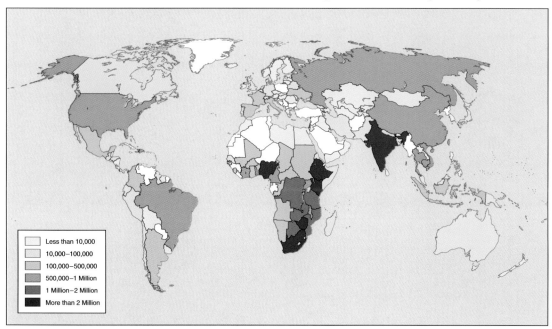

Less than 10,000
10,000–100,000
100,000–500,000
500,000–1 Million
1 Million–2 Million
More than 2 Million

DATA SOURCE: World Health Organization

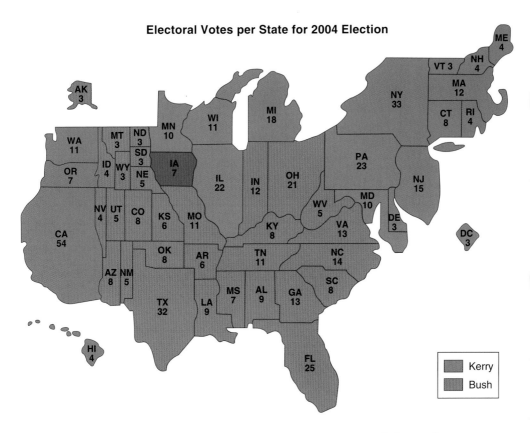

Electoral Votes per State for 2004 Election

AK 3
WA 11
OR 7
MT 3
ID 4
WY 3
ND 3
SD 3
NE 5
MN 10
WI 11
MI 18
NY 33
VT 3
NH 4
ME 4
MA 12
CT 8
RI 4
PA 23
NJ 15
NV 4
UT 5
CO 8
KS 6
MO 11
IL 22
IN 12
OH 21
WV 5
MD 10
DE 3
DC 3
CA 54
OK 8
AR 6
KY 8
VA 13
NC 14
AZ 8
NM 5
TX 32
LA 9
MS 7
AL 9
GA 13
SC 8
HI 4
FL 25
IA 7

Kerry
Bush

Note: States drawn in proportion to number of electoral votes. Total electoral votes: 538

(Source: Based on a map that originally appeared in New York Times. November 5, 2002. Reprinted by permission of NYT Graphics. From O'Connor and Sabato, American Government © 2002; published by Allyn and Bacon, Boston, MA Copyright © 2002 by Pearson Education. Updated for the 2004 election by the author.)

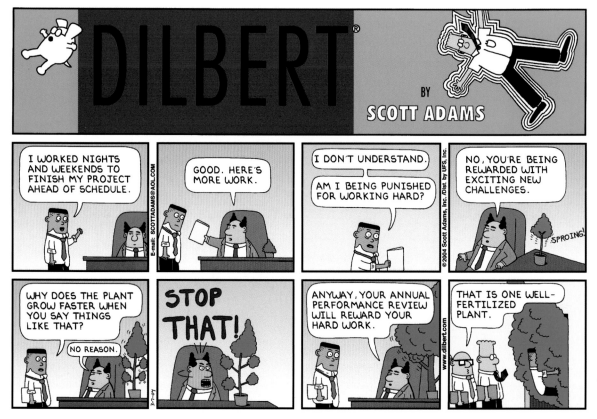

DILBERT: © Scott Adams/Dist. by United Features Syndicate, Inc.

Search for:

| flights | hotels | cars | vacation packages | cruises | deals | maps |

Whatever it is you're looking for in a hotel, find it at Expedia. From the everyday to the out of this world, Expedia offers you great low rates, photos, amenity lists and more. So you can find the hotel that's right for you.

Expedia.com
Don't just travel. Travel Right:

Courtesy of Expedia.com

HP FTD/Creative i

PIERCE BROSNAN'S CHOICE

Seamaster Aqua Terra
Co-Axial Escapement
3 year extended warranty

The name Omega has always been closely associated with quality and reliability. The Seamaster Aqua Terra upholds this pioneering spirit. Its classic design houses the latest in watchmaking technology: the unique Co-Axial Escapement movement, which offers unrivalled long-term accuracy.

Ω
OMEGA
www.omegowatches.com

Courtesy of the Swatch Group

Courtesy of Lowe Worldwide Inc.

Every year, more than 3 million students like Bryson Donaldson are sus-   3
pended and nearly 100,000 more are expelled, from kindergarten through
twelfth grade. Of those, untold thousands like Daniel Brion increasingly face
police action for disciplinary problems that were previously handled in school,
because forty-one states now require that certain acts committed in school be
reported to the police. Boys in general are the targets, with African-American
males bearing a disproportionate brunt of suspensions and disciplinary actions. Together, these trends are the poisonous by-product of a decade of so-
called zero tolerance policies in public schools, from urban enclaves to rural
outposts alike.

Youth advocates and education experts are increasingly alarmed about the   4
toll of zero tolerance policies. While school administrators may believe suspensions and get-tough policies make schools safe and improve student behavior, the research shows otherwise. Excluding kids from school for two days
or two months increases the odds of academic failure and dropping out. What's
more, suspensions and academic failure are strong predictors of entry into the
criminal justice system, especially for African-American males. That's why legal
and education experts are blaming zero tolerance for what they call the
"school to prison pipeline." If yesteryear's prank got a slap on the wrist, today
those wrists could be slapped with handcuffs. "We are breeding a generation
of children who think they are criminals for the way they are being treated in
school," said Judith Browne, senior attorney at the Advancement Project, in
Washington, DC. "School used to be a refuge. Now it's a lockdown environment. We are bringing the practices of criminal justice into the schools."

THE ZERO TOLERANCE JUGGERNAUT

Zero tolerance was born during the Reagan Administration's war on drugs,   5
back in the mid-1980s. But it was Bill Clinton who gave it new currency in the
schools when he signed the Gun Free Schools Act of 1994, mandating expulsion of students who bring weapons to school. It was a time of public hysteria
about youth crime, hyped by pop criminologists like James Q. Wilson, who predicted a violent juvenile crime wave, and John Dilulio, who coined the term
"superpredator" to describe a new, vicious young criminal—the face of whom
was implicitly a black or Latino urban male. Racial coding and stereotypes in-
fused such theories and fed the public's rampant fear of young minority males.
The real dimensions of juvenile crime were far milder: a spike in violent crime
that began in the late 1980s, crested in the early 1990s and has been falling
ever since. At the time of the infamous 1999 Columbine High School shootings,
incidents of school violence, including homicides, were at their lowest point in
a decade. But by then, fear of African-American and Latino "ghetto gangstas"
had expanded to include youth of all demographics, whether they lived in affluent white suburbs or poor black cities. Columbine only accelerated the zero
tolerance juggernaut already in motion.

In the four years since then, states and localities have enacted policies in   6
public schools that make the federal mandates look tepid. Broadened definitions of weapons and threatening behavior can turn a spitball into a deadly

missile and a playground pushing match into an assault. What's more, zero tolerance is getting a boost from President Bush's No Child Left Behind Act of 2001 and its focus on standardized-testing-as-educational-reform. "The wave of school shootings fed [the public's] concerns and states went wild with zero tolerance, giving principals total discretion to kick out any student they wanted," said Mark Soler, president of the Youth Law Center. "Now zero tolerance is fed less by fear of crime and more by high-stakes testing. Principals want to get rid of kids they perceive as trouble."

7   Daniel Brion's school is typical in Kentucky, where zero tolerance took hold after a few incidents of school violence in the late 1990s, like the 1997 fatal shooting at a West Paducah high school prayer group. Yet school crime is very low in Kentucky, says Soler. For each of the past three years, for example, fewer than forty firearms offenses were reported for a student population of 625,000. But suspensions have multiplied: 65,508 in the 1999-2000 school year, and 68,523 the following year. Many of these were for "defiance of authority," a vaguely defined violation of school rules that was reported more than 25,000 times in the 2000-01 school year. "Defiance of authority is talking in class, talking back to teachers; it's irritating behavior. You can't have kids disturbing class, but schools have abdicated responsibility for finding a middle ground," said Soler. "The Kentucky data is clear. If you stop suspensions for minor behaviors, it would reduce the total number dramatically."

WHAT'S RACE GOT TO DO WITH IT?

8   Zero tolerance cheerleaders cite high rates of suspension and expulsion as the reason school violence is low. But no research supports that claim or the theory that zero tolerance improves academic outcomes. If anything, zero tolerance breeds failure among the most vulnerable students and puts kids on a path to prison, according to Russell Skiba, associate professor of education and director of the Safe and Responsive Schools Project at Indiana University. "Students suspended in elementary school are more likely to act out in middle school, and there is some correlation with dropouts. If one of the potent predictors of achievement is time spent learning, then expulsion's effect on achievement is not surprising," said Skiba. "Even if we say these are bad kids, zero tolerance doesn't do anything to help them. It's placing a higher proportion of students at risk for jail."

9   Skiba looked at zero tolerance policies in thirty-seven states using data from 2000 to gauge their relationship to achievement, behavior and youth incarceration. Schools with high out-of-school suspension rates had lower achievement in eighth-grade math, writing and reading. And states with higher school suspension rates were also more likely to have higher juvenile incarceration rates. Perhaps most sobering was the racial disparity: In almost every state, suspension, expulsion and incarceration rates were higher for African-Americans than for the general student population. In Minnesota 6 percent of all students were suspended in the 2000-01 school year, while 34 percent of African-American students were. African-American youth were more likely to

be suspended and incarcerated than white children across the country, with many states guilty of staggering disproportion.

Southern states tend to have the highest absolute rates of suspension and juvenile incarceration, Skiba found, but the racial disparity is highest in the Midwest. In Minnesota, for example, African-American youth are nine times as likely to be suspended from school as white children and nine times as likely to be in jail. Skiba attributes the regional differences to the demographics and teacher quality of Midwestern urban areas, where African-Americans are concentrated. But the overall pattern of racial differences in school exclusion is another matter. "I'm beginning to think of this as an unplanned conspiracy," Skiba said. "When there is racial disparity, it reflects institutional behaviors perpetuated over time." National statistics on suspensions from the US Education Department for 2000 indicate the depth of the disparity: African-American students are 17 percent of the entire public school population but account for 34 percent of all out-of-school suspensions and 30 percent of expulsions. White students, by contrast, are 62 percent of the student population but account for 48 percent of out-of-school suspensions and 49 percent of expulsions.

African-American males face a double jeopardy with zero tolerance policies because they are often overrepresented in special education classes, where the federal Individuals With Disabilities Education Act doesn't always protect them from punitive discipline, according to Linda Raffaele Mendez, an associate professor in the department of school psychology at the University of South Florida. She looked at a thirteen-year study of schoolkids in Pinellas County, Florida, and found deep racial disparities in how suspensions were meted out. During their sixth-grade year, more than 66 percent of poor, black males with disabilities were suspended once, and many were suspended multiple times. "Special ed classes aren't much smaller, and teachers are often on emergency certification. They aren't prepared to work with these kids," Mendez said. "The Zeitgeist now is zero tolerance, and that says you get the kid out when there is an infraction." Like Skiba, Mendez found a connection between suspensions and dropouts for all students. In the Pinellas cohort, a third of students disappeared between ninth and twelfth grades. "Kids are on a path. If they are suspended frequently at the end of elementary school, it's likely that will continue in middle school. And when they get to high school, it's very likely they will drop out."

CRIMINAL INTENTS

The school-to-prison pipeline often starts because teachers and principals are calling 911 and criminalizing student behaviors that in more tolerant times they would have handled themselves. "We're seeing very minor conduct becoming a criminal act. Things a police officer might not arrest someone for in a bar fight, we're seeing schools calling in police to make arrests for," said the Advancement Project's Browne.

Browne studied zero tolerance policies in Miami-Dade, Palm Beach, Houston and Baltimore schools, and found many arrests for disorderly conduct. "It could be a student who refuses to sit down in class, or the spitball," she said. "In addition to getting the three-to-five-day suspension, these kids are getting arrested." Browne said there are no statistics on the arrest trend nationally, and many districts don't keep data. But in Miami-Dade, Florida's largest district, arrests at school nearly tripled between 1999 and 2001, from 820 to 2,435 arrests. Of those, 28 percent were for "miscellaneous" offenses, and 29 percent were for simple assaults.

14   Texas schools have also elevated the trivial transgression to criminal levels. Students can be suspended and placed in an alternative program for cheating, violating dress codes, horseplay, excessive noise and failure to bring homework to class. When students are removed from school, it must be reported to the county juvenile justice board. That surprised Augustina Reyes, associate professor of education at the University of Houston and a former Houston school board member. "I knew there were a few alternative programs for difficult students, but I'd never seen the school disciplinary system become part of the juvenile justice system," said Reyes. "It concerned me that a 14-year-old could be removed from school and all of a sudden, he has a criminal record."

15   Reyes looked at statewide data on disciplinary actions for 2000-01 and found that almost half a million children from kindergarten through twelfth grade had been suspended from their classes, with a total of 1.1 million suspensions. What shocked her most, though, was the nature of school discipline: Of the total 1.7 million disciplinary actions that year, 95 percent were for discretionary reasons. "I thought I was going blind with the numbers," Reyes said. "When you see that only 5 percent of all kids are reported for mandatory reasons—cigarette smoking is a mandatory reason—I couldn't believe it."

TESTING, TESTING—AND INTOLERANCE

16   Zero tolerance critics believe the current emphasis on standardized testing is one reason harsh policies continue even as school crime plummets. Central to No Child Left Behind are state and local mandates for annual testing of students in reading and math, and sanctions for those schools that fail to increase achievement. Reyes says the fixation on testing and a growing population of lower-income, mostly Latino, children in Texas public schools are incentives for suspension and exclusion. "I've seen how life on campus revolves around testing. If teachers are told, 'Your scores go down, you lose your job,' all of a sudden your values shift very quickly," she said. "Teachers think, 'With bad kids in my class. I'll have lower achievements on my tests, so I'll use discretion and remove that kid.'"

17   Judith Browne would like to see longitudinal studies on the relationship between high-stakes testing and the school-to-prison pipeline. "It makes sense that kids who don't pass these tests are being punished by being retained in a grade and are more likely to drop out and more likely to enter the criminal justice system," she said. Politically, zero tolerance reflects a steady

and purposeful divestment in the public education system, and No Child Left Behind continues that political agenda with its underfunded and punitive mandates, according to Browne. "If we're right about what No Child Left Behind means, it is really a call for vouchers," she said. "It means, 'Let's set our schools up to fail so we can go to vouchers,' and there is language that allows transfers for schools that fail or are persistently violent, and each state can define what that means."

For Mark Soler, the fallout from zero tolerance policies extends far beyond 18 the schoolhouse walls. "The great tragedy is, we're looking at losing an entire generation of children, particularly African-American," Soler said. "If we're going to kick kids out of school and put them on the pathway to prison, we'll end up with a whole generation of African-American men who cannot support themselves by lawful means and are less likely to be present husbands and fathers. The consequences for our communities are horrible."

QUESTIONS FOR READING

1. What is Fuentes's subject? Be precise.
2. How many students each year are suspended? Expelled?
3. What does the term *zero tolerance* mean? How has it changed school discipline?
4. What did the Columbine shootings add? What did the No Child Left Behind mandate add?
5. What do studies tell us about the role of race in suspensions and expulsions?
6. What reasons are given for many of the suspensions and arrests of schoolchildren?

QUESTIONS FOR REASONING AND ANALYSIS

1. What does Fuentes gain by beginning her essay with the examples of Bryson and Daniel?
2. What is the author's claim, the primary point of her argument?
3. Throughout the essay, Fuentes also seeks to establish two causal patterns. What do suspensions appear to be causing? And, why do they appear to be happening in such large numbers?
4. Fuentes presents many statistics. How effective are the numbers in supporting her claim and making a convincing argument?

QUESTIONS FOR REFLECTING AND WRITING

1. What statistics surprise you the most? Why? Which ones trouble you the most? Why?
2. Disruptive students do make learning difficult for willing students. If suspensions are too harsh, what should schools do to maintain order?

3. Fuentes suggests that Bush's educational mandate may be having serious, if unintended, consequences. Have you seen evidence of expulsions as a strategy to improve a school's test scores? Is this idea too cynical? Or, are we naïve to think that educators would not use suspensions to secure their jobs? Reflect on these tough questions for class discussion.

SUGGESTIONS FOR DISCUSSION AND WRITING

For all investigative essays—inductive arguments—follow the guidelines in this chapter and use the student essay as your model. Remember that you will need to explain your methods for collecting data, to classify evidence and present it in several formats, and also to explain its significance for readers. Just collecting data does not create an argument. Here are some possible topics to explore:

1. Study print ads for one type of product (e.g., cars, cosmetics, cigarettes) to draw inferences about the dominant techniques used to sell that product. Remember that the more ads you study, the more support you have for your inferences. You should study at least twenty-five ads.

2. Study print ads for one type of product as advertised in different types of magazines clearly directed to different audiences to see how (or if) selling techniques change with a change in audience. (Remember: To demonstrate no change in techniques can be just as interesting a conclusion as finding changes.) Study at least twenty-five ads, in a balanced number from the different magazines.

3. Select a major figure currently in the news and conduct a study of bias in one of the news magazines (e.g., *Time, U.S. News & World Report,* or *Newsweek*) or a newspaper. Use at least eight issues of the magazine or newspaper from the last six months and study all articles on your figure in each of those issues. To determine bias, look at the amount of coverage, the location (front pages or back pages), the use of photos (flattering or unflattering), and the language of the articles.

4. Conduct a study of amounts of violence on TV by analyzing, for one week, all prime-time programs that may contain violence. (That is, eliminate sitcoms and decide whether you want to include or exclude news programs.) Devise some classification system for types of violence based on your prior TV viewing experience before beginning your study—but be prepared to alter or add to your categories based on your viewing of shows. Note the number of times each violent act occurs. You may want to consider the total length of time (per program, per night, per type of violent act) of violence during the week you study. Give credit to any authors in this text or other publications for any ideas you borrow from their articles.

5. As an alternative to topic 4, study the number and types of violent acts in children's programs on Saturday mornings. (This and topic 4 are best handled if you can record and then replay the programs several times.)

6. Conduct a survey and analyze the results on some campus issue or current public policy issue. Prepare questions that are without bias and include questions to get information about the participants so that you can correlate answers with the demographics of your participants (e.g., age, gender, race, religion, proposed major in college, political affiliation, or whatever else you think is important to the topic studied). Decide whether you want to survey students only or both students and faculty. Plan how you are going to reach each group.

© 2000 by Herblock in *The Washington Post*

Read: What is the scene? Who do the two figures in the front look like? Who speaks the words at the top?

Reason: What causes are suggested by the words? What causes are implied visually?

Reflect/Write: What conclusion are we to draw from the cartoon?

CHAPTER 8

Reading, Analyzing,
and
Writing Causal
and
Problem/Solution
Arguments

In the last chapter of this section on argument, we examine two more types of arguments—types that can address both philosophical issues and also public policy debates. Arguments about cause and arguments that offer solutions to perceived problems demand our attention as readers and as writers.

ARGUMENTS ABOUT CAUSE

Because we want to know *why* things happen, arguments about cause abound. We want to understand past events (Why was President Kennedy assassinated?); we want to explain current situations (Why do some teens use drugs?); we want to predict the future (Will the economy improve if there is a tax cut?). All three questions ask for a causal explanation, including the last one. To answer the last question with a yes is to assert that a tax cut is a cause of economic improvement.

Characteristics of Causal Arguments

Assigning cause is tricky business. Perhaps that is the first and most important point to make about issues of causation. Here are some other points about causal arguments.

- *Causal arguments are similar in their purpose but can vary considerably in their subject matter and structure.* Some causal arguments are about a particular situation; others seek explanations for a general state of affairs. However, in either case there may be one or there may be several causes, as illustrated here:

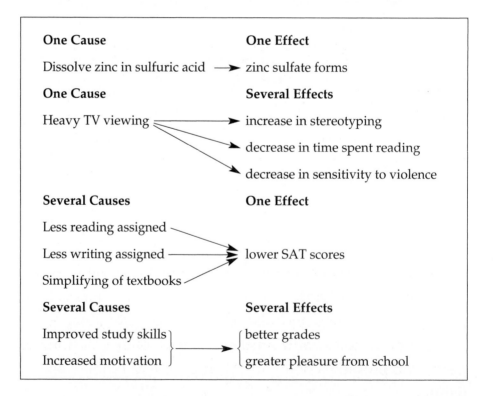

- *There are specific terms related to the discussion of causation that provide useful distinctions in our thinking about why something has happened (or not happened).* First, when looking for the cause of an event, we look for an *agent*—a person, a situation, another event that caused the event to take place. A lit cigarette dropped in a bed caused a house fire; the lit cigarette is the agent. But why, we ask, did someone drop a lit cigarette on a bed? The person, old and ill, took a sleeping pill and dropped the cigarette when he fell asleep. Where do we stop in this chain of causes? Second, we learn that most events do not occur in a vacuum with a single cause. There are *conditions* surrounding the event, making the assigning of only one cause often difficult. In our example, the man's age and health were conditions. Third, we can also speak of *influences.* The sleeping pill certainly influenced the man to drop the cigarette and cause the fire. Some conditions and influences may qualify as *remote causes. Proximate causes* are more immediate, usually closer in time to the event or situation. The man's dozing off with a lighted cigarette is a proximate cause of the fire. Finally, we come to the *precipitating cause,* the triggering event—in our example, the cigarette's igniting the combustible mattress fabric. Isolating a precipitating cause is usually necessary to prevent events from recurring, but often we need to go further back to determine remote causes or conditions, especially if we are interested in assigning responsibility for what has occurred.

- *Because of the long chains of causes that can be found for some complex situations, arguers about cause need to decide on their focus—based on their purpose in writing.* Suppose, for example, your concern is global warming. Cows contribute to global warming. Factories contribute to global warming. Car emissions contribute to global warming. Are we going to give up cattle farms? Not likely. Are we going to tear down factories? Not likely—but we can get factories to put filters on their smokestacks. Are we going to get rid of cars? Not likely—but we can try to get rid of the harmful emissions from cars. So, you argue for eliminating or controlling those causes that society is most likely to agree to and you ignore other causes that may be less practical to eliminate.

Mill's Methods for Investigating Causes

John Stuart Mill, a nineteenth-century British philosopher, explained in detail some important ways of investigating and demonstrating causal relationships: commonality, difference, and process of elimination. We can benefit in our study of cause by understanding and using his methods.

1. *Commonality.* One way to isolate cause is to demonstrate that one agent is *common* to similar outcomes. For instance, twenty-five employees attend a company luncheon. Late in the day, ten report to area hospitals, and another four complain the next day of having experienced vomiting the night before. Public health officials will soon want to know what these people ate

for lunch. Different people during the same 12-hour period had similar physical symptoms of food poisoning. The common factor may well have been the tuna salad they ate for lunch.

2. *Difference.* Another way to isolate cause is to recognize one key *difference.* If two situations are alike in every way but one, and the situations result in different outcomes, then the one way they differ must have caused the different outcome. Studies in the social sciences are often based on the single-difference method. To test for the best teaching methods for math, an educator could set up an experiment with two classrooms similar in every way except that one class devotes 15 minutes three days a week to instruction by drill. If the class receiving the drill scores much higher on a standard test given to both groups of students, the educator could argue that math drills make a measurable difference in learning math. But the educator should be prepared for skeptics to challenge the assertion of only one difference between the two classes. Could the teacher's attitude toward the drills also make a difference in student learning? If the differences in student scores are significant, the educator probably has a good argument, even though a teacher's attitude cannot be controlled in the experiment.

3. *Process of elimination.* One can develop a causal argument around a technique we all use for problem solving: *the process of elimination.* When something happens, we examine all possible causes and eliminate them, one by one, until we are satisfied that we have isolated the actual cause (or causes). When the Federal Aviation Administration has to investigate a plane crash, it uses this process, exploring possible causes such as mechanical failure, weather, human error, or terrorism. Sometimes the process isolates more than one cause or points to a likely cause without providing absolute proof. You will see how Lester Thurow uses the process of elimination method in his article at the end of this chapter (pages 242–44).

EXERCISE: Understanding Causal Patterns

From the following events or situations, select the one you know best and list as many conditions, influences, and causes—remote, proximate, precipitating—as you can think of. You may want to do this exercise with your class partner or in small groups. Be prepared to explain your causal pattern to the class.

1. Teen suicide
2. Global warming
3. Increase in the numbers of women elected to public office
4. High salaries of professional athletes
5. Increased interest in soccer in the United States
6. Comparatively low scores by U.S. students on international tests in math and science

GUIDELINES for Analyzing Causal Arguments

When analyzing causal arguments, what should you look for? The basics of good argument apply to all arguments: a clear statement of claim, qualified if appropriate, a clear explanation of reasons and evidence, and enough relevant evidence to support the claim. How do we recognize these qualities in a causal argument? Use the following points as guides to analyzing:

- **Does the writer carefully distinguish among types of causes?** Word choice is crucial. Is the argument that A and A alone caused B or that A was one of several contributing causes?

- **Does the writer recognize the complexity of causation and not rush to assert only one cause for a complex event or situation?** The credibility of an argument about cause is quickly lost if readers find the argument oversimplified.

- **Is the argument's claim clearly stated, with qualifications as appropriate?** If the writer wants to argue for one cause, not the only cause, of an event or situation, then the claim's wording must make this limited goal clear to readers. For example, one can perhaps build the case for heavy television viewing as *one* cause of stereotyping, loss of sensitivity to violence, and increased fearfulness. But we know that the home environment and neighborhood and school environments also do much to shape attitudes.

- **What reasons and evidence are given to support the argument?** Can you see the writer's pattern of development? Does the reasoning seem logical? Are the data relevant? This kind of analysis of the argument will help you evaluate it.

- **Does the argument demonstrate causality, not just a time relationship or correlation?** A causal argument needs to prove *agency:* A is the cause of B, not just something that happened before B or something that is present when B is present. March precedes April, but March does not cause April to arrive.

- **Does the writer present believable causal agents, agents consistent with our knowledge of human behavior and scientific laws?** Most educated people do not believe that personalities are shaped by astrological signs or that scientific laws are suspended in the Bermuda Triangle, allowing planes and ships to vanish or enter a fourth dimension.

- **What are the implications for accepting the causal argument?** If A and B clearly are the causes of C, and we don't want C to occur, then we presumably must do something about A and B—or at least we must do something about either A or B and see if reducing or eliminating one of the causes significantly reduces the incidence of C.

- **Is the argument convincing?** After analyzing the argument and answering the questions given in the previous points, you need to decide if, finally, the argument works.

Preparing a Causal Argument

In addition to the guidelines for writing arguments presented in Chapter 4, you can use the following advice specific to writing causal arguments.

Planning

1. **Think:** What are the focus and limits of your causal argument? Do you want to argue for one cause of an event or situation? Do you want to argue for several causes leading to an event or situation? Do you want to argue for a cause that others have overlooked? Do you want to show how one cause is common to several situations or events? Diagramming the relationship of cause to effect may help you see what you want to focus on. (See box, page 226).

2. **Think:** What reasons and evidence do you have to support your tentative claim? Consider what you already know that has led to your choice of topic. A brainstorming list may be helpful.

3. **Think:** How, then, do you want to word your claim? As we have discussed, wording is crucial in causal arguments. Review the discussion of characteristics of causal arguments if necessary.

4. **Think:** What, if any, additional evidence do you need to develop a convincing argument? You may need to do some reading or online searching to obtain data to strengthen your argument. Readers expect relevant, reliable, current statistics in most arguments about cause. Assess what you need and then think about what sources will provide the needed information.

5. **Think:** What assumptions (warrants) are you making in your causal reasoning? Do these assumptions hold up to logical scrutiny? Will readers be likely to agree with your assumptions, or will you need to defend them as part of the development of your argument? For example: One reason to defend the effects of heavy TV watching on viewers is the commonsense argument that what humans devote considerable time to will have a significant effect on their lives. Will your readers be prepared to accept this commonsense reasoning, or will they remain skeptical, looking for stronger evidence of a cause/effect relationship?

Drafting

1. Begin with an opening paragraph or two that introduces your topic in an interesting way. Lester Thurow in "Why Women Are Paid Less Than Men" writes:

    > In the 40 years from 1939 to 1979 white women who work full time have with monotonous regularity made slightly less than 60 percent as much as white men. Why?

    This opening establishes the topic and Thurow's purpose in examining causes. The statistics get the reader's attention.

2.   Do not begin by announcing your subject. Avoid openers such as: In this essay I will explain the causes of teen vandalism.

3.   Decide where to place your claim statement. You can conclude your opening paragraph with it, or you can place it in your conclusion, after you have shown readers how best to understand the causes of the issue you are examining. Thurow uses the second approach effectively in his essay.

4.   Present reasons and evidence in an organized way. If you are examining a series of causes, beginning with background conditions and early influences, then your basic plan will be time sequence. Readers need to see the chain of causes unfolding. Use appropriate terms and transitional words to guide readers through each stage in the causal pattern. If you are arguing for an overlooked cause, begin with the causes that have been put forward and show what is flawed in each one. Then present and defend your explanation of cause. This process of elimination structure works well when readers are likely to know what other causes have been offered in the past. You can also use one of Mill's other two approaches, if one of them is relevant to your situation. That is, you can present the points of commonality or difference that show your explanation of cause to be valid.

5.   Address the issue of correlation rather than cause, if appropriate. After presenting the results of a study of marriage that reveals many benefits (emotional, physical, financial) of marriage, Linda Waite examines the question that she knows skeptical readers may have: Does marriage actually *cause* the benefits, or is the relationship one of *correlation* only—that is, the benefits of marriage just happen to come with being married; they are not caused by being married.

6.   Conclude by discussing the implications of the causal pattern you have argued for, if appropriate. Lester Thurow ends by asserting that if he is right about the cause of the gender pay gap, then there are two approaches society can take to remove the pay gap. If, in explaining the causes of teen vandalism, you see one cause as "group behavior," a gang looking for something to do, it then follows that you can advise young readers to stay out of gangs. Often with arguments about cause, there are personal or public policy implications in accepting the causal explanation.

A CHECKLIST FOR REVISION

☐   Do I have a clear statement of my claim? Is it appropriately qualified and focused?

☐   Have I organized my argument so that readers can see my pattern for examining cause?

☐   Have I used the language for discussing causes correctly, distinguishing among conditions and influences and remote and proximate causes? Have I selected the correct word—either *affect* or *effect*—as needed?

☐ Have I avoided the *post hoc* fallacy and the confusing of correlation and cause?

☐ Have I carefully examined my assumptions and convinced myself that they are reasonable and can be defended? Have I defended them when necessary to clarify and thus strengthen my argument?

☐ Have I found relevant facts and examples to support and develop my argument?

☐ Have I used the basic checklist for revision in Chapter 4 (see page 110)?

Read and study the following annotated argument. Complete your analysis of and response to the essay by answering the questions that follow.

A SPECIOUS "EXPERIMENT" | EUGENE ROBINSON

A graduate of the University of Michigan where he was the first black student to be co-editor-in-chief of the university's student newspaper, Eugene Robinson joined the *Washington Post* in 1980. He has served as city reporter, foreign correspondent, and managing editor in charge of the paper's style section. He is now an associate editor and twice-weekly columnist. Robinson focuses on the mix of culture and politics as the following column, published October 4, 2005, reveals.

PREREADING QUESTIONS What does the word *specious* mean? (If you do not know, look it up.) Why does Robinson put *experiment* in quotation marks?

<table>
<tr>
<td valign="top" width="20%">

Attention-getting opening—how the author will deal with the situation.

</td>
<td valign="top">

1   There's no need to pillory William Bennett for his "thought experiment" about how aborting all black children would affect the crime rate. I believe him when he says he wasn't actually advocating genocide, just musing about it to make a point. Instead of going into high-dudgeon mode, let's put him on the couch.

</td>
</tr>
<tr>
<td valign="top">

Explanation of the situation— what Bennett did and how he defended his actions.

</td>
<td valign="top">

2   Bennett, the former education secretary and anti-drug czar who has found a new calling in talk radio, told his audience last week that "if you wanted to reduce crime, you could—if that were your sole purpose—you could abort every black baby in this country, and your crime rate would go down." He quickly added that doing so would be "impossible, ridiculous and morally reprehensible," which is certainly true.

3   So why would such a horrible idea even cross his mind? How could such an evil notion ever pass his lips?

4   Bennett was referring to research done by Steven D. Levitt, a University of Chicago economist and lead author of the best-selling book *Freakonomics*. The iconoclastic Levitt, something of an academic rock star, argues that the steep drop in crime in the United States over the past 15 years resulted in part from the *Roe v. Wade* decision legalizing abortion.

5   In defending his words, Bennett has said he was citing *Freakonomics*. So why did his "thought experiment" refer only to *black* children?

</td>
</tr>
</table>

Levitt's thesis is essentially that unwanted children who grow up poor in single-parent households are more likely than other children to become criminals, and that *Roe v. Wade* resulted in fewer of these children being born. What he doesn't do in the book is single out black children.

Perhaps the ostentatiously intellectual Bennett went back and read Levitt's original 2001 paper on the subject, co-authored with John J. Donohue III. The authors do mention race briefly, in a discussion of the falling homicide rate, but attribute most of the decline to those race-neutral factors that Levitt later cited in *Freakonomics*. To bolster their argument, they cite research on abortion and lowered crime rates in Scandinavia and Eastern Europe—not places where you're likely to find a lot of black people.

If he was citing Levitt's work, Bennett could have said that to lower the crime rate "you could abort every white baby" or "you could abort every Hispanic baby" or "you could abort every Asian baby," since every group has unwanted, poor children being raised by single mothers.

So now that we have Bennett on the couch, shouldn't we conclude that he mentioned only black children because, perhaps on a subconscious level, he associates "black" with "criminal"?

That's what it sounds like to me. I grew up in the South in the days when we had to drink at "colored" water fountains and gas stations had separate "colored" restrooms; I know what a real racist is like, and Bennett certainly doesn't fit the description. But that's what's so troubling about his race-specific "thought experiment"—that such a smart, well-meaning opinion maker would so casually say something that translates, to African American ears, as "blacks are criminals."

What makes it worse is that his words came in the context of abortion. That Bennett staunchly opposes abortion is beside the point. He should know enough history to understand why black Americans would react strongly when whites start imagining experiments to limit black reproduction. For hundreds of years, this country was obsessed with the supposed menace of black sexuality and fertility. Bennett's remarks have to make you wonder whether that obsession has really vanished or just been deemed off-limits in polite discourse.

I've heard people argue—mostly in discussions of affirmative action—that the nation's problem of racial discrimination has mostly been solved. The issue now is class, they say, not race. I'd like to believe that, but I don't.

Bennett is too intelligent not to understand why many of us would take his mental experiment as a glimpse behind the curtain—an indication that old assumptions, now unspoken, still survive. He ought to understand how his words would be taken as validation by the rapper Kanye West, who told a television audience that "George Bush doesn't care about black people," or by the New Orleans survivors who keep calling me with theories of how "they" dynamited selected levees to flood the poor, black Lower Ninth Ward and save the wealthy French Quarter and Garden District.

I have a thought experiment of my own: If we put our racial baggage on the table and talk about it, we'll begin to take care of a lot of unfinished business.

6

7 — Possible cause for Bennett's "experiment" and Robinson's rejection of this cause.

8

9 — Robinson's explanation of the cause of Bennett's "thought experiment."

10

11 — Historical cause for the reactions of blacks to Bennett's remarks.

12

13

Robinson's solution to the problem exposed by Bennett's remarks.

14

QUESTIONS FOR READING

1. What is the occasion for Robinson's column? That is, what has led him to write this particular essay?
2. What does the author want to "do" with Bennett, instead of "going into high-dudgeon mode"? What does the expression in quotation marks mean?
3. What was Bennett's explanation for his comments?
4. Why does Robinson reject Bennett's explanation? How does he explain Bennett's "thought experiment"?

QUESTIONS FOR REASONING AND ANALYSIS

1. What is Robinson's claim? What does he assert about Bennett? About America?
2. How does the author support his claim? What Mill strategy does he use?
3. How would you describe the essay's tone? How does the tone help Robinson with readers?
4. Can you think of any other reasonable cause for Bennett's "thought experiment"? Evaluate the argument.

QUESTIONS FOR REFLECTING AND WRITING

1. Do you agree with Robinson that Bennett probably holds some racist views? Why or why not?
2. Do you agree with Robinson that American society still has issues with racism? Why or why not?
3. Does Robinson have a good suggestion in his conclusion? Why or why not?

THE PROBLEM/SOLUTION ARGUMENT: EXPLORING PUBLIC POLICY ISSUES

Many of the arguments over public policy can be understood as arguments over solutions to problems. Consider the following policy claims.

1. Drunk drivers should receive mandatory six-month suspensions of their licenses.
2. We need to spend whatever is necessary to stop the flow of drugs into this country.
3. The school year in the United States should be extended by at least thirty days.

Each one of these policy claims offers a solution to a problem, as we can see:

1. Fewer people will drink and drive, causing accidents, if they know they will lose their licenses.
2. The way to address the drug problem in this country is to eliminate the supply of drugs.

3.   For America to compete in the world, new generations will have to be bet-
     ter educated; to reach that goal a longer school year is necessary.

Let's think about the characteristics of claims of policy as problem/solution
arguments.

Characteristics of Problem/Solution Arguments

- *Claims of policy usually focus on the nature of the problem, for how we define a
  problem has much to do with what kinds of solutions become appropriate.* For example, some people are concerned about our ability to feed a growing
  world population. But many will argue that the problem is not an agricultural one (how much food we can produce) so much as a political one (to
  whom will the food be distributed and at what cost). If the problem is agricultural, we need to worry about available farmland, water supply, and
  farming technology. If the problem is political, we need to worry about price
  supports, distribution to poor countries, and grain embargoes imposed for
  political leverage. To support a policy claim, you first need to define the
  problem.
- *How the problem is defined also affects what you think are the causes of the problem.*
  Cause is often a part of the debate and may need to be addressed, particularly if solutions are tied to eliminating what you consider to be the causes.
- *Successful problem/solution arguments present viable solutions, solutions that are
  connected to what can realistically be accomplished.* Consider Prohibition, for example. This was a solution to problem drinking—except that it didn't work,
  couldn't be enforced, because the majority of Americans wouldn't accept
  the law.
- *Claims of policy need to be developed with an understanding of the processes of
  government, from college administrations to federal structures.*

GUIDELINES for Analyzing Problem/Solution Arguments

When analyzing problem/solution arguments, what should you look for?
In addition to the basics of good argument, use the following points as
guides to analyzing:

- **Is the writer's claim not just clear but appropriately qualified and focused?** For example, if the school board in the writer's community is not
  doing a good job of communicating its goals as a basis for its funding
  package, the writer needs to focus just on that particular school board, not
  on school boards in general.
- **Does the writer show an awareness of the complexity of most public
  policy issues?** There are many different kinds of problems with American
  schools and many more causes for those problems. A simple solution—a
  longer school year, more money spent, vouchers—is not likely to solve the
  mixed bag of problems. Oversimplified arguments quickly lose credibility.

- **How does the writer define and explain the problem?** Is the way the problem is stated clear? Does it make sense to you? If the problem is being defined differently than most people have defined it, has the writer argued convincingly for looking at the problem in this new way?

- **What reasons and evidence are given to support the writer's solutions?** Can you see how the writer develops the argument? Does the reasoning seem logical? Is the data relevant? This kind of analysis will help you evaluate the proposed solutions.

- **Does the writer address the feasibility of the proposed solutions?** Does the writer make a convincing case for the realistic possibility of achieving the proposed solutions?

- **Is the argument convincing?** Will the solutions solve the problem as it has been defined? Has the problem been defined accurately? Can the solutions be achieved?

Preparing a Problem/Solution Argument

In addition to the guidelines for writing arguments presented in Chapter 4, you can use the following advice specific to defending claims of policy.

Planning

1. **Think:** What should be the focus and limits of your argument? There's a big difference between presenting solutions to the problem of physical abuse of women by men and presenting solutions to the problem of date rape on your college campus. Select a topic that you know something about that you can realistically handle.

2. **Think:** What reasons and evidence do you have to support your tentative claim? Think through what you already know that has led you to select your particular topic. Suppose you want to write on the issue of campus rapes. Is this choice due to a recent event on the campus? Was this event the first in many years, or the last in a trend? Where and when are they occurring? A brainstorming list may be helpful.

3. **Think:** Is there additional evidence that you need to obtain to develop your argument? If so, where can you look for that evidence? Are there past issues of the campus paper in your library? Will the campus police grant you an interview?

4. **Think:** What about the feasibility of each solution you plan to present? Are you thinking in terms of essentially one solution with several parts to it or several separate solutions, perhaps to be implemented by different people? Will coordination be necessary to achieve success? How will this be accomplished? For the problem of campus rape, you may want to consider several solutions as a package to be coordinated by the counseling service or an administrative vice president.

Drafting

1. Begin by either reminding readers of the existing problem you will address or arguing that a current situation should be recognized as a problem. In many cases, you can count on an audience who sees the world as you do and recognizes the problem you will address. But in some cases, your first task will be to convince readers that a problem exists that should worry them. If they are not concerned, they won't be interested in your solutions.

2. Be sure, early in your essay, to define the problem—as you see it—for readers. Do not assume that they will necessarily accept your way of seeing the issue. You may need to defend your assessment of the nature of the problem before moving on to solutions.

3. If appropriate, explain the cause or causes of the problem. If your proposed solution is tied to removing the cause or causes of the problem, then you need to establish cause and prove it early in your argument. If cause is important, argue for it; if it is irrelevant, move to your solution.

4. Explain your solution. If you have several solutions, think about how best to order them. If several need to be developed in a sequence, then present them in that necessary sequence. If you are presenting a package of diverse actions that together will solve the problem, then consider presenting them from the simplest to the more complex. With a problem of campus rape, for example, you may want to suggest better lighting on campus paths at night plus an escort service for women who are afraid to walk home alone plus sensitivity training for male students. Following that order might be the best. Adding more lampposts is much easier than getting students to take sensitivity classes.

5. Explain the process for achieving your solution. If you have not thought through the political or legal steps necessary to implement your solution, then this step cannot be part of your purpose in writing. However, anticipating a skeptical audience that says "How are we going to do that?" you would be wise to have precise steps to offer your reader. You may have obtained an estimate of costs for new lighting on your campus and want to suggest specific paths that need the lights. You may have investigated escort services at other colleges and can spell out how such a service can be implemented on your campus. Showing readers that you have thought ahead to the next steps in the process can be an effective method of persuasion.

6. Support the feasibility of your solution. Be able to estimate costs. Show that you know who would be responsible for implementing. Explain how your solutions can be sold to people who may be unwilling to accommodate your proposals. All of this information will strengthen your argument.

7. Show how your solution is better than others. Anticipate challenges by including in your paper reasons for adopting your program rather than another program. Explain how your solution will be more easily adopted or more effective when implemented than other possibilities. Of course, a less practical but still viable defense is that your solution is the right thing to do. Values also belong in public policy debates, not just issues of cost and acceptability.

A CHECKLIST FOR REVISION ■•■•■•■•■•■•■•■•■•■•■•■•■•■•■•■•■•■•■•■

- ☐ Do I have a clear statement of my policy claim? Is it appropriately qualified and focused?
- ☐ Have I clearly explained how I see the problem to be solved? If necessary, have I argued for seeing the problem that way?
- ☐ Have I presented my solutions—and argued for them—in a clear and logical structure? Have I explained how these solutions can be implemented and why they are better than other solutions that have been suggested?
- ☐ Have I used data that are relevant and current?
- ☐ Have I used the basic checklist for revision in Chapter 4? (See page 110.)

Read and study the following annotated argument. Complete your analysis of and response to the essay by answering the questions that follow.

A NEW STRATEGY FOR THE WAR ON DRUGS | JAMES Q. WILSON

Author of *The Moral Sense*, James Q. Wilson is a professor of public policy at Pepperdine University. His solution to America's drug problem was published on April 13, 2000, in the *Wall Street Journal*.

Opening presents two solutions that Wilson will challenge.

1   The current Senate deliberation over aid to Colombia aimed at fighting narcotics reminds us that there are two debates over how the government ought to deal with dangerous drugs. The first is about their illegality and the second is about their control. People who wish to legalize drugs and those who wish to curtail their supply believe that their methods will reduce crime. Both these views are mistaken, but there is a third way.

2   Advocates of legalization think that both buyers and sellers would benefit. People who can buy drugs freely and at something like free-market prices would no longer have to steal to afford cocaine or heroin; dealers would no longer have to use violence and corruption to maintain their market share. Though drugs may harm people, reducing this harm would be a medical problem not a criminal-justice one. Crime would drop sharply.

PRICES WOULD FALL

Wilson rebuts first solution.

3   But there is an error in this calculation. Legalizing drugs means letting the price fall to its competitive rate (plus taxes and advertising costs). That market price would probably be somewhere between one-third and 1/20th of the illegal price. And more than the market price would fall. As Harvard's Mark Moore has pointed out, the "risk price"—that is, all the hazards associated with buying drugs, from being arrested to being ripped off—would also fall, and this decline might be more important than the lower purchase price.

4   Under a legal regime, the consumption of low-priced, low-risk drugs would increase dramatically. We do not know by how much, but the little evidence we have suggests a sharp rise. Until 1968 Britain allowed doctors to prescribe

heroin. Some doctors cheated, and their medically unnecessary prescriptions helped increase the number of known heroin addicts by a factor of 40. As a result, the government abandoned the prescription policy in favor of administering heroin in clinics and later replacing heroin with methadone.

When the Netherlands ceased enforcing laws against the purchase or pos- 5 session of marijuana, the result was a sharp increase in its use. Cocaine and heroin create much greater dependency, and so the increase in their use would probably be even greater.

The average user would probably commit fewer crimes if these drugs 6 were sold legally. But the total number of users would increase sharply. A large fraction of these new users would be unable to keep a steady job. Unless we were prepared to support them with welfare payments, crime would be one of their main sources of income. That is, the number of drug-related crimes *per user* might fall even as the total number of drug-related crimes increased. Add to the list of harms more deaths from overdose, more babies born to addicted mothers, more accidents by drug-influenced automobile drivers and fewer people able to hold jobs or act as competent parents.

Treating such people would become far more difficult. As psychiatrist Sally 7 Satel has written on this page, many drug users will not enter and stay in treatment unless they are compelled to do so. Phoenix House, the largest national residential drug treatment program, rarely admits patients who admit they have a problem and need help. The great majority are coerced by somebody— a judge, probation officer or school official—into attending. Phoenix House CEO Mitchell Rosenthal opposes legalization, and for good reason. Legalization means less coercion, and that means more addicts and addicts who are harder to treat.

Douglas Anglin, drawing on experiences in California and elsewhere, has 8 shown that people compelled to stay in treatment do at least as well as those who volunteer for it, and they tend (of necessity) to stay in the program longer. If we legalize drugs, the chances of treatment making a difference are greatly reduced. And as for drug-use prevention, forget it. Try telling your children not to use a legal substance.

But people who want to keep drugs illegal have problems of their own. 9 The major thrust of government spending has been to reduce the supply of drugs by cutting their production overseas, intercepting their transfer into the U.S. and arresting dealers. Because of severe criminal penalties, especially on handlers of crack cocaine, our prisons have experienced a huge increase in persons sentenced on drug charges. In the early 1980s, about 1/12th of all prison inmates were in for drug convictions; now well over one-third are.

No one can be certain how imprisoning drug suppliers affects drug use, 10 but we do know that an arrested drug dealer is easily replaced. Moreover, the government can never seize more than a small fraction of the drugs entering the country, a fraction that is easily replaced.

Emphasizing supply over treatment is dangerous. Not only do we spend 11 huge sums on it; not only do we drag a reluctant U.S. military into the campaign;

Wilson rebuts second solution.

we also heighten corruption and violence in countries such as Colombia and Mexico. The essential fact is this: Demand will produce supply.

12   We can do much more to reduce demand. Some four million Americans are currently on probation or parole. From tests done on them when they are jailed, we know that half or more had a drug problem when arrested. Though a lot of drug users otherwise obey the law (or at least avoid getting arrested), probationers and parolees constitute the hard core of dangerous addicts. Reducing their demand for drugs ought to be our highest priority.

Wilson presents his solution.

13   Mark Kleiman of UCLA has suggested a program of "testing and control": Probationers and parolees would be required to take frequent drug tests— say, twice weekly—as a condition of remaining on the street. If you failed the test, you would spend more time in jail; if you passed it, you would remain free. This approach would be an inducement for people to enter and stay in treatment.

14   This would require some big changes in how we handle offenders. Police, probation and parole officers would be responsible for conducting these tests, and more officers would have to be hired. Probation and parole authorities would have to be willing to sanction a test failure by immediate incarceration, initially for a short period (possibly a weekend), and then for longer periods if the initial failure were repeated. Treatment programs at little or no cost to the user would have to be available not only in every prison, but for every drug-dependent probationer and parolee.

Challenges of implementing his solution.

15   These things are not easily done. Almost every state claims to have an intensive community supervision program, but few offenders are involved in them, the frequency with which they are contacted is low, and most were released from supervision without undergoing any punishment for violating its conditions.

16   But there is some hope. Our experience with drug courts suggests that the procedural problems can be overcome. In such courts, several hundred of which now exist, special judges oversee drug-dependent offenders, insisting that they work to overcome their habits. While under drug-court supervision, offenders reduce drug consumption and, at least for a while after leaving the court, offenders are less likely to be arrested.

How solution can work.

17   Our goal ought to be to extend meaningful community supervision to all probationers and parolees, especially those who have a serious drug or alcohol problem. Efforts to test Mr. Kleiman's proposals are under way in Connecticut and Maryland.

18   If this demand-reduction strategy works, it can be expanded. Drug tests can be given to people who apply for government benefits, such as welfare and public housing. Some critics will think this is an objectionable intrusion. But giving benefits without conditions weakens the character-building responsibility of society.

PREVENT HARM TO OTHERS

19   John Stuart Mill, the great libertarian thinker, argued that the only justifiable reason for restricting human liberty is to prevent harm to others. Serious

drug abuse does harm others. We could, of course, limit government action to remedying those harms without addressing their causes, but that is an up-hill struggle, especially when the harms fall on unborn children. Fetal drug syndrome imposes large costs on infants who have had no voice in choosing their fate.

Even Mill was clear that full liberty cannot be given to children or barbar-   20   ians. By "barbarians" he meant people who are incapable of being improved by free and equal discussion. The life of a serious drug addict—the life of someone driven by drug dependency to prostitution and crime—is the life of a barbarian.

Defense of his solution based on practicality and values.

QUESTIONS FOR READING

1.   What are the two solutions to the drug problem presented by others?
2.   Why, according to Wilson, will legalizing drugs not be a good solution? What are the specific negative consequences of legalization?
3.   Government strategies for controlling illegal drugs have included what activities?
4.   What percentage of prisoners are now in prison on drug charges?
5.   What problems do we face trying to reduce the supply of drugs? What, according to Wilson, drives supply?
6.   What is Wilson's proposed solution? Explain the details of his solution.
7.   What are some of the difficulties with the author's solution? What does he gain by bringing up possible difficulties?

QUESTIONS FOR REASONING AND ANALYSIS

1.   What does Wilson seek to accomplish in his concluding two paragraphs? What potential counterargument does he seek to rebut in his conclusion?
2.   On what argument might one agree that Wilson's solution is workable and still object to it? (Think about his concluding comments.)

QUESTIONS FOR REFLECTING AND WRITING

1.   Has Wilson convinced you that legalizing drugs will not reduce crime? Why or why not?
2.   Is his argument against the supply-reduction approach convincing? Why or why not?
3.   Has Wilson's defense of his solution convinced you that it is workable?
4.   Do you have a solution to the drug problem?

FOR ANALYSIS AND DEBATE

WHY WOMEN ARE PAID LESS THAN MEN | LESTER C. THUROW

A professor at the MIT Sloan School of Management and consultant to both government and private corporations, Lester C. Thurow has written extensively on economic and public policy issues. His books include *The Political Economy of Income Redistribution Policies* (1977) and *Dangerous Currents* (1983). "Why Women Are Paid Less Than Men," published in the *New York Times* (March 8, 1981), offers an explanation for the discrepancy between the incomes of men and women.

PREREADING QUESTIONS When he asks "why" at the end of paragraph 1, what kind of analysis or argument does Thurow signal he will develop? Were you aware that women still earn less than men?

1   In the 40 years from 1939 to 1979 white women who work full time have with monotonous regularity made slightly less than 60 percent as much as white men. Why?

2   Over the same time period, minorities have made substantial progress in catching up with whites, with minority women making even more progress than minority men.

3   Black men now earn 72 percent as much as white men (up 16 percentage points since the mid-1950s) but black women earn 92 percent as much as white women. Hispanic men make 71 percent of what their white counterparts do, but Hispanic women make 82 percent as much as white women. As a result of their faster progress, fully employed black women make 75 percent as much as fully employed black men while Hispanic women earn 68 percent as much as Hispanic men.

4   This faster progress may, however, end when minority women finally catch up with white women. In the bible of the New Right, George Gilder's *Wealth and Poverty*, the 60 percent is just one of Mother Nature's constants like the speed of light or the force of gravity.

5   Men are programmed to provide for their families economically while women are programmed to take care of their families emotionally and physically. As a result men put more effort into their jobs than women. The net result is a difference in work intensity that leads to that 40 percent gap in earnings. But there is no discrimination against women—only the biological facts of life.

6   The problem with this assertion is just that. It is an assertion with no evidence for it other than the fact that white women have made 60 percent as much as men for a long period of time.

7   "Discrimination against women" is an easy answer but it also has its problems as an adequate explanation. Why is discrimination against women not declining under the same social forces that are leading to a lessening of discrimination against minorities? In recent years women have made more use of the enforcement provisions of the Equal Employment Opportunities Com-

mission and the courts than minorities. Why do the laws that prohibit discrimination against women and minorities work for minorities but not for women?

When men discriminate against women, they run into a problem. To discriminate against women is to discriminate against your own wife and to lower your own family income. To prevent women from working is to force men to work more.   8

When whites discriminate against blacks, they can at least think that they are raising their own incomes. When men discriminate against women they have to know that they are lowering their own family income and increasing their own work effort.   9

While discrimination undoubtedly explains part of the male-female earnings differential, one has to believe that men are monumentally stupid or irrational to explain all of the earnings gap in terms of discrimination. There must be something else going on.   10

Back in 1939 it was possible to attribute the earnings gap to large differences in educational attainments. But the educational gap between men and women has been eliminated since World War II. It is no longer possible to use education as an explanation for the lower earnings of women.   11

Some observers have argued that women earn less money since they are less reliable workers who are more apt to leave the labor force. But it is difficult to maintain this position since women are less apt to quit one job to take another and as a result they tend to work as long, or longer, for any one employer. From any employer's perspective they are more reliable, not less reliable, than men.   12

Part of the answer is visible if you look at the lifetime earnings profile of men. Suppose that you are asked to predict which men in a group of 25-year-olds would become economically successful. At age 25 it is difficult to tell who will be economically successful and your predictions are apt to be highly inaccurate.   13

But suppose that you were asked to predict which men in a group of 35-year-olds would become economically successful. If you are successful at age 35 you are very likely to remain successful for the rest of your life. If you have not become economically successful by age 35, you are very unlikely to do so later.   14

The decade between 25 and 35 is when men either succeed or fail. It is the decade when lawyers become partners in the good firms, when business managers make it onto the "fast track," when academics get tenure at good universities, and when blue-collar workers find the job opportunities that will lead to training opportunities and the skills that will generate high earnings.   15

If there is any one decade when it pays to work hard and to be consistently in the labor force, it is the decade between 25 and 35. For those who succeed, earnings will rise rapidly. For those who fail, earnings will remain flat for the rest of their lives.   16

But the decade between 25 and 35 is precisely the decade when women are most apt to leave the labor force or become part-time workers to have children. When they do, the current system of promotion and skill acquisition will extract an enormous lifetime price.   17

18   This leaves essentially two avenues for equalizing male and female earnings.

19   Families where women who wish to have successful careers, compete with men, and achieve the same earnings should alter their family plans and have their children either before 25 or after 35. Or society can attempt to alter the existing promotion and skill acquisition system so that there is a longer time period in which both men and women can attempt to successfully enter the labor force.

20   Without some combination of these two factors, a substantial fraction of the male-female earnings differentials are apt to persist for the next 40 years, even if discrimination against women is eliminated.

QUESTIONS FOR READING

1. What situation is the subject of Thurow's argument?
2. Briefly explain why Thurow rejects each of the possible explanations that he covers.
3. What is the author's explanation for the discrepancy between the earnings of white women and white men?

QUESTIONS FOR REASONING AND ANALYSIS

1. What questions should you ask about Thurow's numbers? Do you know the answer to the question?
2. What is Thurow's claim?
3. What evidence does the author provide for his claim? Is it convincing?
4. What strategy for determining cause does Thurow use?

QUESTIONS FOR REFLECTING AND WRITING

1. Do you agree that most people who are going to be successful are so by age 35? Can you think of people who did not become successful until after 35? Is this the kind of assumption that can create its own reality?
2. Evaluate the two solutions Thurow proposes. Do they follow logically from his causal analysis?
3. Thurow's figures are based on the total earnings of workers; they are not comparisons by job category. What are other facts about jobs that men and women hold that may account for some of the discrepancy in pay?

FOUR MYTHS, 30 MILLION POTENTIAL VOTES | BETH SHULMAN

A lawyer, Beth Shulman is vice president, director, and executive board member of the United Food and Commercial Workers Union of the AFL-CIO. She is the author of *The Betrayal of Work: How Low-Wage Jobs Fail 30 Million Americans* (2003). The following article appeared in the *Washington Post* on August 17, 2003.

PREREADING QUESTIONS What meaning of the word myth does the author use? What percentage of American families earn $18,000 a year or less? Are you surprised by this figure?

As the presidential campaigns seek definition, one pivotal issue remains 1 hidden from view. It is potentially huge, especially for Democrats, because it involves their natural constituents, and it addresses core issues of the economy, social justice and fairness. The issue is low-wage work.

Fully 30 million Americans—one in four U.S. workers—earn $8.70 an hour 2 or less, a rate that works out to $18,100 a year, which is the current official poverty level in the United States for a family of four. These low-wage jobs usually lack health care, child care, pensions and vacation benefits. Their working conditions are often grueling, dangerous, even humiliating.

At the same time, more and more middle-class jobs are taking on many of 3 these same characteristics, losing the security and benefits once taken for granted.

The shameful reality of low-wage work in America should be on every 4 Democrat's cue card as a potential weapon to be used against the Republicans' rosy economic scenario. But so far it isn't. Why not? One reason may be four long-standing myths that have for years drowned out a rational discussion of what should be a national call to conscience:

MYTH #1: LOW-WAGE WORK IS MERELY A TEMPORARY STEP ON THE LADDER TO A BETTER JOB

According to the American dream, if you work hard, apply yourself and 5 play by the rules, you will be able to earn a decent living for yourself and your family. If you fail to move up, you must be lazy or incompetent.

THE TRUTH

Low-wage job mobility is minimal. Low-wage workers have few career lad- 6 ders. Those of us lucky enough to have better-paying employment depend on them every day. They are nursing home and home health care workers who care for our parents; they are poultry processors who bone and package our chicken; they are retail clerks in department stores, grocery stores and convenience stores; they are housekeepers and janitors who keep our hotel rooms and offices clean; they are billing and telephone call center workers who take our complaints and answer our questions; and they are teaching assistants in our schools and child care workers who free us so that we can work ourselves.

In a recent study following U.S. adults through their working careers, eco- 7 nomics professors Peter Gottschalk of Boston College and Sheldon Danziger of the University of Michigan found that about half of those whose earnings ranked in the bottom 20 percent in 1968 were still in the same group in 1991. Of those who had moved up, nearly two-thirds remained below the median income. The U.S. economy provides less mobility for low-wage earners, according to an Organization for Economic Cooperation and Development study, than the economies of France, Italy, the United Kingdom, Germany, Denmark, Finland or Sweden.

Today's economy is even more rigid. In many industries, such as insurance, 8 retail and financial services, wealthier clients are served by different employees than lower-status customers. This makes it harder for the lowest wage earners to move up. Some do, but this happens primarily in the manufacturing sector, where the number of jobs continues to decline.

MYTH #2: TRAINING AND NEW SKILLS SOLVE THE PROBLEM

9   Low-wage workers are said to lack the necessary skills for better-paying work in our changing economy. What's needed is retraining and better education for everyone.

THE TRUTH

10   The problem is that there are fewer better jobs to move into. The percentage of low-wage jobs is growing, not shrinking. The growing sectors of our economy are the labor-intensive industries. The two-lowest-paid work categories, retail and service, increased their share of the job market from 30 percent to 48 percent between 1965 and 1998. By the end of the decade, the low end of the job market will account for more than 30 percent of the American workforce. There will be about 1.8 million software engineers and computer support specialists, but more than 3.8 million cashiers.

11   According to the U.S. Bureau of Labor Statistics, half of all new jobs by 2010 will require relatively brief on-the-job training. Only three of every 10 positions currently require more than a high school diploma. Certainly, raising skills and education levels will lead some workers to higher wages and better jobs. But that approach will do little to improve the lives of most of the hardworking women and men in the jobs that will continue to grow as a proportion of our economy.

12   Just as important, those who denigrate low-wage work as "low-skilled" ignore the reality of these jobs. A nursing-home worker must be compassionate, must pay attention to detail and must possess psychological and emotional strength; a call-center worker must have patience and must be able to command enough information to handle questions and complaints; a security guard must be dedicated, alert and conscientious. To say these workers need retraining to earn more lets their employers off the hook for failing to compensate them appropriately for their existing skills and duties.

MYTH #3: GLOBALIZATION STOPS US FROM DOING ANYTHING ABOUT THIS PROBLEM

13   Between 1979 and 1999, 3 million manufacturing jobs vanished as global trade brought in textiles, shoes, cars and steel produced by overseas labor. In June 2003 alone, 56,000 manufacturing jobs were lost. American employers must keep wages and benefits low if they are to compete in the global marketplace.

THE TRUTH

14   Very few low-wage jobs are now in globally competitive industries. It is true that global trade has had a profound impact on our economy and on American workers. But companies in Beijing are not competing with child care providers, nursing homes, restaurants, security guard firms and janitorial services in the United States. Checking out groceries, waiting on tables, servicing office equipment and tending the sick cannot be done from overseas.

Employers and politicians use globalization as an excuse to do nothing for 15
low-wage workers, scaring them into accepting lower pay, fewer benefits and
less job security. It is invoked to justify reduced social spending and less workplace regulation, and workers believe they are powerless to object. Yet not
only does globalization fail to apply to most of America's low-wage jobs, other
industrialized countries facing the same global competition have chosen differently: They provide social safety nets, notably including guaranteed health
care. As a result, according to a 1997 study by Timothy Smeeding of Syracuse
University, Americans in the lowest income brackets have living standards that
are 13 percent below those of low-income Germans and 24 percent below the
bottom 20 percent of Swedes.

MYTH #4: LOW-WAGE JOBS ARE MERELY THE RESULT
OF AN EFFICIENT MARKET

The economy is a force of nature, and we as a society have little control 16
over whatever difficulties it creates.

THE TRUTH

The economic world we live in is the result of our creation, not natural law. 17
America's low-wage workers have little power to change their conditions because of a series of political, economic and corporate decisions over the past
quarter-century that undercut the bargaining power of workers, especially
those in lower pay grades.

Those decisions included the push to increase global trade and open 18
global markets, changes in immigration law, the deregulation of industries that
had been highly unionized, Federal Reserve policies focused on reducing inflation threats, and a corporate ideological shift that eliminated America's postwar social contract with workers and emphasized maximizing shareholder
value. Those decisions worsened conditions in low-wage jobs and exaggerated
disparities in income and wealth.

America's most vulnerable workers have also lost many institutions, laws 19
and political allies that could have helped counterbalance these forces. In the
1950s, the number of American workers who were fired, harassed or threatened for trying to organize a union was in the hundreds a year. According to
Human Rights Watch, by 1990 that number exceeded 20,000. In 1979, one-
fourth of private-sector workers were unionized; only 11 percent are today.
At the same time, the purchasing power of the federal minimum wage fell 30
percent during the 1980s. Despite minimal increases in the 1990s, according
to calculations by the Economic Policy Institute, the value of the current minimum wage of $5.15 per hour is still 21 percent less than it was in 1979.

The richest country in the world should not tolerate such treatment of 20
more than a fourth of its workers. The myths of upward mobility and inevitable
market forces blind too many people to the grim reality of low-wage work. A
presidential campaign is the right time to begin a conversation on how to
change it.

QUESTIONS FOR READING

1. What is Shulman's subject?

2. Shulman presents four myths. What are they about—in general—and what problem are they creating?

3. Explain each of the four myths and the author's rebuttal of each one. In particular: What kinds of low-paying jobs are not affected by global competition?

QUESTIONS FOR REASONING AND ANALYSIS

1. What kinds of evidence does Shulman provide? Do the numbers seem logical, their sources credible?

2. The author argues, in response to myth #4, that our economy is one that we have created, not something out of our control. How does she defend this assertion? Is her argument convincing to you?

3. What type of support does Shulman present in her conclusion? Do you find her ending persuasive?

QUESTIONS FOR REFLECTING AND WRITING

1. Have you believed one or more of the myths Shulman lists? If so, has she convinced you that your perceptions have been incorrect? Why or why not?

2. If you are still convinced that one of the myths is accurate, how would you rebut Shulman's argument and defend that myth?

1. Think of a problem on your campus or in your community for which you have a workable solution. Organize your argument to include all relevant steps as described in this chapter. Although your primary concern will be to present your solution, depending on your topic you may need to begin by convincing readers of the seriousness of the problem or the causes of the problem—if your solutions involve removing those causes.

2. Think of a problem in education—K–12 or at the college level—that you have a solution for and that you are interested in. You may want to begin by brainstorming to develop a list of possible problems in education about which you could write—or look through Chapter 17 for ideas. Be sure to qualify your claim and limit your focus as necessary to work with a problem that is not so broad and general that your "solutions" become general and vague comments about "getting better teachers." (If one problem is a lack of qualified teachers, then what specific proposals do you have for solving that particular problem?) Include as many steps as are appropriate to develop and support your argument.

3. Think of a situation that you consider serious but that apparently many people do not take seriously enough. Write an argument in which you emphasize, by providing evidence, that the situation is a serious problem. You may conclude by suggesting a solution, but your chief purpose in writing will be to alert readers to a problem.

The Researched and Formally Documented Argument

CHAPTER 9

Getting Started and Locating Sources: in the Library, Online, in the Field

We do research all the time. You would not select a college or buy a car without doing research: gathering relevant information, analyzing that information, and drawing conclusions from your study. You may already have done some research in this course: using sources in this text or finding data online to strengthen an argument—and then acknowledging your sources informally in your essay. And, if your instructor has required formal documentation for even one source, then you have already explored this section for documentation guidelines.

When you are assigned a more formal research essay, you will need to use a number of sources and to document them according to a specific style. You may be required to produce a longer essay and to demonstrate skill in finding a variety of sources. Remember that you have been doing research, in some ways, all along, and use this section to guide you to success in the particular demands of your research essay assignment.

TYPES OF RESEARCH PROJECTS

Not all research projects have the same purpose. Different purposes lead to papers that can be classified as primarily *expository, analytic,* or *argumentative.*

Expository

An expository or informative paper, often called a report, is an account of your study of a specific topic. The purpose is to share information, to explain to readers what the researcher has learned from the study. Market and technical reports are important kinds of informative writing in business. A good report reflects your critical judgment in the selection and arrangement of information. Instructors assign expository research papers when they want students to read widely on a topic, gain greater understanding of complex topics, or learn about the process of research.

Analytic

The analytic paper goes beyond an organized reporting of information to an examination of the implications of that information. A report on problems in education may assemble recent test scores and other data. An analysis will examine possible causes of the problem. Many literary studies are analyses.

Argumentative/Persuasive

The argumentative paper (often called an opinion or thesis paper) uses information and analysis to argue for a claim. In an argumentative paper you cannot just report conflicting positions on your topic. You need to evaluate conflicting positions and refute those at odds with your position. To illustrate, compare the following topics to see how they differ in purpose:

EXPOSITORY	Report of recent literature on infant speech development.
ANALYTIC	Explanation of the process of infant speech development.
ARGUMENTATIVE	Argument for specific actions by parents to aid infant speech development.

Examining types of research projects can help us recognize what will not meet research paper expectations. The following is a cautionary list of kinds of writing to avoid when a research paper has been assigned:

1. A paper that merely strings together quotations from sources.
2. An essay drawn entirely from personal experiences and thoughts.

3. An entirely theoretical paper without any specifics from sources.
4. A paper in which information drawn from sources is not properly documented.

Be sure to understand what *type* of essay you have been assigned.

FINDING A WORKABLE TOPIC

To get started you need to select and limit a topic. One key to success is finding a *workable* topic. No matter how interesting or clever the topic, it is not workable if it does not meet the guidelines of your assignment. Begin with a thorough understanding of the writing context created by the assignment.

What Type of Paper Am I Preparing?

Study your assignment to understand the type of project. Is your purpose expository, analytic, or argumentative? How would you classify each of the following topics?

1. Explain the chief solutions proposed for increasing the Southwest's water supply.
2. Compare the Freudian and behavioral models of mental illness.
3. Find the best solutions to a current environmental problem.
4. Consider: What twentieth-century invention has most dramatically changed our personal lives?

Did you recognize that the first topic calls for a report? The second topic requires an analysis of two schools of psychology, so you cannot report on only one, but you also cannot argue that one model is better than the other. Both topics 3 and 4 require an argumentative paper: You must select and defend a claim.

Who Is My Audience?

If you are writing in a specific discipline, imagine your instructor as a representative of that field, a reader with knowledge of the subject area. If you are learning about the research process in a composition course, your instructor may advise you to write to a general reader, someone who reads newspapers but may not have the exact information and perspective you have. For a general reader, specialized terms and concepts need definition.

> **NOTE:** Consider the expectations of readers of research papers. A research essay is not like a personal essay. A research essay is not about you; it is about a subject, so keep yourself more in the background than you might in a more informal piece of writing.

What Are the Assignment's Time and Length Constraints?

The required length of the paper, the time you have to complete the assignment, and the availability of sources are three constraints you must consider when selecting a research topic. Most instructors will establish guidelines regarding length. Knowing the expected length of the paper is crucial to selecting an appropriate topic, so if an instructor does not specify, be sure to ask.

Suppose, for example, that you must argue for solutions to either an educational or environmental problem. Your paper needs to be about six pages and is due in three weeks. Do you have the space or the time to explore solutions to all the problems caused by overpopulation? Definitely not. Limit your study to one issue such as coping with trash. You could further limit this topic by exploring waste management solutions for your particular city or county.

What Kinds of Topics Should I Avoid?

Here are several kinds of topics that are best avoided because they usually produce disasters, no matter how well the student handles the rest of the research process:

1. *Topics that are irrelevant* to your interests or the course. If you are not interested in your topic, you will not produce a lively, informative paper. If you select a topic far removed from the course content, you may create some hostility in your instructor, who will wonder why you are unwilling to become engaged in the course.
2. *Topics that are broad subject areas.* These result in general surveys that lack appropriate detail and support.
3. *Topics that can be fully researched with only one source.* You will produce a summary, not a research paper.
4. *Biographical studies.* Short undergraduate papers on a person's life usually turn out to be summaries of one or two major biographies.
5. *Topics that produce a strong emotional response in you.* If there is only one "right" answer to the abortion issue and you cannot imagine counterarguments, don't choose to write on abortion. Probably most religious topics are best avoided.
6. *Topics that are too technical for you* at this point in your college work. If you do not understand the complexities of the federal tax code, then arguing for a reduction in the capital gains tax may be an unwise topic choice.

How Can I Select a Good Topic?

Choosing from assigned topics. At times students are unhappy with topic restriction. Looked at another way, your instructor has eliminated a difficult step in the research process and has helped you avoid the problem of selecting an unworkable topic. If topics are assigned, you will still have to choose from the list and develop your own claim and approach.

Finding a course-related topic. This guideline gives you many options and requires more thought about your choice. Working within the guidelines, try to write about what interests you. Here are examples of assignments turned into topics of interest to the student:

ASSIGNMENT	INTEREST	TOPIC
1. Trace the influence of any twentieth-century event, development, invention.	Music	The influence of the Jazz Age on modern music
2. Support an argument on some issue of pornography and censorship.	Computers	Censorship of pornography on the Internet
3. Demonstrate the popularity of a current myth and then discredit it.	Science fiction	The lack of evidence for the existence of UFOs

How Do I Get Started When There Are Few Restrictions?

When you are free to write on any course-related topic or any topic at all, you may need to use some strategies for topic selection. Here are some strategies to consider:

- Look through your text's table of contents or index for subject areas that can be narrowed or focused.
- Look over your class notes and think about subjects covered that have interested you.
- Consider college-based or local issues.
- Do a subject search in an electronic database to see how a large topic can be narrowed—for example, type in "dinosaur" and observe such subheadings as *dinosaur behavior* and *dinosaur extinction.*
- With a possible broad topic needing focus, use one or more invention strategies:
  - Freewriting
  - Brainstorming
  - Asking questions about a broad subject, using the reporter's *who, what, where, when,* and *why.*

What Is the "Right" Size for a Topic?

Part of selecting a workable topic is making sure that the topic is sufficiently narrowed and focused. Students sometimes have trouble narrowing topics. Somehow it seems easier to write on a broad subject, such as education. You know there will be enough sources, all easy to find. But this line of thinking overlooks your purpose in doing research and what you know about good writing. Consider the following list of increasingly narrower topics about education:

1. Education
2. Problems in education today
3. Problems in K–12 education today
4. Problems with testing students
5. Why standardized tests aren't fair for all students

The first three items are clearly too broad for a short research project. Do you recognize that topic 4 is also too broad? Remember that the more limited and focused your topic, the more concrete and detailed—and thus convincing and engaging—your study will be.

WRITING A TENTATIVE CLAIM OR RESEARCH PROPOSAL

Once you have selected and narrowed a topic, you need to write a tentative claim, research question, or research proposal. Some instructors will ask to see a statement—from a sentence to a paragraph long—to be approved before you proceed. Others may require as much as a one-page proposal that includes a tentative claim, a basic organizational plan, and a description of types of sources to be used. Even if your instructor does not require anything in writing, you need to write something for your benefit—to direct your reading and thinking. Here are three possibilities.

1. **SUBJECT:**   Computers
   TOPIC: The impact of computers on the twentieth century
   CLAIM: Computers had the greatest impact of any technological development in the twentieth century.

   RESEARCH PROPOSAL: I propose to show that computers had the greatest impact of any technological development in the twentieth century. I will show the influence of computers at work, in daily living, and in play to emphasize the breadth of influence. I will argue that other possibilities (such as cars) did not have the same impact as computers. I will check the library's book catalog and databases for sources on technological developments and on computers specifically. I will also interview a family friend who works with computers at the Pentagon.

This example illustrates several key ideas. First, the initial subject is both too broad and unfocused (What about computers?). Second, the claim is more focused than the topic statement because it asserts a position, a claim the student must support. Third, the research proposal is more helpful than the claim only because it includes some thoughts on developing the thesis and finding sources.

2. Less sure of your topic? Then write a research question or a more open-ended research proposal. Take, for example, a history student studying the effects of Prohibition. She is not ready to write a thesis, but she can write a research proposal that suggests some possible approaches to the topic:

TOPIC:	The effect of Prohibition
RESEARCH QUESTION:	What were the effects of Prohibition on the United States?
RESEARCH PROPOSAL:	I will examine the effects of Prohibition on the United States in the 1920s (and possibly consider some long-term effects, depending on the amount of material on the topic). Specifically, I will look at the varying effects on urban and rural areas and on different classes in society.

3. Asking questions and working with fields of study (think of college departments) offers a third approach. Suppose your assignment is to defend a position on a current social issue. You think you want to do something "on television." Using an electronic database to search for a narrowed topic, you decide on the following:

TOPIC:	Television and violence
RESEARCH PROPOSAL:	I will explore the problem of violence on TV. I will read articles in current magazines and newspapers and see what's on the Internet.

Do you have a focused topic and a proposal that will guide your thinking and research? Not yet. Raise questions by field of study.

LITERARY/ HUMANITIES:	What kinds of violence are found on TV? Children's cartoons? Cop and mystery shows? The news? How are they alike? How different?
SOCIOLOGY:	What are the consequences to our society of a continual and heavy dose of violence on television?
PSYCHOLOGY:	What are the effects of television violence on children? Why are we drawn to violent shows?
POLITICS/ GOVERNMENT:	Should violence on TV be controlled in any way? If so, how?
EDUCATION:	What is the impact on the classroom when children grow up watching a lot of violence on TV? Does it impede social skills? Learning?

Now your thinking is more focused. After reflecting, you choose:

TOPIC:	The negative effects of television violence on children and some solutions

RESEARCH
PROPOSAL: I will demonstrate that children suffer from their exposure to so much violence on TV and propose some solutions. Until I read more, I am not certain of the solutions I will propose; I want to read arguments for and against the V-chip and ratings and other possibilities.

PREPARING A WORKING BIBLIOGRAPHY

To begin this next stage of your research, you need to know three things:

1. *Your search strategy.* If you are writing on a course-related topic, your starting place may be your textbook for relevant sections and possible sources (if the text contains a bibliography). For this course, you may find some potential sources among the readings in this text. Think about what you already know or have in hand as you plan your search strategy.

2. *A method for recording bibliographic information.* You have two choices: the always reliable 3 × 5 index cards or a bibliography file in your personal computer.

3. *The documentation format you will be using.* You may be assigned the Modern Language Association (MLA) format, or perhaps given a choice between MLA and the American Psychological Association (APA) documentation styles. Once you select the documentation style, skim the appropriate pages in either Chapter 10 (for MLA) or Chapter 12 (for APA) to get an overview of both content and style.

A list of possible sources is only a *working* bibliography because you do not yet know which sources you will use. (Your final bibliography will include only those sources you cite—actually refer to—in your paper.) A working bibliography will help you see what is available on your topic, note how to locate each source, and contain the information needed to document your paper. Whether you are using cards or computer files, follow these guidelines:

1. Check all reasonable catalogues and indexes for possible sources. (Use more than one reference source even if you locate enough sources there; you are looking for the best sources, not the first ones you find.)

2. Complete a card or prepare an entry for every potentially useful source. You won't know what to reject until you start a close reading of sources.

3. Copy (or download from an online catalog) all information needed to complete a citation and to locate the source. (When using an index that does not give all needed information, leave a space to be filled in when you actually read the source.)

4. Put bibliographic information in the correct format for every possible source; you will save time and make fewer errors. Do not mix or blend styles. When searching for sources, have your text handy and use the model in Chapter 10 or in Chapter 12 as a guide.

FIGURE 9.1 Bibliography Card for a Book

The following brief guide to correct form will get you started. Illustrations are for cards, but the information and order will be the same in your PC file. Guidelines are for MLA style only; use Chapter 12 if you have selected a different style.

Basic Form for Books

As Figure 9.1 shows, the basic MLA form for books includes the following information in this pattern:

1. The author's full name, last name first.
2. The title (and subtitle if there is one) of the book, underlined.
3. The facts of publication: the city of publication (followed by a colon), the publisher (followed by a comma), and the date of publication.

Note that periods are placed after the author's name, after the title, and at the end of the citation. Other information, when appropriate (e.g., the number of volumes), is added to this basic pattern. (See pages 294–300 for many sample citations.) Include, in your working bibliography, the book's classification number so that you can find it in the library.

Basic Form for Articles

Figure 9.2 shows the simplest form for magazine articles. Include the following information, in this pattern:

1. The author's full name, last name first.
2. The title of the article, in quotation marks.
3. The facts of publication: the title of the periodical (underlined), the volume number (if the article is from a scholarly journal), the date (followed by a colon), and inclusive page numbers.

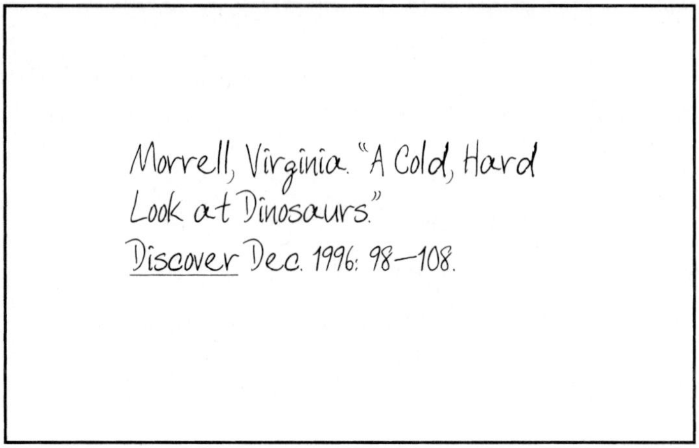

Morrell, Virginia. "A Cold, Hard Look at Dinosaurs." Discover Dec. 1996: 98–108.

FIGURE 9.2 Bibliography Card for a Magazine Article

You will discover that indexes rarely present information in MLA format. Here, for example, is a source on animal rights found in an online database:

Planet of the free apes? Gail Vines.
    New Scientist June 5, 1993 vl38 n1876 p39(4)

If you read the article in the journal itself, then the correct citation, for MLA, will look like this:

Vines, Gail. "Planet of the Free Apes?" New Scientist 5 June 1993: 39–42.

However, if you obtain a full-text copy of the article from the electronic database, your citation will require additional information about the database. (See pages 306–07 for guidelines and examples.)

> **NOTE:** A collection of printouts, slips of paper, and backs of envelopes is not a working bibliography! You may have to return to the library for missing information, and you risk making serious errors in documentation. Know the basics of your documentation format and follow that format faithfully.

KNOWING YOUR LIBRARY

All libraries contain books and periodicals, and a system for accessing them. A *book collection* contains the *general collection* (books that circulate), the *reference collection* (books of a general nature essential to research), and the *reserve book collection*. The library's *periodicals collection* consists of popular magazines, scholarly journals, and newspapers. Electronic databases with full texts of articles provide alternatives to the print periodicals collection.

The book and periodicals collections are supplemented by audiovisual materials, including works on CD, tape, microfilm or microfiche, and online. Many libraries store back issues of periodicals on microfilm, so learn where the microfilm readers are and how to use them. In addition, articles from electronic databases and Internet sources can be printed or, in many cases, e-mailed directly to your own PC.

REMEMBER: All works, regardless of their source or the format in which you obtain them—and this includes online sources—must be fully documented in your paper. Also, there are certain restrictions on copyrighted materials; know the rules to avoid infringing on a copyright.

Locating Books

Your chief guide to the book (and audiovisual) collection is the catalogue, probably a computer database.

In a catalog there are at least three entries for each book: the author entry, the title entry, and one or more subject entries. Online catalogues continue to use these same access points plus a keyword option and possibly others, such as the book's International Standard Book Number (ISBN). When you go to your library's home screen and select the catalogue, you will come to the search screen. Usually, keyword is the default. If you know the exact title, switch to title, type in the title, and click on "submit search." If instead you want a list of all of the library's books by Hemingway, for example, click on author and type in "Hemingway." Keep in mind:

- With a title search, do not type any initial article (a, an, the). Thus, to locate *The Great Gatsby*, type in "Great Gatsby."
- Use correct spelling. If you are unsure of a spelling, use a keyword instead of an author or title search.
- If you are looking for a list of possible books on your subject, do a keyword or subject search.

Reading Entries: Brief and Long View Screens

If you do an author search by last name only, you will get a list of all of the library's books written by writers with that last name. A keyword search will provide a list of all book titles containing your keyword. These "brief view" lists provide enough information to locate a book in the library: author, title, and classification number—the number by which the book is shelved (Figure 9.3).

For books that look promising for your research, click on *View Record* to obtain the "long view" screen. This screen (Figure 9.4) provides additional

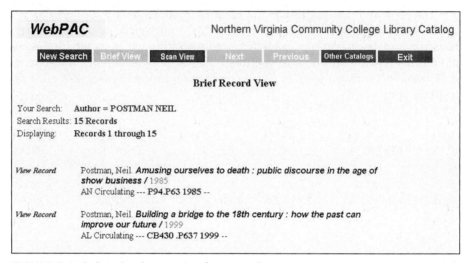

FIGURE 9.3 Online Catalogue—Brief View Author List

WebPAC   Northern Virginia Community College Library Catalog

New Search | Brief View | Scan View | Next | Previous | Other Catalogs | Exit

Long record view

Your Search: Author = POSTMAN NEIL
Displaying Record: 1 of 15

Author:	Postman, Neil.
Title:	Amusing ourselves to death : public discourse in the age of show business / Neil Postman.
Published:	New York : Viking, 1985.
Description:	viii, 184 p. ; 22 cm.
Subject:	Mass media --Influence.
Notes:	"Elisabeth Sifton books."
	Includes index.
	Bibliography: p. 173-175.

Location	Call Number
AN Circulating	P94.P63 1985

FIGURE 9.4 Online Catalogue Entry—Long View of One Book

information, including bibliographic details needed for documentation and one or more subject listings that you can use to find other books on the same subject. For potentially useful books, copy all needed information into your working bibliography.

Using the Reference Collection

The research process often begins with the reference collection. You will find atlases, dictionaries, encyclopedias, general histories, critical studies, and biographies. In addition, various reference tools such as bibliographies and indexes are part of the reference collection.

Many tools in the reference collection once only in print form are now also online. Some are now only online. Yet online is not always the way to go. Let's consider some of the advantages of each of the formats:

Advantages of the Print Reference Collection

1. The reference tool may be only in print—use it.
2. The print form covers the period you are studying. (Most online indexes and abstracts cover only from 1980 to the present.)
3. In a book, with a little scanning of pages, you can often find what you need without getting spelling or commands exactly right.
4. If you know the best reference source to use and are looking for only a few items, the print source can be faster than the online source.
5. All computer terminals are in use—or down—open a book!

Advantages of Online Reference Materials

1. Online databases are likely to provide the most up-to-date information.
2. You can usually search all years covered at one time.
3. Full texts (with graphics) are sometimes available, as well as indexes with detailed summaries of articles. Both can be printed or e-mailed to your PC.
4. Through links to the Internet, you have access to an amazing amount of material. (Unless you focus your keyword search, however, you may be overwhelmed.)

Before using any reference work, take a few minutes to check its date, purpose, and organization. If you are new to online searching, take a few minutes to learn about each reference tool by working through the online tutorial. (Go to the Help screen.) These strategies can supplement the following brief review of some key reference tools.

Basic Reference Tools

Use your library's reference collection as you need to for facts, for background information, and for indexes to possible sources.

Dictionaries

For the spelling of specialized words not found in your PC's dictionary, consult an appropriate subject dictionary; for foreign words, the appropriate foreign-language dictionary. If you need a word's origin or its definitions from an earlier time, use one of the unabridged dictionaries. Here are two to know:

> *Webster's Encyclopedic Unabridged Dictionary of the English Language.* 1996.
> *The Oxford English Dictionary.* 20 volumes in print. Also online.

General Encyclopedias

Two multivolume encyclopedias to know are the *Encyclopedia Americana* and the *Encyclopaedia Britannica.* The *Britannica,* the *World Book,* and other encyclopedias are available online as well as in print.

Atlases

Atlases provide much more than simple maps showing capital cities and the names of rivers. Historical atlases show changes in politics, economics, and culture. Topographical atlases support studies in the earth sciences and many environmental issues. Here are just two:

> *Historical Atlas of the United States.* National Geographic Society, 1988.
> *The Times Atlas of the World.* 9th ed. 1992.

Check to see what atlases your library has on CD-ROM.

Quotations, Mythology, and Folklore

Use the following works to understand unfamiliar references:

> *Bartlett's Familiar Quotations.* 16th ed. 1992. In print and online.
> *Funk and Wagnall's Standard Dictionary of Folklore, Mythology, and Legend.*

Almanacs and Yearbooks

The following sources answer all kinds of questions about current events and provide statistical information on just about anything. Many of these works—and others like them—are both in print and online. Check to see which format your library offers.

> *Congressional Record.* 1873 to date. Issued daily during sessions. Online.
> *Facts on File.* 1940 to date. Digest of important news events. Online.
> *Statistical Abstract of the United States.* 1978 to date. Annual publication of the Bureau of the Census. Online.

Biographical Dictionaries

Most libraries have an array of biographical dictionaries, important tools for investigating authors with whom you are unfamiliar.

> *Contemporary Authors.* 1962 to date. A multivolume guide to current fiction and nonfiction writers and their books. Online.

International Who's Who. 1935 to date. Contains brief biographies of important persons from almost every country.

American Men and Women of Science. Provides brief sketches of more than 150,000 scientists. Lists degrees held and fields of specialization. Regularly updated.

Who's Who. 1849 to date. English men and women.

Who's Who in America. 1899 to date.

Who's Who in American Women. 1958 to date.

USING INDEXES TO PERIODICALS: IN PRINT AND ONLINE

Periodicals (magazines, journals, and newspapers) provide good sources for research projects, especially for projects on current issues. The best way to access articles on your topic is to use one or more periodical indexes. To be efficient, you want to select the most useful indexes for your particular study. Your library will maintain some print indexes to popular magazines, some for scholarly journals, and some to newspapers. In addition, your library probably provides many online databases. Online databases are more likely than older print indexes to blend magazines, journals, and newspaper articles, and many online databases include full texts of the articles. Learn which of the indexes provide full texts and which indexes provide only lists of possibly useful articles that you must then locate in your library's paper collection of periodicals.

The Reader's Guide to Periodical Literature

Probably the most-used paper index, *The Reader's Guide to Periodical Literature* (1900 to date) combines author and subject headings that guide users to articles in about 200 popular magazines. As the sample entries in Figure 9.5 show, the information is heavily abbreviated. When using this index, study the explanation provided and check the list of periodicals found in the front of each volume for the complete title of each magazine. Use this index if you want articles written prior to 1980.

The New York Times Index

Newspapers are a good source of information about both contemporary topics and historical events and issues. Because it is one of the most thorough and respected newspapers, the *New York Times* is available in most libraries. So, when your topic warrants it, become familiar with the *New York Times Index,* for it can guide you to articles as far back as the mid-nineteenth century. (Back issues of the newspaper are on microfilm.) The print *NYT Index* is a subject index, cumulated and bound annually, with articles

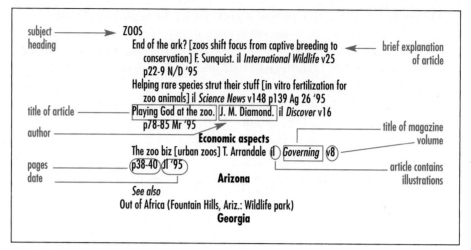

FIGURE 9.5 Entries in *The Reader's Guide to Periodical Literature*

arranged chronologically under each subject heading. The *NYT Index* is also online, and articles in the *New York Times* are often indexed in other online databases.

Online Databases

You will probably access online databases by going to your library's home page and then clicking on the appropriate term or icon. (You may have found the book catalogue by clicking on "library catalog"; you may find the databases by clicking on "library resources" or some other descriptive label.) You will need to choose a particular database and then type in your keyword for a basic search or select "advanced search" to limit your search by date or periodical or to search for articles by a specific author. Each library will create somewhat different screens, but the basic process of selecting among choices provided and then typing in your search commands remains the same. Figure 9.6 shows a first screen in response to the choice to search for magazine and newspaper articles. Notice that the librarians are suggesting seven databases that are useful for many undergraduate research projects. If you do not want to work in one of these seven, you can click on the alphabetical list of databases or search by subject. Select the database that seems most useful for your topic.

Suppose you select Expanded Academic. Observe the first screen, shown in Figure 9.7. You can do a basic keyword search or modify your search in a number of ways. The basic keyword search for "zoos and animal rights" yielded twelve articles. Figure 9.8 shows a partial list of those "hits."

Library Databases:
Magazines, Newspapers & Reference

NVCC

| Library Home | Alexandria | Annandale | Loudoun | Manassas | Medical | Woodbridge |

📷 Note:From off campus you will need to log in--See Remote Access

Library Catalog
Internet
Ask a Librarian
Remote Access
Citing Sources

• **Alphabetical List** of all available Databases

• General Full-text Databases: **cover many different topics and can be a good starting point** :

OneFile▲   Factiva▲
Expanded Academic▲   CQ Researcher
Proquest   Reference Center Gold▲
SIRS   ▲Access Provided by VIVA

• Indexes & Databases by Subject: **specialized databases recommended for different subject areas**

◾ Art   ◾ History
◾ Biography   ◾ Humanities
◾ Business and Economics   ◾ Journals
◾ Computers &   ◾ Language and Literature
Information Technology   ◾ Math
◾ Conferences and Proceedings   ◾ Music
◾ Education   ◾ News and Newspapers
◾ Encyclopedias, Dictionaries &   ◾ Political Science, Public
Reference   Affairs & Law
◾ Engineering and Technology   ◾ Psychology
◾ General   ◾ Science
◾ Health and Medicine   ◾ Social Sciences
                                         ◾ Statistics

[alt]

FIGURE 9.6 Beginning Screen to Search for Articles in Online Databases

GUIDELINES for Using Online Databases

Keep these points in mind as you use online databases.

- **Although some online databases provide full texts of all articles, others provide full texts of only some of the articles indexed.** The articles not in full text will have to be located in a print collection of periodicals.

- **Articles indexed but not available in full text often come with a brief summary or abstract.** This allows you to decide whether the article looks useful for your project. *Do not treat the abstract as the article. Do not use material from it and cite the author. If you want to use the article, find it in your library's print collection or obtain it from another library.*

- **The information you need for documenting material used from an article is not in correct format for any of the standard documentation styles.** You will have to reorder the information and use the correct style for writing titles. If your instructor wants to see a list of possible sources in MLA format, do not hand in a printout of articles from an online database.

- **Because no single database covers all magazines, you may want to search several databases that seem relevant to your project.**

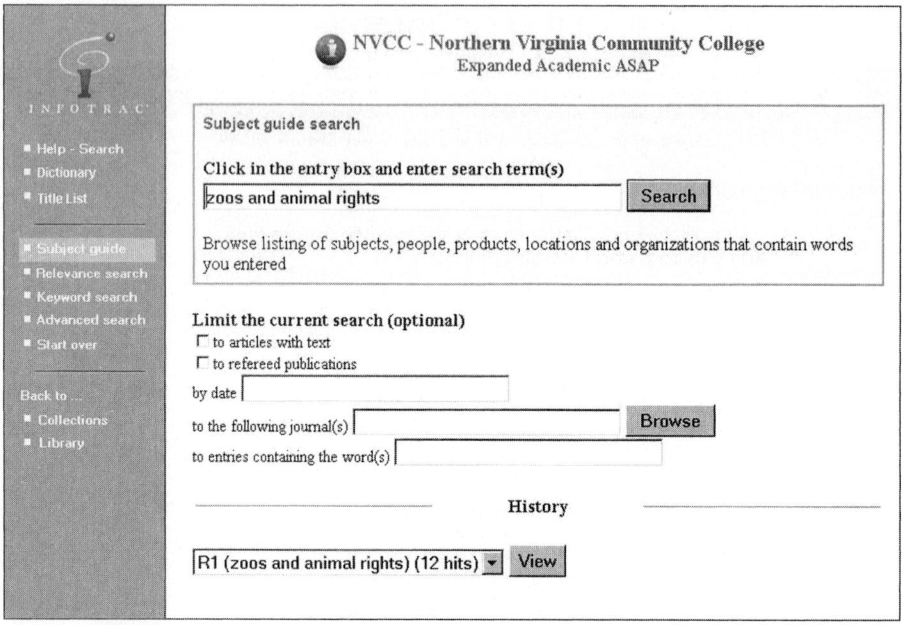

FIGURE 9.7 Search Screen for Online Database

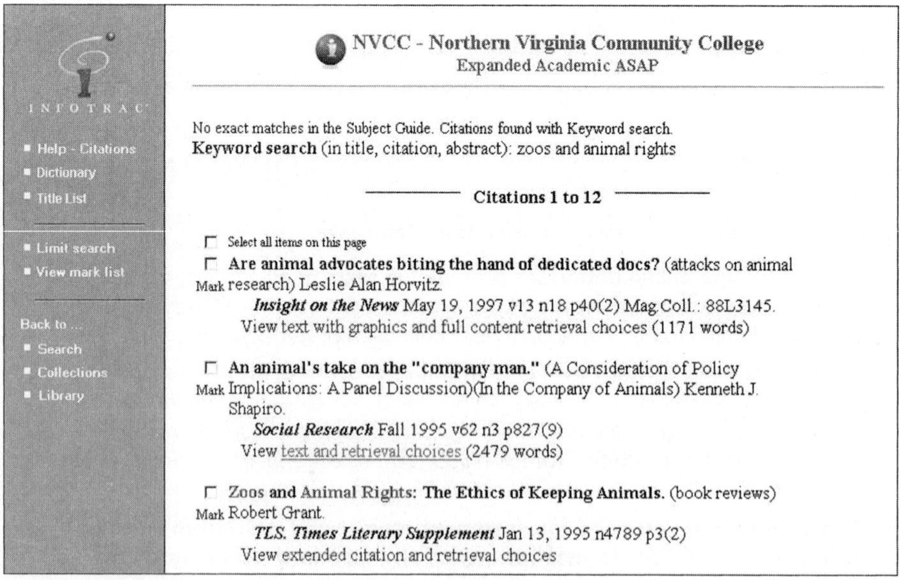

FIGURE 9.8 Partial List of Articles Found on Search Topic

Indexes to Academic Journals: In Print and Online

The indexes to magazines and journals just reviewed provide many good articles for undergraduate research. At times, though, you may need to use articles exclusively from scholarly journals. Many of the more specialized indexes to journals began as print indexes but are now online as well. The following is a brief list of some of the more academic indexes students frequently use. Your reference librarian can recommend others appropriate to your study.

APPLIED SCIENCE AND TECHNOLOGY INDEX	An index to periodicals covering engineering, data processing, earth sciences, space science, and more. Online through FirstSearch.
BOOK REVIEW DIGEST	Begun in 1905, this index is arranged by author of the book reviewed. It contains brief reviews of both fiction and non-fiction works. Online.
ESSAY AND GENERAL LITERATURE INDEX	From 1900, this author and subject index includes references to both biographical and critical materials. Its chief focus is literary criticism.
EDUCATIONAL RESEARCH INFORMATION CENTER (ERIC)	In its print form, there are two sections, Current Index to Journals in Education and Resources in Education, a collection of unpublished reports on educational issues. ERIC is also online.
THE GPO PUBLICATIONS REFERENCE FILE OR GPO ACCESS (ON THE WEB)	The former has been replaced by the regularly updated index on the Internet. You can reach GPO Access at **www.access.gpo.gov/su_docs**.
HUMANITIES INDEX	This index lists articles on art, literature, philosophy, folklore, history, and related topics. Online.
MLA INTERNATIONAL BIBLIOGRAPHY	The annual listing by the Modern Language Association of books, articles, and dissertations on language and literature. Online.
PUBLIC AFFAIRS INFORMATION SERVICE (PAIS)	This index covers books, pamphlets, reports, and articles on economics, government, social issues, and public affairs. It is international in scope and emphasizes works that are strong on facts and statistics. Online.
SCIENCE CITATION INDEX	An index of more than 3,000 journals in mathematics and the natural, physical, and behavioral sciences. It includes an index to articles, a subject index based on keywords appearing in titles of articles indexed, and a citation index, arranged by author, that reveals which articles are referred

to by other authors in their papers. The online version is SciSearch or through Web of Science.

SOCIAL SCIENCES CITATION INDEX	Like the Science Citation Index, this index includes a source index, a subject index by keywords, and a citation index. The online version is Social SciSearch or through Web of Science.

SEARCHING THE INTERNET

In addition to using the online databases to find sources, you can search the Internet directly. If you are new to Internet searching, you may want to study online tutorials to be efficient in your search. Also, your college library may conduct workshops—check it out.

Keep in mind these facts about the Internet:

- The Internet is both disorganized and huge, so you can waste time trying to find information that is easily obtained in a reference book in your library.
- The Internet is best at providing current information, such as news and movie reviews. It is also a great source of government information.
- Because anyone can create a Web site and put anything on it, you will have to be especially careful in evaluating Internet sources. Remember that articles in magazines and journals have been selected by editors and are often peer reviewed as well, but no editor selects or rejects material on a personal Web site. (More on evaluating sources can be found in Chapter 10.)

Access to the Internet provides information in a variety of ways, including:

- *E-mail.* E-mail can be used instead of a printed letter to request information from a government agency or company.
- *Mailing Lists (Listservs).* You can sign up to receive, via your e-mail, continually updated bulletins on a particular subject. Listservs are essentially organized mailing lists. If you find one relevant to your project, you can subscribe for a while and unsubscribe when you are no longer interested.
- *Newsgroups.* Newsgroups differ from listservs in that the discussions and exchanges are collected for you to retrieve; they are not sent to your e-mail address. Otherwise they are much the same: Both are a type of discussion group. To find newsgroups on a specific subject, go to **http://groups.google.com**, a research tool sponsored by the search engine Google, that surveys all Usenet newsgroups.
- *World Wide Web.* To access the Web from your library terminal or on your own PC through a hookup with your college library, you will, as with the catalogue and online databases, start at your library's home page. Usually selecting "search the Internet" will take you to a menu of various search engines and subject directories. Not all search engines are the same, and peo-

ple differ on which are the best. Here are some sites to visit for help in selecting an appropriate search engine:

- *Librarians' Index to the Internet:* **http://lii.org**
- *Greg R. Notess's search engine comparison pages:* **www.notess.com/search**
- *Search Engine Watch:* **www.searchenginewatch.com**

GUIDELINES for Searching the Web

How much information you may find searching for a specific topic, and how useful it is, will vary from one research project to another. Here are some general guidelines to aid your research on the Internet:

1. **Bookmark sites you expect to use often so that you do not have to remember complicated Web addresses, or uniform resource locators (URLs).**

2. **Make your search as precise as possible to avoid getting overwhelmed with hits.**

3. **If you are searching for a specific phrase, put quotation marks around the words.** This will reduce the number of hits and lead to sites more useful to your research. Examples: "Environmental Protection Agency" or "civil disobedience."

4. **Use Boolean connectors to make your search more precise.**
   - AND: This connector limits results to those sites that contain both terms, for example, "zoos AND animal rights."
   - OR: This connector extends the hits to include all sites that contain one or the other search term. So, "zoos OR animal rights" will generate a list of sites containing either term.
   - NOT: This connector limits the search to only the first term, not the second. Thus, "zoos NOT animal rights" will give you sites only about zoo issues not involving animal rights.

5. **If you are not successful with one search engine, try a different one.** Remember that each search engine searches only a part of the Internet.

6. **If you are not successful with a second search engine, check your spelling.** Search engines cannot guess what you mean; spelling must be exact.

7. **To get the best sites for most college research projects, try a directory of evaluated sites or subject guides rather than, say, Yahoo!** (Yahoo! is better for news, people searches, and commercial sites.) Some of the best academic subject guides include:
   - The Argus Clearinghouse (**www.clearinghouse.net**)
   - The University of California's Infomine (**http://infomine.ucr.edu**)
   - Internet Scout Project (**http://scout.cs.wisc.edu**)

8. **Be certain to complete a bibliography card—including the date you accessed the material—for each separate site from which you take information.** Remember: All sources must be documented, including Internet sources. (See pages 307–09 for documentation guidelines.)

DOING FIELD RESEARCH

Field research can enrich many projects. The following sections give some suggestions.

Federal, State, and Local Government Documents

In addition to federal documents you may obtain through *PAIS* or *GPO Access,* department and agency Web sites, or the Library of Congress's good legislative site, *Thomas* (**http://thomas.loc.gov**), consider state and county archives, maps, and other published materials. Instead of selecting a national or global topic, consider examining the debate over a controversial bill introduced in your state legislature. Use online databases to locate articles on the bill and the debate and interview legislators and journalists who participated in or covered the debates or served on committees that worked with the bill.

You can also request specific documents on a topic from appropriate state or county agencies and nonprofit organizations. One student, given the assignment of examining solutions to an ecological problem, decided to study the local problem of preserving the Chesapeake Bay. She obtained issues of the Chesapeake Bay Foundation newsletter and brochures prepared by them advising homeowners about hazardous household waste materials that end up in the bay. Added to her sources were bulletins on soil conservation and landscaping tips for improving the area's water quality. Local problems can lead to interesting research topics because they are current and relevant to you and because they involve uncovering different kinds of source materials.

Correspondence

Business and government officials are usually willing to respond to written requests for information. Make your letter brief and well written. Either include a self-addressed, stamped envelope for the person's convenience or e-mail your request. If you are not e-mailing, write as soon as you discover the need for information and be prepared to wait several weeks for a reply. It is appropriate to indicate your deadline and ask for a timely response. Three guidelines for either letters or e-mails to keep in mind are:

1. Explain precisely what information you need. Avoid writing a general "please send me anything you have on this topic" kind of letter. Busy professionals are more likely to respond to requests that are specific and reveal a control of the topic.
2. Do not request information that can be found in your library's reference collection.
3. Explain how you plan to use the information. Businesses especially are understandably concerned with their public image and will be disinclined to provide information that you intend to use as a means of attacking them.

Use reference guides to companies and government agencies or their Web sites to obtain addresses and the person to whom your letter or e-mail should be addressed. For companies, address your request to the public information officer. For e-mail addresses, check the organization's home page.

Interviews

Some experts are available for personal interviews. Call or write for an appointment as soon as you recognize the value of an interview. Remember that interviews are more likely to be scheduled with state and local officials than with the president of General Motors. If you are studying a local problem, also consider leaders of the civic association with an interest in the issue. In many communities, the local historian or a librarian will be a storehouse of information about the community. Former teachers can be interviewed for papers on education. Interviews with doctors or nurses can add a special dimension to papers on medical issues.

If an interview is appropriate for your topic, follow these guidelines:

1. Prepare specific questions in advance.
2. Arrive on time, properly dressed, and behave in a polite, professional manner.
3. Take notes, asking the interviewee to repeat key statements so that your notes are accurate.
4. Take a tape recorder with you but ask permission to use it before taping.
5. If you quote any statements in your paper, quote accurately, eliminating only such minor speech habits as "you know's" and "uhm's." (See Chapter 10 for proper documentation of interviews.)
6. Direct the interview with your prepared questions, but also give the interviewee the chance to approach the topic in his or her own way. You may obtain information or views that had not occurred to you.
7. Do not get into a debate with the interviewee. You are there to learn, not to try to change the interviewee's thinking.

Lectures

Check the appropriate information sources at your school to keep informed of visiting speakers. If you are fortunate enough to attend a lecture relevant to a current project, take careful, detailed notes. Because a lecture is a source, use of information or ideas from it must be presented accurately and then documented. (See Chapter 10 for documentation format.)

Films, Tapes, Television

Your library will have audiovisual materials that provide good sources for some kinds of topics. For example, if you are studying *Death of a Salesman,* view a videotaped version of the play. Also pay attention to documentaries on public television and to the many news and political talk shows on both public and commercial channels. In many cases transcripts of shows can be obtained from the TV station. Alternatively, tape the program while watching it so that you can view it several times. The documentation format for such nonprint sources is illustrated in Chapter 10.

Surveys, Questionnaires, and Original Research

Depending on your paper, you may want to conduct a simple survey or write and administer a questionnaire. Surveys can be used for many campus and local issues, for topics on behavior and attitudes of college students and/or faculty, and for topics on consumer habits. Prepare a brief list of questions with space for answers. Poll faculty through their mailboxes or e-mail and students individually on campus or in your classes. When writing questions, keep these guidelines in mind:

- Use simple, clear language.
- Devise a series of short questions rather than only a few that have several parts to them. (You want to separate information for better analysis.)
- Phrase questions to avoid wording that seeks to control the answer. For example, do *not* ask: How did you survive the *horrors* of the Depression? Do *not* write: Did you perform your civic duty by voting in the last election? These are loaded questions that prejudge the respondent's answers.

In addition to surveys and questionnaires, you can incorporate some original research. As you read sources on your topic, be alert to reports of studies that you could redo and update in part or on a smaller scale. Many topics on advertising and television give opportunities for your own analysis. Local-issue topics may offer good opportunities for gathering information on your own, not just from your reading. One student, examining the controversy over a proposed new shopping mall on part of the Manassas Civil War Battlefield in Virginia, made the argument that the mall served no practical need in the community. He supported his position by describing existing malls, including the number and types of stores each contained and the number of miles each was from the proposed new mall. How did he obtain this information? He drove around the area, counting miles and stores. Sometimes a seemingly unglamorous approach to a topic turns out to be an imaginative one.

CHAPTER 10

Exploring Sources, Selecting Support, and Documenting
(Using MLA)

As you study your sources, keep rethinking your purpose and approach. Test your research proposal or tentative claim against what you are learning. Remember: You can always change the direction and focus of your paper as new approaches occur to you, and you can even change your position as you reflect on what you are learning.

USING SOURCES EFFECTIVELY

You will work with sources more effectively if you keep in mind why you are using them. What you are looking for will vary somewhat, depending on your topic and purpose, but there are several basic approaches:

1. *Acquiring information and viewpoints firsthand.* Suppose that you are concerned about the mistreatment of animals kept in zoos. You do not want to just read what others have to say on this issue. First, visit a zoo, taking notes on what you see. Second, before you go, plan to interview at least one person on the zoo staff, preferably a veterinarian who can explain the zoo's guidelines for animal care. Only after gathering and thinking about these *primary sources* do you want to add to your knowledge by reading articles and books—*secondary sources.* Many kinds of topics require the use of both primary and secondary sources. If you want to study violence in children's TV shows, for example, you should first spend some time watching specific shows and taking notes.

2. *Acquiring new knowledge.* Suppose you are interested in breast cancer research and treatment, but you do not know much about the choices of treatment and, in general, where we are with this medical problem. You will need to turn to sources first to learn about the topic. You should begin with sources that will give you an overview, perhaps a historical perspective of how knowledge and treatment have progressed in the last thirty years. Similarly, if your topic is the effects of Prohibition in the 1920s, you will need to read first for knowledge but also with an eye to ways to focus the topic and organize your paper.

3. *Understanding the issues.* Suppose you think that you know your views on gun control or immigration, so you intend to read only to obtain some useful statistical information to support your argument. Should you scan sources quickly, looking for facts you can use? This approach may be too hasty. As explained in Chapter 3, good arguments are built on a knowledge of counterarguments. You are wise to study sources presenting a variety of attitudes on your issue so that you understand—and can refute—the arguments of others. *Remember, too, that with controversial issues often the best argument is a conciliatory one that presents a middle ground and seeks to bring people together.* You may also want to consider interviewing an elected official or administering a questionnaire to fellow students.

EVALUATING SOURCES, MAINTAINING CREDIBILITY

When you use facts and opinions from sources, you are saying to readers that the facts are accurate and the ideas credible. If you do not evaluate your sources before using them, you risk losing your credibility as a writer. (Remember Aristotle's idea of *ethos,* how your character is judged.) Just because they are in print does not mean that a writer's "facts" are reliable or ideas worthwhile. Judging the usefulness and reliability of potential sources is an essential part of the research process.

GUIDELINES for Evaluating Sources

Today, with access to so much material on the Internet, the need to evaluate is even more crucial. Here are some strategies for evaluating sources, with special attention to Internet sources:

- **Locate the author's credentials.** Periodicals often list their writers' degrees, current position, and other publications; books, similarly, contain an "about the author" section. If you do not see this information, check various biographical dictionaries (*Biography Index, Contemporary Authors*) for information about the author. For articles on the Web, look for the author's e-mail address or a link to a home page. *Never use a Web source that does not identify the author or the organization responsible for the material. Critical question:* Is this author qualified to write on this topic? How do I know?

- **Judge the credibility of the work.** For books, read how reviewers evaluated the book when it was first published. For articles, judge the respectability of the magazine or journal. Study the author's use of documentation as one measure of credibility. Scholarly works cite sources. Well-researched and reliable pieces in quality popular magazines will also make clear the sources of any statistics used or the credentials of any authority who is quoted. One good rule: Never use undocumented statistical information. Another judge of credibility is the quality of writing. Do not use sources filled with grammatical and mechanical errors. For Web sources, find out what institution hosts the site. If you have not heard of the company or organization, find out more about it. *Critical question:* Why should I believe information/ideas from this source?

- **Select only those sources that are at an appropriate level for your research.** Avoid works that are either too specialized or too elementary for college research. You may not understand the former (and thus could misrepresent them in your paper), and you gain nothing from the latter. *Critical question:* Will this source provide a sophisticated discussion for educated adults?

- **Understand the writer's purpose.** Consider the writer's intended audience. Be cautious using works designed to reinforce biases already shared by the intended audience. Is the work written to persuade rather than to inform and analyze? Examine the writing for emotionally charged language. For Internet sources, ask yourself why this person or institution decided to have a Web site or contribute to a newsgroup. *Critical question:* Can I trust the information from this source, given the apparent purpose of the work?

- **In general, choose current sources.** Some studies published years ago remain classics, but many older works have become outdated. In scientific and technical fields, the "information revolution" has outdated some works published only five years ago. So look at publication dates (When was the Web site page last updated?) and pass over outdated sources in favor of current studies. *Critical question:* Is this information still accurate?

DOCUMENTING SOURCES TO AVOID PLAGIARISM

Documenting sources accurately and fully is required of all researchers. Proper documentation distinguishes between the work of others and your ideas, shows readers the breadth of your research, and strengthens your credibility. In Western culture, copyright laws support the ethic that ideas, new information, and wording belong to their author. To borrow these without acknowledgment is against the law and has led to many celebrated lawsuits. For students who plagiarize the consequences range from an F on the paper to suspension from college. Be certain, then, that you know what the requirements for correct documentation are; accidental plagiarism is still plagiarism and will be punished.

> **NOTE:** MLA documentation requires that precise page references be given for all ideas, opinions, and information taken from sources—except for common knowledge. Author and page references provided in the text are supported by complete bibliographic citations on the Works Cited page.

In sum, you are required to document the following:

- Direct quotations from sources
- Paraphrased ideas and opinions from sources
- Summaries of ideas from sources
- Factual information, except common knowledge, from sources

Understand that putting an author's ideas in your own words in a paraphrase or summary does not eliminate the requirement of documentation. To illustrate, consider the following excerpt from Thomas R. Schueler's report *Controlling Urban Runoff* (Washington Metropolitan Water Resources Planning Board, 1987: 3–4) and a student paragraph based on the report.

SOURCE

The aquatic ecosystems in urban headwater streams are particularly susceptible to the impacts of urbanization . . . Dietemann (1975), Ragan and Dietemann (1976), Klein (1979) and WMCOG (1982) have all tracked trends in fish diversity and abundance over time in local urbanizing streams. Each of the studies has shown that fish communities become less diverse and are composed of more tolerant species after the surrounding watershed is developed. Sensitive fish species either disappear or occur very rarely. In most cases, the total number of fish in urbanizing streams may also decline.

Similar trends have been noted among aquatic insects which are the major food resource for fish . . . Higher post-development sediment and trace metals can interfere in their efforts to gather food. Changes in water temperature, oxygen levels, and substrate composition can further reduce the species diversity and abundance of the aquatic insect community.

PLAGARIZED STUDENT PARAGRAPH

> Studies have shown that fish communities become less diverse as the amount of runoff increases. Sensitive fish species either disappear or occur very rarely, and, in most cases, the total number of fish declines. Aquatic insects, a major source of food for fish, also decline because sediment and trace metals interfere with their food-gathering efforts. Increased water temperature and lower oxygen levels can further reduce the species diversity and abundance of the aquatic insect community.

The student's opening words establish a reader's expectation that the student has taken information from a source, as indeed the student has. But where is the documentation? The student's paraphrase is a good example of plagiarism: an unacknowledged paraphrase of borrowed information that even collapses into copying the source's exact wording in two places. For MLA style, the author's name and the precise page numbers are needed throughout the paragraph. Additionally, most of the first sentence and the final phrase must be put into the student's own words or be placed within quotation marks. The following revised paragraph shows an appropriate acknowledgment of the source used.

REVISED STUDENT PARAGRAPH TO REMOVE PLAGIARISM

> In *Controlling Urban Runoff,* Thomas Schueler explains that studies have shown "that fish communities become less diverse as the amount of runoff increases" (3). Sensitive fish species either disappear or occur very rarely and, in most cases, the total number of fish declines. Aquatic insects, a major source of food for fish, also decline because sediment and trace metals interfere with their food-gathering efforts. Increased water temperature and lower oxygen levels, Schueler concludes, "can further reduce the species diversity and abundance of the aquatic insect community" (4).

What Is Common Knowledge?

In general, common knowledge includes:

- Undisputed dates
- Well-known facts

- Generally known facts, terms, and concepts in a field of study when you are writing in that field

So, do not cite a source for the dates of the American Revolution. If you are writing a paper for a psychology class, do not cite your text when using terms such as *ego* or *sublimation*. However, you must cite a historian who analyzes the causes of England's loss to the Colonies or a psychologist who disputes Freud's ideas. *Opinions* about well-known facts must be documented. *Discussions* of debatable dates, terms, or concepts must be documented. When in doubt, defend your integrity and document.

TAKING NOTES ON SOURCES

As you read and learn, expand your research proposal in two ways. First, draft a claim statement that is as clear and focused as you feel comfortable with at this stage. Second, list possible reasons in support of your claim. Keep this list informal but use it to start thinking about the parts your paper will need. Having an informal outline will guide your search for information and your thinking about how and where to use the information.

How are you going to keep track of information and ideas from your study? You have three possibilities: handwritten notes on cards, keyboarded notes in PC files, and annotations of photocopies of sources. How to choose? If your instructor requires you to hand in notes, then you must use the first or second strategy. (Just print out your files and cut pages into separate note "cards.") Here are guidelines for all three methods plus, in Figure 10.1, an example of good note taking.

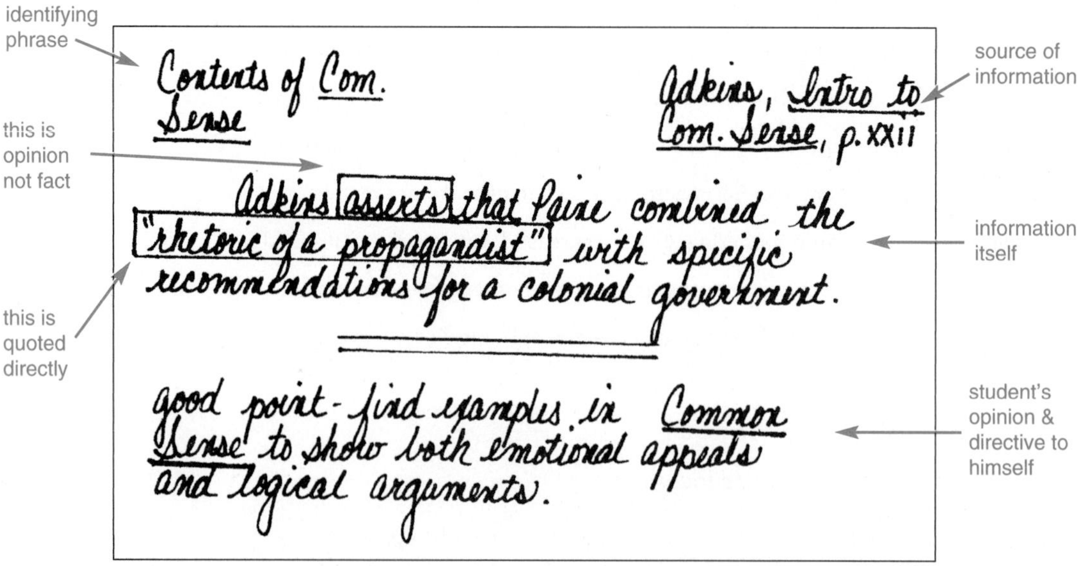

FIGURE 10.1 Sample Note Card

GUIDELINES for Effective Note Taking

Cards

1. **Use either 4 × 6 cards or half sheets of letter-size paper.**
2. **Write in ink.**
3. **Write only one item on each card.** Each card should contain only one idea, piece of information, or group of related facts. The flexibility of cards is lost if you do not follow this procedure. You want to be able to group cards according to your outline when you are ready to draft the paper.

With a Computer

1. **Make one file titled "notes" or make a separate file for each note.**
2. **Use clear headings and subheadings for notes so that you can find particular notes easily.**
3. **Consider printing copies of your notes and cutting them into separate "cards" for organizing prior to drafting.** (When drafting, do not re-keyboard. Just use your printed notes as a guide to placement in the draft.) Use the "cut and paste" or "move" features of your word processor to rearrange notes into the order you want.

Annotating Photocopies

1. **Do not endlessly highlight your photocopies.** Instead, carefully bracket those passages that contain information you want to use.
2. **Write a note in the margin next to bracketed passages indicating how and where you think you want to use that material.** Use the language of your informal outline to annotate marked passages (e.g., "causes," "effects," "rebuttal to counterargument," "solutions").
3. **Keep in mind that you will have to paraphrase most of the marked passages before using the material in your draft.**

Writing Notes: Cards or Keyboarded

1. **Study first; take notes later.** First, do background reading. Second, skim what appear to be your chief sources. Prepare summary notes and annotate photocopies of sources. Read so that you can develop your preliminary outline. Learn what the writers on your topic consider to be important facts, issues, and arguments. Keep in mind that taking too many useless notes is a frustrating, time-wasting activity.
2. **Before preparing any note, identify the source of the note.** Write or type the author's name, a shortened title if necessary, and the precise page number from which the material comes. *Remember: All borrowed information and ideas must be documented with precise page numbers if you are using MLA style—and for all direct quotations if you are using APA style.*
3. **Type or write an identifying word or phrase for each note.** Identifying words or phrases will help you sort cards or find notes when you are ready to draft. Select words carefully to correspond to the sections of your preliminary outline.

4. **Take down the information itself—accurately and clearly.** Be sure to put all directly quoted passages within quotation marks. To treat a direct quotation as a paraphrase in your paper is to plagiarize.

5. **Distinguish between fact and opinion.** Notes that contain opinion should be indicated with such phrases as "Smith believes that" or "Smith asserts that." Alternatively, label the note "opinion."

6. **Distinguish between information from sources and your own opinions, questions, and reactions to the recorded information.** Write notes to yourself so that you do not forget good ideas that come to you as you are reading. Just be certain to label your notes "my notes"—or draw (or type) a line between information from a source and your response.

Should I Quote or Paraphrase Notes or Use Photocopies of Sources?

Here are the arguments:

- Most of your paper should be in your own words, so most of your notes should be paraphrases or summaries. Putting off paraphrasing means just that—putting it off until you are under the pressure of writing the paper.
- Taking direct-quotation notes will give you the exact wording of passages to think about when you draft your paper. At the drafting stage, you can turn the quoted passages into paraphrases.
- The previous point, along with the valid point of convenience, justifies using copies of sources that you annotate to show what passages you want to use. The potential problem is the same as that for direct-quotation notes.

Probably some combination of strategies is a good choice. Photocopy (or download or e-mail to yourself) key articles so that you have the entire article to work with. Initially tab key passages in books with Post-it notes or slips of paper. Then, as you get close to finishing your study of sources, make at least some paraphrased notes to start the process of moving away from the language of original sources. The more sources you are using, the more convenient and efficient notes will be when you are ready to draft your paper.

USING "TAGS" OR "SIGNAL PHRASES" TO AVOID MISLEADING DOCUMENTATION

If you are an honest student, you do not want to submit a paper that is plagiarized, even though that plagiarism was unintentional on your part. What leads to unintentional plagiarism?

- A researcher takes careless notes, neglecting to include precise page numbers on the notes, but uses the information anyway, without any documentation.
- A researcher works in material from sources in such a way that, even with page references, readers cannot tell what has been taken from the sources.

Good note-taking strategies will keep you from the first pitfall. Avoiding the second problem means becoming skilled in ways to include source material in your writing while still making your indebtedness to sources absolutely clear to readers. The way to do this: Give the author's name in the essay. You can also include, when appropriate, the author's credentials ("According to Dr. Hays, a geologist with the Department of Interior, . . ."). These *introductory tags* or *signal phrases* give readers a context for the borrowed material, as well as serving as part of the required documentation of sources. *Make sure that each tag clarifies rather than distorts an author's relationship to his or her ideas and your relationship to the source.*

GUIDELINES for Appropriately Using Borrowed Material

Here are three guidelines to follow to avoid misrepresenting borrowed material:

- **Pay attention to verb choice in tags.** When you vary such standard wording as "Smith says" or "Jones states," be careful that you do not select verbs that misrepresent "Smith's" or "Jones's" attitude toward his or her own work. Do not write "Jones wonders" when in fact Jones has strongly asserted her views. (See page 286 for a discussion of varying word choice in tags.)

- **Pay attention to the location of tags.** If you mention Jones after you have presented her views, be sure that your reader can tell precisely which ideas in the passage belong to Jones. If your entire paragraph is a paraphrase of Jones's work, you are plagiarizing to conclude with "This idea is presented by Jones." Which of the several ideas in your paragraph comes from Jones? Your reader will assume that only the last idea comes from Jones.

- **Paraphrase properly.** Be sure that paraphrases are truly *in your own words.* To use Smith's words and sentence style in your writing is to plagiarize.

> **NOTE:** Putting a parenthetical page reference at the end of a paragraph is not sufficient if you have used the source throughout the paragraph. Use introductory tags or signal phrases to guide the reader through the material.

EXERCISE: Acknowledging Sources

The following paragraph (from Franklin E. Zimring's "Firearms, Violence and Public Policy" [*Scientific American,* Nov. 1991]) provides material for the examples that follow of adequate and inadequate acknowledgment of sources. After reading Zimring's paragraph, study the three examples with these questions in mind: (1) Which example represents adequate acknowledgment? (2) Which examples do not represent adequate acknowledgment? (3) In exactly what ways is each plagiarized paragraph flawed?

SOURCE

Although most citizens support such measures as owner screening, public opinion is sharply divided on laws that would restrict the ownership of handguns to persons with special needs. If the U.S. does not reduce handguns and current trends continue, it faces the prospect that the number of handguns in circulation will grow from 35 million to more than 50 million within 50 years. A national program limiting the availability of handguns would cost many billions of dollars and meet much resistance from citizens. These costs would likely be greatest in the early years of the program. The benefits of supply reduction would emerge slowly because efforts to diminish the availability of handguns would probably have a cumulative impact over time. (page 54)

STUDENT PARAGRAPH 1

One approach to the problem of handgun violence in America is to severely limit handgun ownership. If we don't restrict ownership and start the costly task of removing handguns from our society, we may end up with around 50 million handguns in the country by 2040. The benefits will not be apparent right away but will eventually appear. This idea is emphasized by Franklin Zimring (54).

STUDENT PARAGRAPH 2

One approach to the problem of handgun violence in America is to restrict the ownership of handguns except in special circumstances. If we do not begin to reduce the number of handguns in this country, the number will grow from 35 million to more than 50 million within 50 years. We can agree with Franklin Zimring that a program limiting handguns will cost billions and meet resistance from citizens (54).

STUDENT PARAGRAPH 3

According to law professor Franklin Zimring, the United States needs to severely limit handgun ownership or face the possibility of seeing handgun ownership increase "from 35 million to more than 50 million within 50 years" (54). Zimring points out that Americans disagree significantly on restricting handguns and that enforcing such laws would be very expensive. He concludes that the benefits would not be seen immediately but that the restrictions "would probably have a cumulative impact over time" (54). Although Zimring paints a gloomy picture of high costs and little immediate relief from gun violence, he also presents the shocking possibility of 50 million guns by the year 2040. Can our society survive so much fire power?

Clearly, only the third student paragraph demonstrates adequate acknowledgment of the writer's indebtedness to Zimring. Notice that the placement of the last parenthetical page reference acts as a visual closure to the student's borrowing; then she turns to her response to Zimring and her own views on the problem of handguns.

MLA IN-TEXT (PARENTHETICAL) DOCUMENTATION

The student paragraphs above illustrate the most common form of parenthetical documentation in MLA style: parenthetical references to author and page number, or just to page number if the author has been mentioned in an introductory tag. Because a reference only to author and page number is an incomplete citation (readers could not find the source with such limited information), whatever is cited this way in the essay must refer to a specific source presented fully in a Works Cited list that follows the text of the paper. General guidelines for citing are given below, followed by examples and explanations of the required patterns of documentation.

NOTE: You need a 100 percent correspondence between the sources listed on your Works Cited page(s) and the sources you cite (refer to) in your paper. Do not omit from your Works Cited any sources you refer to in your paper. Do not include in your Works Cited any sources not referred to in your paper.

GUIDELINES for Using Parenthetical Documentation

- **The purpose of documentation is to make clear exactly what material in a passage has been borrowed and from what source the borrowed material has come.**
- **Parenthetical documentation requires specific page references for borrowed material.**
- **Parenthetical documentation is required for both quoted and paraphrased material.**
- **Parenthetical documentation provides as brief a citation as possible consistent with accuracy and clarity.**

The Simplest Patterns of Parenthetical Documentation

The simplest parenthetical reference can be prepared in one of three ways:

1. Give the author's last name (full name in the first reference) in the text of your paper and place the relevant page number(s) in parentheses following the borrowed material.

   Frederick Lewis Allen observes that, during the 1920s, urban tastes spread to

   the country (146).

2. Place the author's last name and the relevant page number(s) in parentheses immediately following the borrowed material.

   During the 1920s, "not only the drinks were mixed, but the company as well"

   (Allen 82).

3. On the rare occasion that you cite an entire work rather than borrowing from a specific passage, give the author's name in the text and omit any page numbers.

   Barbara Tuchman argues that there are significant parallels between the

   fourteenth century and our time.

   Each one of these in-text references is complete *only* when the full citation is found in the Works Cited section of your paper.

   Allen, Frederick Lewis. Only Yesterday: An Informal History of the Nineteen-

   Twenties. New York: Harper, 1931.

   Tuchman, Barbara W. A Distant Mirror: The Calamitous 14th Century. New

   York: Knopf, 1978.

The three patterns just illustrated should be used in each of the following situations:

1. The work is not anonymous—the author is known.
2. The work is by one author.
3. The work cited is the only work used by that author.
4. No other author in your bibliography has the same last name.

Placement of Parenthetical Documentation

The simplest placing of a parenthetical reference is at the end of the appropriate sentence *before* the period, but, when you are quoting, *after* the quotation mark.

   During the 1920s, "not only the drinks were mixed, but the company as well"

   (Allen 82).

Do not put any punctuation between the author's name and the page number.

If the borrowed material ends before the end of your sentence, place the parenthetical reference *after* the borrowed material and before any subsequent punctuation. This placement more accurately shows what is borrowed and what is your own work.

> Sport, Allen observes about the 1920s, had developed into an obsession (66),
>
> another similarity between the 1920s and the 1980s.

If a quoted passage is long enough to require setting off in display form (block quotation), then place the parenthetical reference at the end of the passage, *after* the last period. (Remember that long quotations in display form do not have quotation marks.)

> It is hard to believe that when he writes about the influence of science, Allen is
>
> describing the 1920s, not the 1980s:
>
>> The prestige of science was colossal. The man in the street and the
>>
>> woman in the kitchen, confronted on every hand with new machines and
>>
>> devices which they owed to the laboratory, were ready to believe that
>>
>> science could accomplish almost anything. (164)

And to complete the documentation for all three examples:

Works Cited

> Allen, Frederick Lewis. Only Yesterday: An Informal History of the Nineteen-
>
> Twenties. New York: Harper, 1931.

Parenthetical Citations of Complex Sources

Not all sources can be cited in one of the three simplest forms described above, for not all meet the four criteria listed on page 290. Works by two or more authors, for example, will need somewhat fuller references. Each sample form of parenthetical documentation below would be completed with a full Works Cited reference, as illustrated above and in the next section of this chapter.

Two Authors, Mentioned in the Text

> Richard Herrnstein and Charles Murray contend that it is "consistently . . .
>
> advantageous to be smart" (25).

Two Authors, Not Mentioned in the Text

The advantaged smart group form a "cognitive elite" in our society

(Herrnstein and Murray 26–27).

A Book in Two or More Volumes

Sewall analyzes the role of Judge Lord in Dickinson's life (2: 642–47).

OR

Judge Lord was also one of Dickinson's preceptors (Sewall 2: 642–47).

Note: The number before the colon always signifies the volume number: the number(s) after the colon represents the page number(s).

A Book or Article Listed by Title (Author Unknown)

According to the Concise Dictionary of American Biography, William Jennings

Bryan's 1896 campaign stressed social and sectional conflicts (117).

The Times's editors are not pleased with some of the changes in welfare

programs ("Where Welfare Stands" 4:16).

Always cite the title of the article, not the title of the journal, if the author is unknown.

A Work by a Corporate Author

According to the report of the Institute of Ecology's Global Ecological

Problems Workshop, the civilization of the city can lull us into forgetting our

relationship to the total ecological system on which we depend (13).

Although corporate authors may be cited with the page number within the parentheses, your presentation will be more graceful if corporate authors are introduced in the text. Then only page numbers go in parentheses.

Two or More Works by the Same Author

During the 1920s, "not only the drinks were mixed, but the company as well"

(Allen, Only Yesterday 82).

According to Frederick Lewis Allen, the early 1900s were a period of

complacency in America (The Big Change 4–5).

> In The Big Change, Allen asserts that the early 1900s were a period of
>
> complacency (4–5).

If your Works Cited list contains two or more works by the same author, the fullest parenthetical citation will include the author's last name, followed by a comma, the work's title, shortened if possible, and the page number(s). If the author's name appears in the text—or the author and title both, as in the third example above—omit these items from the parenthetical citation. When you have to include the title, it is best to simplify the citation by including the author's last name in the text.

Two or More Works in One Parenthetical Reference

> Several writers about the future agree that big changes will take place in work
>
> patterns (Toffler 384–87; Naisbitt 35–36).

Separate each author cited with a semicolon. But if the parenthetical citation would be disruptively long, cite the works in a "See also" note rather than in the text.

Complete Publication Information in Parenthetical Reference

Occasionally you may want to give complete information about a source within parentheses in the text of your paper. Then a Works Cited list is not used. Square brackets are used for parenthetical information within parentheses. This approach may be appropriate when you use only one or two sources, even if many references are made to those sources. Literary analyses are one type of paper for which this approach to citation may be a good choice. For example:

> Edith Wharton establishes the bleakness of her setting, Starkfield, not just
>
> through description of place but also through her main character, Ethan, who
>
> is described as "bleak and unapproachable" (Ethan Frome [New York:
>
> Scribner's, 1911] 3. All subsequent references are to this edition.). Later
>
> Wharton describes winter as "shut[ting] down on Starkfield" and negating life
>
> there (7).

Additional Information Footnotes or Endnotes

At times you may need to provide additional useful information, explanation, or commentary that is not central to the development of your paper. These additions belong in content footnotes or endnotes. However, use these sparingly and never as a way of advancing your thesis. Many instructors object to content footnotes or endnotes and prefer only parenthetical citations in student papers.

"See Also" Footnotes or Endnotes

More acceptable to most readers is the footnote that refers to other sources of evidence for or against the point to be established. Such footnotes (or endnotes) can be combined with parenthetical documentation. They are usually introduced with "See also" or "Compare," followed by the citation. For example:

Chekhov's debt to Ibsen should be recognized, as should his debt to

Maeterlinck and other playwrights of the 1890s who were concerned with the

inner life of their characters.[1]

[1]See also Eric Bentley, In Search of Theatre (New York: Vintage, 1959) 330; Walter Bruford, Anton Chekhov (New Haven: Yale UP, 1957) 45; and Raymond Williams, Drama from Ibsen to Eliot (New York: Oxford UP, 1953) 126–29.

PREPARING MLA CITATIONS FOR A "WORKS CITED" PAGE

Parenthetical (in-text) citations are completed by a full reference to each source in a list presented at the end of the paper. To prepare your Works Cited page(s), alphabetize, by the author's last name, the sources you have cited and complete each citation according to the forms illustrated and explained in the following pages. The key is to find the appropriate model for each of your sources and then follow the model exactly. (Guidelines for formatting a finished Works Cited page are found on pages 329 and 338.)

Forms for Books: Citing the Complete Book

A Book by a Single Author

Silver, Lee M. Remaking Eden: Cloning and Beyond in a Brave New World.

New York: Avon, 1997.

The subtitle is included, preceded by a colon, even if there is no colon on the book's title page.

A Book by Two or Three Authors

Adkins, Lesley, and Ray Adkins. The Keys of Egypt: The Race to Crack the

Hieroglyph Code. New York: HaperCollins, 2000.

Second (and third) authors' names appear in signature form.

A Book with More Than Three Authors

> Baker, Susan P., et al. The Injury Fact Book. Oxford: Oxford UP, 1992.

Use the name of the first author listed on the title page. The English "and others" may be used instead of "et al." Shorten "University Press" to "UP."

Two or More Works by the Same Author

> Goodall, Jane. In the Shadow of Man. Boston: Houghton, 1971.

> - - -. Through a Window: My Thirty Years with the Chimpanzees of Gombe.
>   Boston: Houghton, 1990.

Give the author's full name with the first entry. For the second (and additional works), begin the citation with three hyphens followed by a period. Alphabetize the entries by the books' titles.

A Book Written under a Pseudonym with Name Supplied

> Wrighter, Carl P. [Paul Stevens]. I Can Sell You Anything. New York:
>   Ballantine, 1972.

Supply the author's name in square brackets.

An Anonymous Book

> Beowulf: A New Verse Translation. Trans. Seamus Heaney. New York: Farrar,
>   2000.

Do not use "anon." Alphabetize by the book's title.

An Edited Book

> Hamilton, Alexander, James Madison, and John Jay. The Federalist Papers. Ed.
>   Isaac Kramnick. New York: Viking-Penguin, 1987.

> Lynn, Kenneth S., ed. Huckleberry Finn: Text, Sources, and Critics. New York:
>   Harcourt, 1961.

If you cite the author's work, put the author's name first and the editor's name after the title, preceded by "Ed." If you cite the editor's work (an introduction or notes), then place the editor's name first, followed by a comma and "ed."

A Translation

> Schulze, Hagen. Germany: A New History. Trans. Deborah Lucas Schneider.
>
>   Cambridge: Harvard UP, 1998.
>
> Cornford, Francis MacDonald, trans. The Republic of Plato. New York: Oxford
>
>   UP, 1945.

If the author's work is being cited, place the author's name first and the translator's name after the title, preceded by "Trans." If the translator's work is the important element, place the translator's name first, as in the second example above. If the author's name does not appear in the title, give it after the title. For example: By Plato.

A Book in Two or More Volumes

> Spielvogel, Jackson J. Western Civilization. 2 vols. Minneapolis: West, 1991.

A Book in Its Second or Subsequent Edition

> O'Brien, David M. Storm Center: The Supreme Court and American Politics.
>
>   2nd ed. New York: Norton, 1990.
>
> Sundqist, James L. Dynamics of the Party System. Rev. ed. Washington:
>
>   Brookings, 1983.

Always include the number of the edition you have used, abbreviated as shown, if it is not the first edition.

A Book in a Series

> Parkinson, Richard. The Rosetta Stone. British Museum Objects in Focus.
>
>   London: British Museum Press, 2005.

The series title—and number, if there is one—follows the book's title but is not underlined.

A Reprint of an Earlier Work

> Cuppy, Will. How to Become Extinct. 1941. Chicago: U of Chicago P, 1983.
>
> Twain, Mark. Adventures of Huckleberry Finn. 1885. Centennial Facsimile
>
>   Edition. Introd. Hamlin Hill. New York: Harper, 1962.
>
> Faulkner, William. As I Lay Dying. 1930. New York: Vintage-Random, 1964.

Since the date of a work is often important, cite the original date of publication as well as the facts of publication for the reprinted version. Indicate any new material that is part of the reprinted book, as in the second example. The third example shows how to cite a book reprinted, by the same publisher, in a paperback version. (Vintage is a paperback imprint of the publisher Random House.)

A Book with Two or More Publishers

> Green, Mark J., James M. Fallows, and David R. Zwick. Who Runs Congress? Ralph
>
> > Nader Congress Project. New York: Bantam; New York: Grossman, 1972.

If the title page lists two or more publishers, give all as part of the facts of publication, placing a semicolon between them, as illustrated above.

A Corporate or Governmental Author

> California State Department of Education. American Indian Education
>
> > Handbook. Sacramento: California State Department of Education,
> >
> > Indian Education Unit, 1991.
>
> Hispanic Market Connections. The National Hispanic Database: A Los
>
> > Angeles Preview. Los Altos, CA: Hispanic Market Connections, 1992.

List the institution as the author even when it is also the publisher.

A Book in a Foreign Language

> Blanchard, Gerard. Images de la musique au cinéma. Paris: Edilig, 1984.

Capitalize only the first word of titles and subtitles and words normally capitalized in that language (e.g., proper nouns in French, all nouns in German). A translation in square brackets may be provided. Check your work carefully for spelling and accent marks.

The Bible

> The Bible. [Always refers to the King James Version.]
>
> The Bible. Revised Standard Version.
>
> The Reader's Bible: A Narrative. Ed. with intro. Roland Mushat Frye.
>
> > Princeton: Princeton UP, 1965.

Do not underline the title. Indicate the version if it is not the King James Version. Provide facts of publication for versions not well known.

A Book with a Title in Its Title

> Piper, Henry Dan, ed. Fitzgerald's The Great Gatsby: The Novel, the Critics,
>
>   the Background. Scribner Research Anthologies. Ed. Martin
>
>   Steinmann, Jr. New York: Scribner's, 1970.

Forms for Books: Citing Part of a Book

A Preface, Introduction, Foreword, or Afterword

> Sagan, Carl. Introduction. A Brief History of Time: From the Big Bang to
>
>   Black Holes. By Stephen W. Hawking. New York: Bantam, 1988. ix–x.

Use this form if you are citing the author of the preface, etc. Provide the appropriate identifying phrase after the author's name and give inclusive page numbers for the part of the book by that author at the end of the citation.

An Encyclopedia Article

> Ostrom, John H. "Dinosaurs." McGraw-Hill Encyclopedia of Science and
>
>   Technology. 1987 ed.
>
> "Benjamin Franklin." Concise Dictionary of American Biography. Ed. Joseph
>
>   G. E. Hopkins. New York: Scribner's, 1964.

When articles are signed or initialed, give the author's name. Complete the name of the author of an initialed article thus: K[enny], E[dward] J. Identify well-known encyclopedias and dictionaries by the year of the edition only. Give the complete facts of publication for less well-known works or those in only one edition.

One or More Volumes in a Multivolume Work

> James, Henry. The Portrait of a Lady. Vols. 3 and 4 of The Novels and Tales of
>
>   Henry James. 26 vols. New York: Scribner's, 1908.

When using a complete work that makes up one or more volumes of a multivolume work, cite the title and volume number(s) of that work followed by the title, editor (if appropriate), total number of volumes, and facts of publication for the multivolume work.

A Work Within One Volume of a Multivolume Work

> Shaw, Bernard. Pygmalion. New York: Dodd, 1963. Vol 1. of The Complete
>
>   Plays with Prefaces. 6 vols.

Cite the author and title of the single work used, the facts of publication for the multivolume work, then the volume number, and title of the complete work. Then give the inclusive publication dates for the work, followed by the total number of volumes.

A Work in an Anthology or Collection

> Hurston, Zora Neale. The First One. Black Female Playwrights: An Anthology
>
> of Plays Before 1950. Ed. Kathy A. Perkins. Bloomington: Indiana UP,
>
> 1989. 80–88.
>
> Comstock, George. "The Medium and the Society: The Role of Television in
>
> American Life." Children and Television: Images in a Changing
>
> Sociocultural World. Eds. Gordon L. Berry and Joy Keiko Asamen.
>
> Newbury Park, CA: Sage, 1993. 117–31.

Cite the author and title of the work you have used. Then give the title, the editor(s), and the facts of publication of the anthology or collection. Conclude by providing inclusive page numbers for the work used.

An Article in a Collection, Casebook, or Sourcebook

> Welsch, Roger. "The Cornstalk Fiddle." Journal of American Folklore 77
>
> (1964): 262–63. Rpt. in Readings in American Folklore. Ed. Jan Harold
>
> Brunvand. New York: Norton, 1979. 106–07.
>
> MacKenzie, James J. "The Decline of Nuclear Power." engage/social April
>
> 1986. Rpt. as "America Does Not Need More Nuclear Power Plants" in
>
> The Environmental Crisis: Opposing Viewpoints. Eds. Julie S. Bach and
>
> Lynn Hall. Opposing Viewpoints Series. St. Paul: Greenhaven, 1986.
>
> 136–41.

Most articles in collections have been previously published, so a complete citation needs to include the original facts of publication (excluding page numbers if they are unavailable) as well as the facts of publication for the collection. End the citation with inclusive page numbers for the article used.

Cross-References

If you are citing several articles from one collection, you can cite the collection and then provide only the author and title of specific articles used, with a cross-reference to the editor(s) of the collection:

Head, Suzanne, and Robert Heinzman, eds. <u>Lessons of the Rainforest</u>. San

Francisco: Sierra Club, 1990.

Bandyopadhyay, J., and Vandana Shiva. "Asia's Forest, Asia's Cultures." Head

and Heinzman 66–77.

Head, Suzanne. "The Consumer Connection: Psychology and Politics." Head

and Heinzman 156–67.

Forms for Periodicals: Articles in Journals

*Article in a Journal with Continuous Paging Throughout
the Issues of Each Year*

Truman, Dana M., David M. Tokar, and Ann R. Fischer. "Dimensions of

Masculinity: Relations to Date Rape, Supportive Attitudes, and Sexual

Aggression in Dating Situations." <u>Journal of Counseling and Development</u>

76 (1996): 555–62.

Give the volume number followed by the year only, in parentheses, followed by
a colon and inclusive page numbers.

Article in a Journal with Separate Paging for Each Issue

Lewis, Kevin. "Superstardom and Transcendence." <u>Arete: The Journal of Sport

Literature</u> 2.2 (1985): 47–54.

When each issue of a journal begins with a new page 1, give the issue number,
immediately following the volume number, separated by a period.

Article in a Journal That Uses Issue Numbers Only

Keen, Ralph. "Thomas More and Geometry." <u>Moreana</u> 86 (1985): 151–66.

If the journal uses only issue numbers, not volume numbers, treat the issue
number as a volume number.

Forms for Periodicals: Articles in Magazines

Article in a Monthly Magazine

Norell, Mark A., and Xu Xing. "The Varieties of Tyrannosaurs." <u>Natural

History</u> May 2005: 35–39.

Do not use volume or issue number. Instead, cite the month(s) and year after the title, followed by a colon and inclusive page numbers. Abbreviate all months except May, June, and July.

Article in a Weekly Magazine

> Stein, Joel. "Eat This, Low Carbers." Time 15 Aug. 2005: 78.

Provide the complete date, using the order of day, month, and year.

An Anonymous Article

> "Death of Perestroika." Economist 2 Feb. 1991: 12–13.

The missing name indicates that the article is anonymous. Alphabetize under D.

A Published Interview

> Angier, Natalie. "Ernst Mayr at 93." Interview. Natural History May 1997: 8–11.

Follow the pattern for a published article, but add the descriptive label "Interview" (followed by a period) after the article's title.

A Review

> Bardsley, Tim. "Eliciting Science's Best." Rev. of Frontiers of Illusion: Science,
>
> Technology, and the Politics of Progress, by Daniel Sarewitz. Scientific
>
> American June 1997: 142.
>
> Shales, Tom. "A Chilling Stop in 'Nuremberg.' " Rev. of the movie Nuremberg,
>
> TNT 16 July 2000. Washington Post 16 July 2000: G1.

If the review is signed, begin with the author's name, then the title of the review article. Give the title of the work being reviewed, a comma, and its author, preceded by "Rev. of." Alphabetize unsigned reviews by the title of the review. For reviews of art shows, videos, or computer software, provide place and date or descriptive label to make the citation clear.

Forms for Periodicals: Newspapers

An Article from a Newspaper

> Arguila, John. "What Deep Blue Taught Kasparov—and Us." Christian Science
>
> Monitor 16 May 1997: 18.

A newspaper's title should be cited as it appears on the masthead, excluding any initial article; thus *New York Times,* not *The New York Times.*

An Article from a Newspaper with Lettered Sections

> Diehl, Jackson. "Inhuman: Yes or No?" Washington Post 12 Sept. 2005:
>
> > A19.

Place the section letter immediately before the page number, without any spacing.

An Article from a Newspaper with Numbered Sections

> Roberts, Sam. "Another Kind of Middle-Class Squeeze." New York Times
>
> > 18 May 1997, sec. 4: 1+.

Place the section number after the date, preceded by a comma and the abbreviation "sec."

An Article from a Newspaper with a Designated Edition

> Pereira, Joseph. "Women Allege Sexist Atmosphere in Offices Constitutes
>
> > Harassment." Wall Street Journal 10 Feb. 1988, eastern ed.: 23.

If a newspaper is published in more than one edition each day, the edition used is cited after the date.

An Editorial

> "Japan's Two Nationalisms." Editorial. Washington Post 4 June 2000: B6.

Add the descriptive label "Editorial" after the article title.

A Letter to the Editor

> Wiles, Yoko A. "Thoughts of a New Citizen." Letter. Washington Post
>
> > 27 Dec. 1995: A22.

If the letter is titled, use the descriptive label "Letter" after the title. If the letter is untitled, place "Letter" after the author's name.

Citing Other Print and Nonprint Sources

The materials in this section, although often important to research projects, do not always lend themselves to documentation by the forms illustrated above. Follow the basic order of author, title, facts of publication as much as possible and add whatever information is needed to make the citation clear and useful to a reader.

Cartoons and Advertisements

> Schulz, Charles M. "Peanuts." Cartoon. Washington Post 10 Dec. 1985: D8.

Give the cartoon title, if there is one; add the descriptive label "Cartoon"; then give the facts of publication. The pattern is similar for advertisements.

> Halleyscope. "Halleyscopes Are for Night Owls." Advertisement. Natural
>
> History Dec. 1985: 15.

Computer Software

> "Aardvark." The Oxford English Dictionary. 2nd ed. CD-ROM. Oxford:
>
> Oxford UP, 1992.

Give author, title, publication medium (CD-ROM, Diskette, or Magnetic Tape), edition or version, publisher, and year of issue.

Dissertation—Unpublished

> Brotton, Joyce D. "Illuminating the Present Through Literary Dialogism: From
>
> the Reformation Through Postmodernism." Diss. George Mason U, 2002.

Dissertation—Published

> Brotton, Joyce D. Illuminating the Present Through Literary Dialogism: From
>
> the Reformation Through Postmodernism. Diss. George Mason U, 2002.
>
> UMI, 2002. ATT3041383.
>
> Sieger, Thomas Martin. "Global Citizenship: A Model for Student Inquiry and
>
> Decision-Making." 1996. Dissertation Abstracts Online Accession No.
>
> AAG9720651. Online. FirstSearch. 1997.

Government Documents

> U.S. President. Public Papers of the Presidents of the United States.
>
> Washington: Office of the Federal Register, 1961.
>
> United States. Senate. Committee on Energy and Natural Resources.
>
> Subcommittee on Energy Research and Development. Advanced Reactor
>
> Development Program: Hearing, May 24, 1988. Washington: GPO, 1988.

- - -. Environmental Protection Agency. <u>The Challenge of the Environment: A</u>

    <u>Primer on EPA's Statutory Authority</u>. Washington: GPO, 1972.

Observe the pattern illustrated here. If the author of the document is not given, cite the name of the government first followed by the name of the department or agency. If you cite more than one document published by the United States government, do not repeat the name but use the standard three hyphens followed by a period instead. If you cite a second document prepared by the Environmental Protection Agency, use the following pattern:

United States. Senate . . .

- - -. Environmental Protection Agency . . .

- - -. - - -. [second source from EPA]

If the author is known, follow this pattern:

Geller, William. <u>Deadly Force</u>. U.S. Dept of Justice National Institute of Justice

    Crime File Study Guide. Washington: U.S. Dept. of Justice, n.d.

If the document contains no date, use the abbreviation "n.d."

Hays, W. W., ed. <u>Facing Geologic and Hydrologic Hazards</u>. Geological Survey

    Professional Paper 1240-B. Washington: GPO, 1981.

Abbreviate the U.S. Government Printing Office thus: GPO.

An Interview

Plum, Kenneth. Personal Interview. 5 Mar. 1995.

A Lecture

Bateson, Mary Catherine. "Crazy Mixed-Up Families." Lecture delivered at

    Northern Virginia Community College, 26 Apr. 1997.

Legal Documents

U.S. Const. Art. 1, sec. 3.

The Constitution is referred to by article and section. Abbreviations are used; do not underline.

Turner v. Arkansas. 407 U.S. 366. 1972.

In citing a court case, give the name of the case (the plaintiff and defendant); the volume, name, and page of the report cited; and the date. The name of a court case is underlined (italicized) in the text but not in the Works Cited.

> Federal Highway Act, as amended. 23 U.S. Code 109. 1970. Labor
>
> Management Relations Act (Taft-Hartley Act). Statutes at Large. 61.
>
> 1947. 34 U.S. Code. 1952.

Citing laws is complicated, and lawyers use many abbreviations that may not be clear to nonexperts. Bills that become law are published annually in *Statutes at Large* and later in the *U.S. Code.* Provide the title of the bill and the source, volume, and year. References to both *Statutes at Large* and the *U.S. Code* can be given as a convenience to readers.

Unpublished Letter/E-Mail

> Usick, Patricia. E-mail to the author. 26 June 2005.

Treat a published letter as a work in a collection.

Maps and Charts

> Hampshire and Dorset. Map. Kent, Eng.: Geographers' A-Z Map, n.d.

The format is similar to that for an anonymous book but add the appropriate descriptive label.

Plays or Concerts

> Mourning Becomes Electra. By Eugene O'Neill. Shakespeare Theater.
>
> Washington, DC. 16 May 1997.

Include title, author, theater, city, and date of performance. Principal actors, singers, musicians, and/or the director can be added as appropriate.

Recordings

> Stein, Joseph. Fiddler on the Roof. Jerry Bock, composer. Original-Cast
>
> Recording with Zero Mostel. RCA, LSO-1093, 1964.

The conductor and/or performers help identify a specific recording. Also include manufacturer, catalogue number, and date of issue.

A Report

> Environment and Development: Breaking the Ideological Deadlock. Report of
>
> the Twenty-first United Nations Issues Conference, 23–25 Feb. 1990.
>
> Muscatine, Iowa: Stanley Foundation, n.d.

Television or Radio Program

> "Breakthrough: Television's Journal of Science and Medicine." PBS series
>
> hosted by Ron Hendren. 10 June 1997.

Citing Electronic Sources

Remember that the purpose of a citation is to provide readers with the information they need to obtain the source you have used. To locate online sources, more information is usually needed than for standard print works. Think in terms of five basic elements, each of which can be expanded or ignored depending on the specific source:

1. Author (or editor or translator, as appropriate), if there is one
2. "Title" of item, in quotation marks (unless you are citing an entire online book)
3. Information about print publication (if the item also has a print form)
4. Information about the electronic publication (usually including the Title of the site—underlined—the publication date or latest update of the site, and the sponsor's name—possibly a university, a company, an organization—if not mentioned in the title)
5. Access information (including the date you viewed the item and then the electronic address—URL)

If you cannot find all of this information, it may be that not every element applies to the site you are using, but do take time to search the home page for as much information as you can find. AND: Don't forget to put the date you accessed the information in your notes. Study the following two examples of citations to see the information needed and the order of that information.

Author. ⟶ Garvin, Glenn. "Reality Rots: Reality TV May Not Be the End of Civilization ⌐ Title of site.

Title of article.⌐   Posting date of

but It's an Incredible Simulation." Herald.com ⟨10 Mar. 2003⟩ Miami Herald.   article to site.

Access date. ⟶   ⟨3 June 2003⟩ <http://www.miami/com/mld/miamiherald/5355104.htm>.   Owner/sponsor of site.

Web address (URL)   All citations end
in side carets.   in a period.

Author. ——▶ Moffat, Anne Simon. "Resurgent Forests Can Be Greenhouse Gas Sponges." ◀—— Title of article.

Print form ——▶ Science 18 July 1997: 315–16. Sirs Researcher on the Web 1997. 24 Jan. ┄ Title of database.
publication
information.   Posting date.

1998 <http://library2.cc.va.us>. ———— Access date.

URL in side carets. ———

This article appeared in print in *Science* magazine, so the original print facts of publication are supplied after author and title. The researcher accessed the article in an electronic database, so the title of the database and the year of posting in the database are also supplied. Then comes the date of access by the researcher, followed by a URL that shows that the database is owned by a specific library and therefore cannot be accessed by all readers of this book. (The student's instructor, with access to the same library's databases, could, of course, access the database and check the student's work.)

Article from a Database of Previously Published Articles

"Breaking the Glass Ceiling." Editorial. The Economist 10 Aug. 1996: 13.

General Business File ASAP. Jan. 1998. 12 Jan. 1998

<http://sbweb2.med.iacnet.com/infotrac/session/460/259-2012624/

131xrn_39&kbm_13>.

Use the descriptive label "Editorial" just as you would if you were citing the print source. Break the URL only at a backslash.

Kumar, Sanjay. "Scientists Accuse Animal Rights Activists of Stifling

Research." British Medical Journal. 23 Nov. 2002: 1192. Expanded

Academic ASAP. InfoTrac. Northern Virginia Community College Library.

12 Sept. 2005 <http://infotrac.galegroup.com>.

If the URL for a specific item is extremely long, or if you are using a database subscribed to by a library or organization, you can list the subscriber, your date of access, and the URL for the database home page only.

Abstracts of Articles in Online Databases

For some articles, electronic databases provide only a citation and an abstract, a brief summary of the article. In most cases, the author of the article did not write the abstract. So, *never attribute these abstracts to the author. Never quote from these abstracts. Find and study the complete article.* If you must paraphrase some facts from the abstract, always indicate that you have used the abstract, not the original article. Place the descriptive label "Abstract" (followed by a period) after the page numbers for the original facts of publication.

Article from a Reference Database

"Prohibition." Encyclopaedia Britannica Online. 1998. Encyclopaedia

Britannica. 24 Jan. 1998 <http://search.eb.com/>.

Douglas, Susan J. "Radio and Television." HistoryChannel.com. 1996–2003.

History Channel. 31 July 2003 <http://historychannel.com/>.

Path: Television; Radio and Television.

Sometimes URLs are quite long, or the particular document you are citing does not have its own precise URL. You can use the database's search page or its home page followed by "Path" and then the sequence of links that took you to the particular document you are citing.

Online News Source

Associated Press. "Parents: Work Hinders Quality Time with Kids." CNN.com

31 July 2003. 31 July 2003 <http://cnn.com/Health>.

Article in an Online Magazine

Lithwick, Dahlia. "Rape Nuts: Kobe Bryant's Trial Will Showcase Our Mixed-

up Rape Laws." Slate 30 July 2003. 11 pars. 31 July 2003

<http://slate.msn.com/>.

An Entire Internet Site

Thomas: Legislative Information on the Internet. 30 June 2003. Lib. of

Congress, Washington. 4 August 2003 <http://thomas.loc.gov/>.

Poem from a Scholarly Project

Keats, John. "Ode to a Nightingale." Poetical Works. 1884. Bartleby.com:

Great Books. Ed. Steven van Leeuwen. 5 May 2002

<http://www.bartleby.com/126/41.htm>.

Information from a Government Site

U.S. Department of Health and Human Services. "The HHS Poverty

Guidelines." 21 Jan. 1998. 23 Jan. 1998 <http://aspe.os/

dhhs.gov/poverty/7/poverty.htm>.

Information from a Professional Site

> "Music Instruction Aids Verbal Memory." APA Press Release. APA Online 27
>
>> July 2003. 4 Aug. 2003 <http://www.apa.org/releases/
>>
>> music_memory.html>.

Use a descriptive label after the title just as you would with an anonymous print source, such as an editorial.

Information from a Professional or Personal Home Page

> Vachss, Andrew. "How Journalism Abuses Children." The Zero. 2 Aug. 2003
>
>> <http://www.andrewvachss.com/av_articles.html>.

For both professional and personal home pages, begin with the name of the person who created the page, and the title of the site (such as The Zero), or if there is no title, use the identifying phrase "Home page" (but not underlined or in quotation marks), the name of any organization associated with the site, access date, and URL.

An Article Published in Print and on CD-ROM (or Diskette, etc.)

> Detweiler, Richard A., "Democracy and Decency on the Internet." Chronicle of
>
>> Higher Education 28 June 1996: A40. General Periodicals Ondisc.
>>
>> CD-ROM. UMI-Proquest. April 1997.

A Work or Part of a Work on CD-ROM, Diskette, or Magnetic Tape

> "Surrealism." Oxford English Dictionary. 2nd ed. CD-ROM. Oxford: Oxford
>
>> UP, 1992.
>
> Eseiolonis, Karyn. "Georgio de Chirico's Mysterious Bathers." A Passion for
>
>> Art: Renoir, Cezanne, Matisse and Dr. Barnes. CD-ROM. Corbis
>>
>> Productions, 1995.
>
> Barclay, Donald. Teaching Electronic Information Literacy. Diskette. New
>
>> York: Neal-Schuman, 1995.

EXERCISES: Presenting and Documenting Borrowed Information and Preparing Citations

1. Read the following passage and then the three plagiarized uses of the passage. Explain why each one is plagiarized and how it can be corrected.

Original Text: Stanley Karnow, *Vietnam, A History. The First Complete Account of Vietnam at War.* New York: Viking, 1983, 319.

Lyndon Baines Johnson, a consummate politician, was a kaleidoscopic personality, forever changing as he sought to dominate or persuade or placate or frighten his friends and foes. A gigantic figure whose extravagant moods matched his size, he could be cruel and kind, violent and gentle, petty, generous, cunning, naïve, crude, candid, and frankly dishonest. He commanded the blind loyalty of his aides, some of whom worshipped him, and he sparked bitter derision or fierce hatred that he never quite fathomed.

   a. LBJ's vibrant and changing personality filled some people with adoration and others with bitter derision that he never quite fathomed (Karnow 319).

   b. LBJ, a supreme politician, had a personality like a kaleidoscope, continually changing as he tried to control, sway, appease, or intimidate his enemies and supporters (Karnow 319).

   c. Often, figures who have had great impact on America's history have been dynamic people with powerful personalities and vibrant physical presence. LBJ, for example, was a huge figure who polarized those who worked for and with him. "He commanded the blind loyalty of his aides, some of whom worshipped him, and he sparked bitter derision or fierce hatred" from many others (Karnow 319).

2. Read the following passages and then each of the four sample uses of the passage. Judge each of the uses for how well it avoids plagiarism and if it is documented correctly. Make corrections as needed.

Original Text: Stanley Karnow, *Vietnam, A History. The First Complete Account of Vietnam at War.* New York: Viking, 1983, 327.

On July 27, 1965, in a last-ditch attempt to change Johnson's mind, Mansfield and Russell were to press him again to "concentrate on finding a way out" of Vietnam—"a place where we ought not be," and where "the situation is rapidly going out of control." But the next day, Johnson announced his decision to add forty-four American combat battalions to the relatively small U.S. contingents already there. He had not been deaf to Mansfield's pleas, nor had he simply swallowed the Pentagon's plans. He had waffled and agonized during his nineteen months in the White House, but eventually this was his final judgment. As he would later explain: "There are many, many people who can recommend and advise, and a few of them consent. But there is only one who has been chosen by the American people to decide."

a. Karnow writes that Senators Mansfield and Russell continued to try to convince President Johnson to avoid further involvement in Vietnam, "a place where we ought not to be" they felt. (327).

b. Though Johnson received advice from many, in particular Senators Mansfield and Russell, he believed the weight of the decision to become further engaged in Vietnam was solely his as the one " 'chosen by the American people to decide' " (Karnow 327).

c. On July 28, 1965, Johnson announced his decision to add forty-four battalions to the troops already in Vietnam, ending his waffling and agonizing of the past nineteen months of his presidency. (Karnow 357).

d. Karnow explains that LBJ took his responsibility to make decisions about Vietnam seriously (327). Although Johnson knew that many would offer suggestions, only he had " 'been chosen by the American people to decide' " (Karnow 327).

3. Turn the information printed below into correct bibliographic citations for each of the works. Pay attention to the order of information, the handling of titles, and punctuation. Write each citation on a separate index card, or, if your instructor requests, prepare the citations as an alphabetical listing of works.

a. On July 14, 1997, Newsweek magazine printed Robert J. Samuelson's article titled Don't Hold Your Breath on page 40.

b. Richard B. Sewell's book The Life of Emily Dickinson was published in 1974. His book was published in two volumes by the New York City publisher Farrar, Straus, & Giroux.

c. Richard D. Heffner has edited an abridged version of Democracy in America by Alexis De Tocqueville. This is a Mentor Book paperback, a division of (New York City's) New American Library. The book was published in 1956.

d. The Object Stares Back: On the Nature of Seeing by James Elkins is reviewed in an article titled Vision Reviewed by Luciano da F. Costa. The review appeared on pages 124 and 125 in the March 1997 issue of Scientific American.

e. Arthur Whimbey wrote the article Something Better Than Binet for the Saturday Review on June 1, 1974. Joseph Rubinstein and Brent D. Slife reprinted the article on pages 102–108 in the third edition of the edited collection Taking Sides. Taking Sides was published in 1984 by the Dushkin Publishing Company located in Guilford, Connecticut.

f. The Discovery of Superconductivity appeared in Physics Today on pages 40–42. The author of the article is Jacobus de Nobel. The article appeared in the September 1996 issue, volume 49, number 9.

g. You used a biographical article, titled Marc Chagall (1887–1985), from Britannica Online which you found on the Internet September 25, 1999. You used the 1998 version, published by Encyclopaedia Britannica and available at <http://www.eb.com:180>.

h. An editorial appeared in the New York Times, on Sunday, September 7, 1997, with the title Protecting Children from Guns. The editorial could be found on page 16 of section 4.

i. Anthony Bozza's article "Moby Porn" appeared in the magazine Rolling Stone on June 26, 1977, on page 26. You obtained the text of the article from the September 1997 "edition" of General Periodicals Ondisc. The vendor is UMI-ProQuest.

j. A Letter to the Editor titled What Can We Do about Global Warming appeared in the Washington Post on July 24, 1997. The letter was written by S. Fred Singer and printed on page A24.

CHAPTER 11

Writing the Researched Essay

As you organize and draft, keep in mind that your argument skills apply to the research paper as well. Do not let documenting of multiple sources distract you from your best use of critical thinking and writing skills.

ORGANIZING THE PAPER

To make decisions about your paper's organization, a good place to begin is with the identifying phrases at the top of your notes or the list of support you developed as you studied sources. They represent subsections of your topic that emerged as you studied sources. They will now help you organize your paper. Here are some guidelines for getting organized to write:

1. *Arrange notes by identifying phrases and read them through.* Read personal notes as well. Work all notes into one possible order as suggested by the identifying phrases. In reading through all notes at one time, you may discover that some now seem irrelevant. Set them aside,

but do not throw them away yet. Some additional note taking may be necessary to fill in gaps that have become apparent. You know your sources well enough by now to be able to find the additional material that you need.

2. *Reexamine your tentative claim or research proposal and the preliminary list that guided your research.* Consider: As a result of reading and reflection, do you need to alter or modify your claim in any way? Or, if you began with a research question, what now is your answer to the question? What, for example, was the impact of Prohibition on the 1920s? Or, is TV violence harmful to children? You need to decide.

3. *Decide on a final claim.* To produce a unified and coherent essay with a clear central idea and a "reason for being," you need a claim that meets the following criteria:

   - *It is a complete sentence, not a topic or statement of purpose.*

TOPIC:	Rape on college campuses.
CLAIM:	There are steps that both students and administrators can take to reduce incidents of campus rape.

   - *It is limited and focused.*

UNFOCUSED:	Prohibition affected the 1920s in many ways.
FOCUSED:	Prohibition was more acceptable to rural than urban areas because of differences in religious values, in patterns of socializing, in cultural backgrounds, and in the economic impact of prohibiting liquor sales.

   - *It can be supported by your research.*

UNSUPPORTABLE:	*Time* magazine does not like George Bush.
SUPPORTABLE:	A study of *Time*'s coverage of President Bush during the 1990–91 winter months reveals a favorable bias during the Persian Gulf War but a negative bias after the war.

   - *It establishes a new or interesting approach to the topic that makes your research worthwhile.*

NOT INVENTIVE:	A regional shopping mall should not be built adjacent to the Manassas Battlefield.
INVENTIVE:	Putting aside an appeal to our national heritage, one can say, simply, that the building of a regional shopping mall adjacent to the Manassas Battlefield has no economic justification.

4. *Write down the organization revealed by the way you have grouped notes and compare this organization with your preliminary plan.* If you have deleted sections or reordered them, justify those changes in your own mind. Consider: Does the new, fuller plan now provide a complete and logical development of your claim?

THE FORMAL OUTLINE

Some instructors expect a formal outline with research essays. Preparing a formal outline requires that you think through the entire structure of your paper and see the relationship of parts. Remember that the more you analyze your topic, the fuller and therefore more useful your outline will be. But do not expect more out of an outline than it can provide. A logical and clear organization does not result from a detailed outline; rather, a detailed outline results from a logical analysis of your topic.

The formal outline uses a combination of numbers and letters to show headings and subheadings. Keep in mind these three points about outlines:

- The parts of the paper indicated by the same *types* of numbers or letters should be equally important.
- Headings and subheadings indicated by the same types of numbers or letters should be written in the same format or structure (e.g., A. Obtain*ing* Good Equipment; B. Tak*ing* Lessons; C. Practic*ing*).
- Headings that are subdivided must contain at least *two* subsections (that is, if there is a 1 under A, there has to be a 2). A sample outline accompanies the first research paper at the end of this chapter.

DRAFTING THE PAPER

Plan Your Time

Consider how much time you will need to draft your essay. Working with notes and being careful about documentation make research paper writing more time-consuming than writing undocumented essays. You will probably need two or three afternoons or evenings to complete a draft. You should start writing, then, at least five days before your paper is due to allow time between drafting and revising. Don't throw away weeks of study by trying to draft, revise, and proof your paper in one day.

Handle Documentation As You Draft

Although you may believe that stopping to include parenthetical documentation as you write will cramp your writing, you really cannot wait until you complete your draft to add the documentation. The risk of failing to document accurately is too great to chance. Parenthetical documentation is brief; take the time to include it as you compose. Then, when your paper is finished and you are preparing your list of works cited, go through your paper carefully to make certain that there is a work listed for *every* parenthetical reference.

Choose an Appropriate Writing Style

Specific suggestions for composing the parts of your paper will follow, but first here are some general guidelines for research paper style.

Use the Proper Person

Research papers are written primarily in the third person *(she, he, it, they)* to create objectivity and to direct attention to the content of the paper. You are not likely to use the second person *(you)* at all, for the second person occurs in instructions. The usual question is over the appropriateness of the first person *(I, we)*. Although you want to avoid writing "as *you* can see," do not try to skirt around the use of *I* if you need to distinguish your position from the views of others. It is better to write "I" than "it is the opinion of this writer" or "the researcher learned" or "this project analyzed." On the other hand, avoid qualifiers such as "I think." Just state your ideas.

Use the Proper Tense

When you are writing about people, ideas, or events of the past, the appropriate tense is the past tense. When writing about current times, the appropriate tense is the present. Both may occur in the same paragraph, as the following paragraph illustrates:

> Fifteen years ago "personal" computers were all but unheard of. Computers were regarded as unknowable, building-sized mechanized monsters that required a precise 68 degree air-conditioned environment and eggheaded technicians with thick glasses and white lab coats scurrying about to keep the temperamental and fragile egos of the electronic brains mollified. Today's generation of computers is accessible, affordable, commonplace, and much less mysterious. A computer that used to require two rooms to house is now smaller than a briefcase. A computer that cost hundreds of thousands of dollars fifteen years ago now has a price tag in the hundreds. The astonishing progress made in computer technology in the last few years has made computers practical, attainable, and indispensable. Personal computers are here to stay.

In the above example when the student moves from computers in the past to computers in the present, he shifts tenses accurately.

When writing about sources, the convention is to use the present tense *even* for works or authors from the past. The idea is that the source, or the author, *continues* to make the point or use the technique into the present—that is, every time there is a reader. Use of the *historical present tense* requires that you write "Lincoln selects the biblical expression 'Fourscore and seven years ago' " and "King echoes Lincoln when he writes 'five score years ago.' "

Avoid Excessive Quoting

Many students use too many direct quotations. Plan to use your own words most of the time for these good reasons:

- Constantly shifting between your words and the language of your sources (not to mention all those quotation marks) makes reading your essay difficult.
- This is your paper and should sound like you.
- When you take a passage out of its larger context, you face the danger of misrepresenting the writer's views.
- When you quote endlessly, readers may begin to think either that you are lazy or that you don't really understand the issues well enough to put them in your own words. You don't want to present either image to your readers.
- You do not prove any point by quoting another person's opinion. All you indicate is that there is someone else who shares your views. Even if that person is an expert on the topic, your quoted material still represents the view of only one person. You support a claim with reasons and evidence, both of which can usually be presented in your own words.

When you must quote, keep the quotations brief, weave them carefully into your own sentences, and be sure to identify the author in a signal phrase. Study the guidelines for handling quotations on pages 21–23 for models of correct form and style.

Write Effective Beginnings

The best introduction is one that presents your subject in an interesting way to gain the reader's attention, states your claim, and gives the reader an indication of the scope and limits of your paper. In a short research essay, you may be able to combine an attention-getter, a statement of subject, and a claim in one paragraph. More typically, especially in longer papers, the introduction will expand to two or three paragraphs. In the physical and social sciences, the claim may be withheld until the conclusion, but the opening introduces the subject and presents the researcher's hypothesis, often posed as a question. Since students sometimes have trouble with research paper introductions in spite of knowing these general guidelines, several specific approaches are illustrated in the following pages:

1. Begin with a brief example or anecdote to dramatize your topic. One student introduced her study of the nightly news with this attention-getter:

   When I watched television in the first weeks after moving to the United States, I was delighted by the relaxing display of the news programs. It was different from what I was used to on German television, where one finds a stern-looking man reading the news without any emotion. Here the commentators laugh or show distress; their tone with each other is amiable. Watching the news in this country was a new and entertaining experience for me initially, but as my reading skills improved, I found that I preferred reading newspapers to watching television news. Then, reading Neil Postman's attack on television news shows in "Television News Narcosis" reminded me of my early experience with American TV and led me to investigate the major networks' presentation of the news.

In her second paragraph, the student completed her introduction by explaining the procedures used for analyzing network news programs.

2.   In the opening to her study of car advertisements, a student, relating her topic to what readers know, reminds readers of the culture's concern with image:

> Many Americans are highly image conscious. Because the "right" look is essential to a prosperous life, no detail is too small to overlook. Clichés about first impressions remind us that "you never get a second chance to make a first impression," so we obsessively watch our weight, firm our muscles, sculpt our hair, select our friends, find the perfect houses, and buy our automobiles. Realizing the importance of image, companies compete to make the "right" products, that is, those that will complete the "right" image. Then advertisers direct specific products to targeted groups of consumers. Although targeting may be labeled as stereotyping, it has been an effective strategy in advertising.

3.   Challenging a popular attitude or assumption is an effective attention-getting opening. For a paper on the advantages of solar energy, a student began:

> America's energy problems are serious, despite the popular belief that difficulties vanished with the end of the Arab oil embargo in 1974. Our problems remain because the world's supply of fossil fuels is not limitless.

4.   Terms and concepts central to your project need defining early in your paper, especially if they are challenged or qualified in some way by your study. The following opening paragraph demonstrates an effective use of definition:

> William Faulkner braids a universal theme, the theme of initiation, into the fiber of his novel <u>Intruder in the Dust</u>. From ancient times to the present, a prominent focus of literature, of life, has been rites of passage, particularly those of childhood to adulthood. Joseph Campbell defines rites of passage as "distinguished by formal, and usually very severe, exercises of severance." A "candidate" for initiation into adult society, Campbell explains, experiences a shearing away of the "attitudes, attachments and life patterns" of childhood (9). This severe, painful stripping away of the child and installation of the adult is presented somewhat differently in several works by American writers.

5.   Begin with a thought-provoking question. A student, arguing that the media both reflect and shape reality, started with these questions:

> Do the media just reflect reality, or do they also shape our perceptions of reality? The answer to this seemingly "chicken-and-egg" question is: They do both.

6. Beginning with important, perhaps startling, facts, evidence, or statistics is an effective way to introduce a topic, provided the details are relevant to the topic. Observe the following example:

   Teenagers are working again, but not on their homework. Over 40 percent of teenagers have jobs by the time they are juniors (Samuelson A22). And their jobs do not support academic learning since almost two-thirds of teenagers are employed in sales and service jobs that entail mostly carrying, cleaning, and wrapping (Greenberger and Steinberg 62–67), not reading, writing, and computing. Unfortunately, the negative effect on learning is not offset by improved opportunities for future careers.

Avoid Ineffective Openings

Follow these rules for avoiding openings that most readers find ineffective or annoying.

1. *Do not restate the title* or write as if the title were the first sentence in paragraph 1. First, the title of the paper appears at the top of the first page of text. Second, it is a convention of writing to have the first paragraph stand independent of the title.
2. *Do not begin with "clever" visuals* such as artwork or fancy lettering.
3. *Do not begin with humor* unless it is part of your topic.
4. *Do not begin with a question that is just a gimmick, or one that a reader may answer in a way you do not intend.* Asking "What are the advantages of solar energy?" may lead a reader to answer "None that I can think of." A straightforward research question ("Is *Death of a Salesman* a tragedy?") is appropriate.
5. *Do not open with an unnecessary definition quoted from a dictionary.* "According to Webster, solar energy means . . . " is a tired, overworked beginning that does not engage readers.
6. *Do not start with a purpose statement:* "This paper will examine . . . " Although a statement of purpose is a necessary part of a report of empirical research, a report still needs an interesting introduction.

Compose Solid, Unified Paragraphs

As you compose the body of your paper, keep in mind that you want to (1) maintain unity and coherence, (2) guide readers clearly through source material, and (3) synthesize source material and your own ideas. Do not settle for paragraphs in which facts from notes are just loosely run together. Review the following discussion and study the examples to see how to craft effective body paragraphs.

Provide Unity and Coherence

You achieve paragraph unity when every sentence in a paragraph relates to and develops the paragraph's main idea. If you have a logical organization, composing unified paragraphs is not a problem. Unity, however, does not automatically produce coherence; that takes attention to wording. Coherence is achieved when readers can follow the connection between one sentence and another and between each sentence and the main idea. Strategies for achieving coherence include repetition of key words, the use of pronouns that clearly refer to those key words, and the use of transition and connecting words. Observe these strategies at work in the following paragraph:

> Perhaps the most important differences between the initiations of Robin and Biff and that experienced by Chick are the facts that Chick's epiphany does not come all at once and it does not devastate him . Chick learns about adulthood—and enters adulthood—piecemeal and with support. His first eye-opening experience occurs as he tries to pay Lucas for dinner and is rebuffed (15–16). Chick learns , after trying again to buy a clear conscience, the impropriety and affront of his actions (24). Lucas teaches Chick how he should resolve his dilemma by setting him "free" (26–27). Later, Chick feels outrage at the adults crowding into the town, presumably to see a lynching, then disgrace and shame as they eventually flee (196–97, 210).

Coherence is needed not only within paragraphs but between paragraphs. You need to guide readers through your paper, connecting paragraphs and showing relationships by the use of transitions. The following opening sentences of four paragraphs from a paper on solutions to rape on the college campus illustrate smooth transitions:

> ¶ 3 Specialists have provided a number of reasons why men rape .
>
> ¶ 4 Some of the causes of rape on the college campus originate with the colleges themselves and with how they handle the problem.
>
> ¶ 5 Just as there are a number of causes for campus rapes , there are a number of ways to help solve the problem of these rapes.
>
> ¶ 6 If these seem like common-sense solutions , why, then, is it so difficult to significantly reduce the number of campus rapes ?

Without awkwardly writing "Here are some of the causes" and "Here are some of the solutions," the student guides her readers through a discussion of causes for and solutions to the problem of campus rape.

Guide Readers Through Source Material

To understand the importance of guiding readers through source material, consider first the following paragraph from a paper on the British coal strike in the 1970s:

> The social status of the coal miners was far from good. The country blamed them for the dimmed lights and the three-day work week. They had been placed in the position of social outcasts and were beginning to "consider themselves another country." Some businesses and shops had even gone so far as to refuse service to coal miners (Jones 32).

Who has learned that the coal miners felt ostracized or that the country blamed them? As readers we cannot begin to judge the validity of these assertions without some context provided by the writer. Most readers are put off by an unattached direct quotation or some startling observation that is documented correctly but given no context within the paper. Using introductory tags that identify the author of the source and, when useful, the author's credentials helps guide readers through the source material. The following revision of the paragraph above provides not only context but also sentence variety:

> The social acceptance of coal miners, according to Peter Jones, British correspondent for Newsweek , was far from good. From interviews both in London shops and in pubs near Birmingham, Jones concluded that Britishers blamed the miners for the dimmed lights and three-day work week. Several striking miners , in a pub on the outskirts of Birmingham, asserted that some of their friends had been denied service by shopkeepers and that they "consider[ed] themselves another country" (32).

When you use introductory tags, try to vary both the words you use and their place in the sentence. Look, for example, at the first sentence in the sample paragraph above. The tag is placed in the middle of the sentence and is set off by commas. The sentence could have been written two other ways:

> The social acceptance of coal miners was far from good, according to Peter Jones, British correspondent for Newsweek
>
>   *OR*
>
> According to Peter Jones, British correspondent for Newsweek, the social acceptance of coal miners was far from good.

Whenever you provide a name and perhaps credentials for your source, you have these three sentence patterns to choose from. Make a point to use all three options in your paper. Word choice can be varied as well. Instead of writing

"Peter Jones says" throughout your paper, consider some of the many options you have:

Jones *asserts*	Jones *contends*	Jones *attests to*
Jones *states*	Jones *thinks*	Jones *points out*
Jones *concludes*	Jones *stresses*	Jones *believes*
Jones *presents*	Jones *emphasizes*	Jones *agrees with*
Jones *argues*	Jones *confirms*	Jones *speculates*

> **NOTE:** Not all the words in this list are synonyms; you cannot substitute *confirms* for *believes*. First, select the term that most accurately conveys the writer's relationship to his or her material. Then, when appropriate, vary word choice as well as sentence structure.

Readers need to be told how they are to respond to the sources used. They need to know which sources you accept as reliable and which you disagree with, and they need to see you distinguish clearly between fact and opinion. Ideas and opinions from sources need introductory tags and then some discussion from you.

Synthesize Source Material and Your Own Ideas

A smooth synthesis of source material is aided by introductory tags and parenthetical documentation because they mark the beginning and ending of material taken from a source. But a complete synthesis requires something more: your ideas about the source and the topic. To illustrate, consider the problems in another paragraph from the British coal strike paper:

> Some critics believed that there was enough coal in Britain to maintain enough power to keep industry at a near-normal level for thirty-five weeks (Jones 30). Prime Minister Heath, on the other hand, had placed the country's usable coal supply at 15.5 million tons (Jones 30). He stated that this would have fallen to a critical 7 million tons within a month had he not declared a three-day work week (Jones 31).

This paragraph is a good example of random details strung together for no apparent purpose. How much coal did exist? Whose figures were right? And what purpose do these figures serve in the paper's development? Note that the entire paragraph is developed with material from one source. Do sources other than Jones offer a different perspective? This paragraph is weak for several reasons: (1) it lacks a controlling idea (topic sentence) to give it purpose and direction; (2) it relies for development entirely on one source; (3) it lacks any discussion or analysis by the writer.

By contrast, the following paragraph demonstrates a successful synthesis:

> Of course, the iridium could have come from other extraterrestrial sources
>
> besides an asteroid. One theory, put forward by Dale Russell , is that the
>
> iridium was produced outside the solar system by an exploding star (500).

Such an explosion, Russell states , could have blown the iridium either off the surface of the moon or directly from the star itself (500–01), while also producing a deadly blast of heat and gamma rays (Krishtalka 19). Even though this theory seems to explain the traces of iridium in the mass extinction, it does not explain why smaller mammals, crocodiles, and birds survived (Wilford 220). So the supernova theory took a backseat to the other extraterrestrial theories: those of asteroids and comets colliding with the earth. The authors of the book The Great Extinction, Michael Allaby and James Lovelock , subtitled their work The Solution to . . . the Disappearance of the Dinosaurs. Their theory : an asteroid or comet collided with earth around sixty-five million years ago, killing billions of organisms, and thus altering the course of evolution (157). The fact that the theory of collision with a cosmic body warrants a book describing itself as the solution to the extinction of dinosaurs calls for some thought: is the asteroid or comet theory merely sensationalism, or is it rooted in fact? Paleontologist Leonard Krishtalka declares that few paleontologists have accepted the asteroid theory, himself calling "some catastrophic theories . . . small ideas injected with growth hormone" (22). However, other scientists, such as Allaby and Lovelock, see the cosmic catastrophic theory as a solid one based on more than guesswork (10–11).

This paragraph's synthesis is accomplished by several strategies: (1) the paragraph has a controlling idea; (2) the paragraph combines information from several sources; (3) the information is presented in a blend of paraphrase and short quotations; (4) information from the different sources is clearly indicated to readers; and (5) the student explains and discusses the information.

You might also observe the very different lengths of the two sample paragraphs just presented. Although the second paragraph is long, it is not unwieldy because it achieves unity and coherence. By contrast, body paragraphs of only three sentences are probably in trouble.

To sum up, good body paragraphs need:

- A controlling idea
- In most cases, information from more than one source
- Analysis and discussion from the student writer

Write Effective Conclusions

Sometimes ending a paper seems even more difficult than beginning one. You know you are not supposed to just stop, but every ending that comes to mind sounds more corny than clever. If you have trouble, try one of the following types of endings.

1. Do not just repeat your claim exactly as it was stated in paragraph 1, but expand on the original wording and emphasize the claim's significance. Here is the conclusion of the solar energy paper:

    The idea of using solar energy is not as far-fetched as it seemed years ago. With the continued support of government plus the enthusiasm of research groups, environmentalists, and private industry, solar energy may become a household word quite soon. With the increasing cost of fossil fuel, the time could not be better for exploring this use of the sun.

2. End with a quotation that effectively summarizes and drives home the point of your paper. Researchers are not always lucky enough to find the ideal quotation for ending a paper. If you find a good one, use it. Better yet, present the quotation and then add your comment in a sentence or two. The conclusion to a paper on the dilemma of defective newborns is a good example:

    Dr. Joseph Fletcher is correct when he says that "every advance in medical capabilities is an increase in our moral responsibility" (48). In a world of many gray areas, one point is clear. From an ethical point of view, medicine is a victim of its own success.

3. If you have researched an issue or problem, emphasize your proposed solutions in the concluding paragraph. The student opposing a mall adjacent to the Manassas Battlefield concluded with several solutions:

    Whether the proposed mall will be built is clearly in doubt at the moment. What are the solutions to this controversy? One approach is, of course, not to build the mall at all. To accomplish this solution, now, with the rezoning having been approved, probably requires an act of Congress to buy the land and make it part of the National Park. Another solution, one that would please the County and the developer and satisfy citizens objecting to traffic problems, is to build the needed roads before the mall is completed. A third approach is to allow the office park of the original plan to be built, but not the mall. The local preservationists had agreed to this original development proposal, but now that the issue has received national attention, they may no longer be willing to compromise. Whatever the future of the William Center, the present plan for a new regional mall is not acceptable.

Avoid Ineffective Conclusions

Follow these rules to avoid conclusions that most readers consider ineffective and annoying.

1. *Do not introduce a new idea.* If the point belongs in your paper, you should have introduced it earlier.
2. *Do not just stop or trail off,* even if you feel as though you have run out of steam. A simple, clear restatement of the claim is better than no conclusion.
3. *Do not tell your reader what you have accomplished:* "In this paper I have explained the advantages of solar energy by examining the costs . . ." If you have written well, your reader knows what you have accomplished.
4. *Do not offer apologies or expressions of hope.* "Although I wasn't able to find as much on this topic as I wanted, I have tried to explain the advantages of solar energy, and I hope that you will now understand why we need to use it more" is a disastrous ending.
5. *Do not end with a vague or confusing one- or two-sentence summary of complex ideas.* The following sentences make little sense: "These authors have similar and different attitudes and ideals concerning American desires. Faulkner writes with the concerns of man toward man whereas most of the other writers are more concerned with man toward money."

Choose an Effective Title

Give some thought to your paper's title since that is what your reader sees first and what your work will be known by. A good title provides information and creates interest. Make your title informative by making it specific. If you can create interest through clever wording, so much the better. But do not confuse "cutesiness" with clever wording. Better to be just straightforward than to demean a serious effort with a "cutesy" title. Review the following examples of acceptable and unacceptable titles:

VAGUE:	A Perennial Issue Unsolved
	(There are many; which one is this paper about?)
BETTER:	The Perennial Issue of Press Freedom Versus Press Responsibility
TOO BROAD:	Earthquakes
	(What about earthquakes? This title is not informative.)
BETTER:	The Need for Earthquake Prediction
TOO BROAD:	The Scarlet Letter
	(Never use just the title of the work under discussion; you can use the work's title as a part of a longer title of your own.)
BETTER:	Color Symbolism in The Scarlet Letter
CUTESY:	Babes in Trouble
	(The slang "Babes" makes this title seem insensitive rather than clever.)
BETTER:	The Dilemma of Defective Newborns

REVISING THE PAPER: A CHECKLIST

After completing a first draft, catch your breath and then gear up for the next step in the writing process: revision. Revision actually involves three separate steps. *Revising,* step 1, means *rewriting*—adding or deleting text, or moving parts of the draft around. Next comes *editing,* a rereading to correct errors from misspellings to incorrect documentation format. Finally, you need to *proofread* the typed copy. If you treat these as separate steps, you will do a more complete job of revision—and get a better grade on the completed paper!

Rewriting

Read your draft through and make changes as a result of answering the following questions:

Purpose and Audience

- ☐ Is my draft long enough to meet assignment requirements and my purpose?
- ☐ Are terms defined and concepts explained appropriately for my audience?

Content

- ☐ Do I have a clearly stated thesis—the claim of my argument?
- ☐ Have I presented sufficient evidence to support my claim?
- ☐ Are there any irrelevant sections that should be deleted?

Structure

- ☐ Are paragraphs ordered to develop my topic logically?
- ☐ Does the content of each paragraph help develop my claim?
- ☐ Is everything in each paragraph on the same subtopic to create paragraph unity?
- ☐ Do body paragraphs have a balance of information and analysis, of source material and my own ideas?
- ☐ Are there any paragraphs that should be combined? Are there any very long paragraphs that should be divided? (Check for unity.)

Editing

Make revisions guided by your responses to the questions, make a clean copy, and read again. This time, pay close attention to sentences, words, and documentation format. Use the following questions to guide revisions.

Coherence

- ☐ Have connecting words been used and key terms repeated to produce paragraph coherence?
- ☐ Have transitions been used to show connections between paragraphs?

Sources

☐ Have I paraphrased instead of quoted whenever possible?
☐ Have I used signal phrases to create a context for source material?
☐ Have I documented all borrowed material, whether quoted or paraphrased?
☐ Are parenthetical references properly placed after borrowed material?

Style

☐ Have I varied sentence length and structure?
☐ Have I used my own words instead of quotations whenever possible?
☐ Have I avoided long quotations?
☐ Do I have correct form for quotations? For titles?
☐ Is my language specific and descriptive?
☐ Have I avoided inappropriate shifts in tense or person?
☐ Have I removed any wordiness, deadwood, trite expressions, or clichés?
☐ Have I used specialized terms correctly?
☐ Have I avoided contractions as too informal for most research papers?
☐ Have I maintained an appropriate style and tone for academic work?

Proofreading

When your editing is finished, prepare a completed draft of your paper according to the format described and illustrated below. Then proofread the completed copy, making any corrections neatly in ink. If a page has several errors, print a corrected copy. Be sure to make a copy of the paper for yourself before submitting the original to your instructor.

THE COMPLETED PAPER

Your research paper should be double-spaced throughout (including the Works Cited page) with 1-inch margins on all sides. Your project will contain the following parts, in this order:

1. *A title page,* with your title, your name, the course name or number, your instructor's name, and the date, neatly centered, if an outline follows. Alternatively, place this information at the top left of the first page.
2. *An outline,* or statement of purpose, if required.
3. *The body or text of your paper.* Number all pages consecutively, including pages of works cited, using arabic numerals. Place numbers in the upper right-hand corner of each page. Include your last name before each page number.
4. *A list of Works Cited,* placed on a separate page(s) after the text. Title the first page "Works Cited." (Do not use the title "Bibliography.")

SAMPLE STUDENT RESEARCH ESSAY

The following paper illustrates MLA style of documentation for an argument that is developed using sources. The paper shows a separate title page and outline, the appropriate pattern if an outline is required. (If you do not include an outline, use the sample research essay in the Appendix as your model for placement of your name and the paper's title.) Study the student's blending of information and arguments from sources with her own experience and views on TV to build her argument.

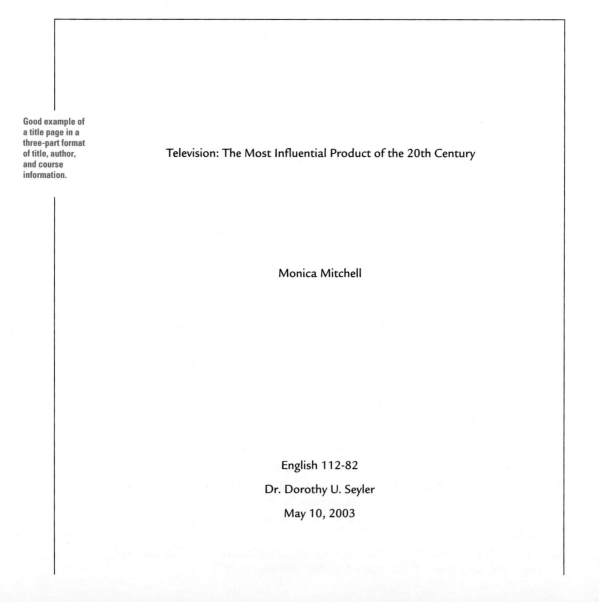

Good example of a title page in a three-part format of title, author, and course information.

Television: The Most Influential Product of the 20th Century

Monica Mitchell

English 112-82

Dr. Dorothy U. Seyler

May 10, 2003

Mitchell 2

Outline

Thesis: The 20th century product with the most widespread, psychological, and enduring impact is television.

Begin with thesis statement and use one standard pattern consistently.

I. Breadth of Television's Influence

    A. Adaptability to Users

    B. Range of Influence

II. Ways Television Influences Lives

    A. World Coverage

    B. Coverage of Sex and Violence

        1. Scary Nature of Violence for Children

        2. Power to Shape Behavior

    C. Restrictions in Some Countries Because of Its Power

    D. Influence on Elections and Images of Politicians

III. Defense of TV Against Other 20th Century Inventions

    A. Defense Against Computers

    B. Defense Against Flight and Space Travel

Last name and
page number in
upper right corner.

Repeat title on
first page of text.

Student introduces
topic with
attention-getting
quotation.

Double-space
throughout.

Student defines
key term and ends
¶ 1 with her
thesis—her
claim.

Student gives
examples of
adaptability of TV.

Television: The Most Influential Product of the 20th Century

"Never before have I witnessed compressed into a single device so much
ingenuity, so much brainpower, so much development, and such phenomenal
results."

(David Sarnoff as qtd. in Fisher and Fisher, xiii)

The 20th century enjoyed—or suffered—more inventions and developments
than all previous centuries combined. Many of these innovations represented
freedom, such as freedom of movement because of cars and airplanes, and
freedom for women as a result of modern birth control. Out of such an
impressive selection, labeling one development of the 1900s the most
influential is at least in part a matter of definition. The inventions of the nuclear
bomb and the space shuttle were certainly tremendously significant. The
Holocaust and the Cold War will forever be remembered as events of historical
magnitude. However, if we are talking about a *product,* a gadget if you will, an
ordinary device in the ordinary person's life, the 20th century development with
the most widespread, psychological, and enduring impact is television.

The Product of the 20th Century is a relatively simple device: once on, it
does nearly all the work for its viewers. There are no inherent physical or
intellectual requirements to enjoy it; in fact, it almost seems as if TV, unlike
other products, will "adapt" to whatever condition viewers are in, making it an
endlessly accommodating appliance. One could be in a full-body cast, unable to
move, yet watching television would still be possible—and perhaps the only
enjoyable activity in such a situation. If one were unable to read, books and
computers would almost be out of the question, but the Product of the 20th
Century wouldn't be, since no typing is required in using it and reading is rare.
If one cannot *see* TV, one can still *hear* it or—the other way around—look at it
without listening. Television can be a news radio, a music stereo, a portable
sports arena. Its top even offers a convenient extra "shelf" to put things on. It
makes a decent dinner companion. It can provide added lighting, baby sit

Mitchell 4

children, boost moods, bust moods. Television is the ultimate chameleon
product.

Although parts of the "electronic puzzle" of TV were experimented with
before 1900, it was, according to David and Jon Marshall Fisher, David Sarnoff
who developed TV as we know it today, using electrons to transmit images
(278). Television's official U.S. debut took place in 1939, when for the first
time a TV camera recorded a presidential speech (Fisher and Fisher 278). The
next day, as Fisher and Fisher tell the story, a handful of New York merchants
began selling TV sets at the cost of a whopping $1000 (281). Understandably
with such a price tag, only eight hundred TVs were sold in the following three
months (Fisher and Fisher 281), but with reduced prices and continued
marketing, the product gained popularity. As Susan J. Douglas explains in her
HistoryChannel.com essay, in 1949 940,000 homes owned TV's. By 1953, 20
million homes could boast a television set. By 1960, the Product of the 20th
Century, in black and white or now in color, had firmly established itself in
American homes, and by 1978, 97 percent of U.S. homes had at least one set
(Douglas). Today, 99 percent of American homes have at least one TV, a higher
percentage than those homes with phones.

Sarnoff envisioned that television, in addition to providing entertainment,
would offer a new sense of freedom and a deeper global understanding (Fisher
and Fisher 200). To a great extent, TV has accomplished this in its relatively
short lifespan. In his book Seducing America: How Television Charms the
Modern Viewer, Roderick P. Hart confirms that for millions of viewers the
names of key places in the world are loaded with implication, even if the viewers
themselves have never visited them (5). Berlin, Johannesburg, Tiananmen
Square, and Bosnia are just a few examples. The Product of the 20th Century
enabled the rest of the world to share—to live—the moments associated with
these locations (Hart 5). These places are associated with traumatic events,
which we, although outsiders, nonetheless have been part of "virtually," thanks

**Student uses brief
history only as
context for breadth
of influence of TV.**

**¶ blends information
from two sources.**

**Tag makes clear
that citation will
not include a page
number.**

**Last stat is common
knowledge.**

Mitchell 5

to television's instant and realistic delivery. Television's immediacy, in Susan Douglas's view, is both its strength and its weakness. Television powerfully replayed Kennedy's assassination in 1963, Vietnam children burned by napalm, water hoses turned on civil rights marchers, and two more murders before the end of that decade, "providing," Douglas asserts, "some images that unified America and others that reflected, and sometimes exacerbated, the country's deep racial, class, and gender divisions."

Tag placed in middle of quotation for variety.

Television has massively expanded its program offerings over the years. Now more than ever there is "something for everyone" in terms of interest and taste, another possible dilemma for this gadget. Two controversial elements dominating TV are violence and sex, phenomena that, ironically, might well sum up the 20th century. Some argue that if these two elements are everywhere in our culture, why should showing them on the tube cause such alarm? The counter to this view is that TV presents behaviors that many viewers, especially children, are not psychologically adept to experience. Marie Winn, who specializes in child development issues, cautions that excessive television viewing at a young age interferes with children's practicing their budding language skills (90). Karen Wright notes that typically children view two hours of TV daily and that "children's programs average between 20 and 25 violent acts per hour—four times as many as adult programs" (29). Because of the array of channels and shows offered around the clock at the push of a button—a convenience (curse?) that sets TV apart from other media outlets such as movie theaters—it is difficult for even the most responsible parent to control the images streaming out to children. Whether TV programs are labeled as such, they are all "educational" in one way or another because behavior is learned by watching. Whether we realize it or like it, television, next to parents, is often a

Student uses personal experience to illustrate her point.

child's earliest and most constant teacher. Even with caring parental supervision, children are often troubled by TV images. One ten-year-old (this

Mitchell 6

writer!) was so frightened by a movie on TV watched at a friend's house that
she swore never to visit there again. In theaters the movie (Raiders of the Lost
Ark) was restricted for ten-year-olds, but there were no age restrictions for the
television broadcast.

Does the Product of the 20th Century also influence viewers to *act* in
certain ways? Frequently yes, the studies show. Brandon S. Centerwall provides
one telling example in "Television and Violent Crime." He cites a survey of a
small Canadian town that two years after having acquired TV for the first time
noted a 160 percent increase in aggressive behavior among its children (307).
Jerry Mander, author of Four Arguments for the Elimination of Television, is
convinced that the medium is inherently corrupt; he insists that TV promotes
physical and mental isolation and passivity, disconnects viewers from reality,
and facilitates autocracy (27), a scary list if accurate. Wright doesn't state the
problem so dramatically, but she does argue that common sense would suggest
that we are influenced by activities at which we spend a great deal of time (29).
She also reports on a long-term study by Jeffrey G. Johnson, a psychiatric
epidemiologist, who followed over 700 youngsters for 17 years. Wright reports
these results from Johnson's study:

> Kids who spent more than three hours a day watching television at
> age 14 were more than four times as likely to have acted aggressively
> by age 22 than kids who watched TV for less than an hour. The
> connection held up even after researchers accounted for other possible
> culprits, including poverty, neglect, and bad neighborhoods. (29)

Finally, if the Product of the 20th Century doesn't affect us to act in certain
ways, why would companies pay millions of dollars for commercial time during
the Super Bowl, the show that boasts the greatest number of U.S. viewers each
year? Clearly advertisers think the high-stakes gamble pays off; otherwise they
would not continue year after year.

Student synthesizes three sources and her own commentary.

Introductory tag makes clear that Wright is reporting on Johnson's study.

Note format of block quotation, indented 10 spaces from the left margin.

Television, more than any other product, opens the floodgates of information. In this sense, TV is a box of freedom, as long as the medium is indeed open. Unfortunately, in some countries governments strictly control TV, preventing unwanted influence while indoctrinating citizens with the "appropriate" ideology, strategies that further attest to the apparent power of television. Not surprisingly, those restricting others do not often impose the same limitations on themselves. According to Scott MacCleod in TimeEurope, Crown Prince Abdullah of Saudi Arabia has 33 sets in his office, enabling him to watch all satellite news channels at the same time.

Excessive state control is perhaps caused by fear. Modern history suggests that TV has the power to "make or break" public figures. The Product of the 20th Century brought in a new era, one in which political candidates must develop a love affair with the camera or fail. Walter Mondale, in hindsight, understood this and declared: "Modern politics requires the mastery of television" (qtd. in Fisher and Fisher 5). And, was a presidential election decided by TV image? Mander points out that leading up to the famous 1960 Nixon/Kennedy television debate, Nixon was leading in the polls. But his TV appearance turned a likely victory into loss. A sweaty, haggard-looking Nixon notably contrasted with the younger, handsome Kennedy, images that may have turned the election (33).

Politicians have also learned that television provides the best way to influence the greatest number of voters at one time and that the tube provides an ideal medium to present their "informal selves." Hart reports politicians' chatting on the endless talk shows, playing the saxophone, and answering questions from ordinary folks in town hall meetings inspire some to see this as "returning government to the people" (28). In Hart's opinion, though, such "cozy" atmospheres actually shield politicians from the tough questions of journalists (28). The TV images projecting such "personal sides" (Kennedy

Mitchell 8

tossing a football on the beach, Reagan brushing his horse) do seem to sway public opinion, making television an immensely powerful political tool.

What of other groundbreaking products of the 20th century? Some would argue that the computer ruled the century, but the computer has yet to reach its full potential. More than TV, it is geared towards the educated. This country is still a ways away from 99 percent ownership of a home computer. Both products provide information and entertainment, but, for example, when news broke of the September 11 terror attacks, many people who had access to the Internet instantly reached for the remote to watch the live TV coverage. Why? Could it be that no text or photo rivals "real-time" TV? Some who that day relied on the Internet found major news sites inaccessible—swamped by the number of hits. No such problems with television: Instant, Live, Replay, Slow Motion, Freeze Frame, Sound Clip, Sky-Cam, Ground-Cam, NYFD-Cam.

Transition to comparison with computer.

What about airplanes and space shuttles? The technology is awe-inspiring. Is it "smarter" than TV? Certainly. Does it conquer TV as Product of the 20th Century? No. Although thousands fly every day and aeronautics has expanded in ways the Wright Brothers might never have imagined, the technology has not affected our minds in the same way that TV has. Have planes made us aggressive, passive, Republican, Democrat? What does the average American know about NASA compared to Survivor? Television, the wondrous, monstrous box of information, has in the 20th century revolutionized the way we see and experience the world. It enables a butcher in Bangladesh to tour a Beverly Hills boudoir, a seamstress in Somalia to sled across the Alaskan snow. And, one might question, how would we truly behave—how would we kiss, cry, dress, speak, vote, fight—had we not seen it done on TV?

A strong conclusion with clever word choice.

Mitchell 9

Works Cited

Centerwall, Brandon S. "Television and Violent Crime." Public Interest Spring
       1993. Rpt. in Read, Reason, Write. 6th ed. Ed. Dorothy U. Seyler.
       New York: McGraw, 2002. 306–15.

Douglas, Susan J. "Radio and Television." HistoryChannel.com. 1996–2003.
       History Channel. 5 May 2003 <http://historychannel.com/>. Path:
       Television; Radio and Television.

Fisher, David E., and John Marshall Fisher. Tube: The Invention of Television.
       New York: Harcourt, 1997.

Hart, Roderick P. Seducing America: How Television Charms the Modern Voter.
       Oxford: Oxford UP, 1994.

MacCleod, Scott. "How to Bring Change to the Kingdom." TimeEurope 2002. 4
       April 2003 <http://www./time/europe/magazine/
       0,13006,901020304-212732-4,00.html>.

Mander, Jerry. Four Arguments for the Elimination of Television. New York:
       Morrow, 1978.

Winn, Marie. "A Commitment to Language." The Plug-In Drug. 1997. Rpt. in
       Read, Reason, Write. 6th ed. Ed. Dorothy U. Seyler. New York: McGraw,
       2002. 89–90.

Wright, Karen. "Guns, Lies, and Video." Discover April 2003: 28–29.

Start a new page for the Works Cited. Include only works actually cited. Double-space throughout. Alphabetize and use hanging indentation.

Cites an Internet news source.

Cites a passage from a book reprinted in another book.

CHAPTER 12

Using Other Styles
of
Documentation
(APA and More)

Although the research process is much the same regardless of the area of study, documentation varies from one discipline to another. You need to be aware that not all disciplines use MLA. Three common styles of documentation other than MLA are the author/year or APA style, the footnote or endnote style, and the number style. The first two are explained and illustrated in this chapter. The number style, used by some scientists, varies considerably from one group to another. Their style sheets, which you can examine as needed, are listed in the footnote below.[*]

---

[*]*Scientific Style and Format: The CBE Manual for Authors, Editors, and Publishers* (6th ed., 1994), published by the Council of Biology Editors; *ACS Style Guide* (1986), published by the American Chemical Society; *AIP Style Manual* (4th ed., 1990), published by the American Institute of Physics; and *A Manual for Authors of Mathematical Papers* (rev. ed., 1990), published by the American Mathematical Society.

AUTHOR/YEAR OR APA STYLE

The *author/year system* identifies a source by placing the author's last name and the publication year of the source within parentheses at the point in the text where the source is cited. The in-text citations are supported by complete citations in a list of sources at the end of the paper. Most disciplines in the social sciences, biological sciences, and earth sciences use some version of the author/year style. Of the various style manuals presenting this style, the most frequently used is the *Publication Manual of the American Psychological Association* (5th ed., 2002).

APA Style: In-Text Citations

The simplest parenthetical reference can be presented in one of three ways:

1. Place the year of publication within parentheses immediately following the author's name in the text.

   > In a typical study of preference for motherese, Fernald (1985) used an
   >
   > operant auditory preference procedure.

Within the same paragraph, additional references to the source do not need to repeat the year, if the researcher clearly establishes that the same source is being cited.

   > Because the speakers were unfamiliar subjects Fernald's work eliminates
   >
   > the possibility that it is the mother's voice per se that accounts for the
   >
   > preference.

2. If the author is not mentioned in the text, place the author's last name followed by a comma and the year of publication within parentheses after the borrowed information.

   > The majority of working women are employed in jobs that are at least
   >
   > 75 percent female (Lawrence & Matsuda, 1997).

3. Cite a specific passage by providing the page, chapter, or figure number following the borrowed material. *Always* give specific page references for quoted material.

   - A brief quotation:

     > Deuzen-Smith (1988) believes that counselors must be involved with clients
     >
     > and "deeply interested in piecing the puzzle of life together" (p. 29).

- A quotation in display form:

Bartlett (1932) explains the cyclic process of perception:

> Suppose I am making a stroke in a quick game, such as tennis or cricket.
>
> How I make the stroke depends on the relating of certain new experiences,
>
> most of them visual, to other immediately preceding visual experiences,
>
> and to my posture, or balance of posture, at the moment. (p. 201)

Indent a block quotation five spaces from the left margin, do not use quotation marks, and double-space throughout. To show a new paragraph within the block quotation, indent the first line of the new paragraph an additional five spaces. Note the placing of the year after the author's name, and the page number at the end of the direct quotation.

More complicated in-text citations should be handled as follows.

Two Authors, Mentioned in the Text

Kuhl and Meltzoff (1984) tested 4- to 5-month-olds in an experiment . . .

Two Authors, Not Mentioned in the Text

. . . but are unable to show preference in the presence of two mismatched

modalities (e.g., a face and a voice; see Kuhl & Meltzoff, 1984).

Give both authors' last names each time you refer to the source. Connect their names with "and" in the text. Use an ampersand (&) in the parenthetical citation.

More Than Two Authors

For works coauthored by three, four, or five people, provide all last names in the first reference to the source. Thereafter, cite only the first author's name followed by "et al."

As Price-Williams, Gordon, and Ramirez have shown (1969), . . .

OR

Studies of these children have shown (Price-Williams, Gordon, & Ramirez,

1969) . . .

THEN

Price-Williams et al. (1969) also found that . . .

If a source has six or more authors, use only the first author's last name followed by "et al." every time the source is cited.

Corporate Authors

In general, spell out the name of a corporate author each time it is used. If a corporate author has well-known initials, the name can be abbreviated after the first citation.

FIRST IN-TEXT CITATION: (National Institutes of Health [NIH], 1989)

SUBSEQUENT CITATIONS: (NIH, 1989)

Two or More Works Within the Same Parentheses

When citing more than one work by the same author in a parenthetical reference, use the author's name only once and arrange the years mentioned in order, thus:

Several studies of ego identity formation (Marcia, 1966, 1983) . . .

When an author, or the same group of coauthors, has more than one work published in the same year, distinguish the works by adding the letters *a, b, c*, and so on, as needed, to the year. Give the last name only once, but repeat the year, each one with its identifying letters; thus:

Several studies (Smith, 1990a, 1990b, 1990c) . . .

When citing several works by different authors within the same parenthesis, list the authors alphabetically; alphabetize by the first author when citing coauthored works. Separate authors or groups of coauthors with semicolons; thus:

Although many researchers (Archer & Waterman, 1983; Grotevant, 1983;

Grotevant & Cooper, 1986; Sabatelli & Mazor, 1985) study identity

formation . . .

APA STYLE: PREPARING A LIST OF REFERENCES

Every source cited parenthetically in your paper needs a complete bibliographic citation. These complete citations are placed on a separate page (or pages) after the text of the paper and before any appendices included in the paper. Sources are arranged alphabetically, and the first page is titled "References." Begin each source flush with the left margin and indent second and subsequent lines five spaces. Double-space throughout the list of references. Follow these rules for alphabetizing:

1. Organize two or more works by the same author, or the same group of coauthors, chronologically.

    Beck, A. T. (1991).

    Beck, A. T. (1993).

2. Place single-author entries before multiple-author entries when the first of the multiple authors is the same as the single author.

> Grotevant, H. D. (1983).
>
> Grotevant, H. D., & Cooper, C. R. (1986).

3. Organize multiple-author entries that have the same first author but different second or third authors alphabetically by the name of the second author or third and so on.

> Gerbner, G., & Gross, L.
>
> Gerbner, G., Gross, L., Jackson-Beeck, M., Jeffries-Fox, S., & Signorielli, N.
>
> Gerbner G., Gross, L., Morgan, M., & Signorielli, N.

4. Organize two or more works by the same author(s) published in the same year alphabetically by title.

Form for Books

A book citation contains these elements in this form:

> Seligman, M. E. P. (1991). *Learned optimism.* New York: Knopf.
>
> Weiner, B. (Ed.). (1974). *Achievement motivation and attribution theory.*
>
> > Morristown, NJ: General Learning Press.

Authors

Give all authors' names, last name first, and initials. Separate authors with commas, use the ampersand (&) before the last author's name, and end with a period. For edited books, place the abbreviation "Ed." or "Eds." in parentheses following the last editor's name.

Date of Publication

Place the year of publication in parentheses followed by a period.

Title

Capitalize only the first word of the title and of the subtitle, if there is one, and any proper nouns. Italicize the title and end with a period. Place additional information such as number of volumes or an edition in parentheses after the title, before the period.

> Butler, R., & Lewis, M. (1982). *Aging and mental health*
>
> > (3rd ed.).

Publication Information

Cite the city of publication; add the state (using the Postal Service abbreviation) or country if necessary to avoid confusion; then give the publisher's name, after a colon, eliminating unnecessary terms such as *Publisher, Co.,* and *Inc.* End the citation with a period.

> Newton, D. E. (1996). *Violence and the media.* Santa Barbara: ABC-Clio.
>
> Mitchell, J. V. (Ed.). (1985). *The ninth mental measurements yearbook.* Lincoln:
>
>> University of Nebraska Press.
>
> National Institute of Drug Abuse. (1993, April 13). *Annual national high school*
>
>> *senior survey.* Rockville, MD: Author.

Give a corporate author's name in full. When the organization is both author and publisher, place the word *Author* after the place of publication.

Form for Articles

An article citation contains these elements in this form:

> Changeaux, J-P. (1993). Chemical signaling in the brain. *Scientific American,*
>
>> *269,* 58–62.

Date of Publication

Place the year of publication for articles in scholarly journals in parentheses, followed by a period. For articles in newspapers and popular magazines, give the year followed by month and day (if appropriate).

> (1997, March).

See also example below.

Title of Article

Capitalize only the title's first word, the first word of any subtitle, and any proper nouns. Place any necessary descriptive information in square brackets immediately after the title.

> Scott, S. S. (1984, December 12). Smokers get a raw deal [Letter to the Editor].

Publication Information

Cite the title of the journal in full, capitalizing according to conventions for titles. Italicize the title and follow it with a comma. Give the volume number, italicized, followed by a comma, and then inclusive page numbers followed by a period. *If a journal begins each issue with a new page 1, then also cite the issue number in parentheses immediately following the volume number.* Do not use "p." or "pp."

before page numbers when citing articles from scholarly journals; do use "p." or "pp." in citations to newspaper and magazine articles.

> Martin, C. L., Wood, C. H., & Little, J. K. (1990). The development of gender
>
> stereotype components. *Child Development, 61,* 1891–1904.
>
> Leakey, R. (2000, April–May). Extinctions past and present. *Time,* p. 35.

Form for an Article or Chapter in an Edited Book

> Goodall, J. (1993). Chimpanzees—bridging the gap. In P. Cavalieri & P. Singer
>
> (Eds.), *The great ape project: Equality beyond humanity* (pp. 10–18). New
>
> York: St. Martin's.

Cite the author(s), date, and title of the article or chapter. Then cite the name(s) of the editor(s) in signature order after "In," followed by "Ed." or "Eds." in parentheses; the title of the book; the inclusive page numbers of the article or chapter, in parentheses, followed by a period. End with the place of publication and the publisher of the book.

A Report

> U.S. Merit Systems Protection Board. (1988). *Sexual harassment in the federal*
>
> *workplace: An update.* Washington, DC: U.S. Government Printing Office.

Electronic Sources

Many types of electronic sources are available on the Internet, and the variety can make documenting these sources complex. At a minimum, an APA reference for any type of Internet source should include the following information: a document title or description; dates—the date of publication or latest update and the date of retrieval—use (n.d.) for "no date" when a publication date is not available; an Internet address (the URL) that works; and, whenever possible, an author name.

Do not place URLs within angle brackets (< >). Also do not place a period at the end of a reference when a URL concludes it. However, if you need to break an Internet address across lines, you should break the URL only after a slash. Here are some examples:

Electronic Daily Newspaper Article Available by Search

> Schwartz, J. (2002, September 13). Air pollution con game. *Washington*
>
> *Times.* Retrieved September 14, 2002, from
>
> http://www.washtimes.com

Journal Article Available from a Periodical Database

Note that no URL is necessary; just provide the name of the database.

> Dixon, B. (2001, December). Animal emotions. *Ethics & the Environment,*
>
> *6*(2), 22. Retrieved August 26, 2002, from Academic Search Premier
>
> database/EBSCO Host Research Databases.

U.S. Government Report on a Government Web Site

> U.S. General Accounting Office. (2002, March). *Identity theft: Prevalence*
>
> *and cost appear to be growing.* Retrieved September 3, 2002, from
>
> http://www.consumer.gov/idtheft/reports/gao-d02363.pdf

Cite a message posted to a newsgroup or electronic mailing list in the references list. Cite an e-mail from one person to another *only* in the essay, not in the list of references.

SAMPLE STUDENT ESSAY IN APA STYLE

The following essay illustrates APA style. Use 1-inch margins and double-space throughout, including any block quotations. Block quotations should be indented *five* spaces from the left margin (in contrast to the ten spaces required by MLA style). The paper illustrates the following elements of papers in APA style: title page, running head, abstract, author/year in-text citations, subheadings within the text, and a list of references.

Transracial Adoptions 1

Sample title page
for a paper in
APA style.

Adoption: An Issue of Love, Not Race

Connie Childress

Northern Virginia Community College

Transracial Adoptions 2

Observe placement of running head and page number.

Papers in APA style usually begin with an abstract of the paper.

Abstract

Over 400,000 children are in foster care in the United States. The majority of these children are non-white. However, the majority of couples wanting to adopt children are white. While matching race or ethnic background when arranging adoptions may be the ideal, the mixing of race or ethnic background should not be avoided, or delayed, when the matching of race is not possible. Children need homes, and studies of racial adoptees show that they are as adjusted as adoptees with new parents of their own race or ethnicity. Legislation should support speedier adoptions of children, regardless of race or ethnic background.

Adoption: An Issue of Love, Not Race

Nine years ago when my daughter, Ashley, was placed in my arms, it marked the happy ending to a long, exhausting, and, at times, heartbreaking journey through endless fertility treatments and the red tape of adoption procedures. Ironically, she had not been in our home a day before we received a call from another adoption agency that specialized in foreign adoptions. The agency stated that it was ready to begin our home study. As I look at Ashley, with her brown hair, hazel eyes, and fair complexion, I have trouble imagining not having her in my life. I know in my heart that I would have this feeling about my daughter whether she came to us from the domestic agency or the agency bringing us a child from a foreign country. To us the issue was only the child, not his or her race or ethnic background. The issue of race or ethnicity should be considered by adoptive parents along with all the other issues needing thought when they make the decision to adopt. But race or ethnicity alone should not be a roadblock to adoption. It is not society's place to decide for parents if they are capable of parenting a child of a different race or ethnic background.

Transracial adoptions are those adoptions involving a family and a child of a different race or ethnic background. Cultural differences occur when the family is of one racial or ethnic background and the adoptive child is of another. Amy Kuebelbeck (1996) reports that, according to the U.S. Department of Health and Human Services, "about 52 percent of children awaiting adoption through state placement services around the country are black." On average, black children wait longer to be adopted than white, Asian, or Hispanic children. Why should it be more difficult for a white family to adopt an African-American child than a child from China or Russia? Or a Hispanic American or mixed-race child? Any of these combinations still results in a mixed-race adoption.

Student introduces her paper by referring to her adoption experience.

The first paragraph concludes with her thesis.

Observe form of author/year citations.

Transracial Adoptions 4

Adoption Issues and Problems

Although interracial adoptions are "statistically rare in the United States," according to Robert S. Bausch and Richard T. Serpe (1997), who cite a 1990 study by Bachrach et al., the issue continues to receive attention from both social workers and the public (p. 137). A *New Republic* editorial (1994) lists several articles, including a cover story in *The Atlantic* in 1992, to illustrate the attention given to transracial adoptions. All of the popular-press articles as well as those in scholarly journals, the editors explain, describe the country's adoption and foster-care problems. While the great majority of families wanting to adopt are white, about half of the children in foster care waiting to be adopted are black. Robert Jackson (1995) estimates that, in 1995, about 440,000 children are being cared for in foster families. The *New Republic* editorial reports on a 1993 study revealing that "a black child in California's foster care system is three times less likely to be adopted than a white child" (p. 6). In some cases minority children have been in a single foster home with parents of a different race their entire life. They have bonded as a family. Yet, often when the foster parents apply to adopt these children, their petitions are denied and the children are removed from their care. For example, Beverly and David Cox, a white couple in Wisconsin, were asked to be foster parents to two young sisters, both African American. The Coxes provided love and nurturing for five years, but when they petitioned to adopt the two girls, not only was their request denied, but the girls were removed from their home. Can removing the children from the only home they have ever known just because of their skin color really be in the best interest of the children? Cole, Drummond, and Epperson (1995) quote Hillary Clinton as saying that "skin color [should] not outweigh the more important gift of love that adoptive parents want to offer" (p. 50).

The argument against transracial adoption has rested on the concern that children adopted by parents of a different race or ethnic background will lose

Page numbers must be given for direct quotations.

Words added to a quotation for clarity are placed in square brackets.

Transracial Adoptions 5

their cultural heritage and racial identity, and that these losses may result in adjustment problems for the children (Bausch & Serpe, 1997). The loudest voice against mixed-race adoptions has been the National Association of Black Social Workers (NABSW), who passed a resolution in 1972 stating their "vehement opposition to the practice of placing Black children with white families" and reaffirmed their position in 1994 (Harnack, 1995, p. 188). Audrey T. Russell (1993), speaking at the 1972 conference, described white adoption of black children as "a practice of genocide" (p. 189). Fortunately, for both children and families wanting to adopt, the NABSW has now reversed its position and concedes that placement in a home of a different race is far more beneficial to the child than keeping the child in foster care (Jackson, 1995). The NABSW's new position may have come in response to the passage of the Multiethnic Placement Act of 1994, legislation designed to facilitate the placement of minority children into adoptive homes. As Randall Kennedy (1995) explains, while this legislation continues to allow agencies to consider "the child's cultural, ethnic and racial background and the capacity of prospective foster or adoptive parents to meet the needs of a child of this background" (p. 44), it prohibits the delaying of an adoption solely for the purpose of racial matching. Kennedy objects to the law's allowing for even some consideration of race matching because he believes that this results in some children never being adopted, as agencies search for a race match. Sandra Haun (1997), a social worker from Fairfax County, Virginia, said in an interview that she does not oppose transracial adoptions but that the best choice for a child is with a family of the same race, if the choice exists. Providing that both adoptive homes could offer the child the same environment in every aspect, then clearly the same-race home may be the best choice. More often than not, however, placing a child in a home of the same race is not an option. How can we worry about a child's cultural identity when the child doesn't have a home to call his or her own? In the cases of minority children who have been with a foster family of a different race for most of their young lives, the benefits of remaining in a stable home far outweigh the benefits of moving to a family of the same race.

The emotional effects of removing a child from a home that he or she has lived in for an extended period of time is well illustrated in the movie *Losing Isaiah.* In the film, a black child is adopted by a white social worker and her husband after the child's birth mother has placed him in the garbage when he is three days old so that she can be free to search for drugs. When Isaiah is three, the courts return him to his birth mother, who is now off drugs. Is it fair to Isaiah for her reward to be at the expense of his emotional health? The attorney representing the adoptive parents sums up the plight of these children in one sentence: "The child is then wrenched from the only family they've ever known and turned over to strangers because of the color of their skin." In the end, Isaiah's birth mother realizes that this system is unfair to him. She appeals to his adoptive parents to assist him in his adjustment to his new home.

Good transition into discussion of movie.

Subheadings are often used in papers in the social sciences.

Some Consequences of Negative Attitudes toward Transracial Adoptions

To protect themselves from heartbreaking situations such as the one depicted in *Losing Isaiah,* potential adoptive couples in this country are seeking other alternatives. We know that many couples seeking to adopt often adopt children from foreign countries. One of the reasons for this is the assumed shortage of children in the United States available for adoption. What may be less widely known is that many American children of mixed race or African American are placed with adoptive families overseas. One of the reasons for this situation is the continued unwillingness of social workers to place black or mixed-race children with white couples. The NABSW's years of resistance to placing black children with white parents has left its mark, although Edmund Blair Bolles (1984) speculates that the rare placing of black—or American Indian—children with white couples may reflect racial prejudices rather than a great concern to preserve black or Indian identities. Whatever the explanation,

it is ironic that American babies are being "exported" to adoptive homes in
other countries while babies from other countries are being "imported" to
American adoptive homes. The child social services system needs to be
overhauled to remove the stigmas or concerns that keep American children
from being adopted in the country of their birth. If one of the arguments
against transracial adoptions is the possible loss of cultural identity, how can
we tolerate a system which appears to prefer placing African American children
outside their own country—their own cultural heritage?

The argument that adopted children may lose their cultural identity is no
longer a justifiable objection to transracial adoptions. As Randall Kennedy
(1995) asserts, "there exists no credible empirical support that substantiates"
the idea that "adults of the same race as the child will be better able to raise
that child than adults of a different race" (p. 44). Bausch and Serpe (1997) cite
four studies done between 1972 and 1992 that show that "most children of
color adopted by white parents appear to be as well adjusted as children of
color adopted by same-race parents" (p. 137). Perhaps the most important
study is one conducted over twenty years by Rita Simon, American University
sociologist. Davis (1995) reports that she studied 204 interracial adoptees over
the twenty-year period and found that many of the adoptees supported
transracial adoptions. Some did report that they felt isolated from other people
of their own race, but we need to remember that those who participated in this
study were adopted when adoptions were more secretive (and when races were
more separated). At that time, most adoptees, regardless of race, may have felt
isolated because of this lack of openness. Simon (1994), in her book (with
Howard Alstein and Marygold S. Melli) draws these conclusions:

> Transracial adoptees do not lose their racial identities, they do not appear
> to be racially unaware of who they are, and they do not display negative
> or indifferent racial attitudes about themselves. On the contrary, . . .

Transracial Adoptions 8

transracially placed children and their families have as high a success rate

as all other adoptees and their families. (p. 204)

With open adoptions becoming increasingly popular, more adoptees today are

aware of their adopted state and often have knowledge of one or both of their

birth parents. It is not only possible, but probably easier, to provide

opportunities for today's adoptee to learn about his or her racial and cultural

background. The fact that the child is being raised by a family of a different race

or ethnic background does not condemn that child to a life of ignorance

concerning his or her own racial and cultural identity.

Conclusion

There can be only one logical solution to the issues surrounding mixed-race

adoptions. Children and their adoptive parents should be united as a family

because they have passed the background investigations and screening

interviews that show they are emotionally and financially able to provide loving

and nurturing environments for the children. To keep children needing homes

and loving parents apart because they are of different races or ethnic

backgrounds is not fair to the children or the adoptive parents. Preventing or

Student restates her position in a concluding paragraph. delaying such adoptions is detrimental to each child's development. Children

require a consistent home environment to flourish, to grow to be productive

members of society. Legislation needs to support speedier adoptive placements

for minority children to give them the same quality of life afforded other

adoptees. Society needs to protect the right of adoptive parents by not denying

transracial adoptions as an option for couples seeking to adopt.

Transracial Adoptions 9

References

All in the family [Editorial]. (1994, Jan. 24). *New Republic,* pp. 6–7.

Bausch, R. S., & Serpe, R. T. (1997). Negative outcomes of interethnic adoption of Mexican American children. *Social Work, 42.2,* 136–43.

Blackman, A., et al. (1994, Aug. 22). Babies for export. *Time, Time On-disc* [CD-ROM], pp. 64–65.

Bolles, E. B. (1984). *The Penguin adoption handbook: A guide to creating your new family.* New York: Viking.

Cole, W., Drummond, T., & Epperson, S. E. (1995, Aug. 14). Adoption in black and white. *Time,* pp. 50–51.

Davis, R. (1995, Apr. 13). Suits back interracial adoptions. *USA Today,* p. A3.

Harnack, A. (Ed.). (1995). *Adoption: Opposing viewpoints* (p. 188). San Diego: Greenhaven.

Haun, S. (1997, Sept. 30). Personal interview.

Jackson, R. L. (1995, Apr. 25). U.S. stresses no race bias in adoptions. *Los Angeles Times,* p. A26.

Kennedy, R., & Moseley-Braun, C. (1995). At issue: interracial adoption—is the multiethnic placement act flawed? *ABA Journal 81, ABA Journal On-Disc* [CD-ROM], pp. 44–45.

Kuebelbeck, A. (1996, Dec. 31). Interracial adoption debated. *AP US and World.* Retrieved October 10, 1999, from http://www.donet.com/~brandyjc/p6at111.htm

Losing Isaiah (1995) [film].

Russell, A. T. (1995). Transracial adoptions should be forbidden. In A. Harnack, Ed., *Adoption: Opposing viewpoints* (pp. 189–96). San Diego: Greenhaven.

Simon, R. J., Alstein, H., & Melli, M. S. (1995). Transracial adoptions should be encouraged. In A. Harnack (Ed.), *Adoption: Opposing viewpoints* (pp. 198–204). San Diego: Greenhaven.

Title the page "References."

Double-space throughout. In each citation indent all lines, after the first, five spaces. Note APA style placement of date and format for titles.

FOOTNOTE OR ENDNOTE STYLE

Instructors in history, philosophy, and art history frequently prefer the footnote or endnote form of documentation to any pattern using parenthetical documentation. The two chief guides for this pattern are the *MLA Handbook* (6th ed., 2003) and the *Chicago Manual of Style* (15th ed., 2003). The required information and the order of that information in a footnote (or endnote) are the same in the two manuals, but they do differ in minor ways in format. Both manuals state a preference for endnotes (citations placed at the end of the paper) rather than footnotes (citations placed at the bottom of appropriate pages), but some instructors may want to see footnotes, so always be sure to determine the precise guidelines for your assignment. Further learn your instructor's expectations with regard to a bibliography in addition to footnotes or endnotes. If the first footnote (or endnote) reference to a source contains complete bibliographic information, a list of works cited may not be necessary. Still, some instructors want both complete documentation notes and the alphabetized Works Cited page(s) following the text (with footnotes) or after the endnotes.

The following guidelines adhere to the *Chicago Manual of Style*. The few differences in format found in the *MLA Handbook* are explained where appropriate.

In-Text Citations

Use a raised (superscript, such as this [2]) arabic numeral immediately following all material from a source, whether the borrowed material is quoted or paraphrased. The number follows all punctuation except the dash, and it always follows material needing documentation at the end of a sentence or clause. Number footnotes or endnotes consecutively throughout the paper, beginning with "1." Use care to present material from sources with introductory tags and with a placing of superscript numbers so that readers can tell where borrowed material begins and where it ends. Regularly placing citation numbers only at the ends of paragraphs will not result in accurate documentation.

Location and Presentation of Footnotes

1. Place footnotes on the same page as the borrowed material. You need to calculate the number of lines needed at the bottom of the page to complete all the footnotes for that page. (A word processor will make these calculations for you.)

2. Begin the first footnote four lines (two double-spaces) below the last line of text.

3. Indent the first line of each footnote five spaces. Type the online, full-size numeral that corresponds to the superscript numeral in the text, followed by a period. (MLA style calls for indenting the first line five spaces and using a superscript numeral without a period.)

4. If a footnote runs to more than one line of text, single-space between lines and begin the second line flush with the left margin.
5. If more than one footnote appears on a page, double-space between notes.

Location and Presentation of Endnotes

1. List endnotes in consecutive order corresponding to the superscript numbers in the text.
2. Indent the first line of each endnote five spaces. Type the online number followed by a period, leave one space, and then type the reference. (MLA style calls for using a superscript numeral in the text as well as in the notes themselves.)
3. If an endnote runs to more than one line, double-space between lines and begin the second line flush with the left margin.
4. Double-space between endnotes.
5. Start endnotes on a new page titled "Notes." Endnotes follow the text and precede a list of works cited, if such a list is included.

Footnote/Endnote Form: First (Primary) Reference

Each first reference to a source contains all the necessary author, title, and publication information that would be found in a list of works cited or list of references. Subsequent references to the same source use a shortened form. Prepare all first-reference notes according to the following guidelines.

Form for Books

1. Cite the author's full name in signature order, followed by a comma.
2. Cite the title of the book in italics. (MLA style: Underline the title.) Include the complete subtitle, if there is one, unless a list of works cited is also provided. No punctuation follows the title.
3. Give the facts of publication in parentheses: city of publication followed by a colon, publisher followed by a comma, and year of publication.
4. Give the precise page reference. Do not use "p." or "pp." *Chicago Manual* style: Place a comma after the closing parenthesis, before the page number. *MLA Handbook* style: Use no punctuation between the closing parenthesis and the page reference. All notes end with a period.

CHICAGO: 1. Daniel J. Boorstin, *The Americans: The Colonial Experience*

(New York: Vintage-Random, 1958), 46.

MLA: ¹ Daniel J. Boorstin, The Americans: The Colonial Experience

(New York: Vintage-Random, 1958) 46.

Form for Articles

1. Cite the author's full name in signature order, followed by a comma.
2. Cite the title of the article in quotation marks, and place a comma *inside* the closing quotation mark.
3. Give the facts of publication: the title of the journal, italicized; the volume in arabic numerals; and the date followed by a colon. Citations of scholarly journals require the volume number followed by the date in parentheses; citations of popular magazines and newspapers eliminate the volume number, giving the date only, not in parentheses.
4. Provide a precise page reference following the colon, without using "p." or "pp." All notes end with a period.

> 2. Everard H. Smith, "Chambersburg: Anatomy of a Confederate Reprisal,"
>
> *American Historical Review* 96 (April 1991): 434.

Sample Footnotes/Endnotes

Additional information must be added as necessary. Some of the common variations are illustrated here. Note that the examples are presented as endnotes; that is, the lines of each note are double-spaced. Remember that footnotes are single-spaced *within* each note but double-spaced *between* notes. The Chicago style of italicizing title, using an online numeral, and placing a comma after the facts of publication in a book citation has been followed in these examples.

A Work by Two or Three Authors

> 3. Charles A. Beard and Mary R. Beard, *The American Spirit* (New York:
>
> Macmillan, 1942), 63.

A Work by More Than Three Authors

> 4. Lester R. Brown et al., *State of the World 1990: A Worldwatch Institute Report*
>
> *on Progress Toward a Sustainable Society* (New York: Norton, 1990), 17.

An Edited Work

> 5. *The Autobiography of Benjamin Franklin*, ed. Max Farrand (Berkeley:
>
> University of California Press, 1949), 6–8.

(Begin with the title—or the editor's name—if the author's name appears in the title.)

6. Bentley Glass, Orvsei Temkin, and William L. Straus, Jr., eds.,
Forerunners of Darwin: 1745–1859 (Baltimore: Johns Hopkins Press paperback
edition, 1968), 326.

A Translation

7. Allan Gilbert, trans. and ed., *The Letters of Machiavelli* (New York:
Capricorn Books, 1961), 120.

A Preface, Introduction, or Afterword

8. Ernest Barker, introduction to *The Politics of Aristotle,* trans. and ed.
Ernest Barker (New York: Oxford University Press, 1962), xiii.

A Book in Two or More Volumes

9. Paul Tillich, *Systematic Theology,* 3 vols. (Chicago: University of Chicago
Press, 1951–63), 1:52.

(Make the page reference first to the volume number, followed by a colon, and
then the page number.)

A Book in Its Second or Subsequent Edition

10. Frank J. Sorauf and Paul Allen Beck, *Party Politics in America,* 6th ed.
(Glenview, IL: Scott, Foresman/Little, Brown, 1988), 326.

A Book in a Series

11. Charles L. Sanford, ed., *Benjamin Franklin and the American Character,*
Problems in American Civilization (Lexington, MA: D.C. Heath, 1955), 4.

A Work in a Collection

12. George Washington, "Farewell Address, 1796," in *A Documentary
History of the United States*, ed. Richard D. Heffner (New York: New American
Library, 1965), 64–65.

An Encyclopedia Article

13. *The Concise Dictionary of American Biography*, 1964 ed., s.v. "Anthony, Susan Brownell."

(Do not cite a page number for reference works arranged alphabetically; rather, cite the entry in quotation marks after "s.v." [*sub verbo*—"under the word"]. The edition number or year is needed, but no other facts of publication are required for well-known reference works.)

An Article in a Scholarly Journal

14. Ellen Fitzpatrick, "Rethinking the Intellectual Origins of American Labor History," *American Historical Review* 96 (April 1991): 426.

An Article in a Popular Magazine

15. Richard Leakey, "Extinctions Past and Present," *Time,* April–May 2000: 35.

An Editorial

16. "Means of Atonement," editorial, *Wall Street Journal*, 22 May 2000: A38.

A Review

17. Gabriel P. Weisberg, "French Art Nouveau," review of *Art Nouveau in Fin-de-Siècle France: Politics, Psychology, and Style* by Deborah Silverman, *Art Journal* 49 (Winter 1990): 427.

An Online News Service

18. Leslie Gevirtz, "US Leads 100-Year Game of Economic Development," *Reuters*, Nov./Dec. 1999, http://www.reuters.com/magazine/ (accessed January 4, 2000).

An Article from a Reference Database

19. *Encyclopaedia Britannica Online*, s.v. "Prohibition," http://search.eb.com/ (accessed January 24, 1998).

Footnote/Endnote Form: Short Forms

After the first full documentary footnote or endnote, subsequent references to the same source should be shortened forms. The simplest short form for any source with an author or editor is the author's or editor's last name followed by a comma and a precise page reference; thus: 20. Fitzgerald, 425. If there is no author cited, use a short title and page number. If two sources are written by authors with the same last name, then add first names or initials to distinguish between them.

> 21. Henry Adams, 16.

> 22. James T. Adams, 252.

If you use two or more sources by the same author, then add a short title to the note; thus:

> 23. Boorstin, *American Politics*, 167.

> 24. Boorstin, *The Americans*, 65–66.

The Latin abbreviations *loc. cit.* and *op. cit.* are no longer recommended, and ibid. is almost as obsolete, usually replaced now by the simple short form of author's last name and page number. Remember that ibid. can be used only to refer to the source cited in the immediately preceding note. The following footnotes, appearing at the bottom of a page from a history paper, illustrate the various short forms.

Sample Footnotes from a History Paper

While mid-twentieth-century historians may be more accurate, they may have lost the flavor of earlier American historians who had a clear ideology that shaped their writing.[20]

> 11. William Bradford, *Of Plymouth Plantation*, in *The American Puritans: Their Prose and Poetry*, ed. Perry Miller (New York: Anchor-Doubleday, 1956), 5.

> 12. Daniel J. Boorstin, *The Americans: The Colonial Experience* (New York: Vintage-Random, 1958), 16.

> 13. Ibid., 155.

> 14. James T. Adams, 136.

> 15. Henry Adams, *The Education of Henry Adams*, ed. D. W. Brogan (Boston: Houghton Mifflin, 1961), 342.

16. Boorstin, *American Politics*, 167.

17. Henry Adams, "The Tendency of History," 16.

18. Ibid., 71.

19. Henry Adams, *Education*, 408.

20. John Higham, "The Cult of the 'American Consensus': Homogenizing Our History," *Commentary* 27 (Feb. 1959): 94–96.

A Collection of Readings

This section is divided into 11 chapters: each of the first ten chapters on a current topic or set of interrelated issues open to debate and the last chapter a collection of some well-known arguments from the past. Although the number of articles varies in each chapter, all contain at least six articles in order to remind readers that complex issues cannot be divided into simple "for" or "against" positions. This point remains true even for the chapters on a rather specific topic. It is not sound critical thinking to be, simply, for or against any complicated public policy issue.

There are questions following each article to aid your reading, analysis, and critical responses, and each chapter begins with a brief introduction and set of questions to focus your thinking as you read. Each introduction concludes with a list of a few Web sites that are relevant to the chapter's topic and may be of interest to you. However, please keep these two thoughts in mind as you read: (1) there is no way to include all possibly relevant Web addresses, and (2) the Internet is ever-changing. Although every effort has been made to include sites that are expected to last, Web sites in existence when this text was prepared may no longer be available.

Here are some general questions to guide your critical thinking as you read and reflect on the various issues:

- What are my views on this issue? Do I already have a coherent position? If so, what can I gain by studying the writers who present a different point of view?

- Which writers rely primarily on facts to support their claims? Which combine facts and logic? Which also use persuasive strategies? Which ones seem to be primarily interested in "pushing emotional buttons" in readers who are assumed to be in agreement with the author? Do I recognize any logical fallacies?

- Which type of argument usually works best for me? Does my answer to this question depend in part on the particular issue?

© George Tames/The New York Times

Read: What is this a photograph of? Who is the figure?

Reason: What is significant about the figure's pose? What does the photographer gain by his position behind the figure?

Reflect/Write: What message does this photograph communicate to viewers?

CHAPTER 13

The Media:
Image and Reality

Although we may not agree with Marshall McLuhan that the medium is itself the message, we must still recognize the ways that the various media influence us, touching our emotions, shaping our vision of the world, altering our lives. The essays in this chapter explore and debate the effects of advertising, television, and the press on the ways we imagine the world and then construct our lives. Surely we are influenced by media images, by the "reality" they reveal to us. The questions become how extensive is the influence, given the other influences in our lives, and what, if anything, can or should we do about it? The writers in this chapter do not agree on the answers to these questions.

Some of the most powerful messages from the print media—newspapers and magazines—come from the photographs accompanying the news stories. One such photograph opens this chapter; eight more are included in a color insert. For the photos in the insert, follow the pattern we have established with the images opening each chapter: read, reason, reflect/write. That is, what can you identify that are facts in the image, what do you observe that seems significant, and then what does each image add up to—what message does it send to viewers? You may need to do some research or work with a class partner to identify the occasion of each of the photos. Remember that you need to start by "reading" the image, and to do that you need to identify the time and place and figures in the photo.

Prereading Questions

1. How "real" are "reality" shows? Does it matter if they are scripted?
2. How accurate is our press coverage? Do media outlets around the world "see" and show the same world to their viewers? Do bloggers offer another way of "seeing" that is useful?
3. How does advertising shape our images of the world? How realistic are those images? Do we want advertising to be "realistic"?
4. What standards of reliability, objectivity, and fairness should be set for the media? What, if any, distortions are acceptable because they make the journalist's story more compelling?

Web Sites Related to This Chapter's Topic

Media Research Center

www.mediaresearch.org

Studies and reports on "liberal" media bias.

Electronic Databases

Databases such as Proquest and Expanded Academic ASAP plus many others containing articles in the social sciences are available through your library. They will lead you to many articles on the topics relevant to this chapter.

IN YOUR FACE . . . ALL OVER THE PLACE! | JEAN KILBOURNE

Writer and speaker Jean Kilbourne has been a visiting scholar at Wellesley College and an adviser on alcohol and tobacco advertising to two surgeons general. She is the author of *Can't Buy My Love* (2000) and editor of *Media Sharp* (2000). The following excerpt is from her book, *Deadly Persuasion*, published in 1999.

PREREADING QUESTIONS We know that TV shows are filled with stereotypes; what about advertising? Think about print or TV ads; what kinds of stereotypes come to mind?

1   In spite of the fact that we are surrounded by more advertising than ever before, most of us still ridicule the idea that we might be personally influenced by it. The ridicule is often extremely simplistic. The argument essentially is, "I'm no robot marching down to the store to do advertising's bidding and therefore advertising doesn't affect me at all." This argument was made

by Jacob Sullum, a senior editor at *Reason* magazine, in an editorial in the *New York Times*. Writing about "heroin chic," the advertising fad in the mid-1990s of using models who looked like heroin addicts, Sullum says, "Like you, I've seen . . . ads featuring sallow, sullen, scrawny youths. Not once have I had an overwhelming urge to rush out and buy some heroin." He concludes from this in-depth research that all critics of advertising are portraying "people not as independent moral agents but as mindless automatons," as if there were no middle ground between rushing out to buy heroin and being completely uninfluenced by the media images that surround us—or no possibility that disaffected teens are more vulnerable than middle-aged executives. After all, Sullum is *not* the target audience for heroin chic ads.

Of course, most of us feel far superior to the kind of person who would be affected by advertising. *We* are not influenced, after all. We are skeptical, even cynical . . . but ignorant (certainly not stupid, just uninformed). Advertising is familiar, but not known. The fact that we are surrounded by it, that we can sing the jingles and identify the models and recognize the logos, doesn't mean that we are educated about it, that we understand it. As Sut Jhally says, "To not be influenced by advertising would be to live outside of culture. No human being lives outside of culture." 2

Advertisers want us to believe that we are not influenced by ads. As Joseph Goebbels said, "This is the secret of propaganda: Those who are to be persuaded by it should be completely immersed in the ideas of the propaganda, without ever noticing that they are being immersed in it." So the advertisers sometimes play upon our cynicism. In fact, they co-opt our cynicism and our irony just as they have co-opted our rock music, our revolutions and movements for liberation, and our concern for the environment. In a current trend that I call "anti-advertising," the advertisers flatter us by insinuating that we are far too smart to be taken in by advertising. Many of these ads spoof the whole notion of image advertising. A scotch ad tells the reader "This is a glass of Cutty Sark. If you need to see a picture of a guy in an Armani suit sitting between two fashion models drinking it before you know it's right for you, it probably isn't." 3

And an ad for shoes says, "If you feel the need to be smarter and more articulate, read the complete works of Shakespeare. If you like who you are, here are your shoes." Another shoe ad, this one for sneakers, says, "Shoe buying rule number one: The image wears off after the first six miles." What a concept. By buying heavily advertised products, we can demonstrate that we are not influenced by advertising. Of course, this is not entirely new. Volkswagens were introduced in the 1960s with an anti-advertising campaign, such as the ad that pictured the car and the headline "Lemon." But such ads go a lot further these days, especially the foreign ones. A British ad for Easy jeans says, "We don't use sex to sell our jeans. We don't even screw you when you buy them." And French Connection UK gets away with a double-page spread that says "fcuk advertising." 4

Cynicism is one of the worst effects of advertising. Cynicism learned from years of being exposed to marketing hype and products that never deliver the 5 promised goods often carries over to other aspects of life. This starts early: A study of children done by researchers at Columbia University in 1975 found that heavy viewing of advertising led to cynicism, not only about advertising, but about life in general. The researchers found that "in most cultures, adolescents have had to deal with social hypocrisy and even with institutionalized lying. But today, TV advertising is stimulating *preadolescent* children to think about socially accepted hypocrisy. They may be too young to cope with such thoughts without permanently distorting their views of morality, society, and business." They concluded that "7- to 10-year-olds are strained by the very existence of advertising directed to them." These jaded children become the young people whose mantra is "whatever," who admire people like David Letterman (who has made a career out of taking nothing seriously), whose response to almost every experience is "been there, done that," "duh," and "do ya think?" Cynicism is not criticism. It is a lot easier than criticism. In fact, easy cynicism is a kind of naivete. We need to be more critical as a culture and less cynical.

6   Cynicism deeply affects how we define our problems and envision their solutions. Many people exposed to massive doses of advertising both distrust every possible solution *and* expect a quick fix. There are no quick fixes to the problems our society faces today, but there are solutions to many of them. The first step, as always, is breaking through denial and facing the problems squarely. I believe it was James Baldwin who said, "Not everything that is faced can be changed, but nothing can be changed until it is faced." One of the things we need to face is that we and our children are indeed influenced by advertising.

7   Although some people, especially advertisers, continue to argue that advertising simply reflects the society, advertising does a great deal more than simply reflect cultural attitudes and values. Even some advertisers admit to this: Rance Crain of *Advertising Age* said great advertising "plays the tune rather than just dancing to the tune." Far from being a passive mirror of society, advertising is an effective and pervasive medium of influence and persuasion, and its influence is cumulative, often subtle, and primarily unconscious. Advertising performs much the same function in industrial society as myth performed in ancient and primitive societies. It is both a creator and perpetuator of the dominant attitudes, values and ideology of the culture, the social norms and myths by which most people govern their behavior. At the very least, advertising helps to create a climate in which certain attitudes and values flourish and others are not reflected at all.

8   Advertising is not only our physical environment, it is increasingly our spiritual environment as well. By definition, however, it is only interested in materialistic values. When spiritual values or religious images show up in ads, it is only to appropriate them in order to sell us something. Sometimes this is very obvious. Eternity is a perfume by Calvin Klein. Infiniti is an automobile and Hydra Zen a moisturizer. Jesus is a brand of jeans. "See the light," says an ad for wool, while a face powder ad promises "an enlightening experience" and absolute heaven." One car is "born again" and another promises to "energize your soul." In a full-page ad in *Advertising Age,* the online service Yahoo! proclaims, "We've got 60 million followers. That's more than some religions," but

goes on to assure readers, "Don't worry. We're *not* a religion." When Pope John Paul II visited Mexico City in the winter of 1999, he could have seen a smiling image of himself on bags of Sabritas, a popular brand of potato chips, or a giant street sign showing him bowing piously next to a Pepsi logo with a phrase in Spanish that reads, "Mexico Always Faithful." In the United States, he could have treated himself to pope-on-a-rope soap.

But advertising's co-optation of spirituality goes much deeper than this. It is commonplace these days to observe that consumerism has become the religion of our time (with advertising its holy text), but the criticism usually stops short of what is most important, what is at the heart of the comparison. Advertising and religion share a belief in transformation and transcendence, but most religions believe that this requires work and sacrifice. In the world of advertising, enlightenment is achieved instantly by purchasing material goods. As James Twitchell, author of *Adcult USA*, says, "The Jolly Green Giant, the Michelin Man, the Man from Glad, Mother Nature, Aunt Jemima, Speedy Alka-Seltzer, the White Knight, and all their otherworldly kin are descendants of the earlier gods. What separates them is that they now reside in manufactured products and that, although earlier gods were invoked by fasting, prayer, rituals, and penance, the promise of purchase calls forth their modern ilk." 9

Advertising constantly promotes the core belief of American culture: that we *can* re-create ourselves, transform ourselves, transcend our circumstances— but with a twist. For generations Americans believed this could be achieved if we worked hard enough, like Horatio Alger. Today the promise is that we can change our lives instantly, effortlessly—by winning the lottery, selecting the right mutual fund, having a fashion makeover, losing weight, having tighter abs, buying the right car or soft drink. It is this belief that such transformation is possible that drives us to keep dieting, to buy more stuff, to read fashion magazines that give us the same information over and over again. Cindy Crawford's makeup is carefully described as if it could transform us into her. On one level, we know it won't—after all, most of us have tried this approach many times before. But on another level, we continue to try, continue to believe that this time it will be different. This American belief that we can transform ourselves makes advertising images much more powerful than they otherwise would be. 10

The focus of the transformation has shifted from the soul to the body. Of course, this trivializes and cheapens authentic spirituality and transcendence. But, more important, this junk food for the soul leaves us hungry, empty, malnourished. The emphasis on instant salvation is parodied in an ad from *Adbusters* for a product called Mammon, in which a man says, "I need a belief system that serves my needs right away." The copy continues, "Dean Sachs has a mortgage, a family and an extremely demanding job. What he doesn't need is a religion that complicates his life with unreasonable ethical demands." The ad ends with the words, "Mammon: Because you deserve to enjoy life—guilt free." 11

As advertising becomes more and more absurd, however, it becomes increasingly difficult to parody ads. There's not much of a difference between the 12 ad for Mammon and the real ad for cruises that says "It can take several life-times to reach a state of inner peace and tranquillity. Or, it can take a couple of weeks." Of course, we know that a couple of weeks on a cruise won't solve our problems, won't bring us to a state of peace and enlightenment, but it is so tempting to believe that there is some easy way to get there, some ticket we can buy.

13   To be one of the "elect" in today's society is to have enough money to buy luxury goods. Of course, when salvation comes via the sale, it becomes important to display these goods. Owning a Rolex would not impress anyone who didn't know how expensive it is. A Rolex ad itself says the watch was voted "most likely to be coveted." Indeed, one of advertising's purposes is to create an aura for a product, so that other people will be impressed. As one marketer said recently in *Advertising Age,* "It's no fun to spend $100 on athletic shoes to wear to high school if your friends don't know how cool your shoes are."

14   Thus the influence of advertising goes way beyond the target audience and includes those who could never afford the product, who will simply be envious and impressed—perhaps to the point of killing someone for his sneakers or jacket, as has sometimes happened in our poverty-stricken neighborhoods. In the early 1990s the city health commissioner in Philadelphia issued a public health warning cautioning youths against wearing expensive leather jackets and jewelry, while in Milwaukee billboards depicted a chalk outline of a body and the warning, "Dress Smart and Stay Alive." Poor children in many countries knot the laces of their Nikes around their ankles to avoid having them stolen while they sleep.

15   Many teens fantasize that objects will somehow transform their lives, give them social standing and respect. When they wear a certain brand of sneaker or jacket, they feel, "This is important, therefore I am important." The brand gives instant status. No wonder they are willing, even eager, to spend money for clothes that advertise the brands. A *USA Today*–CNN–Gallup Poll found that 61 percent of boys and 44 percent of girls considered brand names on clothes "very important" or "somewhat important." As ten-year-old Darion Sawyer from Baltimore said, "People will tease you and talk about you, say you got on no-name shoes or say you shop at Kmart." Leydiana Reyes, an eighth-grader in Brooklyn, said, "My father always tells me I could buy two pairs of jeans for what you pay for Calvin Klein. I know that. But I still want Calvin Klein." And Danny Shirley, a fourteen-year-old in Santa Fe decked out in Tommy Hilfiger regalia, said, "Kids who wear Levi's don't really care about what they wear, I guess."

16   In the beginning, these labels were somewhat discreet. Today we see sweatshirts with fifteen-inch "Polo" logos stamped across the chest, jeans with four-inch "Calvin Klein" labels stitched on them, and a jacket with "Tommy Hilfiger" in five-inch letters across the back. Some of these outfits are so close to sandwich boards that I'm surprised people aren't paid to wear them. Before too long, the logo-free product probably will be the expensive rarity.

17   What people who wear these clothes are really buying isn't a garment, of course, but an *image.* And increasingly, an image is all that advertising has to

sell. Advertising began centuries ago with signs in medieval villages. In the nineteenth century, it became more common but was still essentially designed to give people information about manufactured goods and services. Since the 1920s, advertising has provided less information about the product and focused more on the lives, especially the emotional lives, of the prospective consumers. This shift coincided, of course, with the increasing knowledge and acceptability of psychology, as well as the success of propaganda used to convince the population to support World War I.

Industrialization gave rise to the burgeoning ability of businesses to mass-   18 produce goods. Since it was no longer certain there would be a market for the goods, it became necessary not just to mass-produce the goods but to mass-produce markets hungry for the goods. The problem became not too little candy produced but not enough candy consumed, so it became the job of the advertisers to *produce consumers*. This led to an increased use of psychological research and emotional ploys to sell products. Consumer behavior became recognized as a science in the late 1940s.

As luxury goods, prepared foods, and nonessential items have prolifer-   19 ated, it has become crucial to create artificial needs in order to sell unnecessary products. Was there such a thing as static cling before there were fabric softeners and sprays? An ad for a "lip renewal cream" says, "I never thought of my lips as a problem area until Andrea came up with the solution."

Most brands in a given category are essentially the same. Most shampoos   20 are made by two or three manufacturers. Blindfolded smokers or beer-drinkers can rarely identify what brand they are smoking or drinking, including their own. Whether we know it or not, we select products primarily because of the image reflected in their advertising. Very few ads give us any real information at all. Sometimes it is impossible to tell what is being advertised. "This is an ad for the hair dryer," says one ad, featuring a woman lounging on a sofa. If we weren't told, we would never know. A joke made the rounds a while ago about a little boy who wanted a box of tampons so that he could effortlessly ride bicycles and horses, ski, and swim.

Almost all tobacco and alcohol ads are entirely image-based. Of course,   21 when you're selling a product that kills people, it's difficult to give honest information about it. Think of all the cigarette ads that never show cigarettes or even a wisp of smoke. One of the most striking examples of image advertising is the very successful and long-running campaign for Absolut vodka. This campaign focuses on the shape of the bottle and the word "Absolut," as in "Absolut Perfection," which features the bottle with a halo. This campaign has been so successful that a coffee-table book collection of the ads published just in time for Christmas, the perfect gift for the alcoholic in your family, sold over 150,000 copies. Collecting Absolut ads is now a common pastime for elementary-school children, who swap them like baseball cards.

How does all this affect us? It is very difficult to do objective research about   22 advertising's influence because there are no comparison groups, almost no people who have not been exposed to massive doses of advertising. In addition, research that measures only one point in time does not adequately capture advertising's real effects. We need longitudinal studies, such as George Gerbner's twenty-five-year study of violence on television.

23   The advertising industry itself can't prove that advertising works. While claiming to its clients that it does, it simultaneously denies it to the Federal Trade Commission whenever the subject of alcohol and tobacco advertising comes up. As an editorial in *Advertising Age* once said, "A strange world it is, in which people spending millions on advertising must do their best to prove that advertising doesn't do very much!" According to Bob Wehling, senior vice-president of marketing at Procter & Gamble, "We don't have a lot of scientific studies to support our belief that advertising works. But we have seen that the power of advertising makes a significant difference."

24   What research can most easily prove is usually what is least important, such as advertising's influence on our choice of brands. This is the most obvious, but least significant, way that advertising affects us. There are countless examples of successful advertising campaigns, such as the Absolut campaign, that have sent sales soaring. A commercial for I Can't Believe It's Not Butter featuring a sculptress whose work comes alive in the form of romance-novel hunk Fabio boosted sales about 17 percent. Tamagotchis—virtual pets in an egg—were introduced in the United States with a massive advertising campaign and earned $150 million in seven months. And Gardenburger, a veggie patty, ran a thirty-second spot during the final episode of *Seinfeld* and, within a week, sold over $2 million worth, a market share jump of 50 percent and more than the entire category sold in the same week the previous year. But advertising is more of an art than a science, and campaigns often fail. In 1998 a Miller beer campaign bombed, costing the company millions of dollars and offending a large segment of their customers. The 1989 Nissan Infiniti campaign, known as the "Rocks and Trees" campaign, was the first ever to introduce a car without showing it and immediately became a target for Jay Leno's monologues. And, of course, the Edsel, a car introduced by Ford with great fanfare in 1957, remains a universal symbol of failure.

25   The unintended effects of advertising are far more important and far more difficult to measure than those effects that are intended. The important question is not "Does this ad sell the product?" but rather "What else does this ad sell?" An ad for Gap khakis featuring a group of acrobatic swing dancers probably sold a lot of pants, which, of course, was the intention of the advertisers. But it also contributed to a rage for swing dancing. This is an innocuous example of advertising's powerful unintended effects. Swing dancing is not binge drinking, after all.

26   Advertising often sells a great deal more than products. It sells values, images, and concepts of love and sexuality, romance, success, and, perhaps most important, normalcy. To a great extent, it tells us who we are and who we should be. We are increasingly using brand names to create our identities. James Twitchell argues that the label of our shirt, the make of our car, and our favorite laundry detergent are filling the vacuum once occupied by religion, education, and our family name.

© Bettmann/Corbis

2

© Bettmann/Corbis

© Reuters/Corbis

Hulshizer-AP-World Wide Photos

© Saul Loeb/epa/epa/Corbis

© Kevin Lamarque/Reuters/Corbis

Even more important, advertising corrupts our language and thus influ- 27
ences our ability to think clearly. Critic and novelist George Steiner once talked
with an interviewer about what he called "anti-language, that which is tran-
scendentally annihilating of truth and meaning." Novelist Jonathan Dee, applying this concept to advertising, writes that "the harm lies not in the ad itself; the
harm is in the exchange, in the collision of ad language, ad imagery, with other
sorts of language that contend with it in the public realm. When Apple reprints
an old photo of Gandhi, or Heineken ends its ads with the words 'Seek the
Truth,' or Winston suggests that we buy cigarettes by proposing (just under the
surgeon general's warning) that 'You have to appreciate authenticity in all its
forms,' or Kellogg's identifies itself with the message 'Simple is Good,' these occasions color our contact with those words and images in their other, possibly
less promotional applications." The real violence of advertising, Dee concludes,
is that "words can be made to mean anything, which is hard to distinguish from
the idea that words mean nothing." We see the consequences of this in much
of our culture, from "art" to politics, that has no content, no connection between language and conviction. Just as it is often difficult to tell what product
an ad is selling, so is it difficult to determine what a politician's beliefs are (the
"vision thing," as George Bush so aptly called it, albeit unintentionally) or what
the subject is of a film or song or work of art. As Dee says, "The men and women
who make ads are not hucksters; they are artists with nothing to say, and they
have found their form." Unfortunately, their form deeply influences all the other
forms of the culture. We end up expecting nothing more.

This has terrible consequences for our culture. As Richard Pollay says, 28
"Without a reliance on words and a faith in truth, we lack the mortar for social
cohesion. Without trustworthy communication, there is no communion, no
community, only an aggregation of increasingly isolated individuals, alone in
the mass."

Advertising creates a worldview that is based upon cynicism, dissatisfaction, 29
and craving. The advertisers aren't evil. They are just doing their job, which is to
sell a product, but the consequences, usually unintended, are often destructive
to individuals, to cultures, and to the planet. In the history of the world, there
has never been a propaganda effort to match that of advertising in the twentieth century. More thought, more effort, and more money go into advertising
than has gone into any other campaign to change social consciousness. The
story that advertising tells is that the way to be happy, to find satisfaction—and
the path to political freedom, as well—is through the consumption of material
objects. And the major motivating force for social change throughout the world
today is this belief that happiness comes from the market.

So, advertising has a greater impact on all of us than we generally real- 30
ize. The primary purpose of the mass media is to deliver us to advertisers.
Much of the information that we need from the media in order to make informed choices in our lives is distorted or deleted on behalf of corporate
sponsors. Advertising is an increasingly ubiquitous presence in our lives, and
it sells much more than products. We delude ourselves when we say we are

not influenced by advertising. And we trivialize and ignore its growing significance at our peril.

NOTES

1. "This argument was made by Jacob Sullum": Sullum, 1997, A31.
2. "As Sut Jhally says": Jhally, 1998.
3. "As Joseph Goebbels": Goebbels, 1933, March 28. Quoted in Jacobson and Mazur, 1995, 15.
4. "A study of children done by researchers at Columbia University": Bever, Smith, Bengen, and Johnson, 1975, 119.
5. " '7- to 10-year-olds are strained' ": Bever, Smith, Bengen, and Johnson, 1975, 120.
6. "Rance Crain of *Advertising Age*": Crain, 1999, 23.
7. "When Pope John Paul II": Chacon and Ribadeneria, 1999. A8.
8. " 'The Jolly Green Giant' ": Twitchell, 1996, 30.
9. " 'It's no fun to spend $100 on athletic shoes' ": Peppers and Rogers, 1997, 32.
10. "the city health commissioner in Philadelphia": Worthington, 1992, 15.
11. "A USA Today–CNN–Gallup Poll": Jacobson and Mazur, 1995, 26.
12. "Leydiana Reyes": Leonhardt, 1997, 65.
13. "Danny Shirley": Espen, 1999, 59.
14. "sweatshirts with fifteen-inch 'Polo' logos": Ryan, 1996, D1.
15. "Consumer behavior": Woods, 1995.
16. "Most shampoos": Twitchell, 1996, 252.
17. "Blindfolded smokers": Twitchell, 1996, 125.
18. " 'A strange world it is' ": Bernstein, 1978, August 7.
19. "According to Bob Wehling": Crain, 1998, 24.
20. "A commercial for I Can't Believe It's Not Butter": Haran, 1996, 12.
21. "Tamagotchis": Goldner, 1998, S43.
22. "And Gardenburger": Gardenburger hits the spot, 1998, 17.
23. "In 1998 a Miller beer campaign": Crain, 1998, 24.
24. "The 1989 Nissan Infiniti": Horton, 1996, S28.
25. "the Edsel": Horton, 1996, S30.
26. "An ad for Gap khakis": Cortissoz, 1998, A10.
27. "James Twitchell argues": University of Florida news release, quoted by Orlando, 1999, *http://www.sciencedaily.com/releases/1999/05/990518114815. htm.*
28. "Critic and novelist George Steiner": Dee, 1999, 65–66.
29. "As Richard Pollay": Pollay, 1986.
30. "there has never been a propaganda effort": Jhally, 1998.

QUESTIONS FOR READING

1. What is Kilbourne's subject? (Be more precise than just "advertising.")
2. How is advertising like propaganda?

3. What is the nature of the "anti-advertising" ad? What is one of the consequences of anti-advertising?

4. What role does advertising play in our society? How does it promote "the core belief of American culture"? How is its message different from what that core belief used to emphasize?

5. How does advertising go beyond the target audience? How do we want others to react to what we have purchased? What are we purchasing with designer-labeled clothing?

6. In the second half of the twentieth century, what became advertising's purpose or task? How did this purpose change ads?

7. How does advertising affect language?

QUESTIONS FOR REASONING AND ANALYSIS

1. What is Kilbourne's claim? What *type* of argument is this—that is, what does it seek to accomplish?

2. Kilbourne provides a brief history of advertising. What does she accomplish by including this in her discussion?

3. List the effects of advertising discussed by Kilbourne. How does her discussion of effects support her claim? What evidence does the author provide throughout her analysis?

4. The author points out that it is difficult to study the effects of ads. Why is it difficult? Why does she include these comments in her argument?

QUESTIONS FOR REFLECTING AND WRITING

1. Evaluate Kilbourne's argument. Does she convince you? If not, what would you need to be convinced?

2. Do you find considerable cynicism today? If so, have you ever connected it to the endless distortions created by ads? If not, does this seem like a reasonable causal connection to you now?

3. Should advertising be banned from children's TV programs? Why or why not?

SOCIAL LUBRICANT: HOW A MARKETING CAMPAIGN BECAME THE CATALYST FOR A SOCIETAL DEBATE | ROB WALKER

Rob Walker is a contributing writer to *Inc.* magazine, the author of *Letters from New Orleans* (2005), and the author of a weekly column, "Consumed," in the *New York Times* magazine. In his "Consumed" column, Walker seeks meaning in the consumer culture, that is, what it has to tell us about ourselves. The following column appeared September 4, 2005.

PREREADING QUESTIONS Have you seen any of the Dove ads? If not, look for them and think about what you find. If yes, what was your initial reaction to the ads?

1   "Fat or Fabulous?" asked a line on the cover of a recent issue of *People* magazine, underneath a small photograph of some of the "Dove Girls." These are the young women appearing on billboards and other advertising on behalf of Dove Body Nourishers Intensive Firming Lotion and related products; they are not the ultrathin fashion-model types common to advertising, and they are dressed only in underwear. They have become a minor sensation, sparking opinion articles in major publications (including a *New York Times* editorial) and showing up as guests on the "Today" show. This is a rare thing and pretty clearly a publicity bonanza for the Dove brand.

2   The debate over whether these images of women are positive (because they are more "real" than many marketing or media depictions of women) or negative (because they are all well within typical beauty norms, practically naked and pushing a product) has offered few surprises. But lurking behind it is the more intriguing fact that it is a marketing campaign—not a political figure, or a major news organization, or even a film—that "opened a dialogue" (as one of the young women said to *People*). The buzziest pop artifact to dwell on the unthin female form in recent memory was the Showtime series "Fat Actress"; the Dove Girls ads seem almost intellectual in comparison.

3   Dove's marketing director, Philippe Harousseau, says the campaign has been in the works for a couple of years. It began with a "global study,"commissioned by Dove (which is owned by Unilever) that posed questions about beauty to thousands of women in many countries. Among other things, the women tended to agree that "the media and advertising" were pushing "unrealistic" beauty standards. It seems likely that if this same not-so-original conclusion were reached by a university or a think tank, the impact would have been minimal. But a giant corporation with a huge marketing budget is not so easily ignored. Early pieces of the campaign, which actually started last year, included images of older women and women with stretch marks and such. But it was challenging the only-thin-is-beautiful stereotype that "really hit a nerve," Harousseau says. "Women were ready to hear this."

4   Why they were ready to hear it from marketers is the puzzle. Maybe it is somehow inevitable that marketing, which caused much of the underlying anxiety in the first place, can offer up a point of view that blithely tries to resolve that anxiety. Moreover, as the entertainment side of the media fragments, marketing becomes the one form of communication that permeates everywhere—and is just as effective whether you've actually seen the campaign or you simply have an opinion about it based on what you've heard.

5   Finally, perhaps there is something here that's a backlash against not just the waif-ing of American media culture but also the self-improvement imperative: enough counting carbs, enough lectures from Dr. Phil, enough pressure to learn to dress well enough for the "Queer Eye" crew and achieve Martha-like aesthetic perfection in bathroom décor. The flip side of "Don't you care enough to do better?" could be "Stop telling me how to live."

6   Unilever will not get specific about the campaign's effect on sales, but ultimately Dove products aren't really the point. The Dove Girls could be selling pretty much anything, since what people are really responding to is the atti-

tude they symbolize: an unapologetic self-confidence so appealing that we're basically willing to overlook the shaky intellectual consistency of linking it to Firming Lotions. In fact, maybe the Dove Girls' next move should be to show up in a Burger King ad, enjoying an Enormous Omelet Sandwich, daring anyone to criticize them for it.

Dove's survey is available on its "Campaign for Real Beauty" Web site, and 7 among its other findings is that the top "attributes of making a woman beautiful" are happiness and kindness. In other words, they had nothing to do with physical appearance at all. But these encouraging insights would not have given Dove much of an opportunity to sell—and would have left everyone else very little to debate and nothing at all to buy.

QUESTIONS FOR READING

1. Who are the "Dove Girls"?
2. What is the debate over them?
3. What is the most "intriguing fact" about the Dove Girls, in Walker's view?
4. What reasons does Walker give for the positive response to the Dove ads?
5. What do the ads encourage us to overlook?

QUESTIONS FOR REASONING AND ANALYSIS

1. What is Walker's purpose in writing? What is his claim?
2. Analyze the author's list of causes; do they make sense to you?

QUESTIONS FOR REFLECTING AND WRITING

1. Do you agree with Dove's survey results that beauty is not based on physical traits? If you disagree, how do you account for these survey results? And, how do you explain all the money spent on beauty products?
2. What is your reaction to the Dove ads?

DOVE LOOK IS REAL, BUT DOES IT INSPIRE? | ROBIN GIVHAN

With a master's in journalism from the University of Michigan, Robin Givhan is a staff writer for the *Washington Post* and fashion editor for the newspaper, one of only a few black writers to cover the fashion industry. She is also a freelancer with other newspapers and magazines. Her reaction to the Dove ads was published August 23, 2005, in the *Los Angeles Times*.

PREREADING QUESTIONS Have you seen any of the Dove ads? If not, look for them and think about what you find. If yes, what was your initial reaction to the ads?

Popular culture is in a tizzy of a debate over the female physique and the 1 way in which it is depicted.

2   Much has been written about the broad concept of beauty and its role in cultural politics, but the current conversation has narrowed the focus, from the woman as a whole to her individual parts: thighs, rear end and stomach.

3   The gang of amateur underwear models in the Dove advertising campaign smile broadly from bus shelters and billboards, their convex tummies and soft thighs serving as righteous protest against skinny models and the media's ruthless campaign to shatter the self-worth of the average woman. (Who knew that a woman was such a delicate creature?) The Dove women have been lavished with praise for being social radicals, posing and preening to further a woman's right to be round rather than angular. They are the antidote to advertisements featuring Gisele Bundchen, with her washboard stomach and narrow hips, in full orgiastic reverie over her new Victoria's Secret Ipex bra.

4   The Dove women are familiar not only because they seem to be grinning from every street corner but also because they look like the vast majority of the women one might encounter at the neighborhood gym—not fat but not buff either. They are commonly referred to as "real women," an infuriating term that suggests a model or an actress or any woman who does measure up to an unspecified standard of svelteness is somehow artificial. Real is equated with big, chubby—not sample size, which is as real as it gets in the fashion industry.

5   It would be more accurate to say that the Dove women are amateur models while the women who regularly appear on the covers of magazines are handsomely paid professionals. Genetics has provided them with extra height and good bone structure, and they have promised to do what they can to remain as thin as a reed. If a roaring metabolism does not accomplish that, they will take their nourishment in the form of a daily multivitamin, a bunless turkey burger and a double shot of espresso.

6   In some ways, these women are like professional athletes, paid to maintain a fighting weight and a breathtaking physique. Yet no one complains that championship marathoners, tennis stars and volleyball players, with their impossibly taut bodies, dominate the covers of sports magazines, posing a threat to the delicate psyche of weekend athletes everywhere.

7   It may be that the athletic physique is celebrated because sports is held in high regard. Sports milestones in diversity, for example, are celebrated in history books. The model figure is maligned because the fashion industry could not be perceived as more frivolous and superficial. Cultural breakthroughs are acknowledged with little more than a shrug.

8   Try, for a moment, to separate the bodies from the business. Marion Jones versus Naomi Campbell. Maria Sharapova versus Carolyn Murphy. Is one figure more or less damaging to women's self-image? Certainly all look as though they have the strength and wherewithal to take care of themselves. (The various drugs sometimes called upon in both industries to increase muscle mass, dull the appetite or otherwise lend an artificial edge are part of another discussion.) The new Nike advertising campaign has been incorrectly lumped into this "real" aesthetic. One ad features a close-up of a woman's thigh in a pair of running shorts. The copy has the owner of that leg proclaiming, "I have thunder thighs. And that is a compliment because they are strong and toned and

muscular." Let's be clear. These are not thunder thighs. These are runner's thighs. Biker's legs. They are not "real." And there is nothing average about them. They are spectacular and inspiring. They make one want to rush out and buy a new pair of Nike sneakers and start training for next year's Marine Corps Marathon.

Nike is selling a fantasy just as surely as Victoria's Secret is. Perhaps Nike's 9 next ad blitz should include a chubby lady with wobbly thighs. Her arms could be raised in victory as she wheezes across the one-mile marker. Is that the reality of the female physique that should be displayed?

Fashion thrives by constructing stories, building images and weaving fan- 10 tasies. Should the fashion media portray women as they are? Or as they might imagine themselves?

In the September issue of *Glamour* magazine, the editors ask whether there 11 is such a thing as too much perfection. A seemingly unblemished photograph of the actress Aisha Tyler is covered with notes for retouching. A second photograph shows Tyler after her thighs have been slimmed, her tummy flattened, her cleavage enhanced and her jaw line narrowed. The retouching was exaggerated to make a point: No one is perfect. And, in fact, perfection can look a little weird.

"Women are increasingly perceptive about the way media images are 12 manipulated," says *Glamour* Editor in Chief Cindi Leive. "There's a real level of sophistication about what's done to an image."

"You can retouch your own wedding photos online. And if you happen to 13 have a breakout on your wedding day, who's to say you shouldn't get in there and retouch? That's using the technology for good," Leive says, with a laugh. "But sometimes women like to look at other women who have imperfect features and quirks. I think the problem is not with idealized images. I think the problem, what women react to, is when they see only one type of woman."

It's healthy to occasionally pull back the curtain and remind readers of what 14 most of them already know. Fashion is not truth. That has always been the operating principle of the business. Fashion is extravagance and incongruity, elegance and rebellion. It is envy and exclusivity. All of that may have been epitomized by Richard Avedon's 1955 image of the lithe model Dovima posing in a Christian Dior gown in front of a line of elephants.

It is reassuring to occasionally see the machinations of the magician. It's 15 nice to be presented with a female physique that is a little more accessible. And it is good to see the beauty fantasy broadened to include attributes such as strength and endurance. But no one wants to feel as though they've stumbled into the ladies locker room or caught their neighbors in their skivvies.

QUESTIONS FOR READING

1. How do the Dove women differ from professional models?
2. How have they been referred to? What is Givhan's view of this response?
3. How should the Dove models be viewed? To whom does the author compare professional models?

4. Why do we celebrate the professional athlete's body more than the professional model's?

5. What are Nike and high fashion both selling?

QUESTIONS FOR REASONING AND ANALYSIS

1. What is Givhan's purpose in writing? (Consider how it differs from Rob Walker's.)

2. What is Givhan's claim? Write a claim statement that mentions both the Dove models and professional fashion models.

3. What is clever about Givhan's opening paragraphs?

4. How does the author use analogy to support her argument? Where does she present a conciliatory approach?

QUESTIONS FOR REFLECTING AND WRITING

1. Are you surprised by Givhan's response to the Dove women? Do you like the idea of the Dove ads, or do you share Givhan's response? Explain and defend your reaction.

2. Do you agree that the fantasy of advertising inspires us—or does it damage our self-worth? Or, is it just one of many selling strategies that has little or no lasting impact? Explain and defend your position.

TURNING GOYS INTO GIRLS | MICHELLE COTTLE

A graduate of Vanderbilt University, Michelle Cottle was an editor for two years at the *Washington Monthly* prior to becoming a senior editor, in 1999, at *The New Republic*. She is also a panelist on the PBS political talk show "Tucker Carlson Unfiltered." Her essay on men's magazines was published in the May 1998 issue of the *Washington Monthly*.

PREREADING QUESTIONS What does the word *goys* mean? If you do not know, look it up before reading further.

1   I love *Men's Health* magazine. There, I'm out of the closet, and I'm not ashamed. Sure, I know what some of you are thinking: What self-respecting '90s women could embrace a publication that runs such enlightened articles as "Turn Your Good Girl Bad" and "How to Wake Up Next to a One-Night Stand"? Or maybe you'll smile and wink knowingly: What red-blooded hetero chick wouldn't love all those glossy photo spreads of buff young beefcake in various states of undress, ripped abs and glutes flexed so tightly you could bounce a check on them? Either way you've got the wrong idea. My affection for *Men's Health* is driven by pure gender politics—by the realization that this magazine, and a handful of others like it, are leveling the playing field in a way that *Ms.* can only dream of. With page after page of bulging biceps and Gillette jaws, robust hairlines and silken skin, *Men's Health* is peddling a standard of male beauty as unforgiving and unrealistic as the female version sold by those dewy-eyed pre-teen waifs draped across the covers of *Glamour* and

Elle. And with a variety of helpful features on "Foods That Fight Fat," "Banish Your Potbelly," and "Save Your Hair (Before It's Too Late)," *Men's Health* is well on its way to making the male species as insane, insecure, and irrational about physical appearance as any *Cosmo* girl.

Don't you see, ladies? We've been going about this equality business all 2 wrong. Instead of battling to get society fixated on something besides our breast size, we should have been fighting spandex with spandex. Bra burning was a nice gesture, but the greater justice is in convincing our male counterparts that the key to their happiness lies in a pair of made-for-him Super Shaper Briefs with the optional "fly front endowment pad" (as advertised in *Men's Journal,* $29.95 plus shipping and handling). Make the men as neurotic about the circumference of their waists and the whiteness of their smiles as the women, and at least the burden of vanity and self-loathing will be shared by all.

This is precisely what lads' mags like *Men's Health* are accomplishing. The 3 rugged John-Wayne days when men scrubbed their faces with deodorant soap and viewed gray hair and wrinkles as a badge of honor are fading. Last year, international market analyst Euromonitor placed the U.S. men's toiletries market—hair color, skin moisturizer, tooth whiteners, etc.—at $3.5 billion. According to a survey conducted by DYG researchers for *Men's Health* in November 1996, approximately 20 percent of American men get manicures or pedicures, 18 percent use skin treatments such as masks or mud packs, and 10 percent enjoy professional facials. That same month, *Psychology Today* reported that a poll by Roper Starch Worldwide showed that "6 percent of men nationwide actually use such traditionally female products as bronzers and foundation to create the illusion of a youthful appearance."

What men are putting on their bodies, however, is nothing compared to 4 what they're doing to their bodies: While in the 1980s only an estimated one in 10 plastic surgery patients were men, as of 1996, that ratio had shrunk to one in five. The American Academy of Cosmetic Surgery estimates that nationwide more than 690,000 men had cosmetic procedures performed in '96, the most recent year for which figures are available. And we're not just talking "hair restoration" here, though such procedures do command the lion's share of the male market. We're also seeing an increasing number of men shelling out mucho dinero for face peels, liposuction, collagen injections, eyelid lifts, chin tucks, and of course, the real man's answer to breast implants: penile enlargements (now available to increase both length and diameter).

Granted, *Men's Health* and its journalistic cousins (*Men's Journal, Details,* 5 *GQ,* etc.) cannot take all the credit for this breakthrough in gender parity. The fashion and glamour industries have perfected the art of creating consumer "needs," and with the women's market pretty much saturated, men have become the obvious target for the purveyors of everything from lip balm to lycra. Meanwhile, advances in medical science have made cosmetic surgery a quicker, cleaner option for busy executives (just as the tight fiscal leash of managed care is driving more and more doctors toward this cash-based specialty). Don't have several weeks to recover from a full-blown facelift? No problem. For a few hundred bucks you can get a microdermabrasion face peel on your lunch hour.

6   Then there are the underlying social factors. With women growing ever more financially independent, aspiring suitors are discovering that they must bring more to the table than a well-endowed wallet if they expect to win (and keep) the fair maiden. Nor should we overlook the increased market power of the gay population—in general a more image-conscious lot than straight guys. But perhaps most significant is the ongoing, ungraceful descent into middle age by legions of narcissistic baby boomers. Gone are the days when the elder statesmen of this demographic bulge could see themselves in the relatively youthful faces of those insipid yuppies on "Thirtysomething." Increasingly, boomers are finding they have more in common with the parents of today's TV, movie, and sports stars. Everywhere they turn some upstart Gen Xer is flaunting his youthful vitality, threatening boomer dominance on both the social and professional fronts. (Don't think even Hollywood didn't shudder when the Oscar for best original screenplay this year went to a couple of guys barely old enough to shave.) With whippersnappers looking to steal everything from their jobs to their women, post-pubescent men have at long last discovered the terror of losing their springtime radiance.

7   Whatever combo of factors is feeding the frenzy of male vanity, magazines such as *Men's Health* provide the ideal meeting place for men's insecurities and marketers' greed. Like its more established female counterparts, *Men's Health,* is an affordable, efficient delivery vehicle for the message that physical imperfection, age, and an underdeveloped fashion sense are potentially crippling disabilities. And as with women's mags, this cycle of insanity is self-perpetuating: The more men obsess about growing old or unattractive, the more marketers will exploit and expand that fear; the more marketers bombard men with messages about the need to be beautiful, the more they will obsess. Younger and younger men will be sucked into the vortex of self-doubt. Since 1990, *Men's Health* has seen its paid circulation rise from 250,000 to more than 1.5 million; the magazine estimates that half of its 5.3 million readers are under age 35 and 46 percent are married. And while most major magazines have suffered sluggish growth or even a decline in circulation in recent years, during the first half of 1997, *Men's Health* saw its paid circulation increase 14 percent over its '96 figures. (Likewise, its smaller, more outdoorsy relative, Wenner Media's *Men's Journal,* enjoyed an even bigger jump of 26.5 percent.) At this rate, one day soon, that farcical TV commercial featuring men hanging out in bars, whining about having inherited their mothers' thighs will be a reality. Now that's progress.

VANITY, THY NAME IS MAN

8   Everyone wants to be considered attractive and desirable. And most of us are aware that, no matter how guilty and shallow we feel about it, there are certain broad cultural norms that define attractive. Not surprisingly, both men's and women's magazines have argued that, far from playing on human insecurities, they are merely helping readers be all that they can be—a kind of training camp for the image impaired. In recent years, such publications have embraced the tenets of "evolutionary biology," which argue that, no matter

how often we're told that beauty is only skin deep, men and women are hard-wired to prefer the Jack Kennedys and Sharon Stones to the Rodney Danger-fields and Janet Renos. Continuation of the species demands that specimens with shiny coats, bright eyes, even features, and other visible signs of ruddy good health and fertility automatically kick-start our most basic instinct. Of course, the glamour mags' editors have yet to explain why, in evolutionary terms, we would ever desire adult women to stand 5'10" and weigh 100 pounds. Stories abound of women starving themselves to the point that their bodies shut down and they stop menstruating—hardly conducive to reproduction—yet Kate Moss remains the dish du jour and millions of Moss wannabes still struggle to subsist on a diet of Dexatrim and Perrier.

Similarly, despite its title, *Men's Health* is hawking far more than general   9
fitness or a healthful lifestyle. For every half page of advice on how to cut your stress level, there are a dozen pages on how to build your biceps. For every update on the dangers of cholesterol, there are multiple warnings on the horrors of flabby abs. Now, without question, gorging on Cheetos and Budweiser while your rump takes root on the sofa is no way to treat your body if you plan on living past 50. But chugging protein drinks, agonizing over fat grams, and counting the minutes until your next Stairmaster session is equally unbalanced. The line between taking pride in one's physical appearance and being obsessed by it is a fine one—and one that disappeared for many women long ago.

Now with the lads' mags taking men in that direction as well, in many cases   10
it's almost impossible to tell whether you're reading a copy of *Men's Health* or of *Mademoiselle:* "April 8. To commemorate Buddha's birthday, hit a Japanese restaurant. Stick to low-fat selections. Choose foods described as yakimono, which means grilled," advised the monthly "to do list" in the April *Men's Health.* (Why readers should go Japanese in honor of the most famous religious leader in India's history remains unclear.) The January/February list was equally thought provoking: "January 28. It's Chinese New Year, so make a resolution to custom-order your next takeout. Ask that they substitute wonton soup broth for oil. Try the soba noodles instead of plain noodles. They're richer in nutrients and contain much less fat." The issue also featured a "Total Body Workout Poster" and one of those handy little "substitution" charts (loathed by women everywhere), showing men how to slash their calorie intake by making a few minor dietary substitutions: mustard for mayo, popcorn for peanuts, seltzer water for soda, pretzels for potato chips. . . .

As in women's magazines, fast results with minimum inconvenience is a   11
central theme. Among *Men's Health's* March highlights were a guide to "Bigger Biceps in 2 Weeks," and "20 Fast Fixes" for a bad diet; April offered "A Better Body in Half the Time," along with a colorful four-page spread on "50 Snacks That Wont Make You Fat." And you can forget carrot sticks—this think-thin eating guide celebrated the wonders of Reduced Fat Cheez-its, Munch 'Ems, Fiddle Faddle, Oreos, Teddy Grahams, Milky Ways, Bugles, Starburst Fruit Twists, and Klondike's Fat Free Big Bear Ice Cream Sandwiches. Better nutrition is not the primary issue. A better butt is. To this end, also found in the

pages of *Men's Health,* is the occasional, tasteful ad for liposuction—just in case nature doesn't cooperate.

12   But a blueprint to rock-hard buns is only part of what makes *Men's Health* the preeminent "men's lifestyle" magazine. Nice teeth, nice skin, nice hair, and a red-hot wardrobe are now required to round out the ultimate alpha male package, and *Men's Health* is there to help on all fronts. In recent months it has run articles on how to select, among other items, the perfect necktie and belt, the hippest wallet, the chicest running gear, the best "hair-thickening" shampoo, and the cutest golfing apparel. It has also offered advice on how to retard baldness, how to keep your footwear looking sharp, how to achieve different "looks" with a patterned blazer, even how to keep your lips from chapping at the dentist's office: "[B]efore you start all that 'rinse and spit' business, apply some moisturizer to your face and some lip balm to your lips. Your face and lips won't have that stretched-out dry feeling. . . . Plus, you'll look positively radiant!"

13   While a desire to look good for their hygienists may be enough to spur some men to heed the magazine's advice (and keep 'em coming back for more), fear and insecurity about the alternatives are generally more effective motivators. For those who don't get with the *Men's Health* program, there must be the threat of ridicule. By far the least subtle example of this is the free subscriptions for "guys who need our help" periodically announced in the front section of the magazine. April's dubious honoree was actor Christopher Walken:

> Chris, we love the way you've perfected that psycho persona. But now you're taking your role in "Things to do in Denver When You're Dead" way too seriously with that ghostly pale face, the "where's the funeral?" black clothes, and a haircut that looks like the work of a hasty undertaker. . . . Dab on a little Murad Murasun Self-Tanner ($21). . . . For those creases in your face, try Ortho Dermatologicals' Renova, a prescription antiwrinkle cream that contains tretinoin, a form of vitamin A. Then, find a barber.

14   Or how the March "winner," basketball coach Bobby Knight: "Bob, your trademark red sweater is just a billboard for your potbelly. A darker solid color would make you look slimmer. Also, see 'The Tale of Two Bellies' in our February 1998 issue, and try to drop a few pounds. Then the next time you throw a sideline tantrum, at least people won't say, 'look at the crazy fat man.' "

15   Just as intense as the obsession with appearance that men's (and women's) magazines breed are the sexual neuroses they feed. And if one of the ostensible goals of women's mags is to help women drive men wild, what is the obvious corollary objective for men's magazines? To get guys laid—well and often. As if men needed any encouragement to fixate on the subject, *Men's Health* is chock full of helpful "how-tos" such as, "Have Great Sex Every Day Until You Die" and "What I Learned From My Sex Coach," as well as more cursory explorations of why men with larger testicles have more sex ("Why Big Boys Don't Cry"), how to maintain orgasm intensity as you age ("Be one of the geysers"), and how to achieve stronger erections by eating certain foods ("Bean counters make better lovers"). And for those having trouble even getting to the starting line, last month's issue offered readers a chance to "Win free love lessons."

THE HIGH PRICE OF PERFECTION

Having elevated men's physical and sexual insecurities to the level of grand 16
paranoia, lads' mags can then get down to what really matters: moving merchandise. On the cover of *Men's Health* each month, in small type just above
the magazine's title, appears the phrase "Tons of useful stuff." Thumbing
through an issue or two, however, one quickly realizes that a more accurate description would read: "Tons of expensive stuff." They're all there: Ralph Lauren,
Tommy Hilfiger, Paul Mitchell, Calvin Klein, Clinique, Armani, Versace, Burber-
rys, Nautica, Nike, Omega, Rogaine, The Better Sex Video Series. . . . The magazine even has those annoying little perfume strips guaranteed to make your
nose run and to alienate everyone within a five-mile radius of you.

Masters of psychology, marketers wheel out their sexiest pitches and 17
hottest male models to tempt/intimidate the readership of *Men's Health.* Not
since the last casting call for "Baywatch" has a more impressive display of firm,
tanned, young flesh appeared in one spot. And just like in women's magazines,
the articles themselves are designed to sell stuff. All those helpful tips on
choosing blazers, ties, and belts come complete with info on the who, where,
and how much. The strategy is brilliant: Make men understand exactly how far
short of the ideal they fall, and they too become vulnerable to the lure of high-
priced underwear, cologne, running shoes, workout gear, hair dye, hair
straightener, skin softener, body-fat monitors, suits, boots, energy bars, and
sex aids. As Mark Jannot, the grooming and health editor for *Men's Journal,*
told "Today" show host Matt Lauer in January, "This is a huge, booming
market. I mean, the marketers have found a group of people that are ripe
for the picking. Men are finally learning that aging is a disease." Considering
how effectively *Men's Health* fosters this belief, it's hardly surprising that the
magazine has seen its ad pages grow 510 percent since 1991 and has made it
onto *Adweek's* 10 Hottest Magazines list three of the last five years.

To make all this "girly" image obsession palatable to their audience, lads' 18
mags employ all their creative energies to transform appearance issues into "a
guy thing." *Men's Health* tries to cultivate a joking, macho tone throughout
("Eat Like Brando and Look Like Rambo" or "Is my tallywhacker shrinking?")
and tosses in a handful of Y-chromosome teasers such as "How to Stay Out of
Jail," "How to Clean Your Whole Apartment in One Hour or Less," and my personal favorite, "Let's Play Squash," an illustrated guide to identifying the bug-
splat patterns on your windshield. Instead of a regular advice columnist, which
would smack too much of chicks' magazines, *Men's Health* recently introduced
"Jimmy the Bartender," a monthly column on "women, sex, and other stuff that
screws up men's lives."

It appears that, no matter how much clarifying lotion and hair gel you're 19
trying to sell them, men must never suspect that you think they share women's
insecurities. If you want a man to buy wrinkle cream, marketers have learned,
you better pitch it as part of a comfortably macho shaving regime. Aramis, for
example, assures men that its popular Lift Off! Moisture Formula with alpha hy-
droxy will help cut their shave time by one-third. "The biggest challenge for
products started for women is how to transfer them to men," explained

George Schaeffer, the president of OPI cosmetics, in the November issue of SoapCosmetics-Chemical Specialties. Schaeffer's Los Angeles based company is the maker of Matte Nail Envy, an unobtrusive nail polish that's proved a hit with men. And for the more adventuresome shopper, last year Hard Candy cosmetics introduced a line of men's nail enamel, called Candy Man, that targets guys with such studly colors as Gigolo (metallic black) and Testosterone (gunmetal silver).

20   On a larger scale, positioning a makeover or trip to the liposuction clinic as a smart career move seems to help men rationalize their image obsession. "Whatever a man's cosmetic shortcoming, it's apt to be a career liability," noted Alan Farnham in a September 1996 issue of *Fortune.* "The business world is prejudiced against the ugly." Or how about *Forbes'* sad attempt to differentiate between male and female vanity in its Dec. 1 piece on cosmetic surgery: "Plastic surgery is more of a cosmetic thing for women. They have a thing about aging. For men's it's an investment that pays a pretty good dividend." Whatever you say, guys.

21   The irony is rich and bittersweet. Gender equity is at last headed our way—not in the form of women being less obsessed with looking like Calvin Klein models, but of men becoming hysterical over the first signs of crows-feet. Gradually, guys are no longer pumping up and primping simply to get babes, but because they feel it's something everyone expects them to do. Women, after all, do not spend $400 on Dolce & Gabbana sandals to impress their boyfriends, most of whom don't know Dolce & Gabbana from Beavis & Butthead (yet). They buy them to impress other women—and because that's what society says they should want to do. Most guys haven't yet achieved this level of insanity, but with grown men catcalling the skin tone and wardrobe of other grown men (Christopher Walken, Bobby Knight) for a readership of still more grown men, can the gender's complete surrender to the vanity industry be far behind?

22   The ad for *Men's Health's* web site says it all: "Don't click here unless you want to look a decade younger . . . lose that beer belly . . . be a better lover . . . and more! *Men's Health* Online: The Internet Site For Regular Guys." Of course, between the magazine's covers there's not a "regular guy" to be found, save for the occasional snapshot of one of the publication's writers or editors—usually taken from a respectable distance. The moist young bucks in the Gap jeans ads and the electric-eyed Armani models have exactly as much in common with the average American man as Tyra Banks does with the average American woman. Which would be fine, if everyone seemed to understand this distinction. Until they do, however, I guess my consolation will have to be the image of thousands of once-proud men, having long scorned women's insecurities, lining up for their laser peels and trying to squeeze their middle-aged asses into a snug set of Super Shaper Briefs—with the optional fly front endowment pad, naturally.

QUESTIONS FOR READING

1.   What is Cottle's subject?
2.   What are men's magazines doing to men?
3.   How are women achieving "gender equity," according to Cottle?
4.   What anxieties do the men's magazines feed?
5.   What is it the magazines are ultimately seeking to accomplish?

QUESTIONS FOR REASONING AND ANALYSIS

1.   What is the author's claim?
2.   What *kind* of evidence does Cottle provide? Is it convincing?
3.   Examine the author's word choice. What "voice" does she create? What is the essay's tone?

QUESTIONS FOR REFLECTING AND WRITING

1.   Does Cottle's analysis of men's magazines surprise you with new information and ideas? If so, what is most surprising to you? If you are not surprised, why not?
2.   Has the author convinced you with her details and analysis of strategies in the men's magazines? Why or why not?
3.   Does Cottle actually believe that women have achieved gender equity? Is she pleased with what the men's magazines are doing? Support your answer.
4.   How do we resist the anxieties created by advertising—or the unnecessary purchases? What advice do you have?

THE BLOGS MUST BE CRAZY | PEGGY NOONAN

A contributing editor of the *Wall Street Journal* and weekly columnist for the *Journal*'s editorial page Web site, Peggy Noonan is the author of seven books, including *The Case Against Hillary Clinton* (2000) and *A Heart, a Cross, and a Flag* (2003). The following column appeared February 17, 2005.

PREREADING QUESTIONS Do you regularly read a newspaper? If not, why not? And, how do you obtain news?

"Salivating morons." "Scalp hunters." "Moon howlers." "Trophy hunters." 1
"Sons of Sen. McCarthy." "Rabid." "Blogswarm." "These pseudo-journalist lynch mob people."

This is excellent invective. It must come from bloggers. But wait, it was the 2 mainstream media and their maidservants in the elite journalism reviews, and they were talking about bloggers!

Those MSMers have gone wild, I tell you! The tendentious language, the low 3 insults. It's the Wild Wild West out there. We may have to consider legislation.

4   When you hear name-calling like what we've been hearing from the elite media this week, you know someone must be doing something right. The hysterical edge makes you wonder if writers for newspapers and magazines and professors in J-schools don't have a serious case of freedom envy.

5   The bloggers have that freedom. They have the still pent-up energy of a liberated citizenry, too. The MSM doesn't. It has lost its old monopoly on information. It is angry.

6   But MSM criticism of the blogosphere misses the point, or rather points.

7   Blogging changes how business is done in American journalism. The MSM isn't over. It just can no longer pose as if it is The Guardian of Established Truth. The MSM is just another player now. A big one, but a player.

8   The blogosphere isn't some mindless eruption of wild opinion. That isn't their power. This is their power:

9   1. They use the tools of journalists (computer, keyboard, a spirit of inquiry, a willingness to ask the question) and of the Internet (Google, LexisNexis) to look for and find facts that have been overlooked, ignored or hidden. They look for the telling quote, the ignored statistic, the data that have been submerged. What they are looking for is information that is true. When they get it they post it and include it in the debate. This is a public service.

10   2. Bloggers, unlike reporters at elite newspapers and magazines, are independent operators. They are not, and do not have to be, governed by mainstream thinking. Nor do they have to accept the directives of an editor pushing an ideology or a publisher protecting his friends. Bloggers have the freedom to decide on their own when a story stops being a story. They get to decide when the search for facts is over. They also decide on their own when the search for facts begins. It was a blogger at the World Economic Forum, as we all know, who first reported the Eason Jordan story. It was bloggers, as we all know, who pursued it. Matt Drudge runs a news site and is not a blogger, but what was true of him at his beginning (the Monica Lewinsky story, he decided, is a story) is true of bloggers: It's a story if they say it is. This is a public service.

11   3. Bloggers have an institutional advantage in terms of technology and form. They can post immediately. The items they post can be as long or short as they judge to be necessary. Breaking news can be one sentence long: "Malkin gets Barney Frank earwitness report." In newspapers you have to go to the editor, explain to him why the paper should have another piece on the Eason Jordan affair, spend a day reporting it, only to find that all that's new today is that reporter Michelle Malkin got an interview with Barney Frank. That's not enough to merit 10 inches of newspaper space, so the *Times* doesn't carry what the blogosphere had 24 hours ago. In the old days a lot of interesting information fell off the editing desk in this way. Now it doesn't. This is a public service.

12   4. Bloggers are also selling the smartest take on a story. They're selling an original insight, a new area of inquiry. Mickey Kaus of Kausfiles has his bright take, Andrew Sullivan had his, InstaPundit has his. They're all selling their shrewdness, experience, depth. This too is a public service.

5. And they're doing it free. That is, the *Times* costs me a dollar and so 13
does the *Journal,* but Kausfiles doesn't cost a dime. This too is a public service.
Some blogs get their money from yearly fund-raising, some from advertisers,
some from a combination, some from a salary provided by *Slate* or *National Review.* Most are labors of love. Some bloggers—a lot, I think—are addicted to
digging, posting, coming up with the bright phrase. OK with me. Some get
burned out. But new ones are always coming up, so many that I can't keep track
of them and neither can anyone else.

But when I read blogs, when I wake up in the morning and go to About Last 14
Night and Lucianne and Lileks, I remember what the late great Christopher
Reeve said on "The Tonight Show" 20 years ago. He was the second guest, after Rodney Dangerfield. Dangerfield did his act and he was hot as a pistol.
Then after Reeve sat down Dangerfield continued to be riotous. Reeve looked
at him, gestured toward him, looked at the audience and said with grace and
delight, "Do you believe this is free?" The audience cheered. That's how I feel
on their best days when I read blogs.

That you get it free doesn't mean commerce isn't involved, for it is. It is in- 15
tellectual commerce. Bloggers give you information and point of view. In return you give them your attention and intellectual energy. They gain influence
by drawing your eyes; you gain information by lending your eyes. They become
well-known and influential; you become entertained or informed. They get
something from it and so do you.

6. It is not true that there are no controls. It is not true that the blogosphere 16
is the Wild West. What governs members of the blogospheres is what governs
to some degree members of the MSM, and that is the desire for status and respect. In the blogosphere you lose both if you put forward as fact information
that is incorrect, specious or cooked. You lose status and respect if your take
on a story that is patently stupid. You lose status and respect if you are unpro-
fessional or deliberately misleading. And once you've lost a sufficient amount
of status and respect, none of the other bloggers link to you anymore or raise
your name in their arguments. And you're over. The great correcting mecha-
nism for people on the Web is people on the Web.

There are blogs that carry political and ideological agendas. But everyone 17
is on to them and it's mostly not obnoxious because their agendas are mostly
declared.

7. I don't know if the blogosphere is rougher in the ferocity of its personal at- 18
tacks than, say, Drew Pearson. Or the rough boys and girls of the great American
editorial pages of the 1930s and '40s. Bloggers are certainly not as rough as the
splenetic pamphleteers of the 18th and 19th centuries, who amused themselves
accusing Thomas Jefferson of sexual perfidy and Andrew Jackson of having married a whore. I don't know how Walter Lippmann or Scotty Reston would have
seen the blogosphere; it might have frightened them if they'd lived to see it. They
might have been impressed by the sheer digging that goes on there. I have seen
friends savaged by blogs and winced for them—but, well, too bad. I've been attacked. Too bad. If you can't take it, you shouldn't be thinking aloud for a living.

The blogosphere is tough. But are personal attacks worth it if what we get in return is a whole new media form that can add to the true-information flow while correcting the biases and lapses of the mainstream media? Yes. Of course.

19   I conclude with a few predictions.

20   Some brilliant rising young reporter with a growing reputation at the *Times* or *Newsweek* or *Post* is going to quit, go into the blogging business, start *The Daily Joe,* get someone to give him a guaranteed ad for two years, and become a journalistic force. His motive will be influence, and the use of his gifts along the lines of excellence. His blog will further legitimize blogging.

21   Most of the blogstorms of the past few years have resulted in outcomes that left and right admit or bray were legitimate. Dan Rather fell because his big story was based on a fabrication, Trent Lott said things that it could be proved he said. But coming down the pike is a blogstorm in which the bloggers turn out to be wrong. Good news: They'll probably be caught and exposed by bloggers. Bad news: It will show that blogging isn't nirvana, and its stars aren't foolproof. But then we already know that, don't we?

22   Some publisher is going to decide that if you can't fight blogs, you can join them. He'll think like this: *We're already on the Internet. That's how bloggers get and review our reporting. Why don't we get our own bloggers to challenge our work? Why don't we invite bloggers who already exist into the tent? Why not take the best things said on blogs each day and print them on a Daily Blog page? We'd be enhancing our rep as an honest news organization, and it will further our branding!*

23   Someone is going to address the "bloggers are untrained journalists" question by looking at exactly what "training," what education in the art/science/craft/profession of journalism, the reporters and editors of the MSM have had in the past 60 years or so. It has seemed to me the best of them never went to J-school but bumped into journalism along the way—walked into a radio station or newspaper one day and found their calling. Bloggers signify a welcome return to that old style. In journalism you learn by doing, which is what a lot of bloggers are doing.

24   Finally, someday in America the next big bad thing is going to happen, and lines are going to go down, and darkness is going to descend, and the instant communication we now enjoy is going to be compromised. People in one part of the country are going to wonder how people in another part are doing. Little by little lines are going to come up, and people are going to log on, and they're going to get the best, most comprehensive, and ultimately, just because it's there, most heartening information from . . . some lone blogger out there. And then another. They're going to do some big work down the road.

QUESTIONS FOR READING

1.   Why are mainstream journalists so upset? About whom are they complaining?

2.   What are the specific sources of power for bloggers? State Noonan's seven points in your own words.

3. What predictions does the author make about the future of bloggers? State her five predictions in your own words.

QUESTIONS FOR REASONING AND ANALYSIS

1. What is Noonan's claim? State it so as to include both the idea of bloggers' strengths and their predicted future.

2. What makes Noonan's opening effective? What organizational and other rhetorical strategies are used to good effect?

3. How would you describe the author's tone? How does her tone support her purpose?

QUESTIONS FOR REFLECTING AND WRITING

1. Do you read bloggers? If so, how often? If not, has Noonan sparked your interest in checking them out? Explain.

2. Should mainstream journalists feel threatened by bloggers—or inspired to work harder? Or, should they ignore them as a curiosity that will not last? Defend your position.

INSTANT REVISIONISM | EUGENE ROBINSON

A graduate of the University of Michigan where he was the first black student to be co-editor-in-chief of the university's student newspaper, Eugene Robinson joined the *Washington Post* in 1980. He has served as city reporter, foreign correspondent, and managing editor in charge of the paper's style section. He is now an associate editor and twice-weekly columnist. The following column appeared October 7, 2005.

PREREADING QUESTIONS What are possible consequences for readers of news stories that change significantly as they are reported in the first few hours or days?

1 The story line was a classic: Beauty and the Beast. Remember the Atlanta courthouse shootings a few months ago? Brian Nichols was the ogre whose homicidal rampage led him to the apartment of an attractive young woman named Ashley Smith, who soothed his savage beast by speaking gently of God and redemption. That he was black and she was white seemed to deepen the narrative and give it the status of myth.

2 Oh, did I say myth? I meant meth.

3 It turns out that Smith did more than read to Nichols from *The Purpose-Driven Life* about God's master plan. She also gave him some of her stash of the illegal drug methamphetamine, or "ice" as she has called it in the publicity campaign for her new book.

4 Now, on one level, all you can say is good for her. Smith's imperative was to survive, and if what that took was giving Nichols drugs, then that's what she

had to do. In those circumstances, I would have offered him the whole medicine cabinet. Everyone would have done the same thing.

5   But not everyone would have had some crystal meth lying around. The fact that Smith wasn't a fairy princess but a struggling woman who'd lived a hard-knocks life, including a history of drug abuse, doesn't diminish her bravery. But it does change the narrative from Beauty and the Beast to something more like Two Lost Souls.

6   The whole episode struck me as a good illustration of the dizzying speed with which the story of our times gets written and rewritten in the digital age. It's no wonder that public opinion is so jittery over just about everything, no mystery that *Time* and *Newsweek* tell us every few weeks how desperate we are for spiritual connection and some kind of eternal truth. The worldly truth we know keeps changing on us.

7   I witnessed this warp-speed process in New Orleans following Hurricane Katrina. I got there five days after the deluge, when the story, as the whole world understood it, was one of "Mad Max" depravity and violence. Hoodlums were raping and pillaging, I just "knew"—even shooting at rescue helicopters trying to take hospital patients to safety. So it was a surprise when I rolled into the center of the city, with all my foreign-correspondent antennae bristling, and found the place as quiet as a tomb.

8   The next day I drove into the French Quarter and was struck by how pristine St. Louis Cathedral looked, almost like the castle at Disney World. I got out of the car and walked around the whole area, and I wrote in my notebook that except for the absence of tourists, it could have been just an ordinary Sunday morning in the Big Easy. Then I got back into the car, and on the radio a caller was breathlessly reporting that, as she spoke, a group of policemen were "pinned down" by snipers at the cathedral.

9   I was right there; nobody was sniping at anybody. But the reigning narrative was Mad Max, not Magic Kingdom. Thanks to radio, television and the Internet, everyone "knew" things that just weren't true.

10   That was a month ago. Last week the New Orleans story shifted to the other extreme: There weren't but a handful of murders after the flood, about what the city would expect in a normal week; there were no documented cases of rape at the Superdome or the convention center; "hoodlums" in baggy pants helped with rescues instead of hindering them; and most of the "snipers" were stranded people firing in the air to try to attract the attention of helicopters, not chase them away.

11   I'll bet the truth is more subtle and complicated than either of those extreme versions. It is always so; the path of history is obscured by the weeds of ambiguity. But it used to take a while for the initial version of events to become embedded, and then months or years for historians to come along and dislodge it. Nowadays the 24-7 flood of information gives us the illusion of knowing, then quickly jars us with the revelation that everything we "knew" is wrong.

This isn't a complaint against the media—what are reporters to do, except   12
tell us what they think they have learned? And it certainly isn't a complaint
against information technology, since machines just say and do what they're told.

It's a warning to consumers: You'll sleep better if you remember that the   13
truth is never simple, and that the first story you hear surely won't be the last.

QUESTIONS FOR READING

1. What was "the rest of the story" with Ashley Smith?
2. What was actually happening at the cathedral in New Orleans on the Sunday morning that Robinson was there?
3. What was probably happening during the first days after Katrina?
4. Why don't we get the "truth" of each story from the media the first time they report?

QUESTIONS FOR REASONING AND ANALYSIS

1. How does Robinson account for differences in the media's coverage of events from one day to the next?
2. What is Robinson's claim? What do we need to learn about the "truth"?

QUESTIONS FOR REFLECTING AND WRITING

1. Can you think of another story that was revised from one day to the next? What was your reaction to the instant revisionism?
2. To what extent does the 24/7 demand for news coverage in the press, on TV, and on the Internet contribute to the distortions and revisions that we so often experience?
3. What may be the psychological consequences of our experiencing the revisions of the "truth"? And, what can we do to reduce the impact of the consequences?

OF LOSERS AND MOLES: YOU THINK REALITY TV JUST WRITES ITSELF? | DERRICK SPEIGHT

Derrick Speight is, as he tells us in his essay, a reality TV writer based in Los Angeles, with a dozen TV series to his credit, as story writer or supervising story producer. His scoop on the reality of reality TV shows was published in the *Washington Post,* July 24, 2005.

PREREADING QUESTIONS Do you enjoy watching reality TV shows—or know people who do? Why do you—or they—like these shows? What are the reasons usually given for enjoying these types of TV shows?

A couple of summers ago, I found myself living out a high school fan-   1
tasy. I was running across the hot white sands of a Mexican beach in Playa

del Carmen, chasing after stunning Playboy playmate Angie Everhart. As her bright orange bikini disappeared into the Caribbean surf, I closed my eyes and smiled—then quickly snapped back to reality. I was there as a writer for ABC's "Celebrity Mole: Yucatan," and my job was to find out what Everhart was saying about the show's other beauty, former MTV VJ Ananda Lewis. Would they be dueling divas, headed for a catfight by day's end? I needed to find out. So I sighed, put on the earpiece that picked up the two women's microphones, and began taking notes.

2   Reality TV writers like me are at the heart of a lawsuit filed by the Writers Guild of America, West about two weeks ago. On behalf of 12 such scribes, the union is charging four reality production companies and four networks with unfair labor practices, including providing pay and benefits for below those earned by writers of traditional drama and sitcoms. The suit says a lot about the rise of reality TV, a formerly disreputable format that last year contributed half of the 20 top-rated shows on TV. But in hearing about it, I imagine that people across America were asking the same question members of my own family have voiced ever since I started down this career path: "How exactly do you *write* reality? Isn't it already real?"

3   Yes, Grandma, it is—in all its undigested, contextless, boring glory. What I do is shape that mass into something that'll make viewers want to tune in week after week. Like a journalist, I sniff out what I *think* the story will be, then craft the interviews or situations that'll draw it out. Like a paperback writer, I'm all about highlighting character and plot. Simply put, drama is the pursuit of a goal, with obstacles. Both by developing promising story lines and by pulling out the zingy moments burned in hours upon hours of ho-hum footage, reality TV writers like me—who go under various titles, including story editor and story producer—create it. As I tell my family, having a reality TV show without writers would be like having a countertop of cake ingredients but no idea how to put them together. So, yes, I consider myself a writer.

4   My voyage into reality TV began by accident. Seven years ago, I was new to Hollywood, and sure that I was destined to direct the next film version of *Superman.* But by the time I finished my first fresh-out-of-film-school internship with DreamWorks' Mark Gordon Productions, I was both slightly peeved about not meeting Steven Spielberg and badly in need of a paying job. Luckily, a friend of a friend was looking for production assistants to work on "World's Most Amazing Videos." Hired for roughly $400 a week (and on top of the world about it), I was quickly promoted to logger—basically the guy who looks through all the footage and makes notes on what happens and when. That led to a job at a new company, Actual Reality Pictures, which would end up completely redirecting my career.

5   Actual Reality is the production company of Academy Award nominee R.J. Cutler, whose documentary *The War Room* followed Bill Clinton's 1992 presidential campaign. The building was an intellectual hothouse, packed with scores of Ivy League grads who loved nothing more than to ruminate over the most minuscule story points. As we worked on Cutler's latest project, a docudrama about suburban Chicago teens called *American High,* staff meetings

were virtual master classes in narrative structure. Whole walls of multicolored index cards were dedicated to the deconstruction of an episode, inviting constant rearranging until the optimal narrative was found. And through it all, Cutler, the faintly aloof, greatly admired genius among us, wandered the office hallways yelling, "What's the story?!" My job was to rummage through film footage looking to answer that question. Apparently, our process worked: *American High* went on to win an Emmy.

After I left Actual Reality, I would never again encounter that type of intense, 6 academic scrutiny of story structure. I had risen through the ranks, though, from logger to story assistant to story producer, overseeing other writers. So I ended up going to work on a whole slew of reality TV shows, both Nielsen-topping and not, including "The Bachelor," "The Mole," "The Surreal Life," "The Benefactor" and "The Biggest Loser." On every one of them, whether I was dealing with desperately weeping single gals or former parachute pant wearer MC Hammer, the main question was always the same: "What is the story?"

Some of the crafting of these shows took place on set, as on "Celebrity 7 Mole: Yucatan." While filming is taking place, writers keep track of all the issues that may arise and anticipate which will yield the strongest narrative. Teams of us are on location, assigned to different characters. The uniform: a good pen, steno notepads, an audio monitoring device (to overhear comments and conversations), a digital watch, walkie-talkies and a comfortable pair of shoes—in case anyone takes off running. We typically stand within earshot of what's being filmed, noting mumbled quips, telling looks and memorable exchanges. At the end of the day, we all regroup, compare notes and decide which stories have evolved, or are evolving. These are the situations to which we'll pay particular attention, and in the days following, we'll make sure the right interview questions are asked to round out what appear to be the prominent stories. Like nonfiction writers, we do not script lines—but if we have a hunch, we ask the right questions to follow it up.

Preparation of this kind is, of course, half the battle, but the magic really 8 happens after the filming is done, in post-production. In its one- to four-week scripting phase, the story producers pinpoint scenes, moments and interviews from a mountain of VHS tapes, then structure them to tell the strongest story. After it's approved by the executive producer, this script is given to an editor, who cuts it together. Six-day workweeks and long hours are expected—and get longer midway through editing, when a decision is invariably made to change the direction of the show. As story producers, the responsibility for that reshaping falls to us. Sometimes it's for the better, but sometimes it's for worse. "The Benefactor," for example, began as an exciting, conceptually strong show led by billionaire Mark Cuban and dubbed the Anti-"Apprentice," to contrast with the Donald Trump hit. It was quickly mired by second guessing on all our parts, and we ended up giving in to some Trumpian gimmicks. In the end, the show floundered, suffering dismal ratings and was widely perceived as the very thing it was striving not to be . . . another "Apprentice."

The current lawsuit isn't the Writer's Guild's first attempt to reach out to 9 reality TV crew members. Since this spring, they've been on a major campaign to unionize, gathering up union authorization cards from over 1,000 writers, editors and producers. Despite the many logistics associated with unionizing, at the core, I believe the WGA's gesture to be quite complimentary: By their actions, they are recognizing us as legitimate creative contributors, I like that. It's also a sign that they expect reality TV to be more than just a passing fad. Reality is evolving, and I look forward to its next chapter.

QUESTIONS FOR READING

1. Who has recently filed a lawsuit? What is their issue?
2. What do reality TV writers "do" for reality TV shows? What do they try to find?
3. What strategies do these writers use during the filming? After the filming?
4. What do the lawsuit and unionizing attempts suggest about the future of reality TV?

QUESTIONS FOR REASONING AND ANALYSIS

1. The author gives much information about his job. Is providing information his primary purpose—or not? If not, why does he give us all of the details?
2. If this is not primarily or exclusively informative, then what is Speight's claim?
3. What is effective about Speight's opening paragraph?
4. Why does he include the information in the second half of paragraph 8?

QUESTIONS FOR REFLECTING AND WRITING

1. Are you surprised to learn about reality TV writers—and their complex jobs? Why or why not?
2. Are you shocked or disappointed in reading this essay? Why might some be disappointed?
3. Although some never watch them, many people are "hooked" on reality TV. Why? What is the appeal? Would the appeal be less if viewers understood how these shows are constructed?

"*Great PowerPoint, Kevin, but the answer is no.*"

Read: What is the situation? Who speaks the words in quotations?

Reason: What do you infer to be on the laptop screen?

Reflect/Write: What is the cartoonist's attitude toward PowerPoint presentations? Toward modern society?

CHAPTER 14

Society
and Values
in an
iPod World

New technologies bring changes, not all of them unquestionably good. Seven writers in this chapter examine some of the characteristics—or problems, depending on your perspective—of modern electronic technology and the changes it has produced in the way we live today. Technology and privacy and homeland security issues all "bump into one another" in this new, wired century. Writers in this chapter look at the loss of privacy made possible by the computer, at the downloading of music from the Internet, and, more broadly, at the significant lifestyle changes resulting from modern technology. We can all list the advantages of information at our fingertips, of e-mailing and BlackBerrys; most of the writers here offer a cautionary tale regarding the less positive changes in the ways we live with the electronic gadgets we have made for ourselves.

Prereading Questions

1. Is it possible for the code makers to stay ahead of the hackers, or will "secure" sites always be reachable by gifted "techies"? And, should we care?

2. Even though we are all now a part of the global economy, that seems an abstract concept to many people. How does the computer affect your life in more immediate ways? Try listing the many ways that computers affect our daily lives.

3. Do you shop online? Do you believe that your credit card is secure? Do you download music from a "free" site? Do you think this is right? Why or why not?

4. Do you miss any of the "older" way of doing things? If so, what? If not, why not?

5. How do you envision computer applications affecting your life in the next twenty years? In the next fifty years? Will the effects be good or bad—or both? Why?

Web Sites Related to This Chapter's Topic

Electronic Privacy Information Center: Internet Censorship

www.epic.org/free_speech/censorship

This site focuses on legislation and court cases related to Internet censorship.

The Privacy Pages

www.2020tech.com/maildrop/privacy.html

Sponsored by the Orlando Mail Drop, this site contains many links to organizations and periodicals; it gives current news updates and information on security software and other privacy issues.

Recording Industry Association of America

www.riaa.org

Contains current information on piracy and First Amendment issues.

WE'RE ONLY HUMAN: AND NONE OF US ARE MADE TO RUN LIKE MACHINES | PATRICIA DALTON

A clinical psychologist with a practice in Washington, DC, Patricia Dalton's essays occasionally appear in the *Washington Post*'s "Outlook" section, including a study of some of the consequences of the feminist revolution on women. The following sobering look at the impact of modern technology appeared June 26, 2005.

PREREADING QUESTIONS How many different activities do you try to pack into one day? Do you delight in the variety, or do you feel stretched and stressed by it all?

1   When I read about the recent government-sponsored study of mental illness, I wasn't surprised. It indicates that half of all Americans will, at some point

in their lives, meet the criteria for mental illness (which includes substance abuse), and that those problems are starting at younger ages. I'm well aware of the argument that these rates must be exaggerated, but as a clinical psychologist, there is no doubt in my mind that there has been a real increase in the number of mood and anxiety disorders during the 20-plus years I have been in practice.

I believe I know one reason. As I listen to my patients and to the stories 2 other therapists tell, it is clear that technological change—the blessing and curse of our era—has led many of us to tax the human body and psyche in ways that our species has not had time to accommodate. Not only do adults, adolescents and even little kids have so much activity crammed into the course of a day that it's tiring just to hear them talk, but each generation is experiencing the world quite differently from their parents and grandparents.

The scale of that change came home to me last week, when Jack Kilby, 3 inventor of the microchip, died. Putting his achievements into perspective, the chairman of Texas Instruments said that "there are only a handful of people whose works have truly transformed the world and the way we live in it— Henry Ford, Thomas Edison, the Wright Brothers, and Jack Kilby."

Just think about that statement. Those men's innovations "transformed the 4 world and *the way we live in it*." It's as if we have forgotten the lesson that Charles Darwin taught us: Evolution and biological adaptation take time, usually long periods of time. Yet people seem to assume that we can keep the pace the machine has set. (Remember Charlie Chaplin going round and round, caught in the gears of a giant machine, in his satire *Modern Times*?) Many of the patients I see reveal just how much we've overestimated our flexibility and underestimated the price we pay for how we live in these modern times.

Ever since the first electric bulb shed artificial light, we have been detach- 5 ing ourselves from our natural rhythms. Business travelers cross time zones and go right back to work; adults extend their hours by bringing work home with them; teenagers contact their friends anywhere at any time of the day or night. Until, that is, they end up in therapists' offices having been stopped in their tracks by physical or psychological dysfunction. Many blame themselves when things go wrong. They minimize the impact of our super-charged environment on their psychological well-being.

It's hard to believe that not long ago, most people actually went to bed 6 when the sun went down and got up when the sun came up. They were born, lived and died within short distances of their childhood homes. They communicated face to face most of the time, or else by letter or telegram. They gathered frequently at home, in places of worship and in civic organizations.

Even the movers and shakers kept to a saner schedule. In her book, *No 7 Ordinary Time,* historian Doris Kearns Goodwin describes President Franklin D. Roosevelt's daily schedule. It included eight hours of sleep a night, and an evening cocktail hour when he gathered with friends to talk, laugh and relieve the pressures of the day. President Bush was the butt of his wife's jokes for keeping a similar schedule. Neither exemplified the lives described by many of my patients who work in government, law firms, medical practices and businesses in the D.C. area. With longer work weeks and commutes, they have fewer of the quiet restorative moments that nature requires to recharge and renew.

8   From depressed patients, therapists frequently hear about symptoms that psychiatrists term "vegetative." These concern the most basic biological functions, including sleep; appetite, for food as well as sex; and enjoyment. My children's babysitter, just back from a two-week vacation, once described her own restoration succinctly: "I feel good in my body." Too many people today do not know what it means to feel good in their bodies.

9   Part of the problem is simply lack of sleep. I sometimes fantasize that if I had a magic wand and could ensure that everyone would sleep eight hours a night, visits to therapists would drop by, perhaps, a quarter. Sleep—particularly REM sleep and dreaming—helps discharge tensions, restore energy and rebuild a foundation for stable functioning. I heard a lecture during my student days in which a psychiatrist said, "It is unclear whether depression is primarily a disorder of mood, or primarily a disorder of sleep." People who are sleep-deprived for any length of time are out of whack. Once sleep is seriously disordered, it can be difficult to restore the normal circadian rhythm essential to well-being.

10   I can think of a successful young couple with demanding jobs who found out the hard way. They fully expected to take the demands of children in stride, as well as a move to a new home. In time, the wife developed major depression with serious sleep disruption when child-care problems became for her the proverbial last straw. Only then did they wake up to the forced march their lives had become.

11   Another modern problem is *when* people sleep. Early to bed and early to rise really *is* a good idea, because it maximizes light exposure, which in turn boosts mood. Factories have largely stopped scheduling shifts with employees working days, then afternoons, and then nights at two-week or monthly intervals, because of the resulting physical and psychological strain.

12   Every summer, I talk with the mood-disordered teenagers who are heading off to college about trying to go to bed early and get up early as a hedge against depression. Students on so-called "college time" are without a doubt the most intransigent group when it comes to decent sleep habits. (My oldest child, newly home from college one summer, asked her father and me why we were going to bed so early—at midnight.)

13   A healthy appetite is a sign of a healthy animal. For an increasing number of Americans, appetite disturbance takes the form of eating too much or too little. And how many people take time to eat lunch away from their desk, with another human being? Much less away from the office, at a restaurant or at home? My now 88-year-old father was busy during his middle years running a lumber business, but he always found time to go to the little deli nearby for lunch, and to play golf.

14   Another casualty of turbo-charged lifestyles is sex. There are surprising numbers of people, even in committed relationships, who report having sex infrequently. Lack of sexual desire is occurring at younger ages, sometimes in

relationships that are otherwise sound, and it seems to be due to exhaustion. There is no cure except guarding time and energy. After all, sex is play. We all know how Jack becomes a dull boy!

Anxiety disorders, like depressive ones, are on the rise. (Interestingly, 15 obsessive-compulsive disorder, considered by some psychiatrists to be heavily based in biology, is not increasing.) Noting the increase in the number of children being diagnosed with and treated for attention-deficit hyperactivity disorder, there are experts who believe that regular bombardment by electronic stimuli and the new habit of multi-tasking is fragmenting the attention spans of some kids who may already be at risk.

When teenagers say, "You don't understand," as teenagers have always 16 said, they may be literally as well as figuratively accurate today. Those of us who grew up before instant messaging, for example, don't know what it's like to chat with friends or break up with a boyfriend online. This generation is also more deracinated than the last, having to devise a new set of cultural and social rules to fit new circumstances.

I don't mean to underestimate the benefits of technology: We can stay in 17 touch with relatives and friends who live at a distance. We can get work done more efficiently. Huge amounts of information are at our fingertips. But the angst and dysfunction I've described are real. I can recall one family in need of time and togetherness who decided to take a hike in Great Falls Park, only to have the dad spend most of the time on his BlackBerry. The teenage son muttered under his breath, "Some togetherness."

It is the simple moments that bring our blood pressure down and our spir- 18 its up. I remember one workday when I had a killer headache, and a close friend called unexpectedly. We talked, we laughed, and in 10 minutes my headache was gone.

Are we destined to be the driven in our modern world, or can we be- 19 come the drivers? What we often forget is that we can make deliberate decisions to improve the quality of our lives. The early-20th-century English writer G. K. Chesterton was probably right when he said, "New roads, new ruts." But we have more freedom than we realize to choose which ruts to avoid, given the changes that have already come and will keep coming to our high-tech world.

QUESTIONS FOR READING

1. What is Dalton's subject? Be precise.
2. Who are the people listed as having transformed our lives?
3. What is the key characteristic of change in modern times, as opposed to change over the course of life on earth?
4. What are some of the changes produced by the work of the inventors listed?
5. What are some of the problems produced by a lack of sleep? What group of people is especially prone to sleep deprivation?

QUESTIONS FOR REASONING AND ANALYSIS

1. What is Dalton's claim? State it as a problem that needs to be addressed.
2. What evidence does Dalton provide in support of her claim?
3. What, in the author's view, is causing the problem?
4. What, if any, solutions does she offer?
5. What are some marks of the conciliatory argument in her essay?

QUESTIONS FOR REFLECTING AND WRITING

1. Are your experiences revealing the same dysfunctions that Dalton is seeing in her patients and reading about in mental health studies? If you do not see the problems that she sees, can you account for that difference?
2. Do you see yourself described in this essay in any way? If so, do you see your lifestyle as in any way a problem? Why or why not? If you are not described here, how have you avoided the stress and anxiety Dalton described?

PRIVACY UNDER ATTACK | SIMSON GARFINKEL

Simson Garfinkel is the author of a number of articles and books on Internet privacy issues, including *PGP—Pretty Good Privacy* (1994), *Web Security, Commerce, and Privacy* (2002), *Architects of the Information Society* (a 1999 brief history of MIT's technological achievements), and *Database Nation: The Death of Privacy in the 21st Century* (2001). The following passage is from Chapter 1 of *Database Nation.*

PREREADING QUESTION Some are observing that we live in a "transparent society," a world in which we are constantly watched by cameras and monitored by electronic surveillance strategies when we phone or use the Internet or shop. Does this concern you, or do you see a transparent society as a safer society?

1   You wake to the sound of a ringing telephone—but how could that happen?

2   Several months ago, you reprogrammed your home telephone system so the phone would never ring before the civilized hour of 8:00 a.m. But it's barely 6:45 a.m. Who could be calling at this time? More importantly, who was able to bypass your phone's programming?

3   You pick up the telephone receiver, then slam it down a moment later. It's one of those marketing machines playing a prerecorded message. Computerized telemarketing calls have been illegal within the United States for more than a decade now, but ever since international long-distance prices dropped below 10 cents a minute, calls have been pouring in to North America from all over the world. And they're nearly all marketing calls—hence the popularity of programmable phones today. What's troubling you now is how this call got past the filters you set up. Later on, you'll discover how: the company that sold you the phone created an undocumented "back door"; last week, the phone codes were sold in an online auction. Because you weren't paying attention, you lost the chance to buy back your privacy.

4   Oops.

Now that you're awake, you decide to go through yesterday's mail. There's 5
a letter from the neighborhood hospital you visited last month. "We're pleased
that our emergency room could serve you in your time of need," the letter begins. "As you know, our fees (based on our agreement with your HMO) do not
cover the cost of treatment. To make up the difference, a number of hospitals
have started selling patient records to medical researchers and consumer marketing firms. Rather than mimic this distasteful behavior, we have decided to
ask you to help us make up the difference. We are recommending a tax-
deductible contribution of $275 to help defray the cost of your visit."

The veiled threat isn't empty, but you decide you don't really care who finds 6
out about your sprained wrist. You fold the letter in half and drop it into your
shredder. Also into the shredder goes a trio of low-interest credit card offers.

Why a shredder? A few years ago you would have never thought of shred- 7
ding your junk mail—until a friend in your apartment complex had his identity
"stolen" by the building's superintendent. As best as anybody can figure out,
the super picked one of those preapproved credit-card applications out of the
trash, called the toll-free number, and picked up the card when it was delivered. He's in Mexico now, with a lot of expensive clothing and electronics, all
at your friend's expense.

On that cheery note, you grab your bag and head out the door, which 8
automatically locks behind you.

When you enter the apartment's elevator, a hidden video camera scans 9
your face, approves your identity, and takes you to the garage in the basement.
You hope nobody else gets in the elevator—you don't relish a repeat of what
happened last week to that poor fellow in 4G. It turns out that a neighbor recently broke up with her violent boyfriend and got a restraining order against
him. Naturally, the elevator was programmed to recognize the man and, if he
was spotted, to notify the police and keep the doors locked until they arrived.
Too bad somebody else was in the elevator when it happened. Nobody realized the boyfriend was an undiagnosed (and claustrophobic) psychotic. A
hostage situation quickly developed. Too bad for Mr. 4G. Fortunately, everything was captured on videotape.

Your car computer suggests three recommended approaches to your office 10
this morning. You choose wrong, and a freak accident leaves you tied up in
traffic for more than half an hour. As you wait, the computer plays an advertisement for a nearby burger joint every five minutes. You can't turn it off, of
course: your car computer was free, paid for by the advertising.

Arriving late at work, you receive a polite email message from the com- 11
pany's timecard system; it knows when you showed up, and it gives you several
options for making up the missed time. You can forgo lunch today, work an
extra 45 minutes this evening, or take the 45 minutes out of your ever-dwindling
vacation time. The choice is yours.

You look up and force a smile. A little video camera on your computer 12
screen records your smile and broadcasts it to your boss and your coworkers.
They've told you that Workplace Video Wallpaper™ builds camaraderie—but
the company that sells the software also claims that the pervasive monitoring

cuts down on workplace violence, romances, and even drug use. Nowadays, everybody smiles at work—it's too dangerous to do otherwise.

13   The cameras are just one of the ways you're being continually monitored at work. It started with electronic tags in all the company's books and magazines, designed to stop the steady pilferage from the library. Then, in the aftermath of a bomb scare, employees were told they'd have to wear badges at all times, and that desks and drawers would be subject to random searches. (Rumor has it that the chief of security herself called in the bomb threat—a ploy to justify the new policies.)

14   Next month, the company is installing devices in the bathrooms to make sure people wash their hands. Although the devices were originally intended for the healthcare and food industries, a recent study found that routine washing can also cut down on disease transmission among white-collar workers. So the machines are coming, and with them you'll lose just a little bit more of your privacy and your dignity.

15   This is the future—not a far-off future, but one that's just around the corner. It's a future in which what little privacy we now have will be gone. Some people call this loss of privacy "Orwellian," harking back to *1984*, George Orwell's classic work on privacy and autonomy. In that book, Orwell imagined a future in which privacy was decimated by a totalitarian state that used spies, video surveillance, historical revisionism, and control over the media to maintain its power. But the age of monolithic state control is over. The future we're rushing towards isn't one where our every move is watched and recorded by some all-knowing "Big Brother." It is instead a future of a hundred kid brothers that constantly watch and interrupt our daily lives. George Orwell thought that the Communist system represented the ultimate threat to individual liberty. Over the next 50 years, we will see new kinds of threats to privacy that don't find their roots in totalitarianism, but in capitalism, the free market, advanced technology, and the unbridled exchange of electronic information.

WHAT DO WE MEAN BY PRIVACY?

16   The concept of privacy is central to this . . . [essay], yet I wish I had a better word to express the aspect of individual liberty that is under attack by advanced technology as we enter the new millennium.

17   For decades, people have warned that pervasive databanks and surveillance technology are leading inevitably to the death of privacy and democracy. But these days, many people who hear the word "privacy" think about those kooks living off in the woods with their shotguns: these folks get their mail at post office boxes registered under assumed names, grow their own food, use cash to buy what they can't grow for themselves, and constantly worry about being attacked by the federal government—or by space aliens. If you are not one of these people, you may well ask, "Why should I worry about my privacy? I have nothing to hide."

18   The problem with this word "privacy" is that it falls short of conveying the really big picture. Privacy isn't just about hiding things. It's about self-possession, autonomy, and integrity. As we move into the computerized world

of the twenty-first century, privacy will be one of our most important civil rights. But this right of privacy isn't the right of people to close their doors and pull down their window shades—perhaps because they want to engage in some sort of illicit or illegal activity. It's the right of people to control what details about their lives stay inside their own houses and what leaks to the outside.

To understand privacy in the next century, we need to rethink what privacy   19
really means today:

- It's not about the man who wants to watch pornography in complete anonymity over the Internet. It's about the woman who's afraid to use the Internet to organize her community against a proposed toxic dump—afraid because the dump's investors are sure to dig through her past if she becomes too much of a nuisance.

- It's not about people speeding on the nation's highways who get automatically generated tickets mailed to them thanks to a computerized speed trap. It's about lovers who will take less joy in walking around city streets or visiting stores because they know they're being photographed by surveillance cameras everywhere they step.

- It's not about the special prosecutors who leave no stone unturned in their search for corruption or political misdeeds. It's about good, upstanding citizens who are now refusing to enter public service because they don't want a bloodthirsty press rummaging through their old school reports, computerized medical records, and email.

- It's not about the searches, metal detectors, and inquisitions that have become a routine part of our daily lives at airports, schools, and federal buildings. It's about a society that views law-abiding citizens as potential terrorists, yet does little to effectively protect its citizens from the real threats to their safety.

Today, more than ever before, we are witnessing the daily erosion of per-   20
sonal privacy and freedom. We're victims of a war on privacy that's being waged by government eavesdroppers, business marketers, and nosy neighbors.

Most of us recognize that our privacy is at risk. According to a 1996 nation-   21
wide poll conducted by Louis Harris & Associates, one in four Americans (24%) has "personally experienced a privacy invasion"[1]—up from 19% in 1978. In 1995, the same survey found that 80% of Americans felt that "consumers have lost all control over how personal information about them is circulated and used by companies."[2] Ironically, both the 1995 and 1996 surveys were paid for by Equifax, a company that earns nearly two billion dollars each year from collecting and distributing personal information.

We know our privacy is under attack. The problem is that we don't know   22
how to fight back.

THE ROLE OF TECHNOLOGY

Today's war on privacy is intimately related to the dramatic advances in tech-   23
nology we've seen in recent years. As we'll see time and again . . . , unrestrained

technology ends privacy. Video cameras observe personal moments; computers store personal facts; and communications networks make personal information widely available throughout the world. Although some specialty technology may be used to protect personal information and autonomy, the overwhelming tendency of advanced technology is to do the reverse.

24   Privacy is fundamentally about the power of the individual. In many ways, the story of technology's attack on privacy is really the story of how institutions and the people who run them use technology to gain control over the human spirit, for good and ill. That's because technology by itself doesn't violate our privacy or anything else: it's the people using this technology and the policies they carry out that create violations.

25   Many people today say that in order to enjoy the benefits of modern society, we must necessarily relinquish some degree of privacy. If we want the convenience of paying for a meal by credit card, or paying for a toll with an electronic tag mounted on our rear view mirror, then we must accept the routine collection of our purchases and driving habits in a large database over which we have no control. It's a simple bargain, albeit a Faustian one.

26   I think this tradeoff is both unnecessary and wrong. It reminds me of another crisis our society faced back in the 1950s and 1960s—the environmental crisis. Then, advocates of big business said that poisoned rivers and lakes were the necessary costs of economic development, jobs, and an improved standard of living. Poison was progress: anybody who argued otherwise simply didn't understand the facts.

27   Today we know better. Today we know that sustainable economic development *depends* on preserving the environment. Indeed, preserving the environment is a prerequisite to the survivability of the human race. Without clean air to breathe and clean water to drink, we will all surely die. Similarly, in order to reap the benefits of technology, it is more important than ever for us to use technology to protect personal freedom.

28   Blaming technology for the death of privacy isn't new. In 1890, two Boston lawyers, Samuel Warren and Louis Brandeis, argued in the *Harvard Law Review* that privacy was under attack by "recent inventions and business methods." They contended that the pressures of modern society required the creation of a "right of privacy," which would help protect what they called "the right to be let alone."[3] Warren and Brandeis refused to believe that privacy had to die for technology to flourish. Today, the Warren/Brandeis article is regarded as one of the most influential law review articles ever published.[4] And the article's significance has increased with each passing year, as the technological invasions that worried Warren and Brandeis have become more commonplace.

29   Privacy-invasive technology does not exist in a vacuum, of course. That's because technology itself exists as a junction between science, the market, and society. People create technology to fill specific needs, real or otherwise. And technology is regulated, or not, as people and society see fit.

30   Few engineers set out to build systems designed to crush privacy and autonomy, and few businesses or consumers would willingly use or purchase

these systems if they understood the consequences. What happens more often is that the privacy implications of a new technology go unnoticed. Or if the
privacy implications are considered, they are misunderstood. Or if they are understood correctly, errors are made in implementation. In practice, just a few
mistakes can turn a system designed to protect personal information into one
that destroys our secrets.

How can we keep technology and the free market from killing our privacy? 31
One way is by being careful and informed consumers. But I believe that government has an equally important role to play.

THE ROLE OF GOVERNMENT

With everything we've heard about Big Brother, how can we think of gov- 32
ernment as anything but the enemy of privacy? While it's true that federal laws
and actions have often damaged the cause of privacy, I believe that the federal
government may be our best hope for privacy protection as we move into the
new millennium.

The biggest privacy failure of American government has been its failure to 33
carry through with the impressive privacy groundwork that was laid in the
Nixon, Ford, and Carter administrations. It's worth taking a look back at that
groundwork and how it may serve us today.

The 1970s were a good decade for privacy protection and consumer rights. 34
In 1970, Congress passed the Fair Credit Reporting Act. Elliot Richardson, who
at the time was President Nixon's secretary of health, education, and welfare
(HEW), created a commission in 1972 to study the impact of computers on privacy. After [months] of testimony in Congress, the commission found all the
more reason for alarm and issued a landmark report in 1973.

The most important contribution of the Richardson report was a bill of 35
rights for the computer age, which it called the Code of Fair Information Practices (see the shaded box). That Code remains the most significant American
thinking on the topic of computers and privacy to this day.

CODE OF FAIR INFORMATION PRACTICES

The Code of Fair Information Practices is based on five principles:

- There must be no personal data record-keeping systems whose very
  existence is secret.

- There must be a way for a person to find out what information about
  the person is in a record and how it is used.

- There must be a way for a person to prevent information about the
  person that was obtained for one purpose from being used or made
  available for other purposes without the person's consent.

- There must be a way for a person to correct or amend a record of
  identifiable information about the person.

(continued)

- Any organization creating, maintaining, using, or disseminating records of identifiable personal data must assure the reliability of the data for their intended use and must take precautions to prevent misuses of the data.

Source: Department of Health, Education, and Welfare, 1973.

36   The biggest impact of the HEW report wasn't in the United States, but in Europe. In the years after the report was published, practically every European country passed laws based on these principles. Many created data protection commissions and commissioners to enforce the laws.[5] Some believe that one reason for this interest in electronic privacy was Europe's experience with Nazi Germany in the 1940s. Hitler's secret police used the records of governments and private organizations in the countries he invaded to round up people who posed the greatest threat to the German occupation; postwar Europe realized the danger of allowing potentially threatening private information to be collected, even by democratic governments that might be responsive to public opinion.

37   But here in the United States, the idea of institutionalized data protection faltered. President Jimmy Carter showed interest in improving medical privacy, but he was quickly overtaken by economic and political events. Carter lost the election of 1980 to Ronald Reagan, whose aides saw privacy protection as yet another failed Carter initiative. Although several privacy protection laws were signed during the Reagan/Bush era, the leadership for these bills came from Congress, not the White House. The lack of leadership stifled any chance of passing a nationwide data protection act.

38   In fact, while most people in the federal government were ignoring the cause of privacy, some were actually pursuing an antiprivacy agenda. In the early 1980s, the federal government initiated numerous "computer matching" programs designed to catch fraud and abuse. (Unfortunately, because of erroneous data, these programs often penalized innocent individuals.[6]) In 1994, Congress passed the Communications Assistance to Law Enforcement Act, which gave the government dramatic new powers for wiretapping digital communications. In 1996, Congress passed a law requiring states to display Social Security numbers on driver's licenses, and another law requiring that all medical patients in the U.S. be issued unique numerical identifiers, even if they paid their own bills. Fortunately, the implementation of those 1996 laws has been delayed, largely thanks to a citizen backlash.

39   Continuing the assault, both the Bush and Clinton administrations waged an all-out war against the rights of computer users to engage in private and secure communications. Starting in 1991, both administrations floated proposals for use of "Clipper" encryption systems that would have given the government access to encrypted personal communications. President Clinton also backed

the Communications Decency Act (CDA), which made it a crime to transmit sexually explicit information to minors—and, as a result, might have required Internet providers to deploy far-reaching monitoring and censorship systems. When a court in Philadelphia found the CDA unconstitutional, the Clinton administration appealed the decision all the way to the Supreme Court—and lost.

Finally, the U.S. government's restrictions on the export of encryption tech- 40 nology have effectively restrained the widespread use of this technology for personal privacy protection within the United States.

As we move forward. . . , the United States needs to take personal privacy 41 seriously again. . . .

FIGHTING BACK

Privacy is certainly on the ropes in America today, but so was the environ- 42 ment in 1969. Thirty years ago, the Cuyahoga River in Ohio caught on fire and Lake Erie was proclaimed dead. Times have certainly changed. Today it's safe to eat fish that are caught in the Cuyahoga, Lake Erie is alive again, and the overall environment in America is the cleanest it's been in decades.

There are signs around us indicating that privacy is getting ready to make 43 a comeback as well. The war against privacy is commanding more and more attention in print, on television, and on the Internet. People are increasingly aware of how their privacy is compromised on a daily basis. Some people have begun taking simple measures to protect their privacy, measures like making purchases with cash and refusing to provide their Social Security numbers—or providing fake ones. And a small but growing number of people are speaking out for technology *with* privacy, and putting their convictions into practice by developing systems or services that protect, rather than attack, our privacy.

Over the past few decades, we've learned that technology is flexible, and 44 that when it invades our privacy, the invasion is usually the result of a conscious choice. We now know, for instance, that when a representative from our bank says:

> I'm sorry that you don't like having your Social Security number printed on your bank statement, but there is no way to change it.

that representative is actually saying:

> Our programmers made a mistake by telling the computer to put your Social Security number on you bank statement, but we don't think it's a priority to change the program. Take your business elsewhere.

Today we are relearning this lesson and discovering how vulnerable busi- 45 ness and government can be to public pressure. . . .

Technology is not autonomous; it simply empowers choices made by gov- 46 ernment, business, and individuals. One of the big lessons of the environmental movement is that it's possible to shape these choices through the political process. This, I believe, justifies the involvement of government on the privacy question.

NOTES

1. Harris-Equifax, *Consumer Privacy Survey.* Conducted for Equifax by Louis Harris and Associates in association with Dr. Alan Westin of Columbia University, Equifax, Atlanta, GA, 1996.

2. Harris-Equifax, *Consumer Privacy Survey.* Conducted for Equifax by Louis Harris and Associates in association with Dr. Alan Westin of Columbia University, Equifax, Atlanta, GA, 1995.

3. Samuel Warren and Louis Brandeis, "The Right of Privacy," *Harvard Law Review* 4 (1980), 193. Although the phrase "the right to be let alone" is commonly attributed to Warren and Brandeis, the article attributes the phrase to the nineteenth-century judge Thomas M. Cooley.

4. Turkington et al., *Privacy: Cases and Materials.*

5. David H. Flaherty, *Protecting Privacy in Surveillance Societies* (University of North Carolina Press, 1989).

In 1989, David H. Flaherty, the privacy commissioner of British Columbia, published a revised set of 12 Data Protection Principles and Practices for Government Personal Information Systems. These 12 principles are (emphasis supplied by David Flaherty in May 1997):

The principles of *publicity and transparency* (openness) concerning government personal information systems (no secret databanks).

The principles of *necessity* and relevance governing the collection and storage of personal information.

The principle of reducing the collection, use, and storage of personal information to the maximum extent possible.

The principle of *finality* (the purpose and ultimate administrative uses for personal information need to be established in advance).

The principle of establishing and requiring *responsible keepers* for personal information systems.

The principle of controlling *linkages*, transfers, and interconnections involving personal information.

The principle of requiring informed *consent* for the collection of personal information.

The principle of requiring accuracy and completeness in personal information systems.

The principle of *data trespass*, including civil and criminal penalties for unlawful abuses of personal information.

The requirement of special rules for protecting sensitive personal information.

The right of access to, and correction of, personal information systems.

The *right to be forgotten*, including the ultimate anonymization or destruction of almost all personal information.

6. One federal match program compared a database that had the names of people who had defaulted on their student college loans with another database that had the names of federal employees. The match

then automatically garnished the wages of the federal employees to pay for the defaulted loans. The problem with this match, and others, was that there were many false matches that were the result of incorrect data or similar-sounding names. And because the wages were automatically garnished, victims of this match were required to prove their innocence—that is, to prove that the match was erroneous.

QUESTIONS FOR READING

1. What is Garfinkel's subject? What is the problem he explores?
2. How do some people define privacy? How does the author define it as it applies to our lives in the twenty-first century?
3. What is the primary cause of the invasion of privacy in our time? How does Garfinkel qualify and explain the exact nature of this cause? (What is, in and of itself, not the villain?)
4. What solution does Garfinkel present?
5. What are the key points in the Code of Fair Information Practices?
6. Why hasn't the federal government established laws and commissions to oversee personal privacy similar to those established in some European countries?

QUESTIONS FOR REASONING AND ANALYSIS

1. What is Garfinkel's claim? Where does he state it?
2. Examine Garfinkel's long introduction. What does he accomplish with his futuristic scenario?
3. In paragraphs 26 and 27, and again in paragraph 42, the author develops an analogy. What is the analogy and what is the point he wants to make through the comparison?
4. Solutions to the loss of privacy because of technology are possible only if one believes a basic assumption that Garfinkel repeats throughout his chapter. What is the key assumption about technology on which his argument rests?

QUESTIONS FOR REFLECTING AND WRITING

1. Do you agree with Garfinkel's basic assumption? Or would you argue that computer technology is not just faster and easier but so much so that it is different in kind from previous strategies for collecting data about individuals? That is, is the technology itself a significant part of the problem, or is it a matter of how it is used? Be prepared to debate this point.
2. Do you agree with the problem—has modern technology created the invasion of privacy and autonomy that Garfinkel asserts? David Brin, in his 1998 book *The Transparent Society*, has argued that we need less rather than more privacy, that privacy has usually benefited the rich and powerful or the government, not the average person. Who has the better sense of the situation? Why?

3. If you agree with the problem and the cause, do you agree with the author's solutions? Why or why not?

THE ISSUE IS PIRACY, NOT PRIVACY | CARY SHERMAN

A graduate of Harvard Law School, Cary Sherman is now the president of the Recording Industry Association of America. Sherman is a musician and songwriter as well as an expert on intellectual property law. His article appeared in *USA Today*, January 29, 2003.

PREREADING QUESTIONS Have you downloaded music, movies, or texts from the Internet? Do you think doing so is breaking the law? Do you think it is immoral?

1   Today's debate: Online music files.

2   Opposing view: First Amendment does not protect the theft of other people's property.

3   Ever since a federal court ordered Verizon to identify a subscriber who illegally distributed hundreds of hit songs on the Internet, the company has claimed the ruling somehow violates the individual's right to privacy.

4   Strangely, when it was arguing its case in court, Verizon never uttered a word about privacy. Indeed, Verizon acknowledged that it will identify certain infringers when it suits Verizon. That's because it knows the issue here isn't about privacy; it's about piracy.

5   The fact is, our right to privacy does not include a right to commit illegal acts anonymously. You or I may have a right to keep our banking transactions private, but when we stick a gun in a teller's face and ask for the contents of the cash drawer, the bank is more than entitled to take our picture with a security camera.

6   The same is true on the Internet. Offering to upload music files without permission so millions of strangers can copy them off the Internet is neither a private act nor a legal one. Should those who engage in this gratuitous giveaway of other people's property be able to conceal their identity behind computer numbers or made-up screen names?

7   The Recording Industry Association of America is a stalwart defender of the First Amendment. But music piracy is not the kind of expression the First Amendment seeks to protect. In the words of the opinion, we're not talking about a consumer who "is anonymously using the Internet to distribute speeches of Lenin, biblical passages . . . or criticisms of the government." Rather we're talking about someone who is distributing illegal copies of popular songs—the very antithesis of protected activity.

8   There is a good reason Congress enacted the Digital Millennium Copyright Act, the law that requires Internet service providers to promptly identify the infringer when copyright owners file a sworn declaration that a subscriber is illegally distributing copyrighted materials: In a digital age, when anyone with a decent computer and a shortage of scruples can instantaneously flood the world with an infinite number of perfect copies of any song, movie or text he can get his hands on, copyrights would be worthless without this most basic level of protection.

QUESTIONS FOR READING

1. What is Sherman's subject?

2. What has the court ruled that Verizon must do? What is Verizon's position on the issue?

3. What law relevant to this debate has the Congress passed?

QUESTIONS FOR REASONING AND ANALYSIS

1. What is Sherman's claim?

2. In paragraph 7, Sherman asserts that the RIAA supports the First Amendment. Why does he make this point?

3. In paragraph 5, the author uses an analogy; what is the analogy and what point does he make with it?

QUESTIONS FOR REFLECTING AND WRITING

1. What is the idea of copyrights? How do they work? Why do we have them? Should people be able to copyright their music, movies, and texts? Why or why not?

2. If you agree with the idea of copyrights, then presumably you agree with Sherman's view that downloading music from the Internet is stealing, right? Or not right?

3. What is your review on music "sharing"? Can you justify it? Why or why not? Can you justify it and be consistent with a support for copyrights? Why or why not? Be prepared to debate this issue on practical and ethical grounds, not on emotion.

4. Think back to Simson Garfinkel's argument. Is the technology in control of this problem, or can (and should) we make choices about using the technology—or finding a technological way to block music sharing? Or will the new policing of this activity and the issuing of fines be the only deterrent strategy we need? Explain your position.

IPOD'S MISSED MANNERS | GEORGE F. WILL

A syndicated columnist since 1974, George Will is the author of a number of books, including ones about his great love—baseball. He is also a regular participant in television shows of political analysis. The following column appeared November 20, 2005.

PREREADING QUESTIONS Are you inclined to talk on your cell phone in the midst of a crowd of strangers? Do you consider this bad manners? Should others be offended by your behavior?

Let's be good cosmopolitans and offer sociological explanations rather 1 than moral judgments about students having sex during the day in high schools, as *The Post* reported. Sociology discerns connections, and there may be one between the fact that teenagers are relaxing from academic rigors by enjoying sex in the school auditorium and the fact that Americans soon will be able to watch pornography and prime-time television programs such as "Desperate Housewives"—and, for the high-minded, C-SPAN—on their cell phones and video iPods in public.

2   The connection is this: Many people have no notion of propriety when in the presence of other people, because they are not actually in the presence of other people, even when they are in public.

3   With everyone chatting on cell phones when not floating in iPod-land, "this is an age of social autism, in which people just can't see the value of imagining their impact on others." We are entertaining ourselves into inanition. (There are Web sites for people with Internet addiction. Think about that.) And multiplying technologies of portable entertainments will enable "limitless self-absorption," which will make people solipsistic, inconsiderate and antisocial. Hence manners are becoming unmannerly in this "age of lazy moral relativism combined with aggressive social insolence."

4   So says Lynne Truss in her latest trumpet-blast of a book, *Talk to the Hand: The Utter Bloody Rudeness of the World Today, or Six Good Reasons to Stay Home and Bolt the Door.* Her previous wail of despair was *Eats, Shoots & Leaves: The Zero Tolerance Approach to Punctuation,* which established her as—depending on your sensibility—a comma and apostrophe fascist (the liberal sensibility) or a plucky constable combating anarchy (the conservative sensibility).

5   Good punctuation, she says, is analogous to good manners because it treats readers with respect. "All the important rules," she writes, "surely boil down to one: *remember you are with other people; show some consideration.* Manners, which have been called "quotidian ethics," arise from real or—this, too, is important in lubricating social frictions—feigned empathy.

6   "People," says Truss, "are happier when they have some idea of where they stand and what the rules are." But today's entitlement mentality, which is both a cause and a consequence of the welfare state, manifests itself in the attitude that it is all right to do whatever one has a right to do. Which is why acrimony has enveloped a coffee shop on Chicago's affluent North Side, where the proprietor posted a notice that children must "behave and use their indoor voices." The proprietor, battling what he calls an "epidemic" of antisocial behavior, told the *New York Times* that parents protesting his notice "have a very strong sense of entitlement."

7   A thoroughly modern parent, believing that children must be protected from feelings injurious to self-esteem, says: "Johnny, the fact that you did something bad does not mean you are bad for doing it." We have, Truss thinks, "created people who will not stand to be corrected in any way." Furthermore, it is a brave, or foolhardy, man who shows traditional manners toward women. In today's world of "hair-trigger sensitivity," to open a door for a woman is to play what Truss calls Gallantry Russian Roulette: You risk a high-decibel lecture on gender politics.

8   One writer on manners has argued that a nation's greatness is measured not only by obedience of laws but also by "obedience to the unenforce-

able." But enforcement of manners can be necessary. The well-named David Stern, commissioner of the NBA, recently decreed a dress code for players. It is politeness to the league's customers who, weary of seeing players dressed in "edgy" hip-hop "street" or "gangsta" styles, want to be able to distinguish the Bucks and Knicks from the Bloods and Crips. Stern also understands that players who wear "in your face" clothes of a kind, and in a manner, that evokes Sing Sing more than Brooks Brothers might be more inclined to fight on the floor and to allow fights to migrate to the stands, as happened last year.

Because manners are means of extending respect, especially to strangers, 9 this question arises: Do manners and virtue go together? Truss thinks so, in spite of the possibility of "blood-stained dictators who had exquisite table manners and never used their mobile phones in a crowded train compartment to order mass executions."

Actually, manners are the practice of a virtue. The virtue is called civility, a 10 word related—as a foundation is related to a house—to the word civilization.

QUESTIONS FOR READING

1. What are the "missed manners" of Will's title?
2. What, according to Lynne Truss, has been the result of people plugged into cell phones and iPods? What does she mean by "an age of social autism"?
3. What is Truss's reason for valuing good punctuation?
4 What is the connection between manners and civilization?

QUESTIONS FOR REASONING AND ANALYSIS

1. What is the claim of Will's argument? Where does he state it?
2 What are the causes of the problem, in Will's view? What evidence does he provide for his causal analysis? Has he made his case, in your view?
3. Will offers both liberal and conservative explanations. From the essay as a whole, where do you place the author along with political spectrum?
4. What makes his opening effective?

QUESTIONS FOR REFLECTING AND WRITING

1. Do you agree with truss that people are happier—or less anxious—when they know the rules? Why or why not?
2. Whether you accept Will's causal analysis or not, do you agree with his description of today's lack of manners? Why or why not?
3. Can you explain Internet addiction? Or cell phone addiction?

POWERPOINT: KILLER APP? | RUTH MARCUS

Ruth Marcus is a member of the *Washington Post* editorial board, and she occasionally has a column on the op-ed page of the *Post.* The following column was published August 30, 2005.

PREREADING QUESTIONS Do you think that PowerPoint improves presentations? If so, why? What objections to PowerPoint presentations might someone have?

1   Did PowerPoint make the space shuttle crash? Could it doom another mission? Preposterous as this may sound, the ubiquitous Microsoft "presentation software" has twice been singled out for special criticism by task forces reviewing the space shuttle disaster.

2   Perhaps I've sat through too many PowerPoint presentations lately, but I think the trouble with these critics is that they don't go far enough: The software may be as much of a mind-numbing menace to those of us who intend to remain earthbound as it is to astronauts.

3   PowerPoint's failings have been outlined most vividly by Yale political scientist Edward Tufte, a specialist in the visual display of information. In a 2003 *Wired* magazine article headlined "PowerPoint Is Evil" and a less dramatically titled pamphlet, "The Cognitive Style of PowerPoint," Tufte argued that the program encourages "faux-analytical" thinking that favors the slickly produced "sales pitch" over the sober exchange of information.

4   Exhibit A in Tufte's analysis is a PowerPoint slide presented to NASA senior managers in January 2003, while the space shuttle Columbia was in the air and the agency was weighing the risk posed by the tile damage on the shuttle wings. Key information was so buried and condensed in the rigid PowerPoint format as to be useless.

5   "It is easy to understand how a senior manager might read this PowerPoint slide and not realize that it addresses a life-threatening situation," the Columbia Accident Investigation Board concluded, citing Tufte's work. The board devoted a full page of its 2003 report to the issue, criticizing a space agency culture in which, it said, "the endemic use of PowerPoint" substituted for rigorous technical analysis.

6   But NASA—like the rest of corporate and bureaucratic America—seems powerless to resist PowerPoint. Just this month a minority report by the latest shuttle safety task force echoed the earlier concerns: Often, the group said, when it asked for data it ended up with PowerPoints—without supporting documentation.

7   These critiques are, pardon the phrase, on point, but I suspect that the insidious influence of PowerPoint goes beyond the way it frustrates scientific analysis. The deeper problem with the PowerPointing of America—the PowerPointing of the planet, actually—is that the program tends to flatten the most complex, subtle, even beautiful, ideas into tedious, bullet-pointed bureaucratese.

I experienced a particularly dreary example of this under a starry Hawaiian 8
sky this year, listening to a talk on astronomy. It was the perfect moment for
magical images of distant stars and newly discovered planets. Yet, instead of
using technology to transport, the lecturer plodded point-by-point through
cookie-cutter slides.

The soul-sapping essence of PowerPoint was captured perfectly in a spoof 9
on the Gettysburg Address by computer whiz Peter Norvig of Google. It featured Abe Lincoln fumbling with his computer ("Just a second while I get this
connection to work. Do I press this button here? Function-F7?") and collapsing
his speech into six slides, complete with a bar chart depicting four score and
seven years.

For example, Slide 4:   10

"Review of Key Objectives & Critical Success Factors
- What makes nation unique
  — Conceived in liberty
  — Men are equal
- Shared vision
  — New birth of freedom
  — Gov't of/by/for the people."

If NASA managers didn't recognize the safety problem, perhaps it's be- 11
cause they were dazed from having to endure too many presentations like
this—the inevitable computer balkiness, the robotic recitation of bullet points,
the truncated language of a marketing pitch. Hence the *New Yorker* cartoon in
which the devil, seated at his desk in Hell, interviews a potential assistant: "I
need someone well versed in the art of torture—do you know PowerPoint?"

Like all forms of torture, though, PowerPoint degrades its practitioners as 12
well as its victims. Yes, boring slides were plentiful in the pre-PowerPoint era—
remember the overhead projector? Yes, it can help the intellectually inept organize their thoughts. But the seductive availability of PowerPoint and the
built-in drive to reduce all subjects to a series of short-handed bullet points
eliminates nuances and enables, even encourages, the absence of serious
thinking. Really, why think at all when the auto-content wizard can do it for you?

The most disturbing development in the world of PowerPoint is its migra- 13
tion to the schools—like sex and drugs, at earlier and earlier ages. Now we
have second-graders being tutored in PowerPoint. No matter that students
who compose at the keyboard already spend more energy perfecting their
fonts than polishing their sentences—PowerPoint dispenses with the need to
write any sentences at all. Perhaps the politicians who are so worked up about
the ill effects of violent video games should turn their attention to PowerPoint
instead.

In the meantime, Tufte, who's now doing consulting work for NASA, has a 14
modest proposal for its new administrator: Ban the use of PowerPoint. Sounds
good to me. After all, you don't have to be a rocket scientist to see the perils
of PowerPoint.

QUESTIONS FOR READING

1. What is Marcus's subject?
2. What is Tufte's objection to the slide used during a discussion of *Columbia*'s damaged tiles?
3. What is "seductive" about PowerPoint?
4. What, in the author's view, does PowerPoint allow people to avoid doing?

QUESTIONS FOR REASONING AND ANALYSIS

1. What is Marcus's claim; that is, what is the problem with PowerPoint?
2. Analyze her use of examples, considering their range and effectiveness. Do they provide good support for her claim?
3. Find examples of the author's clever use of language. How does her cleverness serve her purpose?

QUESTIONS FOR REFLECTING AND WRITING

1. Have you ever heard/read anyone objecting to PowerPoint—or is this a new idea for you? Does it make sense, on reflection?
2. On what assumption about the nature or role of language does this argument rest? How do we think? (Consider Marcus's assertion that PowerPoint "flatten[s]" ideas.)

SOCIETY IS DEAD: WE HAVE RETREATED INTO THE IWORLD | ANDREW SULLIVAN

A native of England with a doctorate in political science from Harvard, Andrew Sullivan is editor of Andrewsullivan.com, an online source of commentary on current issues; a *Time* magazine essayist; and a columnist for the *Sunday Times* of London. He also lectures widely and appears frequently on both radio and television programs. The following appeared on *TimesOnline* on February 20, 2005.

PREREADING QUESTIONS Do you frequently "plug in" to a Walkman or iPod? If so, do you think that you may be missing something?

1   I was visiting New York last week and noticed something I'd never thought I'd say about the city. Yes, nightlife is pretty much dead (and I'm in no way the first to notice that). But daylife—that insane mishmash of yells, chatter, clatter, hustle and chutzpah that makes New York the urban equivalent of methamphetamine—was also a little different. It was quieter.

2   Manhattan's downtown is now a Disney-like string of malls, riverside parks and pretty upper-middle-class villages. But there was something else. And as I looked across the throngs on the pavements, I began to see why.

3   There were little white wires hanging down from their ears, or tucked into pockets, purses or jackets. The eyes were a little vacant. Each was in his or her

own musical world, walking to their soundtrack, stars in their own music video, almost oblivious to the world around them. These are the iPod people.

Even without the white wires you can tell who they are. They walk down 4 the street in their own MP3 cocoon, bumping into others, deaf to small social cues, shutting out anyone not in their bubble.

Every now and again some start unconsciously emitting strange tuneless 5 squawks, like a badly tuned radio, and their fingers snap or their arms twitch to some strange soundless rhythm. When others say "Excuse me" there's no response. "Hi," ditto. It's strange to be among so many people and hear so little. Except that each one is hearing so much.

Yes, I might as well own up. I'm one of them. I witnessed the glazed New 6 York looks through my own glazed pupils, my white wires peeping out of my ears. I joined the cult a few years ago: the sect of the little white box worshippers.

Every now and again I go to church—those huge, luminous Apple stores, 7 pews in the rear, the clerics in their monastic uniforms all bustling around or sitting behind the "Genius Bars," like priests waiting to hear confessions.

Others began, as I did, with a Walkman—and then a kind of clunkier MP3 8 player. But the sleekness of the iPod won me over. Unlike other models it gave me my entire music collection to rearrange as I saw fit—on the fly, in my pocket.

What was once an occasional musical diversion became a compulsive 9 obsession. Now I have my iTunes in my iMac for my iPod in my iWorld. It's Narcissus heaven: we've finally put the "i" into Me.

And, like all addictive cults, it's spreading. There are now 22m iPod own- 10 ers in the United States and Apple is becoming a mass-market company for the first time.

Walk through any airport in the United States these days and you will see 11 person after person gliding through the social ether as if on autopilot. Get on a subway and you're surrounded by a bunch of Stepford commuters staring into mid-space as if anaesthetized by technology. Don't ask, don't tell, don't overhear, don't observe. Just tune in and tune out.

It wouldn't be so worrying if it weren't part of something even bigger. 12 Americans are beginning to narrow their lives.

You get your news from your favourite blogs, the ones that won't challenge 13 your view of the world. You tune into a satellite radio service that also aims directly at a small market—for new age fanatics, liberal talk or Christian rock. Television is all cable. Culture is all subculture Your cell phones can receive e-mail feeds of your favourite blogger's latest thoughts—seconds after he has posted them—to get sports scores for your team or stock quotes of your portfolio.

Technology has given us a universe entirely for ourselves—where the 14 serendipity of meeting a new stranger, hearing a piece of music we would never choose for ourselves or an opinion that might force us to change our mind about something are all effectively banished.

Atomisation by little white boxes and cell phones. Society without the so- 15 cial. Others who are chosen—not met at random. Human beings have never lived like this before. Yes, we have always had homes, retreats or places where we went to relax, unwind or shut out the world.

16   But we didn't walk around the world like hermit crabs with our isolation surgically attached.

17   Music was once the preserve of the living room or the concert hall. It was sometimes solitary but it was primarily a shared experience, something that brought people together, gave them the comfort of knowing that others too understood the pleasure of a Brahms symphony or that Beatles album.

18   But music is as atomised now as living is. And it's secret. That bloke next to you on the bus could be listening to heavy metal or a Gregorian chant. You'll never know. And so, bit by bit, you'll never really know him. And by his white wires, he is indicating he doesn't really want to know you.

19   What do we get from this? The awareness of more music, more often. The chance to slip away for a while from everydayness, to give our lives its own soundtrack, to still the monotony of the commute, to listen more closely and carefully to music that can lift you up and keep you going.

20   We become masters of our own interests, more connected to people like us over the internet, more instantly in touch with anything we want, need or think we want and think we need. Ever tried a Stairmaster in silence? But what are we missing? That hilarious shard of an overheard conversation that stays with you all day; the child whose chatter on the pavement takes you back to your early memories; birdsong; weather; accents; the laughter of others. And those thoughts that come not by filling your head with selected diversion, but by allowing your mind to wander aimlessly through the regular background noise of human and mechanical life.

21   External stimulation can crowd out the interior mind. Even the boredom that we flee has its uses. We are forced to find our own means to overcome it.

22   And so we enrich our life from within, rather than from white wires. It's hard to give up, though, isn't it.

23   Not so long ago I was on a trip and realised I had left my iPod behind. Panic. But then something else. I noticed the rhythms of others again, the sound of the airplane, the opinions of the taxi driver, the small social cues that had been obscured before. I noticed how others related to each other. And I felt just a little bit connected again and a little more aware.

24   Try it. There's a world out there. And it has a soundtrack all its own.

QUESTIONS FOR READING

1.   What is the "addictive cult" that Sullivan writes about?
2.   How has the iPod changed New York City?
3.   How has it changed people's lives?
4.   How did humans use to experience music? How has this changed?

QUESTIONS FOR REASONING AND ANALYSIS

1.   What is Sullivan's claim? State it as a problem.
2.   Why, according to the author, do people choose to be wired into a private musical world? What are they seeking? Is his argument convincing?

3. Sullivan develops his claim in large part by creating pictures and reflecting on causes and consequences. Analyze his writing strategies, considering examples, figurative language, sentence patterns, and word choice.

4. How would you describe the tone of the essay? Compare Sullivan and Will: How are their points similar? How do their writing styles differ?

QUESTIONS FOR REFLECTING AND WRITING

1. On a recent trip to New York City, I saw many people walking with little white wires; I also saw many, often together, talking on cell phones. I even saw tourists on Fifth Avenue taking pictures of people walking and talking on their phones. Dalton, Will, and Sullivan are all troubled by such images. Are you? Why or why not?

2. Sullivan concludes by inviting readers to turn off their iPods and listen to the "soundtrack" of the world around them. Does he mean this literally? Does he mean it *only* literally? Should we take his advice? Why or why not?

OUT OF THE WOODS: TODAY'S KIDS CAN'T SEE THE FOREST FOR THE MTV | JOEL ACHENBACH

For years the author of the *Washington Post* Sunday magazine column "Rough Draft," a column of humor and ideas, Joel Achenbach now writes for the paper's style section and maintains his blog, achenblog, on Washingtonpost.com. The following "Rough Draft" column was published May 29, 2005.

PREREADING QUESTIONS How do you spend your playing time—using electronic "toys" or exercising or playing sports or enjoying the outdoors? Do you think you have a good balance of activities in your life? Do you think most American young people do?

Because we need more to worry about, here comes a new ailment: Nature- 1 Deficit Disorder. It's the subject of a new book, by Richard Louv, called *Last Child in the Woods*, which basically says our children stay indoors too much, are alienated from nature and are going a little crazy.

Certainly every parent today has had the experience of begging a child to 2 go outside. The child always asks, "And do what?" And we always say, "Climb a tree!" From the way we talk about it, all we did as children was climb trees, build treehouses and swing on vines. We are arboreal. But these days, when you ask a child to climb a tree, there's a pause while the child tries to figure out a tactful way to point out that *people don't do that anymore*. It's like you've asked the kid to churn butter or boil up a vat of lye.

At some point you'll deliver the entire canned speech how, as a child, you 3 were always building forts, exploring forest trails, roasting squirrels over a fire, and so on, the classic Huck Finn sort of existence, and the only thing you'll forget to mention is that you were nearly fatally bored.

4   Face it, we had no choice but to play in the woods, because civilization hadn't yet invented Nintendo. Kids today don't know the crippling intensity of stupefaction that afflicted young people before the coming of personal computers and MTV. The boredom was like the ocean, and we were all at the bottom, our entire corpuscular beings compressed to 1/100th the normal size. Those "lazy summer days" were lazy for the reason that our blood had stopped circulating altogether.

5   During summer we had nothing to do all day other than eat Fritos and watch that zany Richard Dawson host "Family Feud." Or maybe it was Gene Rayburn over on "Match Game." Our parents' generation survived the Great Depression and World War II, but we survived "Love, American Style." Back then you got three channels, and a fourth if you could pull in that snowy station on the UHF band. The dreadfulness of the programs was commensurate with the absurd measures taken to improve their reception—tinfoil on the rabbit-ear antennae, someone climbing on the roof to adjust the aerial, turning the broken TV knob with pliers. (Younger readers: Whaaa??)

6   Our toys were also dysfunctional, particularly the electric race cars, which invariably fishtailed out of control and off the track entirely. We also had Hot Wheels cars that could roll down a plastic track, over and over, demonstrating for anyone who might doubt it the amazing force of gravity. We would try to filibuster away the boredom with Risk or Stratego or Clue, but eventually even that got dull, and we'd soon be digging up ant beds, trying to get red ants and black ants to fight one another.

7   I would use a metal curtain rod to whack a plastic ball around the yard as though I were Arnold Palmer. Once I decided to dig a swimming pool. It took me hours of hacking through the roots of pine trees and excavating the sandy Florida soil. Finally, I had my pool. I added water from a hose and got into it, and for a moment had a sense of the good life, of living it up, of being the kind of person who owns a pool.

8   And then I was just a boy up to his neck in muddy water.

9   My own kids are going to know what nature is about. I take them on long hikes. "Is this going to be a long hike?" they ask with trepidation. "A death march," I assure them. This may be one reason they associate nature with torture. Sometimes I ask them to help me work in the yard, and they always say, "Doing what?" and I say, "Maybe a little weeding," and they react as though I said we were going to skin and gut a rabbit. Children don't weed, which is just as well, because when you do persuade them to weed, they do it slower than the weeds actually grow.

10   They love the outdoors when it's sunny and the temperature is between 67 and 73 degrees and there are no bugs other than butterflies. They would prefer that there be less dirt, less earth, maybe Astro Turf instead of a lawn.

11   Untimely it's our fault, as parents, that we've let our kids get so soft and indoorsy. We overprotect. We hint, constantly, that the outside world is dangerous, that it's the land of speeding cars, heatstroke, lightning and creepy strangers. We've got to stop sending a message that says, in essence, "Go play outside, and watch out for serial killers."

Children need to get in touch with their inner animals. They need to go 12
wild. As soon as I'm done typing this column, I'm ordering my critters outside
to climb a tree. But, you know, not too high up.

QUESTIONS FOR READING

1. What is Achenbach's subject?
2. What is the author's view of childhood activities from the past?
3. What does he want his children to experience?
4. What anxieties are faced by today's parents?

QUESTIONS FOR REASONING AND ANALYSIS

1. What is the author's claim? Does he agree with Richard Louv that children are alienated from nature? How do you know?
2. Why is it perhaps difficult to know what Achenbach's position is? Note all points in the essay at which Achenbach seems to shift perspectives. Why does he do this? What does it accomplish?
3. What elements of humor are most amusing? Why?

QUESTIONS FOR REFLECTING AND WRITING

1. How do we get more children to love the outdoors and sports activities? What advice do you have for parents?
2. What are the advantages of activities in the outdoors? What are the disadvantages of playing electronic games and watching TV?

Michael Newman/PhotoEdit

Read: What is the boy doing? What toys does he have with him?

Reason: This photo appeared in a psychology textbook. Why do you suppose it appeared there?

Reflect/Write: How do children learn? Should they watch violent TV shows?

Violence and American Society

Are we a violent society? Is the United States any different from other countries? These are two good questions with which to begin this chapter's exploration. Richard Harwood has written ("America's Unchecked Epidemic," 12/1/97) that statistics show that U.S. cities have no more crime than other similar cities in western Europe but that we do have more violence, that is, a higher murder rate. Some social analysts argue that violence in the media is the cause, whereas others defend the media as only one of many influences on our lives and point out that although many watch violent television shows or listen to rap music, only a few act violently. Some argue that it is the American's love affair with guns that generates the violence—whereas gun owners insist that most handle their guns safely. One problem is agreeing on the causes; the other, even more difficult, problem is agreeing on solutions, because solutions are likely to mean restrictions of some sort. Emotions run high on the topics explored in this chapter; try to keep yours in check and read critically.

Prereading Questions

1. Are those concerned about the influence of media violence overreacting or should we be worried?
2. What groups seem especially vulnerable to the influences of media violence?
3. Do you have a position on "gun control"? Do you think that what you mean by this term is about the same as what most people mean?
4. What are the main sources of influence on your thinking about guns—family, friends, religion, reading on the topic? How strong are these influences—that is, how willing are you to listen to someone whose views may differ from yours?

Web Sites Related to This Chapter's Topic

Baby Bag

www.babybag.com/articles/amaviol.htm

Facts about media violence directed to parents but useful for others as well.

Interact/Jesuit Communication Project Site at the University of Oregon

http://interact.uoregon.edu/MediaLit/JCP/violence.html

Contains bibliographies and a list of video resources on media violence.

Handgun Control and the Center to Prevent Handgun Violence

www.handguncontrol.org

An organization founded in 1974 by Sarah Brady; the home page provides links to recent articles, news headlines, and facts about guns.

Center for Responsive Government

www.opensecrets.org/news/guns/index/htm

The center's Web page, called Gun Control vs. Gun Rights, provides information on congressional votes and contributions by lobbies to representatives.

National Rifle Association

www.nra.org

This large gun lobby provides commentary and news updates on gun-control issues.

GUNS, LIES, AND VIDEO | KAREN WRIGHT

Karen Wright is a freelance writer whose articles have appeared in *Discover*, the *New York Times Magazine, Scientific American*, and *Science*. The following article was published in the April 2003 issue of *Discover* magazine.

PREREADING QUESTIONS Have you played violent video games? Which do you think may have the greater influence on children: violence on television or violent video games? Why?

In a survey published earlier this year, seven of 10 parents said they would   1
never let their children play with toy guns. Yet the average seventh grader
spends at least four hours a week playing video games, and about half of those
games have violent themes, like Nuclear Strike. Clearly, parents make a distinction between violence on a screen and that acted out with plastic M-16s.
Should they?

Psychologists point to decades of research and more than a thousand stud-   2
ies that demonstrate a link between media violence and real aggression. Six
formidable public-health organizations, including the American Academy of
Pediatrics and the American Medical Association (AMA), issued a joint statement of concern in 2000. According to one expert's estimate, aggressive acts
provoked by entertainment media such as TV, movies, and music could account
for 10 percent of the juvenile violence in society. And scientists say they have
reason to believe that video games are the most provocative medium yet.

"With video games, you're not only passively receiving attitudes and be-   3
haviors, you're rehearsing them," says pediatrician Michael Rich, a former film-
maker and the current head of the Center on Media and Child Health at
Harvard University.

But the case isn't quite closed. Last year, psychologist Jonathan Freedman   4
of the University of Toronto published an outspoken indictment of some of the
field's most influential studies. The "bulk of the research does not show that
television or movie violence has any negative effects," he argues in *Media Violence and Its Effect on Aggression.* In a 1999 editorial titled "Guns, Lies, and
Videotape," the redoubtable British medical journal *The Lancet* admitted that
"experts are divided on the subject," and that "both groups can support their
views with a sizable amount of published work."

Those who grew up with the Three Stooges or Super Mario Brothers may   5
have trouble seeing their youthful pastimes in a sinister light. But televised violence has been a topic of national consternation almost from the first broadcast. Congressional hearings on the subject date back to 1952; the first
surgeon general's report addressing it was published in 1972. "We've been
studying it at least since then, but the studies haven't given us definite answers," says Kimberly Thompson, director of the Kids Risk Project at the School
of Public Health at Harvard. Thompson and others believe that the rise of TV
viewing in American households may be at least partly responsible for the
eightfold increase in violent crime in this country between 1960 and 1990. Today a typical kid spends two hours a day watching television, and children's
programs average between 20 and 25 violent acts per hour—four times as
many as adult programs. "The message that's going out to children is that
violence is OK or it's funny or it's somehow heroic," says Jeffrey G. Johnson,
a psychiatric epidemiologist at the College of Physicians and Surgeons at
Columbia University in New York.

6   Common sense argues that such exposure must have *some* effect. Designing studies to measure it is another story. So far, for example, there aren't any universal standards defining or quantifying violent content. Many early investigations simply proved that aggressive kids like to watch aggressive TV, without illuminating which tendency leads to which. And it's obvious that poverty, abuse, and ready access to weapons can put a child on the wrong path too.

7   One way to distinguish among the potential causes of juvenile violence is by studying large numbers of people over long periods of time. Last year, Johnson and his colleagues published results of a 17-year study following more than 700 kids from an average age of 6 to adulthood. They tallied the hours each subject spent in front of the tube and compared those numbers with subsequent acts of aggression, ranging from threats to criminal assault. The trends are clear, says Johnson: Kids who spent more than three hours a day watching television at age 14 were more than four times as likely to have acted aggressively by age 22 than kids who watched TV for less than an hour. The connection held up even after researchers accounted for other possible culprits, including poverty, neglect, and bad neighborhoods—and even among tube-addled females, who, like the rest of the subjects, were predominantly white and Catholic.

8   "It's not that TV just triggers aggression in aggressive people," Johnson says. "We saw this in 'nice' girls too."

9   Some laboratory studies hint that violent programming may lead to a malevolent state of mind. In one classic example, 5- to 9-year-olds were told they could press buttons that would either further or foil their playmates' attempts to win a game. Children who watched segments of the 1970s crime drama *The Untouchables* beforehand showed more willingness to hinder their peers' efforts than did those who watched a track race.

10   A recent analysis asserts that the correlation between virtual and actual aggression is stronger than those linking passive smoke and lung cancer, calcium intake and bone density, and exposure to lead and IQ. "The correlation between media violence and aggression is stronger than many of these things that we accept as fact—such as that if you eat lead paint chips, you'll become mentally retarded," says Rich.

11   Rich and others think video games could have an even greater effect than TV because they're interactive. The genre term "first-person shooter" says it all. "Often the interface that the child has with the game is a gun," says Rich. "A very realistic gun."

12   Yet only a handful of video-game studies have been published so far. At Iowa State University in Ames, social psychologist Craig Anderson tested college students' willingness to provide help to others after playing 20 minutes of benign games like Glider Pro or malignant ones like the pedestrian-plowing Carmageddon. Anderson timed how long his subjects waited before responding to a person left whimpering in the hallway after a staged attack. "The people who played a violent video game took about four times as long to come to the aid of the victim than people who played a nonviolent game," says Anderson.

Skeptics like Freedman say such correlations don't amount to causation 13 and that other, well-established risk factors such as poverty and neglect are important to consider. All true, Rich concedes. "But it's only correlations that suggest we should all wear seat belts," he says. "And [exposure to media violence] is one of the few risk factors that is easily controllable."

Laboratory studies have also been criticized for attributing to violent con- 14 tent behavior that could be a result of general physiological arousal. Any exciting program will cause an increase in heart rate, for example, and it's known that a racing heart can make an individual more bellicose. So Anderson took care to compare only video games that elevated his subject's heart rates to the same degree. And child psychologist John Murray of Kansas State University in Manhattan has used realtime MRI scans to observe whether violent content triggers unique patterns of brain activity. One group of Murray's kids watched fight scenes from *Rocky IV*; the other, an action-packed mystery called *Ghostwriter*. Only the boxing bouts activated an area in the right hemisphere called the right posterior cingulate, which may store long-term memories of trauma.

"We were surprised to find this, and worried," says Murray. He fears that 15 violent programs may pack the same emotional punch as actual violence. "It's not 'just' entertainment," he says. "It becomes a story about how life is."

The advertising industry is built on the faith that media content and con- 16 sumption can change human behavior, Rich points out. So why does society question the influence of dramatized violence? The obvious answer is that, despite the reams of paper devoted to its pernicious influence, violent entertainment remains entertaining. Americans appear to regard its consequences, whatever they may be, as an acceptable risk. Even hard-liners like Anderson, Rich, and the AMA don't recommend banning violent content. Instead, they lobby for greater parental awareness and control.

But maybe parents themselves should beware. The effect of violent media 17 on adults is still unexplored territory. And television news, a staple of grown-up media consumption, carries some of the nastiest carnage on the airwaves.

"There is some evidence that violent media has a bigger effect on children." Anderson says. "But there's no age group that's immune."

QUESTIONS FOR READING

1. Which may be the most "provocative medium," TV or video games? Why?
2. What is the "state of affairs" with regard to studies of TV violence?
3. How does violence in children's programs compare with violence in adult programs?
4. Why is it difficult to get a good study of the effect of TV violence?
5. What are some other possible causes of juvenile aggression?
6. What were the results of Johnson's long-term study of TV watching and adult aggression?

7. What did John Murray's studies reveal about increased brain activity?

8. Why do we seem unwilling to respond to what the studies seem to suggest?

QUESTIONS FOR REASONING AND ANALYSIS

1. What is Wright's subject? What is her claim?

2. Does Wright take a strong stand on the topic? Does she have a clear "leaning" on the issue? How do you know? What seems to be her primary purpose in writing?

3. What *kind* of evidence is offered to support the claim?

4. How does Wright qualify her position on the effects of media violence? Why is the qualification important?

5. One can see this as a problem/solution argument. What solutions does the author offer? What solutions are not being pushed by those concerned about the effects of media violence?

QUESTIONS FOR REFLECTING AND WRITING

1. Are you convinced by all the studies that there is at least a strong correlation between experiencing a lot of media violence and increased aggression? Why or why not? If you disagree, how would you rebut the evidence that Wright presents?

2. If the correlation is stronger than that between wearing seat belts and surviving an accident, why aren't we doing something to reduce the amount of violence to which children are exposed? If you were media czar, what would you do?

3. Who is put in charge of controlling children's access to media violence? Is this approach working? If not, why not?

HOLLOW CLAIMS ABOUT FANTASY VIOLENCE | RICHARD RHODES

A graduate of Yale University, fiction writer and journalist Richard Rhodes is the author of 18 books, has won many fellowships and awards, and has been a consultant to public television on nuclear issues. His study *The Making of the Atomic Bomb* (1986) won a Pulitzer Prize for nonfiction. One of his most recent books is *Why They Kill: The Discoveries of a Maverick Criminologist* (1997). The following column was published September 17, 2000, in the *New York Times*.

PREREADING QUESTIONS Given his title, what do you anticipate Rhodes's position on media violence and aggression to be? If media violence has little or no effect on violent behavior, what may be the causes of such behavior?

1   The moral entrepreneurs are at it again, pounding the entertainment industry for advertising its Grand Guignolesque confections to children. If exposure to this mock violence contributes to the development of violent behavior, then our political leadership is justified in its indignation at what the Federal Trade Commission has reported about the marketing of violent fare

to children. Senators John McCain and Joseph Lieberman have been especially quick to fasten on the FTC report as they make an issue of violent offerings to children.

But is there really a link between entertainment and violent behavior?   2

The American Medical Association, the American Psychological Association, the American Academy of Pediatrics and the National Institute of Mental Health all say yes. They base their claims on social science research that has been sharply criticized and disputed within the social science profession, especially outside the United States. In fact, no direct, causal link between exposure to mock violence in the media and subsequent violent behavior has ever been demonstrated, and the few claims of modest correlation have been contradicted by other findings, sometimes in the same studies.   3

History alone should call such a link into question. Private violence has been declining in the West since the media-barren late Middle Ages, when homicide rates are estimated to have been 10 times what they are in Western nations today. Historians attribute the decline to improving social controls over violence—police forces and common access to courts of law—and to a shift away from brutal physical punishment in child-rearing (a practice that still appears as a common factor in the background of violent criminals today).   4

The American Medical Association has based its endorsement of the media violence theory in major part on the studies of Brandon Centerwall, a psychiatrist in Seattle. Dr. Centerwall compared the murder rates for whites in three countries from 1945 to 1974 with numbers for television set ownership. Until 1975, television broadcasting was banned in South Africa, and "white homicide rates remained stable" there, Dr. Centerwall found, while corresponding rates in Canada and the United States doubled after television was introduced.   5

A spectacular finding, but it is meaningless. As Franklin E. Zimring and Gordon Hawkins of the University of California at Berkeley subsequently pointed out, homicide rates in France, Germany, Italy and Japan either failed to change with increasing television ownership in the same period or actually declined, and American homicide rates have more recently been sharply declining despite a proliferation of popular media outlets—not only movies and television, but also video games and the Internet.   6

Other social science that supposedly undergirds the theory, too, is marginal and problematic. Laboratory studies that expose children to selected incidents of televised mock violence and then assess changes in the children's behavior have sometimes found more "aggressive" behavior after the exposure—usually verbal, occasionally physical.   7

But sometimes the control group, shown incidents judged not to be violent, behaves more aggressively afterward than the test group; sometimes comedy produces the more aggressive behavior; and sometimes there's no change. The only obvious conclusion is that sitting and watching television stimulates subsequent physical activity. Any kid could tell you that.   8

As for those who claim that entertainment promotes violent behavior by desensitizing people to violence, the British scholar Martin Barker offers this   9 critique: "Their claim is that the materials they judge to be harmful can only influence us by trying to make us be the same as them. So horrible things will make us horrible—not horrified. Terrifying things will make us terrifying—not terrified. To see something aggressive makes us feel aggressive—not aggressed against. This idea is so odd, it is hard to know where to begin in challenging it."

10   Even more influential on national policy has been a 22-year study by two University of Michigan psychologists, Leonard D. Eron and L. Rowell Huesmann, of boys exposed to so-called violent media. The Telecommunications Act of 1996, which mandated the television V-chip, allowing parents to screen out unwanted programming, invoked these findings, asserting, "Studies have shown that children exposed to violent video programming at a young age have a higher tendency for violent and aggressive behavior later in life than children not so exposed."

11   Well, not exactly. Following 875 children in upstate New York from third grade through high school, the psychologists found a correlation between a preference for violent television at age 8 and aggressiveness at age 18. The correlation—0.31—would mean television accounted for about 10 percent of the influences that led to this behavior. But the correlation only turned up in one of three measures of aggression: the assessment of students by their peers. It didn't show up in students' reports about themselves or in psychological testing. And for girls, there was no correlation at all.

12   Despite the lack of evidence, politicians can't resist blaming the media for violence. They can stake out the moral high ground confident that the First Amendment will protect them from having to actually write legislation that would be likely to alienate the entertainment industry. Some use the issue as a smokescreen to avoid having to confront gun control.

13   But violence isn't learned from mock violence. There is good evidence—causal evidence, not correlational—that it's learned in personal violent encounters, beginning with the brutalization of children by their parents or their peers.

14   The money spent on the all the social science research I've described was diverted from the National Institute of Mental Health budget by reducing support for the construction of community mental health centers. To this day there is no standardized reporting system for emergency-room findings of physical child abuse. Violence is on the decline in America, but if we want to reduce it even further, protecting children from real violence in their real lives—not the pale shadow of mock violence—is the place to begin.

QUESTIONS FOR READING

1. What is Rhodes's subject?
2. Who claims that "mock violence" causes violent behavior? On what basis?
3. What has been in decline since the Middle Ages? What causes do historians find for the decline?

4. How does Rhodes challenge Centerwall's studies?
5. What is the author's objection to lab studies of children's behavior after watching violence on TV?
6. How does Rhodes account for the politicians' desire to blame the media for violence?

QUESTIONS FOR REASONING AND ANALYSIS

1. What is Rhodes's claim? Where does he state it?
2. How is his argument organized? What is he doing in paragraphs 3–11? In paragraphs 12–14?
3. What does the author think is the primary cause of violence? What, then, should we do to reduce violence?
4. Analyze the author's word choice in paragraph 1. How does his language create tone and express his attitude?

QUESTIONS FOR REFLECTING AND WRITING

1. Karen Wright (page 440) argues that common sense tells us that we must be influenced by media violence. Rhodes, in paragraph 9, presents the argument that the opposite should be true—we should react negatively to media violence. Who makes more sense to you? Why? How would you defend your view?
2. Rhodes argues that child abuse, especially by their parents, is the single most powerful cause of aggression; we learn violence from experiencing real violence. Do you agree? Why? Disagree? Why? You may want to do an Internet and/or electronic database search to find information on this topic.

WHAT'S UP DOC? A BLOODY OUTRAGE, THAT'S WHAT | KATHERINE ELLISON

A Pulitzer Prize-winning former foreign correspondent for Knight-Ridder Newspapers, Katherine Ellison is the author of three nonfiction books. Her latest is *The Mommy Brain: How Motherhood Makes Us Smarter* (2005). Her reaction to violent Internet cartoons appeared on October 23, 2005, in the *Washington Post*.

PREREADING QUESTIONS Do you use the Internet for "fun": games, porn, violent cartoons? Do you see any problems with such Internet sites?

The other day I found my 6-year-old son watching an Internet cartoon 1 called "Happy Tree Friends."

Purple daisies danced, high-pitched voices sang and animals with heart- 2 shaped noses waved cheerily. But then the music changed, and a previously merry green bear, wearing dog tags and camouflage, suffered an apparent psychotic breakdown.

Crrrrack!! went the neck of a purple badger, as the bear snapped off its 3 head. Blood splashed and continued flowing as the bear gleefully garroted a hedgehog, then finished off a whimpering squirrel already impaled on metal spikes by placing a hand grenade in its paw.

4   Joshua turned to me with a sheepish grin. He clearly had a sense that I wasn't happy about his new friends, but he couldn't have known what I was really thinking. Which was this: I'm a longtime journalist who reveres the First Amendment, and I live in California's liberal bastion of Marin County. Yet I would readily skip my next yoga class to march with right-wing fundamentalists in a cultural war against "Happy Tree Friends."

5   Just when parents thought we knew who our electronic enemies were—the shoot-'em-up video games, the TVs hawking trans fats, the pedophile e-mail stalkers and teenage-boobs Web sites—here comes this new swamp-thing mass entertainment: the Internet "Flash cartoon," pared down to pure shock value. Its music and animation are tuned to the Teletubbies set—that's its "joke." Its faux warning, "Cartoon Violence: Not for Small Children or Big Babies" is pure come-on—for those who can read. And it's easy to watch over and over again, reinforcing its empathy-dulling impact. That makes it particularly harmful to young psyches, UCLA neuroscientist Marco Iacoboni told me, because children are prompted to copy what they see—especially what they see over and over again. "Not only do you get exposed and desensitized; you're primed, facilitated, almost invited to act that way," maintains Iacoboni, whose expertise in the brain dynamics of imitation makes him an outspoken critic of media mayhem.

6   "Happy Tree Friends" appears tailor-made to sneak under the radar of blocking software (which can't filter images), unless parents are somehow Internet-savvy enough to know about the site and specifically ban it in advance. And it's certainly suited for the kind of viral contagion that caught up with my 6-year-old, who learned of the site from his 9-year-old brother, who first saw it over the shoulder of a teenage summer camp counselor.

7   But the bottom line is, well, the bottom line. In its web-cartoon class, "Happy Tree Friends" is a humongous moneymaker, as irresistible to big advertisers as it is to 6-year-olds. At last count, the site was drawing 15 million unique viewers a month, reaping $300,000 or more in ads for each new episode. It recently snagged a place on cable TV, while spawning DVDs, trademark mints, T-shirts and, inevitably, a planned video game.

8   Internet cartoons had their defining moment with the hilarious "This Land Is Your Land" 2004 election-year parody, featuring George W. Bush calling John Kerry a "liberal wiener" and Kerry calling Bush a "right-wing nut job" to the famous Woody Guthrie tune. By then, the beaten-down Web ad industry was already starting to ride a dramatic recovery, thanks to burgeoning new content and the increasing prevalence of high-quality, high-speed connections. The trend has brought some truly interesting material—and also such savage fare as the graphic cartoon "Gonads & Strife" and another inviting you to repeatedly electrocute a gerbil in a light socket. The Bush-Kerry feature by some reports was the most popular cartoon ever. "Happy Tree Friends," now in its fifth, most successful, year may well be the most lucrative.

Its narrative is as primitive as its business plan. In every episode, the cute   9
creatures are introduced, after which something awful happens to them, either
by gruesome accident, or at the paws of the psychopathic bear. The wordless
content appeals to a global audience, enhancing an already remarkably efficient delivery system for advertising. There's a running ad before each episode,
while banners flash below and beside the cartoons.

The show itself reportedly began as a potential ad—ironically, *against* media   10
violence according to Kenn Navarro, its co-creator. Navarro came up with the
idea while designing an eight-second spot for an educational company, to illustrate what kids *shouldn't* be watching. Indeed, 30 years of extensive research
underscores the link between TV violence and increased violent behavior
among viewers. One study equates the impact as larger than that of asbestos
exposure to cancer—a health risk that certainly moved our society to act. But
try telling that to "Happy Tree Friends" Executive Producer John Evershed,
CEO of Mondo Media in San Francisco.

Evershed, the father of three children, the youngest aged 2, told me dur-   11
ing a phone conversation that he wouldn't let them watch "Happy Tree
Friends." But then he argued that the cartoon wasn't really harmful. "It's like
'Tom & Jerry,'" he said. "I grew up on 'Tom & Jerry,' and I don't think I'm particularly aggressive."

Aggressive? AGGRESSIVE? Much as I'd like to, I can't fairly speak for Ever-   12
shed on this point, but I certainly do worry about the impact on my children.
As for "Tom & Jerry," I know "Tom & Jerry," and this is no "Tom & Jerry." "Tom
& Jerry" never pulled knives or tore heads off or used someone's intestines to
strangle a third party, just for starters.

"Tom & Jerry" also had creativity, with surprising plot twists and a richly   13
emotive score. Most importantly, "Tom & Jerry" had a conscience. Routinely,
Tom attacks Jerry and is punished for his aggression. In terms of human evolution, the 1940s classic is light-years ahead of "Happy Tree Friends," whose authors, Navarro and Rhode Montijo, have been quoted as saying, "If we are in
a room brainstorming episodes and end up laughing at the death scene, then
it's all good!"

Mad as I am, I'm actually not suggesting that the feds step in and ban this   14
cartoon. The basic freedom of the Internet is too precious, and government censorship too risky and probably not even feasible. The current rules—restrictions
on the major airwaves, but anything goes on the Web—will have to do.

But what about the big mainstream advertisers who've made "Happy Tree   15
Friends" such a wild success? I was startled, while watching the cartoon, to see
banner ads for companies including Toyota and Kaiser Permanente (which has
a new campaign they call "Thrive." Thrive, indeed!). Consumers ought to be
able to raise a stink, threaten a reputation, even wage boycotts in the face of
such irresponsibility. But many Internet ads enjoy the escape clause of being
random and ephemeral, as I found out when I called Hilary Weber, Kaiser's San
Francisco-based head of Internet marketing. Weber said she couldn't even
confirm that her company's ad had appeared.

16   "I can't replicate it," she said, adding that it would "take a lot of research" to establish whether Kaiser indeed had purchased such an ad. That, she explained, is because Kaiser, like many other big corporations, buys bulk ads through third parties—saving money, yet relinquishing control over where the ads end up.

17   Weber said she was concerned about Kaiser's reputation and planned to investigate further, yet declined to tell me the names of the third-party companies placing the firm's ads. So I then turned to Mika Salmi, CEO of Atom-Shockwave, which manages the ads on "Happy Tree Friends." Salmi, on his cell phone, said he couldn't, with confidence, name the third-party companies with whom he contracts, though he thought one "might" be Advertising.com. But when I contacted Lisa Jacobson, Advertising.com's spokeswoman, she declined to name advertisers not already listed on her firm's Web page. "We actually don't think we're the best fit for this piece," Jacobson wrote me by e-mail. "You'll probably need to speak with companies like Kaiser and Toyota directly. But thanks for thinking of us . . ."

18   In our brief telephone conversation, Evershed told me he thinks parents have the ultimate responsibility to shield their kids from media violence. In the abstract, I certainly agree with that, but I admit I sometimes wonder if I'm actually doing my kids a disservice by spending so much time and energy chasing them off the Internet, while coaching them in empathy, manners and the Golden Rule. Because if most of their peers, who lack the luxury of moms with time to meddle, are gorging on "Happy Tree Friends," it would probably serve them better to be trained to defend themselves with firearms and karate.

19   Still, for now at least, I refuse to be overwhelmed by the sheer magnitude of what society expects from parents, with so little support in return.

20   So I'd like to offer just two public suggestions. Why can't summer camps and afterschool programs more closely supervise Internet use? And why can't Kaiser and other big companies start crafting contracts that specifically stipulate that their ads never, ever end up on sites like "Happy Tree Friends"?

21   Meanwhile, I'm talking to other parents because the first step in this peaceful war is to realize we're not alone. Together, we may even manage to subvert our culture's embrace of shock for shock's sake, one gory excess at a time.

QUESTIONS FOR READING

1.   "Happy Tree Friends" is Ellison's primary example; what is her subject?

2.   What is the problem with "Happy Tree Friends"? How does it differ from "Tom & Jerry"?

3.   How did the author's 6-year-old discover the cartoon?

4.   What did the author's research reveal about the Web site's advertisers?

5.   What suggestions for change does Ellison propose?

QUESTIONS FOR REASONING AND ANALYSIS

1. What does Ellison *not* want to happen to the Internet? Why?
2. What is her claim?
3. In paragraph 18, Ellison writes that her sons might be better off with "firearms and karate" than encouragement in empathy and the Golden Rule. Does she really mean this? Why does she write it?

QUESTIONS FOR REFLECTING AND WRITING

1. Do you think that Ellison's suggestions will be helpful? Why or why not?
2. Should there be federal controls on Internet content? Why or why not?
3. If there are no controls, how will we protect youngsters from unhealthy sites? Or, should we not worry about protecting them? Explain and defend your position.

HOW HIP-HOP MUSIC LOST ITS WAY AND BETRAYED ITS FANS | BRENT STAPLES

Holding a doctorate in psychology from the University of Chicago, Brent Staples is currently an editorial writer, specializing in politics and culture, for the *New York Times.* He has written a memoir, *Parallel Time: Growing Up in Black and White* (1994), and his essays and columns are widely published. The following column appeared on nytimes.com on May 12, 2005.

PREREADING QUESTIONS Do you listen to hip-hop music? If yes, what is its appeal for you? If no, why not? Whether yes or no, are you ever bothered by either the lyrics or the public personas of some of the rappers?

African-American teenagers are beset on all sides by dangerous myths 1 about race. The most poisonous one defines middle-class normalcy and achievement as "white," while embracing violence, illiteracy and drug dealing as "authentically" black. This fiction rears its head from time to time in films and literature. But it finds its most virulent expression in rap music, which started out with a broad palette of themes but has increasingly evolved into a medium for worshiping misogyny, materialism and murder.

This dangerous narrowing of hip-hop music would be reason for concern 2 in any case. But it is especially troubling against the backdrop of the 1990's, when rappers provoked a real-world gang war by using recordings and music videos to insult and threaten rivals. Two of the music's biggest stars—Tupac Shakur and the notorious B.I.G.—were eventually shot to death.

People who pay only minimal attention to the rap world may have thought 3 the killings would sober up the rap community. Not quite. The May cover of the hip-hop magazine *Vibe* was on the mark when it depicted fallen rappers standing among tombstones under the headline: "Hip-Hop Murders: Why Haven't We Learned Anything?"

4   The cover may have been prompted in part by a rivalry between two rappers that culminated in a shootout at a New York radio station, Hot 97, earlier this spring. The events that led up to the shooting show how recording labels now exploit violence to make and sell recordings.

5   At the center of that Hot 97 shootout was none other than 50 Cent, whose given name is Curtis Jackson III. Mr. Jackson is a confessed former drug dealer who seems to revel in the fact that he was shot several times while dealing in Queens. He has also made a career of "beef" recordings, in which he whips up controversy and heightens tension by insulting rival artists.

6   He was following this pattern in a radio interview in March when a rival showed up at the station. The story's murky, but it appears that the rival's entourage met Mr. Jackson's on the street, resulting in gunfire.

7   Mr. Jackson's on-air agitation was clearly timed to coincide with the release of "The Massacre," his grotesquely violent and misogynist compact disc. The CD cover depicts the artist standing before a wall adorned with weapons, pointing what appears to be a shotgun at the camera. The photographs in the liner notes depict every ghetto stereotype—the artist selling drugs, the artist in a gunfight—and includes a mock autopsy report that has been seen as a covert threat aimed at some of his critics.

8   "The Massacre" promotion raises the ante in a most destructive way. New artists, desperate for stardom, will say or do anything to win notice—and buzz—for their next projects. As the trend escalates, inner-city listeners who are already at risk of dying prematurely are being fed a toxic diet of rap cuts that glorify murder and make it seem perfectly normal to spend your life in prison.

9   Critics who have been angered by this trend have pointed at Jimmy Iovine, the music impresario whose Interscope Records reaped millions on gangster rap in the 90's. Mr. Iovine makes a convenient target as a white man who is lording over an essentially black art form. But also listed on "The Massacre" as an executive producer is the legendary rapper Dr. Dre, a black man who happens to be one of the most powerful people in the business. Dr. Dre has a unique vantage point on rap-related violence. He was co-founder of Death Row Records, an infamous California company that marketed West Coast rap in the 1990's and had a front-row seat for the feud that led to so much bloodshed back then.

10   The music business hopes to make a financial killing on a recently announced summer concert tour that is set to feature 50 Cent and the mega-selling rap star Eminem. But promoters will need to make heavy use of metal detectors to suppress the kind of gun-related violence that gangster artists celebrate. That this lethal genre of art has grown speaks volumes about the industry's greed and lack of self-control.

11   But trends like this reach a tipping point, when business as usual becomes unacceptable to the public as a whole. Judging from the rising hue and cry, hip-hop is just about there.

QUESTIONS FOR READING

1. What seems to be the dominant message of today's hip-hop music?

2. What continues to go on in the rap world? How does this affect the studios? How are some rappers contributing to the situation?

3. How is the public reacting to rappers' behavior and their music, in Staples's view?

QUESTIONS FOR REASONING AND ANALYSIS

1. What is Staples's claim?

2. Staples's argument rests upon a key assumption; what is that assumption? Is it one that Staples can expect readers to accept?

3. What is to be gained by not addressing a perhaps controversial assumption upon which your argument rests? What is risked by this strategy?

QUESTIONS FOR REFLECTING AND WRITING

1. Staples blames the music industry along with specific rappers for "greed and lack of self-control." Ellison blames companies for providing ad money for violent Internet cartoons. Is there any way to reduce violent media by going after the companies that make money off of this violence? What suggestions do you have?

2. Some would argue that the world created by rap music is a fantasy, and listeners know this. Thus the violence has no real impact on listeners. What is your position on the impact of violent rap on listeners? Explain and defend your position.

SUPREMACY CRIMES | GLORIA STEINEM

Editor, writer, and lecturer, Gloria Steinem has been cited in *World Almanac* as one of the 25 most influential women in America. She is the cofounder of *Ms.* magazine and of the National Women's Political Caucus and is the author of a number of books and many articles. The following article appeared in *Ms.* in the August/September 1999 issue.

PREREADING QUESTIONS Who are the teens who commit most of the mass shootings at schools? Who are the adults who commit most of the hate crimes and sadistic killings? What generalizations can you make about these groups based on your knowledge from media coverage?

You've seen the ocean of television coverage, you've read the headlines: "How to Spot a Troubled Kid," "Twisted Teens," "When Teens Fall Apart." 1

After the slaughter in Colorado that inspired those phrases, dozens of 2 copycat threats were reported in the same generalized way: "Junior high students charged with conspiracy to kill students and teachers" (in Texas); "Five honor students overheard planning a June graduation bombing" (in New York); "More than 100 minor threats reported statewide" (in Pennsylvania). In response, the White House held an emergency strategy session titled "Children, Violence, and Responsibility." Nonetheless, another attack was soon reported: "Youth With 2 Guns Shoots 6 at Georgia School."

3   I don't know about you, but I've been talking back to the television set, waiting for someone to tell us the obvious: it's not "youth," "our children," or "our teens." It's our sons—and "our" can usually be read as "white," "middle class," and "heterosexual."

4   We know that hate crimes, violent and otherwise, are overwhelmingly committed by white men who are apparently straight. The same is true for an even higher percentage of impersonal, resentment-driven, mass killings like those in Colorado; the sort committed for no economic or rational gain except the need to say, "I'm superior because I can kill." Think of Charles Starkweather, who reported feeling powerful and serene after murdering ten women and men in the 1950s; or the shooter who climbed the University of Texas Tower in 1966, raining down death to gain celebrity. Think of the engineering student at the University of Montreal who resented females' ability to study that subject, and so shot to death 14 women students in 1989, while saying, "I'm against feminism." Think of nearly all those who have killed impersonally in the workplace, the post office, McDonald's.

5   White males—usually intelligent, middle class, and heterosexual, or trying desperately to appear so—also account for virtually all the serial, sexually motivated, sadistic killings, those characterized by stalking, imprisoning, torturing, and "owning" victims in death. Think of Edmund Kemper, who began by killing animals, then murdered his grandparents, yet was released to sexually torture and dismember college students and other young women until he himself decided he "didn't want to kill all the coeds in the world." Or David Berkowitz, the Son of Sam, who murdered some women in order to feel in control of all women. Or consider Ted Bundy, the charming, snobbish young would-be lawyer who tortured and murdered as many as 40 women, usually beautiful students who were symbols of the economic class he longed to join. As for John Wayne Gacy, he was obsessed with maintaining the public mask of masculinity, and so hid his homosexuality by killing and burying men and boys with whom he had had sex.

6   These "senseless" killings begin to seem less mysterious when you consider that they were committed disproportionately by white, non-poor males, the group most likely to become hooked on the drug of superiority. It's a drug pushed by a male-dominant culture that presents dominance as a natural right; a racist hierarchy that falsely elevates whiteness; a materialist society that equates superiority with possessions; and a homophobic one that empowers only one form of sexuality.

7   As Elliott Leyton reports in *Hunting Humans: The Rise of the Modern Multiple Murderer,* these killers see their behavior as "an appropriate—even 'manly'— response to the frustrations and disappointments that are a normal part of life."

In other words, it's not their life experiences that are the problem, it's the impossible expectation of dominance to which they've become addicted.

This is not about blame. This is about causation. If anything, ending the 8 massive cultural cover-up of supremacy crimes should make heroes out of boys and men who reject violence, especially those who reject the notion of superiority altogether. Even if one believes in a biogenetic component of male aggression, the very existence of gentle men proves that socialization can override it.

Nor is this about attributing such crimes to a single cause. Addiction to the 9 drug of supremacy is not their only root, just the deepest and most ignored one. Additional reasons why this country has such a high rate of violence include the plentiful guns that make killing seem as unreal as a video game; male violence in the media that desensitized viewers in much the same way that combat killers are desensitized in training; affluence that allows maximum access to violence-as-entertainment; a national history of genocide and slavery; the romanticizing of frontier violence and organized crime; not to mention extremes of wealth and poverty and the illusion that both are deserved.

But it is truly remarkable, given the relative reasons for anger at injustice 10 in this country, that white, non-poor men have a near-monopoly on multiple killings of strangers, whether serial and sadistic or mass and random. How can we ignore this obvious fact? Others may kill to improve their own condition, in self-defense, or for money or drugs; to eliminate enemies; to declare turf in drive-by shootings; even for a jacket or a pair of sneakers—but white males addicted to supremacy kill even when it worsens their condition or ends in suicide.

Men of color and females are capable of serial and mass killing, and com- 11 mit just enough to prove it. Think of Colin Ferguson, the crazed black man on the Long Island Railroad, or Wayne Williams, the young black man in Atlanta who kidnapped and killed black boys, apparently to conceal his homosexuality. Think of Aileen Carol Wuornos, the white prostitute in Florida who killed abusive johns "in self-defense," or Waneta Hoyt, the upstate New York woman who strangled her five infant children between 1965 and 1971, disguising their cause of death as sudden infant death syndrome. Such crimes are rare enough to leave a haunting refrain of disbelief as evoked in Pat Parker's poem "jonestown": "Black folks do not/Black folks do not/Black folks do not commit suicide." And yet they did.

Nonetheless, the proportion of serial killings that are not committed by 12 white males is about the same as the proportion of anorexics who are not female. Yet we discuss the gender, race, and class components of anorexia, but not the role of the same factors in producing epidemics among the powerful.

The reasons are buried deep in the culture, so invisible that only by revers- 13 ing our assumptions can we reveal them.

Suppose, for instance, that young black males—or any other men of color— 14 had carried out the slaughter in Colorado. Would the media reports be so willing to describe the murderers as "our children"? Would there be so little discussion about the boys' race? Would experts be calling the motive a mystery, or condemning the high school cliques for making those young men feel like "outsiders"? Would there be the same empathy for parents who gave the murderers luxurious homes, expensive cars, even rescued them from brushes with the law? Would there be as much attention to generalized causes, such as the dangers of violent video games and recipes for bombs on the Internet?

15   As for the victims, if racial identities had been reversed, would racism remain so little discussed? In fact, the killers themselves said they were targeting blacks and athletes. They used a racial epithet, shot a black male student in the head, and then laughed over the fact that they could see his brain. What if that had been reversed?

16   What if these two young murderers, who were called "fags" by some of the jocks at Columbine High School, actually had been gay? Would they have got the same sympathy for being gay-baited? What if they had been lovers? Would we hear as little about their sexuality as we now do, even though only their own homophobia could have given the word "fag" such power to humiliate them?

17   Take one more leap of the imagination: suppose these killings had been planned and executed by young women—of any race, sexuality, or class. Would the media still be so disinterested in the role played by gender-conditioning? Would journalists assume that female murderers had suffered from being shut out of access to power in high school, so much so that they were pushed beyond their limits? What if dozens, even hundreds of young women around the country had made imitative threats—as young men have done—expressing admiration for a well-planned massacre and promising to do the same? Would we be discussing their youth more than their gender, as is the case so far with these male killers?

18   I think we begin to see that our national self-examination is ignoring something fundamental, precisely because it's like the air we breathe: the white male factor, the middle-class and heterosexual one, and the promise of superiority it carries. Yet this denial is self-defeating—to say the least. We will never reduce the number of violent Americans, from bullies to killers, without challenging the assumptions on which masculinity is based: that males are superior to females, that they must find a place in a male hierarchy, and that the ability to dominate someone is so important that even a mere insult can justify lethal revenge. There are plenty of studies to support this view. As Dr. James Gilligan concluded in *Violence: Reflections on a National Epidemic,* "If humanity is to evolve beyond the propensity toward violence . . . then it can only do so by recognizing the extent to which the patriarchal code of honor and shame generates and obligates male violence."

19   I think the way out can only be found through a deeper reversal: just as we as a society have begun to raise our daughters more like our sons—more like whole people—we must begin to raise our sons more like our daughters—that is, to value empathy as well as hierarchy; to measure success by other people's welfare as well as their own.

20   But first, we have to admit and name the truth about supremacy crimes.

QUESTIONS FOR READING

1. What kinds of crimes is Steinem examining? What kinds of crimes is she excluding from her discussion?

2. What messages, according to Steinem, is our culture sending to white, non-poor males?

3. How does Elliott Leyton explain these killers' behavior?

4. What is the primary reason we have not examined serial and random killings correctly, in the author's view? What is keeping us from seeing what we need to see?

5. What do we need to do to reduce "the number of violent Americans, from bullies to killers"?

QUESTIONS FOR REASONING AND ANALYSIS

1. What is Steinem's claim? Where does she state it?

2. What kind of argument is this; that is, what *type* of claim is the author presenting?

3. What is her primary type of evidence?

4. How does Steinem qualify her claim and thereby anticipate and answer counterarguments? In what paragraphs does she present qualifiers and counterarguments to possible rebuttals?

5. How does the author seek to get her readers to understand that we are not thinking soundly about the mass killings at Columbine High School? Is her strategy an effective one? Why or why not?

QUESTIONS FOR REFLECTING AND WRITING

1. Steinem concludes by writing that we must first "name the truth" about supremacy violence before we can begin to address the problem. Does this make sense to you? How can this be good advice for coping with most problems? Think of other kinds of problems that this approach might help solve.

2. Do you agree with Steinem's analysis of the causes of serial and random killings? If yes, how would you add to her argument? If no, how would you refute her argument?

SMALL WEAPONS POSE A GLOBAL THREAT | ROBERT F. DRINAN

A Jesuit friar, Robert F. Drinan is a professor at Georgetown University law school whose specialties include constitutional law, legal ethics, and international human rights. He has published articles in law reviews and opinion journals and is the author of a number of books including *The Mobilization of Shame: A World View of Human Rights* (2001). The following article was published September 30, 2005, in the *National Catholic Reporter.*

PREREADING QUESTIONS How many Americans die of AIDS each year? How many die in car accidents? How many die from murder, accidents, and suicides caused by handguns? If you don't know which number is the highest, do some research.

1   The United Nations has scheduled another meeting on the proliferation of small weapons around the world to be held in Vienna Oct. 10–21. This is the continuation of a program initiated by the world community to do something about the estimated 640 million small guns and pistols currently in circulation.

2   The first global conference on the dangers of unregulated small arms was held in 2001. The United Nations Firearms Protocol adopted by the U.N. General Assembly in 2001 is the first legally binding convention on small weapons to be adopted at the global level. The protocol that emerged entered into force in 2005: It criminalizes certain illicit trafficking. But it failed to provide criteria for the transfer of weapons or even for the civilian possession of such weapons. The 2001 protocol will be discussed and updated at the conference in Vienna.

3   While the legal framework to limit or curb the manufacture or transfer of pistols, shotguns or rifles is still not clear, the awareness of the dangers of these weapons has increased remarkably. Some 1,300 people are killed daily by small arms and light weapons. A large number of these casualties are refugees or other unprotected people.

4   The impact of unregulated small arms is tragic in the United States, where citizens possess millions of handguns. More than 20,000 persons are killed in the United States each year by small weapons. About 11 children in America are murdered by guns every day.

5   At a recent meeting on the topic of handgun possession throughout the globe, sparked in part by the activities of a significant number of nongovernmental organizations, it was pointed out that the civilian population of Iraq now has countless handguns and small weapons after the military disbanded and their weapons ended up in the hands of civilians. The situation contributed to the death of about 170,000 Iraqi civilians and the disabling of many more. The use of handguns in the assault and rape of women in the Balkans is well documented.

6   U.N. Secretary-General Kofi Annan has worked diligently to implement the 2001 U.N. accord on combating illegal trade in small weapons. Mr. Annan has praised Africa, which has been trying to agree on a moratorium on the importation, manufacture and transfer of light weapons. He has also appointed a committee on small arms made up of the 16 U.N. entities.

7   Pakistan estimated that it is awash with small arms and light weapons and that it may have the largest number of guns per capita in the world; the government has estimated that some 5 million people have been killed there as a result of gun violence during the past 20 years. Pakistan has signed the U.N. Firearms Protocol, but it has not yet ratified it.

8   The government of Canada is seeking to place restrictions on the manufacture and export of guns from that country. Officials in Ottawa have asserted that supplying the arms fueling Third-World conflicts also adds to the arsenals of criminal groups operating in developing countries. Some gun owners in Canada are protesting the proposed requirements that all firearms manufactured in Canada be marked and that their export be regulated.

9   The ever more vigorous efforts around the world to curb the violence of the 640 million handguns in use will not find much encouragement in the

United States. A large number of the guns in the world were manufactured in whole or in part in the United States. A significant number of the guns used in civil wars, in violence against women and by groups of criminals can be traced to the United States.

The antigun groups in the United States favor restrictions, but they have 10 little encouragement from the White House or Congress.

A sample of the resistance to any such move can be seen in the filing of a 11 bill by the new Republican senator from Louisiana, David Vitter. His bill would cut back the financing of the United Nations by the United States if the United Nations curbs the international trafficking of guns. The National Rifle Association has in effect endorsed the bill filed by Sen. Vitter.

The danger in the proliferation of small arms around the world has been 12 compared to the presence of land mines in more than 50 countries. That threat has been significantly curtailed by the work of an aggressive and creative nongovernmental organization, the International Campaign to Ban Landmines, which received the Nobel Peace Prize in 1997.

Could other private groups curtail the awful dangers of the presence of 13 640 million guns on the planet? Perhaps America's bishops could speak to this problem with the prophetic voice that was present in their 1983 pastoral on the threats of nuclear war. The U.S. government isn't going to do it.

QUESTIONS FOR READING

1. How many small guns are in circulation worldwide?
2. What groups of people are at greatest risk from these guns?
3. How many have been killed in Pakistan in the last 20 years from small guns?
4. What are the UN and Canada doing to address the issue?
5. What is the United States doing?

QUESTIONS FOR REASONING AND ANALYSIS

1. What is Drinan's claim? Where does he state it?
2. What *type* of argument is this? Does it work?
3. What is the tone of this argument? What kind of voice do you "hear"? What makes Drinan's approach compelling?

QUESTIONS FOR REFLECTING AND WRITING

1. Which statistic most surprises you? Why?
2. Should the United States take responsibility for reducing the number of small arms in the world: Why or why not?
3. If you wanted to curb small arms, how would you proceed? What steps would you take?

FALSE CHOICES ON GUN SAFETY | JONATHAN COWAN

> Jonathan Cowan is the president of Americans for Gun Safety, a nonprofit organization that supports the rights of Americans to own guns but seeks to improve gun safety. His article was published in the *Washington Post* on October 10, 2002.
>
> **PREREADING QUESTION** What was happening in the greater Washington, DC, area in the fall of 2002 that might have led to a debate on gun safety or stricter enforcement of gun laws?

1   A sniper has taken aim, spreading death and fear in Maryland, Virginia and the District of Columbia. Yet despite this terror campaign, there is no movement from Congress or the administration for tougher gun safety laws. This is in sharp contrast to the congressional response to the 1999 Columbine shootings, which led to an immediate Senate vote to require background checks for purchasers at gun shows. Why the difference, and what does it say about the future of gun safety in America?

2   Unfortunately, after the 2000 elections, most Democrats concluded that calling for new gun laws could cost them critical white male votes. Meanwhile, the Bush White House sought to extend its balancing act on guns, taking specific steps to please the gun lobby but publicly maintaining support for limited new gun safety measures to preserve its "compassionate conservative" identity. Thus the bipartisan consensus on guns: Back a narrow agenda that emphasizes the protection of gun rights and tougher enforcement of existing laws, rather than the need for new gun laws.

3   While such an approach may seem to make political sense, it represents an abdication of a critical responsibility of the national government: public safety. Moreover, it offers voters a false choice on two counts—gun rights or gun safety, and new gun laws or tougher enforcement. America can protect gun rights and promote gun responsibility only with new laws and vigorous enforcement of existing laws.

4   With more than 500,000 gun-related crimes each year, America cannot focus exclusively on punishing people once they commit gun-related crimes. It must also attempt to stop guns from falling into the wrong hands in the first place—which means breaking up the black market in illegal guns. According to data from the Bureau of Alcohol, Tobacco and Firearms (ATF), this market—a chain of crooked dealers and petty street traffickers—supplies most of the guns used in crime. Congress and the Bush administration must design a real national strategy aimed at waging a war against this mostly American illegal gun cartel.

5   A comprehensive national gun-trafficking strategy would have three components;

6   (1) A federal enforcement effort focused not just on punishing criminals after the fact—the thrust of the administration's worthy but one-sided Project Safe Neighborhoods—but also on busting up the chain of illegal guns, from manufacturers to dealers to street merchants. The president ought to create a

fully staffed and funded national gun-trafficking task force, similar to the corporate fraud effort launched months ago.

(2) New federal enforcement tools that would beef up the ability of ATF to crack down on gun trafficking, including more tracing of crime guns and ballistics fingerprinting to link slugs and casings to the owners of the guns that fired them. Despite the bipartisan calls for tough enforcement, ATF is hamstrung by laws—such as the one limiting unannounced inspections of gun dealers to one a year—that appear to be intended to make it difficult to punish those at the top of the gun-trafficking chain.

(3) Legislation to close the most glaring loopholes in federal law. This would include requiring background checks at all gun shows for all gun sales and fixing the deeply flawed background check system—a system that has allowed thousands of criminals to obtain guns because they were among the 35 million prohibited buyers whose names were not yet in an instant-check database. During the 2000 campaign, candidate George W. Bush supported some version of these measures, and gun rights and gun safety supporters such as Sens. John McCain, Chuck Schumer, Joe Lieberman and Larry Craig and Reps. Carolyn McCarthy and John Dingell have bipartisan bills to do exactly this. Compromise in closing these dangerous loopholes ought to be achievable.

Opponents will say that new gun laws—or vigorous enforcement of existing laws—violate gun rights. But America has passed six major federal gun laws since the 1930s, and the number of guns in private hands has quintupled. They will say that gun laws don't work, but the Brady law has already stopped 700,000 prohibited buyers from purchasing guns. They will say that guns don't kill, people do—and they are right—but that doesn't mean we shouldn't try to keep guns out of the hands of people who are most likely to commit a crime or kill with a gun.

The country deserves a war on illegal guns, not empty rhetoric about tough enforcement and silence in the face of senseless shootings. Such a war may not have saved the lives lost in the Washington area during the past week, but it will save others—without taking away the guns or diminishing the gun rights of a single law-abiding American.

QUESTIONS FOR READING

1. What is Cowan's subject?
2. What has been the post-2000-election bipartisan consensus on guns?
3. How has the political response to the sniper been different from the response to the Columbine shootings?
4. How many gun-related crimes occur each year in the United States?
5. How do most criminals obtain their guns?
6. What is Cowan's recommendation? Summarize his three-step plan in your own words.

QUESTIONS FOR REASONING AND ANALYSIS

1. What is Cowan's claim? Where does he state it? How does it challenge the current bipartisan consensus on guns?

2. What two points does the author present in paragraphs 3 and 4 as the primary defense of his proposed plan? Do these points make sense to you? Why or why not?

3. What rebuttals of his proposal does he anticipate? How does he answer them?

QUESTIONS FOR REFLECTING AND WRITING

1. Evaluate Cowan's proposal. Does his three-step plan seem sensible? Feasible? If you agree with Cowan, how would you try to sell the plan to your representative and senators? If you disagree with the proposal, what argument would you present to your elected officials to dissuade them from supporting the plan?

2. The powerful gun lobby seems to be a major stumbling block to new gun safety laws and to better enforcement of existing laws. What do you think of this situation? Should powerful lobbies control the ways that elected officials vote or the bills that are presented for consideration? Are lobbies and political action committees, with their money and single-issue approach, significantly altering a party system of compromise and consensus? If so, is this good or bad for our political system? These are some key questions on which to reflect and write.

Read: What is "happening" in the cartoon? Which figure speaks the caption? Who is Hootie?

Reason: What actions and elements of the cartoonist's style make the cartoon funny? What is the point of the cartoon?

Reflect/Write: Should the PGA play at clubs that discriminate in their memberships?

CHAPTER 16

Sports Talk— Sports Battles

Title IX changed the appearance of the playing field. Not only has professional soccer achieved new status and appeal in this country, but women's soccer teams also have been front-page news. But has Title IX leveled the playing field? Rick Reilly and award-winning cartoonist Pat Oliphant look at the place of women in professional tennis and golf—where it seems that the "paying field" is either not level or not even available to women.

Part of the issue with Title IX is that it funnels money for athletics away from men's college sports, and yet men's college sports is big business, bringing, for Division I schools at any rate, both fame and big bucks through television coverage of their men's football and basketball teams. To garner the fame and dollars, though, one must have great teams—not teams that have fun, build strong bodies, and enhance school spirit but teams that win championships. Some would argue that men's college football and basketball teams have become farm leagues for the pros with the loss of the original idea of the college athlete and such romantic goals as building body, mind, and spirit. If this is true, is it a problem? If it is a problem, is there any way to return to an earlier time when college athletes were also expected to take serious courses and get a degree? And, is this competitive emphasis ruining kids' sports?

Prereading Questions

1. What are the requirements of Title IX for college athletic departments? Has Title IX been successful in giving women greater opportunities to participate in sports, not just in college but in high schools and recreation youth leagues as well?

2. Should professional athletes be given equal pay in a sport or be paid according to their popularity or draw, regardless of gender?

3. Should the PGA play at clubs that restrict women from membership? Should private clubs—which get a tax break—be allowed to discriminate in membership selection on the basis of gender, race, or religion?

4. Should the NCAA demand higher academic credentials for would-be college athletes and expect college players to carry typical course loads leading to graduation?

Web Sites Related to This Chapter's Topic

NCAA Online

http://www.ncaa.org

All about the organization and about college sports—stats galore.

Gender Equity in Sports

http://balliwick.lib.uiowa.edu/ge/index.html#200

Site sponsored by the University of Iowa contains information on legal issues connected to Title IX plus resources and links.

There are also Web sites for the PGA (Professional Golf Association) and USTA (United States Tennis Association), in addition to ESPN.com and all of your favorite sports sites.

WHO'S KILLING KIDS' SPORTS? | DAVID OLIVER RELIN

An award-winning journalist, David Relin is a contributing editor to both *Parade* and *Skiing* magazines. He collaborated with Greg Mortenson in the writing of *Three Cups of Tea* (2006), the story of Mortenson's struggles in Pakistan to build schools. The following article was published in *Parade* on August 7, 2005.

PREREADING QUESTIONS Did you participate in sports as a youngster? If so, was it fun or highly competitive? Are youth sports too competitive today?

Two years ago, when he was still in high school, pro basketball prospect   1
LeBron James inked an endorsement contract with Nike worth between $90
million and $100 million. Five days later, the $1 million contract Nike offered to
Maryland soccer prodigy Freddy Adu seemed almost ordinary, except for one
detail—Freddy was just 13 years old.

In the summer of 2003, Jeret Adair, a 15-year-old pitcher from Atlanta,   2
started 64 games with his elite traveling baseball team—more than most pro
players pitch in an entire season. After the ligament in his elbow snapped, he
had to undergo reconstructive surgery, a process once reserved for aging
professional pitchers. In 2004, his doctor, James Andrews, performed similar
surgery on 50 other high school pitchers.

Last March, Valerie Yianacopolus of Wakefield, Mass., was sentenced to   3
one year of probation, including 50 hours of community service, and ordered
to watch a sportsmanship video after she was found guilty of assaulting an 11-
year-old boy who was cheering for the opposing team at her son's Little
League game.

And in June, according to state police, Mark Downs, the coach of a youth   4
T-ball team near Uniontown, Pa., allegedly offered one of his players $25 to
throw a baseball at the head of a 9-year-old disabled teammate so the injured
boy wouldn't be able to play in an upcoming game. League rules mandate that
every healthy child play at least three innings. "The coach was very competitive," said State Trooper Thomas B. Broadwater. "He wanted to win."

A SPORTS CULTURE RUN AMOK

Across the country, millions of children are being chewed up and spit out by   5
a sports culture run amok. With pro scouts haunting the nation's playgrounds in
search of the next LeBron or Freddy, parents and coaches are conspiring to run
youth-sports leagues like incubators for future professional athletes. Prepubescent
athletes are experimenting with performance-enhancing drugs. Doctors are reporting sharp spikes in injuries caused by year-round specialization in a single
sport at an early age. And all too often, the simple pleasure of playing sports is
being buried beneath cutthroat competition.

"If I had to sum up the crisis in kids' sports," says J. Duke Albanese, Maine's   6
former commissioner of education, "I'd do it in one word—adults."

Some adults, Albanese says, are pushing children toward unrealistic goals   7
like college sports scholarships and pro contracts. According to National Collegiate Athletic Association (NCAA) statistics, fewer than 2% of high school
athletes will ever receive a college athletic scholarship. Only one in 13,000 high
school athletes will ever receive a paycheck from a professional team.

"There is a terrible imbalance between the needs kids have and the needs   8
of the adults running their sports programs," says Dr. Bruce Svare, director of
the National Institute for Sports Reform. "Above all, kids need to have fun. Instead, adults are providing unrealistic expectations and crushing pressure."

As a result, Svare says, at a time when an epidemic of obesity is plaguing   9
the nation's youth, 70% of America's children are abandoning organized sports

by age 13. "The only way to reverse this crisis," Svare argues, "is to fundamentally rethink the way America's kids play organized sports."

IS CHANGE POSSIBLE?

10   Many communities *are* trying to change the way they approach children's sports. Florida's Jupiter-Tequesta Athletic Association, facing a rash of violent behavior by sports parents, now requires them to take an online course on how to behave at their children's athletic events. School officials in Connecticut, concerned about the toll of too much focus on a single sport, instituted a statewide ban on students playing on a private travel team during the same season they play their sport in high school.

11   But no reform effort is more aggressive than that of the state of Maine, where educators, student athletes and others have teamed up to launch a counterrevolution called Sports Done Right. Led by J. Duke Albanese and Robert Cobb, dean of the University of Maine's College of Education, and funded by a federal grant secured by U.S. Sen. Susan M. Collins, the project aims to radically remake Maine's youth-sports culture and provide a model that the rest of America might emulate.

THE MAINE CHALLENGE

12   Their first step is a sweeping campaign to dial down the kind of competition that leads many kids to drop out of sports at an early age. "I was a high school football coach—I know how badly communities want their teams to win," Albanese says. "We're not saying there's anything wrong with competition. We're saying what's appropriate at the varsity level is out of bounds in grade school and middle school. That's a time to encourage as many children as possible to play. Period."

13   To do that, the Sports Done Right team held statewide summit meetings before producing an action plan. It chose 12 school districts as the program's pilot sites, but so many other districts clamored to participate that it is now under way in dozens more.

14   The program has identified core principles that it insists must be present in a healthy sports environment for kids, including good sportsmanship, discouragement of early specialization and the assurance that teams below the varsity level make it their mission to develop the skills of every child on every team, to promote a lifelong involvement with sports.

15   Sports Done Right's second task is to attack the two problems it says are most responsible for the crisis in kids' sports—the behavior of parents and coaches.

PROBLEM #1: OUT-OF-CONTROL ADULTS

16   The behavior of adults has been at the center of the debate about reforming kids' sports ever since 2002, when Thomas Junta of Reading, Mass., was convicted of beating Michael Costin to death during an argument at their sons' youth hockey practice. "I've watched adult civility in youth sports spiral downward since the early 1990s," says Doug Abrams, a law professor at the Univer-

sity of Missouri, who has tracked media reports of out-of-control sports parents for more than a decade. "At one time, adults who acted like lunatics were shunned as outcasts. But today, they are too often tolerated."

The nearly 100 Maine students *Parade* interviewed recited a litany of inci- 17 dents involving adults behaving badly, including examples of their own parents being removed from sporting events by police. Nate Chantrill, 17—a shot-putter and discus thrower at Edward Little High School in Auburn and a varsity football player—volunteers to coach a coed fifth-grade football team. "One game, a parent flipped out that we didn't start his daughter," Chantrill recalls. "He was screaming, using bad language and saying she's the best player out there. Parents take this stuff way too seriously. Fifth-grade football is not the Super Bowl. It's a place for your kid to learn some skills and have fun. One parent can ruin it for all the kids."

That's why each Sports Done Right district is holding training sessions to 18 define out-of-bounds behavior at sporting events and requiring the parents of every student who plays to sign a compact promising to abide by higher standards of sportsmanship.

PROBLEM #2: POOR COACHING

Dan Campbell, who has coached Edward Little's track team to two state 19 championships, says he sees too many of his peers pressing to win at all costs and neglecting their primary responsibility—to educate and inspire children. "One coach can destroy a kid for a lifetime," he says. "I've seen it over and over."

"I was at an AAU basketball game where the ref gave the coach a techni- 20 cal and threw him out of the game," says Doug Joerss, who was the starting center on Cony High School's basketball team. "Then the coach swung at the ref. The kids ended up on the floor, getting into a huge brawl. You look up to coaches. Kids think, 'If it's OK for them to do it, it's OK for me to do it.'"

A campaign to improve the quality of coaching is at the center of Sports 21 Done Right. "The most powerful mentors kids have are coaches," J. Duke Albanese says. "Coaches don't even realize the extent of their influence." He disparages the national trend to offer coaches salary incentives based on their won-lost records. Instead, Sports Done Right recommends compensation based on their level of training. And each pilot school district is encouraged to send coaches to continuing-education classes in subjects like leadership and child psychology.

EXPORTING GOOD SENSE

Educators in 30 states have requested more information from Sports Done 22 Right. "We think a small place like Maine is a perfect place to get kids' sports culture under control," said Albanese. "And if we can do that, maybe we can export the good sense Maine is famous for to the rest of the country."

An example of that good sense recently occurred at a Sports Done Right 23 pilot site. "An influential parent, a guy who volunteers to coach sixth-grade basketball, wanted the kids divided into an A and a B team so he could coach just the elite kids," says Stephen Rogers, the principal of Lyman Moore Middle School. "I said we weren't going to separate the kids and discourage half of them. We were going to encourage all of our interested kids to play."

24   "But we won't win the championship," the parent complained.

25   "I don't really care," Rogers said. "We're not talking about the Celtics. We're talking about sixth-graders."

QUESTIONS FOR READING

1. What is Relin's subject? State it as a problem.
2. What seems to be the major cause of the problem?
3. How many high school athletes go on to pro careers?
4. How many youngsters are playing sports after age 13?
5. What are the steps in Maine's Sports Done Right program?

QUESTIONS FOR REASONING AND ANALYSIS

1. What is the author's claim? Where does he state it?
2. What type of argument is this?
3. What strategy does Relin use in his opening four paragraphs? What makes this an effective opening?

QUESTIONS FOR REFLECTING AND WRITING

1. Do you agree with Relin that we have a serious problem in youth sports? If not, why not?
2. Do you agree that the behavior of many parents is unacceptable? If so, what must be done to give the game back to kids?
3. Why do parents and coaches and kids get so competitive? What sources in our culture may be influencing the situation?

MY PLAN TO PUT THE COLLEGE BACK IN COLLEGE SPORTS | GORDON GEE

With degrees in both law and education from Columbia University, Gordon Gee is currently president of Vanderbilt University. Active on many commissions and boards, Gee is also the former president of Brown University, Ohio State University, the University of Colorado, and West Virginia University. His views on college football were published in the *Washington Post* on September 21, 2003.

PREREADING QUESTIONS How important is college football to you? Why is it important to many students and alums? Is it *too* important—especially at Division I colleges?

1   I like to win. I also like to sleep at night. But after 23 years leading universities, I find it increasingly hard to do both.

This has been the most ignominious year in recent memory for college ² sports. We've seen coaches behaving badly, academic fraud, graft, possibly even murder. Clearly, the system is broken, and fixing it will require more than sideline cheering.

That's why, last week, we at Vanderbilt announced that we would replace our ³ traditional athletic department with a new body that is more connected to the mission of the university and more accountable to the institution's academic leadership. We'll no longer need an athletic director. We're not eliminating varsity sports, mind you, or relinquishing our membership in the highly competitive Southeastern Conference. Rather, we're making a clear statement that the "student-athlete"—a term invented decades ago when college sports was faced with another seemingly endless parade of scandals—belongs back in the university.

Many athletic departments exist as separate, almost semi-autonomous ⁴ fiefdoms within universities and there is the feeling that the name on the football jersey is little more than a "franchise" for sports fans. As Bill Bowen and Sarah Levin point out in their new book, *Reclaiming the Game: College Sports and Educational Values*, student-athletes are increasingly isolated, even at the best schools in the country. They do not participate in the extracurricular activities that are so important for personal growth. They miss out on opportunities to study abroad or have internships. They spend too much time in special athletic facilities that are off-limits to the rest of the student body. And their world can too often be defined by coaches' insatiable demands for practice and workout sessions.

True, this is the cost of staying competitive in college sports, where tens of ⁵ millions of dollars are at stake. But should it be? Over the years I have gotten to know thousands of student-athletes. They are as different as any group of individuals could be. What they have in common, though, is a sense that they missed out on an important part of the college experience by focusing only on sports. They also lose out by being stripped of their responsibilities as citizens of the university when we say that "all will be forgiven" as long as their performance on the field is up to snuff.

This must change. At Vanderbilt, that means ensuring that every student, ⁶ every athlete, is part of a vibrant academic and social community.

Shifting Vanderbilt's athletics program to our division of student life and ⁷ university affairs is merely a step—perhaps bold, perhaps quixotic—in the much-needed reform of intercollegiate athletics. We took this step mindful that Vanderbilt is in an unusual position. It is a highly selective private university with an athletics program untarnished by scandal; our student-athletes graduate at rates that are among the best in the country; and we have loyal, generous supporters who have blessed us with excellent facilities. We can do things here that other universities can't or won't.

I will say this: After our announcement, I received many phone calls from ⁸ college presidents who said, "You go, Gordon. Walk off the cliff, and if you succeed, we will be right behind."

In recent years, there have been a number of well-meaning and forceful ⁹ efforts to reform college athletics, but they have not gone far enough. It is time for all those who are concerned about the future of our enterprise to get serious about addressing the crisis of credibility we now face. College presidents, working together, should commit themselves to the following reforms:

10   First, all students who participate in intercollegiate sports should be required to meet the requirements of a core curriculum. The "permanent jockocracy" has for too long made a mockery of academic standards when it comes to athletes. We need to end sham courses, manufactured majors, degree programs that would embarrass a mail-order diploma mill, and the relentless pressure on faculty members to ease student-athletes through their classes.

11   Second, colleges should make a binding four-year commitment to students on athletic scholarships. One of the dirty secrets of intercollegiate athletics is that such scholarships are renewed year-to-year. A bad season? Injury? Poor relationship with a coach? Your scholarship can be yanked with very little notice. Rather than cynically offering the promise of academic enrichment, colleges should back up the promise so long as a student remains in good academic standing.

12   Third, the number of athletic scholarships a school can award should be tied to the graduation rates of its athletes in legitimate academic programs. If a school falls below a threshold graduation rate, it should be penalized by having to relinquish a certain number of scholarships for the next year's entering class. A version of this proposal is part of a reform package now snaking its way through the NCAA.

13   Fourth, graduation rates should be tied to television and conference revenues. If money is the mother's milk of college athletics, then access to it should be contingent on fulfilling the most basic mission of a university—educating students.

14   Finally, college presidents and others need to take a good look at the system we have created for ourselves, in which the professional sports leagues have enjoyed a free feeder system that exploits young people and corrupts otherwise noble institutions. We have maintained the fantasy for far too long that a big-time athletics program is for the students, the alumni, and, at public universities, even for the legislators. It is time for us to call it what it has sadly become: a prep league for the pros, who have taken far more than they have given back. We should demand nothing less than a system in which student-athletes are an integral part of the academic institutions whose names and colors they so proudly wear on game day.

QUESTIONS FOR READING

1. What is Gee's subject? (State it as a problem.)
2. Why, according to Gee, are there problems in college athletics? What, specifically, are the problems for the athletes themselves?
3. What is Gee changing at Vanderbilt?
4. What are the five reforms he recommends for all colleges?

QUESTIONS FOR REASONING AND ANALYSIS

1. What is Gee's claim? (State it as a problem/solution assertion.)

2. In paragraph 7, Gee explains the first move toward reform that he has made at Vanderbilt. He then describes his university. Why? How are his remarks conciliatory? What does he seek to accomplish?

3. Examine Gee's grounds. He does not provide statistics and refers to current problems in only a general way. Why? What does he expect his readers to know?

4. What is Gee's reasoning in support of his claim? What values have been lost in the development of college athletics? Why must they be reinstated?

QUESTIONS FOR REFLECTING AND WRITING

1. Do you agree with the author that many college athletes are shortchanged in their college experience and education? Do you agree that this is a problem? Why or why not?

2. If you agree with President Gee that there are problems, do you agree with his reform proposals? Study them both individually and as a package. Do you accept them all? If so, why? If not, how would you challenge his proposed solution? Do you think that some of the package is useful and workable, but not the whole package? If so, why? What would you support? What reject? Think of yourself as in a debate with Gee, discussing each item of his reform package, one at a time.

3. What is the role or purpose of the university? What is the role or purpose of sports as a part of the university?

EDUCATION, ATHLETICS: THE ODD COUPLE | SALLY JENKINS

A sportswriter for the *Washington Post* for a number of years, Sally Jenkins left in 1990 to work at *Sports Illustrated* and write a number of books, mostly about sports figures. She has a book written with Dean Smith about his years in college basketball. In 2000 she published, with Lance Armstrong, *It's Not about the Bike: My Journey Back to Life*. She has also written *Men Will Be Boys: The Modern Woman Explains Football and Other Amusing Male Rituals* (1996). In 2000 Jenkins returned to the *Post*. The following column appeared there on September 13, 2002.

PREREADING QUESTIONS Explain Jenkins's title; what does it suggest her attitude will be toward college and athletics? How big are the problems with college athletics?

It's knee-jerk time in college athletics again. Ohio State and Maurice 1
Clarett are examples of everything wrong, while Vanderbilt has preserved the sanctity of the academic temple. For days now, we've enjoyed black and white thinking, moral certainty, and stern reform-mindedness. But the last thing we can apply to college sports any more is absolutism. Nothing is as good or bad as it seems—nor is the Ivy League, as it turns out.

Whatever you're sure of on the subject of college sports, you will certainly 2
question it after the publication of a book called *Reclaiming the Game*, by

William G. Bowen and Sarah A. Levin. The book, which will appear next week from Princeton University Press, takes a hard-eyed look at the Ivies and other so-called "elite" colleges and reaches some startling conclusions: Recruited athletes are four times more likely to be admitted to the Ivies than other students, they have lower SAT scores than their peers by 119–165 points, and they chronically under-perform academically. Seem familiar? It sounds like Division I-A.

3   In other words, even the Ivies are getting it wrong?

4   It depends on your view. Every scandal, controversy and ill in the NCAA always boils down to the same question: What are college athletics really for? What are they supposed to be, and what values should they represent? This is where the real trouble begins, because college athletics have increasingly become a matter of competing moralities. And they have always been extremely human, corrupt, and mistaken-prone endeavors, too.

5   People who want to apply pat reforms or even a consistent philosophy to college athletics are simply barking up the wrong tree—and perhaps the worst tree we can bark up these days is to assume that some schools have found the higher moral ground.

6   One of the more interesting conclusions reached by Bowen, a former president of Princeton who is now head of the Andrew W. Mellon Foundation, and co-author Levin, is that academic hypocrisy is rampant.

7   "Truth-telling is important, especially for institutions that pride themselves, as colleges and universities should, on inculcating respect for evidence and for their own unequivocal commitments to honest rendering of facts and to faithful reporting," they write. "But there is something unsettling about reading stories describing the 'purity' of athletics at the non-scholarship schools when so many of their leaders are well aware of the compromises that are being made in fielding teams. There is enough cynicism today about the capacity of institutions (whether they be corporations, churches, colleges and universities, governmental entities, or foundations) to be what they claim to be . . ."

8   It's difficult to read that passage and not think about Vanderbilt, which has presented itself as a paragon of academic virtue this week, while Ohio State, a very good school, is having a difficult time fighting off the taint of academic scandal. Ohio State Athletic Director Andy Geiger suspended Clarett for accepting money against NCAA rules. Meantime, Vanderbilt Chancellor Gordon Gee announced he was doing away with his athletic department.

9   But it turns out Gee's great reform basically amounts to a symbolic name change—he's not cutting any sports, or scholarships. He accompanied it with a speech that smacked of grandstanding. "For too long, college athletics has been segregated from the core mission of the university," Gee intoned.

10   Gee sounds like a personable, well-intentioned guy. But he doesn't sound anymore personable or well-intentioned than Geiger, who insists Ohio State is basically clean and the Clarett affair was isolated.

11   "I hope we get investigated up the yin-yang," Geiger said. "I'd submit we don't have a systemic issue, we have a maverick deal, and it's been more than difficult. But it's not because we're corrupt."

The funny thing is, Gee wasn't always so reform-minded and he's no stranger 12
to big athletic programs. He once was president of Ohio State, where he actually
hired Geiger, and he also presided over West Virginia, and Colorado, when the
Buffaloes enjoyed both national championship and scandal under Bill McCartney.
You have to wonder if, now that he's at Vandy, he's simply playing to a new crowd.

Geiger has a varied resume too; he's been all over Division I-A, and his record 13
for integrity is pretty good. He was the former athletic director at Stanford University, until he got tired of what he calls "Stanford-speak" and decided he
wanted to work for public universities. He went to Maryland, and then Ohio State.

Here is the central problem with any reform of college athletes: The proper 14
role of college sports on a campus depends entirely on what group is evaluating the question. Is the athletic scholarship a scam, or a tool of affirmative action? Some say Ohio State was wrong to give a scholarship to Clarett, a guy
who didn't even want to be there. Others such as Geiger argue that to do away
with scholarships and academic exceptions would be to kill opportunity. He
also maintains that "athletics have some intellectual content unto themselves."

There are differences even within the same programs. Ohio State, for in- 15
stance, will have 105,000 people at the football stadium on Saturday, and
about 200 at a women's soccer game. Yet both sports are supposed to be part
of the same school, program, values, effort, and management.

Any truly intelligent discussion of college athletics may require what Ger- 16
maine Greer once called, in a discussion completely unrelated to football,
"myriad-mindedness." Increasingly, if we're going to solve the "problem" of
athletics we have to accept differing value systems and accept the tension between competing moralities. The NCAA is comprised of public schools, and
private, of large corporatized universities and small precious intellectual
havens, of Northeastern industrials and Midwestern agriculturals—and it's the
clash between them that makes their games so interesting.

What are college sports for? Maybe we should first ask what a college is for. 17
The chief event that occurs in college is the emancipation of your head. The main
undertaking of a student is understanding, and this is why no one expects him or
her to come up with anything resembling consistency; they're too busy questioning and rejecting. College is also where scruple and low-level crime duel. Youth
carouses un-enforced by parents or much else in the way of authority. Hopefully,
the outcome of this formative emancipation is the development of one's own interior hall monitor. But sometimes it produces a communist, or a car wreck.

This is the risk we take by having colleges at all. The same principle could 18
be applied to games that undergraduates play.

QUESTIONS FOR READING

1. What is Jenkins's subject? (Be more precise than "college sports.")
2. What does the book *Reclaiming the Game* reveal? From the title, what do you think
   is the authors' view regarding college sports?

3.   What, according to Jenkins, is at the core of all debates over college athletics?

4.   Who are Andy Geiger and Maurice Clarett? What happened at Ohio State?

5.   What is the connection between Geiger at Ohio State and Chancellor Gee at Vanderbilt? What seems to be the author's attitude toward Gee?

6.   Why is discussion of reforming college athletics difficult, in Jenkins's view?

7.   What, in her view, are colleges for?

QUESTIONS FOR REASONING AND ANALYSIS

1.   What is Jenkins's claim? What are the main points in her argument?

2.   Why does Jenkins present information about Gee's past positions and appointments? How does this serve as evidence in support of her thesis?

3.   Explain the concept of "myriad-mindedness" as it applies to solving problems of college sports.

4.   Examine Jenkins's images in paragraph 17. What makes them effective in support of her concept of college?

QUESTIONS FOR REFLECTING AND WRITING

1.   Evaluate Jenkins's argument. Do you agree with her approach to problems in college athletics? If yes, why? If no, how would you rebut her argument?

2.   The sports pages offer an almost continual flow of rule breaking and scandals (including, in 2003, murder and attempted cover-up at Baylor University) in college athletics, yet Jenkins argues that it is not as bad as it seems. How might you defend her assessment? If you disagree, how would you respond to her?

3.   What is the role or purpose of the university? What is the role or purpose of sports as part of the university? Do we have to "accept the tension between competing moralities," or can (should?) we agree on the basic values and goals of college and college sports?

DISADVANTAGE, WOMEN | RICK REILLY

A graduate of the University of Colorado, Rick Reilly is an award-winning sports writer and columnist. He is a senior writer for *Sports Illustrated* and has coauthored several autobiographies of sports figures. He has also written two novels, including *Missing Links* (1996). His latest nonfiction book is *Who's Your Caddy?* (2003). The following column was posted on SI.com July 10, 2001.

PREREADING QUESTIONS At the four major tennis tournaments, where the men and women are playing at the same time and the purses are the largest, are the players paid equally or not? Does this issue matter to you? Should it?

Did you hear what happened to Venus Williams after she won Wimbledon 1
on Sunday? She was robbed! She had $52,923 ripped right out of her purse! In
broad daylight!

Instead of getting $705,109, which men's winner Goran Ivanisevic received 2
on Monday, she earned about a new Lexus less. You talk about a grass ceiling.
Not only that, but it also happened to Jennifer Capriati this year at the French
Open. The dinosaurs who run that tournament gave her $29,306 less than the
men's winner, Gustavo Kuerten.

Leave it to tennis to jack the only group of players anybody wants to see. 3
You don't believe me? Let's compare, shall we?

In the women's Top 10, you have the riveting Slam Sisters—Venus and Ser- 4
ena Williams—the tempestuous Martina Hingis, the sports story of the year in
Capriati, the tragic Monica Seles and the big Teddette bear, Lindsay Daven-
port, not to mention, at No. 11, the world's leading cause of whiplash, Anna
Kournikova. In the men's Top 10 you have nine guys you couldn't pick out of a
Pinto full of Domino's delivery men, plus Andre Agassi. Combined, most of the
Top 10 men have the Q rating of a lamp. Seriously, is Yevgeny Kafelnikov a ten-
nis player or something you cure with penicillin?

The women play amazing, long, topsy-turvy, edge-of-your-seat points. The 5
men hit 140-mph aces nobody can see, and then ask for a towel. Everything is
serve and towel, serve and towel. It's like being at a cocktail party with Boris
Yeltsin. In a third-round Wimbledon match Ivanisevic had 41 aces against Andy
Roddick, who had 20. It is unclear how the rest of the points were won because
the official statistician fell asleep. If men's tennis is to be saved, somebody had
better start decompressing these guys' balls. Then something has to be done
about the equipment.

The women we know by first names: *Can you believe what Martina said* 6
about Serena? They hate one another, insult one another's fathers, insult their
own fathers, bump each other on changeovers, wear body-hugging Technicolor
dresses designed by Edward Scissorhands and generally provide more story
lines than six months' worth of *All My Children,* all of which will come splatter-
ing out later this month in a new book about the women's tour, *Venus Envy.*

The men, on the other hand, stand around killing the grass. Except for 7
Agassi, they all look like the slackers you have to shoo away from the door of
your Starbucks. They are so dull, they make tennis writers bang their heads
against their laptops. From what we know, there are no books coming out
about the men. They are lucky to make the white pages.

Did you know that the French Open women's final on NBC last month drew 8
almost twice as many viewers as the men's? Did you know that Capriati's quar-
terfinal Wimbledon match last week pulled in 25% more viewers than Pete
Sampras's fourth-rounder the day before? Did you know that of the 10 most-
searched-for athletes on Lycos during one week leading up to Wimbledon, four
were women's tennis stars: Kournikova (No. 1), Hingis (5), Jelena Dokic (7) and
Serena Williams (8)? None were male tennis players. Did you know that John
McEnroe has said, "*Men* may eventually have to sue for equal pay"?

9   Did you know that last year, for the first time in history, more women's matches were played on the Stadium court at the U.S. Open than men's matches? Did you know that this year the U.S. Open, for the first time, has scheduled a final for prime time, and it's the women's, not the men's? Did you know that in an MSNBC survey last year, almost 70% of respondents preferred women's tennis to men's?

10   So what if the men play five sets to the women's three? *Ishtar* is longer than *Casablanca*. Which would you rather see? The pooh-bahs at the Australian Open and U.S. Open figured all this out long ago and raised their women's prize money to match the men's.

11   To recap, the women are more popular, make more headlines and play more entertaining tennis than the men, yet the women made $790,919 less over the Wimbledon fortnight than the men and $428,637 less at the French.

12   Wait, I take it all back. The women should not make as much as the men—they should make *more*.

QUESTIONS FOR READING

1. What is Reilly's subject? What is the issue?
2. What is Reilly's view of the women tennis stars? What is his view of the male players? How do their games differ?
3. Which majors pay the players equally? Which do not?

QUESTIONS FOR REASONING AND ANALYSIS

1. Analyze Reilly's argument. What is his claim? What type of evidence does he provide? What are his reasons for defending his claim?
2. What counterargument does Reilly anticipate? How does he rebut it?
3. Examine his style and tone. What is clever about his opening? What rhetorical strategies does he use?

QUESTIONS FOR REFLECTING AND WRITING

1. Has Reilly presented a convincing argument? If yes, what makes it convincing to you? If no, how would you rebut his argument? (Think: What type of audience might accept your counterargument? What readers might reject your reasoning?)
2. If tennis players should get equal pay at the major tournaments, does it follow that all professional players should get equal pay in their sports, regardless of gender? Consider other sports—soccer or golf or basketball, for example. Plan your argument, using one or more of these other sports. (You may want to go online to seek some current stats similar to Reilly's.)

SOLVING THE TITLE IX PROBLEM | FRANK DEFORD

A native of Baltimore, Maryland, Frank Deford is a sportswriter, biographer, and novelist. He has written biographies of athletes such as Billie Jean King, Bill Tilden, and Arthur Ashe. His eighth novel is *An American Summer.* A member of the Hall of Fame of the National Sportscasters and Sportswriters Association, Deford is a senior contributing columnist for *Sports Illustrated,* a commentator for NPR's *Morning Edition,* and a correspondent on HBO's *RealSports with Bryant Gumbel.* His column on Title IX appeared on *SI Online* June 19, 2002.

PREREADING QUESTIONS   What is good about the enforcing of Title IX? What problems have come with its enforcement? Are these problems that can be solved?

1 No question about equality is more nettlesome than Title IX's application to athletics. The law says, indisputably, that equally proportionate amounts of athletic department money must be spent on both sexes. Because of that, in the years since the law started to be rigorously enforced, the number of girls playing sports in high school is up almost tenfold and the number of young women playing sports in college is up five times.

2 But this great advance in female participation has come at a price for *male* athletes. College wrestling has been emasculated: 170 teams cut. Collegiate male gymnastics is headed for extinction, and the elimination of men's tennis, track and swimming—even baseball—continues apace. Critics of Title IX—which is 30 years old this week—call it reverse discrimination and "affirmative androgyny."

3 Look, goes the men's argument, more boys than girls care about sports. To demand matching amounts of athletic funding for females is a tortured distortion of fairness. Would it make any sense to require equal funding for males in, say, dress making?

4 But then the counter argument: The reason fewer girls want to play sports is that they never had the opportunity before. Give them the same chances as boys, and just as many of them will want to play.

5 For me, that's a more persuasive case. In this professed land of opportunity, where discrimination against women in sports was overwhelming for so long, it's simply dog-in-the-manger to deny females the option of organized athletics because they haven't had the chance to find out if they'd like it.

6 Anyway, all this obscures the elephant in the room: football. It is that rare male sport that has no female analogue. It also uses far more bodies and gobbles up far more money than any other sport. No schools would have to eliminate wrestling and gymnastics if they'd just trim some of the fat off football.

7 But football is a favored sport and politically powerful. Alumni love it and old-boy athletic directors protect it. Football is a banner that schools wave at the beginning of the educational year to rally the troops, students and alumni alike. It identifies and unifies and helps fund-raise . . . if for all the wrong reasons. So,

even if school football is indefensibly expensive as a *sport,* it is a distinct part of our American culture that serves various non-athletic purposes. Not even basketball fulfills those, and, anyway, basketball requires fewer players and there are women's teams as well as men's.

8   No, football is the cheese that stands alone, and it would make sense for it to be separated from all other sports. Football is primarily a spectator sport. It's show biz. It has nothing to do with wrestling, men's or women's track, tennis, gymnastics or all other sports, which are intended primarily to be *played* by students, not *watched* by ticket buyers. Call football what it is: either an arm of annual giving or a form of institutional advertising. But get it out of the athletic department. Then, for both men and women, Title IX would have what it doesn't have now: a level playing field.

QUESTIONS FOR READING

1. What is Deford's subject?
2. What has been the result of Title IX for females? For males?
3. Which college sport creates the biggest problem for college athletic departments needing to achieve gender equity?
4. What are the apparent purposes of football? How does it differ from other college sports?

QUESTIONS FOR REASONING AND ANALYSIS

1. What is Deford's claim? Where does he state it? What does he gain by the placing of his claim?
2. What is the argument against Title IX? What is the argument for Title IX? Which is the more persuasive for Deford? Why?
3. Evaluate Deford's solution to the problems caused by Title IX given the cost of college football. How does he defend his solution?

QUESTIONS FOR REFLECTING AND WRITING

1. Has the author offered, in your view, a sensible, feasible solution to the conflicts created by Title IX demands? If yes, why? If not, how would you refute his argument?
2. Before Deford's solution could be implemented, it would have to stand a court test—that it does not violate the equity standard established by Title IX. How would you defend the solution in court?
3. To implement Deford's solution, college administrators and athletic directors would also have to accept the idea of separating football from the other college sports. Why might they have trouble accepting this solution? How would you try to convince them to embrace the solution?

THE GREATNESS GAP | CHARLES KRAUTHAMMER

A graduate of Harvard Medical School and board certified in psychiatry, Charles Krauthammer is a syndicated columnist and a regular on the political talk show *Inside Washington.* He has won a Pulitzer Prize for political commentary. The following column appeared in *Time* magazine on July 1, 2002.

PREREADING QUESTIONS   What does Krauthammer mean by the "greatness gap"? Who would you list as among the world's greatest athletes?

1   There is excellence, and there is greatness—cosmic, transcendent, Einsteinian. We know it when we see it, we think. But how to measure it? Among Tiger Woods' varied contributions to contemporary American life is that he shows us how.

2   As just demonstrated yet again at the U.S. Open, Woods is the greatest golfer who ever lived. How do we know? You could try Method 1: Compare him directly with the former greatest golfer, Jack Nicklaus. For example, take their total scores in their first 22 major championships (of which Nicklaus won seven, Woods eight). Nicklaus was 40 strokes over par; Tiger was 81 under—an astonishing 121 strokes better.

3   But that is not the right way to compare. You cannot compare greatness directly across the ages. There are so many intervening variables: changes in technology, training, terrain, equipment, often rules and customs.

4   How then do we determine who is greatest? Method 2: The Gap. Situate each among his contemporaries. Who towers? Who is, like the U.S. today, a hyperpower with no second in sight?

5   The mark of true transcendence is running alone. Nicklaus was great, but he ran with peers: Palmer, Player, Watson. Tiger has none. Of the past 11 majors, Woods has won seven. That means whenever and wherever the greatest players in the world gather, Woods wins twice and the third trophy is distributed among the next, oh, 150.

6   In 2000–01, Woods won four majors in a row. The *Washington Post*'s Thomas Boswell found that if you take these four and add the 2001 Players Championship (considered the next most important tournament), Tiger shot a cumulative 1,357 strokes—55 strokes better than the next guy.

7   To find true greatness, you must apply the "next guy" test. Then the clouds part and the deities appear. In 1921 Babe Ruth hit 59 home runs. The next four hit 24, 24, 23, and 23. Ruth alone hit more home runs than half the teams in the major leagues.

8   In the 1981–82 season, Wayne Gretzky scored 212 points. The next two guys scored 147 and 139. Not for nothing had he been known as the Great One—since age 9.

9   Gaps like these are rare as the gods that produce them. By 1968, no one had ever long-jumped more than 27 ft. 4¾ in. In the Mexico City Olympics that year, Bob Beamon jumped 29 ft. 2½ in.—this in a sport in which records are

broken by increments of a few inches, sometimes fractions. (Yes, the air is thin in Mexico City, but it was a legal jump and the record stood for an astonishing 23 years.)

10   In physics, a quantum leap means jumping to a higher level without ever stopping—indeed, without even traveling through—anywhere in between. In our ordinary understanding of things, that is impossible. In sports, it defines greatness.

11   Not only did Michael Jordan play a game of basketball so beautiful that it defied physics, but he racked up numbers that put him in a league of his own. Jordan has averaged 31 points a game, a huge gap over the (future) Hall of Famers he played against (e.g., Karl Malone, 25.7; Charles Barkley, 22.1).

12   The most striking visual representation of the Gap is the photograph of Secretariat crossing the finish line at the Belmont Stakes, 31(!) lengths ahead of the next horse. You can barely see the others—the fastest horses in the world, mind you—in the distance.

13   In 1971, Bobby Fischer played World Championship elimination rounds against the best players on the planet. These were open-ended matches that finished only when one player had won six games. Such matches could take months, because great chess masters are so evenly matched that 80% of tournament games end in draws. Victories come at rare intervals; six wins can take forever. Not this time. Fischer conducted a campaign unrivaled since Scipio Africanus leveled Carthage. He beat two challengers six games in a row, which combined with wins before and after, produced a streak of 20 straight victories against the very best—something never seen before and likely never to be seen again.

14   That's a Gap. To enter the pantheon—any pantheon—you've got to be so far above and beyond your contemporaries that it is said of you, as Jack Nicklaus once said of Tiger Woods, "He's playing a game I'm not familiar with."

15   The biologist and philosopher Lewis Thomas was asked what record of human achievements he would launch into space to be discovered one day by some transgalactic civilization. A continual broadcast of Bach would do, Thomas suggested, though "that would be boasting."

16   Why not make it a music video? A Bach fugue over Tiger hitting those miraculous irons from the deep rough onto the greens at Bethpage Black. Nah. The aliens will think we did it all with computer graphics.

QUESTIONS FOR READING

1. What, exactly, is Krauthammer's topic?
2. What is Method 1 for judging Tiger Woods's greatness? Why is it not a good method?
3. How is Method 2 applied?
4. Who are Krauthammer's greats, using Method 2?

QUESTIONS FOR REASONING AND ANALYSIS

1. What is the author's primary purpose in writing? To argue for Woods's greatness? Something else?

2. What is the claim of the argument?

3. When Krauthammer concludes that aliens would not believe a music video of a Bach fugue playing while Woods hits irons from the rough, what is his point? What writing strategy is he using? What makes this an effective conclusion?

4. Evaluate Krauthammer's argument. Has he defined and illustrated his Method 2 adequately? Does his evidence support his claim effectively? Why or why not?

QUESTIONS FOR REFLECTING AND WRITING

1. Which of Krauthammer's examples do you admire the most? Why? Select one and see what more you can learn about that person or horse. Write a one-page biography that focuses on the stats that support the "gap" concept.

2. Do you agree that the gap is the best way to define greatness in sports? Why? If you disagree, explain what other elements you would include to measure greatness. If you agree, think about other elements some would include and devise a way to challenge that counterargument.

FAREWELL TO A TRUE CHAMPION | JOHN FEINSTEIN

A graduate of Duke University, John Feinstein was a reporter for the *Washington Post* for 11 years. He is the author of a number of books on sports, including *A Good Walk Spoiled: Days and Nights on the PGA Tour* (1995) and *Caddy for Life* (2004). His essay on Nicklaus appeared in the *Washington Post* on July 18, 2005.

PREREADING QUESTIONS What sports figures do you admire most? Why do you admire them?

There's nothing quite like a farewell in golf. For the truly great players, they 1 come much later in life than for other athletes, meaning that their impact is spread across multiple generations. Jack Nicklaus was 20 years old when he first contended in a major championship, the 1960 U.S. Open. Forty-five years later, in what he says will be his last major championship, he still played the game well enough to birdie the final hole and give anyone who has ever cared about golf one last great thrill.

The scene on Friday afternoon at golf's birthplace, the Old Course at St. 2 Andrews, was one of those moments when sports gets it exactly right. There was no script, as is so often the case during retirement ceremonies; no presentations and no speeches. Nicklaus departed exactly the way he wanted to: as a golfer, competing in the British Open on a course where he twice won the game's oldest major championship. He went out—literally—swinging, missing by two shots the 36-hole cut that would have allowed him to play on the weekend. Not bad for a man with 17 grandchildren.

3   There was far more to Nicklaus than longevity, more even than the 18 professional major championships he won—seven more than any player in history. Nicklaus was one of those special athletes who knew both how to win and how to lose. In addition to his 18 victories in majors, he also finished second 19 times and never once whined or complained or talked about bad luck in defeat. It was fitting that he played his final round Friday with longtime rival and friend Tom Watson. It was Watson who inflicted several of Nicklaus's most painful defeats, including the 1977 British Open, when they staged one of the great duels in golf history the last two days, and the 1982 U.S. Open, when Watson's miraculous chip-in on the second-to-last hole stole the championship from Nicklaus.

4   On that day, Nicklaus waited for Watson to finish. When he walked off the 18th green, he grabbed Watson and said, "You did it to me again, you little SOB." And then he added, "I'm proud of you."

5   Tiger Woods was playing three holes behind Nicklaus on Friday, methodically grinding his way to his 10th major title (which he won by five shots yesterday) at the age of 29. It is very possible, even likely, that Woods will someday surpass Nicklaus's 18 majors. He has often said that is his goal and that Nicklaus has been his inspiration since childhood.

6   Except for one thing: Woods seems to think that Nicklaus's legacy is only about numbers, that winning golf tournaments is the only thing that measures a champion. Nothing could be further from the truth, especially in golf.

7   Woods already holds many records. One of them, which is unofficial, is that he has been fined for using profanity publicly more than any player in history. While using profanity in the crucible of competition is hardly a great crime, it is indicative of Woods's attitude that, rather than try to curb his use of language, he has complained that he is being treated unfairly since there are always microphones following him when he plays. Last month, during the U.S. Open, Woods missed a putt and childishly dragged his putter across the green, damaging it as he did so. When he was asked about the incident later, he shrugged and said, "I was frustrated," (no apology) as if he was the only player among 156 dealing with frustration. In recent years he has allowed his caddie, Steve Williams, to frequently treat spectators and members of the media rudely, not only defending him but also appearing to sanction his misbehavior.

8   Woods is extremely popular with the golfing public, in part because of his extraordinary play and in part because of a carefully crafted image built around a series of commercials that show him to be a funny and friendly guy. Sadly, that's not the Woods most people encounter. He is the master of the TV sound bite, but he rarely shares any of his real thoughts with the public.

9   We tend to embrace our sports heroes not just for their greatness but also for allowing us to see that they are fragile. Arnold Palmer is the most popular player in golf history because he always shared his emotions in victory and defeat with his fans. Nicklaus and Watson both warmed to the role of icons as they grew older. Woods still doesn't seem to understand how to be a champion off the golf course. When Phil Mickelson put the green jacket on him during the TV ceremony after his victory at this year's Masters, Woods didn't even glance

back at his longtime rival. As one player put it, "He treated Phil like a butler, not a fellow champion."

Someday, Tiger Woods will walk across the Swilcan Bridge on the 18th fair- 10 way at St. Andrews and say farewell the way Nicklaus did on Friday. No doubt he will be cheered for his greatness as a golfer, just as Nicklaus was. But those cheers—and the tears—were not just for a golfer, they were for a man; one who has always won and always lost with grace and dignity. As a golfer, Woods will no doubt continue to close the gap inexorably on Nicklaus's records. He has a much longer road to travel to match him as a true champion.

QUESTIONS FOR READING

1. What is the occasion for Feinstein's essay?
2. In what ways is Nicklaus a champion?
3. Who might surpass Nicklaus's record?
4. How does Woods differ from Nicklaus, in Feinstein's view?

QUESTIONS FOR REASONING AND ANALYSIS

1. What is Feinstein's claim? State it as a contrast assertion.
2. What evidence does Feinstein provide to establish his contrast? Is it effective?
3. What does Feinstein mean by a "true champion"?

QUESTIONS FOR REFLECTING AND WRITING

1. Do you agree with the author's definition of a champion? Why or why not?
2. If you disagree, are you saying that Woods's behavior is acceptable because he is so good a player? Explain and defend your position.
3. Does our culture tolerate uncivil or unsporting behavior from superstars? If so, is this a problem in your view? If it is a problem, what is the solution? Be prepared to explain and defend your views on these issues.

Read: What is the situation in the cartoon? Who speaks? What is she reading?

Reason: What is significant about the words on the blackboard? The words in the bottom right corner?

Reflect/Write: What do you conclude to be the cartoonist's point about American education?

CHAPTER 17

Quality and Fairness in the American Classroom

To say that the issues in education are both numerous and serious is certainly an understatement. Clinton wanted to be the "education president." Bush has his No Child Left Behind initiative. And yet criticism continues amid a few voices defending U.S. schools. America's best schools and colleges attract students from around the world. But the variation in funding, facilities, teachers, and test scores from one school to another are often unacceptable to politicians and parents alike. Elite colleges have demanding entrance requirements, but the majority of colleges have few requirements beyond a high school diploma. At many colleges, up to one-third of the freshman class is taking at least one remedial course, and fewer than half of those who start college actually graduate. Are we failing at the goal of universal education? Is this goal unrealistic? Can we make changes that will improve

K–12 education? If we don't, will we be able to continue to compete in a global economy? These questions—and others raised by the authors in this chapter—should be the concern of all citizens, for we all benefit, economically and socially, by a well-educated workforce.

In this chapter the first five authors explore problems of both quality and fairness and offer some solutions for those problems. The final two authors debate the new and connected issue of the digital library.

Prereading Question

The topics of these authors are connected to one another and to the questions about U.S. education in general. Think about each author's particular argument, but also reflect on the ways that each one contributes to the larger debate about quality and fairness in America's schools.

Web Sites Related to This Chapter's Topic

U.S. Department of Education

www.ed.gov

This government site contains links to many resources on educational issues.

National Education Association

www.nea.org

This site contains definitions, resources on education, links to debates on bilingual education, charter schools, vouchers, and more.

American Federation of Teachers

www.aft.org

This union's site contains many resources and links. Go to their higher education page for resources on college issues, including distance learning.

Educational Policy Studies

http://w3.ed.uiuc.edu/EPS/Ed_Resources/category.lasso

This site, maintained by the University of Illinois, contains a wealth of information on the many philosophies of education.

DOING THE NUMBERS ON PUBLIC SCHOOLS ADDS UP TO ZERO | DANIEL HENNINGER

A graduate of Georgetown University's School of Foreign Service, Daniel Henninger is deputy editor of the *Wall Street Journal*'s editorial page. Henninger has received numerous awards for his commentary, including sharing in the *Wall Street Journal*'s Pulitzer Prize (2002) for coverage of the 9/11 attacks. The following column appeared May 2, 2003.

PREREADING QUESTIONS Based on his title, what do you expect Henninger's opinion of public schools to be? How do you know?

What with Americans being such an opinionated people, it isn't often that   1
an issue of public policy ever arrives at the steady state of national agreement.
Even as skulls were brought up from Saddam's torture chambers, e-mails still
rolled in from the war's opponents to re-argue the wrongness of the effort. So
imagine how surprising it was to discover this past week that there is one subject about which the people of this country are in about as much agreement as
statistical science ever achieves: America's public schools. They are widely and
deeply regarded as awful.

Public Agenda, a New York-based nonprofit that does opinion surveys on   2
a range of issues, compiled an analysis of a decade of polling on public education, and news reports about the study were eye-catching. Mainly the message was that while accountability matters in the public mind, what really
upsets people is the generalized disorderliness in public schools. Having opinions of my own on what caused many schools to shift from being temples of
learning to temples for having-fun-with-my-friends, I thought the Public
Agenda report, "Where We Are Now," deserved a closer look.

Please join me for a tour of the second circle of hell. George Bush has a   3
plan of action called No Child Left Behind, but if Saddam's weapons of mass
destruction were sufficient reason to invade Iraq, he should now send in the
Marines to occupy and reconstruct the nation's dysfunctional public schools.

Teachers, principals, parents, employers, college professors and students   4
all have a uniformly low opinion of what's going on in our schools. Unless
bracketed, the language here is taken largely from the study's own wording of
questions and results:

Some 71% of respondents believe most public-school students do the bare   5
minimum to get by; 83% of teachers say parents who fail to set limits and create structure at home are a serious problem, and 81% think parents who refuse
to hold their kids accountable for behavior or academic performance are a serious problem. Of teachers, 43% say they spend more time keeping order than
teaching. Instead of more pay (12%), 86% of teachers said they'd rather have
a school where student behavior and parental support were better.

Some 61% of African-American parents think inner-city kids should be   6
expected to achieve the same standards as wealthier kids. Priorities: 82% of
African-American parents think the biggest priority is raising academic standards; 8% want more focus on diversity and integration. Nearly all parents,
92%, think you should have to pass a standardized test to be promoted—and,
if you fail, you should have to go to summer school or repeat the grade.

Employers who think local public schools are doing a good or excellent   7
job: 42%. Some 59% of college professors rate public schools as fair or poor.
Professors who say a high-school diploma means students have learned the basics: 31%. [In the 1970s, a friend who began teaching at the University of Texas
told me most of his freshmen thought they were A students; "they're not."]
Only 47% of professors and 41% of employers think public-school graduates

have the skills to succeed in the work world. About 74% of employers and professors think public-school graduates' writing skills are fair or poor; same number for grammar and spelling. About 64% say graduates' basic math is fair or poor; 69% of employers feel personal organization is fair or poor.

8   Only 19% of teachers say parental involvement is strong in their school [parental involvement is one of the established keys to a successful school]; 87% of teachers think parents ought to limit their kids' TV time or should check their homework [clearly the inference is most parents do neither].

9   Disrespect is pandemic.

10   Of all Americans surveyed, 9% say, "The kids I see in public are respectful toward adults." Only 18% of teachers and 30% of students say, "Students treat each other with respect in my high school"; 19% of students say, "In my high school, most students treat teachers with respect." Americans who feel their schools have a serious discipline problem: 76%.

11   Any stairwell of public-school hell we've left off the tour? Oh yes, we've left off the politics from hell.

12   Asked why talented teachers quit, school superintendents say: low pay and prestige—5%; politics and bureaucracy—81%. Sixty-seven percent of principals wish they were able to reward good teachers and remove bad ones [that is, they can't do either now]. Over 80% of principals and superintendents say they have more new mandates and responsibilities than they can handle. Eighty-four percent of superintendents say they spend too much time on special ed., and 50% say they spend too much on legal issues and litigation.

13   A wag might ask: If we're so stupid, how come the U.S. earned an A in technology and human performance in Iraq? Short answer: The armed services don't let stupid people enlist anymore. The army now provides it own education, which is largely what most employers do as well today. A job is now a re-education camp for many public-school grads.

14   How the schools got this way—how respect for teachers died, disorder rose, basic learning fell, bureaucracy rose, why the best teachers quit, parents stopped caring and why professors think freshmen are academically delusional—is a subject for another column and maybe another lifetime (it takes more than one paragraph to explain how Supreme Court Justices with high IQs render legal decisions reflecting no common sense).

15   But for now, amid the overwhelming agreement found in the Public Agenda surveys, I have one small, recurring question: Tell me again why we're supposed to think charter schools and school choice are bad ideas.

QUESTIONS FOR READING

1.   What is America's attitude toward public schools?

2.   What matters most to teachers? What, in the eyes of teachers, are serious problems?

3.   What do African American parents want?

4.   What are the views of employers and college professors with regard to high school graduates' preparation for college or the workforce?

5.   What view do students and teachers both hold with regard to the showing of respect in their schools?

6.   What bothers principals and superintendents?

7.   Where are most grads now getting "educated"?

QUESTIONS FOR REASONING AND ANALYSIS

1.   Much of Henninger's column is a report of a report—by Public Agenda—on public schools. What is his claim? Or, what claim seems to be implied? On what evidence do you draw your implications?

2.   List the several distinct problems that emerge from the survey. What seem to be at least some of the causes for these problems, as stated or implied by the results of the surveys? What examination of causes requires another column—or lifetime? (For example, why have parents stopped caring?)

3.   What solutions are stated or implied by the author?

QUESTIONS FOR REFLECTING AND WRITING

1.   What statistic surprises you the most? Why?

2.   Select one of the issues listed by the author in paragraph 14 and discuss what you think are the causes of and possible solutions for that particular problem.

3.   Are charter schools and school choice good or bad ideas? Why? Be prepared to defend your position. If these are not solutions to problems in public education, what solutions do you recommend? Why?

PUT TEACHERS TO THE TEST | DIANE RAVITCH

Educated at Wellesley College and Columbia University, Diane Ravitch has been an adjunct professor at Columbia's Teachers College and an assistant secretary in the Department of Education in the first Bush administration. Currently she teaches at New York University and is a visiting fellow at the Brookings Institution. Ravitch has written extensively on the problems in American schools. The following article was published on February 25, 1998, in the *Washington Post*.

PREREADING QUESTIONS How important are teachers in the education process? How well do we train and certify our K–12 teachers?

Last summer, a suburban school district in New York advertised for 35 new   1 teachers and received nearly 800 applications. District officials decided to narrow the pool by requiring applicants to take the 11th-grade state examination in English. Only about one-quarter of the would-be teachers answered 40 of the 50 multiple-choice questions correctly.

As Congress considers reauthorization of the Higher Education Act,   2 teacher education has emerged as a major issue. Many states—and now

President Clinton—are clamoring to reduce class size, but few are grappling with the most important questions: If we are raising standards for students, don't we also need to raise standards for teachers? Shouldn't state and local officials make sure that teachers know whatever they are supposed to teach students?

3   Almost every state claims that it is strengthening standards for students, but the states have been strangely silent when it comes to ensuring that teachers know what they are supposed to teach. Most instead certify anyone with the right combination of education courses, regardless of their command of the subject they expect to teach, and many states require future teachers to pass only a basic skills test.

4   Today, in some states it may be harder to graduate from high school than to become a certified teacher. Something is wrong with this picture.

5   Last summer the U.S. Department of Education reported that approximately one-third of the nation's public school teachers of academic subjects in middle school and high school were teaching "out of field," which means that they had earned neither an undergraduate major nor a minor in their main teaching field.

6   Fully 39.5 percent of science teachers had not studied science as a major or minor; 34 percent of mathematics teachers and 25 percent of English teachers were similarly teaching "out of field." The problem of unqualified teachers was particularly acute in schools where 40 percent or more of the students were from low-income homes; in these schools, nearly half the teaching staff was teaching "out of field."

7   Many states now routinely certify people who do not know what they are supposed to teach. No one should get a license to teach science, reading, mathematics or anything else unless he or she has demonstrated a knowledge of what students are expected to learn.

8   A majority of the nation's teachers majored in education rather than an academic subject. This is troubling, even though most of those who majored in education are elementary teachers. There is a widely accepted notion that people who teach little children don't need to know much other than pedagogical methods and child psychology; that is wrong. Teachers of little children need to be well-educated and should love learning as much as they love children. Yes, even elementary school teachers should have an academic major.

9   The field of history has the largest percentage of unqualified teachers. The Department of Education found that 55 percent of history teachers are "out of field," and that 43 percent of high school students are studying history with a teacher who did not earn either a major or minor in history. This may explain why nearly 60 percent of our 17-year-olds scored "below basic" (the lowest possible rating) on the most recent test of U.S. history administered by the federally funded National Assessment of Educational Progress. Only one out of every five teachers of social studies has either a major or minor in history. Is it any wonder that today's children have no idea when the Civil War occurred, what Reconstruction was, what happened during the progressive era, who FDR

was, what the *Brown* decision decided, or what Stalin did? Many of their teachers don't know those things either.

There are many conditions over which school officials have no control, but 10 they have complete control over who is allowed to teach. Why should anyone be certified to teach science or history who doesn't know what he or she is expected to teach the children?

Many state officials say that they have an abundance of people who want 11 to teach and that this is actually an excellent time to raise standards. For career-changers with a wealth of experience in business or the military, however, obsolete certification requirements get in the way. Instead of requiring irrelevant education courses, states should examine prospective teachers for their knowledge of their academic field and then give them a chance to work in the schools as apprentice teachers.

As Congress ponders ways to improve the teaching profession, it should 12 consider incentives for colleges of liberal arts to collaborate with schools of education in preparing future teachers. Representatives from both parts of the same campus should sit down together, study state academic standards and figure out how to prepare teachers who know both their subject and how to teach it well. Teachers need a strong academic preparation as well as practical classroom experience to qualify for one of the toughest jobs in America.

Every classroom should have a well-educated, knowledgeable teacher. We 13 are far from that goal today. Congress can address this problem by focusing on the quality, not quantity, of the nation's teaching corps.

QUESTIONS FOR READING

1. What kinds of evidence does Ravitch provide to support her claim? What key assumption is a part of her argument?
2. What solutions does the author present? What should school officials do? The states? Congress? How does she defend the feasibility of her solutions?

QUESTIONS FOR REASONING AND ANALYSIS

1. What strategy does Ravitch use in her opening paragraph? What makes her opening effective?
2. What is the claim of Ravitch's argument? What type of argument is this?

QUESTIONS FOR REFLECTING AND WRITING

1. Are you surprised by any of Ravitch's statistics? Why or why not?
2. Did you have any teachers teaching "out of field"? If so, how effective were they?
3. Do you agree that K–6 teachers should have a major in an academic subject? Why or why not? (What does Ravitch think they will gain from an academic major?)

4.   Should all teachers have to pass a basic test in reading, writing, math, history, and science? If not, why not? If so, at what level? Think of some representative types of questions that you would put on such a test.

LEFT BEHIND, WAY BEHIND | BOB HERBERT

An op-ed columnist for the *New York Times* since 1993, Bob Herbert has also been a national correspondent for NBC and a founding panelist for *Sunday Edition*. He writes on politics, urban issues, and social trends, as we see in the following column from the August 29, 2005, nytimes.com.

PREREADING QUESTIONS What does Herbert's title refer to? What groups of students are most behind in K–12?

1   First the bad news: Only about two-thirds of American teenagers (and just half of all black, Latino and Native American teens) graduate with a regular diploma four years after they enter high school.

2   Now the worse news: Of those who graduate, only about half read well enough to succeed in college.

3   Don't even bother to ask how many are proficient enough in math and science to handle college-level work. It's not pretty.

4   Of all the factors combining to shape the future of the U.S., this is one of the most important. Millions of American kids are not even making it through high school in an era in which a four-year college degree is becoming a prerequisite for achieving (or maintaining) a middle-class lifestyle.

5   The Program for International Assessment, which compiles reports on the reading and math skills of 15-year-olds, found that the U.S. ranked 24th out of 29 nations surveyed in math literacy. The same result for the U.S.—24th out of 29—was found when the problem-solving abilities of 15-year-olds were tested.

6   If academic performance were an international athletic event, spectators would be watching American kids falling embarrassingly behind in a number of crucial categories. A new report from a pair of Washington think tanks—the Center for American Progress and the Institute for America's Future—says an urgent new commitment to public education, much stronger than the No Child Left Behind law, must be made if that slide is to be reversed.

7   This would not be a minor task. In much of the nation the public education system is in shambles. And the kids who need the most help—poor children from inner cities and rural areas—often attend the worst schools.

8   An education task force established by the center and the institute noted the following:

> Young low-income and minority children are more likely to start school without having gained important school readiness skills, such as recognizing letters and counting. . . . By the fourth grade, low-income students read about three grade levels behind nonpoor students. Across the nation, only 15 percent of low-income fourth graders achieved proficiency in reading in 2003, compared to 41 percent of nonpoor students.

How's that for a disturbing passage? Not only is the picture horribly bleak 9
for low-income and minority kids, but we find that only 41 percent of nonpoor
fourth graders can read proficiently.

I respectfully suggest that we may be looking at a crisis here. 10

The report, titled "Getting Smarter, Becoming Fairer," restates a point that 11
by now should be clear to most thoughtful Americans: too many American kids
are ill equipped educationally to compete successfully in an ever-more competitive global environment.

Cartoonish characters like Snoop Dogg and Paris Hilton may be good for 12
a laugh, but they're useless as role models. It's the kids who are logging long
hours in the college labs, libraries and lecture halls who will most easily remain
afloat in the tremendous waves of competition that have already engulfed
large segments of the American work force.

The report makes several recommendations. It says the amount of time 13
that children spend in school should be substantially increased by lengthening
the school day and, in some cases, the school year. It calls for the development
of voluntary, rigorous national curriculum standards in core subject areas and a
consensus on what students should know and be able to do by the time they
graduate from high school.

The report also urges, as many have before, that the nation take seriously 14
the daunting (and expensive) task of getting highly qualified teachers into all
classrooms. And it suggests that an effort be made to connect schools in low-
income areas more closely with the surrounding communities. (Where necessary, the missions of such schools would be extended to provide additional
services for children whose schooling is affected by such problems as inadequate health care, poor housing, or a lack of parental support.)

The task force's recommendations are points of departure that can be dis- 15
cussed, argued about and improved upon by people who sincerely want to
ramp up the quality of public education in the U.S. What is most important
about the report is the fact that it sounds an alarm about a critical problem that
is not getting nearly enough serious attention.

QUESTIONS FOR READING

1. What is the source of Herbert's data?
2. In what three ways are American students "behind"? (That is, who is most
   behind, whom do we trail, and what other standards are we not meeting?)
3. What solutions are suggested in the report?

QUESTIONS FOR REASONING AND ANALYSIS

1. What is the author's view of the report's proposed solutions? What must be
   the first step to improvement, implied by Herbert?
2. State the author's claim.
3. What is clever about the opening two paragraphs?

4. How would you describe Herbert's tone? How does it contribute to his argument?

QUESTIONS FOR REFLECTING AND WRITING

1. What statistic is most surprising to you? Why?

2. Do you agree with Herbert that the report presents a crisis in American education? Why or why not?

3. If you agree that we have a problem, what solutions would you propose? Do you embrace any of the report's solutions? Do you object to any of them? Be prepared to explain and defend your position.

BACK-TO-SCHOOL BLUES | BOB SOMERBY

Described as a "topical comedian" who offers "jokes built on ideas," Bob Somerby began his career as a fifth-grade teacher in the Baltimore public schools and then moved to the op-ed pages of the *Baltimore Sun* newspaper. He now does a stand-up comedy act and is editor of *The Daily Howler,* his blog, from which the following article, a response to Bob Herbert's op-ed piece, is taken.

PREREADING QUESTIONS What does reading proficiency mean to you? Do you think that educators can agree on the meaning of "proficiency"?

1   Here in Baltimore, children return to school today. And Bob Herbert, to his credit, discusses their unending bad prospects. "Left Behind, Way Behind," reads the headline on his *Times* op-ed column. In the piece, Herbert cites a new study commissioned by two liberal think tanks:

> HERBERT (9/29/05): An education task force established by the center and the institute noted the following:
>
> "Young low-income and minority children are more likely to start school without having gained important school readiness skills, such as recognizing letters and counting . . . **By the fourth grade, low-income students read about three grade levels behind non-poor students.** Across the nation, only 15 percent of low-income fourth graders achieved proficiency in reading in 2003, compared to 41 percent of non-poor students."

2   "How's that for a disturbing passage?" Herbert asks. "Not only is the picture horribly bleak for low-income and minority kids, but we find that only 41 percent of non-poor fourth graders can read proficiently. I respectfully suggest that we may be looking at a crisis here."

3   For starters, a note about the concept of "proficiency." To a large extent, "proficiency" is in the eye of the beholder. That is, researchers can set the standard for "proficiency" wherever they please, producing various results in the process. In the study by this task force, what did fourth-graders have to do to show they were "proficient" in reading? Herbert doesn't attempt to say. Therefore, when we read that "only 41 percent of non-poor fourth graders can read proficiently," we don't really know what is being said. Nor is it clear that the non-poor fourth-graders are really involved in a "crisis."

Beyond that, the quoted passage might seem a bit puzzling. If most non-   4
poor fourth graders can't read "proficiently," then Herbert's readers might assume that these kids read at third grade level or below. If so, what exactly does
it mean when we're told that "low-income students read about three grade levels behind" *that?* We haven't looked at this study yet. But as often happens
when mainstream scribes write about public ed, Herbert's column draws
sweeping conclusions on the basis of poorly-parsed data.

On the other hand, Herbert's column reminded us of what we saw, with our   5
own eyes, during twelve years in the Baltimore schools—a dozen years in which
we taught the world's most deserving children. As we've noted before, many low-
income kids are already several years below traditional "grade level" in reading
by the time they reach fourth or fifth grade. A fair number aren't really reading at
all. And yes, this is an educational disaster—"crisis" barely does it justice. That is
why we searched Herbert's column for advice about what the nation should do.
And when we did, our analysts groaned as they saw the same tired "solutions":

> HERBERT: The report makes several recommendations. It says the amount of
> time that children spend in school should be substantially increased by
> lengthening the school day and, in some cases, the school year. **It calls for
> the development of voluntary, rigorous national curriculum standards in
> core subject areas** and a consensus on what students should know and be
> able to do by the time they graduate from high school.
>
>   The report also urges, as many have before, that the nation take seriously
> the daunting (and expensive) task of getting highly qualified teachers into all
> classrooms. And it suggests that an effort be made to connect schools in
> low-income areas more closely with the surrounding communities.

For our money, none of those familiar old saws address the leading cor-   6
rectable problems in the nation's urban schools. But we especially groaned at
the recommendation we've highlighted. Low-income fourth graders can't read
at all—*so we need to make our standards more rigorous!* This absurd "solution"
to a human disaster has now been pushed by three successive presidents—by
Bush, by Clinton and then Bush again. We've challenged its groaning illogic
each time—and we'll do so again, all this week.

Poor fourth-grade kids can't read at all. *So we need to set our standards*   7
higher! Poor kids are light-years behind the non-poor. *So we need to define*
one set of graduation standards! In our view, such "recommendations" tend to
come from people who have never set foot in urban schools—and think tanks
funded by both major parties sometimes seem to be full of such people.

QUESTIONS FOR READING

1. What is Somerby's first objection to Herbert's argument?
2. What objections, to both Herbert and the studies, are given in paragraph 4?
3. On what does Somerby agree with Herbert?
4. What are his objections to the report's proposed solutions?

QUESTIONS FOR REASONING AND ANALYSIS

1. Does Somerby disagree with Herbert about a crisis in education? If not, then what is his problem with Herbert's column? State a claim for Somerby's essay that establishes that it is a refutation.

2. The author establishes that he has not yet read the reports referred to by Herbert, but he concludes that Herbert "draws sweeping conclusions on the basis of poorly-parsed data." How effective is this part of Somerby's refutation?

3. Somerby's greatest attention is given to the report's proposed solutions. Is it "absurd" to call for more rigorous standards to respond to the lack of reading proficiency? What does Somerby seem to mean by objecting to higher standards? In what way can higher standards be understood to be helpful, not absurd?

4. Do you find a logical fallacy in paragraph 7?

QUESTIONS FOR REFLECTING AND WRITING

1. Do you agree with Somerby's refutation of Herbert's argument? Are his objections clear? Fair? Supported by logic and evidence? Evaluate both arguments.

2. If one were to establish higher standards, what might these include for poorer students in public schools?

3. Should there be more than one set of graduation standards? If not, why not? If so, how should they differ—and how should the differences be made clear?

A GRAND COMPROMISE | JAMES P. PINKERTON

A senior fellow at the New America Foundation, James Pinkerton is also a columnist for *Newsday*. Previously he worked in the White House as a domestic policy advisor to Presidents Reagan and George H. W. Bush. He is the author of *What Comes Next: The End of Big Government—and the New Paradigm Ahead* (1995). "A Grand Compromise" was published in the January/February 2003 issue of *Atlantic Monthly*.

PREREADING QUESTIONS To have a grand compromise on education requires reconciling the views of what two groups? How do their views on education differ, particularly with regard to some of the issues raised in the previous essays in this chapter?

1   In 1983 a federal education commission warned that "a rising tide of mediocrity" threatened the well-being of the republic. That tide has not ebbed. Nearly two decades later, in 2000, the Program for International Student Assessment found that American fifteen-year-olds ranked fourteenth in science literacy and eighteenth in mathematics literacy among the thirty-two countries administering the test, scoring below the average for developed countries in both categories. And although President George W. Bush and Congress recently united behind the grandiosely titled No Child Left Behind Act of 2001, few observers outside Washington, D.C., believe that the legislation will have anything more than a marginal effect on student performance.

All Presidents claim to be "education Presidents," but the schools drift 2 along, up a bit, down a bit, always costing more money, but never making the sort of dramatic gains witnessed elsewhere in American life. Why should this be?

U.S. schools today are the product of three different educational eras: the 3 agricultural (which produced the nine-month school year), the industrial (which emphasized rote learning and regimentation to fit the rhythms of mass production), and what might be called the experimental (which promoted a range of nostrums, from sex education to Whole Language, often at the expense of basic skills). Each of these has left its own layer of sediment to muck things up in the present. The worst legacy of the past, however, is localized school funding, which not only produces great regional inequalities in spending per pupil but also nurtures the persistent incompetence of many schools.

Today about 45 percent of school funding comes from local sources, such 4 as property taxes. In Virginia, for example, average per-pupil spending in rural Hanover County is only half that in suburban Arlington County. In New Jersey, which has been struggling to equalize school funding for three decades, the schools in Elizabeth spend 70 percent more per pupil than do the schools in Toms River.

Beyond state lines the disparities grow even worse: among school districts 5 with enrollments of 15,000 or more, spending ranges from $3,932 per pupil in DeSoto County, Mississippi, to $14,244 in Elizabeth, New Jersey. Rectifying such imbalances requires a national solution. "Most of the resource inequality cannot be resolved at the state level," David Grissmer and Ann Flanagan, analysts for the Rand Corporation, have written. "States spending the least are southern and western states that also have a disproportionate share of the nation's minority and disadvantaged students." Yet the federal government does little to address this systemic inequality, and continues to contribute only about seven percent of the total spent on elementary and secondary schools.

So what's an "education President" to do? Happily, the means of reform- 6 ing elementary and secondary education does not lie in some obscure theory, or in some other country. It has been right in front of our eyes for decades: the model of the Pell Grant program.

Colleges and universities compete, in effect, in a single national market. 7 The federal government pumps $10 billion a year into college education through Pell Grants. The GI Bill and other aid programs add billions more. Pell Grants have an inherently equalizing effect on per-student funding: every qualifying student in the country has access to the same amount—a maximum of $4,000 a year—and can spend it at the accredited college of his or her choice. Thus much of higher education is more equitably funded than K–12 education. Moreover, because Pell recipients decide where their grants are applied, the program is driven by students, not administrators.

Why not build on the Pell model, and apply it to elementary and secondary 8 education? Total K–12 public school spending, for some 47 million students, is currently about $350 billion a year, slightly more than $7,000 per pupil per year. Expanding on the Pell model would mean giving every American elementary and secondary school student $7,000 to spend at the school of his or her choice. Unlike Pell Grants, this money would be given to all students, regardless of the level of need. This would create, in effect, a grand compromise between left and right, guaranteeing more-equal funding (which the left wants) and more choice for students (which the right wants).

9   Making this happen, of course, would require a radical reshuffling of financial responsibilities among the various levels of government. But such a reshuffling is not unprecedented; after all, though states and localities once bore the cost of raising militias, national defense is now a federal responsibility. Since 9/11, of course, federal responsibility for homeland defense has increased, to the point where a new Cabinet department has been legislated.

10   Education is no less a national priority than defense. Education reformers should not shrink from the full implications of their goals; it's time for the federal government to do more for education—and for state and local governments to do less. It is true that the $350 billion a year in spending that the federal government would have to take on from state and local governments is no small amount. But at three percent of GDP, it is less than the annual U.S. military budget, and less than what the federal government spends on health care each year. And because state and local governments would be able either to spend the money currently allotted to education on other priorities or to rebate money to taxpayers, any federal tax increases or spending cuts made to accommodate this new system would be at least partially offset.

11   Of course, many conservatives and some liberals might object to the loss of local control over schools. But local control is in some ways detrimental to education and to equity. In the Jim Crow South, after all, local control was synonymous with "separate but equal"; today an insistence on local funding ought not to be a cover for maintaining separate and obviously unequal schools.

12   Moreover, conservatives ought to be pleased with the second element of the grand compromise: expanded choice. The current method of funding K–12 education balkanizes school districts into pockets of excellence or indifference; a federal grant program would make all schools part of a national system, in which no child would be forced by accident of region or neighborhood to attend a bad school.

13   Because students in such a system could attend the schools of their choice, they would create a self-correcting market. If a given school was inadequate, students could go elsewhere, taking their funding with them. The fragmentary evidence of the past few years suggests that schools faced with competition will struggle to retain "market share."

14   Of course, if schools in Mississippi are substandard at $4,000 per pupil, there is no guarantee that they would be better at $7,000 per pupil. One of the bitter lessons of the twentieth-century welfare state is that a bureaucracy has an apparently infinite capacity to absorb extra money without producing additional output. But under this proposal schools would have a compelling interest in responding to an exodus of students; a school that failed to respond positively would lose its financial base.

Critics of this plan will say that it is a form of vouchers—and they will be cor- 15
rect. But this plan can't be derided as an attempt to undermine the public
schools by bleeding away their students. Rather, it's an attempt to lift all schools
into the mainstream by equalizing funding across the country, improving the
odds that every child receives an education appropriate for this century.

What schools would be eligible to receive this grant money? Public schools 16
only? Religious schools? Home schools? Ideally, every kind of school, though as a
practical matter certain schools would not be made eligible right away. The politics of reform must sometimes yield to the slower-moving politics of the possible.
But once the principle of federally funded choice was established, its application
would expand as the education market reacted to the new incentives.

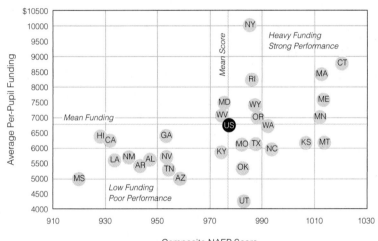

Composite NAEP Score
Sum of most recent math and reading scores for 4th and 8th graders

PUBLIC SCHOOL FUNDING VS. PERFORMANCE Funding disparities between
states partly explain the gaps in student achievement (Source: Census Bureau; National
Center for Educational National Assessment of Educational Progress).

This is just the outline of a grand compromise on education. If the right cel- 17
ebrates "liberty" untrammeled by bureaucracy and the left celebrates "rights"
guaranteed, if necessary, by the government, the two can come together in
behalf of a system of federally funded equal opportunity. Although neither side
will like everything about this proposal, both might yet decide they like the
status quo even less. And federally funded choice is a bold assault on the ortho-
doxies of the status quo.

QUESTIONS FOR READING

1. What are the legacies of the three educational eras? What is the fourth and
    worst legacy, according to the author?

2. What are the elements of the Pell Grant program for colleges?

3. What is Pinkerton's compromise? What does he propose?

4. What changes will be needed to make the compromise work?

5. What financial challenge does the author anticipate? How does he rebut it?

6. What other counterarguments does Pinkerton bring up and rebut?

QUESTIONS FOR REASONING AND ANALYSIS

1. What are the values and goals of the right? Of the left? Does Pinkerton's grand compromise give each side what it wants to see in education? Why or why not?

2. Explain the graph. What does it show? What can we learn from this visual?

3. Analyze Pinkerton's argument that education should be financed and controlled primarily at the federal, not the local, level. What are his reasons? Does he make a convincing case for change? Why or why not?

4. How does the author's "voucher" plan differ from current plans? Do you agree with Pinkerton that his is a better "voucher" plan? Why or why not?

QUESTIONS FOR REFLECTING AND WRITING

1. What statistic surprises you the most? Why?

2. Should students be allowed to use vouchers at private and parochial schools? Why or why not?

3. Is Pinkerton's plan feasible? Can we get people to give up local funding and control of schools? If so, how? If not, why not? *Should* we seek the changes Pinkerton argues for? Why or why not?

THE DIGITAL LIBRARY PLAN: RICHES WE MUST SHARE | MARY SUE COLEMAN

A professor of biochemistry for many years, Mary Sue Coleman has been president of the University of Michigan since 2002. She led the university to a successful case in the Supreme Court defending college affirmative action policies. Her university is now one of the five working with Google to digitize its holdings. Her argument and its counter by Nick Taylor that follows were published in the *Washington Post* on October 22, 2005.

PREREADING QUESTION What are your views on digital libraries? Reflect on the pros and cons on your own and then read both arguments.

1   Some authors and publishers have cried foul regarding Google's digital library initiative, sparking debate about intellectual property rights in an online age. Beyond the specific legal challenges emerging in the wake of such a sea change, there are deeply important public policy issues at stake. We must not lose sight of the transformative nature of Google's plan or the public good that can come from it.

Throughout history, most of the world's printed knowledge has been cre- 2
ated, preserved and used only by society's elites—those for whom education
and power meant access to the great research libraries. Now, groundbreaking
tools for mass digitization are poised to change that paradigm. We believe the
result can be a widening of human conversation comparable to the emergence
of mass literacy itself.

Google plans to make its index searchable to every person in the world 3
who enjoys access to the Internet. For those works that remain in copyright, a
search will reveal brief excerpts along with information about how to buy the
work or borrow it from a public library. Searches of work in the public domain
will yield access to complete texts online.

Imagine what this means for scholars and the general public, who, until 4
now, might have discovered only a fraction of the material written on a subject.
Or picture a small, impoverished school—in America or anywhere in the
world—that does not have access to a substantial library but does have an
Internet connection.

This enormous shift is already upon us. Students coming to my campus to- 5
day belong to the Net Generation. By the time they were in middle school, the
Internet was a part of their daily lives. As we watch the way our students search
for and use information, this much is clear: If information is not digitized, it will
not be found.

Libraries and educational institutions are the only entities whose mission is 6
to preserve knowledge through the centuries. It is a crucial role, one outside
the interest of corporate entities and separate from the whims of the market.
If libraries do not archive and curate, there is substantial risk that entire bodies
of work will be lost.

Universities and the knowledge they offer should be accessible by all. 7

We must continue to ensure access to the vast intellectual opportunity and 8
knowledge we generate and preserve. The digitization of information is a profound gesture that holds open our doors. Limiting access to information is tan-
tamount to limiting the opportunities of our citizens.

Criticism of the Google library project revolves around questions of intel- 9
lectual property. Universities are no strangers to the responsible management
of complex copyright, permission and security issues; we deal with them every
day in our classrooms, libraries, laboratories and performance halls. We will
continue to work within the current criteria for fair use as we move ahead with
digitization.

But we believe deeply that this endeavor exemplifies the spirit under which 10
our nation's copyright law was developed: to encourage the free exchange of
ideas in the service of innovation and societal progress. The protections of copyright are designed to balance the rights of the creator with the rights of the
public. At its core is the most important principle of all: to facilitate the sharing
of knowledge, not to stifle such exchange.

No one believed more fervently in the diffusion of knowledge than Thomas 11
Jefferson, who resurrected the Library of Congress, using his own books, after
its predecessor was destroyed by fire. We must continue to heed his message:

And it cannot be but that each generation succeeding to the knowledge acquired by all those who preceded it, adding to it their own acquisitions and discoveries, and handing the mass down for successive and constant accumulation, must advance the knowledge and well-being of mankind, not infinitely, as some have said, but indefinitely, and to a term which no one can fix and foresee.

12   I worry that we are unnecessarily fearful of a world where our libraries can be widely accessed and that our fear will strangle the exchange of ideas so critical to our Founders. As these technologies are developed, our policies must help ensure that people can find information and that printed works are preserved for future generations.

QUESTIONS FOR READING

1. What is Coleman's subject?
2. What change will the Google digital library produce?
3. How will Google handle works under copyright?
4. What is the ultimate goal of copyright laws, according to the author?
5. What role does the university have that bears on this issue?

QUESTIONS FOR REASONING AND ANALYSIS

1. What is Coleman's claim?
2. What are her primary reasons? State them in your own words.
3. How does she counter the copyright issue?

QUESTIONS FOR REFLECTING AND WRITING

1. Coleman suggests that our "online age" has made a difference in the debate on copyright. Has it? That is, just because we can digitize books, does that mean that it is right to ignore intellectual property rights? Can this argument be defended? Why or why not?
2. What is your position on this debate? Why? Has Coleman influenced your position? If so, how? If not, why not?

THE DIGITAL LIBRARY PLAN: BUT NOT AT WRITERS' EXPENSE | NICK TAYLOR

Nick Taylor is president of the Authors Guild, a member of PEN, and the author of many articles and nonfiction books, including a memoir of astronaut and Senator John Glenn. He is currently working on a book about the Depression-era public works program. His argument was published with the previous one in the *Washington Post* on October 22, 2005.

PREREADING QUESTIONS What potential problems can you identify in plans to digitize large numbers of books? Are these problems avoidable?

I am a writer. 1

For some time now—too much time, I suspect my editor believes—I have 2 been working on a history of the Works Progress Administration. This has taken me to states from Maine to California, into archives and libraries, and on long and occasionally fruitful searches for survivors of the Depression-era program.

I have invested a small fortune in books chronicling the period and copies 3 of old newspapers, spent countless hours on Internet searches, paid assistants to dig up obscure bits of information, and then sat at my keyboard trying to spin a mountain of facts into a compelling narrative. Money advanced by my publisher has made this possible.

Except for a few big-name authors, publishers roll the dice and hope that 4 a book's sales will return their investment. Because of this, readers have a wealth of wonderful books to choose from. Most authors do not live high on their advances; my hourly return at this point is laughable.

Only if my book sells well enough to earn back its advance will I make ad- 5 ditional money, but the law of copyright assures me of ongoing ownership. With luck, income will flow to my publisher and me for a long time, but if my publisher loses interest, I will still own my book and be able to make money from it.

So my question is this: When did we in this country decide that this kind of 6 work and investment isn't worth paying for?

That is what Google, the powerful and extremely wealthy search engine, 7 with co-founders ranking among the 20 richest people in the world, is saying by declining to license in-copyright works in its library scanning program, which has the otherwise admirable aim of making the world's books available for search by anyone with Web access.

Google says writers and publishers should be happy about this: It will in- 8 crease their exposure and maybe lead to more book sales.

That's a devil's bargain. 9

We'd all like to have more exposure, obviously. But is that the only form of 10 compensation Google can come up with when it makes huge profits on the ads it sells along the channels its users are compelled to navigate?

Now that the Authors Guild has objected, in the form of a lawsuit, to 11 Google's appropriation of our books, we're getting heat for standing in the way of progress, again for thoughtlessly wanting to be paid. It's been tradition in this country to believe in property rights. When did we decide that socialism was the way to run the Internet?

The New York Public Library and Oxford University's Bodleian Library, two 12 of the five libraries in the Google program, have recognized the problem. They are limiting the books scanned from their collections to those in the public domain, on which copyright protections have expired.

13   That is not the case with the others—the libraries of the University of Michigan, Harvard and Stanford. Michigan's librarian believes that the authors' insistence on their rights amounts to speed bumps in the road of progress. "We cannot lose sight of the tremendous benefits this project will bring to society," he said in a news release.

14   In other words, traffic is moving too slowly, so let's remove the stop signs.

15   Google contends that the portions of books it will make available to searchers amount to "fair use," the provision under copyright that allows limited use of protected works without seeking permission. That makes a private company, which is profiting from the access it provides, the arbiter of a legal concept it has no right to interpret. And they're scanning the entire books, with who knows what result in the future.

16   There is no argument about the ultimate purpose of Google's initiative. Great value lies in a searchable, online "library at Alexandria" containing all the world's books, at least to that fraction of society that has computers, the electricity to run them and Internet connections. It would make human knowledge available on an unprecedented scale. But it must be done correctly, by acquiring the rights to the resources it wishes to exploit.

17   The value of Google's project notwithstanding, society has traditionally seen its greatest value in the rights of individuals, and particularly in the dignity of their work and just compensation for it.

18   The people who cry that information wants to be free don't address this dignity or this aspect of justice. They're more interested in ease of assembly. The alphabet ought to be free, most certainly, but the people who painstakingly arrange it into books deserve to be paid for their work. This, at the core, is what copyright is all about. It's about a just return for work and the dignity that goes with it.

QUESTIONS FOR READING

1. What must writers and publishers do to make money?
2. What is Google's response to writers?
3. What is the position of the New York Public and Bodleian libraries on copyrighted books?
4. What is Google doing in spite of the copyright lawsuit?

QUESTIONS FOR REASONING AND ANALYSIS

1. What is Taylor's claim?
2. What are his reasons? State them in your own words.
3. How does Taylor rebut Coleman's primary defense of the Google project?
4. What does Taylor seek to accomplish in his opening six paragraphs?

QUESTIONS FOR REFLECTING AND WRITING

1. How does Coleman depict Google? How does Taylor depict Google? Who seems more accurate and fair in your view? Why?

2. Who has the best argument? Why?

3. Do we, as a culture, fail to value the time, effort, and creativity that writing a book demands? If so, why? What is your view of the work of writers? Why do you hold that view?

Read: What does this visual show?

Reason: Where do we find a provision for basic freedoms of speech? What is the exact wording? (If you don't know, look it up.)

Reflect/Write: What reasons are given for our democratic governmental structure? How do these reasons affect our thinking about free speech *and* censorship?

CHAPTER 18

Censorship
and
Free Speech Debates

Seven writers in this chapter explore contemporary situations that generate debates about censorship—and First Amendment rights. These situations include removing some controversial passages in assigned books, "policing" the Internet, and restricting student "speech." As you explore these issues, keep in mind that the Supreme Court continues to hand down rulings that shape our interpretation of First Amendment rights, so what is protected speech under the First Amendment is never absolute—it continues to evolve or be reinterpreted, depending on your point of view. Also keep in mind that many would argue that there is no such thing as absolute freedom in any society and that the First Amendment does not pretend to offer absolute freedoms. For example, you cannot go into a crowded theater and yell "Fire!" when there is no fire. You will be arrested for this behavior that puts others at risk.

Prereading Questions

1. Have you considered positions between the extremes of absolutely no censorship of published materials (in any medium) and of laws prohibiting the publication of obscene, pornographic, or treasonable works or hate speech? What are some possible restrictions that may be agreed upon by most people?

2. What are some ways to control what is published (in any medium) without always resorting to legal restrictions? Are any of these possibilities feasible?

Web Sites Related to This Chapter's Topic

MIT Student Association for Freedom of Expression (SAFE)

http://web.mit.edu/safe/www/safe

Good information and links; site opposes censorship.

Index on Censorship

www.oneworld.org/index_oc

A bimonthly magazine supporting freedom of speech.

National Coalition Against Censorship (NCAC)

www.ncac.org

Organization promoting free speech. Site contains articles and news alerts.

The Censorship Pages, Sponsored by Books A to Z

www.booksatoz.com/censorship

Contains links to resources and lists of frequently banned books.

IF YOU ASSIGN MY BOOK, DON'T CENSOR IT | MARK MATHABANE

A former White House Fellow at the Department of Education, Mark Mathabane is best known for his widely read—and at times controversial—novel *Kaffir Boy*. Mathabane lives and writes in North Carolina; his most recent novel is *Ubuntu*. The following article appeared in the *Washington Post* on November 28, 1999.

PREREADING QUESTIONS Should cutting out parts of or changing parts of a book be seen as censorship? Should publishers—or teachers—change texts in these ways?

1   A few weeks ago, school officials at Kearsley High School in Flint, Mich., decided to censor *Kaffir Boy*, my story of growing up in a South African ghetto during apartheid. On the recommendation of a special committee of administrators, teachers and staff, the school has begun taping over several sentences and parts of sentences in its copies of the book after a half-dozen parents objected to my graphic description of one of the most harrowing experiences

of my life: When I was 7 years old and trapped in the poverty-stricken ghetto of the Alexandra township, 10 miles north of Johannesburg, hunger drove me to tag along with a ring of boys who prostituted themselves for food. One parent called my description "pornography," according to the *Flint Journal*, adding that *Kaffir Boy* belonged in an adult bookstore rather than in a 10th-grade English class.

I wasn't altogether surprised by the parents' objections. The raw emotions 2 and experiences in *Kaffir Boy*, which constitute the core of its power and appeal, have made the book controversial ever since its publication in the United States in 1986. When it became required reading for thousands of high school students nationwide several years ago, it was challenged by parents in school districts in a dozen states and, in some cases, withdrawn. No, what surprises—and disturbs—me is the decision at Kearsley to censor the text, altering a passage that marks a crucial turning point in the book—and in my life.

As a parent of three public school students, ages 6, 8 and 10, I pay atten- 3 tion to what they are assigned to read. I've read them portions of *Kaffir Boy* and my other books, which deal with issues of hunger, child abuse, poverty, violence, the oppression of women and racism. I'm always careful to provide context, to talk to them in a language they can understand.

Every year I also talk to thousands of students about my work and my life 4 in South Africa. I tell them how fortunate they are to live in America, how important it is not to take this nation's freedoms for granted. I recall for them how my peers and I were forbidden by the government in Pretoria to read the U.S. Constitution and the Bill of Rights. I recall how empowered I felt after I clandestinely secured a copy of the Declaration of Independence. And I recall how, during the Soweto uprising of 1976, hundreds of students died fighting for recognition of their unalienable rights to "life, liberty and the pursuit of happiness."

When I came to America in 1978, I was stunned—and exhilarated—to find 5 out that I could walk into any library and check out books that were uncensored and read them without fear of being harassed, thrown in jail or killed.

I have that experience in mind when I think about my own children's read- 6 ing lists. In large part, I trust their teachers to have the judgment to assign books that are not only consistent with educational goals, but also with my children's maturity level. Should my children bring home a book I find objectionable, the responsible thing for me to do would be to request that my child be assigned a different one.

That's why I have no problem with parents who make such a request about 7 *Kaffir Boy*. The parents of a sophomore at West Mecklenburg High School in Charlotte, N.C., where the book has also been challenged, did just that. They were not only uncomfortable with the prostitution scene, but also with my use of racially graphic language such as the word "kaffir" (a pejorative term for "black").

But I strongly disagree with censoring portions of the book. They have no 8 right to decide the issue for other students. Should those students be deprived of what I believe is a key scene in order to make a few parents comfortable?

9   I don't think so. Books aren't written with the comfort of readers in mind. I know I didn't write *Kaffir Boy* that way. I wrote it to reflect reality, to show the world the inhumanity of the apartheid system. It wasn't an easy book for me to write. The memories gave me nightmares. What's more, after the book was published in the United States, members of my family in South Africa were persecuted by the Pretoria regime, which subsequently banned the book there.

10   *Kaffir Boy* is disturbing, but it isn't pornographic. As Kari Molter, chairwoman of the English department at Kearsley High, said, the prostitution scene, which makes up three pages, is "frightening," but it is "an important scene." I included it in the book not to titillate readers, but to reveal a disturbing truth about life under apartheid.

11   That disturbing truth included the terror and helplessness I felt as a child during brutal midnight police raids; the grinding, stunting poverty in which I, my family and millions of other blacks were steeped; the emasculation of my father by a system that denied him the right to earn a living in a way that gave him dignity; the hopelessness and psychic pain that led me to contemplate suicide at age 10; the sacrifices and faith of my long-suffering mother as she battled to save me from the dead-end life of the street and its gangs.

12   Not the least disturbing of those truths is the passage about prostitution. My father, the only breadwinner in a family of nine, had been arrested for the crime of being unemployed. There was no food in our shack, and my mother couldn't even get the usual cattle blood from the slaughterhouse to boil as soup. Desperate for food, one afternoon I linked up with a group of 5-, 6- and 7-year-old boys on the way to the nearby men's hostel. Their pimp, a 13-year-old boy named Mphandlani, promised that at the hostel we would get money and "all the food we could eat" in exchange for playing "a little game" with the migrant workers who lived there.

13   Once inside the hostel, I stood by in confusion and fear as the men and boys began undressing. In the book, I give some physical descriptions of what happened. When Mphandlani told me to undress, too, I refused. One of the men came after me, and I bolted out of the hostel. I fled because I knew that what the men were doing to the boys was wrong, and recalled my parents telling me never to do wrong things. I was called a fool—and shunned—by those boys afterward.

14   Resisting peer pressure is one of the toughest things for young people to do. That is the lesson of the prostitution scene. It's a lesson that seems to be lost on the people who want to censor my book. Teenagers understand what peer pressure is. They confront tough choices every day, particularly if they happen to live in environments where child abuse, poverty, violence and death are commonplace, where innocence dies young, and where children can't afford to be children.

15   Many students have connected powerfully with the story of *Kaffir Boy*. The book, they've told me in letters and e-mail, teaches them to never give up in the face of adversity, not to take freedom—or food—for granted, to regard education as a powerful weapon of hope, and always to strive to do the right thing.

16   Could *Kaffir Boy* have had this impact without the prostitution scene? I doubt it. It was an event that changed me forever. Could I have made that point using less graphic language? Perhaps. But language is a very sacred thing for

a writer. When I write, I strive for clarity and directness, so the reader understands precisely what I mean. To fudge language in order to avoid offending the sensibilities of one group or another leads to doublespeak, which is the death of honesty.

That very honesty is what prompted a senior from Sentinel High School in 17
Missoula, Mont., to send me a letter a few days ago. In it she wrote that *Kaffir Boy* made her realize "that no matter what, there is always hope." It is this hope that I'm seeking to keep alive with my books.

I owe my life to books. While I was in the ghetto, groaning under the yoke 18
of apartheid, wallowing in self-pity, believing that I was doomed to die from the sheer agony of frustrated hopes and strangled dreams, books became my best friends and my salvation. Reading broadened my horizons, deepened my sensibilities and, most importantly, made me think. Books liberated me from mental slavery and opened doors of opportunity where none seemed to exist.

Censorship is not the solution to the legitimate concern some parents have 19
about what is appropriate for their children to read. I wish child abuse and racism weren't facts of life, but they are. Only by knowing about them can we combat them effectively.

What's more, there are alternatives to censorship. One possible solution 20
lies in schools developing reading-list guidelines, such as those being drawn up by the Charlotte-Mecklenburg school system in the wake of objections to *Kaffir Boy*. Under the guidelines, teachers will still choose their own books, but they will be required to give students and parents a summary of the contents and potential concerns, such as profanity or sexually explicit scenes. I don't mind if my book doesn't make the list, or if some parents choose another title for their offspring, but if students do read it, let them read it the way I wrote it.

QUESTIONS FOR READING

1. What is the author's occasion for writing? What is the specific issue with regard to *Kaffir Boy*?
2. What does Mathabane approve of parents doing? What does he object to?
3. Why is the prostitution scene disturbing? Why is it not, in the author's view, pornographic? What definition of pornography emerges from Mathabane's discussion?
4. How does the author defend his choice of language in *Kaffir Boy*?
5. What did books do for the author?
6. What can schools do, instead of censoring, to help parents guide their children's reading?

QUESTIONS FOR REASONING AND ANALYSIS

1. What does the author seek to accomplish in paragraphs 3–7 when he writes of his children and the U.S. freedoms that he admired from a distance in South Africa?

2. What is Mathabane's claim?

3. Mathabane would rather students not read his book than read it with parts removed. Can you understand his position? Why does he think it inappropriate to change someone's words?

4. Has the author presented an effective argument against altering books? Against censorship? Explain.

QUESTIONS FOR REFLECTING AND WRITING

1. Have you read *Kaffir Boy*? If so, did you find it disturbing? Did you find it moving and encouraging, as the author suggests?

2. Are there other assigned readings that bothered you—or that your parents did not want you to read? If so, how did you handle the situation?

3. Do you agree with Mathabane's definition of pornography? If not, why not?

WHY THE FIRST AMENDMENT (AND JOURNALISM) MIGHT BE IN TROUBLE

KEN DAUTRICH AND JOHN BARE

Ken Dautrich, chair of the department of public policy at the University of Connecticut, directed the study, "The Future of the First Amendment," with colleague David Yalof. They are coauthors of the book *The First Amendment and the Media in the Court of Public Opinion* (2002). John Bare, Dautrich's coauthor for this article, is vice president for strategic planning and evaluation at the Arthur M. Blank Family Foundation in Atlanta. Their article appeared in the Summer 2005 issue of *Nieman Reports*, published by Harvard University.

PREREADING QUESTIONS Should the government control content on the Internet? Does the First Amendment protect flag burning?

1   Our first-of-its-kind exploration of the future of the First Amendment among American high school students—a highly visible study of 112,000 students and 8,000 teachers in over 300 high schools—suggests a fragile future for key constitutional freedoms while also pointing us to potential remedies. This study, "The Future of the First Amendment," which was released earlier this year, arrived at a timely moment in American history, on the heels of a national election and amid a war the President is using, by his account, to spread democratic freedoms. The results drew remarkable media attention, which tended to focus on one of the more fearful statistics to emerge from the study: Only 51 percent of 9th to 12th graders agree that newspapers should be allowed to publish freely without government approval of stories—in other words, nearly half entertain the idea of newspaper censorship.

2   Beyond that flashpoint finding, the study allows for a more thorough understanding of today's high school students and can point us to potential remedies. The research also suggests ways to improve support for the First

Amendment. While many of the findings raise concern, some are not so bad. Some are even encouraging. Most of all, the results should be viewed within the context of the history of the First Amendment, which faced challenges— some would say it was compromised—as soon as it was adopted.

FIRST AMENDMENT CHALLENGES

One of the first acts of the first Congress in 1789 was to append a Bill of Rights to the U.S. Constitution, which, among other things, explicitly denied Congress the ability to tamper with Americans' rights of free expression. Indeed, through the course of our history, Americans and their leaders have proclaimed a commitment to freedom and liberty. Most recently, President Bush, in his second inaugural address, justified the Iraqi and Afghani military operations as a vehicle to spread freedom and liberty throughout the world. 3

Despite a long history of veneration to these values, freedom of expression has met with a number of challenges. Not long after adoption of the First Amendment, President John Adams and the Federalist Congress passed the Alien and Sedition Acts, severely thwarting the freedom to speak out against government. Abraham Lincoln's suspension of habeas corpus, the internment of Japanese Americans during Franklin Roosevelt's administration after Pearl Harbor, Senator Joseph McCarthy's "red scare," and Attorney General John Ashcroft's aggressive implementation of the USA Patriot Act represent just a few of the more notable breaches to liberty in America. 4

Like any value in our society, the health and vitality of freedom and liberty are largely dependent upon the public's attention to, appreciation for, and support of them. When Americans are willing to compromise freedom of expression in return for a sense of being more secure, then government officials can more readily take action to curtail freedom. Public fear of Communism allowed McCarthy to tread on people's liberty, just as fear of terrorism allowed Ashcroft to curb freedoms. 5

The real protection of free expression rights lies not in the words of the First Amendment. Rather, it lies in the people's willingness to appreciate and support those rights. That idea led the Freedom Forum's First Amendment Center to commission an annual survey on public knowledge, appreciation and support for free expression rights since 1997 to gauge the health and well-being of the First Amendment. 6

If public opinion is a good measure of the First Amendment's well-being, then its annual checkup has been fraught with health problems. 7

- While more than 9-in-10 agree that "people should be allowed to express unpopular opinions," a paltry 4-in-10 believe that high school students should be able to report on controversial issues in school newspapers without the consent of school officials.

- More than one-third say the press has too much freedom.

- Fewer than 6-in-10 say that musicians should be able to sing songs with lyrics that may be offensive to some.

8   These annual checkups have shown over time that half of adults think that flag burning as a method of protest should not be tolerated. In general, the surveys have revealed that the public holds low support for, a lack of appreciation for, and dangerously low levels of knowledge of free expression rights. Is it no wonder, then, that the suspension of liberty in this land of freedom has been so readily accomplished by its leaders from time to time?

9   It was these rather anemic annual checkups that convinced the John S. and James L. Knight Foundation to commission this unique survey of American high school students and to begin a wider discussion about how to strengthen the polity's commitment to the democratic ideal of freedom and liberty.

10   What follows are some findings from the Knight Foundation survey of high school students that explain, in part, why Americans should be considered about the First Amendment's future.

- Thirty-six percent of high school students openly admit that they take their First Amendment rights for granted and another 37 percent say they never thought enough about this to have an opinion.
- Seventy-five percent incorrectly believe that it is illegal to burn the flag as a means of political protest, and 49 percent wrongly think that government has the right to restrict indecent material on the Internet.
- A source of the lack of support for free press rights might be due to the fact that only four percent of students trust journalists to tell the truth all of the time.
- Thirty-five percent say the First Amendment goes too far in the rights it guarantees, and 32 percent think the press has too much freedom to do what it wants.

PROPOSING SOME REMEDIES

11   This is a bleak picture of what may be in store for the First Amendment as this group matures into adulthood. More importantly, however, a number of findings from the study suggest policies or actions that might better prepare students to value and use their constitutional freedoms. While the suggestions below grow out of findings that are based on correlations, not causation, the logic of the policy ideas holds up against both our experience and our understanding of the data.

12   1. Instruction on the First Amendment matters. Education works! Students who have taken classes that deal with journalism, the role of the media in society, and the First Amendment exhibit higher levels of knowledge and support for free expression rights than those who haven't. The problem, of course, is that the strong trend toward math and science and "teaching to the standardized test" has crowded out instruction that could help students develop good citizenship skills. The less the schools focus on developing strong citizens, the weaker our democracy becomes. The positive lesson to learn from this is that through enhancements to the high school curriculum. students can become better prepared to value and use their freedoms.

2. Use leads to greater appreciation. When students are given an oppor- 13 tunity to use their freedoms, they develop a better appreciation for them. The Knight project found that students who are engaged in extracurricular student media (such as school newspaper, Internet sites, etc.) are more aware and much more supportive of free expression rights.

3. School leaders need lessons, too. Most high school principals need to 14 be reminded of the value of experiential learning and its implications for the future of the First Amendment. While 80 percent of principals agree that "newspapers should be allowed to publish freely without government approval of a story," only 39 percent say their students should be afforded the same rights for publishing in the school newspaper. Granted, principals have many issues to deal with (like parents and school board members calling and asking how they could have ever allowed a story to be printed in a school paper). But if we are to expect students to mature into responsible democratic citizens, they should be given the freedom to express themselves and act responsibly while in school.

4. Place the issues in the context of their daily lives. The project suggests 15 that, as with most people, when issues affecting one's freedom are brought close to home, students are best able to discern the true meaning and value of freedom. When asked if they agreed or disagreed with this statement— "Musicians should be allowed to sing songs with lyrics that might be offensive to others"—70 percent agreed (only 43 percent of principals and 57 percent of adults agree with this). Music matters to many young people. When this form of free expression is challenged, most students come to its defense. The lesson, of course, is that in teaching students about the virtues of free expression, showing how it relates to things important to them will best instill in students why it is so important to the life of a democracy.

The future of the First Amendment is, at best, tenuous. As the current 16 group of high school students takes on their important role as citizens in our democracy, their lack of appreciation and support for free expression rights will provide a ripe atmosphere for government to further intrude on these freedoms. Many institutions in society should shoulder part of the responsibility to ensure good citizenship skills for our youth. Parents, religious institutions, the media, as well as leadership from public officials, just to name a few. But the public schools play an especially important role in socializing youngsters in how to be responsible citizens, and through the schools the future health and vitality of the First Amendment might be restored.

QUESTIONS FOR READING

1. What is the occasion for the authors' article? What was the purpose of the study?
2. What is the primary source of protection for free expression? For what reason do Americans allow free expression to be restricted?

3. What views revealed in the nation's "annual checkup" put First Amendment rights at risk, according to the authors? What did the study reveal about high school students' views?

4. State the four remedies proposed by the authors in your own words.

QUESTIONS FOR REASONING AND ANALYSIS

1. What, specifically, is the essay's topic? What is the authors' claim?

2. What assumption about freedom is part of this argument?

3. Analyze the four proposals. Do they seem logical remedies to you? Do some seem more likely to produce change than others?

QUESTIONS FOR REFLECTING AND WRITING

1. What statistic is most surprising to you? Why?

2. Do you share the authors' concerns for the tenuous state of free speech in the United States? If you disagree, how would you rebut them?

3. Can democracy survive without First Amendment rights? Be prepared to debate this issue.

A LITTLE CIVILITY, PLEASE | MARK DAVIS

Mark Davis, a Texas native and graduate of the University of Maryland, is a popular radio talk show host (the "Mark Davis Show") in the Dallas/Fort Worth area and a columnist for the Dallas *Star-Telegram*. The following column was posted on Star-Telegram.com on March 5, 2003.

PREREADING QUESTIONS The courts have established that schools have rights that would seem to violate students' First Amendment rights. Should they? If so, in what areas? If not, why not?

1   Try something for me.

2   Send your teen-ager to school wearing a T-shirt that says, "Martin Luther King Jr. Was Evil" or "Jews Lie: There Was No Holocaust."

3   Then wait for supporters to suggest that your child was not engaged in the spread of hate but rather in the sparking of vigorous debates.

4   First, your kid would have been yanked from school so fast that his eyeballs would have popped out.

5   But just let him (or you) argue that all this does is get people talking about the civil rights era or anti-Semitism, and the shock will be replaced by laughter.

6   That is exactly the argument made by defenders of Bretton Barber, a Michigan high school junior. The intellectual opening salvo he offered in his school on Feb. 17 was a T-shirt bearing the face of President Bush, framed by the words "International Terrorist."

7   A regular William F. Buckley, this kid.

His intent was obviously not to start a constructive discussion. Conversely, 8 the school did not seek to squelch debate by ordering young Barber to turn the shirt inside out or go home.

If his T-shirt was more generalized and less hateful, with a slogan such as 9 "No War" or even the famous Steve Nash shirt, "Shoot for Peace," I'd say the school should relax.

In the 1960s, students wearing black armbands to protest the Vietnam War 10 won U.S. Supreme Court approval. In the case of Tinker v. Des Moines, the court ruled that students "did not shed their constitutional rights to freedom of expression at the schoolhouse gate."

Well, not all of them, anyway. In the years since, we have properly learned 11 that schools do indeed have the right to establish dress guidelines. Most people have shed the absurd notion that an 11th-grader in a public school has the exact same First Amendment rights as an adult in the outside world.

The student newspaper can be barred from calling for the principal's 12 ouster. Student assemblies can be squelched if they feature racial or religious bigotry.

And T-shirts can be nixed if they are—here's the tough word—*disruptive.* 13

Well, how exactly does a T-shirt disrupt? Do the words on the fabric leap from 14 the wearer's chest and block the students' view of the teacher and blackboard?

No, but an atmosphere that fails to preserve a sense of order and decorum 15 sends the message that various other behavioral extremes might also be tolerated. That is bad.

An armband is one thing. Hate speech, even under the guise of political 16 discourse, is quite another.

How bizarre is it that most who would stand up for Barber's hamhanded 17 "protest" condemning the president would recoil in shock if a kid wore a logo for Marlboro cigarettes or a Confederate flag emblem?

Gosh, wouldn't these be lost opportunities to discuss tobacco and the Civil 18 War?

Passionate debate on controversial issues is good for students and should 19 be encouraged. But within that exercise must be rules of decorous speech and behavior.

This should have nothing to do with whether we agree or disagree with the 20 sentiment expressed. A student wearing a "Clinton is a Pervert" shirt around 1999 or so would have received no argument from me with regard to content, but I would have supported any school banning it.

The *Star-Telegram* is not the only newspaper to stick up for Bretton Barber. 21 I would expect a certain First Amendment zeal from journalists, and I am not immune to it myself.

But his scolding is not, as an editorial stated, a missed opportunity for dis- 22 cussion. It is an opportunity far too rarely claimed, namely to teach a kid what is and is not permissible within the borders of civilized debate.

Young Barber should be welcome to suggest and participate in vigorous 23 discussions on important issues on his own time or in an appropriate class.

QUESTIONS FOR READING

1. What is Davis's occasion for writing? That is, what student action has received media attention?
2. What are some of the controls that the courts have given to K–12 schools since the 1960s? What, specifically, can lead to a prohibiting of T-shirts?
3. What is Davis's newspaper's position on Bretton Barber? Why is Davis not surprised by his paper's position?

QUESTIONS FOR REASONING AND ANALYSIS

1. What is Davis's claim? Where does he state it?
2. What is Davis's evidence? How does he defend his position?
3. How does he rebut the potential counterargument that students should be encouraged to debate controversial issues?
4. Study the examples Davis gives of T-shirt slogans that would quickly be squelched. What do they have in common? What is Davis's point in using those examples?
5. What strategy does Davis use in paragraphs 7 and 18?

QUESTIONS FOR REFLECTING AND WRITING

1. Do you agree with Davis's position on T-shirt slogans? If so, why? If not, how would you rebut his argument?
2. Why have the courts defended the right of K–12 schools to limit the First Amendment rights of students? Is this different from the issue of controlling access to certain Web sites through a college server? (See Robert O'Neil, pages 512–16.) Should it be different? Why or why not?

WHAT LIMITS SHOULD CAMPUS NETWORKS PLACE ON PORNOGRAPHY? | ROBERT O'NEIL

A former president of the University of Wisconsin system and the University of Virginia, Robert O'Neil holds a law degree from Harvard University and currently teaches constitutional and commercial law at the University of Virginia. He is also the founding director of the Thomas Jefferson Center for the Protection of Free Expression and an authority on First Amendment issues. His article was published in the *Chronicle of Higher Education* on March 21, 2003.

PREREADING QUESTIONS Should pornography be restricted on the Internet? Should access to pornography be restricted at the office? Do you have a position on these issues?

1   What if you were about to present a PowerPoint lecture to a large undergraduate class, but found instead on your computer a series of sexually explicit ads and material from pornographic Web sites? That's essentially what happened recently to Mary Pedersen, a nutrition-science professor at California

Polytechnic State University at San Luis Obispo. That incident and the increasing presence of such imagery at Cal Poly have led to a novel, although undoubtedly predictable, struggle over computer content—one that is quite likely to be replicated at countless campuses in the coming months.

A concerned faculty group at Cal Poly has announced its intention to bring 2 before the Academic Senate, sometime this spring, a "Resolution to Enhance Civility and Promote a Diversity-Friendly Campus Climate." Specifically, the measure would prohibit using the university's computers or network to access or download digital material generally described as "pornography." The resolution would also forbid the "transmission" of hate literature and obscenity on the Cal Poly network.

The sponsoring faculty members have offered several reasons for propos- 3 ing such drastic action. First and foremost, they contend that the ready availability of sexually explicit imagery can create occasional but deeply disturbing encounters like Pedersen's discovery of unwelcome and unexpected material on her classroom computer. The pervasive presence of such images, proponents of the resolution argue, is inherently demeaning to female faculty members, administrators, and students.

Indeed, they suggest that the university might even be legally liable for 4 creating and maintaining a "hostile workplace environment" if it fails to take steps to check the spread of such offensive material. That concern has been heightened by a putative link to a growing number of sexual assaults in the environs of the university.

Those who call for tighter regulation cite several other factors to support 5 anti-pornography measures. In their view, a college or university must maintain the highest of standards, not only in regard to the integrity of scholarship and relations between teachers and students, but also in the range of material to which it provides electronic access. The clear implication is that the ready availability of sexually explicit and deeply offensive imagery falls below "the ethical standards that the university claims to uphold."

Critics of easy access to such material also claim that it can divert time, tal- 6 ent, and resources from the university's primary mission. Kimberly Daniels, a local lawyer who is advising the resolution's sponsors, told the student newspaper that "it is offensive that Cal Poly is taking the position that it is acceptable for professors to view pornography during work hours in their work office." That risk is not entirely conjectural. In fact, one professor left the institution last year after being convicted on misdemeanor charges for misusing a state-owned computer, specifically for the purpose of downloading in his office thousands of sexually explicit images. Local newspapers have also reported that the FBI is investigating another former Cal Poly professor who allegedly used a campus computer to view child pornography.

Finally, the concerned faculty group insists that the free flow of porno- 7 graphic materials may expose the Cal Poly computer network to a greater risk of virus infection. They cite a student's recent experience in opening a salacious virus-bearing attachment that the student mistakenly believed had been sent by one of his professors.

8   The proposed Academic Senate resolution has touched off an intense debate. The university's existing computer-use policy presumes that access and choice of material are broadly protected, although it adds that "in exceptional cases, the university may decide that such material directed at individuals presents such a hostile environment under the law that certain restrictive actions are warranted." The new proposal would focus more sharply on sexually explicit imagery, and would require those who wish to view such material through the campus network to obtain the express permission of the university's president.

9   Defenders of the current approach, including the senior staff of the university's office of information technology, insist that a public university may not banish from its system material that is offensive, but legal, without violating First Amendment rights. Those familiar with the operations of such systems also cite practical difficulties in the enforcement of any such restrictions, given the immense volume of digital communications that circulate around the clock at such a complex institution.

10   The debate at Cal Poly echoes what occurred some six years ago in Virginia. The General Assembly enacted what remains as the nation's only ban on public employees' use of state-owned or state-leased computers to access sexually explicit material—at least without express permission of a "superior" for a "bona fide research purpose." Six state university professors immediately challenged the law on First Amendment grounds. A district judge struck down the statute, but the U.S. Court of Appeals for the Fourth Circuit reversed that ruling. The law had been modified before that judgment, and many Virginia professors have since received exemptions or dispensations, but the precedent created by the appeals-court decision remains troubling for advocates of free and open electronic communications.

11   The Virginia ruling complicates the Cal Poly situation. The First Amendment challenge of those who oppose the Academic Senate resolution is less clear than it might at first appear. Two premises underlying that resolution— the need to protect government-owned hardware and the imperative to combat sexual hostility in the public workplace—contributed both to the passage of the Virginia ban, and to its eventual success in the federal courts. What's more, the U.S. Equal Employment Opportunity Commission some months ago gave its blessing to a hostile-workplace complaint filed by Minneapolis Public Library staff members who were offended by persistent display of graphic sexual images on reading-room terminals.

12   Thus, there is more than a superficial basis for the claims of Cal Poly's porn-banishers that (in the words of one faculty member) "the First Amendment doesn't protect . . . subjecting others to inappropriate material in the workplace." Even the information-technology consultant who has championed the current computer-use policy at the university has conceded that access to controversial material is fully protected only "as long as it isn't offending others."

13   Although the desire to reduce the potential for offense and affront to other users of a campus computer network seems unobjectionable, its implications

deserve careful scrutiny. In the analogous situation of public terminals in a library reading room, it is one thing to ask a patron who wishes to access and display sexually explicit material—or racially hateful material, for that matter—to use a terminal facing away from other users and staff members. It is quite another matter to deny access to such material altogether on the plausible premise that, if it can be obtained at all, there is a palpable risk that its visible display will offend others. To invoke an analogy that is now before the U.S. Supreme Court in a challenge to the Children's Internet Protection Act: It is one thing for a library to provide—even be compelled to provide—filtered access for parents who wish it for their children, but quite another to deny all adult patrons any unfiltered access.

What Cal Poly should seek to do, without impairing free expression, is to 14 protect people from being gratuitously assaulted by digital material that may be deeply offensive, without unduly restricting access of those who, for whatever reason, may wish to access and view such material without bothering others. The proposal in the resolution that permission may be obtained from the university's president, for bona-fide research purposes, is far too narrow. Among other flaws, such a precondition might well deter sensitive or conscientious scholars, whether faculty members or students, who are understandably reluctant to reveal publicly their reasons for wishing to access sexually explicit images or hate literature.

A responsible university, seeking to balance contending interests of a high 15 order, might first revisit and make more explicit its policies that govern acceptable computer use and access, by which all campus users are presumably bound. Such policies could condemn the flaunting of thoughtless dissemination of sexually explicit material and digital hate literature, expressing institutional abhorrence of such postings, without seeking to ban either type of material. The computer network might also establish a better warning system through which to alert sensitive users to the occasional and inevitable presence of material that may offend. Finally, a broader disclaimer might be in order, recognizing the limited practical capacity of a university server to control (or even enable users to avoid) troubling material.

What is needed is a reasonable balance that avoids, as Justice William O. 16 Douglas warned a half-century ago, "burning down the house to roast the pig." That aphorism has special felicity here; in the offensive flaunting of sexually explicit imagery, there is a "pig" that doubtless deserves to be roasted. But there is also a house of intellect that must remain free and open, even to those with aberrant tastes and interests.

QUESTIONS FOR READING

1. What is the occasion for O'Neil's article? What is he responding to?
2. What is the resolution some Cal Poly faculty want passed by their Academic Senate? How do they want to limit access?
3. List the arguments for their resolution in your own words.

4. What are the arguments of those supporting the current Cal Poly Internet guidelines?

5. What arguments were used to support the Virginia ban?

6. How do these First Amendment debates affect terminals in public libraries? What is the current ruling on public libraries?

QUESTIONS FOR REASONING AND ANALYSIS

1. What is O'Neil's claim? Where does he state it? What, specifically, does he think that a university's position or strategy should be regarding "offensive" materials obtained through the university's server?

2. What organization does O'Neil use in the development of his argument? (Note where he states his claim.) What does he gain by his approach?

3. Where, essentially, does the author stand on censorship versus First Amendment freedoms?

4. Examine O'Neil's conclusion. How does he use Justice Douglas's metaphor effectively to conclude his argument?

QUESTIONS FOR REFLECTING AND WRITING

1. Evaluate O'Neil's argument. Is he clear and thorough in his analysis of the conflicting positions in this debate? Does he, in your view, have the stronger argument? If so, why? If not, why not?

2. Analyze the author's use of a conciliatory approach. Where does he acknowledge the merits of the opponents' views? How does his claim seek common ground? What might you conclude about the effectiveness of the conciliatory approach when engaged in First Amendment issues?

ONLINE LESSONS ON UNPROTECTED SEX | ANDREW J. MCCLURG

A graduate of the University of Florida, Andrew McClurg is a law professor at Florida International University and author of many law review articles and two legal humor books. He has frequently been recognized as an outstanding teacher. He maintains a Web site: lawhaha.com. His essay was published August 15, 2005, in the *Washington Post*.

PREREADING QUESTIONS Have you posted personal information online? If so, why? Should you post personal details that expose the private lives of others?

1   Kiss-and-tell is as old as love itself. Fortunately, most indiscreet paramours limit their blabbing to a few confidants. Not Jessica Cutler. In May 2004, she spilled out the graphic details of her sexual exploits on Capitol Hill on a blog accessible to hundreds of millions of Internet users.

Now a federal lawsuit by one of her past lovers has set up a potentially 2
high-stakes battle between privacy and speech rights and could give new
meaning to the idea of safe sex in a wired world.

Cutler's blog, written under the pseudonym Washingtonienne, was a daily 3
diary of her sex life while working as a staffer for Sen. Mike DeWine (R-Ohio).
It recounted, entertainingly and in considerable—sometimes embarrassing—
detail, her ongoing relationships with six men, including plaintiff Robert Steinbuch, a lawyer who also worked for DeWine. Although Cutler never used his
full name, and usually referred to the plaintiff by his initials, Steinbuch alleges
the blog revealed sufficient information, including his first name, physical description and where he worked, to identify him.

The Internet gossip site Wonkette published excerpts from Cutler's blog, 4
touching off a media "feeding frenzy" in which Steinbuch was repeatedly identified by his full name. Cutler capitalized on the publicity. She gave print, broadcast and online interviews, posed nude for *Playboy* and reportedly received a
$300,000 advance for her just-published book, a veiled fictional account of
a Senate staffer's sexual adventures on Capitol Hill.

Steinbuch's argument is compelling. By any normative standard, he suf- 5
fered a genuine wrong. As he asserts in his complaint, "It is one thing to be
manipulated and used by a lover, it is another thing to be cruelly exposed to
the world."

The law, however, appears to be against him. This is because Steinbuch 6
does not allege that any of the statements about him are untrue. False statements that damage one's reputation can be actionable as defamation. The
essence of Steinbuch's claim is: You humiliated me by publicizing these true
details about my private life.

His case hinges on a century-old privacy tort claim known as "public dis- 7
closure of private facts." In theory, the tort provides a remedy when one pub-
licizes private, embarrassing, non-newsworthy facts about a person in a manner
that reasonable people would find highly offensive. But while Cutler's actions
may meet this standard, courts have long been hostile to such lawsuits because
of a fear of inhibiting free speech. The Supreme Court has never upheld punishment, based on a privacy theory, for the publication of true information.

In 1989 the court tossed out a lawsuit against a newspaper for publishing 8
a rape victim's name in violation of Florida law. While it stopped short of ruling
that a state may never punish true speech, the test it adopted for when that
can be done without violating the First Amendment is so stringent Justice
Bryon White lamented in dissent that the court had "obliterate[d]" the public
disclosure tort.

One might think the non-newsworthiness of Steinbuch's sex life would save 9
his privacy claim from a free-speech defense. It could, but newsworthiness has
proved to be a broad and elusive legal test in privacy lawsuits. The rape victim's name in the 1989 Florida case, for example, was deemed to be sufficiently
related to the public's interest in crime to doom her claim.

10   Steinbuch's case spotlights the inadequacy of privacy law—developed back when gossip mostly traveled across backyard fences—for responding to the challenges of the Internet age. Today's technology grants any person—no matter how selfish, irresponsible or malicious—the power to invade privacy globally, at almost no cost. All it takes is a computer and Internet access. Some blogging companies offer free services.

11   And blogs are just the tip of the iceberg. In May an Oregon woman sued Yahoo after her ex-boyfriend posted nude pictures of her on the site and Yahoo failed to remove them. Expect more litigation.

12   While we wait to see if old law can adapt to new realities, don't forget the C-word when making safe-sex inquiries. No, not condoms or contraceptives. Ask potential partners if they own a computer.

QUESTIONS FOR READING

1. Who is Jessica Cutler? What did she do?
2. Who is Robert Steinbuch? What has been his response to Cutler's Web disclosures?
3. What laws protect Cutler? What legal precedent is Steinbuch using? What two issues will affect the outcome of his case?

QUESTIONS FOR REASONING AND ANALYSIS

1. McClurg can be expected to be interested in this situation because of the technical legal debate. What else about this modern example of gossip interests the author?
2. Is the author just reporting on a current legal debate—or does he have a position? What, if any, is his claim?
3. What is clever about McClurg's opening and closing paragraphs?

QUESTIONS FOR REFLECTING AND WRITING

1. The Internet poses interesting questions regarding free speech. If you were the judge, how would you rule on Steinbuch's suit? Why?
2. Even if the law supports Cutler, does that make her "wired gossip" right? Defend your position.

LET A THOUSAND FILTERS BLOOM | ANNE APPLEBAUM

Currently a columnist and editorial board member of the *Washington Post,* Anne Applebaum was a journalist and writer in Poland and London for 20 years before returning to the United States. She is the author of *Gulag: A History* (2003). The following *Post* column appeared July 20, 2005.

PREREADING QUESTION What controls, if any, should governments have over the Internet?

In 1949, when George Orwell rote his dystopian novel *1984,* he gave its 1 hero, Winston, a job at the Ministry of Truth. All day long, Winston clips politically unacceptable facts, stuffs them into little pneumatic tubes, and then pushes the tubes down a chute. Beside him sits a woman in charge of finding and erasing the names of people who have been "vaporized." And their office, Orwell wrote, "with its fifty workers or thereabouts, was only one sub-section, a single cell, as it were, in the huge complexity of the Records Department."

It's odd to read *1984* in 2005, because the politics of Orwell's vision aren't 2 outdated. There are still plenty of governments in the world that go to extraordinary lengths to shape what their citizens read, think and say, just like Orwell's Big Brother. But the technology envisioned in *1984* is so—well, 1980s. Paper? Pneumatic tubes? Workers in cubicles? Nowadays, none of that is necessary: It can all be done electronically, especially if, like the Chinese government, you seek the cooperation of large American companies.

Without question, China's Internet filtering regime is "the most sophisti- 3 cated effort of its kind in the world," in the words of a recent report by Harvard Law School's Berkman Center for Internet and Society. The system involves the censorship of Web logs, search engines, chat rooms and e-mail by "thousands of public and private personnel." It also involves Microsoft Inc., as Chinese bloggers discovered last month. Since early June, Chinese bloggers who post messages containing a forbidden word—"Dalai Lama," for example, or "democracy"—receive a warning: "This message contains a banned expression, please delete." It seems Microsoft has altered the Chinese version of its blog tool, MSN Spaces, at the behest of Chinese government. Bill Gates, so eloquent on the subject of African poverty, is less worried about Chinese free speech.

But he isn't alone: Because Yahoo Inc. is one of several companies that have 4 signed a "public pledge on self-discipline," a Yahoo search in China doesn't turn up all of the (politically sensitive) results. Cisco Systems Inc., another U.S. company, has also sold hundreds of millions of dollars of equipment to China, including technology that blocks traffic not only to banned Web sites, but even to particular pages within an otherwise accessible site.

Until now, most of these companies have defended themselves on the 5 grounds that there are side benefits—a Microsoft spokesman has said that "we're helping millions of people communicate, share stories, share photographs and build relationships"—or on the grounds that they can't control technology anyway. A Cisco spokesman told me that this is the "same equipment technology that your local library uses to block pornography," and besides, "we're not doing anything illegal."

But as U.S. companies become more deeply involved in China, and as tech- 6 nology itself progresses, those lines may begin to sound weaker. Over the past couple of years, Harry Wu, a Chinese human rights activist and former political prisoner, has carefully tracked Western corporate cooperation with Chinese police and internal security, and in particular with a Chinese project called "Golden Shield," a high-tech surveillance system that has been under construction for the past five years. Although the company won't confirm it, Wu says. Cisco representatives in China have told him that the company has contracts to provide technology to the police departments of at least 31 provinces. Some of that technology may be similar to what the writer and former businessman Ethan Gutmann describes in his recent book, *Losing the New China: A Story of American Commerce, Desire and Betrayal*. Gutmann—whose account is also bitterly disputed by Cisco ("He's getting a lot of press out of this," complained the spokesman)—claims to have visited a Shanghai trade fair where Cisco was advertising its ability to "integrate judicial networks, border security, and vertical police networks" and more generally its willingness to build Golden Shield.

7   If this isn't illegal, maybe it should be. After the Tiananmen Square massacre in 1989, the United States passed a law prohibiting U.S. firms from selling "crime control and detection" equipment to the Chinese. But in 1989, the definition of police equipment ran to truncheons, handcuffs and riot gear. Has it been updated? We may soon find out: A few days ago, Rep. Dan Burton of the House Foreign Relations Committee wrote a letter to the Commerce Department asking exactly that. In any case, it's time to have this debate again. There could be other solutions—such as flooding the Chinese Internet with filter-breaking technology.

8   Beyond legality, of course, there's morality. And here the judgment of history will prove more important than whatever Congress does or does not do today. Sixty years after the end of World War II, IBM is still battling lawsuits from plaintiffs who accuse the company of providing the "enabling technologies" that facilitated the Holocaust. Sixty years from now, will Microsoft, Cisco and Yahoo by doing the same?

QUESTIONS FOR READING

1.   What is this column about? Be precise.

2.   What U.S. companies are involved? What are they doing?

3.   How do the U.S. companies defend their business in China?

QUESTIONS FOR REASONING AND ANALYSIS

1.   What does Applebaum seek to accomplish in her opening paragraphs? How is *1984* still relevant? How is it outdated?

2.   What is Applebaum's attitude toward the sales of censorship technology to the Chinese government? How do you know?

3.   Explain the meaning of the title.

QUESTIONS FOR REFLECTING AND WRITING

1.   Do you think sales of censorship technology to China should be illegal? Why or why not?

2.   Should these sales by U.S. companies be viewed as immoral and judged in the court of public opinion? Why or why not?

BUSINESS IS BUSINESS | DAVID MCHARDY REID

A professor at the Rochester Institute of Technology, David Reid is director of the Center of International Business. He regularly consults on strategy with companies all over the world and is the author of numerous articles and books on business management and international strategy. Reid's argument was published June 20, 2005, in *USA Today*.

PREREADING QUESTION The United States does restrict the sales of some products to some nations. Should it control the sale of electronic products that restrict freedom on the Internet?

Readers shouldn't be surprised by Microsoft's recent agreement to ban 1 words such as "democracy" and "freedom" from use by bloggers on its China Web portal.

It is not the role of major corporations to police the behavior of other cul- 2 tures. Companies of all hues regularly adjust their positions to meet the acceptable standards of the countries in which they operate. Adaptation is intrinsic to the reality of doing business around the globe. Brands and products must be adapted and trade-offs made.

For example, a tire manufacturer has to choose whether a particular tire will 3 deliver road-holding performance or longevity. The two are in counterpoint. Similarly, the whitening ingredients in toothpaste may deliver a brighter smile but serve to weaken teeth. When information is available, consumers and manufacturers have to choose what to consume and what properties to deliver.

U.S.-based consumer products companies operating in Bangkok, for instance, 4 fill the trucks of cash-paying customers arriving at their distribution facilities. They neither ask the source of their customers' funds nor the destination of the merchandise; nor should they. These companies are not government agents. They have a fiduciary duty to their stockholders to focus on their businesses. Yet the funds may stem from narcotics trafficking through the Golden Triangle, and the goods may be destined for Burma, also known as Myanmar. In this way, critics might argue these companies are subsidizing the corrupt anti-democratic Myanmar regime.

As for Microsoft, its primary role is to sell software and other products in 5 the context of the political environments in which it operates. It is preferable that it concentrates on selling its products. In so doing, it makes the trade-off between accepting potential damage to its brand, in the longer term, by being perceived as kowtowing to a nondemocratic regime, but benefiting by satisfying the needs of Chinese consumers.

Good works are on a different agenda. The Bill and Melinda Gates Foun- 6 dation, created on the vast wealth of Microsoft, is able to support much noble work, including promising to wipe out malaria. That's appropriate. Let's not confuse necessary business practices with charity or political objectives.

QUESTIONS FOR READING

1. What is Reid's subject?
2. What do businesses do to sell products in different countries? What choices do consumers as well as companies make all of the time?

3. What is the point of the example of selling in Bangkok?

QUESTIONS FOR REASONING AND ANALYSIS

1. What is Reid's claim? What are the specific points of support for his claim?
2. Analyze his argument. Would you challenge any of his points? If so, how?
3. Some might rebut by asserting that Reid uses a false analogy. What point of his might be viewed as a false analogy?
4. What does the author want to accomplish in his concluding paragraph?

QUESTIONS FOR REFLECTING AND WRITING

1. Compare Reid's and Applebaum's arguments. Who has the more compelling argument, in your view? Why?
2. Is business always business only? Are there no ethical restrictions in business? If there are some, then how do we decide what they are? When they apply? Be prepared to debate these issues.

© Rick Fowler/Corbis

Read: What is the situation shown in this photo? Who are the figures? What are they doing?

Reason: What can you infer to be the specific situation depicted in this photo? On what do you base your inference?

Reflect/Write: Are demonstrations helpful? Do they serve any purpose?

CHAPTER 19

Ethics and the Law—Current and Enduring Debates

The following eight articles explore and debate four current criminal justice issues: the law and the ethics of the Terri Schiavo case, trying juveniles as adults, the use of animals in medical research, and capital punishment as a sentencing option in some crimes. Much was written about the Schiavo case, both in terms of the ethics of removing her feeding tube and the powers, if any, of government to intervene. One response to teenagers committing murder has been to try them as adults so that adult sentencing, rather than juvenile detention, can be applied. We need to think, as individuals and as a society, about our handling of juvenile offenders. The abuse of animals continues to concern many, and, within that broad context, is the issue of using animals in medical research. Here you will find an argument and a rebuttal to that specific argument, originally published together. Finally, two highly regarded writers debate the social, moral, and philosophical questions relevant to capital punishment.

Prereading Questions

1. Under what circumstances, if any, should family members cease life-sustaining strategies for a patient in a comatose state?
2. Why have we separated juveniles from the adult penal system? Why have some people changed their views on trying juveniles as adults?
3. Do advances in medical research ever outweigh the cruelty associated with the use of animals to achieve those advances?
4. What are the current laws on the use of capital punishment? In capital cases, what kinds of evidence should be presented to decide on guilt beyond a reasonable doubt?
5. If you wanted to change any of the current laws on these issues to make them reflect your views, how would you go about trying to get the laws changed?

Web Sites Related to this Chapter's Topic

www.internationaltaskforce.org

Site with information and links on broad issues of euthanasia.

www.blogsforterri.com

Site with articles and links to many blogs on the Schiavo case.

Fund for the Placement of Animals in Medical Experiments

www.frame.org.uk

Site of a British charity that contains useful links on animals in research.

Association of the British Pharmaceutical Industry

www.abpi.org.uk/amric/amric.asp

Site of an association that supports the use of animals in medical research.

Justice Center Focus on the Death Penalty

http://justice.uaa.alaska.edu/just/death/index.html

From the University of Alaska, a site that provides statistics and court decisions as well as good links.

University of San Diego, Ethics Across the Curriculum

http://ethics.acusd.edu/death_penalty.html

Site with legislative information, statistics, and links.

Cornell Law School—Cornell Death Penalty Project

www.lawschool.corenll.edu/library/death

Contains information on court decisions and results of relevant studies.

Website of Child Defense Attorney Andrew Vachss

http://www.vachss.com

Links to agencies and Web sites that deal with trying juveniles as adults.

CONGRESS SHOULD STAY OUT OF PRIVATE FAMILY MATTERS | MOLLY IVINS

A graduate of Smith College and Columbia University, Molly Ivins began her career as a reporter. She has been a syndicated columnist since 1980. She is also a contributor to magazines and has a collection of her columns published under the title *Molly Ivins Can't Say That, Can She?* The following article was published on March 24, 2005.

PREREADING QUESTION What do you know about the Terri Schiavo case? If you need information, do some online research before reading this and the next essay.

I write about the Terri Schiavo case as one who has personally confronted 1 the "pull-the-plug" question on several levels in recent years and as a staggered observer of this festival of political hypocrisy, opportunism and the trashing of constitutional law, common sense and common decency.

Look, the fundamental question in such cases is, "Who decides?" Prefer- 2 ably, the dying themselves, with a living will. In this case, evidence that Terri Shiavo did not want in her life continued in its current pitiable state has been offered and accepted in several courts of law. Next, the next-of-kin, though in many cases someone else may be closer to the dying person, such as a long-time lover, should be legally designated to make the decision through power of attorney.

Bad cases make bad law, and this is a bad case. In the tragic cases where 3 a family splits on the decision, the case goes to court, where there is a well-established body of law on the subject. The Schiavo case has been litigated for seven years now, the verdict upheld at every level (including the U.S. Supreme Court, by refusing to hear arguments). It is beyond comprehension, not to mention the Constitution, that the Congress of the United States and the president should have involved themselves at this point.

What on Earth makes them think they have the right to do so? Both liber- 4 tarians and constitutional conservatives, including Supreme Court Justice Antonin Scalia, should be having fits over this push by the federal government into a private family matter. Congress has no power to overturn judicial decisions, nor has it any role in such painful personal decisions. This is as arrogant a usurpation of power as we have had since Franklin D. Roosevelt's court-packing plan.

5   As Rep. Barney Frank (D-Mass.) so trenchantly put it, "This is a terribly difficult decision which we are, institutionally, totally incompetent to make." President Bush is neither a neurologist nor a medical ethicist. What on Earth is he doing in this case?

6   For your information, while he was governor of Texas, Bush signed the Advance Directives Act in 1999, which gives hospitals the right to remove life support in cases where there is no possibility of revival or when the family cannot pay, no matter what the family's wishes are in the matter. If Bush is so concerned about the right to life, why didn't he give Texas Death Row inmate Karla Faye Tucker, executed in 1998, more than 10 minutes' consideration and some cheap mockery?

7   The very Republicans who pushed for this arrogant, interfering bill, which if used across the board would take away everyone's right to make his or her own decisions in these awful cases, are the same people who voted to cut Medicaid, which pays for the care of people like Terri Schiavo across the country.

8   That the main player in this fiasco is House Majority Leader Tom DeLay (R-Texas)—who is in the midst of yet another scandal himself—is enough to make anyone throw up. This is a man whose sense of morality is so deformed that upon being admonished three times by the House Ethics Committee, his response was to change the rules and stack the committee.

9   What a despicable display of pure political pandering. What an insult to everyone who has faced this decision without ever considering asking 535 strangers in Washington what to do.

10   How can anyone want to cede that authority to a bunch of politicians?

11   I am indebted to the blogger called Digby for the following points: Those who passed this bill are the same politicians who want to put financial limitations on medical malpractice suits like the one that provided the care for Terri Schiavo for many years while she was in "a persistent vegetative state." They are the same politicians who have just finished changing bankruptcy law so that it is now much harder for families hit by tragedies like this one to get out from under the staggering medical bills. How dare they talk about morality?

12   How can a bunch of blowhard television pundits with no medical training whatsoever conclude anything about Terri Schiavo's condition from watching a few seconds of edited videotape? Where on Earth do they get the nerve to make any pronouncements about her condition?

13   Who are those professional anti-abortion activists who think they have the right to make decisions about someone else's life?

14   I watched one of the dearest men who ever lived, who had no chance of regaining consciousness, toss for hours in relentless pain before he escaped because the State of New York had such draconian drug laws the doctors were afraid to give him enough morphine to kill the pain. The New York legislature, in all its majesty, made sure the 76-year-old, 90-pound man dying from cancer did not become a morphine addict. Political bodies have no business making medical decisions.

15   Do I believe in miracles? Yes, I do, and I'm praying for one that will let the sanctimonious phonies in Washington realize the gross moral error of their presumption.

QUESTIONS FOR READING

1. What, according to Ivins, is the key legal question in a case such as Schiavo's? How has this question been answered in the Schiavo case?

2. What did the president and the Congress try to do? What is the author's reaction to their actions?

3. What other congressional decisions are cited by Ivins as relevant to her argument?

QUESTIONS FOR REASONING AND ANALYSIS

1. What is Ivins's subject? (Be precise. The "Terri Schiavo case" is not precise enough.)

2. What is Ivins's claim?

3. How would you describe the author's tone? What word choice and other strategies create that tone?

4. Who is the 76-year-old man who dies in New York? How does he contribute to our understanding of the author's position and attitude?

QUESTIONS FOR REFLECTING AND WRITING

1. Evaluate Ivins's argument. Given her particular approach to the issue, are the details about presidential and congressional actions relevant to her argument? Why or why not?

2. Who, in the author's view, should make the decision to end a patient's life? Do you agree? Why or why not? If you disagree with Ivins, how would you rebut her argument?

THE CASE HEARD ROUND THE WEB | WESLEY J. SMITH

An attorney, Wesley J. Smith is a consultant to the International Task Force on Euthanasia and Assisted Suicide and to the Center for Bioethics and Culture. He is also a senior fellow at the Discovery Institute, a frequent speaker, and the author of a number of books, including *Culture of Death: The Assault on Medical Ethics in America* (2000) and *Consumer's Guide to a Brave New World* (2004). His essay on the Schiavo case appeared April 4, 2005, in the *Weekly Standard*.

PREREADING QUESTIONS Do you read blogs? Have a blog site? How did you learn about the Terri Schiavo case? Were you influenced in your views of the case by the source(s) of your information?

The arguments over the fate of Terri Schiavo have sowed distrust among the courts and the political branches of government, and forced a state legislature, a popular governor, both houses of Congress, and the president of the United States into tight, uncomfortable political corners. The pending death-by-dehydration of this disabled, 41-year-old Clearwater, Florida, woman—thanks to a court order sought by her husband—has at the same time become a media event of epic proportion.

2   The big question is why. Why did this story, of all stories, reach such a critical mass; why did Terri Schiavo, of all people, ignite such a deep, visceral emotional response in so many of her fellow citizens; why have so many people devoted so much energy and commitment to this case—some utterly intent upon keeping her alive, others adamantly believing she should be left to die as quickly as possible?

3   After all, hers is hardly the first "food and fluids" case to have bitterly divided a family, and it won't be the last. Nor is it at all uncommon in America for patients who are Terri's age and younger to be deprived of food and water so that they will die, even when there is doubt about what they would choose in such circumstances, and even though they are neither brain dead nor terminally ill.

4   Terri's putative husband (he started a new family in the mid-1990s) isn't the first spouse to fight in court with in-laws over the removal of a feeding tube. Two cases in the 1990s were strikingly similar, albeit the courts ruled in favor of life. Both Michael Martin of Michigan and Robert Wendland of California were unquestionably conscious when their wives fought nasty, protracted court battles through trial, appeal, and final decision by state supreme courts to see them die. Michael Martin had allegedly expressed a desire to live to an examining doctor using a facilitated communication device; Robert Wendland could roll a wheelchair down a hospital corridor. Both cases made the news, yet neither consumed the entire country or caused the deep societal divisions that Terri's case has generated.

5   This controversy hit the stratosphere, I believe, because of one simple but very powerful innovation: the Internet. When the Michael Martin and Robert Wendland families fought almost identical battles in the 1990s, the Internet, especially as a source of news, was still in its infancy. It was difficult to spread facts or perspectives that the mainstream media did not want to present—and the reporting of those cases was as skewed and one-sided in favor of death as has been the coverage of Terri Schiavo.

6   Moreover, and I think more important, the guardian-spouses maintained tight control over the images of their husbands. Almost every contemporary picture of Robert Wendland and Michael Martin that was made public was one that Mary Martin and Rose Wendland's lawyers wanted to be seen. While the parents were telling the world that their sons were responsive and aware, the approved photographs and videos generally depicted them as nonresponsive. Indeed, when despite this tight control a San Francisco television program managed to air an "unapproved" video that showed Wendland taking pegs from a board and replacing them during a therapy session, lawyers for Lodi Memorial Hospital—whose spokeswoman had claimed incorrectly that Robert was as good as comatose—sought (unsuccessfully) to have a gag order imposed in the case.

7   By the time the Schiavo litigation came along, the Internet was booming and becoming ever more sophisticated. Ordinary users had the technical means to view videos uploaded onto websites. Knowing that cases such as these are often won and lost in the sphere of public relations, Terri's parents,

Robert and Mary Schindler, and their supporters created a website, terris-fight.org, which carried news of the case, copies of court documents, the story of Terri's life, and most crucially, powerful videos of Terri Schiavo apparently reacting to the world around her.

In one scene, Terri is asked by a doctor to open her eyes For a moment; nothing. Then, Terri's eyes flutter and she opens them. She seems to be so eager to please—and this really touched my heart when I first saw that she opens her eyes so wide her forehead wrinkles. 8

In another scene, Terri's mother comes into the room. She talks happily to her daughter, "Hi! Hi, it's Mommy. How are you?" As Mary Schindler adjusts Terri on the bed, it sure looks as if she recognizes her mother, and she smiles happily. In a third scene Terri appears to respond happily when music is turned on. And so it goes. 9

These videos made all of the difference. Rather than being an abstract "vegetable" (a truly loathsome word to describe any human being), Terri came to be seen as a real person, obviously alive, and fully human. Michael Schiavo's supporters and proponents of Terri's dehydration within the bioethics community stomped and fussed, insisting that the appearance of interactivity in the videos were actually just reflexes. But many viewers saw these complaints as being akin to the cheating husband who tells his wife after she has caught him in flagrante delicto: "Who are you going to believe—me, or your lying eyes?" The videos told a different story than that of a supposedly vegetative woman unable to interact with others. And for hundreds of thousands, maybe millions of people, the real Terri came out of the shadows, a sub-human no more. 10

The ability of supporters of Terri's life to distribute underreported information via the Internet enabled the Schiavo drama to reach an international stage. Terri's supporters were outraged when the mainstream media first downplayed the story entirely, and then, when the case finally demanded front-page coverage, cherry-picked facts to emphasize those aspects that favored Michael. For example, the *New York Times* routinely omitted what many saw as an acutely relevant fact about Terri's husband in deciding whether he or her parents should control her care: Michael has started a new family with his "fiancée," with whom he has two children. Under any ordinary understanding of the facts, that constitutes marital abandonment. 11

When I wrote a series of stories on the Schiavo case for *The Daily Standard* at weeklystandard.com in late 2003 and early 2004, many focusing on facts and arguments that I believed were being, shall we say, "overlooked" by the elite press, I witnessed the power of Internet information distribution. To my great gratification, my articles were passed from computer to computer, finding their way into readers' hands all over the world. Indeed, this is the first non-Internet article I have written about Terri Schiavo in some time. Yet, in recent weeks, as her tragic story reached its unjust denouement, my old online articles continued to circulate widely, to an enormous online audience, thanks both to direct quotations and links from blogs. The contrast with my early days in the anti-euthanasia movement has been stunning. 12

13   Nor is my experience unique. Check out the blogosphere, and you will find stories and commentary on Terri multiplying beyond the ability of anyone to keep up. They, in turn, echo back to talk radio and coverage in more traditional media, to the point that even the *New York Times* acknowledged Michael Schiavo's marital complications.

14   Terri Schiavo's story is a tragedy, and, for many, an outrage. But it holds a glimmer of hope for those with views that have traditionally received short shrift in the media—a category that decidedly includes those fighting to reverse the presumption of death enshrined in all too many state laws covering cases like Terri Schiavo's. Thanks to the new online media, these cases will never again be one-sided.

QUESTIONS FOR READING

1. What, according to Smith, is the key question about the Schiavo case? How does Smith answer the question?
2. To what other cases does Smith compare the Schiavo case? How are they similar? How do they differ?
3. What were the effects of the Internet's role in this case?

QUESTIONS FOR REASONING AND ANALYSIS

1. Smith's subject, expressed in his title, is the impact of the Internet on the Schiavo case. What is his claim regarding this topic?
2. What is Smith's view of the Schiavo case? Where does he stand on the decision to remove her life support? How do you know? What evidence can you point to in the essay to support your inference about his position?
3. What is Smith's view of the "traditional" media? How do you know?
4. What is the tone of the essay? What makes his tone appropriate for a discussion of his specific topic?

QUESTIONS FOR REFLECTING AND WRITING

1. Were you aware of the role of the Internet in the Schiavo case? Is there still a Web site for this issue? Check online and see—and look for other sites as well. Then consider: Did the Internet change the outcome of the case? Did it make other changes? Do you expect bloggers to influence public policy debates from now on? Explain your position.
2. Compare the Ivins and Smith essays on the Schiavo case. How are they similar? How do they differ? Consider presentation, not just positions. Then consider: For someone without a strong position on this issue, which essay might have the greater impact? Why? Would the answer vary, given the reading audience you have in mind?

ADULT CRIME, ADULT TIME | LINDA J. COLLIER

An attorney, Linda J. Collier is currently dean of public services and social sciences at Delaware County Community College in Pennsylvania. She has been the director of student legal services at Pennsylvania State University and special assistant for legal affairs to two college presidents, in addition to teaching courses in sociology and criminal justice. The following essay, published in the *Washington Post* in 1998, is written in response to the case of a 12-year-old and a 14-year-old shooting four students and a teacher at their school in Jonesboro, Arkansas, that same year.

PREREADING QUESTIONS Why do some think that the juvenile justice system is inadequate? What kinds of cases was it originally designed to handle?

When prosecutor Brent Davis said he wasn't sure if he could charge 11-year-old Andrew Golden and 13-year-old Mitchell Johnson as adults after Tuesday afternoon's slaughter in Jonesboro, Ark., I cringed. But not for the reasons you might think. 1

I knew he was formulating a judgment based on laws that have not had a major overhaul for more than 100 years. I knew his hands were tied by the long-standing creed that juvenile offenders, generally defined as those under the age of 18, are to be treated rather than punished. I knew he would have to do legal cartwheels to get the case out of the juvenile system. But most of all, I cringed because today's juvenile suspects—even those who are accused of committing the most violent crimes—are still regarded by the law as children first and criminals second. 2

As astonishing as the Jonesboro events were, this is hardly the first time that children with access to guns and other weapons have brought tragedy to a school. Only weeks before the Jonesboro shootings, three girls in Paducah, Ky., were killed in their school lobby when a 14-year-old classmate allegedly opened fire on them. Authorities said he had several guns with him, and the alleged murder weapon was one of seven stolen from a neighbor's garage. And the day after the Jonesboro shootings, a 14-year-old in Daly City, Calif., was charged as a juvenile after he allegedly fired at his middle-school principal with a semiautomatic handgun. 3

It's not a new or unusual phenomenon for children to commit violent crimes at younger and younger ages, but it often takes a shocking incident to draw our attention to a trend already in progress. According to the U.S. Department of Justice, crimes committed by juveniles have increased by 60 percent since 1984. Where juvenile delinquency was once limited to truancy or vandalism, juveniles now are more likely to be the perpetrators of serious and deadly crimes such as arson, aggravated assault, rape and murder. And these violent offenders increasingly include those as young as the Jonesboro suspects. Since 1965, the number of 12-year-olds arrested for violent crimes has doubled and the number of 13- and 14-year-olds has tripled, according to government statistics. 4

5   Those statistics are a major reason why we need to revamp our antiquated juvenile justice system. Nearly every state, including Arkansas, has laws that send most youthful violent offenders to the juvenile courts, where they can only be found "delinquent" and confined in a juvenile facility (typically not past age 21). In recent years, many states have enacted changes in their juvenile crime laws, and some have lowered the age at which a juvenile can be tried as an adult for certain violent crimes. Virginia, for example, has reduced its minimum age to 14, and suspects accused of murder and aggravated malicious wounding are automatically waived to adult court. Illinois is now sending some 13-year-olds to adult court after a hearing in juvenile court. In Kansas, a 1996 law allows juveniles as young as 10 to be prosecuted as adults in some cases. These are steps in the right direction, but too many states still treat violent offenders under 16 as juveniles who belong in the juvenile system.

6   My views are not those of a frustrated prosecutor. I have represented children as a court-appointed guardian *ad litem,* or temporary guardian, in the Philadelphia juvenile justice system. Loosely defined, a guardian *ad litem* is responsible for looking after the best interest of a neglected or rebellious child who has come into the juvenile courts. It is often a humbling experience as I try to help children whose lives have gone awry, sometimes because of circumstances beyond their control.

7   My experience has made me believe that the system is doing a poor job at treatment as well as punishment. One of my "girls," a chronic truant, was a foster child who longed to be adopted. She often talked of how she wanted a pink room, a frilly bunk bed and sisters with whom she could share her dreams. She languished in foster care from ages 2 to 13 because her drug-ravaged mother would not relinquish her parental rights. Initially, the girl refused to tolerate the half-life that the state had maintained was in her best interest. But as it became clear that we would never convince her mother to give up her rights, the girl became a frequent runaway. Eventually she ended up pregnant, wandering from place to place and committing adult crimes to survive. No longer a child, not quite a woman, she is the kind of teenage offender for whom the juvenile system has little or nothing to offer.

8   A brief history: Proceedings in juvenile justice began in 1890 in Chicago, where the original mandate was to save wayward children and protect them from the ravages of society. The system called for children to be processed through an appendage of the family court. By design, juveniles were to be kept away from the court's criminal side, the district attorney and adult correctional institutions.

9   Typically, initial procedures are informal, non-threatening and not open to public scrutiny. A juvenile suspect is interviewed by an "intake" officer who determines the child's fate. The intake officer may issue a warning, lecture and release; he may detain the suspect; or, he may decide to file a petition, subjecting the child to juvenile "adjudication" proceedings. If the law allows, the intake officer may make a recommendation that the juvenile be transferred to adult criminal court.

10   An adjudication is similar to a hearing, rather than a trial, although the juvenile may be represented by counsel and a juvenile prosecutor will represent the interests of the community. It is important to note that throughout the pro-

ceedings, no matter which side of the fence the parties are on, the operating principle is that everyone is working in the best interests of the child. Juvenile court judges do not issue findings of guilt, but decide whether a child is delinquent. If delinquency is found, the judge must decide the child's fate. Should the child be sent back to the family—assuming there is one? Declare him or her "in need of supervision," which brings in the intense help of social services? Remove the child from the family and place him or her in foster care? Confine the child to a state institution for juvenile offenders?

This system was developed with truants, vandals and petty thieves in mind. 11 But this model is not appropriate for the violent juvenile offender of today. Detaining a rapist or murderer in a juvenile facility until the age of 18 or 21 isn't even a slap on the hand. If a juvenile is accused of murdering, raping or assaulting someone with a deadly weapon, the suspect should automatically be sent to adult criminal court. What's to ponder?

With violent crime becoming more prevalent among the junior set, it's a 12 mystery why there hasn't been a major overhaul of juvenile justice laws long before now. Will the Jonesboro shootings be the incident that makes us take a hard look at the current system? When it became evident that the early release of Jesse Timmendequas—whose murder of 7-year-old Megan Kanka in New Jersey sparked national outrage—had caused unwarranted tragedy, legislative action was swift. Now New Jersey has Megan's law, which requires the advance notification of a sexual predator's release into a neighborhood. Other states have followed suit.

It is unequivocally clear that the same type of mandate is needed to establish a uniform minimum age for trying juveniles as adults. As it stands now, there is no consistency in state laws governing waivers to adult court. One reason for this lack of uniformity is the absence of direction from the federal government or Congress. The Bureau of Justice Statistics reports that adjacent states such as New York and Pennsylvania respond differently to 16-year-old criminals, with New York tending to treat offenders of that age as adults and Pennsylvania handling them in the juvenile justice system.

Federal prosecution of juveniles is not totally unheard of, but it is uncom- 14 mon. The Bureau of Justice Statistics estimates that during 1994, at least 65 juveniles were referred to the attorney general for transfer to adult status. In such cases, the U.S. attorney's office must certify a substantial federal interest in the case and show that one of the following is true: The state does not have jurisdiction; the state refuses to assume jurisdiction or the state does not have adequate services for juvenile offenders; the offense is a violent felony, drug trafficking or firearm offense as defined by the U.S. Code.

Exacting hurdles, but not insurmountable. In the Jonesboro case, prose- 15 cutor Davis has been exploring ways to enlist the federal court's jurisdiction. Whatever happens, federal prosecutions of young offenders are clearly not the long-term answer. The states must act. So as far as I can see, the next step is clear: Children who knowingly engage in adult conduct and adult crimes should automatically be subject to adult rules and adult prison time.

QUESTIONS FOR READING

1. What are some of the problems with current state laws governing juvenile crimes?

2. Briefly summarize the author's history of the juvenile justice system.

3. In addition to failing to punish properly, in the author's view, what else do juvenile court systems fail to do?

4. Where does Collier look for help in correcting the juvenile justice system?

QUESTIONS FOR REASONING AND ANALYSIS

1. What is Collier's claim? Where does she state it?

2. In paragraph 11, when she writes "What's to ponder?" what response does she want from readers?

3. Although Collier is writing in response to the Jonesboro murders, she refers to other juvenile murders in paragraph 3. What does she seek to gain by this?

4. The author asserts that she is not writing as a "frustrated prosecutor" and describes her experience as a court-appointed guardian. What does she gain by this discussion in paragraphs 6 and 7?

QUESTIONS FOR REFLECTING AND WRITING

1. Could the example of one of Collier's court-appointed "girls" be used to argue for, rather than against, the juvenile justice system? Explain your answer.

2. Do you think that juveniles should be tried as adults? If so, in what situations? If not, why not?

KIDS WHO KILL ARE STILL KIDS | RICHARD COHEN

Richard Cohen is a journalist with a syndicated column. The following column appeared in newspapers on August 3, 2001.

PREREADING QUESTIONS Should we, as a country, have a cutoff age for capital sentencing? If so, what should the cutoff age be?

1 When I was about 12, I heaved a cinder block over my neighbor's fence and nearly killed her. I didn't know she was there. When I was about the same age, I started a small fire in a nearby field that spread until it threatened some nearby houses. I didn't mean to do it. When I was even younger, I climbed on top of a toolshed, threw a brick in the general direction of my sister and sent her, bleeding profusely and crying so that I can still hear her, to the hospital. I didn't mean to do that, either.

2 I tell these stories to remind us all that kids are kids and to suggest that even the worst of them—even the ones who commit murder—are still kids. I would be lying if I said that I knew what to do with them—how long they should

be jailed and where—but I do know that something awful has come over this country. It seems the more incomprehensible the crime, the more likely it is that a child will be treated as an adult.

This is what happened to Nathanial Brazill, 14, who was recently sentenced 3 to 28 years in prison for the murder of a teacher, Barry Grunow. Brazill was only 13 when he shot the teacher on the final day of school. Grunow, a much-beloved teacher, had stopped Brazill from talking to two girls and disrupting the class. Earlier in the day, the boy had been suspended for throwing water balloons. He had gone home, gotten a gun and returned to school. Grunow was Brazill's favorite teacher.

I always feel in columns of this sort the necessity to say something about 4 the victim and how his life was taken from him. I feel a particular need to do so in this case because Grunow seemed to be an exceptional teacher, a good person. Anyway—and this is only me talking—I feel a certain awe, a humility, toward people who dedicate their lives to teaching kids instead of, say, peddling tech stocks or mouthing off on television about Gary Condit.[1]

But Grunow is gone and nothing can be done to bring him back. That is 5 not merely a cliché but also an important point. Because always in these cases when it comes time to justify why a minor was treated as an adult, someone says something about sending a message to other kids. This is absurd.

Consider what Brazill did. He shot his teacher before oodles of witnesses. 6 He shot a man he liked. He shot someone without any chance of his getting away. He shot someone for almost no reason at all. He shot someone not in the course of a robbery or a sex crime or because he put a move on his girlfriend but because he is a screwed-up kid, damaged, full of anger and with not much self-control. He shot someone without fully comprehending the consequences. He shot someone, because, among other things, he was just 13 years old.

And yet, he was prosecuted—and sentenced to three years more than the 7 mandatory minimum—as an adult. If there is one thing he is not, it is an adult. But Brazill and, earlier, 13-year-old Lionel Tate were sentenced as if they were button men for some crime family. Tate was given life without parole for the killing of a 6-year-old girl he maintained died in a wrestling accident. These boys were tried as adults but, I'd guess, their ability to participate in their own defense would be labeled juvenile.

Amnesty International says about 200,000 children have been tried as 8 adults by American courts. Florida alone reports that 3,300 kids were prosecuted as adults in fiscal 1999–2000. This sends a message—but it's to the adult community: We're getting tough. Kids, however, are unlikely to get the message. I mean, you know how kids are.

Where is the deterrence in this policy? Will other 13-year-olds now hesitate 9 before killing their teacher? Hardly. Who is being punished? The child at first, but later the adult he becomes.

---

[1]Former member of Congress from California. —Ed.

10   Brazill will be over 40 when he gets out of jail. When he's, say, 35, will he have anything in common with the child who pulled the trigger? No more, I'd say, than I do with the jerk who nearly killed Richie Miller's mother with a cinder block. I didn't set out to hurt anyone, it's true. But neither did Brazill, he says. He just pulled the trigger and the man, somehow, died. It is, when you think about it, a childish explanation.

QUESTIONS FOR READING

1. How many years was Brazill sentenced to? What was his crime?
2. What is Cohen's explanation of Brazill's behavior?
3. What message is supposed to be sent by trying children as adults? What is Cohen's assessment of the success of this strategy?

QUESTIONS FOR REASONING AND ANALYSIS

1. Cohen tells readers that 200,000 children have been tried as adults. Why does he include this statistic?
2. The author begins by reporting some of his actions as a youngster. What does he seek to gain from this beginning?
3. What is Cohen's claim? Evaluate his argument: Is his evidence convincing? Why or why not?

QUESTIONS FOR REFLECTING AND WRITING

1. The United States and Iran are the only two countries that allow for the execution of juveniles. Forty percent of the U.S. states allow the execution of people as young as 16. What should be the cutoff age for capital punishment regardless of the crime? Be prepared to support your position.
2. When you were young, did you do anything that hurt another person, either accidentally—or not so accidentally? If so, what were the consequences? How do you feel now about the incident?
3. How should the two boys Cohen uses as examples have been tried and sentenced, in your view? Be prepared to support your position.

ANIMAL RIGHTS V. ANIMAL RESEARCH: A MODEST PROPOSAL | JOSEPH BERNSTEIN

Dr. Joseph Bernstein is an assistant professor of orthopedics at the University of Pennsylvania's hospital and a senior fellow at the Leonard Davis Institute of Health Economics, also at the University of Pennsylvania. Bernstein's "modest proposal" for animal research appeared in the *Journal of Medical Ethics* in 1996 along with Timothy Sprigge's response.

PREREADING QUESTIONS What is the source of Bernstein's title? (Hint: Check Chapter 23.) Does the demand for advances in medicine justify the use of animals in research? Is the use of animals ethical so long as they are not abused? What constitutes abuse?

Many people love animals. Some animal lovers, though, in the name of ₁ their love, oppose the use of any animals in any medical research, regardless of the care given, regardless of the cause. Of course, many other animal lovers acknowledge the need for animal subjects in some medical studies, as long as no alternatives exist, and provided that care, respect and dignity are applied at all times. Unhappily, between the opponents of animal research and the researchers themselves lies no common ground, no place for an agreement to disagree: the opponents are not satisfied merely to abstain from animal experimentation themselves—they want everyone else to stop too.

Despite that, I would argue that in this case (to a far greater extent than, ₂ say, in the case of abortion) the animal rights question can be answered by exactly that tactic: the abstention of the opposition. Of course, I do not advocate abstention from debate; and, of course, abstention from performing research by those who are not researchers is not meaningful. Rather, I propose that the protesters—and every citizen they can enlist—abstain from the benefits of animal research. I say let the proponents of animal rights boycott the products of animal research. Let them place fair market-place pressure on ending activities they find reprehensible. Let them mobilise the tacit support they claim. Let the market for therapies derived from animal research evaporate, and with it much of the funding for such work. Let the animal lovers attain their desired goal without clamour, and without violence.

To assist them, I offer a modest proposal.   ₃

I suggest that we adopt a legal release form, readily available to all patients, ₄ which will enable them to indicate precisely which benefits of animal research they oppose—and from which, accordingly, they refuse to benefit. This form could be sent to all hospitals and physicians, and would be included in the patient's chart, much like operative consent forms, or Do Not Resuscitate instructions. It should resolve the issue once and for all.

This "Animal Research Advance Directive" would look something like this: ₅

Dear Doctor: ₆

Animals deserve the basic freedom from serving as experiment subjects against their will. Today, we who are committed to seeing the world's scientific laboratories free from unwilling and innocent animals, hereby refuse to benefit from research performed on these victims.

Accordingly, I ask that you care for me to the best of your abilities, but ₇ request that:

(CHECK ALL THAT APPLY)

☐ You do not perform on me a coronary bypass operation, or fix any heart ₈ defect my child may be born with, as these operations and the heart lung machine used during the procedures were developed using dogs. In fact, since the entire field of cardiology has been polluted by animal research for nearly a century, I cannot in good conscience accept any cardiological care.

9   ☐ You treat my child for any disease she may develop, but do not give her a vaccine that was tried first on a blameless animal. As I am not aware of any vaccines that were not animal-tested, please skip them all.

10   ☐ You avoid offering any suggestions regarding my diet and habits, when that information was derived from animal studies. This includes salt and fat intake, tobacco smoke, and various cancer-causing food additives. Do not bother to test my cholesterol levels, as the association between high cholesterol and heart disease is knowledge stolen from the suffering of the innocent.

11   ☐ Should I develop a malignancy, you do not give me chemotherapy, as those drugs were administered first to animals. I must also decline surgical treatment as well, since modern surgical technique and equipment owes its existence to sinful animal research. Finally, do not treat my disease with radiation, since that field, too, was contaminated by dog studies.

12   ☐ You amputate my leg or arm should I break it in such fashion that it requires surgery. Fracture fixation devices were designed through the suffering of dogs, so I must refuse repair of the bone. That probably will hurt a lot, but since I must refuse all pain medicine studied on rats (and that includes just about all of them), it is best if you just remove the damaged limb.

13   Needless to say, I will not accept an AIDS vaccine should one be developed, as unwilling Rhesus monkeys have been used in AIDS research.

14   Thank you for considering my wishes. Only through the concerted avoidance of these ill-gotten technologies can we halt the barbaric practice of animal research. Of course, I have no objection to studying disease on humans. To that end, I pledge my body to science upon my death. It probably will occur a lot sooner than I'd like.

QUESTIONS FOR READING

1. What is Bernstein "proposing"?
2. Why does he include such a long checklist? What does he want to make clear to readers?

QUESTIONS FOR REASONING AND ANALYSIS

1. Does Bernstein seriously expect to see the use of an "Animal Research Advance Directive"? How do you know the answer to this question?
2. What is the tone of this essay? What language and strategies help to create the tone?

QUESTIONS FOR REFLECTING AND WRITING

1. Has Bernstein presented a convincing argument? Are his persuasive strategies effective? Explain your response.
2. If you wanted to refute Bernstein's argument, how would you proceed?

A REPLY TO JOSEPH BERNSTEIN | TIMOTHY SPRIGGE

Endowment fellow in philosophy at the University of Edinburgh, Timothy Sprigge has contributed articles to scholarly journals of philosophy and published several books of philosophy, including *Theories of Existence* (1985) and *Rational Foundations of Ethics* (1990). His argument on the animal rights debate, a response to Joseph Bernstein's argument, also appeared in the *Journal of Medical Ethics* in 1996.

PREREADING QUESTIONS Does the demand for advances in medicine justify the use of animals in research? Is the use of animals ethical so long as they are not abused? What constitutes abuse?

1   Dr Bernstein's "A modest proposal" lays down a witty challenge to opponents of animal experimentation. However, matters are rather less clear cut than he evidently realises and there are various reasons, which I list below, why an anti-vivisectionist may feel no obligation to sign such directives under present conditions. Things would be different if (1) adequately funded facilities on the National Health Service were introduced which would make no use of further medical advances based on painful animal experimentation; (2) public funding for (painful) animal research and "alternative" research henceforth reflected the proportion of those who would not, and those who would, opt for these facilities.

2   (1) A first point is that Dr Bernstein does not distinguish between the use of animals in research which does, and that which does not, involve serious suffering for them (including that imposed by their housing, such as the extremes of boredom, but obviously not including being painlessly killed). The original anti-vivisection societies were, as their names imply, opposed to the cutting up of conscious live animals rather than to human use of animals in general (as may be the case with many animal rightists nowadays) and it seems to me reasonable to use "vivisection" today in a broader sense to cover all research which involves serious animal suffering (something worse, for example, than we feel when we receive an injection). Opponents of this are not necessarily opponents of all use of animals in medical research and it is not clear how many of the medical procedures Dr Bernstein lists were developed through work involving such serious suffering (as opposed, for example, to painless killing). It would facilitate rational debate if both defenders and critics of animal research were clearer on this point than they usually are.

3   (2) Even if, in practice, most of these procedures have been developed in ways which did involve serious animal suffering, it is another question whether they could have been developed without this. The anti-vivisectionist who believes that they could have been, or even probably could have been, developed (by now) by other means has no reason to avoid them because of their unfortunate and, as he thinks, (probably) unnecessary history. In fact, I suggest, no one really knows how far medicine could have advanced had work of a kind which most anti-vivisectionists would condemn, been avoided.[1] If this is so, there is no bad faith in the anti-vivisectionist making use of advances in medicine which he/she guesses would probably have been gained in other ways had the ethics of the past been more like theirs now.

4   The autobahnen in Germany were originally developed for their utility in transporting troops for aggressive war. Should those against aggressive war therefore not use those built in the Hitler period? Likewise Volkswagen cars were developed as cars for the people in the Third Reich as part of a plan to encourage love of that regime. Is one wrong to drive or travel in one today?

5   Many nations established their present borders in wars which involved all manner of what we would now regard as atrocities. Should its decent citizens refuse loyalty to any country with such a past?

6   Few people would answer these questions affirmatively, doubtless believing that, since we cannot change past history, refusing to benefit from its evils, especially where similar benefits could probably have been won otherwise, would be a pointless sacrifice.

7   In short, one may avail oneself of knowledge and techniques which exist now, however first acquired, with a clear conscience even if they were developed in ways which fall below what one would like to be the moral standards of today. Where procedures rely on very recent research he/she should perhaps avoid benefiting from it, if he/she can, because this is likely to be part of a current research programme which he/she should be attempting to discourage. But even here if one believes that similarly useful developments in medicine could have occurred without such pain for animals it is not unreasonable or inconsistent to avail oneself of it, in the absence of alternatives (either of procedures or research) which might have been developed instead in a society less ready to base itself on animal suffering.

8   (3) If our society had long been based on a culture which outlawed the causing of serious pain to animals for human benefit it would have been so different through and through that no one can tell whether humans would have been better off or worse off now than they are. After all, we are the product of a history which, in innumerable ways, depended on behaviour which we would now dub immoral, and we just have to accept that for better or for worse. The moral question now is whether these practices can be justified in the light of the moral ideals to which we now aspire and the knowledge we now possess. So there is no more call on those of us who argue for the cessation of such animal experimentation as involves serious suffering to reject what was acquired in the past by means of it than there is for us to distance ourselves from most of our institutions with their morally mixed past.

9   (4) Judgments about whether people in the past are to be morally condemned for what they did are highly problematic. People act in a historical context and cannot be expected to live by standards which have been developed since. The anti-vivisectionist thinks that we are now ready for higher standards, in our relations with animals. For one thing the technologies of discovery are more sophisticated and need not be so physically intrusive or painful as perhaps they were bound to be in the past. For another thing, surgery was so dreadful for everyone until the development of anaesthetics, that perhaps people could not be expected to be too sensitive about animals amidst so much inevitable pain for themselves. But, with medical advances meaning so much less pain for us humans of today (when the groups to which we belong behave

themselves, as admittedly too few do), it is surely time to be more sensitive about the suffering of animals for our advantage.

It would clarify the whole debate enormously if the following were sharply distinguished: animal-based research which 1) must involve serious animal suffering; 2) does involve it but which could be replaced by research (whether using animals or not) which does not; 3) does not involve it. All sides might then agree that 2) is wrong (inasmuch as the suffering would be un-contentiously unnecessary) and attention could then be paid to how much falls into the first category and whether the benefits it may bring justify the harm both to animals and those who must render themselves callous to their suffering. As for category 3) that divides into various types the morality of which is, indeed, important but much less urgent. At any rate, I see no reason why an anti-vivisectionist should feel the need to avoid the benefits of research other than what he/she is sure is of the first type.

REFERENCE

[1] Balls M. Recent progress towards reducing the use of animal experimentation in biomedical research. In: Garratini S, van Bekkum DW, eds. *The importance of animal experimentation for safety and biomedical research.* Dordrecht: Kluwer Academic Publishers, 1990: 228–9.

QUESTIONS FOR READING

1. In replying to Bernstein's argument, Sprigge makes several distinctions. What distinctions does he make regarding use of animals in research? What distinction does he make with regard to the past and the present?
2. What does the author assert regarding the behavior of people in the past? Have we opposed the use of animals for human advantages in the past?
3. What distinctions does he recommend for the present use of animals in medical research? How will these distinctions clarify the debate?

QUESTIONS FOR REASONING AND ANALYSIS

1. What is Sprigge's position with regard to the use of medical science based on animal research in the past?
2. To support his argument, Sprigge makes several analogies. Do they provide effective reasoning in support of his argument?

QUESTIONS FOR REFLECTING AND WRITING

1. Does Sprigge make a convincing argument for animal rights activists benefiting from medical science based on animal experiments in the past? Do you agree with him on this point? Why or why not?
2. Is Sprigge effective in establishing some common ground for both sides? If so, what is that common ground? If you think that he has failed to do this, explain why.

3. What are your responses to Sprigge's three categories of current animal-based research? Do you agree that number 2 is wrong? Do you agree that number 3 is not as urgent for debate as number 1? What is your position on number 1? Why?

THE ULTIMATE PUNISHMENT: A DEFENSE
ERNEST VAN DEN HAAG

A naturalized citizen born in 1914 in the Netherlands, Ernest van den Haag holds a doctorate from New York University and has been a psychoanalyst. In addition, he has written many articles in both American and European journals and several books on sociological issues, including violence and crime. "The Ultimate Punishment: A Defense" is reprinted (with some footnotes omitted) from the May 7, 1986, issue of the *Harvard Law Review*. Van den Haag effectively organizes his defense around the arguments put forward by his opponents.

PREREADING QUESTIONS Do you have a position on capital punishment? If so, what is it? If not, do you think you should take a stand on this issue? Why or why not?

1   In an average year about 20,000 homicides occur in the United States. Fewer than 300 convicted murderers are sentenced to death. But because no more than thirty murderers have been executed in any recent year, most convicts sentenced to death are likely to die of old age.[1] Nonetheless, the death penalty looms large in discussions: it raises important moral questions independent of the number of executions.

2   The death penalty is our harshest punishment. It is irrevocable: it ends the existence of those punished, instead of temporarily imprisoning them. Further, although not intended to cause physical pain, execution is the only corporal punishment still applied to adults. These singular characteristics contribute to the perennial, impassioned controversy about capital punishment.

I. DISTRIBUTION

3   Consideration of the justice, morality, or usefulness of capital punishment is often conflated with objections to its alleged discriminatory or capricious distribution among the guilty. Wrongly so. If capital punishment is immoral *in se*, no distribution among the guilty could make it moral. If capital punishment is moral, no distribution would make it immoral. Improper distribution cannot affect the quality of what is distributed, be it punishments or rewards. Discriminatory or capricious distribution thus could not justify abolition of the death penalty. Further, maldistribution inheres no more in capital punishment than in any other punishment.

4   Maldistribution between the guilty and the innocent is, by definition, unjust. But the injustice does not lie in the nature of the punishment. Because of the finality of the death penalty, the most grievous maldistribution occurs when it is imposed upon the innocent. However, the frequent allegations of discrimination and capriciousness refer to maldistribution among the guilty and not to the punishment of the innocent.

Maldistribution of any punishment among those who deserve it is irrele- 5 vant to its justice or morality. Even if poor or black convicts guilty of capital offenses suffer capital punishments, and other convicts equally guilty of the same crimes do not, a more equal distribution, however desirable, would merely be more equal. It would not be more just to the convicts under sentence of death.

Punishments are imposed on persons, not on racial or economic groups. 6 Guilt is personal. The only relevant question is: does the person to be executed deserve the punishment? Whether or not others who deserved the same punishment, whatever their economic or racial group, have avoided execution is irrelevant. If they have, the guilt of the executed convicts would not be diminished, nor would their punishment be less deserved. To put the issue starkly, if the death penalty were imposed on guilty blacks, but not on guilty whites, or, if it were imposed by a lottery among the guilty, this irrationally discriminatory or capricious distribution would neither make the penalty unjust, nor cause anyone to be unjustly punished, despite the undue impunity bestowed on others.

Equality, in short, seems morally less important than justice. And justice is 7 independent of distributional inequalities. The ideal of equal justice demands that justice be equally distributed, not that it be replaced by equality. Justice requires that as many of the guilty as possible be punished, regardless of whether others have avoided punishment. To let these others escape the deserved punishment does not do justice to them, or to society. But it is not unjust to those who could not escape.

These moral considerations are not meant to deny that irrational discrimi- 8 nation, or capriciousness, would be inconsistent with constitutional requirements. But I am satisfied that the Supreme Court has in fact provided for adherence to the constitutional requirement of equality as much as possible. Some inequality is indeed unavoidable as a practical matter in any system.[2] But, *ultra posse neo obligatur.* (Nobody is bound beyond ability.)

Recent data reveal little direct racial discrimination in the sentencing of 9 those arrested and convicted of murder. The abrogation of the death penalty for rape has eliminated a major source of racial discrimination. Concededly, some discrimination based on the race of murder victims may exist; yet, this discrimination affects criminal victimizers in an unexpected way. Murderers of whites are thought more likely to be executed than murderers of blacks. Black victims, then, are less fully vindicated than white ones. However, because most black murderers kill blacks, black murderers are spared the death penalty more often than are white murderers. They fare better than most white murderers. The motivation behind unequal distribution of the death penalty may well have been to discriminate against blacks, but the result has favored them. Maldistribution is thus a straw man for empirical as well as analytical reasons.

II. MISCARRIAGES OF JUSTICE

In a recent survey Professors Hugo Adam Bedau and Michael Radelet 10 found that 7000 persons were executed in the United States between 1900 and 1985 and that 25 were innocent of capital crimes. Among the innocents they list Sacco and Vanzetti as well as Ethel and Julius Rosenberg. Although their data may be questionable, I do not doubt that, over a long enough period, miscarriages of justice will occur even in capital cases.

11   Despite precautions, nearly all human activities, such as trucking, lighting, or construction, cost the lives of some innocent bystanders. We do not give up these activities, because the advantages, moral or material, outweigh the unintended losses. Analogously, for those who think the death penalty just, miscarriages of justice are offset by the moral benefits and the usefulness of doing justice. For those who think the death penalty unjust even when it does not miscarry, miscarriages can hardly be decisive.

III. DETERRENCE

12   Despite much recent work, there has been no conclusive statistical demonstration that the death penalty is a better deterrent than are alternative punishments. However, deterrence is less than decisive for either side. Most abolitionists acknowledge that they would continue to favor abolition even if the death penalty were shown to deter more murders than alternatives could deter. Abolitionists appear to value the life of a convicted murderer or, at least, his nonexecution, more highly than they value the lives of the innocent victims who might be spared by deterring prospective murderers.

13   Deterrence is not altogether decisive for me either. I would favor retention of the death penalty as retribution even if it were shown that the threat of execution could not deter prospective murderers not already deterred by the threat of imprisonment.[3] Still, I believe the death penalty, because of its finality, is more feared than imprisonment, and deters some prospective murderers not deterred by the threat of imprisonment. Sparing the lives of even a few prospective victims by deterring their murderers is more important than preserving the lives of convicted murderers because of the possibility, or even the probability, that executing them would not deter others. Whereas the lives of the victims who might be saved are valuable, that of the murderer has only negative value, because of his crime. Surely the criminal law is meant to protect the lives of potential victims in preference to those of actual murderers.

14   Murder rates are determined by many factors; neither the severity nor the probability of the threatened sanction is always decisive. However, for the long run, I share the view of Sir James Fitzjames Stephen: "Some men probably abstain from murder because they fear that if they committed murder they would be hanged. Hundreds of thousands abstain from it because they regard it with horror. One great reason why they regard it with horror is that murderers are hanged." Penal sanctions are useful in the long run for the formation of the internal restraints so necessary to control crime. The severity and finality of the death penalty is appropriate to the seriousness and the finality of murder.

IV. INCIDENTAL ISSUES: COST, RELATIVE SUFFERING, BRUTALIZATION

15   Many nondecisive issues are associated with capital punishment. Some believe that the monetary cost of appealing a capital sentence is excessive. Yet most

comparisons of the cost of life imprisonment with the cost of execution, apart from their dubious relevance, are flawed at least by the implied assumption that life prisoners will generate no judicial costs during their imprisonment. At any rate, the actual monetary costs are trumped by the importance of doing justice.

Others insist that a person sentenced to death suffers more than his victim 16 suffered, and that this (excess) suffering is undue according to the *lex talionis* (rule of retaliation). We cannot know whether the murderer on death row suffers more than his victim suffered; however, unlike the murderer, the victim deserved none of the suffering inflicted. Further, the limitations of the *lex talionis* were meant to restrain private vengeance, not the social retribution that has taken its place. Punishment—regardless of the motivation—is not intended to revenge, offset, or compensate for the victim's suffering, or to be measured by it. Punishment is to vindicate the law and the social order undermined by the crime. This is why the kidnapper's penal confinement is not limited to the period for which he imprisoned his victim; nor is a burglar's confinement meant merely to offset the suffering or the harm he caused his victim; nor is it meant only to offset the advantage he gained.[4]

Another argument heard at least since Beccaria is that, by killing a mur- 17 derer, we encourage, endorse, or legitimize unlawful killing. Yet, although all punishments are meant to be unpleasant, it is seldom argued that they legitimize the unlawful imposition of identical unpleasantness. Imprisonment is not thought to legitimize kidnapping; neither are fines thought to legitimize robbery. The difference between murder and execution, or between kidnapping and imprisonment, is that the first is unlawful and undeserved, the second a lawful and deserved punishment for an unlawful act. The physical similarities of the punishment to the crime are irrelevant. The relevant difference is not physical, but social.[5]

V. JUSTICE, EXCESS, DEGRADATION

We threaten punishments in order to deter crime. We impose them not only 18 to make the threats credible but also as retribution (justice) for the crimes that were not deterred. Threats and punishments are necessary to deter and deterrence is a sufficient practical justification for them. Retribution is an independent moral justification. Although penalties can be unwise, repulsive, or inappropriate, and those punished can be pitiable, in a sense the infliction of legal punishment on a guilty person cannot be unjust. By committing the crime, the criminal volunteered to assume the risk of receiving a legal punishment that he could have avoided by not committing the crime. The punishment he suffers is the punishment he voluntarily risked suffering and, therefore, it is no more unjust to him than any other event for which one knowingly volunteers to assume the risk. Thus, the death penalty cannot be unjust to the guilty criminal.

There remain, however, two moral objections. The penalty may be re- 19 garded as always excessive as retribution and always morally degrading. To regard the death penalty as always excessive, one must believe that no crime—no matter how heinous—could possibly justify capital punishment. Such a belief can be neither corroborated nor refuted; it is an article of faith.

20   Alternatively, or concurrently, one may believe that everybody, the murderer no less than the victim, has an imprescriptible (natural?) right to life. The law therefore should not deprive anyone of life. I share Jeremy Bentham's view that any such "natural and imprescriptible rights" are "nonsense upon stilts."

21   Justice Brennan has insisted that the death penalty is "uncivilized," "inhuman," inconsistent with "human dignity" and with "the sanctity of life," that it "treats members of the human race as nonhumans, as objects to be toyed with and discarded," that it is "uniquely degrading to human dignity" and "by its very nature, [involves] a denial of the executed person's humanity." Justice Brennan does not say why he thinks execution "uncivilized." Hitherto most civilizations have had the death penalty, although it has been discarded in Western Europe, where it is currently unfashionable probably because of its abuse by totalitarian regimes.

22   By "degrading," Justice Brennan seems to mean that execution degrades the executed convicts. Yet philosophers, such as Immanuel Kant and G.F.W. Hegel, have insisted that, when deserved, execution, far from degrading the executed convict, affirms his humanity by affirming his rationality and his responsibility for his actions. They thought that execution, when deserved, is required for the sake of the convict's dignity. (Does not life imprisonment violate human dignity more than execution, by keeping alive a prisoner deprived of all autonomy?)

23   Common sense indicates that it cannot be death—our common fate—that is inhuman. Therefore, Justice Brennan must mean that death degrades when it comes not as a natural or accidental event, but as a deliberate social imposition. The murderer learns through his punishment that his fellow men have found him unworthy of living; that because he has murdered, he is being expelled from the community of the living. This degradation is self-inflicted. By murdering, the murderer has so dehumanized himself that he cannot remain among the living. The social recognition of his self-degradation is the punitive essence of execution. To believe, as Justice Brennan appears to, that the degradation is inflicted by the execution reverses the direction of causality.

24   Execution of those who have committed heinous murders may deter only one murder per year. If it does, it seems quite warranted. It is also the only fitting retribution for murder I can think of.

NOTES

1. Death row as a semipermanent residence is cruel, because convicts are denied the normal amenities of prison life. Thus, unless death row residents are integrated into the prison population, the continuing accumulation of convicts on death row should lead us to accelerate either the rate of executions or the rate of commutations. I find little objection to integration.

2. The ideal of equality, unlike the ideal of retributive justice (which can be approximated separately in each instance), is clearly unattainable unless all guilty persons are apprehended, and thereafter tried, convicted and

sentenced by the same court, at the same time. Unequal justice is the best we can do; it is still better than the injustice, equal or unequal, which occurs if, for the sake of equality, we deliberately allow some who could be punished to escape.

3. If executions were shown to increase the murder rate in the long run, I would favor abolition. Sparing the innocent victims who would be spared, *ex hypothesi,* by the nonexecution of murderers would be more important to me than the execution, however just, of murderers. But although there is a lively discussion of the subject, no serious evidence exists to support the hypothesis that executions produce a higher murder rate. *Cf.* Phillips, *The Deterrent Effect of Capital Punishment: New Evidence on an Old Controversy,* 86 AM. J. Soc. 139 (1980) (arguing that murder rates drop immediately after executions of criminals).

4. Thus restitution (a civil liability) cannot satisfy the punitive purpose of penal sanctions, whether the purpose be retributive or deterrent.

5. Some abolitionists challenge: If the death penalty is just and serves as a deterrent, why not televise executions? The answer is simple. The death even of a murderer, however well-deserved, should not serve as public entertainment. It so served in earlier centuries. But in this respect our sensibility has changed for the better, I believe. Further, television unavoidably would trivialize executions, wedged in, as they would be, between game shows, situation comedies and the like. Finally, because televised executions would focus on the physical aspects of the punishment, rather than the nature of the crime and the suffering of the victim, a televised execution would present the murderer as the victim of the state. Far from communicating the moral significance of the execution, television would shift the focus to the pitiable fear of the murderer. We no longer place in cages those sentenced to imprisonment to expose them to public view. Why should we so expose those sentenced to execution?

QUESTIONS FOR READING

1. What does van den Haag mean by "distribution"? That is, what issue in the death penalty debate does the author examine in section one?

2. On what grounds does van den Haag dismiss the issue of possible maldistribution of death sentencing among the guilty? State his argument in your own words.

3. Does van den Haag believe that a significant racial bias can be found in the distribution of capital punishment? Does he offer evidence to support his views?

4. According to van den Haag, what kind of logical fallacy is illustrated by the argument of maldistribution?

5. On what two grounds does the author dismiss challenges to the death penalty based on miscarriages of justice?

6. What do studies show about the death penalty's potential as a deterrent to murder?

7. What is the position on deterrence of those who oppose the death penalty? What does van den Haag conclude about the values of abolitionists?

8. Why does van den Haag dismiss deterrence as an issue in the debate?

9. Why should costs be considered an irrelevant issue?

10. What is the purpose of punishing a criminal, according to van den Haag? Why is this purpose important to our understanding of death sentencing?

11. How does the author refute the idea that death sentencing legitimizes murder? Those who make this claim are using what type of argument? What strategy does van den Haag use to reveal a weakness in this type of argument?

12. What, finally, is the author's justification of legal punishment, including the death penalty?

QUESTIONS FOR REASONING AND ANALYSIS

1. To argue that the death penalty is always excessive, what must one believe? Why does van den Haag believe that the death penalty does not degrade? Explain his argument in your own words.

2. Where does the author place his claim, the thesis of his essay? What does he accomplish by this choice?

3. Consider the author's word choice in the second section. What words does he avoid using that a writer opposed to the death penalty might use instead of "miscarriage of justice" or to refer to the persons executed because of the miscarriage?

QUESTIONS FOR REFLECTING AND WRITING

1. Van den Haag is prepared to accept some miscarriages of justice (some innocent people will be punished) to achieve the advantages of capital punishment. Are you? If you agree with the author, explain why. If you disagree, how would you challenge van den Haag?

2. Van den Haag argues that capital punishment is a form of retribution for murder; it is not revenge but justice. Do you agree with his distinction between retribution and revenge? Explain your views.

3. Evaluate van den Haag's argument. Is it reasoned, thorough, and appropriately serious? Is it logical? Do you think he is right? Why or why not?

DEATH IS DIFFERENT | HUGO ADAM BEDAU

A native of Oregon with a doctorate from Harvard University, Hugo Adam Bedau has taught for many years in the philosophy department at Tufts University. He is the author of articles and books on justice and capital punishment, including *The Courts, the Constitution and Capital Punishment* (1977) and *Death Is Different* (1987). In the following essay, the concluding chapter of *Death Is Different*, Bedau provides a thorough review of the debating points in the argument over capital punishment.

PREREADING QUESTIONS On what should a stand on the death penalty be based? On social/political concerns? On moral or religious beliefs? On practical considerations that include human error? Why?

Insofar as fundamental moral questions are raised by the death penalty,   1
their resolution does not turn on what a majority of the Supreme Court says
the Constitution permits or forbids. Nor does it rest on what the tea leaves of
public-opinion polls can be construed to mean. Morally speaking, what are at
stake are the *reasons* that can be brought forward to support or to criticize this
punishment. These reasons—familiar from public debates, letters to the editor,
and radio and television talk shows—have not significantly altered over the
past generation, and perhaps not even during the past century.

In order of increasing importance, the main reasons for support seem to   2
me to be these six: (1) the death penalty is a far less expensive method of
punishment than the alternative of life imprisonment; the death penalty is
more effective in preventing crime than the alternative because (2) it is a
more effective deterrent, and because (3) it more effectively incapacitates;
(4) the death penalty is required by justice; (5) in many cases there is no feasible alternative punishment; and (6) the death penalty vindicates the moral
order and thus is an indispensable symbol of public authority. I want to evaluate each of these reasons and elaborate especially on those of salient current importance.

THE TAXPAYER'S ARGUMENT

Is the death penalty really so much less expensive than long-term impris-   3
onment? The answer depends on how one allocates the costs imposed under
the two alternatives. The few attempts that have been made to do this in a
manner comparable to the way economists try to answer other questions
about the costs of alternative social policies are in agreement. In the words of
the most recent study, "A criminal justice system that includes the death
penalty costs more than a system that chooses life imprisonment."[1] Why this is
true is easily understood. It is mainly a consequence of the commendable desire to afford every protection to a defendant whose life is at stake, and virtually every such defendant avails himself of all these protections. If the
defendant is indigent, as are most of those accused of crimes that put them in
jeopardy of the death penalty, then society has to foot the bill for the defendant's attorney as well as for the costs involved in the prosecution, jury selection, trial, and appeals. Although in theory these costs would need to be paid
even if the defendant were not on trial for his life, in practice the evidence
shows that non-death-penalty trials and appeals are generally less protracted
and therefore less expensive. So the taxpayer's argument, as I have called it, is
simply wrong on the facts.

But, of course, even if it were sound, no decent citizen or responsible leg-   4
islator would support the death penalty by relying on this argument alone.
Those who seriously advance it do so only because they also believe that the
criminals in question ought to be executed whatever the cost to society and
however galling the expenditure may be. As a consequence, the taxpayer's argument is really no more than a side issue, since defenders and critics of the
death penalty agree that economic costs should take a back seat to justice and
social defense where human life is concerned.

UNIQUELY EFFECTIVE DETERRENT

5   No one has ever offered any scientific evidence that the death penalty is an effective deterrent, or more effective than the alternative of long-term imprisonment, to any such crime as rape, arson, burglary, kidnapping, aircraft hijacking, treason, espionage, or terrorism (which itself typically involves one or more of these other crimes). All arguments for the death penalty that rest on belief in its superior deterrent capacity to prevent or reduce the incidence of these crimes depend entirely on guesswork, common sense, or analogy to its allegedly superior deterrent effects on the crime of murder.

6   What, then, is the evidence that the death penalty is an effective deterrent to murder? There is little or none. Murder comes in many different forms (gangland killings, murder among family members, murder during armed robbery or burglary, murder in jail or prison, murder for hire, murder to escape custody or avoid arrest), but very little of the research on deterrence has concentrated exclusively on one of these types to the exclusion of all the rest. The threat of executions is conceivably a much better deterrent to some types of murder than to others; but no research currently exists to confirm such a hypothesis.

7   It doesn't really matter. Deterrence is increasingly a make-weight in the argument for the death penalty. Public opinion surveys indicate that most of those who profess support for the death penalty would support it even if they were convinced—contrary to what they believe—that it is not a better deterrent than life imprisonment.[2] I find this plausible. Although from time to time there is sporadic evidence in favor of the deterrent power of executions (hardly anyone who thinks about it attaches much differential deterrent efficacy to the death penalty *statutes,* all by themselves), none of it survives careful scrutiny very long.[3] If anything, there is a steadily accumulating body of evidence to suggest that on balance the death penalty may cause (or encourage, or set the example for) more homicides than it prevents, because its "brutalizing" effect out-performs its deterrent effect.[4]

8   Furthermore, and quite apart from the status of the evidence on the issue of deterrence vs. brutalization, one would expect that the rationale for deterrence in our society is of slowly declining importance. In previous centuries and up to a generation ago, when our society punished many *non*homicidal crimes with death, deterrence was the most plausible reason for hanging a counterfeiter or a horse thief or a claim jumper. Today, however, with the death penalty applied exclusively to murder, nondeterrent considerations naturally play an increasingly prominent role all the time. Indeed, social science research, public opinion, and Supreme Court rulings all neatly converge at this point. Despite more than a decade of effort to obtain convincing support for rational belief in the superior deterrent power of the death penalty, the evidence points the other way. During the same period, advocates of capital punishment—both those who are and those who are not aware of this lack of evidence—shifted the basis of their support for executions from deterrence to other reasons. Meanwhile, the Supreme Court has said in effect that the death penalty is unconstitutional except where it is not disproportionate to the crime and regardless of its deterrent effects.

From a public-policy perspective, one can say this: During the past fifteen 9 years, the legislative re-enactment of death penalty statutes has been no more than a series of stabs in the dark, insofar as these laws have been predicated on their supposed superior deterrence. A legislature ought to have better reasons than this for trying to protect the life of its citizens by imposing the threat of the death penalty. On moral grounds, general deterrence is certainly a legitimate function of the criminal law and therefore a justifiable basis on which to construct a system of punishments under law. Nevertheless, the choice of more rather than less severity in punishment for particular crimes on grounds of better deterrence alone encounters two different objections. One is that we violate moral principles if we are willing to use punitive methods, regardless of their savagery, in order to secure slight improvements in deterrence; the other is that there simply is no adequate evidence in favor of the superior deterrent efficacy of the death penalty.

INCAPACITATION AND PREVENTION

No one can dispute that capital punishment, when carried out, does effec- 10 tively incapacitate each offender who is executed. (This has nothing to do with deterrence, however, because deterrence operates by threat and intimidation, not by destroying the capacity to break the law.) Does this incapacitation make a significant dent in the crime rate? The Department of Justice has reported that as of the end of 1984 "approximately 2 of every 3 offenders under sentence of death had a prior felony conviction; nearly 1 out of 10 had previously been convicted for homicide."[5] These data indicate that more than a hundred of those currently under sentence of death may be some of the worst offenders in the nation—and that several hundred more served a prison term for robbery, assault, or some other crime, and then, after their release, went on to commit the even graver crime of murder. (Of course, these data simultaneously show that the vast majority of condemned prisoners are *not* recidivist murderers.) But do these data also show that society needs the incapacitating power of death to prevent more crimes from being committed by convicted capital offenders?

If parole boards and release authorities knew in advance which inmates 11 would murder after their release, the inmates in question would obviously be prevented from committing these offenses by being kept in some form of custody. Yet we have no reliable methods for predicting future dangerousness, and especially not for the propensity of a convicted murderer to murder again.[6] Consequently, the only effective general-policy alternatives to the present one are a system of mandatory death penalties and a system of mandatory prison terms for life. Even then, if the Bureau's own statistics are reliable, this would prevent only a tiny fraction of the twenty thousand or so murders committed in this nation each year. The truth is, as all release statistics agree, very few of the persons convicted of homicide and sent to prison are ever convicted of homicide again. Either to kill all those convicted of murder or to keep them all in prison forever, because of a few exceptions that cannot be identified in advance, would be an expensive and unjustified policy that very few of us, on reflection, would want to support.

12   Opponents of the death penalty encounter their stiffest objections when they try to explain why even the multiple or serial or recidivist murderer should not be executed. Few would disagree that "the thirst for revenge is keenest in the case of mass murder, . . . especially when it includes elements of sadism and brutality against innocent victims."[7] Revenge apart, incapacitation probably has its most convincing application in such cases. It is hardly surprising that many who generally oppose the death penalty would be willing to make an exception for such killers.

13   Let us note first that if the death penalty were confined to such cases, abolitionists would have scored a major victory. The immediate consequence of such a policy would be an unprecedented reduction in the annual number of death sentences—a drop from more than two hundred per year to fewer than twenty, if we can rely on the Bureau of Justice Statistics report quoted above. Any policy change that reduced death sentences by more than 90 percent should be welcomed by opponents of the death penalty as a giant step in the right direction.

14   More controversial is whether abolitionists could accommodate such an exception on moral grounds. The best way to do so, it seems to me, is to argue much as George Bernard Shaw did earlier in this century in his little book *The Crime of Imprisonment* that the execution of such murderers is society's only alternative—we have no nonlethal methods of sedation or restraint that suffice to make certain that such offenders will not and cannot kill yet again. However, this is a factual question, and I (unlike Shaw) think that once the offender is in our custody, we are never in the position where our only recourse is to lethal methods. Others who have studied the problem more carefully agree;[8] there are reasonably humane methods at our disposal for coping with the most difficult and dangerous prisoners.

15   In the end, however, I think one must admit that the refusal to execute a murderer who has repeated his crime—not to mention those who embody murderous evil on a gigantic scale, such as an Adolph Eichmann or a Lavrenti Beria—is evidence of a position on the death penalty that owes something to fanatic devotion as well as to cool reason. Dedicated pacifists and devoutly religious opponents of the death penalty may well be able to embrace such categorical opposition to executions without fear of rebuke from reason. Conscientious liberals, however, cannot so easily refuse to compromise. Do they not already compromise on other life-and-death issues—often tolerating suicide, euthanasia, abortion, the use of lethal force in social and self-defense—thereby showing that they refuse to accept any moral principle that categorically condemns all killing? If so, what is so peculiarly objectionable, from the moral point of view as they see it, in an occasional state-authorized killing of that rare criminal, the murderer who has murdered more than once? I cannot point to any clear and defensible moral principle of general acceptability that is violated by such a compromise, a principle that *absolutely forbids* such executions. If one nonetheless opposes all executions, as I do, then it must be on other grounds.

RETRIBUTIVE AND VINDICTIVE JUSTICE

Today there is substantial agreement that retribution is an essential aspect 16 of the criminal justice system, and that a general policy of punishment for convicted criminals is the best means to this end. Less argument exists on whether retribution alone justifies the practice of punishment; and there is no consensus on how to construct a penalty schedule on retributive grounds, matching the severity of punishments to the gravity of crimes. Regrettable confusion of the dangerous (though normal) emotion of anger and the desire for revenge it spawns—neither of which has any reliable connection to justice—with moral indignation at victimization—which does—often clouds the thinking of those who defend the "morality" of capital punishment.[9] There is also disagreement on whether other considerations of justice—such as equality, fairness of administration, and respect for the rights of the accused—should yield or prevail when they conflict with the demands of retribution.

These issues are inescapably philosophical, and I have my own views on 17 them, which I have explained elsewhere.[10] In a word, the most that principles of retribution can do for the death penalty is to *permit* it for murder; principles of retribution are strained beyond their capacity if they are invoked to justify the death penalty for any other crime. Thus if retribution is the moral principle on which defenders of the death penalty want to rest their case, then morality requires that nonhomicidal crimes must be punished in some less severe manner. However, the principles of retribution do not *require* us to punish murder by death; what they require is the severest punishment for the gravest crime consistent with our other moral convictions. Consequently, the appeal to retribution in the present climate of discussion—and it is a widespread appeal—fails to justify the death penalty.

In fact I think there is considerable self-deception among those who think 18 they rest their defense of the death penalty on the moral principles of just retribution. Those principles cannot explain why society actually executes those few whom it does, and why it sentences to death no more than a small percentage of the murderers it convicts. Retribution is another fig leaf to cover our nakedness, I am afraid, even if it appears to be a respectable line of moral reasoning when taken in the abstract.

In recent years, neo-conservative writers of various sorts—such as columnist 19 George F. Will, New York's Mayor Edward Koch, and academicians Walter Berns and Ernest van den Haag—have made much of the vindictive powers of the death penalty and of the civilizing and moralizing influence it thus wields. Van den Haag writes, "The [death] penalty is meant to vindicate the social order."[11] Berns elaborates the point: "The criminal law must be made awful, by which I mean, awe-inspiring. . . . It must remind us of the moral order by which alone we can live as *human* beings, and in our day the only punishment that can do this is capital punishment."[12] The language is resonant, but the claim is unconvincing.

One purpose of *any* system of punishment is to vindicate the moral order 20 established by the criminal law—and properly so, because that order protects the rights of the law-abiding and because in a liberal society those rights are the basis for self-esteem and mutual respect. To go further, however, and insist that lethal punishment is the "only" appropriate response by society to the gravest crimes is wrong on two counts. The claim itself relies on naked moral intuitions about how to fit punishment to crimes, and such intuitions—with their deceptive clarity and superficial rationale—are treacherous. The least bit of historical sophistication would tell us that our forebears used the same kind of intuitive claims on behalf of maiming and other savageries that we would be ashamed to preach today. Furthermore, the claim makes sense only against the background of a conception of the state as a mystical entity of semi-divine authority, a conception that is hardly consistent with our pluralistic, liberal, nontheocratic traditions.

THE ALTERNATIVE

21   Imprisonment as it is currently practiced in this country is anything but an ideal alternative to the death penalty. Life imprisonment without the possibility of parole has been opposed by all experienced prison administrators as a virtually unmanageable option. The more one knows about most American prisons the more one judges long-term imprisonment to be a terrible curse for all concerned.[13] Defenders of the death penalty rightly point out that persons in prison can and sometimes do murder other inmates, guards, or visitors—although such crimes occur much less frequently than some of those defenders imply. (Nor do they occur with greater frequency in the prisons of states that do not punish these crimes with death than in the prisons of states that do.[14]) So imprisonment for ten or twenty years, not to mention for life, is vulnerable to many objections. Indeed, a cynic might even go so far as to say that one of the best reasons for the death penalty is the alternative to it. Nevertheless, I think this alternative is still superior to execution—and will have to suffice until something better is proposed—for at least three important reasons.

22   First, society avoids the unsolvable problem of picking and choosing among the bad to try to find the worst, in order to execute them. Experience ought long ago to have taught us that it is an illusion to expect prosecutors, juries, and courts to perform this task in a fashion that survives criticism. Deciding not to kill any among the murderers we convict enables us to punish them all more equitably, just as it relieves us of the illusion that we can choose the worst among the bad, the irredeemable from the others, those who "deserve to die" from those who really do not.

23   Second, we avoid the risk and costly error of executing the innocent, in favor of the equally risky but far less costly error of imprisoning the innocent. Arresting, trying, convicting, and punishing the innocent is an unavoidable problem, whose full extent in our history is only now beginning to be understood. Recent research on persons erroneously convicted of capital crimes in this century in the United States has identified some 350 such cases.[15] Scores of these convictions occurred in states where there was no death penalty; dozens of these errors were corrected and in some instances the wrongly convicted defendant was indemnified. Not so in all cases in the death penalty states. Where is the necessity—moral or empirical—to run the risk of executing the innocent?[16]

Third, there is a crucial symbolic significance in drawing the line at punish- 24
ments that deprive the offender of his liberty. Just as we no longer permit the
authorities to use torture to secure confessions or to attack the body of the
convicted offender with whips, branding irons, or other instruments that maim
and stigmatize, nor to carry out the death penalty by the cruelest means our
fevered imaginations can devise—even though some still cry out that social
defense and just retribution require it—so we should repudiate the death
penalty. It belongs alongside these other barbaric practices, which our society
has rejected in principle.

For at least these reasons, the alternative of imprisonment is preferable to 25
death as punishment in all cases.[17]

THE SYMBOLISM: DEATH OR LIFE?

During earlier centuries, the death penalty played a plausible, perhaps 26
even justifiable, role in society's efforts to control crime and mete out just
deserts to convicted offenders. After all, the alternative of imprisonment—the
modern form of banishment—had yet to be systematically developed. Consequently, society in an earlier age could tolerate the death penalty with a clearer
conscience than we can today. For us, however, the true dimension in which we
assess this mode of punishment is neither its crime-fighting effectiveness nor
its moral necessity, but its symbolism. Mistaken faith in deterrent efficacy, confusion over the requirements of justice, indifference to unfair administration,
ignorance of nonlethal methods of social control—all these can explain only so
much about the current support for the death penalty. The rest of the explanation lies elsewhere, in what executions symbolize, consciously or unconsciously, for those who favor them.

This symbolism deserves a closer look.[18] The death penalty, today as in the 27
past, symbolizes the ultimate power of the state, and of the government of
society, over the individual citizen. Understandably, the public wants visible
evidence that the authority of its political leaders is intact, their powers competent to deal with every social problem, and their courage resolute in the face
of any danger. Anxiety about war, fear of crime, indignation at being victimized
provoke the authorities to use the power of life and death as a public gesture
of strength, self-confidence, and reassurance. Not surprisingly, many are unwilling to abandon the one symbol a society under law in peacetime has at its
disposal that, above all others, expresses this power with awe-inspiring finality:
the death penalty.

This is precisely why, in the end, we should oppose the death penalty in 28
principle and without exception. As long as capital punishment is available
under law for any crime, it is a temptation to excess. Tyrannical governments,
from Idi Amin's Uganda to the Ayatollah's Iran, teach this lesson. At best the
use of the death penalty here and elsewhere has been and continues to be
capricious and arbitrary. The long history of several of our own states, notably
Michigan and Wisconsin, quite apart from the experience of other nations,
proves that the government of a civilized society does not *need* the death
penalty. The citizenry should not clamor for it. Their political leaders should

know better—as, of course, the best of them do—than to cultivate public approval for capital statutes, death sentences, and executions. Instead a civilized government should explain why such practices are ill-advised, and why they are ineffective in reducing crime, removing its causes, and responding to victimization.

NOTES

1. Comment, "The Cost of Taking a Life: Dollars and Sense of the Death Penalty," *U. C. Davis Law Review* 18 (1985):1221–74, at 1270.
2. See *The Gallup Report*, January-February 1986, nos. 244–45, pp. 10–16; and Phoebe C. Ellsworth and Lee Ross, "Public Opinion and Capital Punishment: A Closer Examination of the Views of Abolitionists and Retentionists," *Crime & Delinquency* 29 (1983):116–69, at 147.
3. The findings reported by Isaac Ehrlich, "The Deterrent Effect of Capital Punishment: A Question of Life and Death," *American Economic Review* 65 (1975):397–417 ("[each] additional execution . . . may have resulted . . . in 7 or 8 fewer murderers") have been extensively criticized; see, e.g., Lawrence R. Klein, Brian Forst, and Victor Filatox, "The Deterrent Effect of Capital Punishment: An Assessment of the Estimates," in Alfred Blumstein, Jacqueline Cohen, and Daniel Nagin, eds., *Deterrence and Incapacitation: Estimating the Effects of Criminal Sanctions on Crime Rates* (1978), pp. 336–60. The findings reported by James A. Yunker, "Is the Death Penalty a Deterrent to Homicide? Some Time Series Evidence," *Journal of Behavioral Economics* 5 (1976): 45–81 ("one execution will deter 156 murders") have been evaluated and found wanting by James Alan Fox, "The Identification and Estimation of Deterrence: An Evaluation of Yunker's Model," *Journal of Behavioral Economics* 6 (1977):225–42. The findings reported by David P. Phillips, "The Deterrent Effect of Capital Punishment: New Evidence on an Old Controversy," *American Journal of Sociology* 86 (1980): 139–48 (". . . in the two weeks following a public execution the frequency of homicide drops by 35.7%") has been refuted by William J. Bowers, "Deterrence or Brutalization: What Is the Truth About Highly Publicized Executions?" (unpublished). The latest claims in this vein are by Stephen K. Layson, "Homicide and Deterrence: A Reexamination of the United States Time-Series Evidence," *Southern Economic Journal* 52 (1985):68–89 ("the tradeoff of executions for murders is approximately—18.5," i.e., each execution results in a net decrease of 18.5 murders); for criticism see James Alan Fox, "Persistent Flaws in Econometric Studies of the Death Penalty: A Discussion of Layson's Findings," testimony submitted to the Subcommittee on Criminal Justice, House of Representatives, U.S. Congress, 7 May 1986.
4. See Bowers, "Deterrence or Brutalization."
5. United States, Department of Justice, Bureau of Justice Statistics, *Capital Punishment* 1984 (1985), p. 1.

6. Mark H. Moore et al., *Dangerous Offenders: The Elusive Target of Justice* (1984), and Ted Honderich et al., "Symposium: Predicting Dangerousness," *Criminal Justice Ethics* 2 (Winter/Spring 1983):3–17.
7. Jack Levin and James Alan Fox, *Mass Murder: America's Growing Menace* (1985), p. 222. The authors do not support the death penalty for serial, mass, or recidivist murderers.
8. See especially Norval Morris, *The Future of Imprisonment* (1974), pp. 85–121.
9. This is especially true of Walter Berns, *For Capital Punishment: Crime and the Morality of the Death Penalty* (1979), pp. 153ff. The arousal of "anger" is not evidence that anything morally wrong is its cause. There is no reason to believe that the punitive policies adopted by a society "angry" at criminals will be fair or effective in reducing crime. The revenge that "anger" can motivate has no claim as such to the title of just retribution. Moral indignation is another matter. As a feeling, it may be indistinguishable from anger, but its claim for a different status rests on its essential connection to a moral principle; one's indignation is aroused only if an important moral principle has been violated. Even when this happens, the policies inspired by moral indignation are not thereby guaranteed to be just or effective; and the capacity for self-deception about the legitimacy of one's indignation is legendary.
10. See Bedau, "Classification-Based Sentencing: Some Conceptual and Ethical Problems," *New England Journal of Criminal and Civil Confinement* 10 (1984):1–26; Bedau, "Prisoners' Rights," *Criminal Justice Ethics* 1 (Winter/Spring 1982):26–41; Bedau, "Retribution and the Theory of Punishment," *Journal of Philosophy* 75 (1978):601–20; Bedau, "Penal Theory and Prison Reality Today," *Juris Doctor* 2 (December 1972):40–83.
11. Ernest van den Haag, "The Death Penalty Vindicates the Law," *American Bar Association Journal* 71 (April 1985):38–42 at 42; cf. van den Haag, "Refuting Reiman and Nathanson," *Philosophy & Public Affairs* 14 (1985):165–76 ("punishment must vindicate the disrupted public order").
12. Berns, *For Capital Punishment*, p. 173.
13. See, e.g., Robert Johnson and Hans Toch, eds., *The Pains of Imprisonment* (1982).
14. See Wendy Phillips Wolfson, "The Deterrent Effect of the Death Penalty upon Prison Murder," in Bedau, ed., *The Death Penalty in America,* 3d ed. (1982), pp. 159–73.
15. Hugo Adam Bedau and Michael L. Radelet, "Miscarriages of Justice in Potentially Capital Cases," presented at the annual meeting of the American Society of Criminology, November 1985.
16. Ernest van den Haag argues, with evident complacency, that the death penalty does "lead to the unintended death of some innocents in the long run"; he goes on to add that this leaves the death penalty

precisely where other things of the same sort are: "in the long run nearly all human activities are likely to lead to the unintended deaths of innocents." Van den Haag, "The Death Penalty Vindicates the Law," p. 42. This tends to obscure three important points. First, lawful activities that take "statistical lives" (e.g., coal mining) are not designed to kill anyone, whereas every death by capital punishment (whether of a guilty or an innocent person) is intentional. Second, society permits dangerous commercial and recreational activities on various grounds—it would be wrongly paternalistic to interfere with what people choose to do at their own risk (e.g., scaling dangerous cliffs), and society can better afford the cost of the risky activity than the cost of its complete prevention or stricter regulation (e.g., public highways crowded with long truck-trailer rigs rather than separate highways for cars and trucks). But these reasons have no bearing on the choice between the death penalty and imprisonment, unless the combined deterrent/incapacitative effects of executions are demonstrably superior to those of the alternative. Since no defender of the death penalty has sustained the burden of the proof on this point— see the papers cited in n. 3 supra—van den Haag's argument is undermined. Van den Haag's position would be less vulnerable to objection if the only executions he favored were of persons convicted of several—serial, multiple, or recidivist—murders. But he does not confine his support for the death penalty to such cases.

17. Michael Davis has recently argued that the death penalty is no more "irrevocable," in any important sense of that term, than many other punishments, including life in prison. See Davis, "Is the Death Penalty Irrevocable?" *Social Theory and Practice* 10 (1984):143–56. Insofar as he addresses the arguments I put forward in Chapter 1, to explain why death is a "more severe" punishment than imprisonment, he does not seem to disagree. On his interpretation, however, the issue of revocability has nothing to do with severity (see p. 147). Basic to his argument that the punishments of death and of life in prison are equally (ir)revocable is the idea that (a) an irrevocable punishment is such that if it is erroneously imposed on someone, then there is no way to compensate the person for the injustice he suffers, and (b) anyone has interests that are not extinguished with the end of natural life (see p. 146). But as compensating a person is not always identical with conferring a benefit on something he is interested in—rather, it is sometimes a matter of benefiting *him,* directly and in his own person—the truth of (a) and (b) do not entail that there is no difference, relative to irrevocability, that distinguishes the punishment of death from a life behind bars.

18. See Barbara Ann Stolz, "Congress and Capital Punishment: An Exercise in Symbolic Politics," *Law & Policy Quarterly* 5 (1983):157–80; and Tom R. Tyler and Renee Weber, "Support for the Death Penalty: Instrumental Response to Crime or Symbolic Attitude?" *Law & Society Review* 17

(1982):21–45. Tyler and Weber bifurcate all defenses of the death penalty into the "instrumental" and the "symbolic." Thus a retributive defense of the death penalty is, for them, merely "symbolic." Nor do they make it clear whether the "symbolic" role of this punishment is a conscious and intentional one. Stolz is concerned with the conscious symbolism of enacting national (more precisely, federal) criminal penalties; how much of what she reports could be transferred without loss to the reasons for enactment of state death penalty laws or to the reasons the public supports executions (state or federal) is not clear.

QUESTIONS FOR READING

1. According to Bedau, on what should the resolution of the death penalty debate rest? Why?

2. How does Bedau organize his discussion?

3. What are the six arguments in support of capital punishment? Compare these to the arguments of van den Haag. Has Bedau covered the arguments presented by van den Haag?

4. What is Bedau's position on deterrence? Is there evidence that the death penalty deters murder? Is deterrence a justifiable use of criminal law? Is capital punishment justifiable as a possible deterrent?

5. What are the facts on recidivist murderers? What kind of murderer do many people want executed, even those who generally oppose the death penalty? What would be accomplished if only this kind of murderer were executed? Which group of people will still be unhappy? Why?

6. What are Bedau's arguments for rejecting capital punishment as the necessary response to grave crimes?

7. The author gives three reasons for preferring imprisonment to death. Explain each in your own words.

8. What does the death penalty symbolize, according to Bedau? Why is that the very reason to oppose the death penalty?

QUESTIONS FOR REASONING AND ANALYSIS

1. Bedau begins his discussion of the alternative to the death penalty by agreeing that it is not an ideal alternative. By so doing, what does he accomplish? How does this strengthen his argument?

2. Does retribution *allow* for the death penalty? Does it *require* it? What distinction does Bedau make between *retribution* and *revenge*? What does the author's distinctions among words illustrate about the nature of good argument?

3. What are two reasons for dismissing the "taxpayer's argument"? Compare Bedau and van den Haag on the role of cost in one's position on the death penalty. Do they agree? What might you conclude from your comparison?

QUESTIONS FOR REFLECTING AND WRITING

1. Compare Bedau's views on deterrence to van den Haag's. Who makes the better case? Why?

2. Which of the three reasons for supporting imprisonment over death sentencing do you think is the strongest? Why?

3. Could you accept the compromise position of death sentencing only for multiple murders? Is this a position we should work to make the practice in this country? Why or why not?

4. Do you think that the motive of revenge justifies the death penalty? If so, how would you refute Bedau on this issue?

5. Has Bedau led you to change your views on capital punishment in any way? Explain.

Read: What happens in the cartoon? How does Marvin characterize the dog's attitude?

Reason: What attitude is reflected in the way the dog is drawn in frame 4? What attitude is reflected in the way the cat is drawn in frame 5?

Reflect/Write: What makes the cartoon a clever way of expressing the artist's opposition to stereotyping?

Marriage and Gender Issues: The Debates Continue

Seven writers provide much for readers to reflect on and debate in this chapter of controversial marriage and gender issues. These writers examine the incredible changes that the twentieth century brought to the institution of marriage—and, by extension, to the family. Some approach these changes—and their effects on our politics, our culture, and our personal lives—from the social science perspective; others take a more jocular or satiric approach. Some write from the perspective of research data; others develop their arguments from emotion or a religious persuasion. Some express strongly held views; others seek common ground. Some focus specifically on marriage—how it affects lives and who should be allowed to participate. Others focus on gender issues—and on the stereotyping that continues to affect women in the classroom, in the workplace, and in the issues over AIDS. However, whatever their specific topic, the source of their arguments, or the basis of their values, all of these writers would certainly agree that the changes of the past thirty years, with regard to how we live and work together as men and women, have had a profound effect on our culture and our personal lives.

Prereading Questions

1. Do you expect to have a career? To have a spouse and children? Should society support both men and women having these choices? If so, how?
2. What role, if any, should the government and the courts have in defining marriage?
3. What has been meant by the "traditional family"? How has it changed in the past thirty years?
4. Do you have a position on gay marriage? On partnership recognition and rights? If you have a position, what is it, and what is its source?
5. Is there anything that you can learn from arguments presenting opposing views on gay rights and/or acceptance of gay marriage? Why or why not?
6. Is there anything you can learn from arguments seeking to alter stereotypic views of women? Why or why not?

Web Sites Related to This Chapter's Topic

Same-Sex Marriage and Domestic Partnerships

http://fullcoverage.yahoo.com/fc/us/same_sex_marriage

This Yahoo Full Coverage site contains news, opinions, and useful links.

http://helping.apa.org/family/index.html

This URL takes you directly to the index of articles on marriage and family made available on the American Psychological Association's information-packed Web site.

SOCIAL SCIENCE FINDS: "MARRIAGE MATTERS" | LINDA J. WAITE

A former senior sociologist at the Rand Corporation, Linda Waite is currently a professor at the University of Chicago. She has coauthored several books, including *Teenage Motherhood* (1979) and *New Families, No Families?* (1991). In this article, published in *The Responsive Community* in 1996, Waite pulls together various studies to explore the effects that marriage has on married people.

PREREADING QUESTIONS Although marriage has declined, what has taken its place? How important is marriage to you? Why?

1   As we are all too aware, the last few decades have witnessed a decline in the popularity of marriage. This trend has not escaped the notice of politicians and pundits. But when critics point to the high social costs and taxpayer bur-

den imposed by disintegrating "family values," they overlook the fact that individuals do not simply make the decisions that lead to unwed parenthood,
marriage, or divorce on the basis of what is good for society. Individuals weigh
the costs and benefits of each of these choices to themselves—and sometimes
their children. But how much is truly known about these costs and benefits,
either by the individuals making the choices or demographers like myself
who study them? Put differently, what are the implications, for individuals, of
the current increases in nonmarriage? If we think of marriage as an insurance
policy—which it is, in some respects—does it matter if more people are unin-
sured, or are insured with a term rather than a whole-life policy? I shall argue
that it does matter, because marriage typically provides important and substantial benefits, benefits not enjoyed by those who live alone or cohabit.

2   A quick look at marriage patterns today compared to, say, 1950 shows the
extent of recent changes. Figures from the Census Bureau show that in 1950,
at the height of the baby boom, about a third of white men and women were
not married. Some were waiting to marry for the first time, some were divorced
or widowed and not remarried. But virtually everyone married at least once at
some point in their lives, generally in their early twenties.

3   In 1950 the proportion of black men and women not married was approximately equal to the proportion unmarried among whites, but since that time
the marriage behavior of blacks and whites has diverged dramatically. By 1993,
61 percent of black women and 58 percent of black men were not married,
compared to 38 percent of white men and 41 percent of white women. So, in
contrast to 1950 when only a little over one black adult in three was not married, now a majority of black adults are unmarried. Insofar as marriage "matters," black men and women are much less likely than whites to share in the
benefits, and much less likely today than they were a generation ago.

4   The decline in marriage is directly connected to the rise in cohabitation—
living with someone in a sexual relationship without being married. Although
Americans are less likely to be married today than they were several decades
ago, if we count both marriage and cohabitation, they are about as likely to be
"coupled." If cohabitation provides the same benefits to individuals as marriage does, then we do not need to be concerned about this shift. But we may
be replacing a valuable social institution with one that demands and offers less.

5   Perhaps the most disturbing change in marriage appears in its relationship
to parenthood. Today a third of all births occur to women who are not married,
with huge but shrinking differences between blacks and whites in this behavior. One in five births to white mothers and two-thirds of births to black mothers currently take place outside marriage. Although about a quarter of the
white unmarried mothers are living with someone when they give birth, so that
their children are born into two-parent—if unmarried—families, very few black
children born to unmarried mothers live with fathers too.

6   I believe that these changes in marriage behavior are a cause for concern,
because in a number of important ways married men and women do better
than those who are unmarried. And I believe that the evidence suggests that
they do better because they are married.

MARRIAGE AND HEALTH

7   The case for marriage is quite strong. Consider the issues of longevity and health. With economist Lee Lillard, I used a large national survey to follow men and women over a 20-year period. We watched them get married, get divorced, and remarry. We observed the death of spouses and of the individuals themselves. And we compared deaths of married men and women to those who were not married. We found that once we took other factors into account, married men and women faced lower risks of dying at any point than those who have never married or whose previous marriage has ended. Widowed women were much better off than divorced women or those who had never married, although they were still disadvantaged when compared with married women. But all men who were not currently married faced significantly higher risks of dying than married men, regardless of their marital history. Other scholars have found disadvantages in death rates for unmarried adults in a number of countries besides the United States.

8   How does marriage lengthen life? First, marriage appears to reduce risky and unhealthy behaviors. For example, according to University of Texas sociologist Debra Umberson, married men show much lower rates of problem drinking than unmarried men. Umberson also found that both married men and women are less likely to take risks that could lead to injury than are the unmarried. Second, as we will see below, marriage increases material well-being—income, assets, and wealth. These can be used to purchase better medical care, better diet, and safer surroundings, which lengthen life. This material improvement seems to be especially important for women.

9   Third, marriage provides individuals—especially men—with someone who monitors their health and health-related behaviors and who encourages them to drink and smoke less, to eat a healthier diet, to get enough sleep and to generally take care of their health. In addition, husbands and wives offer each other moral support that helps in dealing with stressful situations. Married men especially seem to be motivated to avoid risky behaviors and to take care of their health by the sense of meaning that marriage gives to their lives and the sense of obligation to others that it brings.

MORE WEALTH, BETTER WAGES—FOR MOST

10   Married individuals also seem to fare better when it comes to wealth. One comprehensive measure to financial well-being—household wealth—includes pension and Social Security wealth, real and financial assets, and the value of the primary residence. According to economist James Smith, in 1992 married men and women ages 51–60 had median wealth of about $66,000 per spouse, compared to $42,000 for the widowed, $35,000 for those who had never married, $34,000 among those who were divorced, and only $7,600 for those who were separated. Although married couples have higher incomes than others, this fact accounts for only about a quarter of their greater wealth.

11   How does marriage increase wealth? Married couples can share many household goods and services, such as a TV and heat, so the cost to each individual is lower than if each one purchased and used the same items individually.

So the married spend less than the same individuals would for the same style of life if they lived separately. Second, married people produce more than the same individuals would if single. Each spouse can develop some skills and neglect others, because each can count on the other to take responsibility for some of the household work. The resulting specialization increases efficiency. We see below that this specialization leads to higher wages for men. Married couples also seem to save more at the same level of income than do single people.

The impact of marriage is again beneficial—although in this case not for all involved—when one looks at labor market outcomes. According to recent research by economist Kermit Daniel, both black and white men receive a wage premium if they are married: 4.5 percent for black men and 6.3 percent for white men. Black women receive a marriage premium of almost 3 percent. White women, however, pay a marriage *penalty,* in hourly wages, of over 4 percent. In addition, men appear to receive some of the benefit of marriage if they cohabit, but women do not. 12

Why should marriage increase men's wages? Some researchers think that marriage makes men more productive at work, leading to higher wages. Wives may assist husbands directly with their work, offer advice or support, or take over household tasks, freeing husbands' time and energy for work. Also, as I mentioned earlier, being married reduces drinking, substance abuse, and other unhealthy behaviors that may affect men's job performance. Finally, marriage increases men's incentives to perform well at work, in order to meet obligations to family members. 13

For women, Daniel finds that marriage and presence of children together seem to affect wages, and the effects depend on the woman's race. Childless black women earn substantially more money if they are married but the "marriage premium" drops with each child they have. Among white women only the childless receive a marriage premium. Once white women become mothers, marriage decreases their earnings compared to remaining single (with children), with very large negative effects of marriage on women's earnings for those with two children or more. White married women often choose to reduce hours of work when they have children. They also make less per hour than either unmarried mothers or childless wives. 14

Up to this point, all the consequences of marriage for the individuals involved have been unambiguously positive—better health, longer life, more wealth, and higher earnings. But the effects of marriage and children on white women's wages are mixed, at best. Marriage and cohabitation increase women's time spent on housework; married motherhood reduces their time in the labor force and lowers their wages. Although the family as a whole might be better off with this allocation of women's time, women generally share their husbands' market earnings only when they are married. Financial well-being declines dramatically for women and their children after divorce and widowhood; women whose marriages have ended are often quite disadvantaged financially by their investment in their husbands and children rather than in their own earning power. Recent changes in divorce law—the rise in no-fault divorce and the move away from alimony—seem to have exacerbated this situation, 15 even while increases in women's education and work experience have moderated it.

IMPROVED INTIMACY

16   Another benefit of married life is an improved sex life. Married men and women report very active sex lives—as do those who are cohabiting. But the married appear to be more satisfied with sex than others. More married men say that they find sex with their wives to be extremely physically pleasurable than do cohabiting men or single men say the same about sex with their partners. The high levels of married men's physical satisfaction with their sex lives contradicts the popular view that sexual novelty or variety improves sex for men. Physical satisfaction with sex is about the same for married women, cohabiting women, and single women with sex partners.

17   In addition to reporting more active and more physically fulfilling sex lives than the unmarried, married men and women say that they are more emotionally satisfied with their sex lives than do those who are single or cohabiting. Although cohabitants report levels of sexual activity as high as the married, both cohabiting men and women report lower levels of emotional satisfaction with their sex lives. And those who are sexually active but single report the lowest emotional satisfaction with it.

18   How does marriage improve one's sex life? Marriage and cohabitation provide individuals with a readily available sexual partner with whom they have an established, ongoing sexual relationship. This reduces the costs—in some sense—of any particular sexual contact, and leads to higher levels of sexual activity. Since married couples expect to carry on their sex lives for many years, and since the vast majority of married couples are monogamous, husbands and wives have strong incentives to learn what pleases their partner in bed and to become good at it. But I would argue that more than "skills" are at issue here. The long-term contract implicit in marriage—which is not implicit in cohabitation—facilitates emotional investment in the relationship, which should affect both frequency of and satisfaction with sex. So the wife or husband who knows what the spouse wants is also highly motivated to provide it, both because sexual satisfaction in one's partner brings similar rewards to oneself and because the emotional commitment to the partner makes satisfying him or her important in itself.

19   To this point we have focused on the consequences of marriage for adults—the men and women who choose to marry (and stay married) or not. But such choices have consequences for the children born to these adults. Sociologists Sarah McLanahan and Gary Sandefur compare children raised in intact, two-parent families with those raised in one-parent families, which could result either from disruption of a marriage or from unmarried childbearing. They find that approximately twice as many children raised in one-parent families than children from two-parent families drop out of high school without finishing. Children raised in one-parent families are also more likely to have a birth themselves while teenagers, and to be "idle"—both out of school and out of the labor force—as young adults.

Not surprisingly, children living outside an intact marriage are also more   20
likely to be poor. McLanahan and Sandefur calculated poverty rates for children
in two-parent families—including stepfamilies—and for single-parent families.
They found very high rates of poverty for single-parent families, especially
among blacks. Donald Hernandez, chief of marriage and family statistics at the
Census Bureau, claims that the rise in mother-only families since 1959 is an important cause of increases in poverty among children.

Clearly poverty, in and of itself, is a bad outcome for children. In addi-   21
tion, however, McLanahan and Sandefur estimate that the lower incomes of
single-parent families account for only half of the negative impact for children in these families. The other half comes from children's access—or lack
of access—to the time and attention of two adults in two-parent families.
Children in one-parent families spend less time with their fathers (this is not
surprising given that they do not live with them), but they also spend less time
with their mothers than children in two-parent families. Single-parent families
and stepfamilies also move much more frequently than two-parent families,
disrupting children's social and academic environments. Finally, children who
spend part of their childhood in a single-parent family report substantially
lower quality relationships with their parents as adults and have less frequent
contact with them, according to demographer Diane Lye.

CORRELATION VERSUS CAUSALITY

The obvious question, when one looks at all these "benefits" of marriage,   22
is whether marriage is responsible for these differences. If all, or almost all,
of the benefits of marriage arise because those who enjoy better health, live
longer lives, or earn higher wages anyway are more likely to marry, then marriage is not "causing" any changes in these outcomes. In such a case, we as
a society and we as individuals could remain neutral about each person's
decision to marry or not, to divorce or remain married. But scholars from
many fields who have examined the issues have come to the opposite conclusion. Daniel found that only half of the higher wages that married men enjoy could be explained by selectivity; he thus concluded that the other half
is causal. In the area of mental health, social psychologist Catherine Ross—
summarizing her own research and that of other social scientists—wrote,
"The positive effect of marriage on well-being is strong and consistent, and
the selection of the psychologically healthy into marriage or the psychologically unhealthy out of marriage cannot explain the effect." Thus marriage itself can be assumed to have independent positive effects on its participants.

So, we must ask, what is it about marriage that causes these benefits? I   23
think that four factors are key. First, the institution of marriage involves a long-
term contract—"'til death do us part." This contract allows the partners to
make choices that carry immediate costs but eventually bring benefits. The
time horizon implied by marriage makes it sensible—a rational choice is at work
here—for individuals to develop some skills and to neglect others because they
count on their spouse to fill in where they are weak. The institution of marriage
helps individuals honor this long-term contract by providing social support for

the couple as a couple and by imposing social and economic costs on those who dissolve their union.

24   Second, marriage assumes a sharing of economic and social resources and what we can think of as co-insurance. Spouses act as a sort of small insurance pool against life's uncertainties, reducing their need to protect themselves—by themselves—from unexpected events.

25   Third, married couples benefit—as do cohabiting couples—from economies of scale.

26   Fourth, marriage connects people to other individuals, to their social groups (such as in-laws), and to other social institutions (such as churches and synagogues) which are themselves a source of benefits. These connections provide individuals with a sense of obligation to others, which gives life meaning beyond oneself.

27   Cohabitation has some but not all of the characteristics of marriage and so carries some but not all of the benefits. Cohabitation does not generally imply a lifetime commitment to stay together; a significant number of cohabiting couples disagree on the future of their relationship. Frances Goldscheider and Gail Kaufman believe that the shift to cohabitation from marriage signals "declining commitment within unions, of men and women to each other and to their relationship as an enduring unit, in exchange for more freedom, primarily for men." Perhaps as a result, many view cohabitation as an especially poor bargain for women.

28   The uncertainty that accompanies cohabitation makes both investment in the relationship and specialization with this partner much riskier than in marriage and so reduces them. Cohabitants are much less likely than married couples to pool financial resources and more likely to assume that each partner is responsible for supporting himself or herself financially. And whereas marriage connects individuals to other important social institutions, cohabitation seems to distance them from these institutions.

29   Of course, all observations concern only the average benefits of marriage. Clearly, some marriages produce substantially higher benefits for those involved. Some marriages produce no benefits and even cause harm to the men, women, and children involved. That fact needs to be recognized.

REVERSING THE TREND

30   Having stated this qualification, we must still ask, if the average marriage produces all of these benefits for individuals, why has it declined? Although this issue remains a subject of much research and speculation, a number of factors have been mentioned as contributing. For one, because of increases in women's employment, there is less specialization by spouses now than in the past; this reduces the benefits of marriage. Clearly, employed wives have less time and energy to focus on their husbands, and are less financially and emotionally dependent on marriage than wives who work only in the home. In addition, high divorce rates decrease people's certainty about the long-run stability of their marriage, and this may reduce their willingness to invest in it, which in turn increases the chance they divorce—a sort of self-fulfilling prophecy. Also, changes

in divorce laws have shifted much of the financial burden for the breakup of the marriage to women, making investment within the marriage (such as supporting a husband in medical school) a riskier proposition for them.

Men, in turn, may find marriage and parenthood a less attractive option when they know that divorce is common, because they may face the loss of contact with their children if their marriage dissolves. Further, women's increased earnings and young men's declining financial well-being may have made women less dependent on men's financial support and made young men less able to provide it. Finally, public policies that support single mothers and changing attitudes toward sex outside of marriage, toward unmarried childbearing, and toward divorce have all been implicated in the decline in marriage. This brief list does not exhaust the possibilities, but merely mentions some of them. 31

So how can this trend be reversed? First, as evidence accumulates and is communicated to individuals, some people will change their behavior as a result. Some will do so simply because of their new understanding of the costs and benefits, to them, of the choices involved. In addition, we have seen that attitudes frequently change toward behaviors that have been shown to have negative consequences. The attitude change then raises the social cost of the newly stigmatized behavior. 32

In addition, though, we as a society can pull some policy levers to encourage or discourage behaviors. Public policies that include asset tests (Medicaid is a good example) act to exclude the married, as do AFDC programs in most states. The "marriage penalty" in the tax code is another example. These and other policies reinforce or undermine the institution of marriage. If, as I have argued, marriage produces individuals who drink less, smoke less, abuse substances less, live longer, earn more, are wealthier, and have children who do better, we need to give more thought and effort to supporting this valuable social institution. 33

QUESTIONS FOR READING

1. What is Waite's subject?
2. What groups are healthiest and live the longest? What three reasons does Waite list to explain these health facts?
3. In what ways can marriage increase wealth? Who, when married, loses in hourly wages?
4. What may be the causes of increased productivity for married men?
5. What are some effects of single-parent families on children?
6. If marriage has such benefits, why are fewer people getting married and more getting divorced?

QUESTIONS FOR REASONING AND ANALYSIS

1. What is Waite's claim? Where does she state it?
2. How does the author help readers move through and see the parts of her argument?

3. How does the author defend her causal argument—that marriage itself is a cause of the financial, health, and contentment effects found in married people? Do you find her argument convincing? Why or why not?

4. What kind of evidence, primarily, does Waite provide? Is this evidence persuasive? Why or why not?

QUESTIONS FOR REFLECTING AND WRITING

1. Which statistic most surprises you? Why?

2. What can be done to increase marriage benefits for women, the ones who have least benefited?

3. Should the evidence Waite provides encourage people to choose marriage over divorce, cohabitation, or the single life? If so, why? If no, why not? (Do you have a sense that most adults know—or do not know—the data that Waite provides?)

4. What can be done to change the movement away from marriage? What are Waite's suggestions? What are yours?

ABOLISH MARRIAGE | MICHAEL KINSLEY

A member of the bar with a law degree from Harvard, Michael Kinsley is a former editor of both *Harper's* and the *New Republic*. He is the founding editor (1996) of *Slate*, the online magazine, has been a cohost of CNN's *Crossfire*, and currently writes a weekly column for the *Washington Post*. The following column appeared in the *Post*, July 3, 2003.

PREREADING QUESTIONS What are the key issues in the debate over gay marriage? What are gay marriage proponents seeking? What are social conservatives seeking?

1   Critics and enthusiasts of *Lawrence v. Texas*, last week's Supreme Court decision invalidating state anti-sodomy laws, agree on one thing: The next argument is going to be about gay marriage. As Justice Antonin Scalia noted in his tart dissent, it follows from the logic of *Lawrence*. Mutually consenting sex with the person of your choice in the privacy of your own home is now a basic right of American citizenship under the Constitution. This does not mean that the government must supply it or guarantee it. But the government cannot forbid it, and the government also should not discriminate against you for choosing to exercise a basic right of citizenship. Offering an institution as important as marriage to male-female couples only is exactly this kind of discrimination. Or so the gay rights movement will now argue. Persuasively, I think.

2   Opponents of gay rights will resist mightily, although they have been in retreat for a couple of decades. General anti-gay sentiments are now considered a serious breach of civic etiquette, even in anti-gay circles. The current line of defense, which probably won't hold either, is between social toleration of homosexuals and social approval of homosexuality. Or between accepting the

reality that people are gay, even accepting that gays are people, and endorsing something called "the gay agenda." Gay marriage, the opponents will argue, would cross this line. It would make homosexuality respectable and, worse, normal. Gays are welcome to exist all they want, and to do their inexplicable thing if they must, but they shouldn't expect a government stamp of approval.

It's going to get ugly. And then it's going to get boring. So we have two 3 options here. We can add gay marriage to the short list of controversies— abortion, affirmative action, the death penalty—that are so frozen and ritualistic that debates about them are more like kabuki performances than intellectual exercises. Or we can think outside the box. There is a solution that ought to satisfy both camps, and may not be a bad idea even apart from the gay marriage controversy.

That solution is to end the institution of marriage. Or rather (he hastens to 4 clarify, dear) the solution is to end the institution of government-sanctioned marriage. Or, framed to appeal to conservatives: End the government monopoly on marriage. Wait, I've got it: Privatize marriage. These slogans all mean the same thing. Let churches and other religious institutions continue to offer marriage ceremonies. Let department stores and casinos get into the act if they want. Let each organization decide for itself what kinds of couples it wants to offer marriage to. Let couples celebrate their union in any way they choose and consider themselves married whenever they want. Let others be free to consider them not married, under rules these others may prefer. And, yes, if three people want to get married, or one person wants to marry herself, and someone else wants to conduct a ceremony and declare them married, let 'em. If you and your government aren't implicated, what do you care?

In fact, there is nothing to stop any of this from happening now. And a lot 5 of it does happen. But only certain marriages get certified by the government. So, in the United States we are about to find ourselves in a strange situation where the principal demand of a liberation movement is to be included in the red tape of a government bureaucracy. Having just gotten state governments out of their bedrooms, gays now want these governments back in. Meanwhile, social-conservative anti-gays, many of them southerners, are calling on the government in Washington to trample states' rights and nationalize the rules of marriage, if necessary, to prevent gays from getting what they want. The Senate majority leader, Bill Frist of Tennessee, responded to the Supreme Court's *Lawrence* decision by endorsing a constitutional amendment, no less, against gay marriage.

If marriage were an entirely private affair, all the disputes over gay marriage 6 would become irrelevant. Gay marriage would not have the official sanction of government, but neither would straight marriage. There would be official equality between the two, which is the essence of what gays want and are entitled to. And if the other side is sincere in saying that its concern is not what people do in private but government endorsement of a gay "lifestyle" or "agenda," that problem goes away too.

Yes, yes, marriage is about more than sleeping arrangements. There are chil- 7 dren, there are finances, there are spousal job benefits such as health insurance and pensions. In all of these areas, marriage is used as a substitute for other factors that are harder to measure, such as financial dependence or devotion to offspring. It would be possible to write rules that measure the real factors at stake and leave marriage out of the matter. Regarding children and finances, people can set their own rules, as many already do. None of this would be easy. Marriage functions as what lawyers call a "bright line," which saves the trouble of trying to measure a lot of amorphous factors. You're either married or you're not. Once marriage itself becomes amorphous, who-gets-the-kids and who-gets-health-care become trickier questions.

8   So, sure, there are some legitimate objections to the idea of privatizing marriage. But they don't add up to a fatal objection. Especially when you consider that the alternative is arguing about gay marriage until death do us part.

QUESTIONS FOR READING

1. What will the next argument be about? What ruling will bring on this argument? What about the ruling invites the argument?
2. Who will win the argument, in Kinsley's view?
3. According to the author, where are we in the "tug-of-war" over gay rights? Where would allowing gay marriage put us in the battle?
4. What is the author's solution to end the argument?
5. What is ironic about gays fighting for the right to marry? What is ironic about conservatives seeking a constitutional amendment against gay marriage?
6. What problems would emerge if governments stopped sanctioning marriage altogether? Are these problems insurmountable, in the author's view?

QUESTIONS FOR REASONING AND ANALYSIS

1. What is Kinsley's claim? Where does he state it?
2. When Kinsley writes that the argument over gay marriage will "get boring," what does he mean? How does his comparison to kabuki performances or to debates over abortion or the death penalty illustrate his point here?
3. How does Kinsley seek to convince both sides of the argument that his solution should please them?
4. The author anticipates counterarguments in his last two paragraphs. How effective is his rebuttal?
5. Analyze the essay's tone. How serious do you think Kinsley is in presenting his solution to the argument over gay marriage? If he does not think his solution is viable, then why is he proposing it? What is his purpose in writing?

QUESTIONS FOR REFLECTING AND WRITING

1. What is your reaction to Kinsley's proposal? Is the best solution to get government out of certifying marriage? If we wanted to "think outside the box," could we solve the other problems—of finances, child custody, and so forth—if we wanted to? How would you support the proposal or challenge it?

2. Is there any hope of finding common ground on this issue, or are we doomed to live with another issue that generates only ritualistic "debates"? Do you have any new suggestions for thinking outside the box on social issues that are currently so divisive?

THE CONSERVATIVE CASE FOR GAY MARRIAGE
ANDREW SULLIVAN

A native of England with a doctorate in political science from Harvard, Andrew Sullivan is editor of Andrewsullivan.com, an online source of commentary on current issues, a *Time* magazine essayist, and a columnist for the *Sunday Times of London.* While editor-in-chief of the *New Republic,* he was named Editor of the Year. He lectures widely and appears frequently on both radio and television programs. The following is a *Time* essay from June 30, 2003.

PREREADING QUESTIONS What does the word *conservative* in the title suggest to you about the author's position and/or approach to the issue of gay marriage? Why might it be useful to present a *conservative* argument on this topic?

A long time ago, the *New Republic* ran a contest to discover the most bor- 1
ing headline ever written. Entrants had to beat the following snoozer, which had inspired the event: WORTHWHILE CANADIAN INITIATIVE. Little did the contest organizers realize that one day such a headline would be far from boring and, in its own small way, a social watershed.

Canada's federal government decided last week not to contest the rulings 2
of three provincial courts that had all come to the conclusion that denying homosexuals the right to marry violated Canada's constitutional commitment to civic equality. What that means is that gay marriage has now arrived in the western hemisphere. And this isn't some euphemism. It isn't the quasi-marriage now celebrated in Vermont, whose "civil unions" approximate marriage but don't go by that name. It's just marriage—for all. Canada now follows the Netherlands and Belgium with full-fledged marital rights for gays and lesbians.

Could it happen in the U.S.? The next few weeks will give us many clues. The 3
U.S. Supreme Court is due to rule any day now on whether it's legal for Texas and other states to prosecute sodomy among gays but not straights. More critical, Massachusetts' highest court is due to rule very soon on whether the denial of marriage to gays is illicit discrimination against a minority. If Massachusetts rules that it is, then gay couples across America will be able to marry not only in Canada (where there are no residency or nationality requirements for marriage) but also in a bona fide American state. There will be a long process of litigation as various married couples try hard to keep their marriages legally intact from one state to another.

This move seems an eminently conservative one—in fact, almost an emblem 4
of "compassionate conservatism." Conservatives have long rightly argued for the vital importance of the institution of marriage for fostering responsibility, commitment and the domestication of unruly men. Bringing gay men and

women into this institution will surely change the gay subculture in subtle but profoundly conservative ways. When I grew up and realized I was gay, I had no concept of what my own future could be like. Like most other homosexuals, I grew up in a heterosexual family and tried to imagine how I too could one day be a full part of the family I loved. But I figured then that I had no such future. I could never have a marriage, never have a family, never be a full and equal part of the weddings and relationships and holidays that give families structure and meaning. When I looked forward, I saw nothing but emptiness and loneliness. No wonder it was hard to connect sex with love and commitment. No wonder it was hard to feel at home in what was, in fact, my home.

5   For today's generation of gay kids, all that changes. From the beginning, they will be able to see their future as part of family life—not in conflict with it. Their "coming out" will also allow them a "coming home." And as they date in adolescence and early adulthood, there will be some future anchor in their mind-set, some ultimate structure with which to give their relationships stability and social support. Many heterosexuals, I suspect, simply don't realize how big a deal this is. They have never doubted that one day they could marry the person they love. So they find it hard to conceive how deep a psychic and social wound the exclusion from marriage and family can be. But the polls suggest this is changing fast: the majority of people 30 and younger see gay marriage as inevitable and understandable. Many young straight couples simply don't see married gay peers next door as some sort of threat to their own lives. They can get along in peace.

6   As for religious objections, it's important to remember that the issue here is not religious. It's civil. Various religious groups can choose to endorse same-sex marriage or not as they see fit. Their freedom of conscience is as vital as gays' freedom to be treated equally under the civil law. And there's no real reason that the two cannot coexist. The Roman Catholic Church, for example, opposes remarriage after divorce. But it doesn't seek to make civil divorce and remarriage illegal for everyone. Similarly, churches can well decide this matter in their own time and on their own terms while allowing the government to be neutral between competing visions of the good life. We can live and let live.

7   And after all, isn't that what this really is about? We needn't all agree on the issue of homosexuality to believe that the government should treat every citizen alike. If that means living next door to someone of whom we disapprove, so be it. But disapproval needn't mean disrespect. And if the love of two people, committing themselves to each other exclusively for the rest of their lives, is not worthy of respect, then what is?

QUESTIONS FOR READING

1.   What important decision has Canada's government recently made?
2.   What decision did the Supreme Court make on the Texas sodomy case, after Sullivan's essay was published?
3.   Why should these rulings be viewed as conservative?

4.   What view toward gay marriage is held by the majority of people 30 and younger?

QUESTIONS FOR REASONING AND ANALYSIS

1.   What is Sullivan's claim?

2.   In paragraph 4, Sullivan puts the term "compassionate conservatism" in quotation marks. Why? What is he suggesting in the sentence?

3.   Sullivan includes his own feelings about feeling excluded from family because he is gay. How does this discussion in paragraph 4 aid his argument?

4.   How does he rebut the presumed counterargument of religious objections? What analogy does he draw in paragraph 6? Is his rebuttal convincing? Why or why not?

5.   How would you describe the tone of this argument? How is the author seeking to use tone to reach readers who might disagree with him?

QUESTIONS FOR REFLECTING AND WRITING

1.   Were you aware that the Netherlands, Belgium, and Canada all allow gay marriages? If you did not know this, does this new knowledge affect your thinking about gay marriage in any way? If so, how? If not, why not?

2.   What, in your view, is the strongest part of Sullivan's argument? Why?

3.   Sullivan is asking readers to support civil equality even though they may have religious objections to gay marriages. Can you separate church and state on this issue? Why or why not?

GAY MARRIAGE, AN OXYMORON | LISA SCHIFFREN

A speechwriter for former vice president Dan Quayle, Lisa Schiffren began her career at the *Detroit News.* She now writes on public policy and social issues in popular magazines and newspapers. Her article on gay marriage was published in the *New York Times* on March 23, 1996—before Hawaii decided not to sanction gay marriages.

PREREADING QUESTIONS What does the term *oxymoron* mean? What view of gay marriage does the author's title convey?

As study after study and victim after victim testify to the social devastation   1
of the sexual revolution, easy divorce, and out-of-wedlock motherhood, marriage is fashionable again. And parenthood has transformed many baby boomers into advocates of bourgeois norms.

Indeed, we have come so far that the surprise issue of the political season   2
is whether homosexual "marriage" should be legalized. The Hawaii courts will likely rule that gay marriage is legal, and other states will be required to accept those marriages as valid.

Considering what a momentous change this would be—a radical redefi-   3
nition of society's most fundamental institution—there has been almost no real debate. This is because the premise is unimaginable to many, and the

forces of political correctness have descended on the discussion, raising the cost of opposition. But one may feel the same affection for one's homosexual friends and relatives as for any other and be genuinely pleased for the happiness they derive from relationships while opposing gay marriage for principled reasons.

4   "Same-sex marriage" is inherently incompatible with our culture's understanding of the institution. Marriage is essentially a lifelong compact between a man and woman committed to sexual exclusivity and the creation and nurture of offspring. For most Americans, the marital union—as distinguished from other sexual relationships and legal and economic partnerships—is imbued with an aspect of holiness. Though many of us are uncomfortable using religious language to discuss social and political issues, Judeo-Christian morality informs our view of family life.

5   Though it is not polite to mention it, what the Judeo-Christian tradition has to say about homosexual unions could not be clearer. In a diverse, open society such as ours, tolerance of homosexuality is a necessity. But for many, its practice depends on a trick of cognitive dissonance that allows people to believe in the Judeo-Christian moral order while accepting, often with genuine regard, the different lives of homosexual acquaintances. That is why, though homosexuals may believe that they are merely seeking a small expansion of the definition of marriage, the majority of Americans perceive this change as a radical deconstruction of the institution.

6   Some make the conservative argument that making marriage a civil right will bring stability, an end to promiscuity, and a sense of fairness to gay men and women. But they miss the point. Society cares about stability in heterosexual unions because it is critical for raising healthy children and transmitting the values that are the basis of our culture.

7   Whether homosexual relationships endure is of little concern to society. That is also true of most childless marriages, harsh as it is to say. Society has wisely chosen not to differentiate between marriages, because it would require meddling into the motives and desires of everyone who applies for a license.

8   In traditional marriage, the tie that really binds for life is shared responsibility for the children. (A small fraction of gay couples may choose to raise children together, but such children are offspring of one partner and an outside contributor.) What will keep gay marriages together when individuals tire of each other?

9   Similarly, the argument that legal marriage will check promiscuity by gay males raises the question of how a "piece of paper" will do what the threat of AIDS has not. Lesbians seem to have little problem with monogamy or the rest of what constitutes "domestication," despite the absence of official status.

10   Finally, there is the so-called fairness argument. The government gives tax benefits, inheritance rights, and employee benefits only to the married. Again, these financial benefits exist to help couples raise children. Tax reform is an effective way to remove distinctions among earners.

If the American people are interested in a radical experiment with same- 11
sex marriages, then subjecting it to the political process is the right route. For
a court in Hawaii to assume that it has the power to radically redefine marriage
is a stunning abuse of power. To present homosexual marriage as a fait ac-
compli, without national debate, is a serious political error. A society struggling to recover from thirty years of weakened norms and broken families is
not likely to respond gently to having an institution central to most people's
lives altered.

QUESTIONS FOR READING

1. What is Schiffren's topic?
2. What is Schiffren's definition of marriage? What is the source of our society's
    ideas about marriage?
3. What does the Judeo-Christian tradition say about homosexual unions?
4. If same-sex marriages are to be approved, by what process should this occur,
    in the author's view?

QUESTIONS FOR REASONING AND ANALYSIS

1. What is the author's claim? Where does she state it?
2. How does Schiffren organize her argument? Briefly summarize the main points
    of her argument.
3. How does the author use conciliatory strategies in her argument? Are they
    effective?

QUESTIONS FOR REFLECTING AND WRITING

1. The author asserts that "marriage is fashionable again." Does she provide any
    evidence to support this assertion? Has the number of marriages in the United
    States increased in recent years? (How might you obtain such information?)
2. How does the author explain why there has been no debate about same-sex mar-
    riages? Does her explanation match your experience? Has the debate of this topic
    increased since Schiffren wrote in 1996?
3. Schiffren asserts that society does not care about stability in gay relationships,
    only in marriages with children. Does she offer evidence that this is how most
    citizens feel? Or are we to believe that she is speaking in a legal sense—the state's
    interest? Should society—we—care about the stability of all relationships? Why
    or why not? Since "society's" concern has not kept the divorce rate from being
    slightly more than 50 percent, is this a meaningful argument? Why or why not?
4. Schiffren also asserts that gay males are promiscuous, presumably more so than
    both lesbians and heterosexuals. Is there evidence for this assertion? Do
    Schiffren's unsupported assertions affect the quality of her argument? Why or
    why not?

WHO SAYS A WOMAN CAN'T BE EINSTEIN? | AMANDA RIPLEY

Amanda Ripley is a reporter for *Time* magazine. The following article, slightly condensed, was the cover story on March 7, 2005—probably in response to the issue raised by Harvard President Larry Summers over possible reasons for so few women pursuing careers in math, science, and engineering.

PREREADING QUESTIONS What does the title suggest to you about the article's subject matter? About the writer's attitude toward the subject? What may be some of the reasons why women do not choose careers in the sciences in the same numbers as men?

1   Now that scientists are finally starting to map the brain with some accuracy, the challenge is figuring out what to do with that knowledge. The possibilities for applying it to the classroom, workplace and doctor's office are tantalizing. "If something is genetic, it means it must be biological. If we can figure out the biology, then we should be able to tweak the biology," says Richard Haier, a psychology professor who studies intelligence at the University of California at Irvine.

LESSON 1: FUNCTION OVER FORM

2   Scientists have been looking for sex differences in the brain since they have been looking at the brain. Many bold decrees have been issued. In the 19th century, the corpus callosum, a bundle of nerve fibers that connects the two hemispheres of the brain, was considered key to intellectual development. Accordingly, it was said to have a greater surface area in men. Then, in the 1980s, we were told that no, it is larger in women—and that explains why the emotional right side of women's brains is more in touch with the analytical left side. Aha. That theory has since been discredited, and scientists remain at odds over who has the biggest and what it might mean. Stay tuned for more breaking news.

3   But most studies agree that men's brains are about 10% bigger than women's brains overall. Even when the comparison is adjusted for the fact that men are, on average, 8% taller than women, men's brains are still slightly bigger. But size does not predict intellectual performance, as was once thought. Men and women perform similarly on IQ tests. And most scientists still cannot tell male and female brains apart just by looking at them.

4   Recently, scientists have begun to move away from the obsession with size. Thanks to new brain-imaging technology, researchers can get a good look at the living brain as it functions and grows. Earlier studies relied on autopsies or X rays—and no one wanted to expose children or women, who might be pregnant, to regular doses of radiation.

5   The deeper you probe, the more interesting the differences. Women appear to have more connections between the two brain hemispheres. In certain regions, their brain is more densely packed with neurons. And women tend to use more parts of their brain to accomplish certain tasks. That might explain

why they often recover better from a stroke, since the healthy parts of their minds compensate for the injured regions. Men do their thinking in more focused regions of the brain, whether they are solving a math problem, reading a book or feeling a wave of anger or sadness.

Indeed, men and women seem to handle emotions quite differently. While 6 both sexes use a part of the brain called the amygdala, which is located deep within the organ, women seem to have stronger connections between the amygdala and regions of the brain that handle language and other higher-level functions. That may explain why women are, on average, more likely to talk about their emotions and men tend to compartmentalize their worries and carry on. Or, of course, it may not.

"Men and women have different brain architectures, and we don't know 7 what they mean," says Haier. By administering IQ tests to a group of college students and then analyzing scans of their brain structure, Haier's team recently discovered that the parts of the brain that are related to intelligence are different in men and women. "That is in some ways a major observation, because one of the assumptions of psychology has been that all human brains pretty much work the same way," he says. Now that we know they don't, we can try to understand why some brains react differently to, say, Alzheimer's, many medications and even teaching techniques, Haier says.

Even more interesting than the brain's adult anatomy might be the jour- 8 ney it takes to get there. For 13 years, psychiatrist Jay Giedd has been compiling one of the world's largest libraries of brain growth. Every Tuesday evening, from 5 o'clock until midnight, a string of children files into the National Institutes of Health outside Washington to have their brains scanned. Giedd and his team ease the kids through the MRI procedure, and then he gives them a brain tour of their pictures—gently pointing out the spinal cord and the corpus callosum, before offering them a copy to take to show-and-tell.

Most of the kids are all business. Rowena Avery, 6, of Sparks, Nev., arrived 9 last week with a stuffed animal named Sidewalk and stoically disappeared into the machine while her mom, dad and little sister watched. In preparation, she had practiced at home by lying very still in the bathtub. Her picture came out crystal clear. "The youngest ones are the best at lying still. It's kind of surprising," Giedd says. "It must be because they are used to hiding in kitchen cabinets and things like that."

Among the girls in Giedd's study, brain size peaks around age 11 1/2. For 10 the boys, the peak comes three years later. "For kids, that's a long time," Giedd says. His research shows that most parts of the brain mature faster than girls. But in a 1999 study of 508 boys and girls. Virginia Tech researcher Harriet Hanlon found that some areas mature faster in boys. Specifically, some of the regions involved in mechanical reasoning, visual targeting and spatial reasoning appeared to mature four to eight years earlier in boys. The parts that handle verbal fluency, handwriting and recognizing familiar faces matured several years earlier in girls. . . .

LESSON 2: THE SEGREGATION OF THE SENSES

11 So how do we explain why in study after study, boys and men are still on average better at rotating 3-D objects in their minds? As for girls and women, how do we explain why they tend to have better verbal skills and social sensitivities?

12 The most surprising differences may be outside the brain. "If you have a man and a woman looking at the same landscape, they see totally different things," asserts Leonard Sax, a physician and psychologist whose book *Why Gender Matters* came out last month. "Women can see colors and textures that men cannot see. They hear things men cannot hear, and they smell things men cannot smell." Since the eyes, ears and nose are portals to the brain, they directly affect brain development from birth on.

13 In rats, for example, we know that the male retina has more cells designed to detect motion. In females, the retina has more cells built to gather information on color and texture. If the same is true in humans, as Sax suspects, that may explain why, in an experiment in England four years ago, newborn boys were much more likely than girls to stare at a mobile turning above their cribs. It may also help explain why boys prefer to play with moving toys like trucks while girls favor richly textured dolls and tend to draw with a wider range of colors, Sax says.

14 Likewise, women's ears are more sensitive to some noises. Baby girls hear certain ranges of sound better. And the divergence gets even bigger in adults. As for smell, a study published in the journal *Nature Neuroscience* in 2002 showed that women of childbearing age were many times more sensitive than men to several smells upon repeated exposure. (Another study has found that heterosexual women have the most sensitive smell and homosexual men have the least.)

15 Rest assured, Sax says: none of that means women are, overall, better than men at perception. It just means the species is internally diverse, making it more likely to survive. "The female will remember the color and texture of a particular plant and be able to warn people if it's poisonous. A man looking at the same thing will be more alert to what is moving in the periphery," he says. "Which is better? You need both."

LESSON 3: NEVER UNDERESTIMATE THE BRAIN

16 Until recently, there have been two groups of people: those who argue sex differences are innate and should be embraced and whose who insist that they are learned and should be eliminated by changing the environment. Sax is one of the few in the middle—convinced that boys and girls are innately different and that we must change the environment so differences don't become limitations.

17 At a restaurant near his practice in Montgomery County, Md., Sax spreads out dozens of papers and meticulously makes his case. He is a fanatic, but a smart, patient one. In the early 1990s, he says, he grew alarmed by the "parade" of parents coming into his office wondering whether their sons had attention-deficit/hyperactivity disorder. Sax evaluated them and found that, indeed, the boys were not paying attention in school. But the more he studied brain differences, the more he became convinced that the

problem was with the schools. Sometimes the solution was simple: some of the boys didn't hear as well as the girls and so needed to be moved into the front row. Other times, the solution was more complex.

Eventually, Sax concluded that very young boys and girls would be better 18 off in separate classrooms altogether. "[Previously], as far as I was concerned, single-sex education was an old-fashioned leftover. I thought of boys wearing suits and talking with British accents," he says. But coed schools do more harm than good, he decided, when they teach boys and girls as if their brains mature at the same time. "If you ask a child to do something not developmentally appropriate for him, he will, No. 1, fail. No. 2, he will develop an aversion to the subject," he says. "By age 12, you will have girls who don't like science and boys who don't like reading." And they won't ever go back, he says. "The reason women are underrepresented in computer science and engineering is not because they can't do it. It's because of the way they're taught."

So far, studies about girls' and boys' achievements in same-sex grammar 19 schools are inconclusive. But if it turns out that targeting sex differences through education is helpful, there are certainly many ways to carry it out. Says Giedd: "The ability for change is phenomenal. That's what the brain does best." A small but charming 2004 study published in *Nature* found that people who learned how to juggle increased the gray matter in their brains in certain locations. When they stopped juggling, the new gray matter vanished. A similar structural change appears to occur in people who learn a second language. . . .

In a recent experiment with humans at Temple University, women showed 20 substantial progress in spatial reasoning after spending a couple of hours a week for 10 weeks playing *Tetris*, of all things. The males improved with weeks of practice too, says Nora Newcombe, a Temple psychologist who specializes in spatial cognition, and so the gender gap remained. But the improvement for both sexes was "massively greater" than the gender differences. "This means that if the males didn't train, the females would outstrip them," she says.

Of course, we already manipulate the brain through drugs—many of 21 which, doctors now realize, have dramatically different effects on different brains. Drugs for improving intelligence are in the works, says Haier, in the quest to find medication for Alzheimer's. "We're going to get a lot better at manipulating genetic biology. We may even be better at manipulating genetic biology than manipulating the environment."

Until then, one solution to overcoming biological tendencies is to con- 22 sciously override them, to say to yourself, "O.K., I may have a hard time with this task, but I'm going to will myself to conquer it." Some experiments show that baby girls, when faced with failure, tend to give up and cry relatively quickly, while baby boys get angry and persist, says Witelson at Ontario's Michael G. DeGroote School of Medicine at McMaster University. "What we don't know is whether that pattern persists into adulthood," she says. But in her experience in academia, she says she knows of at least a couple of brilliant women who never realized their potential in science because they stopped trying when they didn't get grants or encountered some other obstacle. "It's much better," she says, "for people to understand what the differences are, act on their advantages and be prepared for their disadvantages."

LESSON 4: EXPECTATIONS MATTER

23   We have a tendency to make too much of test-score differences between the sexes (which are actually very small compared with the differences between, say, poor and affluent students). And regardless of what happens in school, personality and discipline can better predict success when it comes to highly competitive jobs.

24   One thing we know about the brain is that it is vulnerable to the power of suggestion. There is plenty of evidence that when young women are motivated and encouraged, they excel at science. For most of the 1800s, for example, physics, astronomy, chemistry and botany were considered gender-appropriate subjects for middle- and upper-class American girls. By the 1890s, girls outnumbered boys in public high school science courses across the country, according to *The Science Education of American Girls,* a 2003 book by Kim Tolley. Records from top schools in Boston show that girls outperformed boys in physics in the mid-19th century. Latin and Greek, meanwhile, were considered the province of gentlemen—until the 20th century, when lucrative opportunities began to open up in the sciences.

25   Today, in Iceland and Sweden, girls consistently outperform boys in math and physics. . . . In Sweden the gap is widest in the remote regions in the north. That may be because women want to move to the big cities farther south, where they would need to compete in high-tech economies, while men are focused on local hunting, fishing and forestry opportunities, says Niels Egelund, a professor of educational psychology at the Danish University of Education. The phenomenon even has a name, the Jokkmokk effect, a reference to an isolated town in Swedish Lapland.

26   Back in the States, the achievement gap in the sciences is closing, albeit slowly. Female professors have been catching up with male professors in their publishing output. Today half of chemistry and almost 60% of biology bachelor of science degrees go to females. Patience is required.

QUESTIONS FOR READING

1. How do the brains of men and women differ in size overall? Is this difference considered significant?
2. What are the key differences in brain functioning? What inferences are drawn from these difference? How confident are researchers about these inferences?
3. What are the differences in brain development?
4. What differences has Sax found among men's and women's senses?
5. What do studies suggest about the effect of teaching?
6. What roles do motivation and social expectations play?

QUESTIONS FOR REASONING AND ANALYSIS

1. This article was motivated by statements by (now) former president of Harvard Larry Summers. How does this article address the question of why more men than women excel in the sciences?

2. What is Ripley's claim?

3. In paragraph 2, Ripley provides a brief history of brain size studies and their conclusions. After studies revealed that women's hemisphere connections were larger, a new inference was drawn. Why does Ripley write "Aha" after providing this information? What does she imply?

4. How has the author organized her material? Look at the four headings in the article. What unites each section? What is significant about the *order* of information and the discussion through the four lessons?

QUESTIONS FOR REFLECTING AND WRITING

1. Did you find new ideas/information here? If so, what new idea/fact seems most important to you? Why?

2. What information is most important for parents to know? For teachers to know? For everyone—society—to know? Why?

LAWSUITS WON'T BREAK THAT GLASS CEILING | SUSAN E. REED

A Columbia University graduate and former Nieman Fellow at Harvard, Susan E. Reed is a freelance journalist who writes on politics and business for numerous newspapers and magazines, including the *New York Times,* the *American Prospect,* and *The New Republic.* The following article appeared August 21, 2005, in the *Washington Post.*

PREREADING QUESTIONS What does the term *the glass ceiling* refer to? What strategies are available to groups who seek to remove discrimination?

How about those working women? Suing companies, lobbying bosses, 1 networking nonstop with other women, taking on the workplaces that have kept them down. It seems the women of today will stop at nothing to try to get ahead in the workplace battle of the sexes.

And yet, where does it get them? Women comprise nearly half of full-time 2 workers and half of managers, but they are only 16 percent of corporate officers and barely 1 percent of CEOs in the nation's richest 500 companies. Why can't they improve those rates?

After reporting on their maneuvers for several years now, I've concluded 3 that these warriors are using the wrong weapons to get ahead. Suing for advancement may make a splash in the news, and women's networks might get women more resources from their employers, but these activities are often perceived as selfish by the very men with whom the women will have to work. To get into the executive suite, women have to show one critical thing—that they can lead men.

4   This reality was underscored by last month's ruling by an arbitration panel in a discrimination case against financial service giant Merrill Lunch. The panel ruled that the firm had to rehire a former financial analyst, Hydie Sumner, and send her through its management assessment program because it had denied her this opportunity more than a decade earlier.

5   If Sumner becomes a manager at Merrill, she might find that she's won the battle, but lost the war for hearts and minds. Companies aren't terribly fond of employees who sue them. Merrill's lawyers argued in a public hearing that if Sumner were rehired, she might sue them again if she didn't get what she wanted. They have reason to wonder. In 1991, the year she started working for Merrill, Sumner sued her previous employer. Her quest for reinstatement at Merrill is part of a 1998 class-action lawsuit that was joined by 900 current and former female financial analysts who claimed that the firm had denied them lucrative accounts and promotions. And her lawyer told me that Sumner has spoken out against discrimination in her current workplace.

6   She's not alone. At least four other women who were involved in the class-action suit against Merrill went on to sue or threaten to sue other companies. Sumner has received $2.2 million in compensation from her case against Merrill. But in trying to teach the companies a lesson in how to treat women, these serial suers may have slowed the cause, by bogging companies and careers down in legal wrangles.

7   Once a woman understands how the courts identify gender discrimination, it's pretty easy to recognize it everywhere she goes. Take a look at your local supermarket. If all the cashiers are female and all the managers are male, it might be a case of statistical discrimination and job segregation. Take a look at the Web sites of America's largest corporations where just a couple of women are listed as executives. All of these organizations are ripe for lawsuits. In fact, I would bet that almost every major corporation in the United States has been sued for gender discrimination. I can't prove it because these suits are often settled in secrecy. But the litigation approach has hardly forced regime change.

8   In 1994, Nancy Hopkins, a biology professor at MIT, suspected that a lawsuit might only alienate her male bosses. So she took a different tack. She formed a lobbying group of other female science professors to try to improve their standing. They compared what the guys got in terms of laboratory and office space, grants, awards and administrative positions with what the gals got. When the president of MIT saw the discrepancy, he announced that the institution had unconsciously discriminated and made amends. Some women got bigger salaries, others got a boost to their 401(k)s, and Hopkins got an enormous laboratory and an ongoing grant to deepen her genetics research. This war booty—I mean, victory in resources—made Hopkins happier and more productive in her day-to-day work, she told me. "Looking back, I sure was lucky," she wrote in a recent e-mail. "Many women who try to take this on are not as lucky, I believe."

9   Yet there's collateral damage in any war. Hopkins herself has never been tapped to hold a top spot in the university's administration. Neither has the *Philadelphia Inquirer's* Jane Eisner, who in 1997 organized an employee salary review when female reporters at the paper suspected—largely incorrectly, it

turned out—that they weren't being paid the same as their male counterparts. Eisner, who was then the editorial page editor and the highest-ranking woman at the paper, tried to be the honest broker. But she said she was extremely disappointed two years later not to be selected as managing editor. Still, she went on to become a columnist, and she frequently writes about women's issues.

Although Hopkins and Eisner showed leadership, I believe that the risks 10 they took were not fully appreciated. They were seen to be looking out for one group instead of the whole organization, and this may have proved key to their inability to rise further. Chief executives have to be trusted to act on behalf of everyone in an organization, men and women.

While men used to complain that women hadn't played in organized sports 11 and didn't know how to work as part of a team, they don't seem to like it when women form their own teams. When women started a networking group at General Electric in 1997, several men at the company whined that the women were trying to gain unfair advantage. These men conveniently overlooked the access they themselves had to informal networks such as playing sports or socializing with the other male higher-ups, and resented the women for helping each other fulfill their ambitions.

It's almost as if women who show leadership in their company by organiz- 12 ing groups that are designed to mentor women become too identified with a "woman's cause"—with being, dare I say, sexist? No one likes to think of herself as sexist. But the men at the top don't like to be told that they are sexist, either. That's why they hire women from the outside, to prove that they are enlightened, and to avoid promoting the activists. The *Inquirer* and MIT both recently hired women for their top jobs, in fact—perhaps in part thanks to Eisner's and Hopkin's activities—but both were brought in from the outside.

In my research to find out how women get to the top, I've found that at 13 least half of the women who are executives at the nation's richest companies were imported from the outside rather than groomed from within. Women's route to the top is different from men's, most of whom come from the inside.

If more women wish to work their way up through an organization, they 14 ought to be aware that their male counterparts may not trust them to lead them after they take an activist stance. For every woman who suffers from frustrated ambition, at least one, if not two, three or four of her male colleagues are also nursing the same disappointment. Men, who tend to be the lifers of an organization, would seem to have an innate commitment to improving its function.

A statistical analysis performed as part of the women's class action against 15 Merrill Lynch showed that men as well as women lost out because of the favoritism that managers used in distributing accounts. Some men weren't anointed with the biggest accounts because they didn't play golf with the manager, or they hadn't gone to the right schools, or they weren't in the same church.

Men have been at war against the forces of career failure much longer than 16 women have. It's time for women to stop seeing the problems of achievement at work merely in terms of men vs. women. A farther-reaching approach would be to join forces with men who also bear the brunt of bosses' inconsistent procedures and unfair practices. Nobody likes to be led by someone who engages in favoritism. It's bad for morale and bad for business. Employees of both genders have to join the same team, the same army if they're going to improve their overall opportunities for success. Women have to prove that they can lead men, by showing that they are willing to tackle the complexities of reward and success that men have struggled with for generations.

17   It's hardly a smooth escalator ride into the executive offices of any company. Rising stars, both men and women, get bumped off or fall off along the way. The climb is not only arduous, but long. It takes an average of 30 years to make chief executive officer.

18   Hydie Sumner, now 49, probably doesn't have enough time left in her career to become a CEO, and we'll never know if she had the right stuff. But according to her lawyer, Merrill Lynch has offered her the opportunity to become a sales manager without going through the management training program. While this would be a boost to her career, the ongoing test for Sumner—and for other women like her—will be to show employees whether her activism can benefit not just herself, but both the men and the women of the company she would serve.

QUESTIONS FOR READING

1.   How many workers are women? How many are CEOs?

2.   What strategies have women been using to try to advance into management?

3.   In what way are women who organize themselves successful? In what way are they unsuccessful?

4.   How does the path of women into management frequently differ from men's?

5.   In the author's view, in what way do women who want to achieve need to identify with and work with the men in the company who also want to achieve?

QUESTIONS FOR REASONING AND ANALYSIS

1.   What is Reed's claim? Where does she state it?

2.   What kinds of evidence does Reed present to support her claim? What assertions does she make about leadership and not being selected? Does her reasoning seem logical?

3.   In paragraph 14, Reed writes that "men, who tend to be the lifers of an organization, would seem to have an innate commitment to improving its function." Does she offer any evidence for either part of this statement? Is it true that men are more likely to stay with a company than women? (See Lester Thurow, page 242.) Is it true that commitment is innate in men—and, by implication, not innate in women?

QUESTIONS FOR REFLECTING AND WRITING

1.   Evaluate Reed's argument. Does the author offer any data of women rising in management by working with men in the company? If not, what kind of

support does she offer? What other information would you like to have to weigh this argument?

2. If only 1 percent of CEOs are women, is it relevant to point out that men are passed over for promotion, too? Playing ball with the guys you want to lead seems reasonable; can it also be a slow way to redress the discrimination against women in positions of leadership? What might this argument be analogous to? Is the analogy legitimate? Why or why not?

3. This is a problem/solution argument. What solutions do you have to offer for the problem—either in addition to Reed's solution or instead of her solution?

THE OVERLOOKED VICTIMS OF AIDS | JUDITH D. AUERBACH

A sociologist and former college professor, Judith Auerbach is now vice president for public policy at the American Foundation for AIDS Research. Auerbach has published on a variety of topics, including AIDS, health research, and family policy and gender. The following column, published in the *Washington Post* during the last presidential campaign (October 14, 2004), deplores our lack of awareness of who is suffering from AIDS.

PREREADING QUESTIONS Who, now, is most often becoming infected with HIV/AIDS? Do you know how most women become infected with AIDS?

1 In last week's vice presidential debate, moderator Gwen Ifill talked about the disproportionate impact of HIV-AIDS on African American women and asked what role the government should play in slowing the growth of this domestic epidemic. Both candidates displayed an alarming ignorance of the reality of the crisis in the United States, choosing instead to focus their comment on AIDS in Africa, which Ifill had explicitly asked them not to do.

2 What is inexcusable among the nation's top policymakers is a persistent problem in the general public as well: a failure to recognize that AIDS now disproportionately affects women.

3 According to the Centers for Disease Control and Prevention, the proportion of all AIDS cases reported among adolescent and adult women in the United States has more than tripled since 1986. AIDS is the fourth-leading cause of death among women in this country between the ages of 25 and 44, and is the *leading* cause of death among African American women ages 25 to 34. Black women represent about two-thirds of all new HIV infections among adult and adolescent females.

4 Globally, about half of the 12,000 people ages 15 to 49 infected every day are women. Sixty-two percent of those ages 15 to 24 living with HIV-AIDS are girls and women. In South Africa, that figure climbs to 77 percent. Most women worldwide, including in the United States, acquire HIV infection through heterosexual intercourse.

5 Why is this "feminization of AIDS" occurring? The answer lies in the complex ways that sex and gender intersect, conferring increased vulnerability to HIV infection on women and girls. Biological, sociological and political factors

interact differently for women and men, leaving women more susceptible to viral transmission, more distant from prevention and care services, farther away from accurate information, and far more vulnerable to human rights violations. Here are some of the specifics:

- Women are more vulnerable to HIV infection than men. The physiology of the female genital tract makes women twice as likely to acquire HIV from men as vice versa. Among adolescent girls, this effect is even more pronounced.
- Poverty is correlated with higher rates of HIV infection all over the world. Globally, more than half of the people living in poverty are women. In the United States, nearly 30 percent are African American women.
- Lack of education is associated with higher HIV infection rates. Girls in developing countries are less likely to complete secondary education than boys, and almost twice as likely to be illiterate.
- Early marriage is a significant risk factor for HIV among women and girls. In developing countries, a majority of sexually active girls ages 15 to 19 are married. Married adolescent girls tend to have higher HIV infection rates than their sexually active unmarried peers.
- A significant risk factor for HIV infection is violence, to which women are more susceptible in virtually all societies. In a South African study, for example, women who were beaten or dominated by their partners were 48 percent more likely to become infected than women who lived in nonviolent households.
- Rape of women has been used as a tool for subjugation and so-called ethnic cleansing in war and conflict situations. Of the 250,000 women raped during the Rwandan genocide, about 70 percent of the survivors are HIV-positive.

6   The experience of women and girls in the HIV-AIDS epidemic in the United States and around the world highlights how social arrangements, cultural norms, laws, policies and institutions contribute to the unequal status of women in society and to the spread of disease. Together they undermine the capacity of women and girls to exercise power over their own lives and to control the circumstances that increase their vulnerability to HIV infection, particularly in the context of sexual relationships. For African American women, gender inequalities are exacerbated by persistent racism.

7   It is only when this unhealthy mix is acknowledged and addressed—particularly by the highest levels of government—that we will be able to stem the alarming increase of HIV-AIDS among more than half the world's population.

QUESTIONS FOR READING

1. What do politicians, and Americans generally, seem not to know about AIDS?
2. How do most women become infected?

3. For what group of Americans is AIDS the leading cause of death?

4. What are six specifics about women's experiences that make them more vulnerable to HIV infection? Explain in your own words.

QUESTIONS FOR REASONING AND ANALYSIS

1. What is Auerbach's purpose in writing? How does she want to affect readers?

2. What is the author's claim?

3. How would you describe Auerbach's style—her sentence structure and word choice?

4. What is effective about the use of bullets in this essay?

5. Is the author's style effective for her subject and purpose? Explain.

QUESTIONS FOR REFLECTING AND WRITING

1. Were you aware of the "feminization of AIDS"? Does this surprise? Shock? Make you wonder how this shift has happened? Explain.

2. Which statistic is most shocking to you? Why?

3. Which one of the six experiences correlating with increased risk for AIDS is most surprising to you? Why?

4. What should be done to address this serious world health problem? If you were the president's "AIDS czar," what specific programs would you seek to put into place in this country? Around the world? Explain your cause/effect reasoning.

Read: What situation is depicted in the cartoon?

Reason: Except for the speaker, what expressions do the figures have? Who are we asked to identify with—the speaker or the others?

Reflect/Write: What is the cartoonist's point? How are we supposed to relate the situation to our own time?

CHAPTER 21

Science—
and the Politics
of Science

Undoubtedly changes in computer technology will dramatically change our lives in this twenty-first century. Just as assuredly will our concepts of the family affect the way we live. But for many the most dramatic—perhaps the most fearful—changes will come from medical research or biotechnology, most particularly from stem cell research and cloning. Will medical science take us into a utopia, a world of longevity without most of the disagreeable elements of aging, a world freed from genetically transmitted diseases? Or will biotechnology deliver us into a nightmarish universe of genetically "enhanced" humans who at some point truly cease to be human as we understand that term today? And will this debate matter in the long run if we destroy the environment? These are tough questions. It is difficult to stop scientific study, even if we should want to, and it is difficult to want to stem the tide of advancements against Parkinson's disease or infertility, to name only two of the many medical problems we hope to solve.

The writers of this chapter debate bioethics, the environment, and the nature of science itself. Two writers offer differing views on the direction of biotechnology. They follow one of the most important documents on this topic, the executive summary of the President's Council on Bioethics. Although longish, this document is worth your careful study and attention as it clearly presents the issues of the debate and presents the Council's recommendations to the president. Before and after the three works on bioethics are articles on the nature and roles of science and issues facing our environment—plenty of food for thought.

Prereading Questions

1. How well do you understand stem cell research and what is referred to as "cloning"? How important is it to understand the science involved in order to have a position on this research?

2. Do you have a position on stem cell research? If so, what are the primary sources on which you base your position? Family? Friends? Biology class?

3. If you don't have a position, do you think that it is important to understand this issue, the points of debate, and then move toward an informed decision? Why or why not?

4. Are you more likely to listen to scientists or to politicians or religious leaders when exploring scientific questions? What is the reasoning behind your choice of expert?

Web Sites Related to This Chapter's Topic

The Environmental Protection Agency

http://www.epa.gov

This agency's Web site has lots of information on environmental issues.

Bioethics Resources on the Web—NIH

http://www.nih.gov/sigs/bioethics

As its name indicates, there are lots of bioethics resources on this site.

Center for Bioethics and Human Dignity

http://www.cbhd.org

Lots of information, but from a perspective of Christian values.

CENSORING SCIENCE WON'T MAKE US ANY SAFER | LAURA K. DONOHUE

A former fellow at Harvard's John F. Kennedy School of Government, Laura Donohue is a fellow at the Center for International Security and Cooperation at Stanford University. She is the author of numerous articles as well as *Counter-Terrorist Law and*

Emergency Powers in the United Kingdom 1922–2000 (2001). The following article was published in the *Washington Post* June 26, 2005.

PREREADING QUESTIONS Should information on building bombs or biological warfare be kept from publication or Internet posting? Why or why not?

In 1920, the Irish Republican Army reportedly considered a terrifying new   1
weapon: typhoid-contaminated milk. Reading from an IRA memo he claimed had been captured in a recent raid, Sir Hamar Greenwood described to Parliament the ease with which "fresh and virulent cultures" could be obtained and introduced into milk served to British soldiers. Although the plot would only target the military, the memo expressed concern that the disease might spread to the general population.

Although the IRA never used this weapon, the incident illustrates that poi-   2
soning a nation's milk supply with biological agents hardly ranks as a new concept. Yet just two weeks ago, the National Academy of Sciences' journal suspended publication of an article analyzing the vulnerability of the U.S. milk supply to botulinum toxin, because the Department of Health and Human Services warned that information in the article provided a "road map for terrorists."

That approach may sound reasonable, but the effort to suppress scientific   3
information reflects a dangerously outdated attitude. Today, information relating to microbiology is widely and instantly available, from the Internet to high school textbooks to doctoral theses. Our best defense against those who would use it as a weapon is to ensure that our own scientists have better information. That means encouraging publication.

The article in question, written by Stanford University professor Lawrence   4
Wein and graduate student Yifan Liu, describes a theoretical terrorist who obtains a few grams of botulinum toxin on the black market and pours it into an unlocked milk tank. Transferred to giant dairy silos, the toxin contaminates a much larger supply. Because even a millionth of a gram may be enough to kill an adult, hundreds of thousands of people die. (Wein summarized the article in an op-ed he wrote for the *New York Times*.[1]) The scenario is frightening, and it is meant to be—the authors want the dairy industry and its federal regulators to take defensive action.

The national academy's suspension of the article reflects an increasing con-   5
cern that publication of sensitive data can provide terrorists with a how-to manual, but it also brings to the fore an increasing anxiety in the scientific community that curbing the dissemination of research may impair our ability to counter biological threats. This dilemma reached national prominence in fall 2001, when 9/11 and the anthrax mailings drew attention to another controversial article. This one came from a team of Australian scientists.

Approximately every four years, Australia suffers a mouse infestation. In   6
1998, scientists in Canberra began examining the feasibility of using a highly contagious disease, mousepox, to alter the rodents' ability to reproduce. Their experiments yielded surprising results. Researchers working with mice naturally resistant to the disease found that combining a gene from the rodent's immune

system (interleukin-4) with the pox virus and inserting the pathogen into the animals killed them—all of them. Plus 60 percent of the mice not naturally resistant who had been vaccinated against mousepox.

7   In February 2001 the American Society for Microbiologists' (ASM) *Journal of Virology* reported the findings. Alarm ensued. The mousepox virus is closely related to smallpox—one of the most dangerous pathogens known to humans. And the rudimentary nature of the experiment demonstrated how even basic, inexpensive microbiology can yield devastating results.

8   When the anthrax attacks burst into the news seven months later, the mousepox case became a lightning rod for deep-seated fears about biological weapons. *The Economist* reported rumors about the White House pressuring American microbiology journals to restrict publication of similar pieces. Samuel Kaplan, chair of the ASM publications board, convened a meeting of the editors in chief of the ASM's nine primary journals and two review journals. Hoping to head off government censorship, the organization—while affirming its earlier decision—ordered its peer reviewers to take national security and the society's code of ethics into account.

9   Not only publications came under pressure, but research itself. In spring 2002 the newly formed Department of Homeland Security developed an information-security policy to prevent certain foreign nationals from gaining access to a range of experimental data. New federal regulations required that particular universities and laboratories submit to unannounced inspections, register their supplies and obtain security clearances. Legislation required that all genetic engineering experiments be cleared by the government.

10   On the mousepox front, however, important developments were transpiring. Because the Australian research had entered the public domain, scientists around the world began working on the problem. In November 2003, St. Louis University announced an effective medical defense against a pathogen similar to—but even more deadly than—the one created in Australia. This result would undoubtedly not have been achieved, or at least not as quickly, without the attention drawn by the ASM article.

11   The dissemination of nuclear technology presents an obvious comparison. The 1946 Atomic Energy Act classifies nuclear information "from birth." Strong arguments can be made in favor of such restrictions: The science involved in the construction of the bomb was complex and its application primarily limited to weapons. A short-term monopoly was possible. Secrecy bought the United States time to establish an international nonproliferation regime. And little public good would have been achieved by making the information widely available.

12   Biological information and the issues surrounding it are different. It is not possible to establish even a limited monopoly over microbiology. The field is too fundamental to the improvement of global public health, and too central to the development of important industries such as pharmaceuticals and plastics, to be isolated. Moreover, the list of diseases that pose a threat ranges from high-end bugs, like smallpox, to common viruses, such as influenza. Where does one draw the line for national security?

Experience suggests that the government errs on the side of caution. In 13 1951, the Invention Secrecy Act gave the government the authority to suppress any design it deemed detrimental to national defense. Certain areas of research—atomic energy and cryptography—consistently fell within its purview. But the state also placed secrecy orders on aspects of cold fusion, space technology, radar missile systems, citizens band radio voice scramblers, optical engineering and vacuum technology. Such caution, in the microbiology realm, may yield devastating results. It is not in the national interest to stunt research into biological threats.

In fact, the more likely menace comes from naturally occurring diseases. In 14 1918 a natural outbreak of the flu infected one-fifth of the world's population and 25 percent of the United States'. Within two years it killed more than 650,000 Americans, resulting in a 10-year drop in average lifespan. Despite constant research into emerging strains, the American Lung Association estimates that the flu and related complications kill 36,000 Americans each year. Another 5,000 die annually from food-borne pathogens—an extraordinarily large number of which have no known cure. The science involved in responding to these diseases is incremental, meaning that small steps taken by individual laboratories around the world need to be shared for larger progress to be made.

The idea that scientific freedom strengthens national security is not new. In 15 the early 1980s, a joint Panel on Scientific Communication and National Security concluded security by secrecy was untenable. Its report called instead for security by accomplishment—ensuring strength through advancing research. Ironically, one of the three major institutions participating was the National Academy of Sciences—the body that suspended publication of the milk article earlier this month.

The government has a vested interest in creating a public conversation 16 about ways in which our society is vulnerable to attack. Citizens are entitled to know when their milk, their water, their bridges, their hospitals lack security precautions. If discussion of these issues is censored, the state and private industry come under less pressure to alter behavior; indeed, powerful private interests may actively lobby against having to install expensive protections. And failure to act may be deadly.

Terrorists will obtain knowledge. Our best option is to blunt their efforts to 17 exploit it. That means developing, producing and stockpiling effective vaccines. It means funding research into biosensors—devices that detect the presence of toxic substances in the environment—and creating more effective reporting requirements for early identification of disease outbreaks. And it means strengthening our public health system.

For better or worse, the cat is out of the bag—something brought home 18 to me last weekend when I visited the Tech Museum of Innovation in San Jose. One hands-on exhibit allowed children to transfer genetic material from one species to another. I watched a 4-year-old girl take a red test tube whose contents included a gene that makes certain jellyfish glow green. Using a pipette, she transferred the material to a blue test tube containing bacteria. She cooled the solution, then heated it, allowing the gene to enter the bacteria. Following instructions on a touch-screen computer, she transferred the contents to a petri dish, wrote her name on the bottom, and placed the dish in an incubator. The next day, she could log on to a Web site to view her experiment, and see her bacteria glowing a genetically modified green.

19   In other words, the pre-kindergartener (with a great deal of help from the museum) had conducted an experiment that echoed the Australian mousepox study. Obviously, this is not something the child could do in her basement. But just as obviously, the state of public knowledge is long past anyone's ability to censor it.

20   Allowing potentially harmful information to enter the public domain flies in the face of our traditional way of thinking about national security threats. But we have entered a new world. Keeping scientists from sharing information damages our ability to respond to terrorism and to natural disease, which is more likely and just as devastating. Our best hope to head off both threats may well be to stay one step ahead.

---

1. Actually the description of a theoretical terrorist obtaining a toxin on the black market appeared only in the *New York Times* article, not in the original article that the National Academy of Sciences refused to publish.

QUESTIONS FOR READING

1. What is the occasion for Donohue's article?
2. What other restrictions have been developed by Homeland Security?
3. How is the scientific community reacting to restrictions? What is their concern?
4. What is probably a greater threat than terrorism?
5. Is it possible to censor information on microbiology?

QUESTIONS FOR REASONING AND ANALYSIS

1. What is Donohue's claim? State it as a problem/solution type of argument.
2. To state her claim as a problem/solution type of argument is to suggest that her argument is more practical than philosophical; is that a fair assessment? Why or why not? What are the two key points of her argument?
3. In paragraph 11, Donohue reminds readers that nuclear information is classified and asserts that it should be. Why does she include this paragraph?

QUESTIONS FOR REFLECTING AND WRITING

1. Donohue reminds readers that scientific knowledge is built up by many contributing a little bit to the knowledge base. And yet a scientific journal suppressed an article. Why? Does Homeland Security have too much power? Have we all become too fearful of terrorists?
2. Has the author convinced you that we are at greater risk by censoring knowledge than by publishing information? Why or why not?

3. Are you fearful of terrorism? Are you fearful of infectious diseases? Statistically, which is more likely to be a threat to you? Why are our fears often disconnected from the facts?

PSYCHOLOGY AND THE ENVIRONMENT | GLEN D. SHEAN

A professor of psychology at the College of William & Mary, Dr. Shean has published research on personality disorders and is interested in social cognition and psychopathology. Two books of his are *Understanding and Treating Schizophrenia* (2004) and *Psychology and the Environmental Crisis* (2005). His article on psychology and the environment appeared in the Fall 2005 issue of the *William & Mary Alumni Magazine*.

PREREADING QUESTIONS What are the views of scientists on environmental changes? Do you have any reason to doubt their research findings? Why or why not?

Today, many of our political and religious leaders ignore or minimize environmental and population issues. They are able to do so because many of us are complacent about these topics. Our natural reluctance to face up to environmental issues is fostered by vested interest groups that work to undermine the credibility of warnings about global warming. Industry financed organizations with misleading names, such as The Center for the Study of CO_2 and Global Change and the Committee for a Constructive Tomorrow, are devoted to clouding public understanding with misinformation and have been effective in raising doubts about the validity of environmental warnings. 1

We are now living as if our environmental problems can be ignored. It is increasingly apparent, however, that human activities are having a significant and lasting negative impact on the global environment. Environmental problems, resource utilization and population growth are increasing at unsustainable rates. Over 1 billion people were added to the world population just during the 1990s, each striving for a healthy and materially satisfying life. Today, the equivalent of the population of France is added to the world every six months, and the number of world citizens grows by the amount of China's population every decade. In parallel, with obviously unsustainable global population growth, resource utilization and environmental degradation have increased dramatically. For example, between A.D. 1000 and 1800, levels of greenhouse gases, such as CO_2 and methane, remained largely unchanged. Since 1800, atmospheric levels of these greenhouse gases have nearly doubled and increases of other more powerful greenhouse gases, such as nitrous oxide and surface level ozone, mirror these increases. Can anyone doubt these changes will have adverse consequences on our climate and on the stability and viability of our economic and social-political systems? 2

We have been able to remain complacent about these matters because most adverse environmental effects have thus far been localized or relatively mild. As a result, there is a "tangibility gap" between immediate wants and long-term consequences. This is the case because the payoff for adopting 3 sustainable lifestyles is incremental, but the costs are immediate. Because of this gap, people have a strong incentive to deny environmental problems as long as possible, and voters sense no compelling reason to move environmental issues, such as climate change, higher on their agendas.

4   In contrast to public attitudes, the world's leading environmental scientists are unanimous in their concern. Two of the world's most prestigious scientific groups, the Royal Society of London and the U.S. National Academy of Sciences, issued the following joint statement in 1992: "There is an urgent need to address economic activity, population growth and environmental protection as interrelated issues and as crucial components affecting the sustainability of human society. The next 30 years will be crucial." Today, in the United States, this warning is largely ignored. Like addicts, we continue to choose short-term payoffs and ignore the long-term consequences of our actions.

5   Resistance to environmental action stems from many sources, including our tendency to avoid discomforting information, a lack of individual accountability for environmentally harmful actions, a natural dislike for making sacrifices, and evolutionary characteristics of the human brain. We are predisposed to make quick judgments based on impressions that are difficult to change and to simplify complex problems in order to make them seem more manageable. Our brains developed to help us process information, to provide a sense of stability and to help create a reality that is comforting. As a consequence, we tend to respond to the short term, to ignore or avoid threatening information, to develop attachments to a limited and immediate group of kinsmen, and to form a relatively fixed set of beliefs. These characteristics that fostered human survival for thousands of years may no longer be adaptive. What can we do?

6   The values associated with pro-environmental behaviors are related to a deep, intuitive appreciation of the connection between the individual, the community and the natural environment. Opportunities to directly experience and connect with the natural world are important building blocks for developing a sense of connection with nature. Direct experiences, parental modeling and values, cultural norms, and social policies all play a role in the formation of pro-environmental values. Values affect attitudes by motivating people to pay attention to information about changes that may adversely affect things they view as important and to seek information and experiences that affirm their views. This self-affirming tendency makes values and beliefs difficult to change once established. Changes in values can occur, however, when people have access to information and experiences that create dissonance with established beliefs, and when they are afforded opportunities to process the implications of these experiences in a supportive context.

7   We must become more effective in encouraging development of pro-environmental values in order to broaden the constituency of individuals committed to advocacy of policies and practices to arrest environmental degradation. Provision of opportunities to directly experience and understand natural processes and to directly observe the environmental effects of excessive consumption, along with opportunities to discuss and process these experiences can foster changes in existing attitudes.

In order for ecological values to be developed, several things must happen: 8

1. Experiences must be provided that foster a strong sense of connection to place through reminders that we are part of and dependent on the integrity and stability of our ecological system.

2. An intuitive sense of connection with and caring about all life must be developed and fostered.

3. People must develop a sense of interrelatedness, community and belonging.

4. People must develop a sense of empowerment, personal responsibility and self-efficacy that fosters active political citizenship.

Over a decade ago, the world's leading scientists told us the next 30 years will 9
be crucial for the future of the global environment. This warning was not based on faulty data, nor was it the self-serving statement of academicians in pursuit of grant money. It was a serious and well-reasoned warning based on a large body of evidence. As potentially rational, future-oriented creatures, it is up to us to choose either to continue with business as usual or respond effectively to these challenges.

QUESTIONS FOR READING

1. What is Shean's subject? (Do not write "the environment"; be more precise.)
2. By how much did the population increase in the 1990s?
3. By how much have greenhouse gases increased since 1800?
4. Why are we complacent about environmental degradation? Explain Shean's "tangibility gap."
5. What is the view of environmental scientists regarding change?
6. What psychological strategies interfere with a needed concern for environmental degradation?
7. What solutions does Shean offer?

QUESTIONS FOR REASONING AND ANALYSIS

1. What is Shean's claim?
2. What *type* of argument is this?
3. Shean's solutions are based on his analysis of the causes of nonaction. Does his analysis of cause seem logical and consistent with your knowledge and experience of human behavior? If yes, are you then prepared to accept his proposed solutions? Why or why not?
4. How would you describe the author's tone? How does his choice of tone contribute to his argument?

QUESTIONS FOR REFLECTING AND WRITING

1. Shean concludes by asserting that "as potentially rational, future-oriented creatures" we can choose to ignore obvious and serious problems, or we can "respond effectively." What makes this an effective ending?

2. Issues of climate change have become highly political, especially in the United States. Why? If scientists are in agreement over the seriousness of climate change, why don't the politicians do something?

3. If you were one of Shean's "rational, future-oriented creatures" and in a position of leadership, what would you do to address environmental degradation? Explain and defend your proposals.

DON'T MESS WITH MOTHER | ANNA QUINDLEN

A syndicated columnist, Anna Quindlen has won the Pulitzer Prize for commentary and has published several volumes of her columns. She has also written novels, including *Black and Blue* (1998) and *Blessings* (2002). Her following "Last Word" *Newsweek* column was published September 19, 2005.

PREREADING QUESTIONS Based on the title alone, what would you guess this essay to be about? Adding the context of its place in this chapter, does that change your anticipation of the essay's subject?

1 The dark aftermath of the frontier, of the vast promise of possibility this country first offered, is an inflated sense of American entitlement today. We want what we want, and we want it now. Easy credit. Fast food. A straight shot down the interstate from point A to point B. The endless highway is crowded with the kinds of cars large enough to take a mountain pass in high snow. Instead they are used to take children from soccer practice to Pizza Hut. In the process they burn fuel like there's no tomorrow.

2 Tomorrow's coming.

3 The cataclysm named Katrina has inspired a Hummer-load of rumination, about class, about race, about the pathetic failure of the Feds after four long years of much-vaunted homeland-security plans. The president made himself foolish, calling for an investigation into who fouled up, perhaps ignorant of Harry Truman's desk plaque reading THE BUCK STOPS HERE. The press rose to the occasion, awakened out of its recent somnambulant state, galvanized into empathy and rage. The public was remarkable, opening their homes and their wallets.

4 But the failure by government, in the midst of a hurricane season forecast early on to be a monstrous one, illustrates once again the lack of a long view. The long view at the moment is not about patching levees, or building houses, or getting oil rigs back up and running, or assigning blame. It's about changing the way we all live now.

5 Both the left, with its endless talk of rights, and the right, with its disdain for government oversight, suggest that you can do what you please. Americans have taken the message to heart, and nowhere is that clearer than in the mess we've made of the natural environment. How many times do we have to watch homes cantilevered over canyons surrender to a river of mud or beach houses on stilts slide into the surf to know that when we do high-stakes battle with Mother Nature, Mother takes all? Once I heard a businessman at a

zoning-board meeting say, "Well, a person can do what he wants with his land." Actually, that's not true; that's why zoning exists. Is any city, town or state brave enough to just say no to waterfront development that destroys dunes, despoils water and creates the conditions that will, when a storm strikes, create destruction?

New Orleans lived for 80 years with the granddaddy of all environmentally 6 misguided plans, the project that straightened out the mighty Mississippi so its banks would be more hospitable to homes and businesses. Little by little the seductive city at the river's mouth became like one of those denuded developments built after clear-cutting. It was left with no natural protection, girded with a jerry-built belt of walled-off water, its marshland and barrier islands gone, a sitting duck for a big storm.

But it was not alone. Everywhere in the country, wetlands disappeared and 7 parking lots bloomed during the past half century of mindless growth, in which bigger was always assumed to be better. While the streets of European cities were filled with tiny compact cars, the SUV took over American roads. Show houses sprang up that will soon present an interesting lesson in what happens when cathedral ceilings meet sky-high fuel prices. In the aftermath of Katrina, one displaced person after another told TV reporters that at least they were alive, their family was safe, the stuff didn't matter. If only that were the ethic for the long haul. Consumption used to be the name for a mortal wasting disease. It still is.

This administration of big-oil guys is the last place to look for leadership on 8 conservation. Many Bush supporters scoff at global warming as a lefty myth, and early on the president made his position clear when he made the United States one of two industrialized nations to reject the Kyoto Protocol, the plan to curtail climate change by cutting down emission levels. But there has been no powerful national leadership from either party on this front in recent memory. Political officials have bowed to the public's thirst for more, more, more.

The effects of disaster fall disproportionately on those who have less, as 9 they did during Hurricane Katrina, when poor families had no cars to flee in, when there were no immediately available means for a second act in another town and another home. But between the blackouts, the fuel costs, the eroding coastlines, the disappearing open spaces, it is going to become harder and harder to overcome the effects of blind overgrowth even for those of means. Get ready for the $100 tank of gas, and an Armageddon of our own making.

New Orleans will be rebuilt, but rebuilt how? In the heedless, grasping 10 fashion in which so much of this country has been built over the past 50 years, which has led to a continuous loop of floods, fires and filth in the air and water? Or could the new New Orleans be the first city of a new era, in which the demands of development and commerce are carefully balanced against the good of the land and, in the long run, the good of its people? We have been crummy stewards of the Earth, with a sense of knee-jerk entitlement that tells us there is always more where this came from.

There isn't. 11

QUESTIONS FOR READING

1. What problems were exposed, what issues raised, as a result of Katrina?
2. What is the long-range issue made clear by Katrina, in the author's view?
3. What groups, for different reasons, contribute to Americans' sense of entitlement?
4. What was done in New Orleans that increased its danger in the face of a big storm?
5. In what other ways, across the United States, have we made bad choices "for the long haul," in the author's words?

QUESTIONS FOR REASONING AND ANALYSIS

1. What is Quindlen's claim? Where does she state it?
2. Analyze the author's style and tone by contrasting her essay with Shean's.
3. Find one or two passages that use rhetorical techniques in especially effective ways. What makes these passages clever?

QUESTIONS FOR REFLECTING AND WRITING

1. Both Quindlen and Shean argue that we are destroying our environment, but their writing is quite different. Which argument do you find more convincing? Why? Are there some readers for whom one approach might be better than the other? Explain.
2. Quindlen does not spell out solutions, but in her warnings of the troubles to come she points to problem areas. What, by implication, must we do to stop messing with Mother? How can we bring about change in these areas?

HUMAN CLONING AND HUMAN DIGNITY: AN ETHICAL INQUIRY | PRESIDENT'S COUNCIL ON BIOETHICS

The following work is the executive summary of the report prepared by the President's Council on Bioethics. The Council's task was to study the ethics of human cloning and make a recommendation to the president. The summary reprinted here has been cut slightly for purposes of length only, and the excluded passages have been indicated with ellipses. The full text of the report is available at the Council's Web site. The chair of the Council is Leon R. Kass, the Hertog Fellow at the American Enterprise Institute. (Names of other members of the Council can be found on the Web site.)

PREREADING QUESTIONS What does the title of the report suggest to you about its approach? About the issues it will examine with regard to human cloning?

1   For the past five years, the prospect of human cloning has been the subject of considerable public attention and sharp moral debate, both in the United States and around the world. Since the announcement in February 1997 of the first successful cloning of a mammal (Dolly the sheep), several other species of mammals have been cloned. Although a cloned human child has yet

to be born, and although the animal experiments have had low rates of success, the production of functioning mammalian cloned offspring suggests that the eventual cloning of humans must be considered a serious possibility.

In November 2001, American researchers claimed to have produced the 2 first cloned human embryos, though they reportedly reached only a six-cell stage before they stopped dividing and died. In addition, several fertility specialists, both here and abroad, have announced their intention to clone human beings. The United States Congress has twice taken up the matter, in 1998 and again in 2001–2002, with the House of Representatives in July 2001 passing a strict ban on all human cloning, including the production of cloned human embryos. As of this writing, several cloning-related bills are under consideration in the Senate. Many other nations have banned human cloning, and the United Nations is considering an international convention on the subject. . . .

The debate over human cloning became further complicated in 1998 when 3 researchers were able, for the first time, to isolate human embryonic stem cells. Many scientists believe that these versatile cells, capable of becoming any type of cell in the body, hold great promise for understanding and treating many chronic diseases and conditions. Some scientists also believe that stem cells derived from cloned human embryos, produced explicitly for such research, might prove uniquely useful for studying many genetic diseases and devising novel therapies. Public reaction to the prospect of cloning-for-biomedical-research has been mixed: some Americans support it for its medical promise; others oppose it because it requires the exploitation and destruction of nascent human life, which would be created solely for research purposes. . . .

THE INQUIRY: OUR POINT OF DEPARTURE

As Members of the President's Council on Bioethics, we have taken up the 4 larger ethical and social inquiry called for in the NBAC [National Bioethics Advisory Commission] and NAS [National Academy of Sciences] reports, with the aim of advancing public understanding and informing public policy on the matter. We have attempted to consider human cloning (both for producing children and for biomedical research) within its larger human, technological, and ethical contexts, rather than to view it as an isolated technical development. We focus first on the broad human goods that it may serve as well as threaten, rather than on the immediate impact of the technique itself. By our broad approach, our starting on the plane of human goods, and our open spirit of inquiry, we hope to contribute to a richer and deeper understanding of what human cloning means, how we should think about it, and what we should do about it.

On some matters discussed in this report, Members of the Council are not 5 of one mind. Rather than bury these differences in search of a spurious consensus, we have sought to present all views fully and fairly, while recording our agreements as well as our genuine diversity of perspectives, including our differences on the final recommendations to be made. By this means, we hope to help policymakers and the general public appreciate more thoroughly the difficulty of the issues and the competing goods that are at stake.

FAIR AND ACCURATE TERMINOLOGY

6   On the basis of (1) a careful analysis of the act of cloning, and its relation to the means by which it is accomplished and the purposes it may serve, and (2) an extensive critical examination of alternative terminologies, the Council has adopted the following definitions for the most important terms in the matter of human cloning:

- *Cloning:* A form of reproduction in which offspring result not from the chance union of egg and sperm (sexual reproduction) but from the deliberate replication of the genetic makeup of another single individual (asexual reproduction).
- *Human cloning:* The asexual production of a new human organism that is, at all stages of development, genetically virtually identical to a currently existing or previously existing human being. It would be accomplished by introducing the nuclear material of a human somatic cell (donor) into an oocyte (egg) whose own nucleus has been removed or inactivated, yielding a product that has a human genetic constitution virtually identical to the donor of the somatic cell. (This procedure is known as "somatic cell nuclear transfer," or SCNT.) We have declined to use the terms "reproductive cloning" and "therapeutic cloning." We have chosen instead to use the following designations:
- *Cloning-to-produce-children:* Production of a cloned human embryo, formed for the (proximate) purpose of initiating a pregnancy, with the (ultimate) goal of producing a child who will be genetically virtually identical to a currently existing or previously existing individual.
- *Cloning-for-biomedical-research:* Production of a cloned human embryo, formed for the (proximate) purpose of using it in research or for extracting its stem cells, with the (ultimate) goals of gaining scientific knowledge of normal and abnormal development and of developing cures for human diseases.
- *Cloned human embryo:* (a) A human embryo resulting from the nuclear transfer process (as contrasted with a human embryo arising from the union of egg and sperm). (b) The immediate (and developing) product of the initial act of cloning, accomplished by successful SCNT, whether used subsequently in attempts to produce children or in biomedical research. . . .

THE ETHICS OF CLONING-TO-PRODUCE-CHILDREN

7   Two separate national-level reports on human cloning (NBAC, 1997; NAS, 2002) concluded that attempts to clone a human being would be unethical at this time due to safety concerns and the likelihood of harm to those involved. The Council concurs in this conclusion. But we have extended the work of these distinguished bodies by undertaking a broad ethical examination of the merits of, and difficulties with, cloning-to-produce-children.

8   Cloning-to-produce-children might serve several purposes. It might allow infertile couples or others to have genetically-related children; permit couples

at risk of conceiving a child with a genetic disease to avoid having an afflicted child; allow the bearing of a child who could become an ideal transplant donor for a particular patient in need; enable a parent to keep a living connection with a dead or dying child or spouse; or enable individuals or society to try to "replicate" individuals of great talent or beauty. These purposes have been defended by appeals to the goods of freedom, existence (as opposed to nonexistence), and well-being—all vitally important ideals.

A major weakness in these arguments supporting cloning-to-produce- 9 children is that they overemphasize the freedom, desires, and control of parents, and pay insufficient attention to the well-being of the cloned child-to-be. The Council holds that, once the child-to-be is carefully considered, these arguments are not sufficient to overcome the powerful case against engaging in cloning-to-produce-children.

First, cloning-to-produce-children would violate the principles of the ethics 10 of human research. Given the high rates of morbidity and mortality in the cloning of other mammals, we believe that cloning-to-produce-children would be extremely unsafe, and that attempts to produce a cloned child would be highly unethical. Indeed, our moral analysis of this matter leads us to conclude that this is not, as is sometimes implied, a merely temporary objection, easily removed by the improvement of technique. We offer reasons for believing that the safety risks might be enduring, and offer arguments in support of a strong conclusion: that conducting experiments in an effort to make cloning-to-produce-children less dangerous would itself be an unacceptable violation of the norms of research ethics. There seems to be no ethical way to try to discover whether cloning-to-produce-children can become safe, now or in the future.

If carefully considered, the concerns about safety also begin to reveal the 11 ethical principles that should guide a broader assessment of cloning-to-produce-children: the principles of freedom, equality, and human dignity. To appreciate the broader human significance of cloning-to-produce-children, one needs first to reflect on the meaning of having children; the meaning of asexual, as opposed to sexual, reproduction; the importance of origins and genetic endowment for identity and sense of self; the meaning of exercising greater human control over the processes and "products" of human reproduction; and the difference between begetting and making. Reflecting on these topics, the Council has identified five categories of concern regarding cloning-to-produce-children. . . .

- *Problems of identity and individuality.* Cloned children may experience serious problems of identity both because each will be genetically virtually identical to a human being who has already lived and because the expectations for their lives may be shadowed by constant comparisons to the life of the "original."
- *Concerns regarding manufacture.* Cloned children would be the first human beings whose entire genetic makeup is selected in advance. They might come to be considered more like products of a designed

manufacturing process than "gifts" whom their parents are prepared to accept as they are. Such an attitude toward children could also contribute to increased commercialization and industrialization of human procreation.

- *The prospect of a new eugenics.* Cloning, if successful, might serve the ends of privately pursued eugenic enhancement, either by avoiding the genetic defects that may arise when human reproduction is left to chance, or by preserving and perpetuating outstanding genetic traits, including the possibility, someday in the future, of using cloning to perpetuate genetically engineered enhancements.

- *Troubled family relations.* By confounding and transgressing the natural boundaries between generations, cloning could strain the social ties between them. Fathers could become "twin brothers" to their "sons"; mothers could give birth to their genetic twins; and grandparents would also be the "genetic parents" of their grandchildren. Genetic relation to only one parent might produce special difficulties for family life.

- *Effects on society.* Cloning-to-produce-children would affect not only the direct participants but also the entire society that allows or supports this activity. Even if practiced on a small scale, it could affect the way society looks at children and set a precedent for future nontherapeutic interventions into the human genetic endowment or novel forms of control by one generation over the next. In the absence of wisdom regarding these matters, prudence dictates caution and restraint.

12   *Conclusion: For some or all of these reasons, the Council is in full agreement that cloning-to-produce-children is not only unsafe but also morally unacceptable, and ought not to be attempted.*

THE ETHICS OF CLONING-FOR-BIOMEDICAL-RESEARCH

13   Ethical assessment of cloning-for-biomedical-research is far more vexing. On the one hand, such research could lead to important knowledge about human embryological development and gene action, both normal and abnormal, ultimately resulting in treatments and cures for many dreaded illnesses and disabilities. On the other hand, the research is morally controversial because it involves the deliberate production, use, and ultimate destruction of cloned human embryos, and because the cloned embryos produced for research are no different from those that could be implanted in attempts to produce cloned children. The difficulty is compounded by what are, for now, unanswerable questions as to whether the research will in fact yield the benefits hoped for, and whether other promising and morally nonproblematic approaches might yield comparable benefits. The Council, reflecting the differences of opinion in American society, is divided regarding the ethics of research involving (cloned) embryos.

14   To make clear to all what is at stake in the decision, Council Members have presented, as strongly as possible, the competing ethical cases for and against cloning-for-biomedical-research in the form of first-person attempts at moral suasion. Each case has tried to address what is owed to suffering humanity, to the human embryo, and to the broader society. Within each case, supporters

of the position in question speak only for themselves, and not for the Council as a whole.

A. THE MORAL CASE FOR CLONING-FOR-BIOMEDICAL-RESEARCH

The moral case for cloning-for-biomedical-research rests on our obligation 15 to try to relieve human suffering, an obligation that falls most powerfully on medical practitioners and biomedical researchers. We who support cloning-for-biomedical-research all agree that it may offer uniquely useful ways of investigating and possibly treating many chronic debilitating diseases and disabilities, providing aid and relief to millions. We also believe that the moral objections to this research are outweighed by the great good that may come from it. Up to this point, we who support this research all agree. But we differ among ourselves regarding the weight of the moral objections, owing to differences about the moral status of the cloned embryo. These differences of opinion are sufficient to warrant distinguishing two different moral positions within the moral case for cloning-for-biomedical-research:

Position Number One. Most Council Members who favor cloning-for- 16 biomedical-research do so with serious moral concerns. Speaking only for ourselves, we acknowledge the following difficulties, but think that they can be addressed by setting proper boundaries.

- *Intermediate moral status.* While we take seriously concerns about the treatment of nascent human life, we believe there are sound moral reasons for not regarding the embryo in its earliest stages as the moral equivalent of a human person. We believe the embryo has a developing and intermediate moral worth that commands our special respect, but that it is morally permissible to use early-stage cloned human embryos in important research under strict regulation.
- *Deliberate creation for use.* We believe that concerns over the problem of deliberate creation of cloned embryos for use in research have merit, but when properly understood should not preclude cloning-for-biomedical-research. These embryos would not be "created for destruction," but for use in the service of life and medicine. They would be destroyed in the service of a great good, and this should not be obscured.
- *Going too far.* We acknowledge the concern that some researchers might seek to develop cloned embryos beyond the blastocyst stage, and for those of us who believe that the cloned embryo has a developing and intermediate moral status, this is a very real worry. We approve, therefore, only of research on cloned embryos that is strictly limited to the first fourteen days of development—a point near when the primitive streak is formed and before organ differentiation occurs.
- *Other moral hazards.* We believe that concerns about the exploitation of women and about the risk that cloning-for-biomedical-research could lead to cloning-to-produce-children can be adequately addressed by appropriate rules and regulations. These concerns need not frighten us into abandoning an important avenue of research.

17   *Position Number Two.* A few Council Members who favor cloning-for-biomedical-research do not share all the ethical qualms expressed above. Speaking only for ourselves, we hold that this research, at least for the purposes presently contemplated, presents no special moral problems, and therefore should be endorsed with enthusiasm as a potential new means of gaining knowledge to serve humankind. Because we accord no special moral status to the early-stage cloned embryo and believe it should be treated essentially like all other human cells, we believe that the moral issues involved in this research are no different from those that accompany any biomedical research. What is required is the usual commitment to high standards for the quality of research, scientific integrity, and the need to obtain informed consent from donors of the eggs and somatic cells used in nuclear transfer.

B. THE MORAL CASE AGAINST CLONING-FOR-BIOMEDICAL-RESEARCH

18   The moral case against cloning-for-biomedical-research acknowledges the possibility—though purely speculative at the moment—that medical benefits might come from this particular avenue of experimentation. But we believe it is morally wrong to exploit and destroy developing human life, even for good reasons, and that it is unwise to open the door to the many undesirable consequences that are likely to result from this research. We find it disquieting, even somewhat ignoble, to treat what are in fact seeds of the next generation as mere raw material for satisfying the needs of our own. Only for very serious reasons should progress toward increased knowledge and medical advances be slowed. But we believe that in this case such reasons are apparent.

- *Moral status of the cloned embryo.* We hold that the case for treating the early-stage embryo as simply the moral equivalent of all other human cells (Position Number Two, above) is simply mistaken: it denies the continuous history of human individuals from the embryonic to fetal to infant stages of existence; it misunderstands the meaning of potentiality; and it ignores the hazardous moral precedent that the routinized creation, use, and destruction of nascent human life would establish. We hold that the case for according the human embryo "intermediate and developing moral status" (Position Number One, above) is also unconvincing, for reasons both biological and moral. Attempts to ground the limited measure of respect owed to a maturing embryo in certain of its developmental features do not succeed, and the invoking of a "special respect" owed to nascent human life seems to have little or no operative meaning if cloned embryos may be created in bulk and used routinely with impunity. If from one perspective the view that the embryo seems to amount to little may invite a weakening of our respect, from another perspective its seeming insignificance should awaken in us a sense of shared humanity and a special obligation to protect it.
- *The exploitation of developing human life.* To engage in cloning-for-biomedical-research requires the irreversible crossing of a very significant moral boundary: the creation of human life expressly and

exclusively for the purpose of its use in research, research that necessarily involves its deliberate destruction. If we permit this research to proceed, we will effectively be endorsing the complete transformation of nascent human life into nothing more than a resource or a tool. Doing so would coarsen our moral sensibilities and make us a different society: one less humble toward that which we cannot fully understand, less willing to extend the boundaries of human respect ever outward, and more willing to transgress moral boundaries once it appears to be in our own interests to do so.

- *Moral harm to society.* Even those who are uncertain about the precise moral status of the human embryo have sound ethical-prudential reasons to oppose cloning-for-biomedical-research. Giving moral approval to such research risks significant moral harm to our society by (1) crossing the boundary from sexual to asexual reproduction, thus approving in principle the genetic manipulation and control of nascent human life; (2) opening the door to other moral hazards, such as cloning-to-produce-children or research on later-stage human embryos and fetuses; and (3) potentially putting the federal government in the novel and unsavory position of mandating the destruction of nascent human life. Because we are concerned not only with the fate of the cloned embryos but also with where this research will lead our society, we think prudence requires us not to engage in this research.

- *What we owe the suffering.* We are certainly not deaf to the voices of suffering patients; after all, each of us already shares or will share in the hardships of mortal life. We and our loved ones are all patients or potential patients. But we are not only patients, and easing suffering is not our only moral obligation. As much as we wish to alleviate suffering now and to leave our children a world where suffering can be more effectively relieved, we also want to leave them a world in which we and they want to live—a world that honors moral limits, that respects all life whether strong or weak, and that refuses to secure the good of some human beings by sacrificing the lives of others.

PUBLIC POLICY OPTIONS

The Council recognizes the challenges and risks of moving from moral assessment to public policy. Reflections on the "social contract" between science and society highlight both the importance of scientific freedom and the need for boundaries. We recognize the special difficulty in formulating sound public policy in this area, given that the two ethically distinct matters—cloning-to-produce-children and cloning-for-biomedical-research—will be mutually affected or implicated in any attempts to legislate about either. Nevertheless, our ethical and policy analysis leads us to the conclusion that some deliberate public policy at the federal level is needed in the area of human cloning.   19

We reviewed the following seven possible policy options and considered their relative strengths and weaknesses: (1) Professional self-regulation but no federal legislative action ("self-regulation"); (2) A ban on   20 cloning-to-produce-children, with neither endorsement nor restriction of cloning-for-biomedical-research ("ban plus silence"); (3) A ban on cloning-to-produce-children, with regulation of the use of cloned embryos for biomedical research ("ban plus regulation"); (4) Governmental regulation, with no legislative prohibitions ("regulation of both"); (5) A ban on all human cloning, whether to produce children or for biomedical research ("ban on both"); (6) A ban on cloning-to-produce-children, with a moratorium or temporary ban on cloning-for-biomedical-research ("ban plus moratorium"); or (7) A moratorium or temporary ban on all human cloning, whether to produce children or for biomedical research ("moratorium on both").

THE COUNCIL'S POLICY RECOMMENDATIONS

21   Having considered the benefits and drawbacks of each of these options, and taken into account our discussions and reflections throughout this report, the Council recommends two possible policy alternatives, each supported by a portion of the Members.

22   *Majority Recommendation:* Ten Members of the Council recommend *a ban on cloning-to-produce-children combined with a four-year moratorium on cloning-for-biomedical-research. We also call for a federal review of current and projected practices of human embryo research, preimplantation genetic diagnosis, genetic modification of human embryos and gametes, and related matters, with a view to recommending and shaping ethically sound policies for the entire field.* Speaking only for ourselves, those of us who support this recommendation do so for some or all of the following reasons:

- By permanently banning cloning-to-produce-children, this policy gives force to the strong ethical verdict against cloning-to-produce-children, unanimous in this council (and in Congress) and widely supported by the American people. And by enacting a four-year moratorium on the creation of cloned embryos, it establishes an additional safeguard not afforded by policies that would allow the production of cloned embryos to proceed without delay.

- It calls for and provides time for further democratic deliberation about cloning-for-biomedical research, a subject about which the nation is divided and where there remains great uncertainty. A national discourse on this subject has not yet taken place in full, and a moratorium, by making it impossible for either side to cling to the status-quo, would force both to make their full case before the public. By banning all cloning for a time, it allows us to seek moral consensus on whether or not we should cross a major moral boundary (creating nascent cloned human life solely for research) and prevents our crossing it without deliberate decision. It would afford time for scientific evidence, now sorely lacking, to be gathered—from animal models and other avenues of human research—that might give us a better sense of whether cloning-for-biomedical-research would work as promised, and whether other morally nonproblematic approaches might be available. It would promote a fuller and better-informed public debate. And it would show respect for the deep moral concerns of the large number of Americans who have serious ethical objections to this research.

- Some of us hold that cloning-for-biomedical-research can never be ethically pursued, and endorse a moratorium to enable us to continue to make our case in a democratic way. Others of us support the moratorium because it would provide the time and incentive required to develop a system of national regulation that might come into use if, at the end of the four-year period, the moratorium were not reinstated or made permanent. Such a system could not be developed overnight, and therefore even those who support the research but want it regulated should see that at the very least a pause is required. In the absence of a moratorium, few proponents of the research would have much incentive to institute an effective regulatory system. Moreover, the very process of proposing such regulations would clarify the moral and prudential judgments involved in deciding whether and how to proceed with this research.

- A moratorium on cloning-for-biomedical-research would enable us to consider this activity in the larger context of research and technology in the areas of developmental biology, embryo research, and genetics, and to pursue a more comprehensive federal regulatory system for setting and executing policy in the entire area.

- Finally, we believe that a moratorium, rather than a lasting ban, signals a high regard for the value of biomedical research and an enduring concern for patients and families whose suffering such research may help alleviate. It would reaffirm the principle that science can progress while upholding the community's moral norms, and would therefore reaffirm the community's moral support for science and biomedical technology.

The decision before us is of great importance. Creating cloned embryos for 23 *any* purpose requires crossing a major moral boundary, with grave risks and likely harms, and once we cross it there will be no turning back. Our society should take the time to make a judgment that is well-informed and morally sound, respectful of strongly held views, and representative of the priorities and principles of the American people. We believe this ban-plus-moratorium proposal offers the best means of achieving these goals. . . .

Minority Recommendation: Seven Members of the Council recommend 24 *a ban on cloning-to-produce-children, with regulation of the use of cloned embryos for biomedical research.* Speaking only for ourselves, those of us who support this recommendation do so for some or all of the following reasons:

- By permanently banning cloning-to-produce-children, this policy gives force to the strong ethical verdict against cloning-to-produce-children, unanimous in this Council (and in Congress) and widely supported by the American people. We believe that a ban on the transfer of cloned embryos to a woman's uterus would be a sufficient and effective legal safeguard against the practice.

- *It approves cloning-for-biomedical-research and permits it to proceed without substantial delay.* This is the most important advantage of this proposal. The research shows great promise, and its actual value can only be determined by allowing it to go forward now. Regardless of how much time we allow it, no amount of experimentation with animal models can provide the needed understanding of human diseases. The special benefits from working with stem cells from cloned human embryos cannot be obtained using embryos obtained by IVF. We believe this research could provide relief to millions of Americans, and that the government should therefore support it, within sensible limits imposed by regulation.

- It would establish, *as a condition of proceeding*, the necessary regulatory protections to avoid abuses and misuses of cloned embryos. These regulations might touch on the secure handling of embryos, licensing and prior review of research projects, the protection of egg donors, and the provision of equal access to benefits.

- Some of us also believe that mechanisms to regulate cloning-for-biomedical-research should be part of a larger regulatory program governing all research involving human embryos, and that the federal government should initiate a review of present and projected practices of human embryo research, with the aim of establishing reasonable policies on the matter.

25   Permitting cloning-for-biomedical-research now, while governing it through a prudent and sensible regulatory regime, is the most appropriate way to allow important research to proceed while insuring that abuses are prevented. We believe that the legitimate concerns about human cloning expressed throughout this report are sufficiently addressed by this ban-plus-regulation proposal, and that the nation should affirm and support the responsible effort to find treatments and cures that might help many who are suffering.

QUESTIONS FOR READING

1. What are the two purposes of human cloning?
2. Sum up in your own words the process for human cloning. Sum up the process used in cloning-for-biomedical-research.
3. What is the Council's position on cloning-to-produce-children? What are the possible merits of such action? What are the possible disadvantages?
4. How does the Council rebut the possible merits of cloning-to-produce-children? What are the problems, both practical and ethical, in the Council's view?
5. What are the possible benefits of cloning-for-biomedical-research? What are the possible disadvantages? What is the Council's position on cloning for research?

6. Of those who favor cloning-for-biomedical-research, how do they differ on the moral issues surrounding this research?

7. What are the moral arguments of those who oppose cloning-for-biomedical-research?

8. What is the majority public policy recommendation of the Council? What are their arguments in support of their recommendation?

9. What is the minority public policy recommendation of the Council? What are their arguments in support of their recommendation?

QUESTIONS FOR REASONING AND ANALYSIS

1. Examine, first, the arguments against cloning for children. Does the Council make a convincing argument? Much of their argument turns on the repeated statement of the "virtual" identity of the cloned child and the original donor. Is it accurate to see the cloned child as a reproduction of the original donor? Why or why not? To what extent, if any, do these subtle but important distinctions affect your view of their argument on this particular point? Explain.

2. Examine the argument supporting cloning for research. This argument turns on the assertion that the embryo in the first fourteen days does not have the same moral significance as it does after those first fourteen days—as well as on the relief of suffering that may result from such research. Does the Council make a convincing argument? How much does the relief of suffering count in your evaluation? How much does the use of embryos only in the earliest stages count in your evaluation? Explain.

QUESTIONS FOR REFLECTING AND WRITING

1. What, in your opinion, is the most critical issue in deciding for or against cloning-for-biomedical-research? Why?

2. One issue is the moral one, but another is the practical public policy issue. Will a four-year moratorium on cloning-for-biomedical-research enlighten the debate meaningfully? Why or why not? Can a moratorium, in practical terms, be implemented? If so, how? If not, why not?

3. If one allows cloning-for-biomedical-research, will it be possible to control cloning-to-produce-children? Should it be? Where do you stand on these parts of the debate?

THE HORROR | JOSEPH BOTTUM

A graduate of Georgetown University and Boston College (with a doctorate in philosophy), Joseph Bottum is books and arts editor of the *Weekly Standard.* His essays, reviews, and poetry have been published in many journals and magazines, and he also hosts *Book Talk,* a syndicated radio program. His collection of poems is *The Fall and Other Poems* (2001). His contribution to a debate on bioethics in *Public Interest* appeared in the Winter 2003 issue.

PREREADING QUESTIONS What does Bottum's title suggest to you about his position in the bioethics debate? What did the Council vote to ban? What did they vote just a moratorium on?

1   There are three directions in which we might take a discussion of the report of the President's Council on Bioethics. We might first talk about the issue of cloning itself. Then again, we might turn to the deliberations of the President's Council, as presented in this . . . [chapter], and talk about the divisions and insights of the council's members. Finally, we might take this discussion to be about politics—which is to say, the impact and the importance, in the real world, of the policy recommendations made by the President's Council. About all three of these, I have enormous amounts to say—more than could ever be fit into the time we have. But here are a few first thoughts.

2   Among the finest features of the report is the perfect civility of its thoughtful deliberations. And yet, that civility comes at a cost, which I am not sure we have fully reckoned. While I applaud nearly all of its work, the council's report does not, for example, sufficiently express the horror and repugnance that the idea of cloning arouses in me.

3   Perhaps an analogy will help make that feeling clear. I once tried to write a poem about an attractive young woman I had seen walking along the street. I suppose she was not beautiful, per se, but then I have reached the age at which youth itself begins to seem beautiful. Those of you who are still young may not understand what I am talking about. But for those of us growing old, there is a lure in youthfulness—the tautness of it, the glow.

4   And there is also a crime: to act upon that lure, to seek one's own youth restored by leeching on the youthfulness of others. This is the mockable widower seeking a young bride in Molière's comedies; it is the sexual sickness expressed by Charles Dickens in *Nicholas Nickleby* when the aged Arthur Gride drools over the young Madeleine after using her father's debts to force her into his power.

5   But I have in mind something more than putting an armful of warm girl in an old man's cold bed. Behind this stands the fantasy of age, that would sacrifice the young to buy its way back from the aches and diseases that age is prone to. There is, for instance, the old witch who wants to fatten up Hansel and Gretel before she bakes them in her oven and devours their youth. And then there is Elizabeth Bathory—the seventeenth-century Hungarian countess and perhaps the most famous figure to come out of Transylvania since Vlad the Impaler. Her trial records estimate that she slaughtered 600 young virgins in a decade, in order to bathe in their youth-restoring blood.

6   Let me bring this analogy home. It seems to me that the proponents of much of the biotech revolution—the supporters and enablers of the Brave New World of eugenic biotechnology—are forced into the uncomfortable position of insisting that the Countess Bathory was absolutely right, at least about her goals. She merely chose the wrong means.

7   I mean that not quite in the provocative sense in which I phrased it. She was obviously wrong about the effects of virgins' blood, and she lacked the help of

Advanced Cell Technology's laboratories in Massachusetts. But she also chose the wrong means when she used living, conscious human beings. The proponents of cloning-for-biomedical-research insist that the objects upon which modern laboratories work are not living human beings but cells—or biological accidents, or bits of human beings—which, because of ancient prejudices, must be spoken of in reverential ways, but which need not be treated any differently than a fingernail clipping or, in that great euphemism of abortionists, "the product of conception."

But I want to think about this in terms of human motivation. Indeed, when the President's Council distinguishes "cloning-for-biomedical-research" from "cloning-to-produce-children," it invites us to notice that the primary distinction between them is, in fact, a matter of human motivation—namely, the purpose for which the biotechnologist created the clone. 8

Much has been made, by Francis Fukuyama and others, about the recent efforts of scientists to complete the Baconian project—the great vision of Francis Bacon that science will finally ameliorate the human condition, so that we will all be happy, diseaseless, and nigh on immortal. I think it is right to notice this impending fulfillment of the promise that Bacon made centuries ago. But there is something else to notice as well—namely, that Bacon required for his dream that we dismiss all notion of purpose and goal for the objects of science. Indeed, Bacon's *New Organon* is filled with attacks upon the Aristotelian idea of final causation, a natural purpose or aim for things. 9

But goals don't actually go away just because we want them to. In the space opened up by the dismissal of final cause from science, there entered the malleability of things to the human will. We give things their purpose; we give them their final cause. The human act is conceived to be the only thing in the universe that has motive, purpose, goal, or aim—and those motives will eventually eat up the reality of everything else. 10

In fact, they have already eaten up reality. There are serious political questions that might be raised about the council's report. But think about this: The council was unanimous in wanting to prohibit forever cloning-to-produce-children, and could only by the barest majority reach the compromise of a temporary moratorium on cloning-for-biomedical-research. This seems to me exactly backwards. However much cloning-to-produce-children proceeds along defective means, it still aims at the natural cause of procreation. It wants to make babies. 11

Cloning-for-biomedical-research, on the other hand, has abandoned the goal. Embryos, fetuses, blastocysts, activated eggs, products of SCNT, whatever euphemism is floating around this week—cloning-for-biomedical-research takes those objects and makes them plastic playthings for the human will. What is worse, it is the human will traveling down a line of motivation that is inherently suspect—if we remember Molière and Dickens, and the old, old stories. We are becoming the people that, once upon a time, our ancestors used fairy tales to warn their children against. 12

Now, Francis Bacon's scientific vision of modernity is not the only one. There is also a literary vision of modernity. And from Mary Shelley's *Frankenstein* to 13

Aldous Huxley's *Brave New World*, the literary imagination has not pictured the prospect of manufactured human beings with much joy. From Robert Louis Stevenson's *Dr. Jekyll and Mr. Hyde* to H. G. Wells' *The Island of Dr. Moreau*, the literary imagination has not been much taken with scientists who manipulate the deep things of life just because they can.

14   The truth is, after reading these authors, I worry about people who reach into the stuff of life and twist it to their will. I worry about people who act simply because they can. If they lived in crumbling castles—their hair standing up on end and their voices howling in maniacal laughter—we'd know them to be mad scientists. But they wear nice white lab coats, and their pleasant-looking chief executive appears on television to assure us that they are really acting for the best of medical motives and, besides, there is a great deal of money to be made in biotech and pharmaceutical stocks.

15   Sometimes the disingenuousness is unbearable. Evading the regulations in France, the French company Clonaid recently opened a laboratory in Ivory Coast, and its spokeswoman announced that they had done so in response to the great demand for cloning in sub-Saharan Africa. Ah, yes, my wife suggested: Those poor, starving Africans, desperate for food, drinking water, and the latest fads in biotechnology.

16   But Clonaid's move to Africa seems to me a final proof of the dangerousness of unlimited human will. The people who say that this technology can be regulated are simply ignorant of human nature. If you were to put up a lever with a sign that said, "Don't touch or the world will be destroyed," the paint wouldn't even be dry before someone's last words were, "I just wanted to see what would happen."

17   We have to applaud the seriousness that Leon Kass has brought to Washington, the tone and tenor of the deliberations, and the report that issued from the President's Council on Bioethics. But I think we must also raise questions about the civility that is the report's finest feature.

QUESTIONS FOR READING

1. What is Bottum's subject?
2. What is his view of the aging trying to regain their youth through the use of others?
3. What is the difference, in the author's view, between cloning-for-biomedical-research and cloning-to-produce-children?
4. What was Francis Bacon's vision of science? What was necessary, in Bacon's eyes, for the achievement of his vision?
5. What is, according to Bottum, backward about the Council's decisions?
6. What dangerous element are we ignoring?

QUESTIONS FOR REASONING AND ANALYSIS

1. What is Bottum's claim? Why does he take exception to the Council's positions?
2. What is his primary reason for disagreeing with the Council's views?

3. What evidence does he offer in support of his primary reason?

4. How would you describe the author's tone? How might his tone help his argument?

QUESTIONS FOR REFLECTING AND WRITING

1. Do you agree that "unlimited human will" is dangerous? Why or why not?

2. If you agree that "unlimited human will" is dangerous, do you agree that this is a good and sufficient reason to ban all research into or using cloning of human cells? Why or why not?

3. Huxley's novel *Brave New World* is repeatedly referred to in debates on bioethics. Have you read the novel? If so, how would you explain its connection to the bioethics debate to someone who has not read the novel? If not, do you think that you should read the novel as part of your research in understanding the issues surrounding bioethics? Why or why not?

THE VIRTUAL CHILD | LEE M. SILVER

Holding a Harvard University doctorate in biophysics, Lee Silver is a professor in the department of molecular biology at Princeton University and in the Woodrow Wilson School of Public and International Affairs. He is the author of many articles and books, including *The Last Taboo, Genetics: From Genes to Genomes*, and *Remaking Eden: Cloning and Beyond in a Brave New World* (1977). The following is from a chapter in *Remaking Eden*.

PREREADING QUESTIONS What does the term *eugenics* mean to you? What connotation does the word have for you? What might be the advantages of selecting and/or rejecting particular genes before they are transmitted to one's children?

There are some people who equate the early embryo with a human be- 1 ing that is deserving of the same respect as a child or adult, based on the idea that each human embryo contains a human spirit, deposited within it at the time of fertilization. These people are generally opposed to the destruction of any embryos at any time, whether it is through the normal practice of IVF or in response to embryo selection. A scientific critique of this viewpoint was presented earlier and will not be considered further here. Instead, I will focus on ethical concerns raised by people who are willing to accept the traditional practice of IVF—where embryos are chosen randomly for introduction into a woman's uterus—but are troubled specifically by genetic selection.

Once people reject the notion that an early human embryo is equivalent 2 to a human being, the reasons for opposing embryo selection are varied, but they can all be classified under the rubric of eugenics. *Eugenics.* The word causes people to shudder. But what exactly is eugenics and why is it considered so bad? We must answer these questions before it is possible to continue our discussion.

3   Unfortunately, answers are not that easy to come by. As the political scientist Diane Paul writes, "'Eugenics' is a word with nasty connotations but an indeterminate meaning. Indeed, it often reveals more about its users' attitudes than it does about the policies, practices, intentions, or consequences labeled. . . . The superficiality of public debate on eugenics is partly a reflection of these diverse, sometimes contradictory meanings, which result in arguments that often fail to engage."

4   In its original connotation, eugenics referred to the idea that a society might be able to improve its gene pool by exerting control over the breeding practices of its citizens. In America, early twentieth-century attempts to put this idea into practice brought about the forced sterilization of people deemed genetically inferior because of (supposed) reduced intelligence, minor physical disabilities, or possession of a (supposed) criminal character. And further "protection of the American gene pool" was endeavored by congressional enactment of harsh immigration policies aimed at restricting the influx of people from Eastern and Southern Europe—regions seen as harboring populations (which included all four grandparents of the author . . .) with undesirable genes. Two decades later, Nazi Germany used an even more drastic approach in its attempt to eliminate—in a single generation—those who carried undesirable genes. In the aftermath of World War II, all of these misguided attempts to practice eugenics were rightly repudiated as discriminatory, murderous, and infringing upon the natural right of human beings to reproductive liberty. *Eugenics* was now clearly a dirty word.

5   While eugenics was defined originally in terms of a lofty *outcome*—the improvement of a society's gene pool—its contemporary usage has fallen to the level of a *process*. In its new meaning, eugenics is the notion of human beings exerting control over the genes that are transmitted from one generation to the next—irrespective of whether the action itself could have any effect on the gene pool, and irrespective of whether it's society as a whole or an individual family that exerts the control. According to this definition, the practice of embryo screening is clearly eugenics. Since eugenics is horrible, it follows logically that embryo screening is horrible.

6   Although the fallacy in this logic is transparent, it is remarkable how often it is used by contemporary commentators to criticize reprogenetic technologies. A recent book entitled *The Quest for Perfection: The Drive to Breed Better Human Beings* uses this theme over and over again to castigate one reproductive practice after another. But simply placing a eugenics label on something does not make it wrong. The Nazi eugenics program was wrong not only because it was mass murder, but also because it was an attempt at genocide. The forced sterilizations in America were wrong because they restricted the reproductive liberties of innocent people. And restrictive immigration policies directed against particular regions of the world are still wrong because they are designed to discriminate directly against particular ethnic groups. Clearly, none of these wrongs can be applied to the voluntary practice of embryo screening by a pair of potential parents.

Once we remove ourselves from the eugenics trap, it becomes possible to 7
consider the ethical concerns that surround embryo screening in the absence of
anxiety-producing labels. Again, I want to emphasize my intent to consider only
those concerns related to genetic selection rather than the random disposal of
embryos during the normal process of IVF. I will start out with five general concerns based on concepts of morality and naturalness. I will move on to concerns
about the negative impact that embryo screening could have on society. . . .

IT IS IMMORAL TO CHOOSE ONE CHILD OVER ANOTHER

When embryo selection is equated with choosing children, there is a pal- 8
pable sense of revulsion. It is not hard to understand this feeling. Often in the
past, and in some places still, genetic choice is exercised through infanticide.
The particular choice made most often in some Third World countries is boy
babies over girl babies, who are suffocated or drowned soon after birth. In
other societies, it is infants with physical disabilities that are most often killed.

But the analogy of embryo screening to infanticide is a false one. What em- 9
bryo screening provides is the ability to select genotypes, not children. Today,
parents can use the technology to make sure that their *one* child—whom they
had always planned on bringing into the world—is not afflicted with Tay-Sachs.

Even in the future, when it becomes possible to draw computer images 10
based on genetic profiles, embryos will still not be *real* children. Virtual children
exist only in one's mind, and the consummation of an actual fertilization event
is not even a prerequisite for their creation. Once genetic profiles have been
obtained for any man and any woman, it becomes possible to determine the
virtual gametes that each might produce. Each combination of a virtual male
gamete and a virtual female gamete will produce a virtual child. And each one
of the trillions upon trillions of virtual children made possible by virtual intercourse between a single man and woman (who may never have met) could be
associated with a computer-generated profile as extensive and detailed as
those presented for the virtual Alices at the start of this chapter. At the end of
the story, however, only one real Alice emerged. And what her parents chose
for her were the alleles that she received from each of them.

IT IS WRONG TO TAMPER WITH THE NATURAL ORDER

This concern is expressed by many who are not particularly religious in the 11
traditional sense. Still, they feel that there is some predetermined goal for the
evolution of humankind, and that this goal can only be achieved by the current
random process through which our genes are transmitted to our children. However, unfettered evolution is never predetermined, and not necessarily associated with progress—it is simply a response to unpredictable environmental
changes. If the asteroid that hit our planet 60 million years ago had flown past
instead, there would never have been any human beings at all. And whatever
the natural order might be, it is not necessarily good. The smallpox virus was
part of the natural order until it was forced into extinction by human intervention. I doubt that anyone mourns its demise.

EMBRYO SELECTION FOR ADVANTAGEOUS TRAITS IS A MISUSE OF MEDICINE

12   The purpose of medicine is to prevent suffering and heal those with disease. Based on this definition, it is clear that embryo selection could be put to uses that lie far outside this scope. But medical doctors have used their knowledge and skills to work in other nonmedical areas such as nontherapeutic cosmetic surgery. If we accept the right of medical doctors to enter into nonmedical business practices, we have to accept their right to develop private programs of embryo selection as well.

13   One could argue that since the embryo screening technology was developed with the use of government funds, it should only be used for societally approved purposes. But government funds have been used in the development of nearly all forms of modern technology, both medical and nonmedical. This association has never been viewed as a reason for restricting the use of any other technology in private profit-making ventures.

EMBRYO SELECTION TAKES THE NATURAL WONDER AWAY FROM THE BIRTH OF A CHILD

14   Many prospective parents choose not to learn the sex of their child before birth, even when it is known to their physician through prenatal testing. There is the feeling that this choice allows the moment of birth to be one of parental discovery. If a child's characteristics were pre-determined in many more ways than just sex, many fear that the sense of awe associated with birth would disappear. For some, this may be true. But this is a personal concern that could play a role in whether an individual couple chooses embryo selection for themselves. It can't be used as a rationale to stop others whose feelings are different.

WHETHER INTENTIONAL OR NOT, EMBRYO SELECTION COULD AFFECT THE GENE POOL

15   If embryo selection were available to all people in the world and there was general acceptance of its use, then the gene pool might indeed be affected very quickly. The first result would be the almost-complete elimination of a whole host of common alleles with lethal consequences such as Tay-Sachs, sickle cell anemia, and cystic fibrosis.

16   There are some who argue that it would be wrong to eliminate these alleles, or others, because they might provide *a hidden advantage to the gene pool.* This is another version of the "natural order" argument, based here on the idea that even alleles with deleterious effects in isolated individuals exist because they provide some benefit to the species as a whole. Those who make this argument believe that all members of a species somehow function together in genetic terms.

17   This point of view has no basis in reality. It results from a misunderstanding of what the gene pool is, and why we should, or should not, care about it. The concept of the gene pool was invented as a tool for developing mathematical models by biologists who study populations of animals or plants. It is calculated

as the frequencies with which particular alleles at particular genes occur across all of the members of a population that interbreed with each other.

Most healthy individuals are not carriers of the Tay-Sachs or cystic fibrosis 18 alleles, and if given the choice, I doubt if anyone would want to have his or her genome changed to become a carrier. So on what basis can we insist that others receive a genotype that we've rejected? There is none. Genes do not function in human populations (except in a virtual sense imagined by biologists), they function within individuals. And there is no species-wide knowledge or storage of particular alleles for use in future generations.

In fact, there is not even a tendency or rationale for a species to preserve 19 itself at all. At each stage throughout the evolution of our ancestors—from rodentlike mammals to apelike primates to *Australopithecus* to *Homo habilis* to *Homo erectus* and, finally, *Homo sapiens*—small groups of individuals gained genetic advantages that allowed them to survive even as they participated in the death of the species from which they arose! Survival and evolution operate at the level of the individual, not the species.

There are some who are not concerned about abstract concepts like the 20 gene pool and evolution so much as they are worried that the genetic elimination of mental illness (an unlikely possibility) would prevent the birth of future Ernest Hemingways and Edgar Allan Poes. This worry is based on the demonstrated association between manic depression (also known as bipolar affective disorder) and creative genius.

This could indeed be a future loss for society. But once again, how can we 21 insist that others be inflicted with a predisposition to mental disease (one we wouldn't want ourselves) on the chance that a brilliant work of art would emerge? And if particular aberrant mental states are deemed beneficial to society, the use of hallucinogenic or other types of psychoactive drugs that could achieve the same effect—in timed doses—would seem preferable to mutant genes. It is also important to point out that the perceived loss of mad genius from future society is virtual, not real. If the manic depressive Edgar Allan Poe were never born, we wouldn't miss *The Raven*. Likewise, we don't miss all of the additional piano concertos that Mozart would have composed if he hadn't died at the age of thirty-four.

EMBRYO SELECTION WILL BRING ABOUT DISCRIMINATION

With the use of embryo selection, prospective parents will be able to en- 22 sure that their children are born without a variety of non-life-threatening disabilities. These will include a wide range of physical impediments, as well as physiological disabilities (such as deafness or blindness) and learning disabilities.

Many people with hereditary disabilities have overcome adversity to live 23 long and fruitful lives. These people are concerned that the widespread acceptance of embryo selection against their disabilities could reinforce the attitude that they are not full-fledged members of society, and not deserving of love and attention.

24   Of course, disabilities can result from either genetic or environmental factors. And one common environmental cause of disability in the past was the polio virus, which resulted in paralysis, muscular atrophy, and often physical deformity. Inoculation of children with the polio vaccine was not generally seen as discriminatory against those who were already disabled. Why should genetic inoculation against disability be viewed any differently?

25   One difference could be in the access of society's members to the inoculation. The polio vaccine was provided to all children, regardless of class or socioeconomic status, while embryo selection may only be available to those families who can afford it. The philosopher Philip Kitcher suggests that as a consequence, "the genetic conditions the affluent are concerned to avoid will be far more common among the poor—they will become 'lower-class' diseases, other people's problems. Interest in finding methods of treatment or for providing supportive environments for those born with the diseases may well wane."

26   This is a serious concern. But it is important to point out that the privileged class already reduces the likelihood of childhood disabilities through their superior ability to control the environment within which a fetus and child develops. People who argue that embryo selection should *not* be used to prevent serious childhood disabilities because it's unfair to those families who are unable to afford the technology should logically want to ban access of the privileged class to environmental advantages provided to their children as well. Political systems based on this premise have not fared well at the end of the twentieth century.

27   The alternative method for preventing inequality is referred to as "utopian eugenics" by Kitcher and is based on the vision of George Bernard Shaw of a society in which all citizens have free and equal access to the same disease-preventing technologies (and environments). Although discrimination would not be based on class differences in this utopian society, it could still be aggravated by the overall reduction in the number of disabled persons.

28   It's important to understand the nature of the relationship that might exist between embryo selection and discrimination against the disabled. Embryo selection will not itself be the cause of discrimination, just as the polio vaccine could not be blamed for discrimination against those afflicted with polio. All it could do, perhaps, is change people's attitudes toward those less fortunate than themselves. An enlightened society would not allow this to happen. Is it proper to blame a technology in advance for the projected moral shortcomings of an unenlightened, future society?

EMBRYO SELECTION WILL BE COERCIVE

29   I distinguished embryo selection from abhorrent eugenic policies of the past with the claim that embryo selection would be freely employed in Western society by prospective parents who were not beholden to the will of the state. As a consequence, the use of the technology would not be associated with any restrictions on reproductive liberty.

30   There are social science critics who say that this claim is naive. They fear that societal acceptance of embryo selection will lead inevitably to its use in a

coercive manner. Coercion can be both subtle and direct. Subtle pressures will exist in the form of societal norms that discourage the birth of children deemed unfit in some way. More direct pressures will come from insurance companies or state regulations that limit health coverage only to children who were embryonically screened for the absence of particular disease and predisposition genotypes.

How coercion of this type is viewed depends on the political sensibilities 31 of the viewer. Civil libertarians tend to see any type of coercion as an infringement on reproductive rights. And liberal libertarians would be strongly opposed to policies that discriminated against those born with avoidable medical conditions.

Communitarians, however, may view the refusal to preselect against such 32 medical conditions as inherently selfish. According to this point of view, such refusal would—by necessity—force society to help the unfortunate children through the expenditure of large amounts of resources and money that would otherwise be available to promote the welfare of many more people.

The communitarian viewpoint is considered shocking to many in America 33 today because, as Diane Paul says, "the notion that individual desires should sometimes be subordinated to a larger social good has itself gone out of fashion, to be replaced by an ethic of radical individualism."

EMBRYO SELECTION COULD HAVE A DRAMATIC
LONG-TERM EFFECT ON SOCIETY

Embryo selection is currently used by a tiny fraction of prospective parents 34 to screen for a tiny number of disease genotypes. For the moment, its influence on society is nonexistent. In fact, there are many critics who think that far too much attention is devoted to a biomedical "novelty item" with no relevance as a solution to any of the problems faced by the world. But with each coming year, the power of the technology will expand, and its application will become more efficient. Slowly but surely, embryo selection will be incorporated into American culture, just as other reproductive technologies have been in the past. And sooner or later, people will be forced to consider its impact on the society within which they live.

The nature of that impact will depend as much on the political *status quo* 35 and social norms of the future as they do on the power of the technology itself. In a utopian society of the kind imagined by George Bernard Shaw, all citizens would have access to the technology, all would have the chance to benefit from it, but none would be forced to use it. In this vision of utopia, embryo selection would take an entire society down the same path, wherever it might lead. Unfortunately, if future protocols of embryo selection remain in any way similar to those used now, the technology will remain prohibitively expensive, and utopian access would bankrupt a country.

A different scenario emerges if Americans hold fast to the overriding importance of personal liberty and personal fortune in guiding what individuals 36 are allowed and able to do. The first effects on society will be small. Affluent parents will have children who are less prone to disease, and even more likely to succeed (on average) than they might have been otherwise as a simple consequence of the affluent environment within which they are raised. But with each generation, the fruits of selection will accumulate. . . . [I]n every subsequent generation, selection could become more and more refined.

37   It is impossible to predict the cumulative outcome of generation upon generation of embryo selection, but some things seem likely. The already wide gap between the rich and the poor could grow even larger as well-off parents provide their children not only with the best education that money can buy, and the best overall environment that money can buy, but the "best cumulative set of genes" as well. Emotional stability, long-term happiness, inborn talents, increased creativity, and healthy bodies—these could be the starting points chosen for the children of the rich. Obesity, heart disease, hypertension, alcoholism, mental illness, and predispositions to cancer—these will be the diseases left to drift randomly among the families of the underclass.

38   But before we rush to ban the use of embryo selection by the privileged, we must carefully consider the grounds on which such a ban would be based. Is this future scenario different—in more than degree—from a present in which embryo selection plays no role at all? If it is within the rights of parents to spend $100,000 for an exclusive private school education, why is it not also within their rights to spend the same amount of money to make sure that a child inherits a particular set of their genes? Environment and genes stand side by side. Both contribute to a child's chances for achievement and success in life, although neither guarantees it. If we allow money to buy an advantage in one, the claim for stopping the other is hard to make, especially in a society that gives women the right to abort for any reason at all.

39   These logical arguments have been tossed aside in some countries like Germany, Norway, Austria, and Switzerland, as well as states like Louisiana, Maine, Minnesota, New Hampshire, and Pennsylvania, where recently passed laws seem to prohibit the use of embryo selection for any purpose whatsoever. In these countries and states, no distinction is made between the prevention of Tay-Sachs disease and selection in favor of so-called positive traits.

40   But if the short history of surrogacy is any guide, all such attempts to limit this technology will be doomed to failure. Many Tay-Sachs-carrying parents will surely feel that it is their "God-given" right to have access to a technology that allowed earlier couples to have nonafflicted children, and just as surely, there will always be a clinic in some open state or country that will accommodate their wishes. And if the technology is available for this one purpose, it will also be available for others.

41   It certainly does seem that embryo selection will be with us forever—whether we like it or not—as a powerful tool to be used by more and more parents to choose which of their genes to give to their children. But . . . the power of this tool pales in comparison to what becomes possible when people gain the ability to choose not only from among their own genes, but from any gene that one can imagine, whether or not it already exists.

QUESTIONS FOR READING

1. What does IVF stand for?
2. What is the source of the negative connotation of the word *eugenics*?
3. Why should eugenics in its negative connotation not apply to embryo screening?
4. Why is embryo screening not choosing one child over another?
5. How does Silver defend embryo screening as within the purview of medicine?
6. In what sense is concern for the gene pool another version of the "natural order" argument? Why is it not a valid argument for rejecting embryo screening?
7. Why is the possible discrimination against the disabled not a good reason for rejecting embryo selection? What advantages do the affluent already have that the poor do not have?
8. What types of coercion to use embryo selection might develop? What is the communitarian response to this anxiety?
9. How will embryo selection affect future generations? Why should the effects not lead us to reject this technological advance?

QUESTIONS FOR REASONING AND ANALYSIS

1. What is Silver's implied claim? What does his reasoning support?
2. Why is defining and discussing eugenics a necessary first step in Silver's argument?
3. Examine the structure of Silver's argument; how is it organized?
4. What *type* of argument can this be classified as? What is Silver "doing" with each of his eight points or concerns about embryo selection?

QUESTIONS FOR REFLECTING AND WRITING

1. What is the most important new idea or new fact in this essay for you? Why did you select that idea or fact?
2. Has Silver responded to each of the ethical concerns in a convincing way? Why or why not? Are some issues more troubling to you than others? If so, which ones and why? Are some rebuttals of Silver more convincing than others? If so, which sections of his argument are, in your view, weakest?
3. If you had the opportunity to remove disease-carrying genes and select genes for health or looks or intelligence for your future child, would you do so? If so, why? If not, why not?

GENES, GENIUS, GENIES | PATRICIA J. WILLIAMS

A professor of law at Columbia University, Patricia Williams is a member of the State Bar in California and a columnist. She has written a number of books, including *The Alchemy of Race & Rights* (1993) and *Seeing a Color-Blind Future: The Paradox of Race* (1997). Her column in *The Nation* appeared November 21, 2005.

PREREADING QUESTION How would you define the relationship between a pregnant woman and the fetus she is carrying?

1   In the beginning, there was a time when doctors treated pregnant women by listening to them tell of their symptoms. There were no visuals, no color glossies, no T-shirts with the sonogram emblazoned. There was a relative quiet in the womb, which took quiet to attend to. It required listening to the woman say, "This is what it feels like." It required a palpating of the body, a laying on of hands. Midwives and doctors used touch, eyes, ears, measuring from the outside to get a sense of what was within—sounds, motions, clues. It was the mother-to-be whose health was indicative of the condition of the embryo or fetus. Whether life was deemed to begin at conception or whether with quickening, the interdependence of the womb and the woman was a given. I'm certainly not advocating that we turn back the clock with regard to obstetric medicine, but it is arresting to recall that inter-connectedness in a time when "life" has become increasingly divorced from tradi-tional contours of the human body. We live in a time when embryos and fetuses are gaining legal rights to sue, are attaining the status of persons, are being en-shrined in a molecularly sized iconography of innocents to be saved. With tech-nology, we can make visual what no generation has been privy to before. Like satellites homing in on a secret bunker from space, we have the spyware to case the joint—the interior of the uterus, the cells, even mitochondria, and now DNA.

2   With all that comes interpretation, and politics, and ideology. And lo, the birth of "the unborn." The magnified fetus becomes an external, a separate entity. Women are no longer imbued with the halo-illuminated metaphors of ripeness and enfolding that underscore so many of our religious notions about women round with child. At least or perhaps especially in the United States, we find ourselves tangled in new definitions of separation and individuation. There has been a re-structuring, of our rhetoric as well as of certain religious ideologies, that expressly pits a woman's body against her fetus. There is, these days, a tendency to conceive of the fetus as an entire person, and a litigious little person at that, with a warrior attitude and a long list of complaints that can be asserted against the madonna in question. We've all read about negligence actions, criminal cases, child welfare cases, all involving fetuses still *in utero*. But the status of the fetus is no longer the most contentious part of the debate. It's moved further and further back in the de-velopmental cycle. Recently the Arizona court of appeals declined to rule that a set of cryogenically frozen fertilized eggs were "persons" for purposes of a wrongful death action, saying that such a designation was for the legislature. The lawsuit was brought by a couple who had sued the Mayo Clinic after its lab lost or possibly de-stroyed some of the eggs. The eggs were days old, still a clump of cells; never-theless the court was careful to craft a special category for them: "pre-embryos." Pre-embryonic status is thus not a biological designation but rather a new legal cat-egory, a way of dodging the political controversy engendered by those who be-lieve embryos are calling out for rescue. As John Jacubczyk, president of Arizona Right to Life, stated the argument: "Life begins at fertilization."

3   Although the Arizona court did not confer personhood in this case, the matter is sure to be appealed; furthermore, an Illinois court ruled this past

February that an embryo is a person, a claim that is likely to make its way to higher authorities—whether courts or legislatures—sometime in the not so distant future. So we should consider carefully the collective narratives that are shaping the debates. At one end we have the Snowflakes Frozen Embryo Adoption Program, a Christian organization that has made it its mission to rescue the unused embryos that have been harvested by fertility clinics and then discarded by couples once they do achieve a successful pregnancy. Snowflakes considers the abandonment and/or destruction of those cells nothing less than murder, and so has set out to "adopt" discarded embryos. It has rounded up women in whom to implant them, and families with whom to place the babies thus brought to term. Mere blastemas are imbued with intent and longing; indeed, the Snowflakes website asserts that it is "helping some of the more than 400,000 frozen embryos reach their ultimate purpose—life."

On the other side of things there is a philosophically inflected concern that 4 if cellular "life" is equated with personhood, and personhood begins at fertilization, then the very notion of the person as an autonomous entity becomes terribly vexed. Eggs fertilized in a petri dish and stored in a freezer are most consistent with our notions of property, of product, of artifice. From this angle, eggs in a dish are relatively artificial, a species of mechanical construct requiring tools, inventory, technology. At the same time, there is also a commercial narrative of altruism, in which those fertilized eggs are, not unlike the Snowflakes website's take, so purposeful, so hyper-autonomous, that they can fight their way out of a petri dish with no help from a womb or a woman or even a mad scientist. Personhood becomes an anthropomorphizing of cellular life—the tiny but strong, the minuscule but mighty, the intelligence with design, the responsible agent, the genie in the jar that imprisons the fully formed perfect child yearning to break free. It is a very seductive story, even if it is questionable as a scientific matter. And more to the point for us in the legal community, it confuses will and determinism, potential and predestination.

But if the power of these narratives has resulted in a kind of cult celebrity 5 status for the pre-born, or prenatal, or pre-conscious or whatever, imagine how much more creative it will get with the emerging overlays of DNA screening, of accumulating commercial interests in profiles for health insurance, in DNA banks as a tool of social engineering. Somewhere between the extremities of the moment, we must remember that there is nothing inevitable in this course; let us not be seduced by an idealized personification of destiny. Let us not forget that one in five American children lives in poverty. And at least 130,000 post-born, not-so-perfect children ("surplus" is how Seventh Circuit Judge Richard Posner once expressed it) are available for domestic adoption at any given time. Aren't they "a person" too?

QUESTIONS FOR READING

1. How was obstetric medicine practiced in the past? How has it changed today?
2. What has been the result of the change in perception of the mother–fetus relationship?

3. What is the new image of the fetus? What can it now "do"?

4. What now is the status of "pre-embryos"?

5. What is the Snowflakes program doing? What traits do they give to embryos? How does this become a legal issue?

QUESTIONS FOR REASONING AND ANALYSIS

1. What is Williams's claim? (Much is implied, little asserted, in this argument, so as readers we need to think carefully about the author's argument.)

2. What kinds of evidence are presented in support of the claim?

3. What is the essay's tone? How is it used as a strategy in the argument? (Pay special attention to the conclusion.)

QUESTIONS FOR REFLECTING AND WRITING

1. Have you considered the legal complications that are the result of defining an embryo or pre-embryo as a person? If yes, what are your reactions? If no, has the author given you good reasons to consider them? Why or why not?

2. How do you understand the author's title?

3. Has Williams presented a convincing argument? If yes, why? If no, how would you rebut her argument?

SHOW ME THE SCIENCE | DANIEL C. DENNETT

Professor of philosophy at Tufts University, Daniel Dennett is also director for the Center of Cognitive Studies at Tufts. He has written over 200 scholarly articles on philosophy, especially mind functioning, and several books, including *Darwin's Dangerous Idea* (1995) and *Freedom Evolves* (2003). His article reprinted here was originally published in the *New York Times* on August 28, 2005.

PREREADING QUESTIONS Given his title and his training, what do you expect Dennett to write about? Or, what do you expect his approach to be?

1   President Bush, announcing this month that he was in favor of teaching about "intelligent design" in the schools, said, "I think that part of education is to expose people to different schools of thought." A couple of weeks later, Senator Brill Frist of Tennessee, the Republican leader, made the same point. Teaching both intelligent design and evolution "doesn't force any particular theory on anyone," Mr. Frist said. "I think in a pluralistic society that is the fairest way to go about education and training people for the future."

2   Is "intelligent design" a legitimate school of scientific thought? Is there something to it, or have these people been taken in by one of the most ingenious hoaxes in the history of science? Wouldn't such a hoax be impossible? No. Here's how it has been done.

3   First, imagine how easy it would be for a determined band of naysayers to shake the world's confidence in quantum physics—how weird it is!—or

Einsteinian relativity. In spite of a century of instruction and popularization by physicists, few people ever really get their heads around the concepts involved. Most people eventually cobble together a justification for accepting the assurances of the experts: "Well, they pretty much agree with one another, and they claim that it is their understanding of these strange topics that allows them to harness atomic energy, and to make transistors and lasers, which certainly do work."

Fortunately for physicists, there is no powerful motivation for such a band 4 of mischief-makers to form. They don't have to spend much time persuading people that quantum physics and Einsteinian relativity really have been established beyond all reasonable doubt.

With evolution, however, it is different. The fundamental scientific idea of 5 evolution by natural selection is not just mind-boggling; natural selection, by executing God's traditional task of designing and creating all creatures great and small, also seems to deny one of the best reasons we have for believing in God. So there is plenty of motivation for resisting the assurances of the biologists. Nobody is immune to wishful thinking. It takes scientific discipline to protect ourselves from our own credulity, but we've also found ingenious ways to fool ourselves and others. Some of the methods used to exploit these urges are easy to analyze; others take a little more unpacking.

A creationist pamphlet sent to me some years ago had an amusing page 6 in it, purporting to be part of a simple questionnaire:

Test Two

Do you know of any building that didn't have a builder? [YES] [NO]

Do you know of any painting that didn't have a painter? [YES] [NO]

Do you know of any car that didn't have a maker? [YES] [NO]

If you answered YES for any of the above, give details:

Take that, you Darwinians! The presumed embarrassment of the test-taker 7 when faced with this task perfectly expresses the incredulity many people feel when they confront Darwin's great idea. It seems obvious, doesn't it, that there couldn't be any designs without designers, any such creations without a creator.

Well, yes—until you look at what contemporary biology has demonstrated 8 beyond all reasonable doubt: that natural selection—the process in which reproducing entities must compete for finite resources and thereby engage in a tournament of blind trial and error from which improvements automatically emerge—has the power to generate breathtakingly ingenious designs.

Take the development of the eye, which has been one of the favorite challenges of creationists. How on earth, they ask, could that engineering marvel be produced by a series of small, unplanned steps? Only an intelligent designer could have created such a brilliant arrangement of a shape-shifting lens, an aperture-adjusting iris, a light-sensitive image surface of exquisite sensitivity, all housed in a sphere that can shift its aim in a hundredth of a second and send megabytes of information to the visual cortex every second for years on end.

10   But as we learn more and more about the history of the genes involved, and how they work—all the way back to their predecessor genes in the sightless bacteria from which multicelled animals evolved more than a half-billion years ago—we can begin to tell the story of how photosensitive spots gradually turned into light-sensitive craters that could detect the rough direction from which light came, and then gradually acquired their lenses, improving their information-gathering capacities all the while.

11   We can't yet say what all the details of this process were, but real eyes representative of all the intermediate stages can be found, dotted around the animal kingdom, and we have detailed computer models to demonstrate that the creative process works just as the theory says.

12   All it takes is a rare accident that gives one lucky animal a mutation that improves its vision over that of its siblings; if this helps it have more offspring than its rivals, this gives evolution an opportunity to raise the bar and ratchet up the design of the eye by one mindless step. And since these lucky improvements accumulate—this was Darwin's insight—eyes can automatically get better and better and better, without any intelligent designer.

13   Brilliant as the design of the eye is, it betrays its origin with a tell-tale flaw: the retina is inside out. The nerve fibers that carry the signals from the eye's rods and cones (which sense light and color) lie on top of them, and have to plunge through a large hole in the retina to get to the brain, creating the blind spot. No intelligent designer would put such a clumsy arrangement in a camcorder, and this is just one of hundreds of accidents frozen in evolutionary history that confirm the mindlessness of the historical process.

14   If you still find Test Two compelling, a sort of cognitive illusion that you can feel even as you discount it, you are like just about everybody else in the world; the idea that natural selection has the power to generate such sophisticated designs is deeply counterintuitive. Francis Crick, one of the discovers of DNA, once jokingly credited his colleague Leslie Orgel with "Orgel's Second Rule": Evolution is cleverer than you are. Evolutionary biologists are often startled by the power of natural selection to "discover" an "ingenious" solution to a design problem posed in the lab.

15   This observation lets us address a slightly more sophisticated version of the cognitive illusion presented by Test Two. When evolutionists like Crick marvel at the cleverness of the process of natural selection they are not acknowledging intelligent design. The designs found in nature are nothing short of brilliant, but the process of design that generates them is utterly lacking in intelligence of its own.

16   Intelligent design advocates, however, exploit the ambiguity between process and product that is built into the word "design." For them, the presence of a finished product (a fully evolved eye, for instance) is evidence of an intelligent design process. But this tempting conclusion is just what evolutionary biology has shown to be mistaken.

17   Yes, eyes are for seeing, but these and all the other purposes in the natural world can be generated by processes that are themselves without purposes

and without intelligence. This is hard to understand, but so is the idea that colored objects in the world are composed of atoms that are not themselves colored, and that heat is not made of tiny hot things.

The focus on intelligent design has, paradoxically, obscured something 18 else: genuine scientific controversies about evolution that abound. In just about every field there are challenges to one established theory or another. The legitimate way to stir up such a storm is to come up with an alternative theory that makes a prediction that is crisply denied by the reigning theory—but that turns out to be true, or that explains something that has been baffling defenders of the status quo, or that unifies two distant theories at the cost of some element of the currently accepted view.

To date, the proponents of intelligent design have not produced anything 19 like that. No experiments with results that challenge any mainstream biological understanding. No observations from the fossil record or genomics or biogeography or comparative anatomy that undermine standard evolutionary thinking.

Instead, the proponents of intelligent design use a ploy that works some- 20 thing like this. First you misuse or misdescribe some scientist's work. Then you get an angry rebuttal. Then, instead of dealing forthrightly with the charges leveled, you cite the rebuttal as evidence that there is a "controversy" to teach.

Note that the trick is content-free. You can use it on any topic. "Smith's 21 work in geology supports my argument that the earth is flat," you say, misrepresenting Smith's work. When Smith responds with a denunciation of your misuse of her work, you respond, saying something like: "See what a controversy we have here? Professor Smith and I are locked in a titanic scientific debate. We should teach the controversy in the classrooms." And here is the delicious part: you can often exploit the very technicality of the issues to your own advantage, counting on most of us to miss the point in all the difficult details.

William Dembski, one of the most vocal supporters of intelligent design, 22 notes that he provoked Thomas Schneider, a biologist, into a response that Dr. Dembski characterizes as "some hair-splitting that could only look ridiculous to outside observers." What looks to scientists—and is—a knockout objection by Dr. Schneider is portrayed to most everyone else as ridiculous hair-splitting.

In short, no science. Indeed, no intelligent design hypothesis has even 23 been ventured as a rival explanation of any biological phenomenon. This might seem surprising to people who think that intelligent design competes directly with the hypothesis of non-intelligent design by natural selection. But saying, as intelligent design proponents do, "You haven't explained everything yet," is not a competing hypothesis. Evolutionary biology certainly hasn't explained everything that perplexes biologists. But intelligent design hasn't yet tried to explain anything.

To formulate a competing hypothesis, you have to get down in the 24 trenches and offer details that have testable implications. So far, intelligent design proponents have conveniently sidestepped that requirement, claiming that they have no specifics in mind about who or what the intelligent designer might be.

25   To see this shortcoming in relief, consider an imaginary hypothesis of intelligent design that could explain the emergence of human beings on this planet:

> About six million years ago, intelligent genetic engineers from another galaxy visited Earth and decided that it would be a more interesting planet if there was a language-using, religion-forming species on it, so they sequestered some primates and genetically re-engineered them to give them the language instinct, and enlarged frontal lobes for planning and reflection. It worked.

26   If some version of this hypothesis were true, it could explain how and why human beings differ from their nearest relatives, and it would disconfirm the competing evolutionary hypotheses that are being pursued.

27   We'd still have the problem of how these intelligent genetic engineers came to exist on their home planet, but we can safely ignore that complication for the time being, since there is not the slightest shred of evidence in favor of this hypothesis.

28   But here is something the intelligent design community is reluctant to discuss: no other intelligent-design hypothesis has anything more going for it. In fact, my farfetched hypothesis has the advantage of being testable in principle: we could compare the human and chimpanzee genomes, looking for unmistakable signs of tampering by these genetic engineers from another galaxy. Finding some sort of user's manual neatly embedded in the apparently functionless "junk DNA" that makes up most of the human genome would be a Nobel Prize-winning coup for the intelligent design gang, but if they are looking at all, they haven't come up with anything to report.

29   It's worth pointing out that there are plenty of substantive scientific controversies in biology that are not yet in the textbooks or the classrooms. The scientific participants in these arguments vie for acceptance among the relevant expert communities in peer-reviewed journals, and the writers and editors of textbooks grapple with judgments about which findings have risen to the level of acceptance—not yet truth—to make them worth serious consideration by undergraduates and high school students.

30   So get in line, intelligent designers. Get in line behind the hypothesis that life started on Mars and was blown here by a cosmic impact. Get in line behind the aquatic ape hypothesis, the gestural origin of language hypothesis and the theory that singing came before language, to mention just a few of the enticing hypotheses that are actively defended but still insufficiently supported by hard facts.

31   The Discovery Institute, the conservative organization that has helped to put intelligent design on the map, complains that its members face hostility from the established scientific journals. But establishment hostility is not the real hurdle to intelligent design. If intelligent design were a scientific idea whose time had come, young scientists would be dashing around their labs, vying to win the Nobel Prizes that surely are in store for anybody who can overturn any significant proposition of contemporary evolutionary biology.

Remember cold fusion? The establishment was incredibly hostile to that 32 hypothesis, but scientists around the world rushed to their labs in the effort to explore the idea, in hopes of sharing in the glory if it turned out to be true.

Instead of spending more than $1 million a year on publishing books and 33 articles for non-scientists and on other public relations efforts, the Discovery Institute should finance its own peer-reviewed electronic journal. This way, the organization could live up to its self-professed image: the doughty defenders of brave iconoclasts bucking the establishment.

For now, though, the theory they are promoting is exactly what George 34 Gilder, a long-time affiliate of the Discovery Institute, has said it is: "Intelligent design itself does not have any content."

Since there is no content, there is no "controversy" to teach about in biol- 35 ogy class. But here is a good topic for a high school course on current events and politics: Is intelligent design a hoax? And if so, how was it perpetrated?

QUESTIONS FOR READING

1. What is Dennett's subject? Be precise.
2. Why is evolution more vulnerable to attack than quantum mechanics? How is it similar to quantum mechanics or relativity?
3. What is ambiguous about the word *design?*
4. What must proponents of intelligent design do to get into biology textbooks?
5. How, instead, do they create theoretical controversy?

QUESTIONS FOR REASONING AND ANALYSIS

1. What is Dennett's claim? Is it helpful to think in terms of two claims that connect?
2. When the author explains the imperfections of evolutionary theory, is he seeking common ground? Explain.
3. Dennett repeatedly uses the word *hypothesis.* What is the difference between a scientific hypothesis and a scientific theory?
4. What is the tone of this essay? How does it contribute to the author's argument?
5. Do you think that Dennett expects to convince proponents of intelligent design that they are not backing a scientific theory? To whom is he writing, primarily?

QUESTIONS FOR REFLECTING AND WRITING

1. What, in your view, is Dennett's best example of support for evolutionary biology? What is his best evidence for rejecting intelligent design? Defend your choices.
2. Evaluate Dennett's argument. Is it likely to influence his primary audience?

"High Note." *Dallas Morning News* (Irwin Thompson)

Read: What is this a photo of? What are the figures reflected in?

Reason: Where might this photo have been taken—given the chapter's topics?

Reflect/Write: What makes this photo effective?

CHAPTER 22

Storm Clouds over America: Where Are We Headed?

The writers in this chapter examine the issues of 2005 that, to them, represent the ways that American society may be losing its unity, its direction, its sense of purpose. Although these issues may not seem obviously related, these writers connect them to America's image of itself, its internal problems, and its role in the world. How should we protect ourselves and fight the war on terror? By continuing to fight in Iraq and to profile at home? Or, is the price of the war going to be a permanent division in American society? How do we respond, individually and as a political entity, to the catastrophe of Katrina, a natural disaster that has been seen by many also as a snapshot of America's unaddressed racial divide and the failure of government, at all levels, to function in a crisis and to make socially correct decisions.

And, so, where are we headed? Can America's status as the only super-power be maintained? Will this century give rise to a worldwide Muslim community? To a more powerful China or India? Can we get our own house in order and find a new role in the world? There are many competing voices today; which ones should we follow? Some of the chapter's writers point to the problems; others offer general solutions or basic road maps; still others are more precise, especially with regard to protections from terrorism. All of the writers will make you ponder some of the key issues and problems of our time.

Sources Related to This Chapter

There are too many issues raised in the essays here to justify listing just a couple of Web sites. To become more informed on the subjects explored in this chapter, read a good newspaper, every day, find a journal of opinion that speaks to you and read it regularly, and explore the world of the blogs to see, day in and day out, what troubles these folks about the actions—or inaction—of government. The writers in this chapter would tell you, if you asked them, that you are obligated to be informed.

THAT FEELING OF BEING UNDER SUSPICION | TUNKU VARADARAJAN

Although he holds a law degree from Oxford University, Tunku Varadarajan has chosen journalism for his career. He has been an editorial writer for the London *Times*, a freelance writer for newspapers and magazines, and a media critic and columnist for the *Wall Street Journal*. Currently he is the *WSJ*'s editorial features editor. The following column appeared at WSJ.com, July 29, 2005.

PREREADING QUESTIONS Have you experienced profiling because either you are, or someone thinks that you look like, a Muslim? If so, how did this make you feel? Are you willing to tolerate profiling to advance the war against terrorism?

1   After the terrorist bombings in London, and the revelations that many of the perpetrators were of Pakistani origin, I find that I am—for the first time in my life—part of a "group" that is under broad but emphatic visual suspicion. In other words, I fit a visual "profile," and the fit is most disconcerting.

2   The fact that I am neither Muslim nor Pakistani is irrelevant: Who except the most absurdly expert physiognomist or anthropologist could tell from my face that I am not an Ali, or a Mohammed, or a Hassan; that my ancestors are all from the deepest South India; and that my line has worshipped not Allah but Lord Shiva—mightiest deity of the Hindu pantheon—for 2,000 years? I *will* be mistaken for Muslim at some point—just as earlier this week in Manhattan five young men were pulled off a sightseeing bus and handcuffed by police on suspicion that they might have been Islamist terrorists. Their names, published in the papers, revealed that they were in fact all Sikhs and Hindus—something few could have established by simply looking at them. (The Sikhs here were short-haired and unturbanned.)

What we had in this incident—what we must get used to—is a not irrational 3 sequence: alarm, provoked by a belief that someone in the vicinity could do everyone around him great harm, followed instinctively by actions in which the niceties of social intercourse, the judgmental taboos that have been drilled into us, are set aside in the interest of self-preservation.

Terrorism has had many effects on society, and the foremost among them 4 are philosophical, or spiritual. We are now called upon to adjust the way we live and think, and to do so we must also adjust the bandwidth of our tolerance. By this I don't mean that we must be less tolerant of others but that some among us must learn to tolerate—or put up with—hardships, inconvenience or a new set of presumptions, given the all-consuming nature of the threat we face, in which "the profiled" and "the profilers" alike are targets.

In evaluating the moral fitness of "profiling," I should stress that we are 5 identifying people for *scrutiny*, not punishment. Recall the fate of Cinna the poet, in the Bard's *Julius Caesar*, who is killed by a mob that believes him, because of his name, to be Cinna the conspirator. When scrutiny becomes stigma, and stigma leads to victimization, a clear jump to evil has occurred. This has not happened in America, and must not.

But what of "profiling" as a forensic tool? Here, one must be satisfied 6 either that profiling *ought* to be done or at least—per Bentham—that it isn't something that "ought *not* to be done." I am satisfied on the second count. The practice cannot be rejected with the old moral clarity. The profiling process is not precisely racial but broadly physical according to "Muslim type." (Does that make it worse or better?) The process under way now does not constitute racial profiling in the classic sense—Muslims, after all, come in flavors other than Pakistani, including white Chechens and black Somalis.

But there is no getting around profiling, surely, because of the life-or- 7 death, instant decisions involved. So we have to ask one section of society to bear up under heightened scrutiny, asking them also to work extra hard— visibly so—to expunge the threat. Meanwhile, and just as important, we must ask the rest of society not to stigmatize those who conform to the broad physical category while also not allowing feelings of racial and moral guilt to slow our society's response to danger.

If I'm sounding overly nuanced on a subject that should, in the view of 8 some, have bright moral outlines, it's because the devil resides in this predicament. We are all facing the quandary of the policeman chasing a suspect who might be armed. Does he shoot or hesitate, shout a warning and possibly get shot? In that situation, society asks that he take the risk of self-harm. In our current situation, large swaths of society might be eradicated. Suddenly we all feel like the cop, and some of us like the suspect.

I am just as concerned about catching terrorists (who may look like me) as 9 anyone else who looks different. I can ask that the searches and scrutiny be done in a professional manner, with no insults and nothing that offends my dignity. I, too, see the absurdity of subjecting Chinese grandmothers to the same level of scrutiny as people from the Indian subcontinent at the airport check-in counter.

10   Do I *like* being profiled? Of course not. But my displeasure is yet another manifestation of the extraordinary power of terrorism. I am not being profiled because of racism but rather because Islamist fanatics have declared war on my society. They are the dark power that leads me to an experience in which my individuality is corroded. This is tragic; but it strengthens my resolve to support the war that seeks to destroy terrorism.

QUESTIONS FOR READING

1. What event has led to Varadarajan's column?
2. What are some effects of terrorism? What must people learn to tolerate?
3. When is profiling morally acceptable? When does it become evil?
4. Why is the current profiling not exactly racial? Why is it acceptable to Varadarajan? (Who is Bentham? If you do not know, look him up.)
5. What, in the author's view, seems absurd about some airport scrutiny?

QUESTIONS FOR REASONING AND ANALYSIS

1. What is Varadarajan's claim? What type of argument is this—that is, what is the author's approach to the issue?
2. Why, in the author's view, is the debate lacking in "bright moral outlines"? Explain his analogy in paragraph 8.
3. Who, for Varadarajan, is the real enemy, if it is not the profiler?
4. Varadarajan's approach to a highly emotional issue is worth your reflection. What is the essay's tone? What voice do we hear "speaking" to us? How does his approach influence his argument?

QUESTIONS FOR REFLECTING AND WRITING

1. Do you agree with the author that profiling is a complex philosophical issue? Why or why not?
2. If profiling is acceptable, under what circumstances is it acceptable? Are there circumstances in which it is unacceptable, in your view? Explain and defend.

NO COMPROMISES: WHY WE'RE GOING TO LOSE THE WAR ON TERROR—AND HOW WE COULD WIN | KARINA ROLLINS

A University of Maryland graduate, Karina Rollins spent much of her youth with her parents in Germany. Included in her journalism career was a spell at the *National Review,* and she has been published in many magazines. Currently she is a senior editor at *The American Enterprise* magazine, a regular on C-SPAN's *Washington Journal,* and a panelist on national German TV. Her article appeared in the January/February 2003 issue of *The American Enterprise.*

PREREADING QUESTIONS Do you have concerns about our security in this country? If so, what are they? If not, why not? What role does—or should—technology play, for good or for bad, in the problem of terrorism?

After 19 terrorists hijacked commercial airplanes, crashed them into the 1
World Trade Center and the Pentagon, and killed over 3,000 Americans, the U.S. government sprang into action: The director of the Federal Bureau of Investigation held a friendly meeting with an American Muslim group with known ties to terrorists. The State Department printed up thousands of copies of a poster series, "Mosques of America," and sponsored an imam-exchange program. None of which attracted any criticism from the attorney general or the President; all of which would be amusing if it were a sketch on *Saturday Night Live*.

The nation's new and improved airport security is a joke; all the stories 2
about little blue-haired ladies' shoes searched for explosives are true. Americans know the hassle and make-work and plastic forks don't add to their safety. One of the biggest laugh lines of a Washington, D.C., political comedy troupe, The Capitol Steps, comes at the beginning of a skit about airport security. A man in a giant turban walks on stage and hangs a big sign that reads simply, "O'Hare Security." It brings down the house.

Former senators Warren Rudman and Gary Hart, cochairmen of the Com- 3
mission on National Security in the 21st Century, concluded that "A year after 9/11, America remains dangerously unprepared to prevent and respond to a catastrophic terrorist attack on US soil." Rudman and Hart lament that enormous amounts of money are spent on airports, while port and cargo security take a back seat; that police, firemen, and emergency medical workers still can't communicate well with each other or their counterparts in nearby cities; that public health facilities are unprepared for a biological or chemical attack; that local police work in an intelligence vacuum and don't have access to terrorist watch lists; and that there has been no national debate about how to protect factories and power plants. Cyberspace is still glaringly unprotected as well.

The Homeland Security bill has now, after many distractions, finally been 4
passed. It will be the job of the new department to close the gaping security holes, and it will surely be successful in implementing some effective safety mechanisms. But it could take years for the department to become operational. Besides, addressing such practical matters is only half the solution; there is an entire worldview in Washington that must change drastically.

The administration publicly characterizes al-Qaeda and its sympathizers as 5
a group of criminals, ignoring the religious nature of their plans to destroy the West. If the government—and the American people—are to win the war on terror, both must understand that our enemies have succeeded in launching a holy war—a war that will most certainly last beyond the lifetime of anyone reading these pages.

More than a year after 9/11, too many clear and present dangers continue 6
to loom over Americans. Following are prescriptions to address some of the biggest problems:

RETURN TO COMMON SENSE AND PURGE POLITICAL CORRECTNESS

7   Transportation Secretary Norman Mineta frets that being more suspicious of Arab males than 12-year-old girls will lead to World War II-style internment camps for Muslims. When asked several months ago on *60 Minutes* if elderly white women and young Muslim men should be treated the same at the airport security gate, he answered "Basically, I would hope so." The President praises Mr. Mineta for outstanding performance.

8   As William Lind of the Free Congress Foundation realizes, "The same government that wants to invade Iraq is too intimidated by political correctness to provide homeland security by profiling terrorists. The government's feeble efforts to protect our own perimeter spread fear and erode loyalties by telling patriotic citizens that their own government does not or cannot differentiate between patriots and terrorists." In a small bit of encouraging news, the government has announced plans to fingerprint and photograph men who are citizens of countries on an adjustable terror watch list. No, racial profiling isn't the answer. But terrorist profiling is. And that means being wary of young Arab-looking men. It's reality.

ELIMINATE TERRORIST TRAINING CAMPS—FOR REAL

9   The United States "should immediately tell all nations that have terrorist training camps on their territory that they should get rid of them," declares Cliff May, president of the Foundation for the Defense of Democracies. "We should tell these countries we would like them to take care of the camps on their own. If they don't, we should tell them: 'We are going to violate your sovereignty to eliminate them if you do not.' We should give them a limited amount of time. If they don't comply, we should have contingency plans to eliminate the camps through bombing or commando raids.

10   "There is a lot of talk about the recruitment of terrorists, but you can't become a terrorist unless you're trained to be one. You need training to become a sniper or a suicide bomber. You have to go someplace where they teach you. It is vital that there be no such places in the world within the next six months."

GIVE SECURITY CLEARANCES TO LOCAL POLICE
AND PLAN STATEWIDE RESPONSES

11   "What's important is trust and inclusion," says Edward Davis, police superintendent of Lowell, Massachusetts.

12   "That only happens through face-to-face contact. It's important that local police have security clearances. I have one and it makes me feel like I'm in the game. The joint task forces are working pretty well here in Massachusetts.

13   "And there has to be more discussion of regional responses to incidents. Jurisdictional issues have to be ironed out. There should be response scenarios that are clear, that can be trained, and that take care of the communications and coordination problems that can happen. If I had 1,000 police officers here tomorrow, I wouldn't really know how to coordinate them. You need a plan in advance. Not a complicated one, but a plan nonetheless. We need to do a better job planning for responses on a statewide level."

ISSUE NATIONAL I.D. CARDS

National I.D. cards are a scary thought for many Americans, conjuring up 14
images of Big Brother and George Orwell's dystopia. Enough with the hysteria
already. "Like it or not," points out my colleague Eli Lehrer, who founded the
Heritage Foundation's Excellence in Policing Project and has written extensively about national identity cards, "Americans already have national I.D.
cards. When they travel overseas, open a bank account, start a new job, or buy
a gun, U.S. citizens need to provide state-issued identification. A citizen who
gets stopped by the police and can't produce a driver's license, passport, or
Social Security card will often have to spend the night in jail." It's hard to argue
that this constitutes government power run amok.

A national I.D. card, far from robbing Americans of freedom or privacy, 15
would simply make it much easier for police to tell the majority of law-abiding
people from the small proportion of criminals and terrorists in our midst who are
capable of doing real harm. It would make us safer—and that makes us freer.

STOP PRETENDING THAT SAUDI ARABIA IS OUR FRIEND

As former assistant secretary of defense Frank Gaffney, Jr., now president 16
of the Center for Security Policy, explains: "Saudi Arabia's alignment with
America's enemies extends far beyond the anti-U.S. and anti-Western propaganda that is also ceaselessly disseminated by the kingdom's government-run
media. For some fifty years, Saudi officials, royal family, and what passes for private sector institutions have been expending untold sums to promote the state
religion—a virulently intolerant strain of Islam known as Wahabism. Washington has long ignored the individual and cumulative effects of such spending
on Wahabi proselytizing, recruiting, indoctrination, training, and equipping of
adherents who embrace the sect's injunction to convert or kill infidels.

"In the wake of terrorism made possible—or at least abetted—at home 17
and abroad by such Saudi-connected activities, the United States can no longer
afford to turn a blind eye to this profoundly unfriendly behavior. That is particularly true insofar as there is reason to believe that Wahabi enterprises are giving rise to perhaps the most insidious enemy of all: an Islamist Fifth Column
operating within this country."

As of the printing of this issue, the White House continues to call the Saudis 18
"good partners" in the war on terror.

PRAY THAT THE STATE DEPARTMENT DOESN'T DESTROY US

The State Department is directly responsible for issuing visas to the 19 Sep- 19
tember 11 hijackers, almost all of which should have been flatly rejected. The
consular officers who issued the visas each received bonuses of $10,000 to
$15,000. The State Department's Visa Express program, which let Saudi citi-
zens apply for visas at Saudi travel agencies and provided even fewer safeguards than the regular system, continued for almost a whole year after 9/11.

The Homeland Security Act includes stricter visa controls for Saudi 20
citizens—but only by accident. If the State Department had had its way, those
controls would have been wiped clear off the bill: State objected to the singling

out of Saudi Arabia—the country from which came 15 of the 19 September 11 hijackers. Joel Mowbray, who first broke the visa scandal story in *National Review*, reports that the department was assured, incredibly, that the Saudi provision would be struck from the legislation. Only due to "the last-minute confusion and the rush to get the mammoth bill passed during the lameduck session," he says, "did the provision stay put."

21   Unfazed by even the most egregious breaches of security, Secretary of State Colin Powell continues to wax poetic: "From the mountains of Afghanistan to the valleys of Bosnia to the plains of Africa to the forests of Asia and around the world we are on the ground working with our Muslim partners to expand the circle of peace, the circle of prosperity, the circle of freedom."

22   Secretary Powell also wants more of these "partners" on the ground right here in the U.S., pledging to expand programs to bring more Islamic political and religious leaders as well as journalists and teachers to America.

GET SERIOUS ABOUT BORDER CONTROL AND IMMIGRATION

23   The Immigration and Naturalization Service is guilty of the same reckless sloppiness in approving documents as the State Department. Of course, the INS is also understaffed and underfunded—something which could start to be fixed immediately (and should have been started on September 12, 2001). The administration seems to lack any real sense of urgency about the country's porous borders, and the lack of cooperation from our Mexican and, especially, Canadian neighbors.

24   "When it comes to immigration, the President's approach is guided by compassion and fairness," says Sharon Castillo, a spokesman for the Republican National Committee. No word on how fair it is to Americans who died at the hands of terrorists who could have been kept out of the country.

RECOGNIZE THE THREAT POSED BY MUSLIM ORGANIZATIONS, ISLAMIC CENTERS, AND MOSQUES IN OUR MIDST

25   Terror expert Steven Emerson founded The Investigative Project to collect data on militant Muslim groups in the U.S. In his book *American Jihad: The Terrorists Living Among Us*, he points to nine "terrorist support networks" based in America: Muslim Arab Youth Association, the American Islamic Group, Islamic Cultural Workshop, the Council on American-Islamic Relations, the American Muslim Council, Islamic Circle of North America, the Muslim Public Affairs Council, the American Muslim Alliance, and the Islamic Society of North America.

26   These groups, Emerson says, use "the laws, freedoms, and loopholes of the most liberal nation on earth to help finance and direct one of the most violent international terrorism groups in the world. Operating in the freewheeling and tolerant environment of the United States, bin Laden was able to set up a whole array of 'cells' in a loosely organized network that included Tucson, Arizona; Brooklyn, New York; Orlando, Florida; Dallas, Texas; Santa Clara, California; Columbia, Missouri; and Herndon, Virginia."

START POINTING FINGERS

No reform or security measure is going to mean very much if the people   27
who egregiously violate the most basic rules, and those in charge of them,
aren't held accountable, which in most cases means being fired. After 9/11, the
administration and members of Congress bent over backwards to insist that no
one was "finger pointing" or "seeking to lay blame." But accountability is precisely what's needed.

Minneapolis FBI special agent Coleen Rowley and her team did everything   28
in their power to get authorization from FBI headquarters merely to search the
computer of Zacarias Moussaoui, the so-called twentieth hijacker. They were
stalled and denied at every turn, despite providing clear evidence for the necessity of the search. One supervisory special agent in particular was responsible for the travesty. FBI Director Robert Mueller's response when Rowley's
memo made the front pages: announcing plans to hire more agents and buy
new computers. Oh, and he promoted that supervisory agent.

Calling for Mueller's resignation back in May, the *Wall Street Journal*   29
pointed out the obvious: "If Mueller had wanted to send a message to change
the FBI mindset he would have fired the supervisory special agent who ignored
the Minneapolis warnings on Moussaoui." To make matters worse, Mueller and
Attorney General John Ashcroft did not inform the President of the debacle for
seven months. As long as Robert Mueller is allowed to keep his job, the FBI's
credibility is non-existent. The White House's response; praise all around.

So, how safe are we?   30

QUESTIONS FOR READING

1. What is Rollins's subject? (State it as a problem.)
2. What specific issues does she see within the larger problem?
3. What two problems concern her with the Department of Homeland Security and
    the current administration?
4. State in your own words each of Rollins's proposed solutions.

QUESTIONS FOR REASONING AND ANALYSIS

1. What is Rollins's claim? Where does she state it?
2. Analyze the author's opening two paragraphs. What rhetorical strategy is she us-
    ing? Does it get your attention? Will it be effective for her anticipated audience?
3. How would you describe the author's style and tone in general throughout her
    essay? What, presumably, does she want to suggest with her style and tone?
4. Evaluate Rollins's eight proposed solutions. She develops each one largely by
    quoting various people. Are her sources credible and relevant? Convincing? Are
    you prepared to accept all eight proposals? Why or why not?

QUESTIONS FOR REFLECTING AND WRITING

1. Would you agree that the author has "done her homework"? If no, why not? If yes, does this make her argument more compelling, or is it what we should expect of anyone presenting a serious argument? Explain your views.

2. If you are not in agreement with one or more of Rollins's proposals, how would you rebut each one? Prepare your counterarguments.

3. Are there actions we should take that Rollins has left out of her agenda? If so, what are they? Note, for example that she mentions in paragraph 3 that "Cyberspace is still glaringly unprotected." However, she does not offer proposals for protecting cyberspace. How does an "unprotected" cyberspace aid terrorism? Do you think that cyberspace needs protecting? If not, why not? If so, what are your recommendations?

WHEN DENIAL CAN KILL | IRSHAD MANJI

Irshad Manji is a Canadian journalist, a Shia Muslim, and an outspoken feminist and lesbian. She has an active Web site, appears on Canadian television, and is a contributing blogger at *The Huffington Post.* Not surprisingly she has received death threats, especially since the publication of her book *The Trouble with Islam Today* (2002), now in paperback and translated into a dozen languages. The following essay was published in *Time* magazine on July 25, 2005.

PREREADING QUESTIONS Given the essay's title and the author's bio, what do you expect her essay to be about? Are you willing to read her essay with an open mind, the mind of a critical thinker? Why or why not?

1   I was surprised last week to learn how easily some Westerners believe terrorism can be explained. The realization unfolded as I looked into the sad face of a student at Oxford University. After giving a speech about Islam, I met this young magazine editor to talk about Islam's lost tradition of critical thinking and reasoned debate. But we never got to that topic. Instead, we got stuck on the July 7 bombings in London and what might have compelled four young, British-raised, observant Muslim men to blow themselves up while taking innocent others with them.

2   She emphasized their "relative economic deprivation." I answered that the lads had immigrant parents who had worked hard to make something of themselves. I reminded her that several of the 9/11 hijackers came from wealthy families, and it's not as if they left the boys out of the will. Finally, I told her about my conversation three years ago with the political leader of Islamic Jihad in Gaza. "What's the difference between suicide, which the Koran condemns, and martyrdom?" I asked. "Suicide," he replied, "is done out of despair. But remember: most of our martyrs today were very successful in their earthly lives." In short, there was a future to live for—and they detonated it anyway.

3   By this time, the Oxford student had grown somber. It was clear I had let her down. I had failed to appreciate that the London bombers were victims of British society. To be fair to her, she is right that marginalization, real or per-

ceived, diminishes self-esteem. Which, in turn, can make young people vulnerable to those peddling a radical message of instant belonging. But suppose the messages being peddled are marinated in religious rhetoric. Then wouldn't you say religion plays some role in motivating these atrocities?

The student shifted uncomfortably. She just couldn't bring herself to examine my suggestion seriously. And I suppose I couldn't expect her to. Not when Muslim leaders themselves won't go there. Iqbal Sacranie, secretary-general for the Muslim Council of Britain, is an example. In the midst of a debate with me, he listed potential incentives to bomb, including "alienation" and "segregation." But Islam? God forbid that the possibility even be entertained. 4

That is the dangerous denial from which mainstream Muslims need to emerge. While our spokesmen assure us that Islam is an innocent bystander in today's terrorism, whose who commit terrorist acts often tell us otherwise. Mohammed Atta, ringleader of the Sept. 11 hijackers, left behind a note asserting that "it is enough for us to know that the Koran's verses are the words of the Creator of the Earth and all the planets." Atta highlighted the Koran's description of heaven. In 2004 the executioners of Nick Berg, an American contractor in Iraq, alluded on tape to a different Koranic passage: "Whoever kills a human being, except as punishment for murder or other villainy in the land, shall be regarded as having killed all mankind." The spirit of that verse forbids aggressive warfare, but the clause beginning with *except* is readily deployed by militant Muslims as a loophole. If you want murder and villainy in the land, they say, look no further than U.S. bootprints in Arab soil. 5

For too long, we Muslims have been sticking fingers in our ears and chanting "Islam means Peace" to drown out the negative noise from our holy book. Far better to own up to it. Not erase or revise, just recognize it and thereby join moderate Jews and Christians in confessing "sins of Scripture," as an American bishop says about the Bible. In doing so, Muslims would show a thoughtful side that builds trust with the wider communities of the West 6

We could then cultivate the support to inspire cross-cultural understanding. For instance, schools throughout the West should teach how Islamic civilization helped give birth to the European Renaissance. Some of the first universities in recorded history sprang up in 3rd century Iran, 9th century Baghdad and 10th century Cairo. The Muslim world gave us mocha coffee, the guitar and even the Spanish expression *olé!* (which has its root in the Arabic word Allah). Muslim students would learn there is no shame in defending the values of pluralism. Non-Muslim students would learn that those values took great inspiration from Islamic culture. All would learn that Islam and the West are more interdependent than divided. 7

Still, as long as Muslims live in pretense, we will be affirming that we have something to hide. It's not enough for us to protest that radicals are exploiting Islam as a sword. Of course they are. Now, moderate Muslims must stop exploiting Islam as a shield—one that protects us from authentic introspection and our neighbors from genuine understanding. 8

QUESTIONS FOR READING

1. What is Manji's subject? Be precise.
2. What has been the economic condition of many terrorists?
3. What role can poverty and discrimination play in terrorism? What role can religion play?
4. What incentive to terrorism are Muslim leaders ignoring, in the author's view?
5. What reasons do terrorists often give for their actions?
6. What must moderate Muslims do? What will they then accomplish?

QUESTIONS FOR REASONING AND ANALYSIS

1. What is Manji's claim?
2. What evidence does she provide? Divide her argument into "what is" and "what would be."
3. What does the author gain by using the context of her Oxford speech as an opening?

QUESTIONS FOR REFLECTING AND WRITING

1. Do you agree that the terrorists have given evidence of religious motivation? Why or why not?
2. Do you agree that moderate Muslims can change the world's view of Islam's beliefs, culture, and history? Why or why not?
3. Do you know moderate Muslims who actively speak out against terrorism? Are you a Muslim who speaks out against terrorism? How important is speaking out? Explain your views.

SAVING AMERICA'S SOUL KITCHEN | WYNTON MARSALIS

Born and raised in New Orleans, Wynton Marsalis is an internationally acclaimed trumpeter. He is jazz trumpeter and artistic director of New York City's Jazz at Lincoln Center. His *Time* magazine essay was published September 19, 2005, shortly after the Katrina disaster.

PREREADING QUESTION Although Marsalis surely wants us to rescue New Orleans from its disaster, what else may the author want readers to "save"?

1   Now the levee breach has been fixed. The people have been evacuated. Army Corps of Engineers magicians will pump the city dry, and the slow (but quicker than we think) job of rebuilding will begin. Then there will be no 24-hour news coverage. The spin doctors' narrative will create a wall of illusion thicker than the new levees. The job of turning our national disaster into sound-bite-size commercials with somber string music will be left to TV. The story will

be sanitized as our nation's politicians congratulate themselves on a job well done. Americans of all stripes will demonstrate saintly concern for one another. It's what we do in a crisis.

This tragedy, however, should make us take an account of ourselves. We ² should not allow the mythic significance of this moment to pass without proper consideration. Let us access the size of this cataclysm in cultural terms, not in dollars and cents or politics. Americans are far less successful at doing that because we have never understood how our core beliefs are manifest in culure—and how culture should guide political and economic realities. That's what the city of New Orleans can now teach the nation again as we are all forced by circumstance to literally come closer to one another. I say teach us again, because New Orleans is a true American melting pot: the soul of America. A place freer than the rest of the country, where elegance met an indefinable wildness to encourage the flowering of creative intelligence. Whites, Creoles and Negroes were strained, steamed, and stewed in a thick, sticky, below-sea-level bowl of musky gumbo. These people produced an original cuisine, an original architecture, vibrant communal ceremonies and an original art form: jazz.

Their music exploded irrepressibly from the forced integration of these ³ castes to sweep the world as the definitive American art form. New Orleans, the Crescent City, the Big Easy—home of Mardi Gras, the second-line parade, the po'boy sandwich, the shotgun house—is so many people's favorite city. But not favorite enough to embrace the integrated superiority of its culture as a national objective. Not favorite enough to digest the gift of supersized soul internationally embodied by the great Louis Armstrong. Over time, New Orleans became known as the national center for frat-party-type decadence and (yeah, boy) great food. The genuine greatness of Armstrong is reduced to his good nature; his artistic triumphs are unknown to all but a handful. So it's time to consider, as we rebuild this great American city, exactly what this bayou metropolis symbolizes for the U.S.

New Orleans has a habit of tweaking the national consciousness at pivotal ⁴ times. The last foreign invasion on U.S. soil was repelled in the Crescent City in 1815. The Union had an important early victory over the South with the capture of the Big Easy in 1862. Homer Plessy, a black New Orleanian, fought for racial equality in 1896, although it took our Supreme Court 58 years to agree with him and, with *Brown v. Board of Education,* to declare segregation unequal. Martin Luther King's Southern Christian Leadership Conference was formally organized in New Orleans in 1957. The problem is that we, all us Americans, have a tendency to rise in that moment of need, but when that moment passes, we fall back again.

The images of a ruined city make it clear that we need to rebuild New ⁵ Orleans. The images of people stranded, in shock, indicate that we need to rebuild a community. The images of all sorts of Americans aiding these victims speak of the size of our hearts. But this time we need to look a little deeper. Let's use the resurrection of the city to reacquaint the country with the gift of New Orleans: a multicultural community invigorated by the arts. Forget about tolerance. What about embracing. This tragedy implores us to re-examine the soul of America. Our democracy from its very beginnings has been challenged by the shackles of slavery. The parade of black folks across our TV screens asking, as if ghosts, "Have you seen my father, mother, sister, brother?" reconnects us all to the still unfulfilled goals of the Reconstruction era. We always back away from fixing our nation's racial problems. Not fixing the city's levees before Katrina struck will now cost us untold billions. Not resolving the nation's issues of race and class has and will cost us so much more.

QUESTIONS FOR READING

1. What does Marsalis expect to happen after Katrina?

2. What does he want Americans to do?

3. What does New Orleans represent? What did the city produce? What historical contributions did it make?

4. What should we not forget as the crisis recedes? What must we still address in America, in the author's view?

QUESTIONS FOR REASONING AND ANALYSIS

1. What is Marsalis's claim? What evidence does he present?

2. Examine his metaphor in paragraph 2. What makes it effective?

3. How does Marsalis use his expertise and stature to develop and inform his argument?

QUESTIONS FOR REFLECTING AND WRITING

1. Look again at paragraph 1. How has Marsalis been incorrect about New Orleans and the country a year or more after Katrina? Has New Orleans been rebuilt? Have the politicians been able to pat themselves on the back? Should we be optimistic about the mechanics of recovery from Katrina?

2. What about the spiritual "recovery" that Marsalis seeks? Have we sought to resolve "the nation's issues of race and class"? If not, how should we go about doing this? What process would you propose?

3. Should New Orleans be rebuilt? As it was? In some more limited way? (See Anna Quindlen, pages 604–06.) Explain and defend your views.

THE BURSTING POINT | DAVID BROOKS

A columnist for the *New York Times* and a commentator on *The NewsHour with Jim Lehrer*, David Brooks has appeared in many newspapers and magazines and has published two books: *Bobos in Paradise: The New Upper Class and How They Got There* (2000) and *On Paradise Drive: How We Live Now (and Always Have) in the Future Tense* (2004). The following *NYT* column was published September 4, 2005.

PREREADING QUESTIONS Did the government manage the Katrina disaster effectively? Is it managing the war against terror effectively?

As Ross Douthat observed on his blog, The American Scene, Katrina was 1 the anti-911.

On Sept. 11, Rudy Giuliani took control. The government response was 2 quick and decisive. The rich and poor suffered alike. Americans had been hit, but felt united and strong. Public confidence in institutions surged.

Last week in New Orleans, by contrast, nobody took control. Authority was 3 diffuse and action was ineffective. The rich escaped while the poor were abandoned. Leaders spun while looters rampaged. Partisans squabbled while the nation was ashamed.

The first rule of the social fabric—that in times of crisis you protect the vul- 4 nerable—was trampled. Leaving the poor in New Orleans was the moral equivalent of leaving the injured on the battlefield. No wonder confidence in civic institutions is plummeting.

And the key fact to understanding why this is such a huge cultural moment 5 is this: Last week's national humiliation comes at the end of a string of confidence-shaking institutional failures that have cumulatively changed the nation's psyche.

Over the past few years, we have seen intelligence failures in the inability 6 to prevent Sept. 11 and find W.M.D.'s in Iraq. We have seen incompetent postwar planning. We have seen the collapse of Enron and corruption scandals on Wall Street. We have seen scandals at our leading magazines and newspapers, steroids in baseball, the horror of Abu Ghraib.

Public confidence has been shaken too by the steady rain of suicide bomb- 7 ings, the grisly horror of Beslan and the world's inability to do anything about rising oil prices.

Each institutional failure and sign of helplessness is another blow to national 8 morale. The sour mood builds on itself, the outraged and defensive reaction to one event serving as the emotional groundwork for the next.

The scrapbook of history accords but a few pages to each decade, and it 9 is already clear that the pages devoted to this one will be grisly. There will be pictures of bodies falling from the twin towers, beheaded kidnapping victims in Iraq and corpses still floating in the waterways of New Orleans five days after the disaster that caused them.

It's already clear this will be known as the grueling decade, the Hobbesian 10 decade. Americans have had to acknowledge dark realities that it is not in our nature to readily acknowledge: the thin veneer of civilization, the elemental violence in human nature, the lurking ferocity of the environment, the limitations on what we can plan and know, the cumbersome reactions of bureaucracies, the uncertain progress good makes over evil.

As a result, it is beginning to feel a bit like the 1970's, another decade in 11 which people lost faith in their institutions and lost a sense of confidence about the future.

"Rats on the West Side, bedbugs uptown/What a mess! This town's in 12 tatters/I've been shattered," Mick Jagger sang in 1978.

13   Midge Decter woke up the morning after the night of looting during the New York blackout of 1977 feeling as if she had "been given a sudden glimpse into the foundations of one's house and seen, with horror, that it was utterly infested and rotting away."

14   Americans in 2005 are not quite in that bad a shape, since the fundamental realities of everyday life are good. The economy and the moral culture are strong. But there is a loss of confidence in institutions. In case after case there has been a failure of administration, of sheer competence. Hence, polls show a widespread feeling the country is headed in the wrong direction.

15   Katrina means that the political culture, already sour and bloody-minded in many quarters, will shift. There will be a reaction. There will be more impatience for something new. There is going to be some sort of big bang as people respond to the cumulative blows of bad events and try to fundamentally change the way things are.

16   Reaganite conservatism was the response to the pessimism and feebleness of the 1970's. Maybe this time there will be a progressive resurgence. Maybe we are entering an age of hardheaded law and order. (Rudy Giuliani, an unlikely G.O.P. nominee a few months ago, could now win in a walk.) Maybe there will be a call for McCainist patriotism and nonpartisan independence. All we can be sure of is that the political culture is about to undergo some big change.

17   We're not really at a tipping point as much as a bursting point. People are mad as hell, unwilling to take it anymore.

QUESTIONS FOR READING

1. How did Katrina differ from 9/11?
2. What "rule of the social fabric" was "trampled" during the Katrina disaster?
3. What events have affected national morale?
4. What will this decade be known as, in Brooks's view? (Who was Hobbes? If you don't know, look him up.) Why?
5. What do polls reveal about American attitudes?
6. What predictions does Brooks make?

QUESTIONS FOR REASONING AND ANALYSIS

1. What is Brooks's claim? Where does he state it?
2. What *type* of argument is this? List the author's evidence in a way that reveals the nature of the argument.
3. Brooks suggests several possible directions for the future, but he does not argue for one precise change. Is his argument weakened by his lack of clear assertion about the future? Explain.

QUESTIONS FOR REFLECTING AND WRITING

1. Brooks's details about present problems are not debatable. Do you agree with his conclusion that Americans in general are "mad as hell"? Why or why not?

2.   Do you agree that there will be some major changes in the political culture? Why or why not?

WHEN GOVERNMENT IS GOOD | E. J. DIONNE, JR.

Holding a doctorate in philosophy from Oxford University, E. J. Dionne is a senior fellow at the Brookings Institution, an adjunct professor at Georgetown University, and a syndicated columnist. Two of his books include *Why Americans Hate Politics* (1991) and *Stand Up Fight Back: Republican Toughs, Democratic Wimps, and the Politics of Revenge* (2004). The following column appeared September 2, 2005.

PREREADING QUESTIONS Do you think government should be "big enough" and "smart enough" to handle an "enormous task"? Does the U.S. government meet your standards?

The sight of rescue workers, the police and the Coast Guard, governors, mayors, and federal officials struggling desperately with the devastation wrought by Hurricane Katrina brings to mind Cohen's Law: "Government is the enemy until you need a friend." 1

Bill Cohen, the former defense secretary, minted the phase nine years ago when he was a Republican senator from Maine. He was speaking then of a plane crash and the public's hankering for more effective safety regulation. Cohen's point was that government-bashing is easy in good times for those doing just fine. But when disaster strikes, many turn around and ask why government didn't do more to prevent a catastrophe—or why it wasn't doing more to relieve its effects. 2

The horrors in New Orleans and on the Mississippi and Alabama coasts are a frightful reminder of the fragility of our personal efforts to build solid and secure lives. 3

The homes people saved for over many years and spent many more years maintaining and improving can be destroyed in an instant. Like so many other Americans, I tried to imagine, after we put our kids to bed, how my wife and I would feel if our own home were inundated with water, permanently ruined. How would we feel if our children found themselves not comfortably asleep but stuck in a rancid stadium with no food or water or plumbing? How would we feel if our neighbors' homes were also wiped out, our streets washed out, our lovely neighborhood rendered uninhabitable? 4

Yes, the communities people built over generations can disappear. Disaster can wipe away intricately constructed social bonds, not just property. Law becomes unenforceable. Some cast aside the social constraints that normally govern their daily lives and take what they can as everything falls apart around them. 5

It turns out that our individual striving goes on within a web of social protections that we take for granted until they disappear. We rely on each other more than we know. The rich, the middle class and the poor—all of us—bank on law, government, collective action and *public* goods more than we ever want to admit. The dreaded word "infrastructure" puts people to sleep at city council meetings and congressional hearings. But when publicly built infrastructure—those 6 levees that held for so many years—breaks down, we realize that the things that seem boring and not worth thinking about are essential.

7   One can hope that our individual generosity will pour forth to our fellow citizens suffering on the Gulf Coast. We can take some solace in the fact that for every looter, there is a sport fisherman who brought a boat up to New Orleans to help in rescue efforts. There is a Red Cross nurse caring for an injured person, a Coast Guard member conducting a daring rescue, a volunteer in a church basement comforting a homeless child.

8   Yet this is a moment in which individual acts of charity and courage, though laudable and absolutely necessary, cannot be enough. It is a time when government is morally obligated to be competent, prepared, innovative, flexible, well-financed—in short, smart enough and, yes, big enough to undertake an enormous task. Not only personal lives but also public things must be put back together.

9   You wonder if this summer, with deteriorating conditions in Iraq and now this terrifying act of God, might make us more serious. This is said not to be a time for politics, and we can surely do without the petty sort. But how we pull out country together, make our government work at a time of great need, and share the sacrifices that war and natural catastrophe have imposed on us— these are inescapably political questions.

10   How can we look Katrina's victims in the eye, say we care and yet not take account of how their needs should affect the other things government does? I'm sorry to raise this, but can it make any sense that one of the early issues the U.S. Senate is scheduled to confront this month is the repeal of the estate tax on large fortunes when we haven't even calculated the costs of Katrina? And why do we keep evading a national debate over who is bearing the burdens of a war that has dragged on far longer than its architects promised?

11   Katrina is the work of nature, but what happens from this point forward is the responsibility of political leadership. Is it possible that in the face of a catastrophe of this magnitude, Washington will not even bother to rethink our nation's priorities?

QUESTIONS FOR READING

1.   What do we need to remember about the things we own?
2.   What are several things that can be lost during a disaster?
3.   What can disasters teach us about our relationships to others and to government?
4.   When do we expect government to be competent?
5.   How should Katrina affect government decisions in Washington?

QUESTIONS FOR REASONING AND ANALYSIS

1.   Who is Dionne's primary audience—whose thinking does he want to influence?
2.   What is the author's claim?
3.   What kind of support (grounds) does Dionne offer? What kind of argument is this, then?

QUESTIONS FOR REFLECTING AND WRITING

1. Did Washington respond competently to Katrina? What grade would you give President Bush? The Congress? Why?

2. Do you agree with Dionne that there is a role for a large, financed, competent government? Why or why not?

3. If you want a government big enough to "do the job," how would you define the job? That is, what do you want government to do? Explain and defend your views.

INTELLIGIBLE DESIGN | KATHA POLLITT

Associate editor at *The Nation*, Katha Pollitt contributes to periodicals, has collected her essays in *Reasonable Creatures: Essays on Women and Feminism* (1994), and has a book of poetry, *Antarctic Traveller* (1982). "Intelligible Design" appeared in *The Nation* on October 3, 2005.

PREREADING QUESTION Given the context of this chapter and her title, what do you expect Pollitt's essay to be about?

Let's say, for example, that the American Empire is just about over. Let's say 1
China and India and other countries as well are set to surge ahead in science and technology, leaving reduced opportunities for upward mobility for the educated, while capital continues to roam the world in search of cheap labor, leaving a shattered working class. Let's say we really are becoming a society of fixed status: the have-nots, an anxious and defensive middle and what George W. Bush famously calls his base, the havemores. What sort of shifts in culture and social structure would prepare us for this looming state of affairs? A resurgence of Christian fundamentalism would fill the bill nicely.

Intellectually, scientifically, even artistically, fundamentalism—biblical 2
liberalism—is a road to nowhere, because it insists on fidelity to revealed truths that are not true. But religious enthusiasm is not all bad. Like love or political activism, it can help troubled souls transform their lives. And if what we're looking at is an America with an ever-larger and boxed-in working class and tighter competition for high-paying jobs among the elite, fundamentalism is exactly the thing to manage decline: It schools the downwardly mobile in making the best of their lot while teaching them to be grateful for the food pantry and day-care over at the church. At the same time, taking advantage of existing currents of anti-intellectualism and school-tax resistance, it removes from the pool of potential scientists and other creative professionals vast numbers of students, who will have had their minds befuddled with creationism and its smooth-talking cousin, intelligent design. Already, according to a study by University of Minnesota biology professor Randy Moore, 40 percent of high school biology teachers don't teach evolution, either because it's socially unacceptable in their communities or because they themselves don't believe in it.

If you think of current behavior as an advance accommodation to what is 3
on the way, some things make sense that otherwise are mysterious. Why, at the

very moment that we are talking obsessively about academic "excellence" and leaving no child behind, are we turning our public schools into factories of rote learning and multiple-choice testing, as if learning how to read and count were some huge accomplishment? Well, if your fate is to be a supermarket checker—and that's a "good job" these days—you won't be needing Roman history or art or calculus. By the same token, cutting state university budgets, burdening students with debt and turning college into a kind of middle-management trade school makes sense, if shrinking opportunities for the professional elite lie ahead. Why create more competition for the graduates of the Ivy League?

4   Another mystery potentially explained: Government's determination to keep working-class women from controlling their fertility. Why does it set a biological trap that dooms them to years of struggle with repercussions for everyone around them, including their children? (It's true that teen pregnancy rates are going down, but they're still astronomical by the standards of any other industrial nation—six times the rate in the Devil's own country, France.) For all our talk about single-parent families—the reason for the terrible poverty of black New Orleans, if we are to believe right-wing columnists Rich Lowry and David Brooks—we act to bring about more of them, and of the most vulnerable, makeshift kind. Somehow single motherhood is supposed to be the fault of the left, but it's the right that has cut public funding for contraception, held up Plan B, restricted abortion, flooded the schools with useless abstinence-only sex ed and now even threatens to bar confidentiality to girls seeking birth control. If you wanted a fatalistic, disorganized working class, a working class too worn out by the day-to-day to do much more than get by, saddling girls with babies is a great idea.

5   Hurricane Katrina was heartbreaking—and it was shocking too. The realities it laid bare—the stark class and race divisions of New Orleans, the callousness and cluelessness and sheer shameless incompetence of the Bush Administration, the long years of ecological mismanagement of the Gulf region—show how far the process of adaptation to decline has already gone. Bush's ownership society turns out to be the on-your-ownership society. The rising tide that was supposed to lift all boats is actually a flood that only those who already have a boat can escape.

6   For decades the right has worked day and night to delegitimize concepts without which no society can thrive, or maybe even survive—the common good, social solidarity, knowledge and expertise, public service. God, abstinence and the market were supposed to solve all our problems. Bad news—climate change, rising poverty, racial and gender disparities, educational failure, the mess in Iraq—was just flimflam from liberals who hate freedom. Is there another world power that lives in such a fantasy world? Now, in old people left to drown in their nursing home beds, in police who reportedly demanded that young women stranded on rooftops bare their breasts in return for rescue, in the contempt for public safety shown by Bush's transformation of FEMA into a pasture for hapless cronies—we can all see what those fantasies obscured. A government that doesn't believe in government was a disaster waiting to happen

That disaster was Katrina, and it's swept us a crucial political moment. It's   7
as if we're being given something people rarely get: a chance to take a hard
look at the future we are preparing for ourselves, an America that has used up
its social and economic and intellectual capital and in which it's every man for
himself, and every woman, too.

Is that the future we want? Because if we let this moment slip away, that is   8
where we are heading.

QUESTIONS FOR READING

1. How does the author describe our class structure?
2. What problems do we have in education, in the author's view?
3. What problem does the government continue to make worse?
4. What problems of society and government were revealed by the Katrina catastrophe?
5. What concepts has the political right worked to devalue? What concepts do they put forward?
6. What does Katrina force us to examine, in the author's view?

QUESTIONS FOR REASONING AND ANALYSIS

1. Pollitt examines many issues, but what is her overriding subject? What is the claim of her argument? (Think about the type of argument this is to help you frame her central assertion.)
2. Examine the essay for examples of the various rhetorical strategies discussed in Chapter 2. Consider especially the various kinds of sentence patterns that she uses and her clever play with words. Where does she use irony? Finally, what is the essay's tone? (Contrast this essay with E. J. Dionne's on style and tone.)
3. Pollitt's and Dionne's styles are quite different, reminding us that there are many ways to write successful arguments. To some extent style is a personal choice, but it must also be shaped by one's intended audience. Who is Pollitt's primary audience? Why are they going to be amused by her approach? Which author might be most successful with the widest audience? Why?

QUESTIONS FOR REFLECTING AND WRITING

1. Pollitt has covered a number of issues that she sees as problems in American society today. Of the issues she includes, which do you think poses the greatest problem for America? Why?
2. Which issue is the least serious problem? Why?
3. Pollitt is not alone in suggesting that the twentieth century was America's century, but the twenty-first will belong to another nation or combination of nations. That is, we are in decline. What evidence do you see that we are in decline? Is there evidence to suggest that we are *not* in decline? How serious a problem do you consider this to be? Explain and defend your views.

THE FIVE STAGES OF CRISIS MANAGEMENT | JACK WELCH

The CEO of General Electric from 1981 to 2001, Jack Welch trimmed the bureaucracy at GE, created more informality, fired the weakest managers and rewarded the best, and increased the value of the company manyfold during his tenure at the top. In 1999 *Fortune* magazine named him "Manager of the Century." He is the author of three books and coauthor, with his wife Suzy Welch, of his latest book *Winning* (2005). His essay in response to Katrina appeared in the *Wall Street Journal* on September 14, 2005.

PREREADING QUESTION Before reading, think about Welch's title; what do you think some of the five stages might be?

1   Our last day in Nantucket this summer, we bumped into a crusty old islander we know, a sea-hand who has seen his share of hurricanes. We asked him about the storm bearing down on New Orleans. "Probably just another overhyped Weather Channel event," he mused. We saw him again the next day, a few hours after the storm's landfall, and he repeated his take, this time with relief. We agreed—the pictures on TV weren't that bad.

2   Then, of course, the levees broke and all hell broke loose with them.

3   In the terrible days since then, there has been a hurricane of debate about what went wrong in New Orleans and who is to blame. Mother Nature, perhaps for the first time in the case of a bona fide natural disaster, has been given a pass. Instead, the shouting has been about crisis-management—or the lack thereof. Everyone from President Bush to the police chief in a small parish on the outskirts of the city has been accused of making shockingly bad mistakes and misjudgments. The Katrina crisis, you would think, is unlike any before it.

4   Unfortunately, that's not completely true.

5   Yes, there has never been a natural disaster of Katrina's magnitude in our history. An entire city has been devastated, hundreds of lives lost, and hundreds of thousands of people displaced. In terms of impact, only an extended catastrophe like the Great Depression can compare in scope.

6   And yet, Hurricane Katrina is practically a case study of the five stages people seem to have to go through during severe crisis. Over the past 40 years, I've seen these stages unfold in companies large and small, of every type, in every part of the world, and I went through them myself at my own company more than a few times.

7   New Orleans, of course, is not a company, but like any city, it is an organization. And there can be no denying that New Orleans' crisis is tragic in a way that company crisis are not. But contrary to the sound and fury out there right now, the Katrina crisis follows a well-worn pattern.

8   The first stage of that pattern is *denial*. The problem isn't that bad, the thinking usually goes, it can't be, because bad things don't happen here, to us. The second is *containment*. This is the stage where people, including perfectly capable leaders, try to make the problem disappear by giving it to someone

else to solve. The third stage is *shame-mongering,* in which all parties with a stake in the problem enter into a frantic dance of self-defense, assigning blame and claiming credit. Fourth comes *blood on the floor.* In just about every crisis, a high profile person pays with his job, and sometimes he takes a crowd with him. In the fifth and final stage, *the crisis gets fixed* and, despite prophecies of permanent doom, life goes on, usually for the better.

We are a way off from the fifth stage in New Orleans, but the first four 9 played out like an old movie.

DENIAL

In the days and even hours before the hurricane struck, officials at every 10 level of the government demonstrated a lack of urgency about the storm that seems crazy now. No one operated out of malice—that can be said for certain. But the facts reveal the kinds of paralysis so often brought on by panic and its ironically common side-effect, inertia. The federal government received hourly updates on the storm, but the head of FEMA, the ill-fated Michael Brown, waited 24 hours, by the most generous estimations, before ordering personnel into the area. The state's governor, in her early communications with the president, mainly asked for financial aid for the city's clean-up efforts. On the local level, the mayor let a critical 12 hours elapse before ordering an evacuation of the city.

Denial in the face of disaster is human. It is the main and immediate emo- 11 tion people feel at the receiving end of any really bad news. That doesn't excuse what happened in New Orleans. In fact, one of the marks of good leadership is the ability to dispense with denial quickly and face into hard stuff with eyes open and fists raised. With particularly bad crises facing them, good leaders also define reality, set direction and inspire people to move forward. Just think of Giuliani after 9/11 or Churchill during World War II. Denial doesn't exactly come to mind—a forthright, calm, fierce boldness does.

All that was in short supply during the disaster in New Orleans. But it might 12 be argued that denial in and about New Orleans started long ago. New Orleans was a city with more than 20% living below the poverty line, a homicide rate almost 10 times higher than New York, and an intractable tradition of political corruption.

Why did it take a hurricane to reveal these unacceptable conditions? 13

New Orleans was also well aware that its levee system was inadequate for 14 a major storm and that the economic plight of its citizenry, with their lack of cars and cash, rendered evacuation plans meaningless.

Why did it take a hurricane to prove those points? 15

In both cases, the only answer is denial, that predictable first phase of cri- 16 sis, which in Katrina's case, happened before, during, and after the actual storm.

CONTAINMENT

For this second predictable phase in crisis, Katrina was no exception. 17 In companies, containment usually plays out with leaders trying to keep the "matter" quiet—a total waste of energy, as all problems, and especially messy ones, eventually get out and explode. In Katrina's case, containment came in a related form, buck-passing—pushing responsibility for the disaster from one part of government to another in hopes of making it go away. The city and state screamed for federal help, the feds said they couldn't send in the troops (literally) until the state asked for them, the state said it wouldn't approve the federal relief plan, and round and round went the baton.

18   No layer is a good layer. Bureaucracy, with its pettiness and formalities, slows action and initiative in any situation, business or otherwise. In a crisis like Katrina, it can be deadly. The terrible part is that Katrina might have avoided some of its bureaucratic bumbling if FEMA had not been buried in the Department of Homeland Security. As an independent entity for decades prior, FEMA fared better. But inside Homeland Security, FEMA was a layer down, twisted in and hobbled by government hierarchy. And to make matters worse, its head, Michael Brown, appears to have been an inexperienced political operative—making his appointment an example of bureaucratic inefficiency at its worst.

SHAME-MONGERING

19   This is a period in which all stakeholders fight to get their side of the story told, with themselves as the heroes at the center. Katrina's shame-mongering had blasted into overdrive by Tuesday, about 48 hours after landfall. I would wager that never before has a storm become so politicized. Very quickly, Katrina wasn't a hurricane—it was a test of George Bush's leadership, it was a reflection of race and poverty in America, it was a metaphor for Iraq. The Democrats used the event to define George Bush for their own purposes; the Republicans—after a delay and with markedly less gusto—used it to define them back. The key word here is delay. Because in any crisis, effective leaders get their message out strongly, clearly—and early. George Bush and his team in Washington didn't do that, and they are paying for it.

BLOOD ON THE FLOOR

20   From the moment it became obvious that Katrina was a crisis-management disaster, you knew someone's head was going to roll. That's what usually happens in the fourth stage of crises. People need to feel that someone has paid, and paid dearly, for what went wrong. Michael Brown was the obvious choice—a guy who had few hard credentials in his bag of defenses. And if Katrina is like most crises, his blood won't be the last spilled. In a few weeks, more personnel changes in FEMA and Homeland Security are sure to come, and politicians in New Orleans and Louisiana will be both made and ruined by what they did during the storm.

21   Eventually, all crises go away, and New Orleans' will too. The waters will recede; people will return and rebuild. In a year, the media will report that progress toward normalcy has been made. In three years, the best levees ever constructed will be completed with great fanfare; the Superdome or its re-

placement will have been outfitted to keep thousands of people housed and fed for a month. In five years, the before-and-after photos of New Orleans will boggle the mind.

History shows us that crises almost always seem to give way to something 22 better. Maybe that's because crises reveal how and where the system is broken in ways that make denial no longer feasible. They have a way of forcing real solutions to happen.

Hurricane Katrina has the potential to do that in New Orleans—to compel 23 leaders in government and business to find ways to break the city's cycle of poverty and corruption. The opportunities are huge because the losses were. There is a blank slate for change to begin, and it most likely will. Just watch the entrepreneurs rush in with ideas and energy, revitalizing old and creating new businesses with the help of the money politicians will be outbidding one another to throw at the problem. Just watch the residents of New Orleans flock to the jobs that are created with a new spirit of optimism. Crises like Katrina have a way of galvanizing people toward a better future. That's the fifth and final part of the pattern—the best part.

Now, you may be wondering that if most every crisis follows a pattern, why 24 can't we manage them better, or even prevent them?

In business, we very often do. Over time, organizations may go through 25 several crises, but very rarely do they go through the same type twice. The reason? Companies typically go to extremes after a crisis. They throw up fortresses of rules, controls and procedures to fix what went wrong in the first place. In that way, they build a kind of immunity to the sickness that felled them. It is very unlikely, for instance, that Johnson & Johnson will ever have another product-tampering disaster like Tylenol.

Immunity to crises comes from learning. Crises teach us where the system 26 is broken and how to repair it so it won't break again. Ultimately, learning is why disasters, in business and in nature, have the potential to make the organizations that survive them so much stronger in the long run. And learning will reveal the crisis management of Katrina for what it was—an age-old pattern meant to be broken.

QUESTIONS FOR READING

1. What is Welch's subject? (Don't write "Katrina"; be more precise.)
2. What are the five stages of response to a crisis?
3. How do leaders get past the denial stage?
4. What are other marks of denial in New Orleans before Katrina?
5. What did the containment stage reveal about FEMA and Homeland Security?
6. What did the shame-mongering stage keep Bush from doing?
7. What are Welch's predictions for the outcome of the Katrina disaster?

QUESTIONS FOR REASONING AND ANALYSIS

1. What is Welch's claim?

2. What is the author's attitude toward bureaucracy? Is it reasonable, in your view, to treat business and government bureaucracies as basically the same? Why or why not?

3. What is the essay's tone? How does it contribute to Welch's argument?

4. Examine Welch's predictions. Has he been on target?

QUESTIONS FOR REFLECTING AND WRITING

1. Evaluate Welch's argument.

2. Should FEMA be a part of Homeland Security or a separate agency? Defend your views.

© Alan Schein/Zefa/Corbis

Read: Do you recognize this building? What might the sculptured figure be holding?

Reason: What *kind* of building would be an appropriate choice for this chapter? Why?

Reflect/Write: Which branch of government has the greatest impact on our daily lives? Why? Defend your choice.

CHAPTER 23

Some Classic Arguments

This final chapter presents six of the many well-known arguments worthy of your study. Your instructor may also recommend Niccolo Machiavelli's *The Prince,* or George Orwell's "Politics and the English Language," or any of the *Federalist Papers.* All of these arguments illustrate excellent persuasive strategies; they also continue to influence the debates of enduring issues. As you read, observe how these authors use language, sentence patterns, metaphors, irony, and other strategies to drive home their claims.

A MODEST PROPOSAL | JONATHAN SWIFT

For Preventing the Children of Poor People in Ireland from Being a Burden to Their Parents or Country, and for Making Them Beneficial to the Public

Born in Dublin, Jonathan Swift (1667–1745) was ordained in the Anglican Church and spent many years as dean of St. Patrick's in Dublin. Swift was also involved in the political and social life of London for some years, and throughout his life he kept busy writing. His most famous imaginative work is *Gulliver's Travels* (1726). Almost as well known is the essay that follows, published in 1729. Here you will find Swift's usual biting satire but also his concern to improve humanity.

PREREADING QUESTIONS Swift was a minister, but he writes this essay as if he were in a different job. What "voice" or persona do you hear? Does Swift agree with the views of this persona?

1   It is a melancholy object to those who walk through this great town[1] or travel in the country, where they see the streets, the roads, and cabin doors crowded with beggars of the female sex, followed by three, four, or six children, all in rags, and importuning every passenger for an alms. These mothers, instead of being able to work for their honest livelihood, are forced to employ all their time in strolling to beg sustenance for their helpless infants, who, as they grow up, either turn thieves for want of work, or leave their dear native country to fight for the pretender[2] in Spain or sell themselves to the Barbados.

2   I think it is agreed by all parties that this prodigious number of children in the arms, or on the backs, or at the heels of their mothers, and frequently of their fathers, is in the present deplorable state of the kingdom a very great additional grievance; and therefore, whoever could find out a fair, cheap, and easy method of making these children sound and useful members of the commonwealth would deserve so well of the public as to have his statue set up for a preserver of the nation.

3   But my intention is very far from being confined to provide only for the children of professed beggars; it is of a much greater extent, and shall take in the whole number of infants at a certain age who are born of parents in effect as little able to support them as those who demand our charity in the streets.

4   As to my own part, having turned my thoughts for many years upon this important subject, and maturely weighed the several schemes of other projectors,[3] I have always found them grossly mistaken in the computation. It is true a child just dropped from its dam may be supported by her milk for a solar year with little other nourishment; at most not above the value of two shillings, which the mother may certainly get, or the value in scraps, by her lawful occupation of begging; and, it is exactly at one year that I propose to provide for them in such a manner as instead of being a charge upon their parents or the parish, or

---

[1] Dublin.—Ed.

[2] James Stuart, claimant to the British throne lost by his father, James II, in 1688.—Ed.

[3] Planners.—Ed.

wanting food and raiment for the rest of their lives, they shall on the contrary contribute to the feeding, and partly to the clothing, of many thousands.

There is likewise another great advantage in my scheme, that it will prevent 5 those voluntary abortions, and that horrid practice of women murdering their bastard children, alas, too frequent among us, sacrificing the poor innocent babes, I doubt, more to avoid the expense than the shame, which would move tears and pity in the most savage and inhuman breast.

The number of souls in this kingdom being usually reckoned one million 6 and a half, of these I calculate there may be about two hundred thousand couples whose wives are breeders; from which number I subtract thirty thousand couples who are able to maintain their own children, although I apprehend there cannot be so many, under the present distress of the kingdom; but this being granted, there will remain a hundred and seventy thousand breeders. I again subtract fifty thousand for those women who miscarry, or whose children die by accident or disease within the year. There only remain a hundred and twenty thousand children of poor parents annually born. The question therefore is, how this number shall be reared and provided for, which, as I have already said, under the present situation of affairs, is utterly impossible by all the methods hereto proposed. For we can neither employ them in handicraft or agriculture; we neither build houses (I mean in the country) nor cultivate land. They can very seldom pick up a livelihood by stealing until they arrive at six years old, except where they are of towardly parts[4]; although I confess they learn the rudiments much earlier, during which time they can, however, be properly looked upon only as probationers, as I have been informed by a principal gentleman in the country of Cavan, who protested to me that he never knew above one or two instances under the age of six, even in the part of the kingdom renowned for the quickest proficiency in that art.

I am assured by our merchants that a boy or girl before twelve years old is 7 no saleable commodity; and even when they come to this age they will not yield above three pounds, or three pounds and a half a crown at most, on the exchange; which cannot turn to account either to the parents or the kingdom, the charge of nutriment and rags having been at least four times that value.

I shall now therefore humbly propose my own thoughts, which I hope will 8 not be liable to the least objection.

I have been assured by a very knowing American of my acquaintance in 9 London that a young healthy child well nursed is at a year old a most delicious, nourishing, and wholesome food, whether stewed, roasted, baked, or boiled; and I make no doubt that it will equally serve in a fricassee or ragout.

I do therefore humbly offer it to public consideration that of the hundred 10 and twenty-thousand children, already computed, twenty thousand may be reserved for breed, whereof only one fourth part to be males, which is more than we allow to sheep, black cattle, or swine; and my reason is that these children are seldom the fruits of marriage, a circumstance not much regarded by our

---

[4] Innate abilities.—Ed.

savages, therefore one male will be sufficient to serve four females. That the remaining hundred thousand may at a year old be offered in sale to the persons of quality and fortune, through the kingdom, always advising the mother to let them suck plentifully in the last month, so as to render them plump and fat for the table. A child will make two dishes at an entertainment for friends; and when the family dines alone, the fore or hind quarter will make a reasonable dish, and seasoned with a little pepper or salt will be very good boiled on the fourth day, especially in winter.

11   I have reckoned upon a medium that a child just born will weigh twelve pounds, and in a solar year if tolerably nursed increaseth to twenty-eight pounds.

12   I grant this food will be somewhat dear, and therefore very proper for landlords, who, as they have already devoured most of the parents, seem to have the best title to the children.

13   Infant's flesh will be in season throughout the year, but more plentiful in March, and a little before and after. For we are told by a grave author, an eminent French physician,[5] that fish being a prolific diet, there are more children born in Roman Catholic countries about nine months after Lent than at any other season; therefore reckoning a year after Lent, the markets will be more gutted than usual, because the number of popish infants is at least three to one in this kingdom; and therefore it will have one other collateral advantage, by lessening the number of Papists among us.

14   I have already computed the charge of nursing a beggar's child (in which list I reckon all cottagers, laborers, and four-fifths of the farmers) to be about two shillings per annum, rags included; and I believe no gentleman would repine to give ten shillings for the carcass of a good fat child, which, as I have said, will make four dishes of excellent nutritive meat, when he hath only some particular friend or his own family to dine with him. Thus the squire will learn to be a good landlord, and grow popular among his tenants; the mother will have eight shillings net profit, and be fit for work until she produces another child.

15   Those who are more thrifty (as I must confess the times require) may flay the carcass; the skin of which artificially dressed will make admirable gloves for ladies and summer boots for fine gentlemen.

16   As to our city of Dublin, shambles[6] may be appointed for this purpose, in the most convenient parts of it, and butchers we may be assured will not be wanting; although I rather recommend buying the children alive, and dressing them hot from the knife as we do roasting pigs.

17   A very worthy person, a true lover of his country, and whose virtues I highly esteem, was lately pleased in discoursing on this matter to offer a refinement upon my scheme. He said that many gentlemen of this kingdom, having of late destroyed their deer, he conceived that the want of venison might be well supplied by the bodies of young lads and maidens, not exceeding fourteen years of age nor under twelve, so great a number of both sexes in every county

---

[5] Francois Rabelais.—Ed.

[6] Butcher shops.—Ed.

being now ready to starve for want of work and service; and these to be disposed of by their parents, if alive, or otherwise by their nearest relations. But with due deference to so excellent a friend and so deserving a patriot, I cannot be altogether in his sentiments. For as to the males, my American acquaintance assured me from frequent experience that their flesh was generally tough and lean, like that of our school-boys, by continual exercise, and their taste disagreeable; and to fatten them would not answer the charge. Then as to the females, it would, I think with humble submission, be a loss to the public, because they soon would become breeders themselves; and besides, it is not probable that some scrupulous people might be apt to censure such a practice (although indeed very unjustly) as a little bordering upon cruelty; which, I confess, hath always been with me the strongest objection against any project, how wellsoever intended.

But in order to justify my friend, he confessed that this expedient was put 18 into his head by the famous Psalmanazar,[7] a native of the island Formosa who came from thence to London above twenty years ago, and in conversation told my friend that in his country when any young person happened to be put to death, the executioner sold the carcass to persons of quality as a prime dainty; and that in his time the body of a plump girl of fifteen, who was crucified for an attempt to poison the emperor, was sold to his Imperial Majesty's prime minister of state, and other great mandarins of the court, in joints from the gibbet, at four hundred crowns. Neither indeed can I deny that if the same use were made of several plump young girls in this town, who without one single groat to their fortunes cannot stir abroad without a chair, and appear at the playhouse and assemblies in foreign fineries which they never will pay for, the kingdom would not be the worse.

Some persons of a desponding spirit are in great concern about that vast 19 number of poor people who are aged, diseased, or maimed, and I have been desired to employ my thoughts what course may be taken to ease the nation of so grievous an incumbrance. But I am not in the least pain upon that matter, because it is very well known that they are every day dying and rotting by cold and famine, and filth and vermin, as fast as can be reasonably expected. And as to the younger laborers, they are now in almost as hopeful a condition. They cannot get work, and consequently pine away for want of nourishment to a degree that if at any time they are accidentally hired to common labor, they have not strength to perform it; and thus the country and themselves are in a fair way of being soon delivered from the evils to come.

I have too long digressed, and therefore shall return to my subject. I think 20 the advantages by the proposal which I have made are obvious and many, as well as of the highest importance.

For, first, as I have already observed, it would greatly lessen the number of 21 Papists, with whom we are yearly overrun, being the principal breeders of the nation as well as our most dangerous enemies; and who stay at home on purpose with a design to deliver the kingdom to the pretender, hoping to take

---

[7] A known imposter who was French, not Formosan as he claimed.—Ed.

their advantage by the absence of so many good Protestants, who have chosen rather to leave their country than stay at home and pay tithes against their conscience to an idolatrous Episcopal curate.

22   Secondly, the poorer tenants will have something valuable of their own, which by law may be made liable to distress,[8] and help their landlord's rent; their corn and cattle being already seized, and money a thing unknown.

23   Thirdly, whereas the maintenance of a hundred thousand children, from two years old upwards, cannot be computed at less than ten shillings a piece per annum, the nation's stock will be thereby increased fifty thousand pounds per annum, besides the profit of a new dish introduced to the tables of all gentlemen of fortune in the kingdom who have any refinement in taste. And the money will circulate among ourselves, the goods being entirely of our own growth and manufacture.

24   Fourthly, the constant breeders, besides the gain of eight shillings sterling per annum by the sale of their children, will be rid of the charge of maintaining them after the first year.

25   Fifthly, this food would likewise bring great custom to taverns, where the vintners will certainly be so prudent as to procure the best receipts for dressing it to perfection, and consequently have their houses frequented by all the fine gentlemen, who justly value themselves upon their knowledge in good eating; and a skillful cook, who understands how to oblige his guests, will contrive to make it as expensive as they please.

26   Sixthly, this would be a great inducement to marriage, which all wise nations have either encouraged by rewards or enforced by laws and penalties. It would increase the care and tenderness of mothers towards their children, when they were sure of a settlement for life to the poor babes, provided in some sort by the public; to their annual profit instead of expense. We should soon see an honest emulation among the married women, which of them could bring the fattest child to the market. Men would become as fond of their wives during the time of their pregnancy as they are now of their mares in foal, their cows in calf, or sows when they are ready to farrow; nor offer to beat or kick them (as it is too frequent a practice) for fear of a miscarriage.

27   Many other advantages might be enumerated. For instance, the addition of some thousand carcasses in our exportation of barrelled beef, the propagation of swine's flesh, and improvement in the art of making good bacon, so much wanted among us by the great destruction of pigs, too frequent at our tables, which are no way comparable in taste or magnificence to a well-grown fat, yearling child, which roasted whole will make a considerable figure at a lord mayor's feast or any other public entertainment. But this and many others I omit, being studious of brevity.

28   Supposing that one thousand families in this city would be constant customers for infants' flesh, besides others who might have it at merry meetings, particularly weddings and christenings, I compute that Dublin would take off annually about twenty thousand carcasses, and the rest of the kingdom

---

[8] Can be seized by lenders.—Ed.

(where probably they will be sold somewhat cheaper) the remaining eighty thousand.

I can think of no one objection that will possibly be raised against this pro- 29 posal, unless it should be urged that the number of people will be thereby much lessened in the kingdom. This I freely own, and it was indeed one principal design in offering it to the world. I desire the reader will observe that I calculate my remedy for this one individual kingdom of Ireland and for no other that ever was, is, or I think ever can be upon earth. Therefore let no man talk to me of other expedients: of taxing our absentees at five shillings a pound: of using neither clothes nor household furniture except what is of our own growth and manufacture: of utterly rejecting the materials and instruments that promote foreign luxury: of curing the expensiveness or pride, vanity, idleness, and gaming in our women: of introducing a vein of parsimony, prudence and temperance: of learning to love our country, wherein we differ even from Laplanders and the inhabitants of Topinamboo[9]: of quitting our animosities and factions, nor act any longer like the Jews, who were murdering one another at the very moment their city was taken[10]: of being a little cautious not to sell our country and consciences for nothing: of teaching landlords to have at least one degree of mercy towards their tenants. Lastly, of putting a spirit of honesty, industry, and skill into our shopkeepers; who, if a resolution could now be taken to buy only our native goods, would immediately unite to cheat and exact upon us in the price, the measure, and the goodness, nor could ever yet be brought to make one fair proposal of just dealing, though often and earnestly invited to it.

Therefore I repeat, let no man talk to me of these and the like expedients, 30 till he hath at least a glimpse of hope that there will ever be some hearty and sincere attempt to put them in practice.

But as to myself, having been wearied out for many years with offering 31 vain, idle, visionary thoughts, and at length utterly despairing of success, I fortunately fell upon this proposal, which, as it is wholly new, so it hath something solid and real, of no expense and little trouble, full in our own power, and whereby we can incur no danger in disobliging England. For this kind of commodity will not bear exportation, the flesh being of too tender a consistence to admit a long continuance in salt, although perhaps I could name a country which would be glad to eat up our whole nation without it.

After all, I am not so violently bent upon my own opinion as to reject any 32 offer proposed by wise men, which shall be found equally innocent, cheap, easy, and effectual. But before something of that kind shall be advanced in contradiction to my scheme, and offering a better, I desire the author, or authors, will be pleased maturely to consider two points. First, as things now stand, how they will be able to find food and raiment for a hundred thousand useless mouths and backs. And secondly, there being a round million of creatures in human figure throughout this kingdom, whose whole subsistence put into a

---

[9] An area in Brazil.—Ed.

[10] Some Jews were accused of helping the Romans and were executed during the Roman siege of Jerusalem in 70 A.D.—Ed.

common stock would leave them in debt two million of pounds sterling, adding those who are beggars by profession to the bulk of farmers, cottagers, and laborers, with their wives and children who are beggars, in effect; I desire those politicians who dislike my overture, and may perhaps be so bold to attempt an answer, that they will first ask the parents of these mortals whether they would not at this day think it a great happiness to have been sold for food at a year old in the manner I prescribe, and thereby have avoided such a perpetual scene of misfortunes as they have since gone through by the oppression of landlords, the impossibility of paying rent without money or trade, the want of common sustenance, with neither house nor clothes to cover them from the inclemencies of weather, and the most inevitable prospect of entailing the like or greater miseries upon their breed forever.

32   I profess, in the sincerity of my heart, that I have not the least personal interest in endeavoring to promote this necessary work, having no other motive than the public good of my country, by advancing our trade, providing for infants, relieving the poor, and giving some pleasure to the rich. I have no children by which I can propose to get a single penny, the youngest being nine years old, and my wife past childbearing.

QUESTIONS FOR READING

1. How is the argument organized? What is accomplished in paragraphs 1–7? In paragraphs 8–16? In paragraphs 17–19? In paragraphs 20–28? In paragraphs 29–33?
2. What specific advantages does the writer offer in defense of his proposal?

QUESTIONS FOR REASONING AND ANALYSIS

1. What specific passages and connotative words make us aware that this is a satirical piece using irony as its chief device?
2. After noting Swift's use of irony, what do you conclude to be his purpose in writing?
3. What can you conclude to be some of the problems in eighteenth-century Ireland? Where does Swift offer direct condemnation of existing conditions in Ireland and attitudes of the English toward the Irish?
4. What actual reforms would Swift like to see?

QUESTIONS FOR REFLECTING AND WRITING

1. What are some of the advantages of using irony? What does Swift gain by this approach? What are possible disadvantages in using irony? Reflect on irony as a persuasive strategy.
2. What are some current problems that might be addressed by the use of irony? Make a list. Then select one and think about what "voice" or persona you might use to bring attention to that problem. Plan your argument with irony as a strategy.

CIVIL DISOBEDIENCE | HENRY DAVID THOREAU

Naturalist, essayist, poet, transcendentalist, Thoreau (1817–1862) was a man of wide interests. His two most famous works—*Walden* (1854) and the essay "Civil Disobedience" (delivered as a lecture in 1848 and published in 1849)—have influenced many readers who have shared his search for "higher laws."

PREREADING QUESTION What should be our response to unjust laws?

I heartily accept the motto,—"That government is best which governs least;"[1] and I should like to see it acted up to more rapidly and systematically. Carried out, it finally amounts to this, which also I believe,—"That government is best which governs not at all;" and when men are prepared for it, that will be the kind of government which they will have. Government is at best but an expedient; but most governments are usually, and all governments are sometimes, inexpedient. The objections which have been brought against a standing army, and they are many and weighty, and deserve to prevail, may also at last be brought against a standing government. The standing army is only an arm of the standing government. The government itself, which is only the mode which the people have chosen to execute their will, is equally liable to be abused and perverted before the people can act through it. Witness the present Mexican war,[2] the work of comparatively a few individuals using the standing government as their tool; for, in the outset, the people would not have consented to this measure.

This American government,—what is it but a tradition, though a recent one, endeavoring to transmit itself unimpaired to posterity, but each instant losing some of its integrity? It has not the vitality and force of a single living man; for a single man can bend it to his will. It is a sort of wooden gun to the people themselves; and, if ever they should use it in earnest as a real one against each other, it will surely split. But it is not the less necessary for this; for the people must have some complicated machinery or other, and hear its din, to satisfy that idea of government which they have. Governments show thus how successfully men can be imposed on, even impose on themselves, for their own advantage. It is excellent, we must all allow; yet this government never of itself furthered any enterprise, but by the alacrity with which it got out of its way. *It* does not keep the country free. *It* does not settle the West. *It* does not educate. The character inherent in the American people has done all that has been accomplished; and it would have done somewhat more, if the government had not sometimes got in its way. For government is an expedient by which men would fain succeed in letting one another alone; and, as has been said, when it is most expedient, the governed are most let alone by it. Trade and commerce, if they were not made of India rubber, would never manage to bounce over the obstacles which legislators are continually putting in their way; and, if one were to judge these men wholly by the effects of their actions, and

---

[1] Motto of the monthly journal *United States Monthly Magazine and Democratic Review.*—Ed.

[2] From 1846 to 1848.—Ed.

not partly by their intentions, they would deserve to be classed and punished with those mischievous persons who put obstructions on the railroads.

3   But, to speak practically and as a citizen, unlike those who call themselves no-government men, I ask for, not at once no government, but *at once* a better government. Let every man make known what kind of government would command his respect, and that will be one step toward obtaining it.

4   After all, the practical reason why, when the power is once in the hands of the people, a majority are permitted, and for a long period continue, to rule, is not because they are most likely to be in the right, nor because this seems fairest to the minority, but because they are physically the strongest. But a government in which the majority rule in all cases cannot be based on justice, even as far as men understand it. Can there not be a government in which majorities do not virtually decide right and wrong, but conscience?—in which majorities decide only those questions to which the rule of expediency is applicable? Must the citizen ever for a moment, or in the least degree, resign his conscience to the legislator? Why has every man a conscience, then? I think that we should be men first, and subjects afterward. It is not desirable to cultivate a respect for the law, so much as for the right. The only obligation which I have a right to assume, is to do at any time what I think right. It is truly enough said, that a corporation has no conscience; but a corporation of conscientious men is a corporation *with* a conscience. Law never made men a whit more just; and, by means of their respect for it, even the well-disposed are daily made the agents of injustice. A common and natural result of an undue respect for law is, that you may see a file of soldiers, colonel, captain, corporal, privates, powder-monkeys and all, marching in admirable order over hill and dale to the wars, against their wills, aye, against their common sense and consciences, which makes it very steep marching indeed, and produces a palpitation of the heart. They have no doubt that it is a damnable business in which they are concerned; they are all peaceably inclined. Now, what are they? Men at all? or small moveable forts and magazines, at the service of some unscrupulous man in power? Visit the Navy Yard, and behold a marine, such a man as an American government can make, or such as it can make a man with its black arts, a mere shadow and reminiscence of humanity, a man laid out alive and standing, and already, as one may say, buried under arms with funeral accompaniments, though it may be

> "Not a drum was heard, nor a funeral note,
> As his corse to the ramparts we hurried;
> Not a soldier discharged his farewell shot
> O'er the grave where our hero we buried."[3]

5   The mass of men serve the State thus, not as men mainly, but as machines, with their bodies. They are the standing army, and the militia, jailers, constables, *posse comitatus*, &c. In most cases there is no free exercise whatever of the judgment or of the moral sense; but they put themselves on a level with

---

[3] By Charles Wolfe, 1791–1823.—Ed.

wood and earth and stones; and wooden men can perhaps be manufactured that will serve the purpose as well. Such command no more respect than men of straw, or a lump of dirt. They have the same sort of worth only as horses and dogs. Yet such as these even are commonly esteemed good citizens. Others, as most legislators, politicians, lawyers, ministers, and office-holders, serve the State chiefly with their heads; and, as they rarely make any moral distinctions, they are as likely to serve the devil, without intending it, as God. A very few, as heroes, patriots, martyrs, reformers in the great sense, and *men*, serve the State with their consciences also, and so necessarily resist it for the most part; and they are commonly treated by it as enemies. A wise man will only be useful as a man, and will not submit to be "clay," and "stop a hole to keep the wind away,"[4] but leave that office to his dust at least:—

> "I am too high-born to be propertied,
> To be a secondary at control,
> Or useful serving-man and instrument
> To any sovereign state throughout the world."[5]

He who gives himself entirely to his fellow-men appears to them useless and selfish; but he who gives himself partially to them is pronounced a benefactor and philanthropist. 6

How does it become a man to behave toward this American government to-day? I answer that he cannot without disgrace be associated with it. I cannot for an instant recognize that political organization as *my* government which is the *slave's* government also. 7

All men recognize the right of revolution; that is, the right to refuse allegiance to and to resist the government, when its tyranny or its inefficiency are great and unendurable. But almost all say that such is not the case now. But such was the case, they think, in the Revolution of '75. If one were to tell me that this was a bad government because it taxed certain foreign commodities brought to its ports, it is most probable that I should not make an ado about it, for I can do without them: all machines have their friction; and possibly this does enough good to counterbalance the evil. At any rate, it is a great evil to make a stir about it. But when the friction comes to have its machine, and oppression and robbery are organized, I say, let us not have such a machine any longer. In other words, when a sixth of the population of a nation which has undertaken to be the refuge of liberty are slaves, and a whole country is unjustly overrun and conquered by a foreign army, and subjected to military law, I think that it is not too soon for honest men to rebel and revolutionize. What makes this duty the more urgent is the fact, that the country so overrun is not our own, but ours is the invading army. 8

Paley,[6] a common authority with many on moral questions, in his chapter on the "Duty of Submission to Civil Government," resolves all civil obligation 9

---

[4] Shakespeare, *Hamlet,* V.i. 236–37.—Ed.

[5] Shakespeare, *King John,* V.i.i. 79–82.—Ed.

[6] British philosopher, William Paley.—Ed.

into expediency; and he proceeds to say, "that so long as the interest of the whole society requires it, that is, so long as the established government cannot be resisted or changed without public inconveniency, it is the will of God that the established government be obeyed, and no longer."—"This principle being admitted, the justice of every particular case of resistance is reduced to a computation of the quantity of the danger and grievance on the one side, and of the probability and expense of redressing it on the other." Of this, he says, every man shall judge for himself. But Paley appears never to have contemplated those cases to which the rule of expediency does not apply, in which a people, as well as an individual, must do justice, cost what it may. If I have unjustly wrested a plank from a drowning man, I must restore it to him though I drown myself. This, according to Paley, would be inconvenient. But he that would save his life, in such a case, shall lose it. This people must cease to hold slaves, and to make war on Mexico, though it cost them their existence as a people.

10   In their practice, nations agree with Paley; but does any one think that Massachusetts does exactly what is right at the present crisis?

> "A drab of state, a cloth-o'-silver slut,
> To have her train borne up, and her soul trail in the dirt."[7]

Practically speaking, the opponents to a reform in Massachusetts are not a hundred thousand politicians at the South, but a hundred thousand merchants and farmers here, who are more interested in commerce and agriculture than they are in humanity, and are not prepared to do justice to the slave and to Mexico, *cost what it may.* I quarrel not with far-off foes, but with those who, near at home, co-operate with, and do the bidding of those far away, and without whom the latter would be harmless. We are accustomed to say, that the mass of men are unprepared; but improvement is slow, because the few are not materially wiser or better than the many. It is not so important that many should be as good as you, as that there be some absolute goodness somewhere; for that will leaven the whole lump. There are thousands who are *in opinion* opposed to slavery and to the war, who yet in effect do nothing to put an end to them; who, esteeming themselves children of Washington and Franklin, sit down with their hands in their pockets, and say that they know not what to do, and do nothing; who even postpone the question of freedom to the question of free-trade, and quietly read the prices-current along with the latest advices from Mexico, after dinner, and, it may be, fall asleep over them both. What is the price-current of an honest man and patriot to-day? They hesitate, and they regret, and sometimes they petition; but they do nothing in earnest and with effect. They will wait, well disposed, for others to remedy the evil, that they may no longer have it to regret. At most, they give only a cheap vote, and a feeble countenance and God-speed, to the right, as it goes by them. There are nine hundred and ninety-nine patrons of virtue to one virtuous man; but it is easier to deal with the real possessor of a thing than with the temporary guardian of it.

---

[7] Tourneur, *The Revengers Tragadie,* IV.iv.—Ed.

All voting is a sort of gaming, like chequers or backgammon, with a slight   11
moral tinge to it, a playing with right and wrong, with moral questions; and
betting naturally accompanies it. The character of the voters is not staked. I
cast my vote, perchance, as I think right; but I am not vitally concerned that
that right should prevail. I am willing to leave it to the majority. Its obligation,
therefore, never exceeds that of expediency. Even voting *for the right* is *doing*
nothing for it. It is only expressing to men feebly your desire that it should prevail. A wise man will not leave the right to the mercy of chance, nor wish it to
prevail through the power of the majority. There is but little virtue in the
action of masses of men. When the majority shall at length vote for the abolition of slavery, it will be because they are indifferent to slavery, or because
there is but little slavery left to be abolished by their vote. *They* will then be
the only slaves. Only *his* vote can hasten the abolition of slavery who asserts
his own freedom by his vote.

I hear of a convention to be held at Baltimore, or elsewhere, for the selec-   12
tion of a candidate for the Presidency, made up chiefly of editors, and men who
are politicians by profession; but I think, what is it to any independent, intelligent, and respectable man what decision they may come to, shall we not have
the advantage of his wisdom and honesty, nevertheless? Can we not count
upon some independent votes? Are there not many individuals in the country
who do not attend conventions? But no: I find that the respectable man, so
called, has immediately drifted from his position, and despairs of his country,
when his country has more reason to despair of him. He forthwith adopts one
of the candidates thus selected as the only *available* one, thus proving that he
is himself *available* for any purposes of the demagogue. His vote is of no more
worth than that of any unprincipled foreigner or hireling native, who may have
been bought. Oh for a man who is a *man,* and, as my neighbor says, has a bone
in his back which you cannot pass your hand through! Our statistics are at fault:
the population has been returned too large. How many *men* are there to a
square thousand miles in this country? Hardly one. Does not America offer any
inducement for men to settle here? The American has dwindled into an Odd
Fellow,—one who may be known by the development of his organ of gregari-
ousness, and a manifest lack of intellect and cheerful self-reliance; whose first
and chief concern, on coming into the world, is to see that the alms-houses are
in good repair; and, before yet he has lawfully donned the virile garb, to collect a fund for the support of the widows and orphans that may be; who, in
short, ventures to live only by the aid of the mutual insurance company, which
has promised to bury him decently.

It is not a man's duty, as a matter of course, to devote himself to the erad-   13
ication of any, even the most enormous wrong; he may still properly have other
concerns to engage him; but it is his duty, at least, to wash his hands of it, and,
if he gives it no thought longer, not to give it practically his support. If I devote
myself to other pursuits and contemplations, I must first see, at least, that I do
not pursue them sitting upon another man's shoulders. I must get off him first,
that he may pursue his contemplations too. See what gross inconsistency is
tolerated. I have heard some of my townsmen say, "I should like to have them

order me out to help put down an insurrection of the slaves, or to march to Mexico,—see if I would go;" and yet these very men have each, directly by their allegiance, and so indirectly, at least, by their money, furnished a substitute. The soldier is applauded who refuses to serve in an unjust war by those who do not refuse to sustain the unjust government which makes the war; is applauded by those whose own act and authority he disregards and sets at nought; as if the State were penitent to that degree that it hired one to scourge it while it sinned, but not to that degree that it left off sinning for a moment. Thus, under the name of order and civil government, we are all made at last to pay homage to and support our own meanness. After the first blush of sin, comes its indifference; and from immoral it becomes, as it were, *unmoral*, and not quite unnecessary to that life which we have made.

14   The broadest and most prevalent error requires the most disinterested virtue to sustain it. The slight reproach to which the virtue of patriotism is commonly liable, the noble are most likely to incur. Those who, while they disapprove of the character and measures of a government, yield to it their allegiance and support, are undoubtedly its most conscientious supporters, and so frequently the most serious obstacles to reform. Some are petitioning the State to dissolve the Union, to disregard the requisitions of the President. Why do they not dissolve it themselves,—the union between themselves and the State,—and refuse to pay their quota into its treasury? Do not they stand in the same relation to the State, that the State does to the Union? And have not the same reasons prevented the State from resisting the Union, which have prevented them from resisting the State?

15   How can a man be satisfied to entertain an opinion merely, and enjoy *it*? Is there any enjoyment in it, if his opinion is that he is aggrieved? If you are cheated out of a single dollar by your neighbor, you do not rest satisfied with knowing that you are cheated, or with saying that you are cheated, or even with petitioning him to pay you your due; but you take effectual steps at once to obtain the full amount, and see that you are never cheated again. Action from principle,—the perception and the performance of right,—changes things and relations; it is essentially revolutionary, and does not consist wholly with any thing which was. It not only divides states and churches, it divides families; aye, it divides the *individual,* separating the diabolical in him from the divine.

16   Unjust laws exist: shall we be content to obey them, or shall we endeavor to amend them, and obey them until we have succeeded, or shall we transgress them at once? Men generally, under such a government as this, think that they ought to wait until they have persuaded the majority to alter them. They think that, if they should resist, the remedy would be worse than the evil. But it is the fault of the government itself that the remedy *is* worse than the evil. *It* makes it worse. Why is it not more apt to anticipate and provide for reform? Why does it not cherish its wise minority? Why does it not cry and resist before it is hurt? Why does it not encourage its citizens to be on the alert to point out its faults, and *do* better than it would have them? Why does it always crucify Christ, and excommunicate Copernicus and Luther, and pronounce Washington and Franklin rebels?

One would think, that a deliberate and practical denial of its authority was   17
the only offence never contemplated by government; else, why has it not assigned its definite, its suitable and proportionate penalty? If a man who has no
property refuses but once to earn nine shillings for the State, he is put in prison
for a period unlimited by any law that I know, and determined only by the discretion of those who placed him there; but if he should steal ninety times nine
shillings from the State, he is soon permitted to go at large again.

If the injustice is part of the necessary friction of the machine of govern-   18
ment, let it go, let it go: perchance it will wear smooth,—certainly the machine
will wear out. If the injustice has a spring, or a pulley, or a rope, or a crank, exclusively for itself, then perhaps you may consider whether the remedy will not
be worse than the evil; but if it is of such a nature that it requires you to be the
agent of injustice to another, then, I say, break the law. Let your life be a counter
friction to stop the machine. What I have to do is to see, at any rate, that I do
not lend myself to the wrong which I condemn.

As for adopting the ways which the State has provided for remedying the   19
evil, I know not of such ways. They take too much time, and a man's life will be
gone. I have other affairs to attend to. I came into this world, not chiefly to
make this a good place to live in, but to live in it, be it good or bad. A man
has not every thing to do, but something; and because he cannot do *every
thing,* it is not necessary that he should do *something* wrong. It is not my business to be petitioning the governor or the legislature any more than it is theirs
to petition me; and, if they should not hear my petition, what should I do then?
But in this case the State has provided no way: its very Constitution is the evil.
This may seem to be harsh and stubborn and unconciliatory; but it is to treat
with the utmost kindness and consideration the only spirit that can appreciate
or deserves it. So is all change for the better, like birth and death which con-
vulse the body.

I do not hesitate to say, that those who call themselves abolitionists should   20
at once effectually withdraw their support, both in person and property, from the
government of Massachusetts, and not wait till they constitute a majority of one,
before they suffer the right to prevail through them. I think that it is enough if
they have God on their side, without waiting for that other one. Moreover, any
man more right than his neighbors, constitutes a majority of one already.

I meet this American government, or its representative the State govern-   21
ment, directly, and face to face, once a year, no more, in the person of its tax-
gatherer; this is the only mode in which a man situated as I am necessarily
meets it; and it then says distinctly, Recognize me; and the simplest, the most
effectual, and, in the present posture of affairs, the indispensablest mode of
treating with it on this head, of expressing your little satisfaction with and love
for it, is to deny it then. My civil neighbor, the tax-gatherer, is the very man I
have to deal with,—for it is, after all, with men and not with parchment that I
quarrel,—and he has voluntarily chosen to be an agent of the government.
How shall he ever know well what he is and does as an officer of the government, or as a man, until he is obliged to consider whether he shall treat me, his
neighbor, for whom he has respect, as a neighbor and well-disposed man, or

as a maniac and disturber of the peace, and see if he can get over this obstruction to his neighborliness without a ruder and more impetuous thought or speech corresponding with his action? I know this well, that if one thousand, if one hundred, if ten men whom I could name,—if ten *honest* men only,—aye, if *one* HONEST man, in this State of Massachusetts, *ceasing to hold slaves*, were actually to withdraw from this copartnership, and be locked up in the county jail therefor, it would be the abolition of slavery in America. For it matters not how small the beginning may seem to be: what is once well done is done for ever. But we love better to talk about it: that we say is our mission. Reform keeps many scores of newspapers in its service, but not one man. If my esteemed neighbor, the State's ambassador,[8] who will devote his days to the settlement of the question of human rights in the Council Chamber, instead of being threatened with the prisons of Carolina, were to sit down the prisoner of Massachusetts, that State which is so anxious to foist the sin of slavery upon her sister,—though at present she can discover only an act of inhospitality to be the ground of a quarrel with her,—the Legislature would not wholly waive the subject the following winter.

22   Under a government which imprisons any unjustly, the true place for a just man is also a prison. The proper place to-day, the only place which Massachusetts has provided for her freer and less desponding spirits, is in her prisons, to be put out and locked out of the State by her own act, as they have already put themselves out by their principles. It is there that the fugitive slave, and the Mexican prisoner on parole, and the Indian come to plead the wrongs of his race, should find them; on that separate, but more free and honorable ground, where the State places those who are not *with* her but *against* her,—the only house in a slave-state in which a free man can abide with honor. If any think that their influence would be lost there, and their voices no longer afflict the ear of the State, that they would not be as an enemy within its walls, they do not know by how much truth is stronger than error, nor how much more eloquently and effectively he can combat injustice who has experienced a little in his own person. Cast your whole vote, not a strip of paper merely, but your whole influence. A minority is powerless while it conforms to the majority; it is not even a minority then; but it is irresistible when it clogs by its whole weight. If the alternative is to keep all just men in prison, or give up war and slavery, the State will not hesitate which to choose. If a thousand men were not to pay their tax-bills this year, that would not be a violent and bloody measure, as it would be to pay them, and enable the State to commit violence and shed innocent blood. This is, in fact, the definition of a peaceable revolution, if any such is possible. If the tax-gatherer, or any other public officer, asks me, as one has done, "But what shall I do?" my answer is, "If you really wish to do any thing, resign your office." When the subject has refused allegiance, and the officer has resigned his office, then the revolution is accomplished. But even suppose blood should flow. Is there not a sort of blood shed when the conscience is wounded?

---

[8] Samuel Hoar (1778–1856) went from Concord to the South Carolina legislature to protest treatment of black seamen.

Through this wound a man's real manhood and immortality flow out, and he bleeds to an everlasting death. I see this blood flowing now.

I have contemplated the imprisonment of the offender, rather than the seizure of his goods,—though both will serve the same purpose,—because they who assert the purest right, and consequently are most dangerous to a corrupt State, commonly have not spent much time in accumulating property. To such the State renders comparatively small service, and a slight tax is wont to appear exorbitant, particularly if they are obliged to earn it by special labor with their hands. If there were one who lived wholly without the use of money, the State itself would hesitate to demand it of him. But the rich man—not to make any invidious comparison—is always sold to the institution which makes him rich. Absolutely speaking, the more money, the less virtue; for money comes between a man and his objects, and obtains them for him; and it was certainly no great virtue to obtain it. It puts to rest many questions which he would otherwise be taxed to answer; while the only new question which it puts is the hard but superfluous one, how to spend it. Thus his moral ground is taken from under his feet. The opportunities of living are diminished in proportion as what are called the "means" are increased. The best thing a man can do for his culture when he is rich is to endeavour to carry out those schemes which he entertained when he was poor. Christ answered the Herodians according to their condition. "Show me the tribute-money," said he;—and one took a penny out of his pocket;—If you use money which has the image of Caesar on it, and which he has made current and valuable, that is, *if you are men of the State,* and gladly enjoy the advantages of Caesar's government, then pay him back some of his own when he demands it; "Render therefore to Caesar that which is Caesar's, and to God those things which are God's,"—leaving them no wiser than before as to which was which; for they did not wish to know.

When I converse with the freest of my neighbors, I perceive that, whatever they may say about the magnitude and seriousness of the question, and their regard for the public tranquility, the long and the short of the matter is, that they cannot spare the protection of the existing government, and they dread the consequences of disobedience to it to their property and families. For my own part, I should not like to think that I ever rely on the protection of the State. But, if I deny the authority of the State when it presents its tax-bill, it will soon take and waste all my property, and so harass me and my children without end. This is hard. This makes it impossible for a man to live honestly and at the same time comfortably in outward respects. It will not be worth the while to accumulate property; that would be sure to go again. You must hire or squat somewhere, and raise but a small crop, and eat that soon. You must live within yourself, and depend upon yourself, always tucked up and ready for a start, and not have many affairs. A man may grow rich in Turkey even, if he will be in all respects a good subject of the Turkish government. Confucius said,—"If a State is governed by the principles of reason, poverty and misery are subjects of shame; if a State is not governed by the principles of reason, riches and honors are the subjects of shame." No: until I want the protection of Massachusetts to be extended to me in some distant southern port, where my liberty is endangered, or until I am bent solely on building up an estate at home by peaceful enterprise, I can afford to refuse allegiance to Massachusetts, and her right to my property and life. It costs me less in every sense to incur the penalty of disobedience to the State, than it would to obey. I should feel as if I were worth less in that case.

25   Some years ago, the State met me in behalf of the church, and commanded me to pay a certain sum toward the support of a clergyman whose preaching my father attended, but never I myself. "Pay it," it said, "or be locked up in the jail." I declined to pay. But, unfortunately, another man saw fit to pay it. I did not see why the schoolmaster should be taxed to support the priest, and not the priest the schoolmaster; for I was not the State's schoolmaster, but I supported myself by voluntary subscription. I did not see why the lyceum should not present its tax-bill, and have the State to back its demand, as well as the church. However, at the request of the selectmen, I condescended to make some such statement as this in writing:—"Know all men by these presents, that I, Henry Thoreau, do not wish to be regarded as a member of any incorporated society which I have not joined." This I gave to the town-clerk; and he has it. The State, having thus learned that I did not wish to be regarded as a member of that church, has never made a like demand on me since; though it said that it must adhere to its original presumption that time. If I had known how to name them, I should then have signed off in detail from all the societies which I never signed on to; but I did not know where to find a complete list.

26   I have paid no poll-tax for six years. I was put into a jail once on this account, for one night; and, as I stood considering the walls of solid stone, two or three feet thick, the door of wood and iron, a foot thick, and the iron grating which strained the light, I could not help being struck with the foolishness of that institution which treated me as if I were mere flesh and blood and bones, to be locked up. I wondered that it should have concluded at length that this was the best use it could put me to, and had never thought to avail itself of my services in some way. I saw that, if there was a wall of stone between me and my towns-men, there was a still more difficult one to climb or break through, before they could get to be as free as I was. I did not for a moment feel confined, and the walls seemed a great waste of stone and mortar. I felt as if I alone of all my towns-men had paid my tax. They plainly did not know how to treat me, but behaved like persons who are underbred. In every threat and in every compliment there was a blunder; for they thought that my chief desire was to stand the other side of that stone wall. I could not but smile to see how industriously they locked the door on my meditations, which followed them out again without let or hinderance, and *they* were really all that was dangerous. As they could not reach me, they had resolved to punish my body; just as boys, if they cannot come at some person against whom they have a spite, will abuse his dog. I saw that the State was half-witted, that it was timid as a lone woman with her silver spoons, and that it did not know its friends from its foes, and I lost all my remaining respect for it, and pitied it.

Thus the State never intentionally confronts a man's sense, intellectual or 27 moral, but only his body, his senses. It is not armed with superior wit or honesty, but with superior physical strength. I was not born to be forced. I will breathe after my own fashion. Let us see who is the strongest. What force has a multitude? They only can force me who obey a higher law than I. They force me to become like themselves. I do not hear of *men* being *forced* to live this way or that by masses of men. What sort of life were that to live? When I meet a government which says to me, "Your money or your life," why should I be in haste to give it my money? It may be in a great strait, and not know what to do: I cannot help that. It must help itself; do as I do. It is not worth the while to snivel about it. I am not responsible for the successful working of the machinery of society. I am not the son of the engineer. I perceive that, when an acorn and a chestnut fall side by side, the one does not remain inert to make way for the other, but both obey their own laws, and spring and grow and flourish as best they can, till one, perchance, overshadows and destroys the other. If a plant cannot live according to its nature, it dies; and so a man.

The night in prison was novel and interesting enough. The prisoners in their 28 shirt-sleeves were enjoying a chat and the evening air in the door-way, when I entered. But the jailer said, "Come, boys, it is time to lock up;" and so they dispersed, and I heard the sound of their steps returning into the hollow apartments. My room-mate was introduced to me by the jailer, as "a first-rate fellow and a clever man." When the door was locked, he showed me where to hang my hat, and how he managed matters there. The rooms were whitewashed once a month; and this one, at least, was the whitest, most simply furnished, and probably the neatest apartment in the town. He naturally wanted to know where I came from, and what brought me there; and, when I had told him, I asked him in my turn how he came there, presuming him to be an honest man, of course; and, as the world goes, I believe he was. "Why," said he, "they accuse me of burning a barn; but I never did it." As near as I could discover, he had probably gone to bed in a barn when drunk, and smoked his pipe there; and so a barn was burnt. He had the reputation of being a clever man, had been there some three months waiting for his trial to come on, and would have to wait as much longer; but he was quite domesticated and contented, since he got his board for nothing, and thought that he was well treated.

He occupied one window, and I the other; and I saw, that if one stayed 29 there long, his principal business would be to look out the window. I had soon read all the tracts that were left there, and examined where former prisoners had broken out, and where a grate had been sawed off, and heard the history of the various occupants of that room; for I found that even here there was a history and a gossip which never circulated beyond the walls of the jail. Probably this is the only house in the town where verses are composed, which are afterward printed in a circular form, but not published. I was shown quite a long list of verses which were composed by some young men who had been detected in an attempt to escape, who avenged themselves by singing them.

30   I pumped my fellow-prisoner as dry as I could, for fear I should never see him again; but at length he showed me which was my bed, and left me to blow out the lamp.

31   It was like travelling into a far country, such as I had never expected to behold, to lie there for one night. It seemed to me that I never had heard the town-clock strike before, nor the evening sounds of the village; for we slept with the windows open, which were inside the grating. It was to see my native village in the light of the middle ages, and our Concord was turned into a Rhine stream, and visions of knights and castles passed before me. They were the voices of old burghers that I heard in the streets. I was an involuntary spectator and auditor of whatever was done and said in the kitchen of the adjacent village-inn,—a wholly new and rare experience to me. It was a closer view of my native town. I was fairly inside of it. I never had seen its institutions before. This is one of its peculiar institutions; for it is a shire town. I began to comprehend what its inhabitants were about.

32   In the morning, our breakfasts were put through the hole in the door, in small oblong-square tin pans, made to fit, and holding a pint of chocolate, with brown bread, and an iron spoon. When they called for the vessels again, I was green enough to return what bread I had left; but my comrade seized it, and said that I should lay that up for lunch or dinner. Soon after, he was let out to work at haying in a neighboring field, whither he went every day, and would not be back till noon; so he bade me good-day, saying that he doubted if he should see me again.

33   When I came out of prison,—for some one[9] interfered, and paid the tax,— I did not perceive that great changes had taken place on the common, such as he observed who went in a youth, and emerged a tottering and gray-headed man; and yet a change had to my eyes come over the scene,—the town, and State, and country,—greater than any that mere time could effect. I saw yet more distinctly the State in which I lived. I saw to what extent the people among whom I lived could be trusted as good neighbors and friends; that their friendship was for summer weather only; that they did not greatly purpose to do right; that they were a distinct race from me by their prejudices and superstitions, as the Chinamen and Malays are; that, in their sacrifices to humanity, they ran no risks, not even to their property; that, after all, they were not so noble but they treated the thief as he had treated them, and hoped, by a certain outward observance and a few prayers, and by walking in a particular straight though useless path from time to time, to save their souls. This may be to judge my neighbors harshly; for I believe that most of them are not aware that they have such an institution as the jail in their village.

34   It was formerly the custom in our village, when a poor debtor came out of jail, for his acquaintances to salute him, looking through their fingers, which were crossed to represent the grating of a jail window, "How do ye do?" My neighbors did not thus salute me, but first looked at me, and then at one another, as if I had returned from a long journey. I was put into jail as I was going

---

[9] Probably Maria Thoreau, his aunt.—Ed.

to the shoemaker's to get a shoe which was mended. When I was let out the next morning, I proceeded to finish my errand, and, having put on my mended shoe, joined a huckleberry party, who were impatient to put themselves under my conduct; and in half an hour,—for the horse was soon tackled,[10]—was in the midst of a huckleberry field, on one of our highest hills, two miles off; and then the State was nowhere to be seen.

This is the whole history of "My Prisons."[11]   35

I have never declined paying the highway tax, because I am as desirous of   36
being a good neighbor as I am of being a bad subject; and, as for supporting schools, I am doing my part to educate my fellow-countrymen now. It is for no particular item in the tax-bill that I refuse to pay it. I simply wish to refuse allegiance to the State, to withdraw and stand aloof from it effectually. I do not care to trace the course of my dollar, if I could, till it buys a man, or a musket to shoot one with,—the dollar is innocent,—but I am concerned to trace the effects of my allegiance. In fact, I quietly declare war with the State, after my fashion, though I will still make what use and get what advantage of her I can, as is usual in such cases.

If others pay the tax which is demanded of me, from a sympathy with the   37
State, they do but what they have already done in their own case, or rather they abet injustice to a greater extent than the State requires. If they pay the tax from a mistaken interest in the individual taxed, to save his property or prevent his going to jail, it is because they have not considered wisely how far they let their private feelings interfere with the public good.

This, then, is my position at present. But one cannot be too much on his   38
guard in such a case, lest his action be biassed by obstinacy, or an undue regard for the opinions of men. Let him see that he does only what belongs to himself and to the hour.

I think sometimes, Why, this people mean well; they are only ignorant;   39
they would do better if they knew how: why give your neighbors this pain to treat you as they are not inclined to? But I think, again, this is no reason why I should do as they do, or permit others to suffer much greater pain of a different kind. Again, I sometimes say to myself, When many millions of men, without heat, without ill-will, without personal feeling of any kind, demand of you a few shillings only, without the possibility, such is their constitution, of retracting or altering their present demand, and without the possibility, on your side, of appeal to any other millions, why expose yourself to this overwhelming brute force? You do not resist cold and hunger, the winds and the waves, thus obstinately; you quietly submit to a thousand similar necessities. You do not put your head into the fire. But just in proportion as I regard this as not wholly a brute force, but partly a human force, and consider that I have relations to those millions as to so many millions of men, and not of mere brute or inanimate things, I see that appeal is possible, first and instantaneously, from them to the Maker of them, and, secondly, from them to themselves. But,

---

[10] Harnessed.—Ed.

[11] Reference to memoirs of Italian patriot Silvio Pellico.—Ed.

if I put my head deliberately into the fire, there is no appeal to fire or to the Maker of fire, and I have only myself to blame. If I could convince myself that I have any right to be satisfied with men as they are, and to treat them accordingly, and not according, in some respects, to my requisitions and expectations of what they and I ought to be, then, like a good Mussulman[12] and fatalist, I should endeavor to be satisfied with things as they are, and say it is the will of God. And, above all, there is this difference between resisting this and a purely brute or natural force, that I can resist this with some effect; but I cannot expect, like Orpheus, to change the nature of the rocks and trees and beasts.

40   I do not wish to quarrel with any man or nation. I do not wish to split hairs, to make fine distinctions, or set myself up as better than my neighbors. I seek rather, I may say, even an excuse for conforming to the laws of the land. I am but too ready to conform to them. Indeed I have reason to suspect myself on this head; and each year, as the tax-gatherer comes round, I find myself disposed to review the acts and position of the general and state governments, and the spirit of the people, to discover a pretext for conformity. I believe that the State will soon be able to take all my work of this sort out of my hands, and then I shall be no better a patriot than my fellow-countrymen. Seen from a lower point of view, the Constitution, with all its faults, is very good; the law and the courts are very respectable; even this State and this American government are, in many respects, very admirable and rare things, to be thankful for, such as a great many have described them; but seen from a point of view a little higher, they are what I have described them; seen from a higher still, and the highest, who shall say what they are, or that they are worth looking at or thinking of at all?

41   However, the government does not concern me much, and I shall bestow the fewest possible thoughts on it. It is not many moments that I live under a government, even in this world. If a man is thought-free, fancy-free, imagination-free, that which *is not* never for a long time appearing *to be* to him, unwise rulers or reformers cannot fatally interrupt him.

42   I know that most men think differently from myself; but those whose lives are by profession devoted to the study of these or kindred subjects, content me as little as any. Statesmen and legislators, standing so completely within the institution, never distinctly and nakedly behold it. They speak of moving society, but have no resting-place without it. They may be men of a certain experience and discrimination, and have no doubt invented ingenious and even useful systems, for which we sincerely thank them; but all their wit and usefulness lie within certain not very wide limits. They are wont to forget that the world is not governed by policy and expediency. Webster never goes behind government, and so cannot speak with authority about it. His words are wisdom to those legislators who contemplate no essential reform in the existing government; but for thinkers, and those who legislate for all time, he never once glances at the subject. I know of those whose serene and wise speculations on this theme would soon reveal the limits of his mind's range and hospitality. Yet, compared

---

[12] A Moslem.—Ed.

with the cheap professions of most reformers, and the still cheaper wisdom and eloquence of politicians in general, his are almost the only sensible and valuable words, and we thank Heaven for him. Comparatively, he is always strong, original, and, above all, practical. Still his quality is not wisdom, but prudence. The lawyer's truth is not Truth, but consistency, or a consistent expediency. Truth is always in harmony with herself, and is not concerned chiefly to reveal the justice that may consist with wrong-doing. He well deserves to be called, as he has been called, the Defender of the Constitution. There are really no blows to be given by him but defensive ones. He is not a leader, but a follower. His leaders are the men of '87. "I have never made an effort," he says, "and never propose to make an effort; I have never countenanced an effort, and never mean to countenance an effort, to disturb the arrangement as originally made, by which the various States came into the Union." Still thinking of the sanction which the Constitution gives to slavery, he says, "Because it was a part of the original compact,—let it stand." Notwithstanding his special acuteness and ability, he is unable to take a fact out of its merely political relations, and behold it as it lies absolutely to be disposed of by the intellect,—what, for instance, it behoves a man to do here in America to-day with regard to slavery, but ventures, or is driven, to make some such desperate answer as the following, while professing to speak absolutely, and as a private man,—from which what new and singular code of social duties might be inferred?—"The manner," says he, "in which the government of those States where slavery exists are to regulate it, is for their own consideration, under their responsibility to their constituents, to the general laws of propriety, humanity, and justice, and to God. Associations formed elsewhere, springing from a feeling of humanity, or any other cause, have nothing whatever to do with it. They have never received any encouragement from me, and they never will."[13]

They who know of no purer sources of truth, who have traced up its stream 43
no higher, stand, and wisely stand, by the Bible and the Constitution, and drink at it there with reverence and humility; but they who behold where it comes trickling into this lake or that pool, gird up their loins once more, and continue their pilgrimage toward its fountain-head.

No man with a genius for legislation has appeared in America. They are 44
rare in the history of the world. There are orators, politicians, and eloquent men, by the thousand; but the speaker has not yet opened his mouth to speak, who is capable of settling the much-vexed questions of the day. We love eloquence for its own sake, and not for any truth which it may utter, or any heroism it may inspire. Our legislators have not yet learned the comparative value of free-trade and of freedom, of union, and of rectitude, to a nation. They have no genius or talent for comparatively humble questions of taxation and finance, commerce and manufactures and agriculture. If we were left solely to the wordy wit of legislators in Congress for our guidance, uncorrected by the seasonable experience and the effectual complaints of the people, America would

---

[13] Quotations are from a speech of Webster's in the Senate. Thoreau notes that these quotations were added for the printed version of the essay.—Ed.

not long retain her rank among the nations. For eighteen hundred years, though perchance I have no right to say it, the New Testament, has been written; yet where is the legislator who has wisdom and practical talent enough to avail himself of the light which it sheds on the science of legislation?

45   The authority of government, even such as I am willing to submit to,—for I will cheerfully obey those who know and can do better than I, and in many things even those who neither know nor can do so well,—is still an impure one: to be strictly just, it must have the sanction and consent of the governed. It can have no pure right over my person and property but what I concede to it. The progress from an absolute to a limited monarchy, from a limited monarchy to a democracy, is a progress toward a true respect for the individual. Is a democracy, such as we know it, the last improvement possible in government? Is it not possible to take a step further towards recognizing and organizing the rights of man? There will never be a really free and enlightened State, until the State comes to recognize the individual as a higher and independent power, from which all its own power and authority are derived, and treats him accordingly. I please myself with imagining a State at last which can afford to be just to all men, and to treat the individual with respect as a neighbor; which even would not think it inconsistent with its own repose, if a few were to live aloof from it, not meddling with it, nor embraced by it, who fulfilled all the duties of neighbors and fellow-men. A State which bore this kind of fruit, and suffered it to drop off as fast as it ripened, would prepare the way for a still more perfect and glorious State, which also I have imagined, but not yet anywhere seen.

QUESTIONS FOR READING

1. Thoreau begins by expressing a desire for less government. After stating these views, he calls for what kind of government?

2. What, according to Thoreau, is everyone's obligation? What is not our obligation, with regard to the law or the government?

3. What does Thoreau want Americans of his time to think about their government? What are his two specific complaints about the government in 1848?

4. How did Thoreau feel about his night in jail?

5. Where does he offer a conciliatory passage? What common ground does he find?

6. In paragraph 42, Thoreau asserts that "the lawyer's truth is not Truth." What does he mean by this statement?

QUESTIONS FOR REASONING AND ANALYSIS

1. What is the central claim of Thoreau's argument?

2. Do you agree with Thoreau that you must be responsible for your conscience before being responsible to the government and the law? Why or why not?

3. Do you agree that unjust laws must be disobeyed as the vehicle for change? Why or why not?

QUESTIONS FOR REFLECTING AND WRITING

1.   What is one statement of Thoreau's that has most surprised or interested you? Why did you select that statement?

2.   Would you demonstrate against an unjust law, risking jail time for your cause? Why or why not? Develop an argument in support of or against action of civil disobedience.

DECLARATION OF SENTIMENTS | ELIZABETH CADY STANTON

Elizabeth Cady Stanton (1815–1902) was one of the most important leaders of the women's rights movement. Educated at the Emma Willard Seminary in Troy, New York, Stanton studied law with her father before her marriage. At the Seneca Falls Convention in 1848 (the first women's rights convention), Stanton gave the opening speech and read her "Declaration of Sentiments." She founded and became president of the National Women's Suffrage Association in 1869.

PREREADING QUESTION As you read, think about the similarities and differences between this document and the "Declaration of Independence." What significant differences in wording and content do you find?

When, in the course of human events, it becomes necessary for one por-   1
tion of the family of man to assume among the people of the earth a position different from that which they have hitherto occupied, but one to which the laws of nature and of nature's God entitle them, a decent respect to the opinions of mankind requires that they should declare the causes that impel them to such a course.

We hold these truths to be self-evident: that all men and women are cre-   2
ated equal; that they are endowed by their Creator with certain inalienable rights; that among these are life, liberty, and the pursuit of happiness; that to secure these rights governments are instituted, deriving their just powers from the consent of the governed. Whenever any form of government becomes destructive of these ends, it is the right of those who suffer from it to refuse allegiance to it, and to insist upon the institution of a new government, laying its foundation on such principles, and organizing its powers in such form, as to them shall seem most likely to effect their safety and happiness. Prudence, indeed, will dictate that governments long established should not be changed for light and transient causes; and accordingly all experience hath shown that mankind are more disposed to suffer, while evils are sufferable, than to right themselves by abolishing the forms to which they were accustomed. But when a long train of abuses and usurpations, pursuing invariably the same object evinces a design to reduce them under absolute despotism, it is their duty to throw off such government, and to provide new guards for their future security. Such has been the patient sufferance of the women under this government, and such is now the necessity which constrains them to demand the equal station to which they are entitled.

3   The history of mankind is a history of repeated injuries and usurpations on the part of man toward woman, having in direct object the establishment of an absolute tyranny over her. To prove this, let facts be submitted to a candid world.

4   He has never permitted her to exercise her inalienable right to the elective franchise.

5   He has compelled her to submit to laws, in the formation of which she had no voice.

6   He has withheld from her rights which are given to the most ignorant and degraded men—both natives and foreigners.

7   Having deprived her of this first right of a citizen, the elective franchise, thereby leaving her without representation in the halls of legislation, he has oppressed her on all sides.

8   He has made her, if married, in the eye of the law, civilly dead.

9   He has taken from her all right in property, even to the wages she earns.

10   He has made her, morally, an irresponsible being, as she can commit many crimes with impunity, provided they be done in the presence of her husband. In the covenant of marriage, she is compelled to promise obedience to her husband, he becoming, to all intents and purposes, her master—the law giving him power to deprive her of her liberty, and to administer chastisement.

11   He has so framed the laws of divorce, as to what shall be the proper causes, and in case of separation, to whom the guardianship of the children shall be given, as to be wholly regardless of the happiness of women—the law, in all cases, going upon a false supposition of the supremacy of man, and giving all power into his hands.

12   After depriving her of all rights as a married woman, if single, and the owner of property, he has taxed her to support a government which recognizes her only when her property can be made profitable to it.

13   He has monopolized nearly all the profitable employments, and from those she is permitted to follow, she receives but a scanty remuneration. He closes against her all the avenues to wealth and distinction which he considers most honorable to himself. As a teacher of theology, medicine, or law, she is not known.

14   He has denied her the facilities for obtaining a thorough education, all colleges being closed against her.

15   He allows her in Church, as well as State, but a subordinate position, claiming Apostolic authority for her exclusion from the ministry, and, with some exceptions, from any public participation in the affairs of the Church.

16   He has created a false public sentiment by giving to the world a different code of morals for men and women, by which moral delinquencies which exclude women from society, are not only tolerated, but deemed of little account in man.

17   He has usurped the prerogative of Jehovah himself, claiming it as his right to assign for her a sphere of action, when that belongs to her conscience and to her God.

He has endeavored, in every way that he could, to destroy her confidence 18
in her own powers, to lessen her self-respect, and to make her willing to lead
a dependent and abject life.

Now in view of this entire disfranchisement of one-half the people of this 19
country, their social and religious degradation—in view of the unjust laws
above mentioned, and because women do feel themselves aggrieved, oppressed, and fraudulently deprived of their most sacred rights, we insist that
they have immediate admission to all the rights and privileges which belong to
them as citizens of the United States.

In entering upon the great work before us, we anticipate no small amount 20
of misconception, misrepresentation, and ridicule; but we shall use every in-
strumentality within our power to effect our object. We shall employ agents,
circulate tracts, petition the State and National legislatures, and endeavor to
enlist the pulpit and the press in our behalf. We hope this Convention will be
followed by a series of Conventions embracing every part of the country.

QUESTIONS FOR READING

1. Summarize the ideas of paragraphs 1 and 2. Be sure to use your own words.
2. What are the first three facts given by Stanton? Why are they presented first?
3. How have women been restricted by law if married or owning property? How have they been restricted in education and work? How have they been restricted psychologically?
4. What, according to Stanton, do women demand? How will they seek their goals?

QUESTIONS FOR REASONING AND ANALYSIS

1. What is Stanton's claim? With what does she charge men?
2. Most—but not all—of Stanton's charges have been redressed, however slowly. Which continue to be legitimate complaints, in whole or in part?

QUESTIONS FOR REFLECTING AND WRITING

1. Do we need a new declaration of sentiments for women? If so, what specific charges would you list? If not, why not?
2. Do we need a declaration of sentiments for other groups—children, minorities, the elderly, animals? If so, what specific charges should be listed? Select one group (that concerns you) and prepare a declaration of sentiments for that group. If you do not think any group needs a declaration, explain why.

FROM "ON LIBERTY" | JOHN STUART MILL

John Stuart Mill (1806–1873) rose to be an important official in the East India
Company. He is now known as one of the world's most influential philosophers. Some
of his important works include: *A System of Logic* (1843), *Principles of Political*

Economy (1848), *The Subjection of Women* (1869), and *On Liberty* (1859), from which the following passages have been taken. In his essay Mill explores the issue of individual freedom in the context of individual good versus social good.

PREREADING QUESTIONS In what two ways can the tyranny of the majority operate in society? Which way may be the most worrisome? Why?

INTRODUCTORY

1   The subject of this Essay is . . . Civil, or Social Liberty: the nature and limits of the power which can be legitimately exercised by society over the individual. A question seldom stated, and hardly ever discussed, in general terms, but which profoundly influences the practical controversies of the age by its latent presence, and is likely soon to make itself recognized as the vital question of the future. It is so far from being new, that, in a certain sense, it has divided mankind, almost from the remotest ages, but in the stage of progress into which the more civilized portions of the species have now entered, it presents itself under new conditions, and requires a different and more fundamental treatment. . . .

2   In political and philosophical theories, as well as in persons, success discloses faults and infirmities which failure might have concealed from observation. The notion, that the people have no need to limit their power over themselves, might seem axiomatic, when popular government was a thing only dreamed about, or read of as having existed at some distant period of the past. Neither was that notion necessarily disturbed by such temporary aberrations as those of the French Revolution, the worst of which were the work of an usurping few, and which, in any case, belonged, not to the permanent working of popular institutions, but to a sudden and convulsive outbreak against monarchical and aristocratic despotism. In time, however, a democratic republic came to occupy a large portion of the earth's surface, and made itself felt as one of the most powerful members of the community of nations; and elective and responsible government became subject to the observations and criticisms which wait upon a great existing fact. It was now perceived that such phrases as "self-government," and "the power of the people over themselves," do not express the true state of the case. The "people" who exercise the power, are not always the same people with those over whom it is exercised, and the "self-government" spoken of, is not the government of each by himself, but of each by all the rest. The will of the people, moreover, practically means, the will of the most numerous or the most active *part* of the people; the majority, or those who succeed in making themselves accepted as the majority: the people, consequently, *may* desire to oppress a part of their number; and precautions are as much needed against this, as against any other abuse of power. The limitation, therefore, of the power of government over individuals, loses none of its importance when the holders of power are regularly accountable to the community, that is, to the strongest party therein. This view of things, recommending itself equally to the intelligence of thinkers and to the inclination of those important classes in European society to whose real or supposed interests democracy is adverse, has

had no difficulty in establishing itself; and in political speculations "the tyranny of the majority" is now generally included among the evils against which society requires to be on its guard.

Like other tyrannies, the tyranny of the majority was at first, and is still vulgarly, held in dread, chiefly as operating through the acts of the public authorities. But reflecting persons perceived that when society is itself the tyrant—society collectively, over the separate individuals who compose it—its means of tyrannizing are not restricted to the acts which it may do by the hands of its political functionaries. Society can and does execute its own mandates: and if it issues wrong mandates instead of right, or any mandates at all in things with which it ought not to meddle, it practises a social tyranny more formidable than many kinds of political oppression, since, though not usually upheld by such extreme penalties, it leaves fewer means of escape, penetrating much more deeply into the details of life, and enslaving the soul itself. Protection, therefore, against the tyranny of the magistrate is not enough; there needs protection also against the tyranny of the prevailing opinion and feeling; against the tendency of society to impose, by other means than civil penalties, its own ideas and practices as rules of conduct on those who dissent from them; to fetter the development, and, if possible, prevent the formation, of any individuality not in harmony with its ways, and compel all characters to fashion themselves upon the model of its own. There is a limit to the legitimate interference of collective opinion with individual independence; and to find that limit, and maintain it against encroachment, is as indispensable to a good condition of human affairs, as protection against political despotism.

But though this proposition is not likely to be contested in general terms, the practical question, where to place the limit—how to make the fitting adjustment between individual independence and social control—is a subject on which nearly everything remains to be done. All that makes existence valuable to any one, depends on the enforcement of restraints upon the actions of other people. Some rules of conduct, therefore, must be imposed, by law in the first place, and by opinion on many things which are not fit subjects for the operation of law. What these rules should be, is the principal question in human affairs; but if we except a few of the most obvious cases, it is one of those which least progress has been made in resolving. No two ages, and scarcely any two countries, have decided it alike; and the decision of one age or country is a wonder to another. Yet the people of any given age and country no more suspect any difficulty in it, than if it were a subject on which mankind had always been agreed. The rules which obtain among themselves appear to them self-evident and self-justifying. This all but universal illusion is one of the examples of the magical influence of custom, which is not only, as the proverb says, a second nature, but is continually mistaken for the first. The effect of custom, in preventing any misgiving respecting the rules of conduct which mankind impose on one another, is all the more complete because the subject is one on which it is not generally considered necessary that reasons should be given, either by one person to others, or by each to himself. People are accustomed to believe and have been encouraged in the belief by some who aspire to the character of philosophers, that their feelings, on subjects of this nature, are better than reasons, and render reasons unnecessary. The practical principle which guides them to their opinions on the regulation of human conduct, is the feeling in each person's mind that everybody should be required to act as he, and those with whom he sympathizes, would like them to act. No one, indeed, acknowledges to himself that his standard of judgment is his own liking; but an opinion on a point of conduct, not supported by reasons, can only count as one person's preference; and if the reasons, when given, are a mere appeal to a similar preference felt by other people, it is still only many people's liking instead of one. To an ordinary man, however, his own preference, thus supported, is not only a perfectly satisfactory reason, but the only one he generally has for any of his notions of morality, taste, or propriety, which are not expressly written in his religious creed; and his chief guide in the interpretation even of that. Men's opinions, accordingly, on what is laudable or blamable, are affected by all the multifarious causes which influence their wishes in regard to the conduct of others, and which are as numerous as those which determine their wishes on any other subject. Sometimes their reason—at other times their prejudices or superstitions: often their social affections, not seldom their anti-social ones, their envy or jealousy, their arrogance or contemptuousness: but most commonly, their desires or fears for themselves—their legitimate or illegitimate self-interest. Wherever there is an ascendant class, a large portion of the morality of the country emanates from its class interests, and its feelings of class superiority. The morality between Spartans and Helots, between planters and negroes, between princes and subjects, between nobles and roturiers, between men and women, has been for the most part the creation of these class interests and feelings: and the sentiments thus generated, react in turn upon the moral feelings of the members of the ascendant class, in their relations among themselves. Where, on the other hand, a class, formerly ascendant, has lost its ascendency, or where its ascendency is unpopular, the prevailing moral sentiments frequently bear the impress of an impatient dislike of superiority. Another grand determining principle of the rules of conduct, both in act and forbearance which have been enforced by law or opinion, has been the servility of mankind towards the supposed preferences or aversions of their temporal masters, or of their gods. This servility though essentially selfish, is not hypocrisy; it gives rise to perfectly genuine sentiments of abhorrence; it made men burn magicians and heretics. Among so many baser influences, the general and obvious interests of society have of course had a share, and a large one, in the direction of the moral sentiments: less, however, as a matter of reason, and on their own account, than as a consequence of the sympathies and antipathies which grew out of them: and sympathies and antipathies which had little or nothing to do with the interests of society, have made themselves felt in the establishment of moralities with quite as great force. . . .

5   The object of this Essay is to assert one very simple principle, as entitled to govern absolutely the dealings of society with the individual in the way of

compulsion and control, whether the means used be physical force in the form of legal penalties, or the moral coercion of public opinion. That principle is, that the sole end for which mankind are warranted, individually or collectively in interfering with the liberty of action of any of their number, is self-protection. That the only purpose for which power can be rightfully exercised over any member of a civilized community, against his will, is to prevent harm to others. His own good, either physical or moral, is not a sufficient warrant. He cannot rightfully be compelled to do or forbear because it will be better for him to do so, because it will make him happier, because, in the opinions of others, to do so would be wise, or even right. These are good reasons for remonstrating with him, or reasoning with him, or persuading him, or entreating him, but not for compelling him, or visiting him with any evil, in case he do otherwise. To justify that, the conduct from which it is desired to deter him must be calculated to produce evil to some one else. The only part of the conduct of any one, for which he is amenable to society, is that which concerns others. In the part which merely concerns himself, his independence is, of right, absolute. Over himself, over his own body and mind, the individual is sovereign.

It is, perhaps, hardly necessary to say that this doctrine is meant to apply 6 only to human beings in the maturity of their faculties. We are not speaking of children, or of young persons below the age which the law may fix as that of manhood or womanhood. Those who are still in a state to require being taken care of by others, must be protected against their own actions as well as against external injury. . . .

It is proper to state that I forego any advantage which could be derived 7 to my argument from the idea of abstract right as a thing independent of utility. I regard utility as the ultimate appeal on all ethical questions; but it must be utility in the largest sense, grounded on the permanent interests of man as a progressive being. Those interests, I contend, authorize the subjection of individual spontaneity to external control, only in respect to those actions of each, which concern the interest of other people. If any one does an act hurtful to others, there is a *prima facie* case for punishing him, by law, or, where legal penalties are not safely applicable, by general disapprobation. There are also many positive acts for the benefit of others, which he may rightfully be compelled to perform; such as, to give evidence in a court of justice; to bear his fair share in the common defence, or in any other joint work necessary to the interest of the society of which he enjoys the protection; and to perform certain acts of individual beneficence, such as saving a fellow-creature's life, or interposing to protect the defenceless against ill-usage, things which whenever it is obviously a man's duty to do, he may rightfully be made responsible to society for not doing. A person may cause evil to others not only by his actions but by his inaction, and in neither case he is justly accountable to them for the injury. The latter case, it is true, requires a much more cautious exercise of compulsion than the former. To make any one answerable for doing evil to others, is the rule; to make him answerable for not preventing evil, is, comparatively speaking, the exception. Yet there are many cases clear enough and grave enough to justify that exception. In all things which regard the external relations of the individual, he is *de jure* amenable to those whose interests are concerned, and if need be, to society as their protector. There are often good reasons for not holding him to the responsibility; but these reasons must arise from the special expediencies of the case: either because it is a kind of case in which he is on the whole likely to act better, when left to his own discretion, than when controlled in any way in which society have it in their power to control him. . . .

8   There is a sphere of action in which society, as distinguished from the individual, has, if any, only an indirect interest; comprehending all that portion of a person's life and conduct which affects only himself, or, if it also affects others, only with their free, voluntary, and undeceived consent and participation. When I say only himself, I mean directly, and in the first instance: for whatever affects himself, may affect others *through* himself; and the objection which may be grounded on this contingency, will receive consideration in the sequel. This, then, is the appropriate region of human liberty. It comprises, first, the inward domain of consciousness; demanding liberty of conscience, in the most comprehensive sense; liberty of thought and feeling; absolute freedom of opinion and sentiment on all subjects, practical or speculative, scientific, moral, or theological. The liberty of expressing and publishing opinions may seem to fall under a different principle, since it belongs to that part of the conduct of an individual which concerns other people; but, being almost of as much importance as the liberty of thought itself, and resting in great part on the same reasons, is practically inseparable from it. Secondly, the principle requires liberty of tastes and pursuits; of framing the plan of our life to suit our own character; of doing as we like, subject to such consequences as may follow; without impediment from our fellow-creatures, so long as what we do does not harm them even though they should think our conduct foolish, perverse, or wrong. Thirdly, from this liberty of each individual, follows the liberty, within the same limits, of combination among individuals; freedom to unite, for any purpose not involving harm to others: the persons combining being supposed to be of full age, and not forced or deceived.

9   No society in which these liberties are not, on the whole, respected, is free, whatever may be its form of government; and none is completely free in which they do not exist absolute and unqualified. The only freedom which deserves the name, is that of pursuing our own good in our own way, so long as we do not attempt to deprive others of theirs, or impede their efforts to obtain it. Each is the proper guardian of his own health, whether bodily, or mental or spiritual. Mankind are greater gainers by suffering each other to live as seems good to themselves, than by compelling each to live as seems good to the rest. . . .

OF THE LIBERTY OF THOUGHT AND DISCUSSION

10   The time, it is to be hoped, is gone by when any defense would be necessary of the "liberty of the press" as one of the securities against corrupt or tyrannical government. No argument, we may suppose, can now be needed against permitting a legislature or an executive, not identified in interest with

the people, to prescribe opinions to them and determine what doctrines or what arguments they shall be allowed to hear. This aspect of the question, besides, has been so often and so triumphantly enforced by preceding writers that it need not be specially insisted on in this place. Though the law of England, on the subject of the press, is as servile to this day as it was in the time of the Tudors, there is little danger of its being actually put in force against political discussion except during some temporary panic when fear of insurrection drives ministers and judges from their propriety; and, speaking generally, it is not, in constitutional countries, to be apprehended that the government, whether completely responsible to the people or not, will often attempt to control the expression of opinion, except when in doing so it makes itself the organ of the general intolerance of the public. Let us suppose, therefore, that the government is entirely at one with the people, and never thinks of exerting any power of coercion unless in agreement with what it conceives to be their voice. But I deny the right of the people to exercise such coercion, either by themselves or by their government. The power itself is illegitimate. The best government has no more title to it than the worst. It is as noxious, or more noxious, when exerted in accordance with public opinion than when in opposition to it. If all mankind minus one were of one opinion, mankind would be no more justified in silencing that one person than he, if he had the power, would be justified in silencing mankind. Were an opinion a personal possession of no value except to the owner, if to be obstructed in the enjoyment of it were simply a private injury, it would make some difference whether the injury was inflicted only on a few persons or on many. But the peculiar evil of silencing the expression of an opinion is that it is robbing the human race, posterity as well as the existing generation—those who dissent from the opinion, still more than those who hold it. If the opinion is right, they are deprived of the opportunity of exchanging error for truth; if wrong, they lose, what is almost as great a benefit, the clearer perception and livelier impression of truth produced by its collision with error. . . .

11   We have now recognized the necessity to the mental well-being of mankind (on which all their other well-being depends) of freedom of opinion, and freedom of the expression of opinion, on four distinct grounds, which we will now briefly recapitulate:

12   First, if any opinion is compelled to silence, that opinion may, for aught we can certainly know, be true. To deny this is to assume our own infallibility.

13   Secondly, though the silenced opinion be an error, it may, and very commonly does, contain a portion of truth; and since the general or prevailing opinion on any subject is rarely or never the whole truth, it is only by the collision of adverse opinions that the remainder of the truth has any chance of being supplied.

14   Thirdly, even if the received opinion be not only true, but the whole truth: unless it is suffered to be, and actually is, vigorously and earnestly contested, it will, by most of those who receive it, be held in the manner of a prejudice, with little comprehension or feeling of its rational grounds. And not only this, but, fourthly, the meaning of the doctrine itself will be in danger of being lost

or enfeebled, and deprived of its vital effect on the character and conduct: the dogma becoming a mere formal profession, inefficacious for good, but cumbering the ground and preventing the growth of any real and heartfelt conviction from reason or personal experience.

QUESTIONS FOR READING

1. Explain the concept of "the tyranny of the majority." Under what kind of government is this potentially an issue?

2. In paragraph 3, Mill writes: "There is a limit to the legitimate interference of collective opinion with individual independence; and to find that limit . . . is as indispensable . . . as protection against political despotism." This statement establishes two principles; what are they? What is asserted and what is implied in the statement?

3. Why, in Mill's view, are limits on individual behavior necessary in a society?

4. In what two ways does a society impose "rules of conduct" on citizens? How difficult do most people think these are? How do most people arrive at their views?

5. What is the one principle that should be the basis for deciding what constraints on individuals are appropriate? What is not a sufficient reason to restrict an individual?

6. What group is excluded from the principle referred to in question 5? Why?

7. What does freedom of the press provide a society?

8. Summarize Mill's four reasons for protecting freedom of expression of opinion.

QUESTIONS FOR REASONING AND ANALYSIS

1. What is Mill's claim?

2. Mill's study of individual liberty is necessarily abstract because his goal is to establish a universal principle. Given his purpose's influence on his writing, has he written persuasively? Why or why not?

3. Mill says that "a person may cause evil to others not only by his actions but by his inaction" and should be held accountable for both kinds of injuries. Apply this idea to a specific case: Should we have a Good Samaritan law that would require motorists to stop to aid a motorist in trouble? (Germany has such a law.) What would Mill say? What would you say? Why?

4. What part of his argument would Mill use to justify prohibiting child pornography? Do you agree with Mill? Why or why not?

QUESTIONS FOR REFLECTING AND WRITING

1. Cigarette advertising is currently banned from television. Should all cigarette advertising be banned? What would Mill say? What do you say? Why?

2. Should individuals be free to act in ways that are "harmful" (in someone else's view) to themselves, so long as they are not harming others? Or should society

seek to legislate on issues of personal morality or personal health? Defend your position.

3.   What one of Mill's reasons for not repressing freedom of expression is, in your view, the most persuasive? Why?

A HANGING | GEORGE ORWELL

George Orwell (1903–1950), the pseudonym of Eric Arthur Blair, was a British essayist and novelist best known for his political satires *Animal Farm* (1945) and *1984* (1949). He is also well known for his essay "Politics and the English Language," the essay that set the standard for the analysis of doublespeak in political language. In the following essay, published in *Shooting an Elephant and Other Essays* (1950), Orwell captures the telling details of a brief scene he witnessed.

PREREADING QUESTIONS   Why might a writer choose to tell the story of a hanging? What kinds of issues might emerge from such a story?

It was in Burma, a sodden morning of the rains. A sickly light, like yellow 1 tinfoil, was slanting over the high walls into the jail yard. We were waiting outside the condemned cells, a row of sheds fronted with double bars, like small animal cages. Each cell measured about ten feet by ten and was quite bare within except for a plank bed and a pot of drinking water. In some of them brown silent men were squatting at the inner bars, with their blankets draped round them. These were the condemned men, due to be hanged within the next week or two.

One prisoner had been brought out of his cell. He was a Hindu, a puny wisp 2 of a man, with a shaven head and vague liquid eyes. He had a thick, sprouting moustache, absurdly too big for his body, rather like a moustache of a comic man on the films. Six tall Indian warders were guarding him and getting him ready for the gallows. Two of them stood by with rifles and fixed bayonets, while the others handcuffed him, passed a chain through his handcuffs and fixed it to their belts, and lashed his arms tight to his sides. They crowded very close about him, with their hands always on him in a careful, caressing grip, as though all the while feeling him to make sure he was there. It was like men handling a fish which is still alive and may jump back into the water. But he stood quite unresisting, yielding his arms limply to the ropes, as though he hardly noticed what was happening.

Eight o'clock struck and a bugle call, desolately thin in the wet air, floated 3 from the distant barracks. The superintendent of the jail, who was standing apart from the rest of us, moodily prodding the gravel with his stick, raised his head at the sound. He was an army doctor, with a grey toothbrush moustache and a gruff voice. "For God's sake hurry up, Francis," he said irritably. "The man ought to have been dead by this time. Aren't you ready yet?"

Francis, the head jailer, a fat Dravidian in a white drill suit and gold spec- 4 tacles, waved his black hand. "Yes sir, yes sir," he bubbled. "All iss satisfactorily prepared. The hangman iss waiting. We shall proceed."

5   "Well, quick march, then. The prisoners can't get their breakfast till this job's over."

6   We set out for the gallows. Two warders marched on either side of the prisoner, with their rifles at the slope; two others marched close against him, gripping him by arm and shoulder, as though at once pushing and supporting him. The rest of us, magistrates and the like, followed behind. Suddenly, when we had gone ten yards, the procession stopped short without any order or warning. A dreadful thing had happened—a dog, come goodness knows whence, had appeared in the yard. It came bounding among us with a loud volley of barks, and leapt round us wagging its whole body, wild with glee at finding so many human beings together. It was a large woolly dog, half Airedale, half pariah. For a moment it pranced round us, and then, before anyone could stop it, it had made a dash for the prisoner, and jumping up tried to lick his face. Everyone stood aghast, too taken aback even to grab at the dog.

7   "Who let that bloody brute in here?" said the superintendent angrily. "Catch it, someone!"

8   A warder, detached from the escort, charged clumsily after the dog, but it danced and gambolled just out of his reach, taking everything as part of the game. A young Eurasian jailer picked up a handful of gravel and tried to stone the dog away, but it dodged the stones and came after us again. Its yaps echoed from the jail walls. The prisoner, in the grasp of the two warders looked on incuriously, as though this was another formality of the hanging. It was several minutes before someone managed to catch the dog. Then we put my handkerchief through its collar and moved off once more, with the dog still straining and whimpering.

9   It was about forty yards to the gallows. I watched the bare brown back of the prisoner marching in front of me. He walked clumsily with his bound arms, but quite steadily, with that bobbing gait of the Indian who never straightens his knees. At each step his muscles slid neatly into place, the lock of hair on his scalp danced up and down, his feet printed themselves on the wet gravel. And once, in spite of the men who gripped him by each shoulder, he stepped slightly aside to avoid a puddle on the path.

10   It is curious, but till that moment I had never realised what it means to destroy a healthy, conscious man. When I saw the prisoner step aside to avoid the puddle, I saw the mystery, the unspeakable wrongness, of cutting a life short when it is in full tide. This man was not dying, he was alive just as we were alive. All the organs of his body were working—bowels digesting food, skin renewing itself, nails growing, tissues forming—all toiling away in solemn foolery. His nails would still be growing when he stood on the drop, when he was falling through the air with a tenth of a second to live. His eyes saw the yellow gravel and the grey walls, and his brain still remembered, foresaw, reasoned—reasoned even about puddles. He and we were a party of men walking together, seeing, hearing, feeling, understanding the same world; and in two minutes, with a sudden snap, one of us would be gone—one mind less, one world less.

11   The gallows stood in a small yard, separate from the main grounds of the prison, and overgrown with tall prickly weeds. It was a brick erection like three

sides of a shed, with planking on top, and above that two beams and a cross-bar with the rope dangling. The hangman, a grey-haired convict in the white uniform of the prison, was waiting beside his machine. He greeted us with a servile crouch as we entered. At a word from Francis the two warders, gripping the prisoner more closely than ever, half led, half pushed him to the gallows and helped him clumsily up the ladder. Then the hangman climbed up and fixed the rope round the prisoner's neck.

We stood waiting, five yards away. The warders had formed in a rough 12 circle round the gallows. And then, when the noose was fixed, the prisoner began crying out on his god. It was a high, reiterated cry of "Ram! Ram! Ram! Ram!," not urgent and fearful like a prayer or a cry for help, but steady, rhythmical, almost like the tolling of a bell. The dog answered the sound with a whine. The hangman, still standing on the gallows, produced a small cotton bag like a flour bag and drew it down over the prisoner's face. But the sound, muffled by the cloth, still persisted, over and over again: "Ram! Ram! Ram! Ram! Ram!"

The hangman climbed down and stood ready, holding the lever. Minutes 13 seemed to pass. The steady, muffled crying from the prisoner went on and on, "Ram! Ram! Ram!" never faltering for an instant. The superintendent, his head on his chest, was slowly poking the ground with his stick; perhaps he was counting the cries, allowing the prisoner a fixed number—fifty, perhaps, or a hundred. Everyone had changed colour. The Indians had gone grey like bad coffee, and one or two of the bayonets were wavering. We looked at the lashed, hooded man on the drop, and listened to his cries—each cry another second of life; the same thought was in all our minds: oh, kill him quickly, get it over, stop that abominable noise!

Suddenly the superintendent made up his mind. Throwing up his head he 14 made a swift motion with his stick. "Chalo!" he shouted almost fiercely.

There was a clanking noise, and then dead silence. The prisoner had vanished, and the rope was twisting on itself. I let go of the dog, and it galloped 15 immediately to the back of the gallows; but when it got there it stopped short, barked, and then retreated into a corner of the yard, where it stood among the weeds, looking timorously out at us. We went round the gallows to inspect the prisoner's body. He was dangling with his toes pointed straight downwards, very slowly revolving, as dead as a stone.

The superintendent reached out with his stick and poked the bare body; it 16 oscillated, slightly. "*He's* all right," said the superintendent. He backed out from under the gallows, and blew out a deep breath. The moody look had gone out of his face quite suddenly. He glanced at his wrist-watch. "Eight minutes past eight. Well, that's all for this morning, thank God."

The warders unfixed bayonets and marched away. The dog, sobered and 17 conscious of having misbehaved itself, slipped after them. We walked out of the gallows yard, past the condemned cells with their waiting prisoners, into the big central yard of the prison. The convicts, under the commend of warders armed with lathis, were already receiving their breakfast. They squatted in long rows, each man holding a tin pannikin, while two warders with buckets marched round ladling out rice; it seemed quite a homely, jolly scene, after the hanging. An enormous relief had come upon us now that the job was done. One felt an impulse to sing, to break into a run, to snigger. All at once everyone began chattering gaily.

18   The Eurasian boy walking beside me nodded towards the way we had come, with a knowing smile: "Do you know, sir, our friend (he meant the dead man), when he heard his appeal had been dismissed, he pissed on the floor of his cell. From fright.—Kindly take one of my cigarettes, sir. Do you not admire my new silver case, sir? From the boxwallah, two rupees eight annas. Classy European style."

19   Several people laughed—at what, nobody seemed certain.

20   Francis was walking by the superintendent, talking garrulously: "Well, sir, all hass passed off with the utmost satisfactoriness. It wass all finished—flick! like that. It iss not always so—oah, no! I have known cases where the doctor wass obliged to go beneath the gallows and pull the prisoner's legs to ensure decease. Most disagreeable!"

21   "Wriggling about, eh? That's bad," said the superintendent.

22   "Ach, sir, it iss worse when they become refractory! One man, I recall, clung to the bars of hiss cage when we went to take him out. You will scarcely credit, sir, that it took six warders to dislodge him, three pulling at each leg. We reasoned with him. 'My dear fellow,' we said, 'think of all the pain and trouble you are causing to me!' But no, he would not listen! Ach, he wass very troublesome!"

23   I found that I was laughing quite loudly. Everyone was laughing. Even the superintendent grinned in a tolerant way. "You'd better all come out and have a drink," he said quite genially. "I've got a bottle of whisky in the car. We could do with it."

24   We went through the big double gates of the prison, into the road. "Pulling at his legs!" exclaimed a Burmese magistrate suddenly, and burst into a loud chuckling. We all began laughing again. At this moment Francis's anecdote seemed extraordinarily funny. We all had a drink together, native and European alike, quite amicably. The dead man was a hundred yards away.

QUESTIONS FOR READING

1. How did Orwell come to witness this hanging? What was his connection?
2. What action by the prisoner made Orwell reflect on what the group was doing?
3. What is the reaction of those watching to the prisoner's cries when he is standing on the gallows?
4. What is the most common reaction as the witnesses leave the gallows and walk back through the main prison yard?

QUESTIONS FOR REASONING AND ANALYSIS

1. What does Orwell accomplish by opening with a description of the row of condemned cells?

2.   Study the description of the prisoner and his guards in paragraph 2. What seems ironic about the picture Orwell draws? How does this help to suggest his attitude toward the hanging?

3.   What is the significance of the dog? Why does Orwell describe this incident as a "dreadful thing" that happened? How is this scene ironic?

4.   Orwell has only one brief passage of general comments; almost all of the essay is narration. What inferences are we encouraged to draw from the details of the event? How would you state Orwell's subject? His thesis? What details from the essay support your assertion of Orwell's thesis?

QUESTIONS FOR REFLECTING AND WRITING

1.   What is your emotional reaction to the essay? Has Orwell moved you in any way? Why or why not?

2.   Is this essay just about capital punishment? What is Orwell suggesting about being human—and inhuman?

3.   Have you had occasion to be distressed or embarrassed by a particular event? If so, what was your reaction? Did you laugh? Or want a drink? Or try to stop what was happening that was upsetting to you? Can you explain why we react to distress by laughter?

I HAVE A DREAM | MARTIN LUTHER KING, JR.

Martin Luther King, Jr. (1929–1968), Baptist minister, civil rights leader dedicated to nonviolence, president of the Southern Christian Leadership Conference, Nobel Peace Prize winner in 1964, was assassinated in 1968. He was an important figure in the August 1963 poor people's march on Washington, where he delivered his speech from the steps of the Lincoln Memorial.

King's plea for equality, echoing the language and cadences of both the Bible and "The Gettysburg Address," has become a model of effective oratory.

PREREADING QUESTION What is the purpose or what are the purposes of King's speech?

Five score years ago, a great American, in whose symbolic shadow we 1 stand, signed the Emancipation Proclamation. This momentous decree came as a great beacon light of hope to millions of Negro slaves who had been seared in the flames of withering injustice. It came as a joyous daybreak to end the long night of captivity.

But one hundred years later, we must face the tragic fact that the Negro is 2 still not free. One hundred years later, the life of the Negro is still sadly crippled by the manacles of segregation and the chains of discrimination. One hundred years later, the Negro lives on a lonely island of poverty in the midst of a vast ocean of material prosperity. One hundred years later, the Negro is still languished in the corners of American society and finds himself an exile in his own land. So we have come here today to dramatize an appalling condition.

3   In a sense we have come to our nation's Capital to cash a check. When the architects of our republic wrote the magnificent words of the Constitution and the Declaration of Independence, they were signing a promissory note to which every American was to fall heir. This note was a promise that all men would be guaranteed the unalienable rights of life, liberty, and the pursuit of happiness.

4   It is obvious today that America has defaulted on this promissory note insofar as her citizens of color are concerned. Instead of honoring this sacred obligation, America has given the Negro people a bad check which has come back marked "insufficient funds." But we refuse to believe that the bank of justice is bankrupt. We refuse to believe that there are insufficient funds in the great vaults of opportunity of this nation. So we have come to cash this check— a check that will give us upon demand the riches of freedom and the security of justice. We have also come to this hallowed spot to remind America of the fierce urgency of *now*. This is no time to engage in the luxury of cooling off or to take the tranquilizing drug of gradualism. *Now* is the time to make real the promises of Democracy. *Now* is the time to rise from the dark and desolate valley of segregation to the sunlit path of racial justice. *Now* is the time to open the doors of opportunity to all of God's children. *Now* is the time to lift our nation from the quicksands of racial injustice to the solid rock of brotherhood.

5   It would be fatal for the nation to overlook the urgency of the moment and to underestimate the determination of the Negro. This sweltering summer of the Negro's legitimate discontent will not pass until there is an invigorating autumn of freedom and equality. 1963 is not an end, but a beginning. Those who hope that the Negro needed to blow off steam and will now be content will have a rude awakening if the nation returns to business as usual. There will be neither rest nor tranquility in America until the Negro is granted his citizenship rights. The whirlwinds of revolt will continue to shake the foundations of our nation until the bright day of justice emerges.

6   But there is something that I must say to my people who stand on the warm threshold which leads into the palace of justice. In the process of gaining our right place we must not be guilty of wrongful deeds. Let us not seek to satisfy our thirst for freedom by drinking from the cup of bitterness and hatred. We must forever conduct our struggle on the high plane of dignity and discipline. We must not allow our creative protest to degenerate into physical violence. Again and again we must rise to the majestic heights of meeting physical force with soul force. The marvelous new militancy which has engulfed the Negro community must not lead us to a distrust of all white people, for many of our white brothers, as evidenced by their presence here today, have come to realize that their destiny is tied up with our destiny and their freedom is inextricably bound to our freedom. We cannot walk alone.

7   And as we walk, we must make the pledge that we shall march ahead. We cannot turn back. There are those who are asking the devotees of civil rights, "When will you be satisfied?" We can never be satisfied as long as the Negro is the victim of the unspeakable horrors of police brutality. We can never be satisfied as long as our bodies, heavy with the fatigue of travel, cannot gain lodg-

ing in the motels of the highways and the hotels of the cities. We cannot be satisfied as long as the Negro's basic mobility is from a smaller ghetto to a larger one. We can never be satisfied as long as a Negro in Mississippi cannot vote and a Negro in New York believes he has nothing for which to vote. No, no, we are not satisfied, and we will not be satisfied until justice rolls down like waters and righteousness like a mighty stream.

I am not unmindful that some of you have come here out of great trials and 8 tribulations. Some of you have come fresh from narrow jail cells. Some of you have come from areas where your quest for freedom left you battered by the storms of persecution and staggered by the winds of police brutality. You have been the veterans of creative suffering. Continue to work with the faith that unearned suffering is redemptive.

Go back to Mississippi, go back to Alabama, go back to South Carolina, go 9 back to Georgia, go back to Louisiana, go back to the slums and ghettos of our northern cities, knowing that somehow this situation can and will be changed. Let us not wallow in the valley of despair.

I say to you today, my friends, that in spite of the difficulties and frustra- 10 tions of the moment I still have a dream. It is a dream deeply rooted in the American dream.

I have a dream that one day this nation will rise up and live out the true 11 meaning of its creed: "We hold these truths to be self-evident; that all men are created equal."

I have a dream that one day on the red hills of Georgia the sons of former 12 slaves and the sons of former slaveowners will be able to sit down together at the table of brotherhood.

I have a dream that one day even the state of Mississippi, a desert state 13 sweltering with the heat of injustice and oppression, will be transformed into an oasis of freedom and justice.

I have a dream that my four little children will one day live in a nation where 14 they will not be judged by the color of their skin but by the content of their character.

I have a dream today. 15

I have a dream that one day the state of Alabama, whose governor's lips 16 are presently dripping with the words of interposition and nullification, will be transformed into a situation where little black boys and black girls will be able to join hands with little white boys and white girls and walk together as sisters and brothers.

I have a dream today. 17

I have a dream that one day every valley shall be exalted, every hill and 18 mountain shall be made low, the rough places will be made plain, and the crooked places will be made straight, and the glory of the Lord shall be revealed, and all flesh shall see it together.

This is our hope. This is the faith with which I return to the South. With this 19 faith we will be able to hew out of the mountain of despair a stone of hope. With this faith we will be able to transform the jangling discords of our nation into a beautiful symphony of brotherhood. With this faith we will be able to

20   work together, to pray together, to struggle together, to go to jail together, to stand up for freedom together, knowing that we will be free one day.

This will be the day when all of God's children will be able to sing with new meaning

My country, 'tis of thee,
Sweet land of liberty,
        Of thee I sing;
Land where my fathers died,
Land of the pilgrims' pride,
From every mountain-side
        Let freedom ring.

21   And if America is to be a great nation this must become true. So let freedom ring from the prodigious hilltops of New Hampshire. Let freedom ring from the mighty mountains of New York. Let freedom ring from the heightening Alleghenies of Pennsylvania!

22   Let freedom ring from the snowcapped Rockies of Colorado!

23   Let freedom ring from the curvaceous peaks of California!

24   But not only that; let freedom ring from Stone Mountain of Georgia!

25   Let freedom ring from Lookout Mountain of Tennessee!

26   Let freedom ring from every hill and molehill of Mississippi. From every mountainside, let freedom ring.

27   When we let freedom ring, when we let it ring from every village and every hamlet, from every state and every city, we will be able to speed up that day when all of God's children, black men and white men, Jews and Gentiles, Protestants and Catholics, will be able to join hands and sing in the words of the old Negro spiritual, "Free at last! thank God almighty, we are free at last!"

QUESTIONS FOR READING

1.   King is directly addressing those participants in the poor people's march who are at the Lincoln Memorial. What other audience did he have as well?

2.   How does the language of the speech reflect King's vocation as a Christian minister? How does it reflect his sense of his place in history?

QUESTIONS FOR REASONING AND ANALYSIS

1.   List all the elements of style discussed in Chapter 2 that King uses. What elements of style dominate?

2.   What stylistic techniques do Lincoln and King share?

3.   Find one sentence that you think is especially effective and explain why you picked it. Is the effect achieved in part by the way the sentence is structured?

4.   Explain each metaphor in paragraph 2.

5.   State the claim of King's argument.

QUESTIONS FOR REFLECTING AND WRITING

1. Which, in your view, is King's most vivid and powerful metaphor? Why do you find it effective?

2. If King were alive today, would he want to see another march on Washington? If so, what would be the theme, or purpose, of the march? If not, why not?

3. Would King have supported the Million Man March? The rally of the Promise Keepers? Why or why not? (If necessary, do some research on these two events.)

Understanding Literature

The same process of reading nonfiction can be used to understand literature—fiction, poetry, and drama. You still need to read what is on the page, looking up unfamiliar words and tracking down references you don't understand. You still need to examine the context, to think about who is writing to whom, under what circumstances, and in what literary format. And, to respond fully to the words, you need to analyze the writer's techniques for developing ideas and expressing attitudes.

Although it seems logical that the reading process should be much the same regardless of the work, not all readers of literature are willing to accept that logic. Some readers want a work of literature to mean whatever they think it means. But what happened to the writer's desire to communicate? If you decide that a Robert Frost poem, for example, should mean whatever you are feeling when you read it, you might as well skip the reading of Frost and just commune with your feelings. Presumably you read Frost to gain some new insight from him, to get beyond just your vision and see something of human experience and emotion from a new vantage point.

Other readers of literature hesitate over the concept of *literary analysis,* or at least over the word *analysis.* These readers complain that analysis will "tear the work apart" and "ruin it." If you are inclined to share this attitude, stop for a minute and think about the last sports event you watched. Do you remember thinking, "Davenport's going to serve wide and come in; she has to against Hingis." Or perhaps a friend explained: "North Carolina is so good at stalling to use up the clock; Duke will have to foul to get the ball and have a chance to tie the game." Both games are being analyzed! And that analysis makes each event more fully experienced by those who understand at least some of the elements of tennis or basketball.

The analogy is clear. You, too, can be a fan of literature. You can enjoy reading and discussing your reading once you learn to use your active reading and analytic skills to open up a poem or story, and once you sharpen your knowledge of literary terms and concepts so that you can "speak the language" of literary criticism with the same confidence with which you discuss the merits of a full court press or a drop volley.

GETTING THE FACTS: ACTIVE READING, SUMMARY, AND PARAPHRASE

Let's begin with the following poem by Paul Dunbar. As you read, make marginal notes, circling a phrase you fancy, putting a question mark next to a difficult line, underscoring words you need to look up. Note, too, your emotional reactions as you read.

PROMISE | PAUL LAWRENCE DUNBAR

Born of former slave parents, Dunbar (1872–1906) was educated in Dayton, Ohio. After a first booklet of poems, *Oak and Ivy,* was printed in 1893, several friends helped Dunbar get a second collection, *Majors and Minors,* published in 1895. A copy was given to author and editor William Dean Howells, who reviewed the book favorably, increasing sales and Dunbar's reputation. This led to a national publisher issuing *Lyrics of Lowly Life* in 1896, the collection that secured Dunbar's fame.

> I grew a rose within a garden fair,
> And, tending it with more than loving care,
> I thought how, with the glory of its bloom,
> I should the darkness of my life illume;
> And, watching, ever smiled to see the lusty bud
> Drink freely in the summer sun to tinct its blood.   5
>
> My rose began to open, and its hue
> Was sweet to me as to it sun and dew;
> I watched it taking on its ruddy flame
> Until the day of perfect blooming came,   10
> Then hasted I with smiles to find it blushing red—
> Too late! Some thoughtless child had plucked my rose and fled!

"Promise" should not have been especially difficult to read, although you may have paused a moment over "illume" before connecting it to "illuminate," and you may have to check the dictionary for a definition of "tint." Test your knowledge of content by listing all the facts of the poem. Pay attention to the poem's basic situation. Who is speaking? What is happening, or what thoughts is the speaker sharing? In this poem, the "I" is not further identified, so you will have to refer to him or her as the "speaker." You should not call the speaker "Dunbar," however, because you do not know if Dunbar ever grew a rose.

In "Promise" the speaker is describing an event that has taken place. The speaker grew a rose, tended to it with care, and watched it begin to bloom; then, when the rose was in full bloom, some child picked the rose and took it away. The situation is fairly simple, isn't it? Too simple, unfortunately, for some readers who decide that the speaker never grew a rose at all. But when anyone writes, "I grew a rose within a garden fair," it is wise to assume that the writer means just that. People do grow roses, most often in gardens, and then the gardens are made "fair" or beautiful by the flowers growing there. Read first for the facts; try not to jump too quickly to broad generalizations.

As with nonfiction, one of the best ways to make certain you have understood a literary work is to write a summary or paraphrase. Since a summary condenses, you are most likely to write a summary of a story, novel, or play, whereas a paraphrase is usually reserved for poems or complex short passages. When you paraphrase a difficult poem, you are likely to end up with more words than in the original because your purpose is to turn cryptic lines into more ordinary sentences with normal word order. For example, Dunbar's "Then hasted I with smiles" can be paraphrased to read: "Then, full of smiles, I hurried."

When summarizing a literary work, remember to use your own words, draw no conclusions, giving only the facts, but focus your summary on the key events in the story. (Of course the selecting you do to write a summary represents preliminary analysis; you are making some choices about what is important in the work. The "steps" of observation, analysis, and interpretation do overlap.) Read the following short story by Langston Hughes and then write your own summary. Finally, compare yours to the summary that follows the story.

EARLY AUTUMN | LANGSTON HUGHES

Like many American writers, Langston Hughes (1902–1967) moved from the Middle West to New York City, lived and worked in France, and then returned to the United States to a career in writing. He was a journalist, fiction writer, and poet, the author of more than sixty books. The success of his novel *Not Without Laughter* (1930) secured his reputation and enabled him to become the first black American to support himself as a professional writer. Known as "the bard of Harlem," Hughes was an important public figure and voice for black writers. "Early Autumn" is reprinted from the collection *Something in Common* (1963).

When Bill was very young, they had been in love. Many nights they had 1 spent walking, talking together. Then something not very important had come between them, and they didn't speak. Impulsively, she had married a man she thought she loved. Bill went away, bitter about women.

2   Yesterday, walking across Washington Square, she saw him for the first time in years.

3   "Bill Walker," she said.

4   He stopped. At first he did not recognize her, to him she looked so old.

5   "Mary! Where did you come from?"

6   Unconsciously, she lifted her face as though wanting a kiss, but he held out his hand. She took it.

7   "I live in New York now," she said.

8   "Oh"—smiling politely. Then a little frown came quickly between his eyes.

9   "Always wondered what happened to you, Bill."

10   "I'm a lawyer. Nice firm, way downtown."

11   "Married yet?"

12   "Sure. Two kids."

13   "Oh," she said.

14   A great many people went past them through the park. People they didn't know. It was late afternoon. Nearly sunset. Cold.

15   "And your husband?" he asked her.

16   "We have three children. I work in the bursar's office at Columbia."

17   "You're looking very . . ." (he wanted to say *old*) ". . . well," he said.

18   She understood. Under the trees in Washington Square, she found herself desperately reaching back into the past. She had been older than he then in Ohio. Now she was not young at all. Bill was still young.

19   "We live on Central Park West," she said. "Come and see us sometime."

20   "Sure," he replied. "You and your husband must have dinner with my family some night. Any night. Lucille and I'd love to have you."

21   The leaves fell slowly from the trees in the Square. Fell without wind. Autumn dusk. She felt a little sick.

22   "We'd love it," she answered.

23   "You ought to see my kids." He grinned.

24   Suddenly the lights came on up the whole length of Fifth Avenue, chains of misty brilliance in the blue air.

25   "There's my bus," she said.

26   He held out his hand. "Good-by."

27   "When . . ." she wanted to say, but the bus was ready to pull off. The lights on the avenue blurred, twinkled, blurred. And she was afraid to open her mouth as she entered the bus. Afraid it would be impossible to utter a word.

28   Suddenly she shrieked very loudly, "Good-by!" But the bus door had closed.

29   The bus started. People came between them outside, people crossing the street, people they didn't know. Space and people. She lost sight of Bill. Then she remembered she had forgotten to give him her address—or to ask him for his—or tell him that her youngest boy was named Bill, too.

Summary of "Early Autumn"

Langston Hughes's short story "Early Autumn" is about two people, Mary and Bill, who were in love once but broke up and did not speak to each other. Mary married someone else "impulsively" and does not see Bill again until one late afternoon, years later, in New York City's Washington Square. When Mary speaks, Bill does not at first recognize her. They discuss their jobs, their marriages, their children. When Mary invites Bill to visit, he says "Sure" and that she should have dinner with his family sometime. When Mary's bus arrives and she gets on, she has trouble speaking. She realizes that they have not set a date or exchanged addresses. She has also forgotten to tell him that her youngest son is named Bill.

Note that the summary is written in the present tense to recount the events that take place during the time of the story. Brevity is achieved by condensing several lines of dialogue into a statement such as "they discuss their jobs." Notice, too, that the summary is not the same as the original; the emotions of the characters, conveyed through what is said—and not said—are missing.

Now for a paraphrase. Read the following sonnet by Shakespeare, looking up unfamiliar words and making notes. Remember to read to the end of a unit of thought, not just to the end of a line. Some sentences continue through several lines; if you pause before you reach punctuation, you will be confused. Write your own paraphrase, not looking ahead in the text, and then compare yours with the one that follows the poem.

SONNET 116 | WILLIAM SHAKESPEARE

Surely the best-known name in literature, William Shakespeare (1564–1616) is famous as both a dramatist and a poet. Rural Warwickshire and the market town of Stratford-on-Avon, where he grew up, showed him many of the character types who were to enliven his plays, as did the bustling life of a young actor in London. Apparently his sonnets were intended to be circulated only among his friends, but they were published nonetheless in 1609. His thirty-seven plays were first published together in 1623. Shakespeare's 154 sonnets vary, some focusing on separation and world-weariness, others on the endurance of love.

> Let me not to the marriage of true minds
> Admit impediments. Love is not love
> Which alters when it alteration finds,
> Or bends with the remover to remove.
> O, no! it is an ever-fixed mark   5
> That looks on tempests and is never shaken;
> It is the star to every wand'ring bark,
> Whose worth's unknown, although his height be taken.
> Love's not Time's fool, though rosy lips and cheeks
> Within his bending sickle's compass come;   10
> Love alters not with his brief hours and weeks,

But bears it out even to the edge of doom.
  If this be error and upon me proved,
  I never writ, nor no man ever loved.

Paraphrase of "Sonnet 116"

I cannot accept barriers to the union of steadfast spirits. We cannot call love love if it changes because it discovers change or if it disappears during absence. On the contrary, love is a steady guide that, in spite of difficulties, remains unwavering. Love can define the inherent value in all who lack self-knowledge, though superficially they know who they are. Love does not lessen with time, though signs of physical beauty may fade. Love endures, changeless, eternally. If anyone can show me to be wrong in this position, I am no writer and no man can be said to have loved.

We have examined the facts of a literary work, what we can call the internal situation. But, as we noted in Chapter 2, there is also the external situation or context of any piece of writing. For many literary works, the context is not as essential to understanding as it is with nonfiction. You can read "Early Autumn," for instance, without knowing much about Langston Hughes, or the circumstances in which he wrote the story, although such information would enrich your reading experience. There is a body of information, however, that is very important, what we can call the external literary situation. Literary externals are those basic elements of a work that readers should take note of before they begin to read.

> **REMEMBER:** Active reading includes looking over a work first and predicting what will come next. Do not just start reading words without first understanding what kind of work you are about to read.

Let's review some of these essentials.

- First, don't make the mistake of calling every work a "story." When you read—and then later discuss—literature, make clear distinctions among stories, novels, plays, and poems.
- Poems can be further divided into narrative, dramatic, and lyric poems.
- A *narrative poem,* such as Homer's *The Iliad,* tells a story in verse. A *dramatic poem* records the speech of at least one character.
- A poem in which only one figure speaks—but clearly addresses words to someone who is present in a particular situation—is called a *dramatic monologue.*
- *Lyric poems,* Dunbar's "Promise," for example, may place the speaker in a situation or may express a thought or feeling with few, if any, situational details, but lyric poems have in common the convention that we as readers are listening in on someone's thoughts, not listening to words directed to a

second, created figure. These distinctions make us aware of how the words of the poem are coming to us. Are we hearing a storyteller or someone speaking? Or, are we overhearing someone's thoughts?

Lyric poems can be further divided into many subcategories or types. Most instructors will expect you to be able to recognize some of these types. You should be able to distinguish between a poem in *free verse* (no prevailing metrical pattern) and one in *blank verse* (continuous unrhymed lines of iambic pentameter.) (Note: A metrical line will contain a particular number—pentameter is five—of one kind of metrical "foot." The iambic foot consists of one unstressed syllable followed by one stressed syllable.) You should also be able to tell if a poem is written in some type of *stanza* form (repeated units with the same number of lines, same metrical pattern, and same rhyme scheme), or if it is a *sonnet* (always fourteen lines of iambic pentameter with one of two complex rhyme schemes labeled either "English" or "Italian"). You want to make it a habit to observe these external elements before you read. To sharpen your observation, complete the following exercise.

EXERCISE: Observing Literary Types and Using Literary Terms

1. After surveying this appendix, make a list of all the works of literature by primary type: short story, poem, play.

2. For each work on your list, add two additional pieces of information: whether the author is American or British, and in what century the work was written. Why should you be aware of the writer's dates and nationality as you read?

3. Further divide the poems into narrative, dramatic, or lyric, as appropriate.

4. List as many of the details of type or form as you can for each poem. For example, if the poem is written in stanzas, describe the stanza form used: the number of lines, the meter, the rhyme scheme. If the poem is a sonnet, determine the rhyme scheme. (Note: Rhyme scheme is indicated by using letters, assigning "a" to the first sound and using a new letter for each new sound. Thus, if two consecutive lines rhyme, the scheme is *aa, bb, cc, dd,* and so on.)

SEEING CONNECTIONS: ANALYSIS

Although we read first for the facts and an initial emotional response, we do not stop there, because as humans we seek meaning. Surely there is more to "Early Autumn" than the summary suggests; emotionally we know this to be true. As with nonfiction, one of the best places to start analysis is with a work's organization or structure. Lyric poems will be shaped by many of the same structures found in essays: chronological, spatial, general to particular, particular to general, a list of particulars with an unstated general point, and so forth. In

"Promise," Dunbar gives one illustration, recounted chronologically, to make a point that is left unstated. "Sonnet 116" contains a list of characteristics of love underscored in the conclusion by the speaker's conviction that he is right.

Analysis of Narrative Structure

In stories (and plays and narrative poems) we are given a series of events, in time sequence, involving one or more characters. In some stories, episodes are only loosely connected but are unified around a central character (Mark Twain's *Adventures of Huckleberry Finn,* for example). Most stories present events that are at least to some extent related causally; that is, action A by the main character leads to event B, which requires action C by the main character. This kind of plot structure can be diagrammed, as in Figure 1.

Figure 1 introduces some terms and concepts useful in analyzing and discussing narratives. The story's *exposition* refers to the background details needed to get the story started, including the time and place of the story and relationships of the characters. In "Early Autumn" Hughes begins by telling us that the action will take place in lower Manhattan, late in the afternoon, between a man and a woman who had once loved each other. The *complication* refers to an event; something happens to produce tension or conflict. In "Early Autumn" the meeting of Mary and Bill, after many years, could be an occasion for joy but seems to cause a complication instead. Mary expects to be kissed but Bill merely offers his hand; Bill smiles "politely" and then frowns. The meeting becomes a complication for both characters because it generates a *conflict* within each character. Bill's conflict seems the more manageable; he turns on his polite behavior to get through the unexpected encounter. Mary is more upset; seeing Bill makes her feel old, and she is hardly able to speak when she boards the bus. A key question arises: Why is Mary so upset?

Although some stories present one major complication leading to a climactic moment of decision or insight for the main character, many actually repeat the pattern, presenting several complications—each with an attempted resolution that generates yet another complication—until we reach the high point of tension, the *climax.* The climax then generates the story's *resolution* and ending. These terms are useful even though some stories end abruptly without having much resolution. An abbreviated resolution is part of the modern writer's view

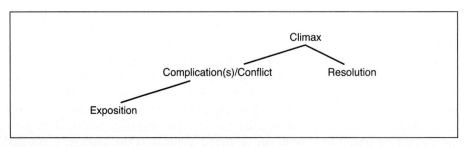

FIGURE 1 Plot Structure

of reality, that life goes on, with problems remaining unresolved. The climax in "Early Autumn" comes when Mary boards her bus and then realizes that she will once again be separated from Bill. This story's climax is muted and merges quickly into the resolution of the last line. The ending offers little genuine resolution; our recognizing this fact helps us better understand the story.

Analysis of Character

An analysis of plot structure has shown that Mary is the more troubled character. You should recognize that Mary is not in conflict *with* Bill but rather is in conflict *over* him, or over her feelings for him, still strong in spite of years of a life without him. Note the close connection between complication (event) and conflict (what the characters are feeling). Fiction requires both plot and character, events and players in those events. In serious literature the greater emphasis is usually on character, on what we learn about human life through the interplay of character and incident.

As we shift attention from the plot of "Early Autumn" to the characters, it helps to consider how writers present character. Writers have several techniques for conveying character:

- Descriptive details. (Bill's polite smile followed by a frown.)
- Dramatic scenes. (Instead of telling us, they show us. Most of "Early Autumn" consists of dialogue between Mary and Bill.)
- Contrast among characters. (We have already observed that Mary and Bill react differently to their encounter.)
- Other elements in the work. (Names can be significant, or characters can become associated with objects, or details of setting can become symbolic.)

Understanding character is always a challenge because we must infer from a few words, gestures, and actions. Looking at all of a writer's options for presenting character will keep us from overlooking important details.

Analysis of Elements of Style and Tone

Important elements in "Early Autumn" include the time of day and the title. How are they connected? What do they suggest about the characters? All the elements, discussed in Chapter 2, that shape a writer's style and create tone can be found in literary works as well and need to be considered as a part of your analysis. Hughes's title is actually a metaphor and, reinforced by the late-in-the-day meeting, suggests that this meeting comes too late for Mary to regain what she has lost—her youth and her youthful love. Shakespeare's "Sonnet 116" develops the speaker's ideas about love through a series of metaphors. The rose in Dunbar's "Promise," is not a metaphor, though, because it is not part of a comparison. Yet, as we read "Promise" we sense that the poem is about something more serious than the nurturing and stealing of one flower, no matter how beautiful. Again, this work's title gives us a clue that the rose stands for something more than itself; it is a symbol. Traditionally the red rose is a symbol of love. To tie the poem together, we will have to see how the title, the usual symbolic value of the rose, and the specifics of the poem connect.

DRAWING CONCLUSIONS: INTERPRETATION

We have studied the facts of several works and analyzed their structures and other key elements. To reach some conclusions from this information and shape it into an organized form is to offer an interpretation of the work. At this point, readers can be expected to disagree somewhat, but if we have all read carefully and applied our knowledge of literature, differences should, most of the time, be ones of focus or emphasis. Presumably no one is prepared to argue that "Promise" is about pink elephants or "Early Autumn" about the Queen of England, because neither work contains any facts to support those conclusions.

What conclusions can we reach about "Promise"? A beautiful flower has been nurtured into bloom by a speaker who expects it to brighten his or her life. The title lets us know that the rose represents great promise. Has a rival stolen the speaker's loved one, represented symbolically by the rose? A thoughtless child would not be an appropriate rival for an adult speaker, so in the context of this poem, the rose represents, more generally, something that the speaker cherishes in anticipation of the pleasure it will bring.

In "Early Autumn" the pain that Mary feels when she meets Bill in Washington Square comes from her awareness that she still loves Bill and that he is lost to her. Bill has gone on to a happy life in which she has no part. The lights blur because Mary's eyes are filled with tears as the conversation makes her aware that Bill has given her little thought over the years, whereas Mary, to keep some part of Bill in her life, has named her youngest son Bill. The details of the story, an analysis of plot and character conflict, and the story's metaphors support these conclusions.

WRITING ABOUT LITERATURE

When you are assigned a literary essay, you will usually be asked to write either an explication or an analysis. An *explication* presents a reading of a complex poem. It will combine paraphrase and explanation to clarify the poem's meaning. A *literary analysis* can take many forms. You may be asked to analyze one element in a work: character conflict, the use of setting, the tone of a poem. Or you could be asked to contrast two works. Usually an analytic assignment requires you to connect analysis to interpretation, for we analyze the parts to better understand the whole. If you are asked to examine the metaphors in a Shakespeare sonnet, for example, you will want to show how understanding the metaphors contributes to an understanding of the entire poem. In short, literary analysis is much the same as a style analysis of an essay, and thus the guidelines for writing about style discussed in Chapter 2 apply here as well.* Successful analyses

---

*Remember: The guidelines for referring to authors, titles, and direct quotations—presented in Chapter 1—also apply.

are based on accurate reading, reflection on the work's emotional impact, and the use of details from the work to support conclusions.

Literary analyses can also incorporate material beyond the particular work. We can analyze a work in the light of biographical information or from a particular political ideology. Or, we can study the social-cultural context of the work, or relate it to a literary tradition. These are only a few of the many approaches to the study of literature, and they depend on the application of knowledge outside the work itself. For undergraduates, topics based on these approaches usually require research. The student research essay at the end of the Appendix is a literary analysis. Alan examines Faulkner's *Intruder in the Dust* as an initiation novel. He connects his analysis to works by Hawthorne and Arthur Miller. What is taken from his research is documented and helps develop and support his own conclusions about the story.

To practice close reading, analysis, and interpretation of literature, read the following works. Use the questions after each work to aid your analysis of and responses to the literature.

TO HIS COY MISTRESS | ANDREW MARVELL

One of the last poets of the English Renaissance, Andrew Marvell (1621–1678) graduated from Cambridge University, spent much of his young life as a tutor, and was elected to Parliament in 1659. He continued in public service until his death. Most of his best-loved lyric poems come from his years as a tutor. "To His Coy Mistress" was published in 1681.

Had we but world enough, and time,
This coyness, lady, were no crime.
We would sit down, and think which way
To walk, and pass our long love's day.
Thou by the Indian Ganges' side   5
Shouldst rubies find; I by the tide
Of Humber would complain. I would
Love you ten years before the Flood,
And you should, if you please, refuse
Till the conversion of the Jews.   10
My vegetable° love should grow   *slowly vegetative*
Vaster than empires, and more slow;
An hundred years should go to praise
Thine eyes, and on thy forehead gaze;
Two hundred to adore each breast,   15
But thirty thousand to the rest;
An age at least to every part,
And the last age should show your heart.
For, lady, you deserve this state,
Nor would I love at lower rate.
  But at my back I always hear   20
Time's wingèd chariot hurrying near;
And yonder all before us lie
Deserts of vast eternity.

Thy beauty shall no more be found,   25
Nor in thy marble vault shall sound
My echoing song; then worms shall try
That long preserved virginity,
And your quaint honor turn to dust,
And into ashes all my lust.   30
The grave's a fine and private place,
But none, I think, do there embrace.
   Now therefore, while the youthful hue
Sits on thy skin like morning dew,
And while thy willing soul transpires   35
At every pore with instant fires,
Now let us sport us while we may,
And now, like amorous birds of prey,
Rather at once our time devour
Than languish in his slow-chapped power.   40
Let us roll all our strength and all
Our sweetness up into one ball,
And tear our pleasures with rough strife
Thorough° the iron gates of life.   *through* 45
Thus, though we cannot make our sun
Stand still, yet we will make him run.

QUESTIONS FOR READING, REASONING, AND REFLECTING

1. Describe the poem's external form.
2. How are the words coming to us? That is, is this a narrative, dramatic, or lyric poem?
3. Summarize the speaker's argument, using the structures *if, but,* and *therefore.*
4. What figure of speech do we find throughout the first verse paragraph? What is its effect on the speaker's tone?
5. Find examples of irony and understatement in the second verse paragraph.
6. How does the tone shift in the second section?
7. Explain the personification in line 22.
8. Explain the metaphors in lines 30 and 45.
9. What is the paradox of the last two lines? How can it be explained?
10. What is the idea of this poem? What does the writer want us to reflect on?

THE PASSIONATE SHEPHERD TO HIS LOVE | CHRISTOPHER MARLOWE

Cambridge graduate, Renaissance dramatist second only to Shakespeare, Christopher Marlowe (1564–1593) may be best known for this lyric poem. Not only is it widely anthologized, it has also spawned a number of responses by such significant writers as the seventeenth-century poet John Donne and the twentieth-century humorous poet Ogden Nash. For the Renaissance period the shepherd was a standard figure of the lover.

Come live with me and be my love,
And we will all the pleasures prove
That valleys, groves, hills, and fields,
Woods, or steepy mountain yields.

And we will sit upon the rocks,　　　　　　　　　　5
Seeing the shepherds feed their flocks,
By shallow rivers to whose falls
Melodious birds sing madrigals.

And I will make thee beds of roses
And a thousand fragrant posies,
A cap of flowers, and a kirtle
Embroidered all with leaves of myrtle;

A gown made of the finest wool　　　　　　　　　10
Which from our pretty lambs we pull;
Fair lined slippers for the cold,
With buckles of the purest gold;

A belt of straw and ivy buds,　　　　　　　　　　15
With coral clasps and amber studs:
And if these pleasures may thee move,
Come live with me, and be my love.

The shepherds' swains shall dance and sing　　　20
For thy delight each May morning:
If these delights thy mind may move,
Then live with me and be my love.

QUESTIONS FOR READING, REASONING, AND REFLECTING

1. Describe the poem's external structure.
2. What is the speaker's subject? What does he want to accomplish?
3. Summarize his "argument." How does he seek to convince his love?
4. What do the details of his argument have in common—that is, what kind of world or life does the speaker describe? Is there anything missing from the shepherd's world?
5. Would you like to be courted in this way? Would you say yes to the shepherd? If not, why?

THE NYMPH'S REPLY TO THE SHEPHERD | SIR WALTER RALEIGH

The renowned Elizabethan courtier, Sir Walter Raleigh (1552–1618) led a varied life as both a favorite of Queen Elizabeth and out of favor at court, as a colonizer and writer, and as one of many to be imprisoned in the Tower of London. In the following poem, Raleigh offers a response to Marlowe, using the nymph as the voice of the female lover.

> If all the world and love were young,
> And truth in every shepherd's tongue,
> These pretty pleasures might me move
> To live with thee and be thy love.
>
> Time drives the flocks from field to fold   5
> When rivers rage and rocks grow cold,
> And Philomel becometh dumb;
> The rest complains of cares to come.
>
> The flowers do fade, and wanton fields   10
> To wayward winter reckoning yields;
> A honey tongue, a heart of gall,
> Is fancy's spring, but sorrow's fall.
>
> Thy gowns, thy shoes, thy beds of roses,
> Thy cap, thy kirtle, and thy posies
> Soon break, soon wither, soon forgotten,—
> In folly ripe, in reason rotten.
>
> Thy belt of straw and ivy buds,   15
> Thy coral clasps and amber studs,
> All these in me no means can move
> To come to thee and be thy love.
>
> But could youth last and love still breed,   20
> Had joys no date nor age no need,
> Then these delights my mind might move
> To live with thee and be thy love.

QUESTIONS FOR READING, REASONING, AND REFLECTING

1. Describe the poem's external structure.
2. What is the context of the poem, the reason the speaker offers her words?
3. Analyze the speaker's argument, using *if* and *but* as your basic structure—and then the concluding, qualifying *but*.
4. What evidence does the speaker provide to support her argument?
5. Who has the more convincing argument: Marlowe's shepherd or Raleigh's nymph? Why?

IS MY TEAM PLOUGHING | A. E. HOUSMAN

British poet A. E. Housman (1859–1936) was a classicist, first a professor of Latin at University College, London, and then at the University of Cambridge. He spent the rest of his life at Trinity College, Cambridge. He is best known for his first volume of poetry, *A Shropshire Lad* (1896), a collection of crystal clear and deceptively simple verses that give expression to a world that has been lost—perhaps the innocence of youth.

"Is my team ploughing,
   That I was used to drive
And hear the harness jingle
   When I was man alive?"

Ay, the horses trample,   5
   The harness jingles now:
No change though you lie under
   The land you used to plough.

"Is football playing
   Along the river shore,
With lads to chase the leather,
   Now I stand up no more?"   10

Ay, the ball is flying,
   The lads play heart and soul;
The goal stands up, the keeper
   Stands up to keep the goal.   15

"Is my girl happy,
   That I thought hard to leave,
And has she tired of weeping
   As she lies down at eve?"   20

Ay, she lies down lightly,
   She lies not down to weep:
Your girl is well contented.
   Be still, my lad, and sleep.

"Is my friend hearty,   25
   Now I am thin and pine,
And has he found to sleep in
   A better bed than mine?"

Yes, lad, I lie easy,   30
   I lie as lads would choose;
I cheer a dead man's sweetheart,
   Never ask me whose.

QUESTIONS FOR READING, REASONING, AND REFLECTING

1. Classify the poem according to its external structure.
2. Is this a narrative, dramatic, or lyric poem? How are we to read the words coming to us?
3. What is the relationship between the two speakers? What has happened to the first speaker? What has changed in the life of the second speaker?
4. What ideas are suggested by the poem? What does Housman want us to take from his poem?

TAXI | AMY LOWELL

Educated at private schools and widely traveled, American Amy Lowell (1874–1925) was both a poet and a critic. Lowell frequently read her poetry and lectured on poetic techniques, defending her verse and that of other modern poets.

> When I go away from you
> The world beats dead
> Like a slackened drum.
> I call out for you against the jutted stars
> And shout into the ridges of the wind.   5
> Streets coming fast,
> One after the other,
> Wedge you away from me,
> And the lamps of the city prick my eyes
> So that I can no longer see your face.   10
> Why should I leave you,
> To wound myself upon the sharp edges of the night?

QUESTIONS FOR READING, REASONING, AND REFLECTING

1. Classify the poem according to its external structure.
2. Is this a narrative, dramatic, or lyric poem?
3. Explain the simile in the opening three lines and the metaphor in the last line of the poem.
4. What is the poem's subject? What seems to be the situation in which we find the speaker?
5. How would you describe the tone of the poem? How do the details and the emotional impact of the metaphors help to create tone?
6. What is the poem's meaning or theme? In other words, what does the poet want us to understand from reading her poem?

THE STORY OF AN HOUR | KATE CHOPIN

Now a highly acclaimed short-story writer, Kate Chopin (1851–1904) enjoyed a decade of publication and popularity from 1890 to 1900 and then critical condemnation followed by sixty years of neglect. Chopin began her writing career after her husband's death, having returned to her home in St. Louis with her six children. She saw two collections of her stories published—*Bayou Folk* in 1894 and *A Night in Acadie* in 1897—before losing her popularity with the publication of her short novel *The Awakening* in 1899, the story of a woman struggling to free herself from years of repression and subservience.

1   Knowing that Mrs. Mallard was afflicted with a heart trouble, great care was taken to break to her as gently as possible the news of her husband's death.

It was her sister Josephine who told her, in broken sentences; veiled hints 2 that revealed in half concealing. Her husband's friend Richards was there, too, near her. It was he who had been in the newspaper office when intelligence of the railroad disaster was received, with Brently Mallard's name leading the list of "killed." He had only taken the time to assure himself of its truth by a second telegram, and had hastened to forestall any less careful, less tender friend in bearing the sad message.

She did not hear the story as many women have heard the same, with a 3 paralyzed inability to accept its significance. She wept at once, with sudden, wild abandonment, in her sister's arms. When the storm of grief had spent itself she went away to her room alone. She would have no one follow her.

There stood, facing the open window, a comfortable, roomy armchair. Into 4 this she sank, pressed down by a physical exhaustion that haunted her body and seemed to reach into her soul.

She could see in the open square before her house the tops of trees that 5 were all aquiver with the new spring life. The delicious breath of rain was in the air. In the street below a peddler was crying his wares. The notes of a distant song which some one was singing reached her faintly, and countless sparrows were twittering in the eaves.

There were patches of blue sky showing here and there through the 6 clouds that had met and piled one above the other in the west facing her window.

She sat with her head thrown back upon the cushion of the chair, quite 7 motionless, except when a sob came up into her throat and shook her, as a child who has cried itself to sleep continues to sob in its dreams.

She was young, with a fair, calm face, whose lines bespoke repression and 8 even a certain strength. But now there was a dull stare in her eyes, whose gaze was fixed away off yonder on one of those patches of blue sky. It was not a glance of reflection, but rather indicated a suspension of intelligent thought.

There was something coming to her and she was waiting for it, fearfully. 9 What was it? She did not know; it was too subtle and elusive to name. But she felt it, creeping out of the sky, reaching toward her through the sounds, the scents, the color that filled the air.

Now her bosom rose and fell tumultuously. She was beginning to recog- 10 nize this thing that was approaching to possess her, and she was striving to beat it back with her will—as powerless as her two white slender hands would have been.

When she abandoned herself a little whispered word escaped her slightly 11 parted lips. She said it over and over under her breath: "free, free, free!" The vacant stare and the look of terror that had followed it went from her eyes. They stayed keen and bright. Her pulses beat fast, and the coursing blood warmed and relaxed every inch of her body.

She did not stop to ask if it were or were not a monstrous joy that held her. 12 A clear and exalted perception enabled her to dismiss the suggestion as trivial.

13   She knew that she would weep again when she saw the kind, tender hands folded in death; the face that had never looked save with love upon her, fixed and gray and dead. But she saw beyond that bitter moment a long procession of years to come that would belong to her absolutely. And she opened and spread her arms out to them in welcome.

14   There would be no one to live for her during those coming years; she would live for herself. There would be no powerful will bending hers in that blind persistence with which men and women believe they have a right to impose a private will upon a fellow-creature. A kind intention or a cruel intention made the act seem no less a crime as she looked upon it in that brief moment of illumination.

15   And yet she had loved him—sometimes. Often she had not. What did it matter! What could love, the unsolved mystery, count for in face of this possession of self-assertion which she suddenly recognized as the strongest impulse of her being!

16   "Free! Body and soul free!" she kept whispering.

17   Josephine was kneeling before the closed door with her lips to the keyhole, imploring for admission. "Louise, open the door! I beg; open the door—you will make yourself ill. What are you doing, Louise? For heaven's sake open the door."

18   "Go away. I am not making myself ill." No; she was drinking in a very elixir of life through that open window.

19   Her fancy was running riot along those days ahead of her. Spring days, and summer days, and all sorts of days that would be her own. She breathed a quick prayer that life might be long. It was only yesterday she had thought with a shudder that life might be long.

20   She arose at length and opened the door to her sister's importunities. There was a feverish triumph in her eyes, and she carried herself unwittingly like a goddess of Victory. She clasped her sister's waist, and together they descended the stairs. Richards stood waiting for them at the bottom.

21   Someone was opening the front door with a latchkey. It was Brently Mallard who entered, a little travel-stained, composedly carrying his grip-sack and umbrella. He had been far from the scene of accident, and did not even know there had been one. He stood amazed at Josephine's piercing cry; at Richards' quick motion to screen him from the view of his wife.

22   But Richards was too late.

23   When the doctors came they said she had died of heart disease—of joy that kills.

QUESTIONS FOR READING, REASONING, AND REFLECTING

1.   Analyze the story's plot structure, using the terms presented in Figure 1 (page 718).

2.   What is Mrs. Mallard's conflict? Explain the opposing elements of her conflict as precisely as you can.

3. When Mrs. Mallard goes to her room, she gazes out the window. Consider the details of the scene; what do these details have in common? How do the details help us understand what Mrs. Mallard experiences?

4. Why is it inaccurate to say that Mrs. Mallard does not love her husband? Cite evidence from the story.

5. The author James Joyce has described a character's moment of insight or intuition as an "epiphany." What is Mrs. Mallard's epiphany?

6. Are we to agree with the doctor's explanation for Mrs. Mallard's death? What term is appropriate to describe the story's conclusion?

THE ONES WHO WALK AWAY FROM OMELAS | URSULA K. LE GUIN

A graduate of Radcliffe College and Columbia University, Ursula K. Le Guin is the author of more than 20 novels and juvenile books, several volumes of poetry, and numerous stories and essays published in science fiction, scholarly, and popular journals. Her fiction stretches the categories of science fiction or fantasy and challenges a reader's moral understanding. First published in 1973, the following story, according to Le Guin, was inspired by a passage in William James's "The Moral Philosopher and the Moral Life" in which he asserts that we could not tolerate a situation in which the happiness of many people was purchased by the "lonely torment" of one "lost soul."

With a clamor of bells that set the swallows soaring, the Festival of Summer came to the city Omelas, bright-towered by the sea. The rigging of the boats in harbor sparkled with flags. In the streets between houses with red roofs and painted walls, between the old moss-grown gardens and under avenues of trees, past great parks and public buildings, processions moved. Some were decorous: old people in long stiff robes of mauve and gray, grave master workmen, quiet, merry women carrying their babies and chatting as they walked. In other streets the music beat faster, a shimmering of gong and tambourine, and the people went dancing, the procession was a dance. Children dodged in and out, their high calls rising like the swallows' crossing flights over the music and the singing. All the processions wound towards the north side of the city, where on the great water-meadow called the Green Fields boys and girls, naked in the bright air, with mudstained feet and ankles and long, lithe arms, exercised their restive horses before the race. The horses wore no gear at all but a halter without bit. Their manes were braided with streamers of silver, gold, and green. They flared their nostrils and pranced and boasted to one another; they were vastly excited, the horse being the only animal who has adopted our ceremonies as his own. Far off to the north and west the mountains stood up half circling Omelas on her bay. The air of morning was so clear that the snow still crowning the Eighteen Peaks burned with white-gold fire across the miles of sunlit air, under the dark blue of the sky. There was just enough wind to make the banners that marked the racecourse snap and flutter now and then. In the silence of the broad green meadows one could hear the music winding through the city streets, farther and nearer and ever approaching, a cheerful faint sweetness of the air that from time to time trembled and gathered together and broke out into the great joyous clanging of the bells.

2   Joyous! How is one to tell about joy? How describe the citizens of Omelas?

3   They were not simple folk, you see, though they were happy. But we do not say the words of cheer much any more. All smiles have become archaic. Given a description such as this one tends to make certain assumptions. Given a description such as this one tends to look next for the King, mounted on a splendid stallion and surrounded by his noble knights, or perhaps in a golden litter borne by great-muscled slaves. But there was no king. They did not use swords, or keep slaves. They were not barbarians. I do not know the rules and laws of their society, but I suspect that they were singularly few. As they did without monarchy and slavery, so they also got on without the stock exchange, the advertisement, the secret police, and the bomb. Yet I repeat that these were not simple folk, not dulcet shepherds, noble savages, bland utopians. They were not less complex than us. The trouble is that we have a bad habit, encouraged by pedants and sophisticates, of considering happiness as something rather stupid. Only pain is intellectual, only evil interesting. This is the treason of the artist: a refusal to admit the banality of evil and the terrible boredom of pain. If you can't lick 'em, join 'em. If it hurts, repeat it. But to praise despair is to condemn delight, to embrace violence is to lose hold of everything else. We have almost lost hold, we can no longer describe a happy man, nor make any celebration of joy. How can I tell you about the people of Omelas? They were not naïve and happy children—though their children were, in fact, happy. They were mature, intelligent, passionate adults whose lives were not wretched. O miracle! But I wish I could describe it better. I wish I could convince you. Omelas sounds in my words like a city in a fairy tale, long ago and far away, once upon a time. Perhaps it would be best if you imagined it as your own fancy bids, assuming it will rise to the occasion, for certainly I cannot suit you all. For instance, how about technology? I think that there would be no cars or helicopters in and above the streets; this follows from the fact that the people of Omelas are happy people. Happiness is based on a just discrimination of what is necessary, what is neither necessary nor destructive, and what is destructive. In the middle category, however—that of the unnecessary but undestructive, that of comfort, luxury, exuberance, etc.—they could perfectly well have central heating, subway trains, washing machines, and all kinds of marvelous devises not yet invented here, floating light-sources, fuelless power, a cure for the common cold. Or they could have none of that: it doesn't matter. As you like it. I incline to think that people from towns up and down the coast have been coming in to Omelas during the last days before the Festival on very fast trains and double-decked trams, and that the train station of Omelas is actually the handsomest building in town, though plainer than the magnificent Farmers' Market. But even granted trains, I fear that Omelas so far strikes

some of you as goody-goody. Smiles, bells, parades, horses, bleh. If so, please add an orgy. If an orgy would help, don't hesitate. Let us not, however, have temples from which issue beautiful nude priests and priestesses already half in ecstasy and ready to copulate with any man or woman, lover or stranger, who desires union with the deep godhead of the blood, although that was my first idea. But really it would be better not to have any temples in Omelas—at least, not manned temples. Religion yes, clergy no. Surely the beautiful nudes can just wander about, offering themselves like divine soufflés to the hunger of the needy and the rapture of the flesh. Let them join the processions. Let tambourines be struck above the copulations, and the glory of desire be proclaimed upon the gongs, and (a not unimportant point) let the offspring of these delightful rituals be beloved and looked after by all. One thing I know there is none of in Omelas is guilt. But what else should there be? I thought that first there were no drugs, but that is puritanical. For those who like it, the faint insistent sweetness of *drooz* may perfume the ways of the city, *drooz* which first brings a great lightness and brilliance to the mind and limbs, and then after some hours a dreamy languor, and wonderful visions at last of the very arcana and inmost secrets of the Universe, as well as exciting the pleasure of sex beyond all belief; and it is not habit-forming. For more modest tastes I think there ought to be beer. What else, what else belongs in the joyous city? The sense of victory, surely, the celebration of courage. But as we did without clergy, let us do without soldiers. The joy built upon successful slaughter is not the right kind of joy; it will not do; it is fearful and it is trivial. A boundless and generous contentment, a magnanimous triumph felt not against some outer enemy but in communion with the finest and fairest in the souls of all men everywhere and the splendor of the world's summer; this is what swells the hearts of the people of Omelas, and the victory they celebrate is that of life. I really don't think many of them need to take *drooz*.

Most of the processions have reached the Green Fields by now. A marvelous smell of cooking goes forth from the red and blue tents of the provisioners. The faces of small children are amiably sticky; in the benign grey beard of a man a couple of crumbs of rich pastry are entangled. The youths and girls have mounted their horses and are beginning to group around the starting line of the course. An old woman, small, fat, and laughing, is passing out flowers from a basket, and tall young men wear her flowers in their shining hair. A child of nine or ten sits at the edge of the crowd, alone, playing on a wooden flute. People pause to listen, and they smile, but they do not speak to him, for he never ceases playing and never sees them, his dark eyes wholly rapt in the sweet, thin magic of the tune. 4

He finishes, and slowly lowers his hands holding the wooden flute. 5

As if that little private silence were the signal, all at once a trumpet sounds 6 from the pavilion near the starting line: imperious, melancholy, piercing. The horses rear on their slender legs, and some of them neigh in answer. Soberfaced, the young riders stroke the horses' necks and soothe them, whispering, "Quiet, quiet, there my beauty, my hope." They begin to form in rank along the starting line. The crowds along the racecourse are like a field of grass and flowers in the wind. The Festival of Summer has begun.

7   Do you believe? Do you accept the festival, the city, the joy? No? Then let me describe this one more thing.

8   In a basement under one of the beautiful public buildings of Omelas, or perhaps in the cellar of one of its spacious private homes, there is a room. It has one locked door, and no window. A little light seeps in dustily between cracks in the boards, secondhand from the cobwebbed window somewhere across the cellar. In one corner of the little room a couple of mops, with stiff, clotted, foul-smelling heads, stand near a rusty bucket. The floor is dirt, a little damp to the touch, as cellar dirt usually is. The room is about three paces long and two wide: a mere broom closet or disused tool room. In the room a child is sitting. It could be a boy or a girl. It looks about six, but actually is nearly ten. It is feeble-minded. Perhaps it was born defective, or perhaps it has become imbecile through fear, malnutrition, and neglect. It picks its nose and occasionally fumbles vaguely with its toes or genitals, as it sits hunched in the corner farthest from the bucket and the two mops. It is afraid of the mops. It finds them horrible. It shuts its eyes, but it knows the mops are still standing there; and the door is locked; and nobody will come. The door is always locked; and nobody ever comes, except that sometimes—the child has no understanding of time or interval—sometimes the door rattles terribly and opens, and a person, or several people, are there. One of them may come in and kick the child to make it stand up. The others never come close, but peer in at it with frightened, disgusted eyes. The food bowl and the water jug are hastily filled, the door is locked, the eyes disappear. The people at the door never say anything, but the child, who has not always lived in the tool room, and can remember sunlight and its mother's voice, sometimes speaks. "I will be good," it says. "Please let me out. I will be good!" They never answer. The child used to scream for help at night, and cry a good deal, but now it only makes a kind of whining, "eh-haa-eh-haa," and it speaks less and less often. It is so thin there are no calves to its legs; its belly protrudes; it lives on a half-bowl of corn meal and grease a day. It is naked. Its buttocks and thighs are a mass of festered sores, as it sits in its own excrement continually.

9   They all know it is there, all the people of Omelas. Some of them have come to see it, others are content merely to know it is there. They all know that it has to be there. Some of them understand why, and some do not, but they all understand that their happiness, the beauty of their city, the tenderness of their friendships, the health of their children, the wisdom of their scholars, the skill of their makers, even the abundance of their harvest and the kindly weathers of their skies, depend wholly upon this child's abominable misery.

10   This is usually explained to children when they are between eight and twelve, whenever they seem capable of understanding; and most of those who come to see the child are young people, though often enough an adult comes, or comes back, to see the child. No matter how well the matter has been explained to them, these young spectators are always shocked and sickened at

the sight. They feel disgust, which they had thought themselves superior to. They feel anger, outrage, impotence, despite all the explanations. They would like to do something for the child. But there is nothing they can do. If the child were brought up into the sunlight out of that vile place, if it were cleaned and fed and comforted, that would be a good thing, indeed; but if it were done, in that day and hour all the prosperity and beauty and delight of Omelas would wither and be destroyed. Those are the terms. To exchange all the goodness and grace of every life in Omelas for that single, small improvement: to throw away the happiness of thousands for the chance of the happiness of one: that would be to let guilt within the walls indeed.

The terms are strict and absolute; there may not even be a kind word spoken to the child. 11

Often the young people go home in tears, or in a tearless rage, when they have seen the child and faced this terrible paradox. They may brood over it for weeks or years. But as time goes on they begin to realize that even if the child could be released, it would not get much good of its freedom: a little vague pleasure of warmth and food, no doubt, but little more. It is too degraded and imbecile to know any real joy. It has been afraid too long ever to be free of fear. Its habits are too uncouth for it to respond to humane treatment. Indeed, after so long it would probably be wretched without walls about it to protect it, and darkness for its eyes, and its own excrement to sit in. Their tears at the bitter injustice dry when they begin to perceive the terrible justice of reality, and to accept it. Yet it is their tears and anger, the trying of their generosity and the acceptance of their helplessness, which are perhaps the true source of the splendor of their lives. Theirs is no vapid, irresponsible happiness. They know that they, like the child, are not free. They know compassion. It is the existence of the child, and their knowledge of its existence, that makes possible the mobility of their architecture, the poignancy of their music, the profundity of their science. It is because of the child that they are so gentle with children. They know that if the wretched one were not there snivelling in the dark, the other one, the flute-player, could make no joyful music as the young riders line up in their beauty for the race in the sunlight of the first morning of summer. 12

Now do you believe in them? Are they not more credible? But there is one more thing to tell, and this is quite incredible. 13

At times one of the adolescent girls or boys who go to see the child, does not go home to weep or rage, does not, in fact, go home at all. Sometimes also a man or woman much older falls silent for a day or two, and then leaves home. These people go out into the street, and walk down the street alone. They keep walking, and walk straight out of the city of Omelas, through the beautiful gates. They keep walking across the farmlands of Omelas. Each one goes alone, youth or girl, man or woman. Night falls; the traveler must pass down village streets, between the houses with yellow-lit windows, and on out into the darkness of the fields. Each alone, they go west or north, towards the mountains. They go on. They leave Omelas, they walk ahead into the darkness, and 14 they do not come back. The place they go towards is a place even less imaginable to most of us than the city of happiness. I cannot describe it at all. It is possible that it does not exist. But they seem to know where they are going, the ones who walk away from Omelas.

QUESTIONS FOR READING, REASONING, AND REFLECTING

1. What is the general impression you get of the city of Omelas from the opening paragraph? To what senses does the author appeal?

2. Describe the people of Omelas. Are they happy? Do they have technology? Guilt? Religion? Soldiers? Drugs?

3. What shocking detail emerges about Omelas? On what does this ideal community thrive?

4. How do the children and teens respond to the locked-up child at first? How do they reconcile themselves to the situation? What do some residents do?

5. Can you understand the reason most residents accept the situation? Can you understand those who walk away? With which group do you most identify? Why?

6. On what does Le Guin want us to reflect? How would you state the story's theme?

TRIFLES | SUSAN GLASPELL

Born in Iowa, Susan Glaspell (1882?–1948) attended Drake University and then began her writing career as a reporter with the *Des Moines Daily News.* She also started writing and selling short stories; her first collection, *Lifted Masks,* was published in 1912. She completed several novels before moving to Provincetown with her husband, who started the Provincetown Players in 1915. Glaspell wrote seven short plays and four long plays for this group, including *Trifles* (1916). The well-known "Jury of Her Peers" (1917) is a short-story version of the play *Trifles.* Glaspell must have recognized that the plot of *Trifles* was a gem worth working with in more than one literary form.

Characters
George Henderson, County Attorney
Henry Peters, Sheriff
Lewis Hale, A Neighboring Farmer
Mrs. Peters
Mrs. Hale

SCENE: *The kitchen in the now abandoned farmhouse of* JOHN WRIGHT, *a gloomy kitchen, and left without having been put in order—unwashed pans under the sink, a loaf of bread outside the bread-box, a dish-towel on the table— other signs of incompleted work. At the rear, the outer door opens and the* SHERIFF *comes in followed by the* COUNTY ATTORNEY *and* HALE. *The* SHERIFF *and* HALE *are men in middle life; the* COUNTY ATTORNEY *is a young man; all are much bundled up and go at once to the stove. They are followed by the two*

women—the SHERIFF's *wife first; she is a slight wiry woman, a thin nervous face.*
MRS. HALE *is larger and would ordinarily be called more comfortable looking,*
but she is disturbed now and looks fearfully about as she enters. The women
have come in slowly, and stand close together near the door.

COUNTY ATTORNEY
[*Rubbing his hands.*] This feels good. Come up to the fire, ladies.

MRS. PETERS
[*After taking a step forward.*] I'm not—cold.

SHERIFF
[*Unbuttoning his overcoat and stepping away from the stove as if to mark*
the beginning of official business.] Now, Mr. Hale, before we move things
about, you explain to Mr. Henderson just what you saw when you came here
yesterday morning.

COUNTY ATTORNEY
By the way, has anything been moved? Are things just as you left them
yesterday?

SHERIFF
[*Looking about.*] It's just the same. When it dropped below zero last night
I thought I'd better send Frank out this morning to make a fire for us—no use
getting pneumonia with a big case on, but I told him not to touch anything except the stove—and you know Frank.

COUNTY ATTORNEY
Somebody should have been left here yesterday.

SHERIFF
Oh—yesterday. When I had to send Frank to Morris Center for that man
who went crazy—I want you to know I had my hands full yesterday. I knew you
could get back from Omaha by today and as long as I went over everything
here myself—

COUNTY ATTORNEY
Well, Mr. Hale, tell just what happened when you came here yesterday
morning.

HALE
Harry and I had started to town with a load of potatoes. We came along
the road from my place and as I got here I said, "I'm going to see if I can't get
John Wright to go in with me on a party telephone." I spoke to Wright about
it once before and he put me off, saying folks talked too much anyway, and all
he asked was peace and quiet—I guess you know about how much he talked

himself; but I thought maybe if I went to the house and talked about it before his wife, though I said to Harry that I didn't know as what his wife wanted made much difference to John—

COUNTY ATTORNEY

Let's talk about that later, Mr. Hale. I do want to talk about that, but tell now just what happened when you got to the house.

HALE

I didn't hear or see anything; I knocked at the door, and still it was all quiet inside. I knew they must be up, it was past eight o'clock. So I knocked again, and I thought I heard somebody say, "Come in." I wasn't sure, I'm not sure yet, but I opened the door—this door [*indicating the door by which the two women are still standing*] and there in that rocker—[*pointing to it*] sat Mrs. Wright.

[*They all look at the rocker.*]

COUNTY ATTORNEY

What—was she doing?

HALE

She was rockin' back and forth. She had her apron in her hand and was kind of—pleating it.

COUNTY ATTORNEY

And how did she—look?

HALE

Well, she looked queer.

COUNTY ATTORNEY

How do you mean—queer?

HALE

Well, as if she didn't know what she was going to do next. And kind of done up.

COUNTY ATTORNEY

How did she seem to feel about your coming?

HALE

Why, I don't think she minded—one way or other. She didn't pay much attention. I said, "How do, Mrs. Wright, it's cold, ain't it?" And she said, "Is it?"—and went on kind of pleating at her apron. Well, I was surprised; she didn't ask me to come up to the stove, or to set down, but just sat there, not even looking at me, so I said, "I want to see John." And then she—laughed. I guess you would call it a laugh. I thought of Harry and the team outside, so I said a little sharp: "Can't I see John?" "No," she says, kind o' dull like. "Ain't he home?" says I. "Yes," says she, "he's home." "Then why can't I see him?" I asked her, out of patience. " 'Cause he's dead," says she. *"Dead?"* says I. She just nodded her head, not getting a bit excited, but rockin' back and forth. "Why—where is he?" says I, not knowing what to say. She just pointed upstairs—like that [*himself pointing to the room above*]. I got up, with the idea of going up there. I walked from there to here—then I says, "Why, what did he die of?" "He died of a rope around his neck," says she, and just went on pleatin' at her apron. Well, I went out and called Harry. I thought I might—need help. We went upstairs and there he was lyin'—

COUNTY ATTORNEY

I think I'd rather have you go into that upstairs, where you can point it all out. Just go on now with the rest of the story.

HALE

Well, my first thought was to get that rope off. It looked . . . [*Stops, his face twitches*] . . . but Harry, he went up to him, and he said, "No, he's dead all right, and we'd better not touch anything." So we went back downstairs. She was still sitting that same way. "Has anybody been notified?" said Harry. He said it business-like—and she stopped pleatin' of her apron. "I don't know," she says. "You don't *know?*" says Harry. "No," says she. "Weren't you sleepin' in the bed with him?" says Harry. "Yes," says she, "but I was on the inside." "Somebody slipped a rope round his neck and strangled him and you didn't wake up?" says Harry. "I didn't wake up," she said after him. We must'a looked as if we didn't see how that could be, for after a minute she said, "I sleep sound." Harry was going to ask her more questions but I said maybe we ought to let her tell her story first to the coroner, or the sheriff, so Harry went fast as he could to Rivers' place, where there's a telephone.

COUNTY ATTORNEY

And what did Mrs. Wright do when she knew that you had gone for the coroner?

HALE

She moved from that chair to this one over here [*Pointing to a small chair in the corner*] and just sat there with her hands held together and looking down. I got a feeling that I ought to make some conversation, so I said I had come in to see if John wanted to put in a telephone, and at that she started to laugh, and then she stopped and looked at me—scared. [*The County Attorney, who has had his notebook out, makes a note.*] I dunno, maybe it wasn't scared. I wouldn't like to say it was. Soon Harry got back, and then Dr. Lloyd came, and you, Mr. Peters, and so I guess that's all I know that you don't.

COUNTY ATTORNEY

[*Looking around.*] I guess we'll go upstairs first—and then out to the barn and around there. [*To the Sheriff.*] You're convinced that there was nothing important here—nothing that would point to any motive.

SHERIFF

Nothing here but kitchen things.

[*The County Attorney, after again looking around the kitchen, opens the door of a cupboard closet. He gets up on a chair and looks on a shelf. Pulls his hand away, sticky.*]

COUNTY ATTORNEY

Here's a nice mess.

[*The women draw nearer.*]

MRS. PETERS

[*To the other woman.*] Oh, her fruit; it did freeze. [*To the Lawyer.*] She worried about that when it turned so cold. She said the fire'd go out and her jars would break.

SHERIFF

Well, can you beat the woman! Held for murder and worryin' about her preserves.

COUNTY ATTORNEY

I guess before we're through she may have something more serious than preserves to worry about.

HALE

Well, women are used to worrying over trifles.

[*The two women move a little closer together.*]

COUNTY ATTORNEY

[*With the gallantry of a young politician.*] And yet, for all their worries, what would we do without the ladies? [*The women do not unbend. He goes to the sink, takes a dipperful of water from the pail and pouring it into a basin, washes his hands. Starts to wipe them on the roller-towel, turns it for a cleaner place.*] Dirty towels! [*Kicks his foot against the pans under the sink.*] Not much of a housekeeper, would you say, ladies?

MRS. HALE

[*Stiffly.*] There's a great deal of work to be done on a farm.

COUNTY ATTORNEY

To be sure. And yet [*with a little bow to her*] I know there are some Dickson County farmhouses which do not have such roller towels.

[*He gives it a pull to expose its full length again.*]

MRS. HALE

Those towels get dirty awful quick. Men's hands aren't always as clean as they might be.

COUNTY ATTORNEY

Ah, loyal to your sex, I see. But you and Mrs. Wright were neighbors. I suppose you were friends, too.

MRS. HALE

[*Shaking her head.*] I've not seen much of her of late years. I've not been in this house—it's more than a year.

COUNTY ATTORNEY

And why was that? You didn't like her?

MRS. HALE

I liked her all well enough. Farmers' wives have their hands full, Mr. Henderson. And then—

COUNTY ATTORNEY

Yes—?

MRS. HALE

[*Looking about.*] It never seemed a very cheerful place.

COUNTY ATTORNEY

No—it's not cheerful. I shouldn't say she had the homemaking instinct.

MRS. HALE

Well, I don't know as Wright had, either.

COUNTY ATTORNEY

You mean that they didn't get on very well?

MRS. HALE

No, I don't mean anything. But I don't think a place'd be any cheerfuller for John Wright's being in it.

COUNTY ATTORNEY

I'd like to talk more of that a little later. I want to get the lay of things upstairs now.

[*He goes to the left, where three steps lead to a stair door.*]

SHERIFF

I suppose anything Mrs. Peters does'll be all right. She was to take in some clothes for her, you know, and a few little things. We left in such a hurry yesterday.

COUNTY ATTORNEY

Yes, but I would like to see what you take, Mrs. Peters, and keep an eye out for anything that might be of use to us.

MRS. PETERS

Yes, Mr. Henderson.
[*The women listen to the men's steps on the stairs, then look about the kitchen.*]

MRS. HALE

I'd hate to have men coming into my kitchen, snooping around and criticizing.
[*She arranges the pans under the sink which the* Lawyer *had shoved out of place.*]

MRS. PETERS

Of course it's no more than their duty.

MRS. HALE

Duty's all right, but I guess that deputy sheriff that came out to make the fire might have got a little of this on. [*Gives the roller towel a pull.*] Wish I'd thought of that sooner. Seems mean to talk about her for not having things slicked up when she had to come away in such a hurry.

MRS. PETERS

[*Who has gone to a small table in the left corner of the room, and lifted one end of a towel that covers a pan.*] She had bread set.
[*Stands still.*]

MRS. HALE

[*Eyes fixed on a loaf of bread beside the breadbox, which is on a low shelf at the other side of the room. Moves slowly toward it.*] She was going to put this in there. [*Picks up loaf, then abruptly drops it. In a manner of returning to familiar things.*] It's a shame about her fruit. I wonder if it's all gone. [*Gets up on the chair and looks.*] I think there's some here that's all right, Mrs. Peters. Yes—here; [*holding it toward the window*] this is cherries, too. [*Looking again.*] I declare I believe that's the only one. [*Gets down, bottle in her hand. Goes to the sink and wipes it off on the outside.*] She'll feel awful bad after all her hard work in the hot weather. I remember the afternoon I put up my cherries last summer.

[*She puts the bottle on the big kitchen table, center of the room. With a sigh, is about to sit down in the rocking-chair. Before she is seated realizes what chair it is; with a slow look at it, steps back. The chair which she has touched rocks back and forth.*]

MRS. PETERS

Well, I must get those things from the front room closet. [*She goes to the door at the right, but after looking into the other room, steps back.*] You coming with me, Mrs. Hale? You could help me carry them.

[*They go in the other room; reappear, Mrs. Peters carrying a dress and skirt, Mrs. Hale following with a pair of shoes.*]

MRS. PETERS

My, it's cold in there.

[*She puts the clothes on the big table, and hurries to the stove.*]

MRS. HALE

[*Examining the skirt.*] Wright was close. I think maybe that's why she kept so much to herself. She didn't even belong to the Ladies Aid. I suppose she felt she couldn't do her part, and then you don't enjoy things when you feel shabby. She used to wear pretty clothes and be lively, when she was Minnie Foster, one of the town girls singing in the choir. But that—oh, that was thirty years ago. This all you was to take in?

MRS. PETERS

She said she wanted an apron. Funny thing to want, for there isn't much to get you dirty in jail, goodness knows. But I suppose just to make her feel more natural. She said they was in the top drawer in this cupboard. Yes, here. And then her little shawl that always hung behind the door. [*Opens stair door and looks.*] Yes, here it is.

[*Quickly shuts door leading upstairs.*]

MRS. HALE

[*Abruptly moving toward her.*] Mrs. Peters?

MRS. PETERS

Yes, Mrs. Hale?

MRS. HALE

Do you think she did it?

MRS. PETERS

[*In a frightened voice.*] Oh, I don't know.

MRS. HALE

Well, I don't think she did. Asking for an apron and her little shawl. Worrying about her fruit.

MRS. PETERS

[*Starts to speak, glances up, where footsteps are heard in the room above. In a low voice.*] Mr. Peters says it looks bad for her. Mr. Henderson is awful sarcastic in a speech and he'll make fun of her sayin' she didn't wake up.

MRS. HALE

Well, I guess John Wright didn't wake when they was slipping that rope under his neck.

MRS. PETERS

No, it's strange. It must have been done awful crafty and still. They say it was such a—funny way to kill a man, rigging it all up like that.

MRS. HALE

That's just what Mr. Hale said. There was a gun in the house. He says that's what he can't understand.

MRS. PETERS

Mr. Henderson said coming out that what was needed for the case was a motive; something to show anger, or—sudden feeling.

MRS. HALE

[*Who is standing by the table.*] Well, I don't see any signs of anger around here. [*She puts her hand on the dish towel which lies on the table, stands looking down at table, one half of which is clean, the other half messy.*] It's wiped to here. [*Makes a move as if to finish work, then turns and looks at loaf of bread outside the breadbox. Drops towel. In that voice of coming-back to familiar things.*] Wonder how they are finding things upstairs. I hope she had it a little more red-up up there. You know, it seems kind of *sneaking*. Locking her up in town and then coming out here and trying to get her own house to turn against her!

MRS. PETERS

But Mrs. Hale, the law is the law.

MRS. HALE

I s'pose 'tis. [*Unbuttoning her coat.*] Better loosen up your things, Mrs. Peters. You won't feel them when you go out.

[*Mrs. Peters takes off her fur tippet, goes to hang it on hook at back of room, stands looking at the under part of the small corner table.*]

MRS. PETERS

She was piecing a quilt.

[*She brings the large sewing basket and they look at the bright pieces.*]

MRS. HALE

It's log cabin pattern. Pretty, isn't it? I wonder if she was goin' to quilt it or just knot it? [*Footsteps have been heard coming down the stairs. The Sheriff enters followed by Hale and the City Attorney.*]

SHERIFF

They wonder if she was going to quilt it or just knot it!
[*The men laugh, the women look abashed.*]

COUNTY ATTORNEY

[*Rubbing his hands over the stove.*] Frank's fire didn't do much up there, did it? Well, let's go out to the barn and get that cleared up.
[*The men go outside.*]

MRS. HALE

[*Resentfully.*] I don't know as there's anything so strange, our takin' up our time with little things while we're waiting for them to get the evidence. [*She sits down at the big table smoothing out a block with decision.*] I don't see as it's anything to laugh about.

MRS. PETERS

[*Apologetically.*] Of course they've got awful important things on their minds. [*Pulls up a chair and joins Mrs. Hale at the table.*]

MRS. HALE

[*Examining another block.*] Mrs. Peters, look at this one. Here, this is the one she was working on, and look at the sewing! All the rest of it has been so nice and even. And look at this! It's all over the place! Why, it looks as if she didn't know what she was about!
[*After she has said this they look at each other, then start to glance back at the door. After an instant Mrs. Hale has pulled at a knot and ripped the sewing.*]

MRS. PETERS

Oh, what are you doing, Mrs. Hale?

MRS. HALE

[*Mildly.*] Just pulling out a stitch or two that's not sewed very good. [*Threading a needle.*] Bad sewing always made me fidgety.

MRS. PETERS

[*Nervously.*] I don't think we ought to touch things.

MRS. HALE

I'll just finish up this end. [*Suddenly stopping and leaning forward.*] Mrs. Peters?

MRS. PETERS

Yes, Mrs. Hale?

MRS. HALE

What do you suppose she was so nervous about?

MRS. PETERS

Oh—I don't know. I don't know as she was nervous. I sometimes sew aw-ful queer when I'm just tired. [*Mrs. Hale starts to say something, looks at Mrs. Peters, then goes on sewing.*] Well I must get these things wrapped up. They may be through sooner than we think. [*Putting apron and other things to-gether.*] I wonder where I can find a piece of paper, and string.

MRS. HALE

In that cupboard, maybe.

MRS. PETERS

[*Looking in cupboard.*] Why, here's a bird-cage. [*Holds it up.*] Did she have a bird, Mrs. Hale?

MRS. HALE

Why, I don't know whether she did or not—I've not been here for so long. There was a man around last year selling canaries cheap, but I don't know as she took one; maybe she did. She used to sing real pretty herself.

MRS. PETERS

[*Glancing around.*] Seems funny to think of a bird here. But she must have had one, or why would she have a cage? I wonder what happened to it.

MRS. HALE

I s'pose maybe the cat got it.

MRS. PETERS

No, she didn't have a cat. She's got that feeling some people have about cats—being afraid of them. My cat got in her room and she was real upset and asked me to take it out.

MRS. HALE

My sister Bessie was like that. Queer, ain't it?

MRS. PETERS

[*Examining the cage.*] Why, look at this door. It's broke. One hinge is pulled apart.

MRS. HALE

[*Looking too.*] Looks as if someone must have been rough with it.

Mrs. Peters

Why, yes.
[*She brings the cage forward and puts it on the table.*]

Mrs. Hale

I wish if they're going to find any evidence they'd be about it. I don't like this place.

Mrs. Peters

But I'm awful glad you came with me, Mrs. Hale. It would be lonesome for me sitting here alone.

Mrs. Hale

It would, wouldn't it? [*Dropping her sewing.*] But I tell you what I do wish, Mrs. Peters. I wish I had come over sometimes when *she* was here. I—[*looking around the room*]—wish I had.

Mrs. Peters

But of course you were awful busy, Mrs. Hale—your house and your children.

Mrs. Hale

I could've come. I stayed away because it weren't cheerful—and that's why I ought to have come. I—I've never liked this place. Maybe because it's down in a hollow and you don't see the road. I dunno what it is, but it's a lonesome place and always was. I wish I had come over to see Minnie Foster sometimes. I can see now—
[*Shakes her head.*]

Mrs. Peters

Well, you mustn't reproach yourself, Mrs. Hale. Somehow we just don't see how it is with other folks until—something comes up.

Mrs. Hale

Not having children makes less work—but it makes a quiet house, and Wright out to work all day, and no company when he did come in. Did you know John Wright, Mrs. Peters?

Mrs. Peters

Not to know him; I've seen him in town. They say he was a good man.

Mrs. Hale

Yes—good; he didn't drink, and kept his word as well as most, I guess, and paid his debts. But he was a hard man, Mrs. Peters. Just to pass the time of day with him—[*Shivers.*] Like a raw wind that gets to the bone. [*Pauses, her eye falling on the cage.*] I should think she would'a wanted a bird. But what do you suppose went with it?

MRS. PETERS

I don't know, unless it got sick and died.
[*She reaches over and swings the broken door, swings it again, both women watch it.*]

MRS. HALE

You weren't raised round here, were you? [*Mrs. Peters shakes her head.*] You didn't know—her?

MRS. PETERS

Not till they brought her yesterday.

MRS. HALE

She—come to think of it, she was kind of like a bird herself—real sweet and pretty, but kind of timid and—fluttery. How—she—did—change. [*Silence; then as if struck by a happy thought and relieved to get back to everyday things.*] Tell you what, Mrs. Peters, why don't you take the quilt in with you? It might take up her mind.

MRS. PETERS

Why, I think that's a real nice idea, Mrs. Hale. There couldn't possibly be any objection to it, could there? Now, just what would I take? I wonder if her patches are in here—and her things.
[*They look in the sewing basket.*]

MRS. HALE

Here's some red. I expect this has got sewing things in it. [*Brings out a fancy box.*] What a pretty box. Looks like something somebody would give you. Maybe her scissors are in here. [*Opens box. Suddenly puts her hand to her nose.*] Why—[*Mrs. Peters bends nearer, then turns her face away.*] There's something wrapped up in this piece of silk.

MRS. PETERS

Why, this isn't her scissors.

MRS. HALE

[*Lifting the silk.*] Oh, Mrs. Peters—it's—
[*Mrs. Peters bends closer.*]

MRS. PETERS

It's the bird.

MRS. HALE

[*Jumping up.*] But, Mrs. Peters—look at it! Its neck! Look at its neck! It's all—other side to.

MRS. PETERS
Somebody—wrung—its—neck.
[*Their eyes meet. A look of growing comprehension, or horror. Steps are heard outside. Mrs. Hale slips box under quilt pieces, and sinks into her chair. Enter Sheriff and County Attorney. Mrs. Peters rises.*]

COUNTY ATTORNEY
[*As one turning from serious things to little pleasantries.*] Well ladies, have you decided whether she was going to quilt it or knot it?

MRS. PETERS
We think she was going to—knot it.

COUNTY ATTORNEY
Well, that's interesting, I'm sure. [*Seeing the bird-cage.*] Has the bird flown?

MRS. HALE
[*Putting more quilt pieces over the box.*] We think the—cat got it.

COUNTY ATTORNEY
[*Preoccupied.*] Is there a cat?
[*Mrs. Hale glances in a quick covert way at Mrs. Peters.*]

MRS. PETERS
Well, not *now*. They're superstitious, you know. They leave.

COUNTY ATTORNEY
[*To Sheriff Peters, continuing an interrupted conversation.*] No sign at all of anyone having come from the outside. Their own rope. Now let's go up again and go over it piece by piece. [*They start upstairs.*] It would have to have been someone who knew just the—
[*Mrs. Peters sits down. The two women sit there not looking at one another, but as if peering into something and at the same time holding back. When they talk now it is in the manner of feeling their way over strange ground, as if afraid of what they are saying, but as if they can not help saying it.*]

MRS. HALE
She liked the bird. She was going to bury it in that pretty box.

MRS. PETERS
[*In a whisper.*] When I was a girl—my kitten—there was a boy took a hatchet, and before my eyes—and before I could get there—[*Covers her face an instant.*] If they hadn't held me back I would have—[*Catches herself, looks upstairs where steps are heard, falters weakly*]—hurt him.

MRS. HALE

[*With a slow look around her.*] I wonder how it would seem never to have had any children around. [*Pause.*] No, Wright wouldn't like the bird—a thing that sang. She used to sing. He killed that, too.

MRS. PETERS

[*Moving uneasily.*] We don't know who killed the bird.

MRS. HALE

I knew John Wright.

MRS. PETERS

It was an awful thing was done in this house that night, Mrs. Hale. Killing a man while he slept, slipping a rope around his neck that choked the life out of him.

MRS. HALE

His neck. Choked the life out of him.
[*Her hand goes out and rests on the bird-cage.*]

MRS. PETERS

We don't know who killed him. We don't *know*.

MRS. HALE

[*Her own feeling not interrupted.*] If there'd been years and years of nothing, then a bird to sing to you, it would be awful—still, after the bird was still.

MRS. PETERS

[*Something within her speaking.*] I know what stillness is. When we homesteaded in Dakota, and my first baby died—after he was two years old, and me with no other then—

MRS. HALE

[*Moving.*] How soon do you suppose they'll be through, looking for the evidence?

MRS. PETERS

I know what stillness is. [*Pulling herself back.*] The law has got to punish crime, Mrs. Hale.

MRS. HALE

[*Not as if answering that.*] I wish you'd seen Minnie Foster when she wore a white dress with blue ribbons and stood up there in the choir and sang. [*A look around the room.*] Oh, I *wish* I'd come over here once in a while! That was a crime! That was a crime! Who's going to punish that?

Mrs. Peters
[*Looking upstairs.*] We mustn't—take on.

Mrs. Hale
I might have known she needed help! I know how things can be—for women. I tell you, it's queer, Mrs. Peters. We live close together and we live far apart. We all go through the same things—it's all just a different kind of the same thing. [*Brushes her eyes, noticing the bottle of fruit, reaches out for it.*] If I was you I wouldn't tell her her fruit was gone. Tell her it *ain't*. Tell her it's all right. Take this in to prove it to her. She—she may never know whether it was broke or not.

Mrs. Peters
[*Takes the bottle, looks about for something to wrap it in; takes petticoat from the clothes brought from the other room, very nervously begins winding this around the bottle. In a false voice.*] My, it's a good thing the men couldn't hear us. Wouldn't they just laugh! Getting all stirred up over a little thing like a—dead canary. As if that could have anything to do with—with—wouldn't they *laugh*!
[*The men are heard coming downstairs.*]

Mrs. Hale
[*Under her breath.*] Maybe they would—maybe they wouldn't.

County Attorney
No, Peters, it's all perfectly clear except a reason for doing it. But you know juries when it comes to women. If there was some definite thing. Something to show—something to make a story about—a thing that would connect up with this strange way of doing it—
[*The women's eyes meet for an instant. Enter Hale from outer door.*]

Hale
Well, I've got the team around. Pretty cold out there.

County Attorney
I'm going to stay here awhile by myself. [*To the Sheriff.*] You can send Frank out for me, can't you? I want to go over everything. I'm not satisfied that we can't do better.

Sheriff
Do you want to see what Mrs. Peters is going to take in?
[*The Lawyer goes to the table, picks up the apron, laughs.*]

County Attorney
Oh, I guess they're not very dangerous things the ladies have picked out. [*Moves a few things about, disturbing the quilt pieces which cover the box.*

Steps back.] No, Mrs. Peters doesn't need supervising. For that matter, a sheriff's wife is married to the law. Ever think of it that way, Mrs. Peters?

MRS. PETERS

Not—just that way.

SHERIFF

[*Chuckling.*] Married to the law. [*Moves toward the other room.*] I just want you to come in here a minute, George. We ought to take a look at these windows.

COUNTY ATTORNEY

[*Scoffingly.*] Oh, windows!

SHERIFF

We'll be right out, Mr. Hale.

[*Hale goes outside. The Sheriff follows the County Attorney into the other room. Then Mrs. Hale rises, hands tight together, looking intensely at Mrs. Peters, whose eyes make a slow turn, finally meeting Mrs. Hale's. A moment Mrs. Hale holds her, then her own eyes point the way to where the box is concealed. Suddenly Mrs. Peters throws back quilt pieces and tries to put the box in the bag she is wearing. It is too big. She opens box, starts to take bird out, cannot touch it, goes to pieces, stands there helpless. Sound of a knob turning in the other room. Mrs. Hale snatches the box and puts it in the pocket of her big coat. Enter County Attorney and Sheriff.*]

COUNTY ATTORNEY

[*Facetiously.*] Well, Henry, at least we found out that she was not going to quilt it. She was going to—what is it you call it, ladies?

MRS. HALE

[*Her hand against her pocket.*] We call it—knot it, Mr. Henderson.

QUESTIONS FOR READING, REASONING, AND REFLECTING

1. Explain the situation as the play begins.
2. Examine the dialogue of the men. What attitudes about themselves—their work, their abilities, their importance—are revealed? What is their collective opinion of women?
3. When Mrs. Hale and Mrs. Peters discover the dead bird, what do they begin to understand?
4. What other "trifles" in the kitchen provide additional evidence as to what has happened?

5. What trifles can be seen as symbols? What do they reveal about Mrs. Wright's life and character?

6. What is the play about primarily? Is it a murder mystery? Does it speak for feminist values? Is it about not seeing—not really knowing—others? In a few sentences, state what you consider to be the play's dominant theme. Then list the evidence you would use to support your conclusion.

7. Is there any sense in which one could argue that Mrs. Wright had a right to kill her husband? If you were a lawyer, how would you plan her defense? If you were on the jury, what sentence would you recommend?

SAMPLE STUDENT LITERARY ANALYSIS

Peterson 1

Alan Peterson

American Literature 242

May 5, 1998

Faulkner's Realistic Initiation Theme

William Faulkner braids a universal theme, the theme of initiation, into the fiber of his novel Intruder in the Dust. From ancient times to the present, a prominent focus of literature, of life, has been rites of passage, particularly those of childhood to adulthood. Joseph Campbell defines rites of passage as "distinguished by formal, and usually very severe, exercises of severance." A "candidate" for initiation into adult society, Campbell explains, experiences a shearing away of the "attitudes, attachments and life patterns" of childhood (9). This severe, painful stripping away of the child and installation of the adult is presented somewhat differently in several works by American writers.

One technique of handling this theme of initiation is used by Nathaniel Hawthorne in his story "My Kinsman, Major Molineaux." The story's main character, Robin, is suddenly awakened to the real world, the adult world, when he sees Major Molineaux "in tar-and-feathery dignity" (Hawthorne 528). A terrified and amazed Robin gapes at his kinsman as the large and colorful crowd laughs at and ridicules the Major; then an acquiescent Robin joins with the crowd in the mirthful shouting (Hawthorne 529). This moment is Robin's epiphany, his sudden realization of reality. Robin goes from unsophisticated rube to resigned cynical adult in one quick scene. Hawthorne does hold out hope that Robin will not let this event ruin his life, indeed that he will perhaps prosper from it.

A similar, but decidedly less optimistic, example of an epiphanic initiation occurs in Arthur Miller's play Death of a Salesman. Miller develops an

Appropriate heading when separate title page is not used. (See page 330.)

Center the title.

Double-space throughout.

Opening ¶ introduces subject, presents thesis, and defines key term— initiation.

Student combines paraphrase and brief quotations in definition.

Summary and analysis combined to explain initiation in Hawthorne's story.

Transition to second example establishes contrast with Hawthorne.

initiation theme within a flashback. A teenaged Biff, shockingly confronted with Willy's infidelity and weakness, has his boyhood dreams, ambitions—his vision—shattered, leaving his life in ruins, a truth borne out in scenes in which Biff is an adult during the play (1083–84, 1101). Biff's discovery of the vices and shortcomings of his father overwhelm him. His realization of adult life is a revelation made more piercing when put into the context of his naive and overly hopeful upbringing. A ravaged and defeated Biff has adulthood wantonly thrust upon him. Unlike Hawthorne's Robin, Biff never recovers.

> ¶ concludes with emphasis on contrast.

> Transition to Faulkner's story by contrast with Hawthorne and Miller.

William Faulkner does not follow these examples when dealing with the initiation of his character Chick in Intruder in the Dust. In Robin's and Biff's cases, each character's passage into adulthood was brought about by realization of and disillusionment with the failings and weaknesses of a male adult playing an important role in his life. By contrast, Chick's male role models are vital, moral men with integrity. Chick's awakening develops as he begins to comprehend the mechanisms of the adult society in which he would be a member.

Faulkner uses several techniques for illustrating Chick's growth into a man. Early in the novel, at the end of the scene in which Chick tries to pay for his dinner, Lucas warns Chick to "stay out of that creek" (Faulkner 16).[1] The creek is an effective symbol: it is both a physical creek and a metaphor for the boy's tendency to slide into gaffes that perhaps a man could avoid. The creek's symbolic meaning is more evident when, after receiving the molasses, Chick encounters Lucas in town. Lucas again reminds Chick not to "fall in no more creeks this winter" (24). At the end of the novel, Lucas meets Chick in Gavin's office and states: "you ain't fell in no more creeks lately, have you?" (241). Although Lucas phrases this as a question, the answer is obvious to Lucas, as

> Footnote first parenthetical reference to inform readers that subsequent citations will exclude the author's name and give only the page number. (See pages 289–90).

---

[1]Subsequent references to Faulkner's novel cite page numbers only.

well as to the reader, that indeed Chick has not blundered into his naive

boyhood quagmire lately. When Lucas asks his question, Chick's actual falling

into a creek does not occur to the reader.

Another image Faulkner employs to show Chick growing into a man is the

Note transition. (See page 332 on transitions.)

single-file line. After Chick gets out of the creek, he follows Lucas into the

house, the group walking in single file. In the face of Lucas's much stronger

adult will, Chick is powerless to get out of the line, to go to Edmonds's house

(7). Later in the novel, when Miss Habersham, Aleck Sander, and Chick are

walking back from digging up the grave, Chick again finds himself in a single-file

line with a strong-willed adult in front. Again he protests, then relents, but

Note interpolation in square brackets.

clearly he feels slighted and wonders to himself "what good that [walking

single file] would do" (130). The contrast between these two scenes illustrates

Chick's growth, although he is not yet a man.

Faulkner gives the reader other hints of Chick's passage into manhood.

Good use of brief quotations combined with analysis. (See page 319.)

As the novel progresses, Chick is referred to (and refers to himself) as a "boy"

(24), a "child" (25), a "young man" (46), "almost a man" (190), a "man"

(194), and one of two "gentlemen" (241). Other clues crop up from time to

time. Chick wrestles with himself about getting on his horse and riding away,

far away, until Lucas's lynching is "all over finished done" (41). But his growing

sense of responsibility and outrage quell his boyish desire to escape, to bury his

head in the sand. Chick looks in the mirror at himself with amazement at his

deeds (125). Chick's mother serves him coffee for the first time, despite the

agreement she has with his father to withhold coffee until his eighteenth

birthday (127). Chick's father looks at him with pride and envy (128–29).

Characteristics of Chick's gradual and positive initiation explained. Observe coherence techniques. (See page 321.)

Perhaps the most important differences between the epiphanic initiations

of Robin and Biff and that experienced by Chick are the facts that Chick's

epiphany does not come all at once and it does not devastate him. Chick learns

about adulthood—and enters adulthood—piecemeal and with support. His first

eye-opening experience occurs as he tries to pay Lucas for dinner and is

Peterson 4

rebuffed (15–16). Chick learns, after trying again to buy a clear conscience, the impropriety and affront of his actions (24). Lucas teaches Chick how he should resolve *his* dilemma by setting him "free" (26–27). Later, Chick feels outrage at the adults crowding into the town, presumably to see a lynching, then disgrace and shame as they eventually flee (196–97, 210). As in most lives, Chick's passage into adulthood is a gradual process; he learns a little bit at a time and has support in his growing. Gavin is there for him, to act as a sounding board, to lay a strong intellectual foundation, to confirm his beliefs. Chick's initiation is consistent with Joseph Campbell's explanation: "all rites of passage are intended to touch not only the candidate, but also every member of his circle" (9). Perhaps Gavin is affected the most, but Chick's mother and father, and Lucas as well, are influenced by the change in Chick.

    In Intruder in the Dust, William Faulkner has much to say about the role of and the actions of adults in society. He depicts racism, ignorance, resignation, violence, fratricide, citizenship, hope, righteousness, lemming-like aggregation, fear, and a host of other emotions and actions. Chick learns not only right and wrong, but that in order to be a part of society, of his community, he cannot completely forsake those with whom he disagrees or whose ideas he challenges. There is much compromise in growing up; Chick learns to compromise on some issues, but not all. Gavin's appeal to Chick to "just don't stop" (210) directs him to conform enough to be a part of the adult world, but not to lose sight of, indeed instead to embrace, his own values and ideals.

> Student concludes by explaining the values Chick develops in growing up.

Works Cited

Paging is continuous.

Place Works Cited on separate page.

Double-space throughout.

Use hanging indentation.

Campbell, Joseph. The Hero with a Thousand Faces. Princeton: Princeton UP, 1949.

Faulkner, William. Intruder in the Dust. New York: Random, 1948.

Hawthorne, Nathaniel. "My Kinsman, Major Molineaux." 1832. The Complete Short Stories of Nathaniel Hawthorne. New York: Hanover/Doubleday, 1959. 517–30.

Miller, Arthur. Death of a Salesman. 1949. An Introduction to Literature. 9th ed. Eds. Sylvan Barnet, Morton Berman, and William Burto. Boston: Little, 1985. 1025–111.

SUGGESTIONS FOR DISCUSSION AND WRITING

1. Prepare an explication of either Amy Lowell's "Taxi" or Sir Walter Raleigh's "The Nymph's Reply to the Shepherd." You will need to explain both what the poem says and what it means—or what it accomplishes.

2. Analyze A. E. Housman's attitudes toward life and human relationships in "Is My Team Ploughing."

3. Analyze Mrs. Mallard's conflict, and decision about that conflict, as the basis for your understanding of the dominant theme in "The Story of an Hour."

4. You are Mrs. Wright's attorney (see *Trifles,* page 734). Write your closing argument in her defense, explaining why only a light sentence is warranted for Mrs. Wright. Select details from the play to support your assertions about Mrs. Wright's character and motivation.

5. Explain what you think are the most important ideas about community in Ursula K. Le Guin's "The Ones Who Walk Away from Omelas."

6. John Donne in "The Bait" and Ogden Nash in "Love Under the Republicans (or Democrats)" also have responses to Marlowe's "The Passionate Shepherd to His Love." Select one of these poems, read and analyze it, and then evaluate its argument as a response to Marlowe's shepherd.

Credits

Achenbach, Joel. "Out of the Woods: Today's Kids Can't See the Forest for the MTV." *The Washington Post,* May 29, 2005. Reprinted by permission.

Applebaum, Anne. "Let a Thousand Filters Bloom." *The Washington Post,* July 20, 2005. Reprinted by permission.

Auerbach, Judith. "The Overlooked Victims of AIDS." Reprinted by permission of the author and amfAR.

Barry, Dave. "Remote Control." Copyright 2003 Tribune Media Services, Inc. All Rights Reserved. Reprinted by permission.

Bedau, Hugo Adam. From *Death Is Different: Studies in the Morality, Law, and Politics of Capital Punishment* by Hugo Adam Bedau. Copyright 1987 by Hugo Adam Bedau. Reprinted with the permission of Northeastern University Press.

Bernstein, Joseph. "Animal Rights vs. Animal Research: A Modest Proposal." 1996, v. 22. BMJ Publishing Group. Reprinted by permission.

Bork, Robert H. "Addicted to Health." *The National Review.* © 1997 by National Review, Inc., 215 Lexington Avenue, New York, NY 10016. Reprinted by permission.

Bottum, J. "The Horror." Reprinted with permission of the author. © National Affairs Inc., The Public Interest, No. 150, Winter 2003, Washington D.C.

Brooks, David. "The Bursting Point." Copyright © 2005 by The New York Times Co. Reprinted with permission.

Brzezinski, Zbigniew. "War and Football." *The Washington Post,* January 7, 2000. Reprinted by permission.

Califano, Joseph A., Jr. "Don't Make Teen Drinking Easier." *The Washington Post,* May 11, 2003. Reprinted by permission.

Cohen, Richard. "Kids Who Kill Are Still Kids." *The Washington Post,* August 3, 2001. Reprinted by permission.

Coleman, Mary. "The Digitial Library Plan: Riches We Must Share." Reprinted by permission of the author.

Cottle, Michelle. "Turning Goys into Girls." *The Washington Monthly.*

Collier, Linda J. "Adult Crime, Adult Time." *The Washington Post,* 1998. Reprinted by permission.

Cowan, Jonathan. "False Choices on Gun Safety." *The Washington Post,* October 10, 2002. Reprinted by permission.

Dalton, Patricia. "We're Only Human: And None of Us Are Made to Run Like Machines." Reprinted by permission of the author.

Dautrich, Ken, and Bare, John. "Why the First Amendment (and Journalism) Might Be in Trouble." Reprinted by permission of Nieman Reports, the Nieman Foundation for Journalism at Harvard University.

Davis, Mark. "A Little Civility, Please." *The Fort Worth Star-Telegram,* March 5, 2003. Reprinted by permission.

Deford, Frank. "Solving the Title IX Problem." CNNSI; Posted June 19, 2002. Reprinted courtesy of the author.

Dennett, Daniel C. "Show Me the Science." Copyright © 2005 by The New York Times Co. Reprinted with permission.

Dionne, E.J., Jr. "When Government Is Good." *The Washington Post,* September 2, 2005. Reprinted by permission.

Donohue, Laura. "Censoring Science Won't Make Us Any Safer." Reprinted by permission of the author.

Mathabane, Mark. "If You Assign My Book, Don't Censor It." *The Washington Post,* November 28, 1999. Reprinted by permission.

McClurg, Andrew. "Online Lessons on Unprotected Sex." Reprinted by permission of the author.

Morin, Richard. "Political Ads and the Voters They Atrract." *The Washington Post,* November 23, 2003. Reprinted by permission.

Morin, Richard. "Paradise Lost." *The Washington Post,* July 9, 2000. Reprinted by permission.

Noonan, Peggy. "The Blogs Must Be Crazy." *The Wall Street Journal.* Dist. by William Morris Agency, Inc.

Norell, Mark A. & Xing, Xu "The Varieties of Tyrannosaurs." Reprinted from *Natural History* May 2005; © Natural History Magazine, Inc., 2005.

O'Neil, Robert. "What Limits Should Campus Networks Place on Pornography." Originally published in *The Chronicle of Higher Education,* March 21, 2003. Reprinted by permission.

Orwell, George. "A Hanging" from *Shooting an Elephant and Other Essays* by George Orwell, copyright 1950 by Sonia Brownell Orwell and renewed by Sonia Pitt-Rivers, reprinted by permission of Harcourt, Inc.

Pinkerton, Jim. "A Grand Compromise." *The Atlantic Monthly,* Jan/Feb 2003. Reprinted by permission.

Pollitt, Katha. "Intelligible Design." First published in *The Nation.* Reprinted by permission of the author.

Quindlen, Anna. "Don't Mess with Mother." Reprinted by permission of International Creative Management, Inc. Copyright © 2005 by Anna Quindlen. First appeared in Newsweek.

Rainer, Peter. "Knightly in Shining Armor." Reprinted by permission of the author.

Ransdell, Lynda. "More Than a Game: One Woman's Fight for Gender Equity in Sport." WSPAJ. Reprinted by permission from the author.

Ravitch, Diane. "Put Teachers to the Test." *The Washington Post,* February 25, 1998. Reprinted by permission.

"Reader's Guide to Periodical Literature" excerpts, 1975. Reprinted by permission of H.W. Wilson Company.

Reid, David. "Business Is Business." Reprinted by permission of the author.

Reilly, Rick. "Disadvantage, Women." Reprinted courtesy of Sports Illustrated: "Disadvantage, Women" by Rick Reilly, *Sports Illustrated,* July 16, 2001, Copyright © 2001. Time Inc. All rights reserved.

Reed, Susan E. "Lawsuits Won't Break That Glass Ceiling." Reprinted by permission of the author.

Relin, David. "Who's Killing Kids' Sports." © 2005 David Oliver Relin. All rights reserved.

Rhodes, Richard. "Hollow Claims About Fantasy Violence." Copyright © 2000 *The New York Times.* Reprinted by permission.

Rieff, David. "Their Hearts and Minds?" First Published in The New York Times Magazine © 2005 by David Rieff, reprinted with permission of the Wylie Agency.

Ripley, Amanda. "Who Says a Woman Can't Be Einstein?" ©2005 Time Inc. Reprinted by permission.

Robinson, Eugene, "Instant Revisionism." *The Washington Post,* October 7, 2005. Reprinted by permission.

Robinson, Eugene. "A Specious 'Expirement.' " *The Washington Post,* October 4, 2005. Reprinted by permission.

Rodriguez, Gregory. "Mongrel America." *The Atlantic Monthly,* Jan/Feb 2003. Reprinted by permission.

Rollins, Karina. "No Compromise: Why We're Going to Lose the War on Terror . . . and How We Could Win." Reprinted with permission of *The American Enterprise,* a magazine of Politics, Business, and Culture. On the web at www.TAEmag.com

Sadker, David. "Gender Games." *The Washington Post,* July 31, 2000. Reprinted by permission.

Samuelson, Robert J. "A Century of Freedom." *The Washington Post,* December 22, 1999. Reprinted by permission.

Sanders, James C. "Beer Commercials Do No Harm" by James C. Sanders, Letter to the editor, *Washington Post,* January 28, 1989. © *The Washington Post.*

Schiffren, L. "Gay Marriage, an Oxymoron." Copyright © 2005 by The New York Times Co. Reprinted with permission.

Schobert, Less. "Let the Zoo's Elephants Go." Reprinted by permission of the author.

Seaman, Barrett. "How Bingeing Became the New College Sport." ©2005 Time Inc. Reprinted by permission.

Shean, Glenn. "Psychology and the Environment." Reprinted by permission of the author.

Sherman, Cary. "The Issue is Piracy, Not Privacy." *USA Today,* January 29, 2003. Reprinted by permission.

Shulman, Beth. "Four Myths, 30 Million Potential Votes." *The Washington Post,* August 17, 2003. Reprinted with permission.

Silver, Lee M. "Remaking Eden." Copyright © 1998 by Lee M. Silver. Reprinted by permisson of HarperCollins Publishers Inc. Avon Books.

Singer, PA and M Siegler. "Euthanasia—A Critique." Copyright © 1990 Massachussetts Medial Society. All rights reserved.

Smith, Wesley. "The Case Heard Round the Web." Reprinted by permission of *The Weekly Standard.*

Somerby, Bob. "Back-to-School Blues." Reprinted by permission of the author.

Speight, Derrick. "Of Losers and Moles . . ." Reprinted by permission of the author.

Sprigge, Timothy. "A Reply to Joseph Bernstein." 1996, v. 22. BMJ Publishing Group. Reprinted by permission.

"Springing a Radioactive Leak." Time, February 8, 1982. Copyright © 1982 by *Time,* Inc. Reprinted by permission.

Staples, Brent. "How Hip-Hop Lost Its Way and Betrayed Its Fans." Copyright © 2005 by The New York Times Co. Reprinted with permission.

Steinem, Gloria. "Supremacy Crimes," Aug/Sep 1999. Reprinted by permission.

Sullivan, Andrew. "The Conservative Case for Gay Marriage." *Time* Magazine, June 30, 2003. Reprinted by permission.

Sullivan, Andrew. "Society Is Dead." Andrew Sullivan, *The Sunday Times,* London.

Tannen, Deborah. "We Need a Higher Quality of Outrage." *The Christian Sciene Monitor,* October 22, 2004, copyright Deborah Tannen. Reprint by permission.

Taylor, Nick. "The Digital Library Plan: But Not at Writers' Expense." Copyright © 2005 by Nick Taylor. Originally published in *The Washington Post.* Reprinted with permission of author.

Thurow, Lester C. "Why Women Are Paid Less Than Men." *The New York Times,* March 8, 1981. Copyright © 1981 by The New York Times Company. Reprinted by permission.

Thurow, Lester. "Why Women Are Paid Less." *The New York Times,* March 8, 1981. Reprinted by permission.

Vachss, Andrew. "Watch Your Language." © 2005 Andrew Vachss. All rights reserved.

van den Haag, Ernest. From "The Ultimate Punishment: A Defense" by Ernest van den Haag, *Harvard Law Review,* May 7, 1986. Copyright © 1986 by the Harvard Law Association. Reprinted by permission of the author.

Varadarajan, Tunku. "That Feeling of Being under Suspicion." Reprinted with permission of *The Wall Street Journal* © 2005 Dow Jones Company. All rights reserved.

Waite, Linda J. "Social Science Finds: Marriage Matters." From *The Responsive Community,* Vol. 6, issue 3, Summer 1996. Copyright © 1996 by *The Responsive Community.* Reprinted with permission.

Walker, Rob. "Social Lubricant: How a Marketing Campaign Became the Catalyst for a Societal Debate." *The New York Times Magazine,* March 8, 1981. Reprinted by permission.

Williams, Patricia. "Genes, Genius, Genies." Reprinted with permission from the November 21, 2005 issue of *The Nation.*

Will, George F. "IPod's Missing Manners." © 2005, The Washington Post Writers Group, Reprinted with permission.

Wilson, James. "A New Strategy in the War on Drugs." *The Wall Street Journal,* April 13, 2000. Reprinted from *The Wall Street Journal* ©2000. Dow Jones & Company, Inc. All rights reserved.

Wright, Karen. "Guns, Lies, and Video." *Discover,* April 2003. © 2003 Karen Wright. This article first appeared in *Discover* magazine.

Index